Little Oxford Dictionary of

Proverbs

SECOND EDITION

Edited by
Elizabeth Knowles

OXFORD
UNIVERSITY PRESS

Great Clarendon Street, Oxford, OX2 6DP,
United Kingdom

Oxford University Press is a department of the University of Oxford.
It furthers the University's objective of excellence in research, scholarship,
and education by publishing worldwide. Oxford is a registered trade mark of
Oxford University Press in the UK and in certain other countries

First Edition published in 2009
Second Edition published in 2016
Impression: 2

Published in the United States of America by Oxford University Press
198 Madison Avenue, New York, NY 10016, United States of America

British Library Cataloguing in Publication Data
Data available

Library of Congress Control Number: 2016943803

ISBN 978-0-19-877837-0

Printed in India by
Replika Press Pvt. Ltd.

❋ Contents

Introduction   vii

Acknowledgements   x

List of Subjects   xi

Little Oxford Dictionary of Proverbs   **1**

Keyword Index   387

Introduction ✤

This new edition of the *Little Oxford Dictionary of Proverbs* once more brings together a wide range of proverbs and sayings, from the traditional Western maxims of biblical and classical tradition, through proverbs from across the wider world, to expressions of contemporary wisdom from popular culture. The selection made is based on the diversity of real usage: when reaching today for a saying to use in advice or admonition, we happily draw material from a broad range of sources. New additions from today's world include the advice to interviewees to 'Dress for the job you want, not for the job you have', and the rueful reflection from the world of computing that in matters of online security, 'There is no patch for stupid.'

The dictionary is arranged by theme, so that a number of sayings on each topic can be found together. Subjects covered range widely, from **Action** ('The shrimp that falls asleep is swept away by the current') to **Cooperation** ('Cross the river in a crowd and the crocodile won't eat you'), and from **Friendship** ('The road to a friend's house is never long') to **Gardens** ('A garden is never finished'). A piece of advice for **Parents** may resonate with anyone seeing a son or daughter off on a gap year: 'Send the beloved child on a journey.' Within each theme, the proverbs and sayings are arranged alphabetically (initial 'a' and 'the' being ignored). There is a keyword index for essential words from the first part of each saying, allowing the reader to trace a saying to its place in its particular theme.

One of the pleasures of proverbs is in seeing how, in different parts of the world, the same idea may be expressed.

Introduction

At **Optimism and Pessimism**, the traditional rueful reflection that 'If wishes were horses, beggars would ride' is now matched by a comment from Senegal: 'If you had teeth of steel, you could eat iron coconuts.' Under **Power**, the reflection from Africa that 'When elephants fight, it is the grass that gets hurt' is echoed by the Korean saying 'When whales fight, the shrimp's back is broken.'

At **Caution**, the traditional English adjuration to 'Look before you leap' is now reinforced by a Chinese saying recommending a different form of careful exploration, 'Cross the river by feeling the stones.' 'Be what you want to seem' at **Behaviour** finds an echo in the more recent, 'Fake it 'til you make it.'

Sometimes, of course, different approaches are emphasized. At **Ability**, the idea that someone not naturally suited to a task will perform poorly is traditionally expressed by the proverb 'A sow may whistle, though it has an ill mouth for it.' The African saying 'If you can talk, you can sing, and if you can walk, you can dance' offers a much more positive approach. Views of **Enemies** range from 'The enemy of my enemy is my friend' to the warning 'Do not call a wolf to help you against the dogs.' The section on **Crises** includes two divergent modern contributions: the advice to 'Keep calm and carry on', and the wryer comment, 'Never waste a good crisis.'

Some new items have come to attention through high profile use. Hillary Clinton, speaking at a fundraising dinner in Arkansas when running for the Democratic nomination, used the saying 'If you see a turtle on a fencepost, it didn't get there by accident': this has now been added to **Causes and Consequences**. President Michael Higgins of Ireland, thanking those who had given help to the injured after the collapse of a balcony in Berkeley had resulted in the death and injury of a number of Irish students, quoted the Irish saying, 'We live in each other's shadow.' This now appears at **Cooperation.** At times, a news item may unexpectedly put us in touch with another culture. In October 2015, news from the British bird reserve of Slimbridge about the annual arrival of whooper swans quoted a Russian proverb associating migrating swans with impending wintry weather: 'The swan brings snow on its bill' (this is now at **Birds**).

One of the fascinating things about language is that we can never really say with certainty that a maxim which has fallen out of use may not reappear. The traditional saying 'A wise man turns chance into good fortune' seemed to have dropped out of use. However, when in November 2015 President Xi Jinping of China was entertained at a Buckingham Palace state banquet, he included it in his speech as a famous British adage. The proverb is now to be found at **Opportunity**.

An Arab proverb advises, 'To understand the people, acquaint yourself with their proverbs'. Working on this book has again been particularly pleasurable because of the opportunity to observe a multiplicity of views, and to enjoy the vigour and creativity of language. I hope that once more some of this pleasure will be shared with the reader.

❄ Acknowledgements

Little Proverbs has once more drawn on the most recent editions of the *Oxford Treasury of Sayings & Quotations* (4/e, 2011) and the *Oxford Dictionary of Proverbs* (6/e, 2015). This material has been augmented by Oxford's Quotations reading programme, the Oxford Corpus, and the Editor's own reading and research. Any book of this kind rests on the research, scholarship, and insight of many others, and I am extremely fortunate to have had such a foundation. I am grateful too to Ben Harris, who had the original idea for this book, and to Joanna Harris and Susan Ratcliffe who have provided valuable editorial support.

ELIZABETH KNOWLES
Oxford 2016

List of Subjects ✳

A

Ability
Absence
Achievement
Action and Inaction
Adversity
Advertising
Advice
Age
Ambition
Anger
Apology and Excuses
Appearance
Architecture
Argument
Armed Forces, The
Art
Autumn

B

Beauty
Beginning
Behaviour
Belief
Birds
Body, The
Books
Borrowing: see
    Debt and
    Borrowing
British Towns and
    Regions
Broadcasting

Business
Buying and Selling

C

Cats
Causes and
    Consequences
Caution
Certainty and
    Doubt
Chance and Luck
Change
Character
Charity
Children
Choice
Christian
    Church, The
Christmas
Circumstance and
    Situation
Cities: see Towns
    and Cities
Clergy
Computing
Conscience
Consequences:
    see Causes and
    Consequences
Cooking
Cooperation
Corruption
Countries and
    Peoples

Country and the
    Town, The
Courage
Crime and
    Punishment
Crises
Criticism
Custom and
    Habit

D

Dance
Danger
Death
Debt and
    Borrowing
Deception
Deeds: see Words
    and Deeds
Defiance
Delay: see Haste
    and Delay
Determination
Difference: see
    Similarity and
    Difference
Discontent: see
    Satisfaction and
    Discontent
Discoveries: see
    Inventions and
    Discoveries
Dislikes: see Likes
    and Dislikes

List of Subjects

Dogs
Doubt: *see* Certainty and Doubt
Dreams
Dress
Drink
Drunkenness

E

Eating
Education
Effort
Employment
Ending
Enemies
Environment, The
Envy
Equality
Evil: *see* Good and Evil
Excellence
Excess
Excuses: *see* Apology and Excuses
Experience
Extravagance: *see* Thrift and Extravagance

F

Fact: *see* Hypothesis and Fact
Failure: *see* Success and Failure

Fame
Familiarity
Family, The
Fate
Fear
Feelings
Flattery: *see* Praise and Flattery
Flowers
Food
Fools
Foresight
Forgiveness
Friendship
Futility
Future, The

G

Games: *see* Sports and Games
Gardens
Generosity
God
Good and Evil
Gossip
Government
Gratitude
Greed
Guilt

H

Habit: *see* Custom and Habit
Happiness
Haste and Delay
Health

History
Home, The
Honesty
Hope
Horses
Hospitality
Housework
Human Race, The
Hypothesis and Fact

I

Idleness
Ignorance
Inaction: *see* Action and Inaction
Indecision
Inventions and Discoveries

J

Journalism: *see* News and Journalism
Justice

K

Knowledge

L

Law, The
Leadership
Leisure

List of Subjects

Letters
Lies
Life
Lifestyles
Likes and Dislikes
Losing: *see* Winning
   and Losing
Love
Loyalty
Luck: *see* Chance
   and Luck

M

Management
Manners
Marriage
Means: *see* Ways
   and Means
Medicine
Meeting and
   Parting
Men
Men and Women
Mind, The
Misfortunes
Mistakes
Moderation
Money
Mourning
Murder
Music

N

Names
Nature
Necessity

Neighbours
News and
   Journalism

O

Opinion
Opportunity
Optimism and
   Pessimism

P

Parents
Parting: *see*
   Meeting and
   Parting
Past, The
Patience
Peace
Pessimism: *see*
   Optimism and
   Pessimism
Politics
Possessions
Poverty
Power
Practicality
Praise and
   Flattery
Prejudice and
   Tolerance
Preparation and
   Readiness
Present, The
Pride
Problems and
   Solutions

Punctuality
Punishment: *see*
   Crime and
   Punishment

Q

Quantities and
   Qualities

R

Rank
Readiness: *see*
   Preparation and
   Readiness
Reading
Rebellion: *see*
   Revolution and
   Rebellion
Relationships
Religion
Reputation
Responsibility
Revenge
Revolution and
   Rebellion
Rivers
Royalty

S

Satisfaction and
   Discontent
Sayings
Science
Sea, The
Secrecy

List of Subjects

Self-Esteem and
  Self-Assertion
Self-Interest
Selling: *see* Buying
  and Selling
Sex
Sickness
Silence
Similarity and
  Difference
Situation: *see*
  Circumstance
  and Situation
Sleep
Smoking
Solitude
Solutions: *see*
  Problems and
  Solutions
Sorrow
Speech
Sports and Games
Spring
Strength and
  Weakness
Success and Failure
Suffering
Summer

Surprise
Sympathy

T

Teaching
Technology
Temptation
Thinking
Thoroughness
Thrift and
  Extravagance
Time
Tolerance: *see*
  Prejudice and
  Tolerance
Town: *see* The
  Country and the
  Town
Towns and Cities
Transience
Travel
Treachery: *see*
  Trust and
  Treachery
Trees
Trust and Treachery
Truth

V

Value
Virtue

W

Warfare
Ways and Means
Weakness: *see*
  Strength and
  Weakness
Wealth
Weather, The
Weddings
Winning and Losing
Winter
Wisdom
Women
Words
Words and Deeds
Work
Worry
Writing

Y

Youth

Ability

The consensus of proverbial wisdom is that ability (or the lack of it) is innate, although aptitudes may be developed: If you can talk, you can sing; if you can walk, you can dance.

Genius is an infinite capacity for taking pains.
English proverb, late 19th century.

Horses for courses.
originally (in horse-racing) meaning that different horses are suited to different racecourses, but now used more generally to mean that different people are suited to different roles; English proverb, late 19th century.

If you can talk, you can sing; if you can walk, you can dance.
often used as an encouragement to undertake something new; African (Shona) proverb.

Inside the forest there are many birds.
people are of many different kinds and abilities ('many birds' here = 'birds of many kinds'); Chinese proverb.

Is Saul also among the prophets?
a rhetorical question asked when someone displays unexpected abilities; from the biblical account (1 Samuel 10:11), in which the young Saul's prophesying became one of the signs that he had been chosen as king of Israel.

Absence

A sow may whistle, though it has an ill mouth for it.
someone not naturally suited to a task will perform it badly;
English proverb, early 19th century.

 # Absence

See also MEETING AND PARTING

Despite the saying that Absence *makes the heart
grow fonder, it is possible that an absent person who
is not present to defend themselves may be blamed for
something, or simply forgotten.*

Absence is the mother of disillusion.
American proverb, mid 20th century.

Absence makes the heart grow fonder.
affection for a person is strengthened by missing them;
English proverb, mid 19th century, derived from a Latin
proverb recorded from the 1st century BC.

Absence of evidence is not evidence of absence.
traditional saying, recorded from the 19th century.

The absent get farther away every day.
Japanese proverb.

He who is absent is always in the wrong.
someone who is not present cannot defend themselves;
English proverb, mid 15th century.

A little absence does much good.

American proverb, mid 20th century.

Out of sight, out of mind.

someone who is not present is easily forgotten; English
proverb, mid 13th century.

Achievement

See also AMBITION, EFFORT, PROBLEMS AND SOLUTIONS,
SUCCESS AND FAILURE

*Effort and aspiration are both needed for achievement,
but even if the goal is reached the outcome may
not be satisfactory, since* While the grass grows,
the steed starves.

Behind an able man there are other able men.

modern saying, said to be a Chinese proverb.

The difficult is done at once.

slogan of the US Armed Forces; recorded earlier as a
comment by the French statesman Charles Alexandre
de Calonne (1734–1802), 'Madam, if a thing is possible,
consider it done; the impossible?—that will be done.'

**The hand will not reach what the heart does not
long for.**

desire is essential for achievement; Welsh proverb.

3

Achievement

He who likes cherries soon learns to climb.
achievement seen as the result of motivation;
German proverb.

In a calm sea every man is a pilot.
apparent achievement may not have been tested by
circumstances; English proverb, recorded from the early
19th century.

***Palmam qui meruit, ferat* [Let him who has won it
bear the palm].**
Latin, adopted by Lord Nelson (1758–1805) as his motto,
from John Jortin *Lusus Poetici* (3rd ed., 1748), 'Ad Ventos'.

***Per ardua ad astra* [Through struggle to the stars].**
Latin, motto of the Mulvany family, quoted and translated
by Rider Haggard in his novel *The People of the Mist* (1894),
and still in use as a motto of the Royal Air Force, having
been approved by King George V in 1913.

Seekers are finders.
success is the result of effort; Persian proverb; compare **Seek
and ye shall find** at ACTION AND INACTION.

Still achieving, still pursuing.
American proverb, mid 20th century, from Henry
Wadsworth Longfellow's adjuration, 'Let us, then, be up
and doing, With a heart for any fate; Still achieving, still

pursuing, Learn to labour and to wait' from the poem
'A Psalm of Life' (1838).

Whatever man has done, man can do.

anything that has been achieved once can be achieved again;
English proverb, mid 14th century.

While the grass grows, the steed starves.

by the time hopes or expectations can be satisfied, it may be
too late; English proverb, mid 14th century.

You cannot have your cake and eat it.

you cannot have things both ways; English proverb, mid
16th century.

Action and Inaction

See also IDLENESS, WORDS AND DEEDS

*While setting out on a planned course is likely to be
rewarded, since we are told that* Seek and ye shall find,
there are also dangers in not thinking things through:
Action without thought is shooting without aim.

Action is worry's worst enemy.

advocating the control of fruitless worry by taking a
decision and acting upon it; American proverb, mid
20th century.

Action and Inaction

Action this day.
annotation as used by Winston Churchill at the Admiralty
in 1940.

Action without thought is shooting without aim.
American proverb, mid 20th century.

A barking dog never bites.
noisy threats often do not presage real danger; English
proverb, 16th century; recorded earlier in French in the
13th century.

**Better to light one candle than to curse the
darkness.**
motto of the American Christopher Society, founded
in 1945.

If it ain't broke, don't fix it.
warning against interference with something that is working
satisfactorily; late 20th-century saying.

If you want something done, ask a busy person.
implying that a busy person is most likely to have
learned how to manage their time efficiently; late 20th
century saying.

It is as cheap sitting as standing.
often used literally; English proverb, mid 17th century.

Action and Inaction

Lookers-on see most of the game.

those who are not participating are able to take an overall view; English proverb, early 16th century.

The road to hell is paved with good intentions.

often used as a comment on well-intentioned actions that have turned out badly; English proverb, late 16th century (earlier forms omit the first three words).

Seek and ye shall find.

an active search for something wanted is likely to be rewarded; English proverb, mid 16th century, from the Bible (Matthew 7:7), 'Ask, and it shall be given you: seek, and ye shall find'; compare **Seekers are finders** at ACHIEVEMENT.

The shrimp that falls asleep is swept away by the current.

if you get distracted you will fall behind; Spanish proverb, *Camarón que se duerme se lo lleva la corriente.*

When in doubt, do nowt.

advising against taking action when one is unsure of one's ground; English proverb, mid 19th century.

7

✾ Adversity

See also MISFORTUNES, SUFFERING

*Adversity is unavoidable, and may in fact be salutary;
a modern saying advises making the best of it:* If life
hands you lemons, make lemonade. *We also, according
at least to a Swahili proverb, have the comfort that
adversity is finite:* After hardship comes relief.

Adversity introduces a man to himself.

modern saying, implying that experiencing difficult
circumstances leads to self-knowledge.

Adversity is the foundation of virtue.

Japanese proverb.

Adversity makes strange bedfellows.

shared difficulties may bring together very different people;
English proverb, mid 19th century.

After hardship comes relief.

African proverb (Swahili).

A dose of adversity is often as needful as a dose of medicine.

American proverb, mid 20th century.

If life hands you lemons, make lemonade.

an adjuration to make the best of difficult circumstances;
late 20th century saying.

Advertising

It is tempting to think of advertising as a modern phenomenon, but the awareness that It pays to advertise *goes back a considerable way, as* Good wine needs no bush *shows.*

Any publicity is good publicity.
it is always preferable to have attention focused on a name than to be unnoticed; English proverb, early 20th century.

Blow your own horn, even if you don't sell a clam.
American saying.

Don't advertise what you can't fulfil.
American proverb, mid 20th century.

Good wine needs no bush.
there is no need to advertise or boast about something of good quality as people will always discover its merits, referring to the bunch of ivy that was formerly the sign of a vintner's shop; English proverb, early 15th century.

It pays to advertise.
American proverb, mid 20th century.

Let's run it up the flagpole and see if anyone salutes it.
recorded as an established expression in the 1960s, suggesting the testing of a new idea or product.

Advice

Caution should be exercised in the giving and receiving of advice: against the warning Don't teach your grandmother to suck eggs, *we have the reminder that* A fool may give a wise man counsel.

Ask advice, but use your common sense.
American proverb, mid 20th century.

Don't teach your grandmother to suck eggs.
a caution against offering advice to the wise and experienced; English proverb, early 18th century.

A fool may give a wise man counsel.
sometimes used as a warning against overconfidence in one's judgement; English proverb, mid 14th century.

Never give advice unless asked.
German proverb.

Night brings counsel.
sometimes used as a warning against overconfidence in one's judgement; English proverb, mid 14th century.

A nod's as good as a wink to a blind horse.
the slightest hint is enough to convey one's meaning in a particular case; English proverb, late 18th century.

A word to the wise is enough.

only a very brief warning is necessary to an intelligent person; English proverb, early 16th century; earlier in Latin *verbum sat sapienti* [a word is sufficient to a wise man].

Age

See also YOUTH

The consensus on the latter part of life is that experience is likely to have brought wisdom: the 'fool at forty' is an exception to the view that The older the ginger the more pungent its flavour.

Age is just a number.

modern saying.

A fool at forty is a fool indeed.

someone who has not learned wisdom by the age of forty will never learn it; in this form from Edward Young's *Universal Passions* (1725), 'Be wise with speed; A fool at forty is a fool indeed'; English proverb, early 16th century.

For the unlearned, old age is winter; for the learned, it is the season of harvest.

Jewish saying.

Age

The fox may grow grey, but never good.
ageing will not change a person's essential nature; English
proverb; compare **The wolf may lose his teeth, but never
his nature** below.

The gods send nuts to those who have no teeth.
opportunities or pleasures often come too late to be
enjoyed; English proverb, early 20th century.

Life begins at forty.
English proverb, mid 20th century, from the title of a book
(1932) by Walter B. Pitkin.

Like fine wine,—gets better with age.
modern saying.

The older the ginger the more pungent its flavour.
older people have more knowledge and experience than the
young; Chinese proverb.

An old horse does not spoil the furrow.
Russian proverb; compare **There's many a good tune
played on an old fiddle** below.

There's many a good tune played on an old fiddle.
someone's abilities do not depend on their being young;
English proverb, early 20th century; compare **An old horse
does not spoil the furrow** above.

There's no fool like an old fool.

often used to suggest that folly in an older person, who should be wiser, is particularly acute; English proverb, mid 16th century.

When an elder dies, it is as if a whole library has burned down.

African proverb.

The wolf may lose his teeth, but never his nature.

age may affect physical strength, but not a dangerous nature; English proverb; compare **The fox may grow grey, but never good** above.

Ambition

See also ACHIEVEMENT, SUCCESS AND FAILURE

Although There is always room at the top *is encouraging, proverbial wisdom warns that the results of pursuing one's goals may be less than happy:* Many go out for wool and come home shorn.

Aut Caesar, aut nihil [Caesar or nothing].

motto coined by Cesare Borgia (1476–1507), and inscribed on his sword.

Ambition

Hasty climbers have sudden falls.
the over-ambitious often fail to take necessary precautions;
English proverb, mid 15th century.

**The higher the monkey climbs the more he shows
his tail.**
the further an unsuitable person is advanced, the more their
inadequacies are apparent; English proverb, late 14th century.

It's ill waiting for dead men's shoes.
often used of a situation in which one is hoping for a
position currently occupied by another; English proverb,
mid 16th century; compare **A bloody war and a sickly
season** at ARMED FORCES.

Many go out for wool and come home shorn.
many who seek to better themselves or make themselves
rich end by losing what they already have; English proverb,
late 16th century.

**The smaller the lizard, the greater its hopes of
becoming a crocodile.**
lack of power may be a spur to ambition; African proverb.

There is always room at the top.
as a response to being advised against joining the
overcrowded legal profession, it is also attributed to the
American politician and lawyer Daniel Webster (1782–1852);
English proverb, early 20th century.

Anger ✿

Losing your temper is unproductive, since Anger
improves nothing but the arch of a cat's back;
*traditional advice suggests using soft answers to deflect
the anger of others, and counting to a hundred to avoid
becoming angry yourself.*

Anger improves nothing but the arch of a cat's back.
American proverb, mid 20th century.

He that will be angry for anything will be angry for nothing.
frequent anger is likely to be prompted by petty reasons;
Scottish proverb.

A little pot is soon hot.
a small person soon becomes angry or passionate; English
proverb, mid 16th century.

A soft answer turneth away wrath.
with allusion to the Bible (Proverbs 15:1); English proverb,
late Middle English.

When angry count a hundred.
advising against precipitate response (the number proposed
varies, and sometimes the advice is '…recite the alphabet');
English proverb, late 16th century.

Apology and Excuses

Making excuses to avoid blame is regarded poorly, since He who excuses himself, accuses himself, *and we are told that* A bad workman blames his tools. *However, it may be right to try to make some kind of explanation:* A bad excuse is better than none.

Apology is only egoism wrong side out.
American proverb, mid 20th century.

A bad excuse is better than none.
It is better to attempt to give some kind of explanation, even a weak one; English proverb, mid 16th century.

A bad workman blames his tools.
often used as a comment on someone's excuses for their lack of success; English proverb, early 17th century, late 13th century in French; (compare **One who cannot dance blames the uneven floor** at DANCE).

Don't make excuses, make good.
American proverb, mid 20th century.

He who excuses himself, accuses himself.
often used to mean that attempts to excuse oneself show a guilty conscience; English proverb, early 17th century.

It is easy to find a stick to beat a dog.

it is easy to find reasons to criticize someone who is
vulnerable; English proverb, mid 16th century.

When you are in a hole, stop digging.

complicated explanations and attempts to exculpate
oneself often make a bad situation worse; late 20th century
saying; often associated with the British Labour politician
Denis Healey.

Appearance

See also BEAUTY, THE BODY

The idea that Appearances are deceptive *is reflected
in a number of sayings. While it may be true that* A
carpenter is known by his chips, *we are cautioned in a
number of ways against judging by the outward look.*

Appearances are deceptive.

the outward form of something may not be a true guide to
its real nature; English proverb, mid 17th century.

A blind man's wife needs no paint.

there is no point in making efforts that cannot be appreciated;
English proverb, mid 17th century.

Appearance

A carpenter is known by his chips.

the nature of a person's occupation or interest is
demonstrated by the traces left behind; English proverb,
mid 16th century.

The cowl does not make the monk.

warning against judging nature and moral character by
appearance; English proverb, late 14th century.

Distance lends enchantment to the view.

English proverb, late 18th century, from the lines
''Tis distance lends enchantment to the view, and robes
the mountain in its azure hue', by Thomas Campbell
(1777–1844) in *Pleasures of Hope* (1799).

Do not judge a tree by its bark.

a warning against making assumptions based on the
outward appearance; Italian proverb.

A fair skin hides seven defects.

Japanese proverb; compare **Beauty is only skin deep**
at BEAUTY.

A good horse cannot be of a bad colour.

colour is not an indicator of a horse's quality; English
proverb, early 17th century.

A man without culture is like a zebra without stripes.

African proverb (Masai).

Merit in appearance is more rewarded than merit itself.

American proverb, mid 20th century.

Never choose your women or linen by candlelight.

warning against being deceived by apparent attractions seen in a poor light; English proverb, late 16th century.

What you see is what you get.

used generally to mean that the function and value of something can be deduced from its outward appearance, and that there are no hidden drawbacks or advantages; late 20th century computing expression, from which the acronym *wysiwyg* derives.

You can't tell a book by its cover.

outward appearance is not a guide to a person's real nature; English proverb, early 20th century.

Architecture

Building is likely to involve expense, although the 17th-century view that Building and marrying of children are great wasters *may be thought too severe.*

The arch never sleeps.

saying, meaning that an arch constantly thrusts against keystone and walls.

Architecture

Building and marrying of children are great wasters.
comparing two major sources of expense for the head of a household; English proverb.

In settling an island, the first building erected by a Spaniard will be a church; by a Frenchman, a fort; by a Dutchman, a warehouse; and by an Englishman, an alehouse.
English proverb, late 18th century.

It is easier to build two chimneys than to maintain one.
the cost of using and maintaining a building may be much greater than the cost of building it; English proverb, mid 16th century.

No good building without a good foundation.
English proverb, late 15th century.

__Si monumentum requiris, circumspice__ [If you seek a monument, gaze around].
Latin inscription in St Paul's Cathedral, London, applied to Sir Christopher Wren, its architect, and attributed to Wren's son.

Argument

See also OPINION

Positive injunctions to avoid quarrelling, such as
Birds in their little nests agree, *are reinforced by*
pragmatic reflections as to the dangers of indulging in
disagreement: While two dogs are fighting for a bone,
a third runs away with it.

Birds in their little nests agree.

used as a direction that young children should not argue
among themselves; a nursery proverb from Isaac Watts
Divine Songs (1715).

Do not argue against the sun.

there is no point in disputing what is obvious; saying, of
Latin origin.

It takes two to make a quarrel.

some responsibility for a disagreement rests with each party
to it; English proverb, early 18th century.

The more arguments you win, the less friends you will have.

American proverb, mid 20th century.

The only thing a heated argument ever produced is coolness.

American proverb, mid 20th century.

The Armed Forces

While two dogs are fighting for a bone, a third runs away with it.
while the attention of two disputants is on their quarrel, they may lose possession of what they are fighting over to a third party; English proverb, late 14th century, which gave rise to the phrase 'bone of contention'.

 # The Armed Forces

See also WARFARE

A number of sayings reflect life within the armed forces over several centuries, from the naval toast A bloody war and a sickly season from the time of the Napoleonic wars, to the advice to soldiers in the Second World War: If it moves, salute it; if it doesn't move, pick it up; and if you can't pick it up, paint it.

The army knows how to gain a victory but not how to make proper use of it.
American proverb, mid 20th century.

An army of stags led by a lion would be more formidable than one of lions led by a stag.
courage and tenacity can be negated by poor leadership, while a strong leader can provide crucial encouragement for weak forces; English military saying, of classical origin.

A bloody war and a sickly season.

naval toast in the time of Nelson, when an increased death rate meant more rapid promotion; compare **It's ill waiting for dead men's shoes** at AMBITION and **a willing foe and sea room** below.

The first duty of a soldier is obedience.

English proverb, mid 19th century.

If it moves, salute it; if it doesn't move, pick it up; and if you can't pick it up, paint it.

1940s military saying.

Old soldiers never die.

English proverb, early 20th century.

Providence is always on the side of the big battalions.

English proverb, early 19th century; a similar thought can be found earlier in other languages, as the words of the Roman senator and historian Tacitus, *'Deos fortioribus adesse* [The gods are on the side of the stronger]', and the comment in a letter of the French soldier and poet the Comte de Bussy Rabutin (1618–93), 'As you know, God is usually on the side of the big squadrons against the small.'

A singing army and a singing people can't be defeated.

American proverb, mid 20th century.

Art

A soldier of the Great War known unto God.
adopted by the War Graves Commission as the standard
epitaph for the unidentified dead of the First World War.

A willing foe and sea room.
naval toast in the time of Nelson (compare **a bloody war
and a sickly season** above).

Your King and Country need you.
1914 recruiting advertisement, showing Lord Kitchener
with pointing finger.

**Your soul may belong to God, but your ass belongs
to the army.**
American saying to new recruits, mid 20th century.

 # Art

*Even a talented painter needs to practise their art:
the advice* Not a day without a line *goes back to the
classical world.*

Every painter paints himself.
Italian proverb, said to be of Renaissance origin.

A good painter can draw a devil as well as an angel.
English proverb, late 16th century.

Not a day without a line.
traditional saying, attributed to the Greek artist Apelles
(fl. 325 BC) by Pliny the Elder.

Autumn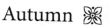

See also SPRING, SUMMER, WINTER

There are notably fewer proverbs about Autumn than the other seasons, and those in use today sound a cautionary note.

All autumns do not fill granaries.
Estonian proverb.

Chickens are counted in the autumn.
Russian proverb; compare **Don't count your chickens before they are hatched** at OPTIMISM, and **May chickens come cheeping** at SPRING.

If you do not sow in the spring, you will not reap in the autumn.
Irish proverb.

September blow soft till the fruit's in the loft.
expressing the hope that fine weather often customary in September will hold until a crop of apples or other fruit has been picked and stored; English proverb, late 16th century.

September dries up wells or breaks down bridges.
traditional saying, suggesting that September can see either drought or flood.

Beauty

See also APPEARANCE, THE BODY

The early 20th-century advertising slogan Beauty is
power *reflects a traditional awareness of the force of
physical attraction, but as far back as the 17th century
we have also been warned that* Beauty is only
skin deep.

Beauty draws with a single hair.

asserting the powerful attraction of a woman's beauty
(often shown as outdoing great physical strength); English
proverb, late 16th century.

Beauty is a good letter of introduction.

American proverb, mid 20th century.

Beauty is in the eye of the beholder.

beauty is not judged objectively, but according to the
beholder's estimation; English proverb, early 17th century.

Beauty is only skin deep.

physical beauty is no guarantee of a good character or
temperament; English proverb, early 17th century; compare
A fair skin hides seven defects at APPEARANCE.

Beauty is power.

advertising slogan for Helena Rubinstein's Valaze Skin
Food, 1904.

Black is beautiful.

slogan of American civil rights campaigners, mid 1960s.

It is the beautiful bird that gets caged.

beauty has its own dangers; Chinese proverb.

Monday's child is fair of face.

first line of a traditional rhyme, mid 19th century (compare qualities associated with birth on other days at entries under GIFTS, SORROW, TRAVEL, and WORK).

Please your eye and plague your heart.

contrasting the pleasure given by the appearance of a beautiful person with the heartache they may cause; English proverb, early 17th century.

The prettiest girl in the world can only give what she has.

French proverb, *La plus belle fille du monde ne peut donner que ce qu'elle a.*

Beginning

See also CHANGE, ENDING

Starting well is important, as we are told that A good beginning makes a good ending, *but it is also wise to consider whether the course on which you are embarking is a wise one:* It is easier to raise the Devil than to lay him.

Beginning

Beginning is easy; continuing is hard.
a good start is not enough, since success requires
pertinacity; modern saying, said to be a Japanese proverb.

First impressions are the most lasting.
English proverb, early 18th century.

The golden rule of life is, make a beginning.
American proverb, mid 20th century.

A good beginning makes a good ending.
getting things right at the outset is likely to ensure success;
English proverb, early 14th century.

It is easier to raise the Devil than to lay him.
sometimes used to mean that it is easier to start a process
than to stop it; English proverb, mid 17th century.

It is the first step that is difficult.
English proverb, late 16th century.

The longest journey begins with a single step.
often used to emphasize how important a single decision
may be; late 20th-century saying, ultimately derived from
words of the Chinese philosopher Lao Tzu (*c.*604–*c.*531 BC)
in the *Tao-te Ching*, 'A tower of nine storeys begins with a
heap of earth. The journey of a thousand *li* starts from
where one stands.'

The sooner begun, the sooner done.
used as a warning against putting off a necessary but
unwanted task; English proverb, late 16th century.

There is always a first time.
English proverb, late 16th century.

Well begun is half done.
emphasizing the importance of a successful beginning
to the completion of a project; English proverb, early
15th century.

Behaviour

See also MANNERS, WORDS AND DEEDS

*While there is a traditional emphasis on the importance
of right action, as in* Do as I say, not as I do, *there is
also a certain scepticism about what may be only the
appearance of good behaviour:* Handsome is as
handsome does.

Be what you would seem to be.
English proverb, late 14th century; earlier in classical
sources, as in *Seven against Thebes* by the Greek tragedian
Aeschylus (*c.*525–456 BC), 'He wishes not to appear but to
be the best.'

Behaviour

By a sweet tongue and kindness, you can drag an elephant by a hair.
Middle Eastern proverb, commonly found in this form in Arabic; the equivalent proverb in Persian has 'drag a snake'.

Cleanliness is next to godliness.
next here means 'immediately following', as in serial order, and is now often used humorously to mean 'the second most desirable quality possible'; English proverb, late 18th century.

Do as I say, not as I do.
often used with an imputation of hypocrisy; English proverb, mid 16th century.

Evil communications corrupt good manners.
proper conduct is harmfully influenced by false information or knowledge; the saying is also sued to assert the deleterious effect of bad example; English proverb, early 15th century, from the Bible (1 Corinthians 15:33).

Fake it 'til you make it.
self-help motto from the 1970s, now often associated with Alcoholics Anonymous.

Good behaviour is the last refuge of mediocrity.
American proverb, mid 20th century.

Handsome is as handsome does.

handsome here referred to chivalrous or genteel behaviour, although it is often popularly taken to refer to good looks; English proverb, late 16th century; compare **Pretty is as pretty does** below.

He is a good dog who goes to church.

good character is shown by moral custom and practice; English proverb, early 19th century.

It is one thing to keep your morals on high plane; it's another to keep up with them.

American proverb, mid 20th century.

Never do evil that good may come of it.

the prospect of a good outcome cannot justify wrongdoing; English proverb, late 16th century.

Pretty is as pretty does.

American proverb, mid 19th century, equivalent of **Handsome is as handsome does** above.

When in Rome, do as the Romans do.

English proverb, late 15th century; ultimately deriving from a passage in a letter of St Ambrose, AD *c*.400, 'When I go to Rome, I fast on Saturday, but here [Milan] I do not. Do you also follow the custom of whatever church you attend, if you do not want to give or receive scandal.'

Belief

See also CERTAINTY AND DOUBT

Belief may relate to religious faith as in Faith will move mountains, *but some traditional sayings deal with more general questions of how you should approach the world around you:* Believe nothing of what you hear, and only half of what you see.

Believe nothing of what you hear, and only half of what you see.

English proverb, mid 19th century; a related Middle English saying warns that you should not believe everything that is said or that you hear.

A believer is a songless bird in a cage.

American proverb, late 19th century.

Believing has a core of unbelieving.

American proverb, mid 19th century.

Don't strain at a gnat, and swallow a camel.

do not make difficulties over a small matter, when you have already accepted something of much greater importance; saying with biblical allusion, to Matthew 23:24, 'Ye blind guides, which strain at a gnat, and swallow a camel.'

Faith will move mountains.
with the help of faith something naturally impossible can be
achieved; English proverb, late 19th century, in allusion to
the Bible (Matthew 17:20, 'If ye have faith as a grain of
mustard seed, ye shall say unto this mountain, Remove
hence to yonder place; and it shall remove').

Pigs may fly, but they are very unlikely birds.
English proverb, mid 19th century.

Seeing is believing.
acceptance of the existence of something depends on actual
demonstration; English proverb, early 17th century.

Birds

*Sayings relating to birds are likely to reflect the
associations of particular species, from the English
magpies whose gathering may foretell sorrow or mirth,
to the rare white heron of New Zealand.*

Birds of prey do not sing.
German proverb.

**The cuckoo comes in April, He sings his song in May;
In the middle of June He changes his tune, And then
he flies away.**
traditional rhyme.

Birds

A mockingbird has no voice of his own.
the mockingbird is known for its mimicry of the calls and
songs of other birds; American proverb, mid 19th century.

**One for sorrow; two for mirth; three for a wedding,
four for a birth.**
a traditional rhyme found in a variety of forms, referring to
the number of magpies seen on a particular occasion;
English proverb, mid 19th century.

**The robin and the wren are God's cock and hen;
the martin and the swallow are God's mate
and marrow.**
there was a traditional belief that the robin and the wren
were sacred birds, and that to harm them in any way would
be unlucky (*marrow* = 'companion'); English proverb, late
18th century.

The swan brings snow on its bill.
the arrival of migrating swans may be the harbinger of
wintry weather; Russian proverb.

The white heron is a bird of a single flight.
the white heron is very rare; Maori proverb.

The Body

See also APPEARANCE, BEAUTY, THE SENSES

Physical characteristics may give a clue to inner qualities, from Cold hands, warm heart *to* The larger the body, the bigger the heart.

Cold hands, warm heart.

an outward sign may contradict an inward reality; English proverb, early 20th century.

The eyes are the window of the soul.

it is in the eyes that a person's true nature may be discerned; English proverb, mid 16th century.

The larger the body, the bigger the heart.

American proverb, mid 20th century.

Books

See also READING, WRITING

While not every book is admirable (A great book is a great evil), *the consensus of proverbial wisdom is in favour of the written word:* A book is like a garden carried in the pocket.

Borrowing

Beware of the man of one book.
warning against the person who places too much
confidence in a single authority; Latin proverb.

A book is like a garden carried in the pocket.
Middle Eastern saying.

A great book is a great evil.
a long book is likely to be verbose and badly written;
English proverb, early 17th century; a contraction of
Callimachus (*c*.305–*c*.240 BC), 'The great book is equal
to a great evil.'

A library is a repository of medicine for the mind.
American proverb, mid 20th century.

 Borrowing
See DEBT AND BORROWING

 British Towns and Regions

*Local pride is an enduring quality, whether expressed in
a traditional saying such as* Kirton was a borough
town when Exon was a vuzzy down, *or a 20th-century
slogan such as* Glasgow's miles better.

Essex stiles, Kentish miles, Norfolk wiles, many a man beguiles.

traditional saying, early 17th century.

From Hell, Hull, and Halifax, good Lord deliver us.

traditional saying, late 16th century.

Glasgow's miles better.

slogan introduced by Provost Michael Kelly, 1980s.

Kirton was a borough town when Exon was a vuzzy down.

on the relative ages of Crediton (*Kirton*) and Exeter (*Exon*); traditional saying.

Lincoln was, London is, and York shall be.

referring to which is the greatest city; traditional saying, late 16th century.

May God in His mercy look down on Belfast.

traditional refrain.

Northamptonshire for squires and spires.

traditional saying, late 19th century.

Peebles for pleasure.

the town of Peebles in the Scottish Borders has traditionally been a favoured holiday resort; traditional saying, late 19th century.

British Towns and Regions

Some places of Kent have health and no wealth, some wealth and no health, some health and wealth.
referring to the north and east part of the county, Romney Marsh, and the Weald respectively; traditional saying, late 16th century.

Sussex won't be druv.
asserting that Sussex people have minds of their own, and cannot be forced against their will (*druv* is a dialect version of *drove*, meaning *driven*); English proverb, early 20th century.

Take away Aberdeen and twelve miles round, and where are you?
Scottish saying, reflecting local pride in the city.

There are more saints in Cornwall than in heaven.
traditional saying, relating to the number of West Country saints known through their local cult.

What Manchester says today, the rest of England says tomorrow.
English proverb, late 19th century, occurring in a variety of forms.

Yorkshire born and Yorkshire bred, strong in the arm and weak in the head.
the names of other (chiefly northern) English counties and towns are also used instead of Yorkshire; English proverb, mid 19th century.

Broadcasting

The early days of broadcasting are associated with the high-minded aspirations of Nation shall speak peace unto nation; *later years brought a somewhat more flippant approach, as in the American advice* Always turn the radio on before you listen to it.

Always turn the radio on before you listen to it.
American saying, mid 20th century.

Assistant heads must roll!
traditional solution to management problems in broadcasting.

Nation shall speak peace unto nation.
motto of the BBC, adapted from the Bible (Isaiah 2:4, 'Nation shall not lift up sword against nation, neither shall they learn war any more') by Montague John Rendall (1862–1950).

To inform, educate, and entertain.
traditional expression of the mission of the BBC, associated with Lord Reith (1889–1971).

Business

See also BUYING AND SELLING

While not all sayings go as far as the modern Business
is war, *there is a consensus in favour of determined
application:* Business before pleasure, *and* Business
neglected is business lost.

Bull markets climb a wall of worry.

signs of recovery from a recession are treated with
scepticism; modern saying.

Business before pleasure.

often used to encourage a course of action; English proverb,
mid 19th century.

Business goes where it is invited and stays where it is well treated.

American proverb, mid 20th century.

Business is like a car: it will not run by itself except downhill.

American proverb, mid 20th century.

Business is war.

modern saying, sometimes said to be of Japanese origin.

Business neglected is business lost.

North American proverb, mid 20th century.

The customer is always right.

English proverb, early 20th century; compare a saying of the Swiss hotel proprietor César Ritz (1850–1918), '*Le client n'a jamais tort* [The customer is never wrong].'

He that cannot abide a bad market does not deserve a good one.

to be successful in business you must be able to deal with bad times as well as good; English proverb, late 17th century.

If you don't speculate, you can't accumulate.

outlay (and some degree of risk) is necessary if real gain is to be achieved; English proverb, mid 20th century.

Keep your own shop and your shop will keep you.

recommending attention to what is essential to one's livelihood; English proverb, early 17th century.

Never try to catch a falling knife.

do not invest in a failing business; figurative use of health and safety advice for caterers.

No cure, no pay.

known principally from its use on Lloyd's of London's Standard Form of Salvage Agreement; English proverb, late 19th century.

Buying and Selling

No penny, no paternoster.
if you want a thing you must pay for it (the allusion is to
priests insisting on being paid for performing services);
English proverb, late 16th century.

Pay beforehand was never well served.
payment in advance removes the incentive to finish the
work; English proverb, late 16th century.

Pile it high, sell it cheap.
slogan coined by Jack Cohen (1898–1979), founder of the
Tesco supermarket chain.

There are tricks in every trade.
the practice of every skill is likely to involve some trickery
or dishonesty; English proverb, mid 17th century.

Trade follows the flag.
commercial development is likely to follow military
intervention; English proverb, late 19th century.

 # Buying and Selling

See also BUSINESS

The warning Let the buyer beware, *drawn ultimately
from the classical world, enshrines a core belief about
the world of commerce. More explicit advice along the
same lines is found in the saying,* The buyer has need
of a hundred eyes, the seller of but one.

The bulls make money, the bears make money, but the hogs get slaughtered.

money can be made through buying or selling stock, but greed is fatal; modern saying.

The buyer has need of a hundred eyes, the seller of but one.

stressing the responsibility of a purchaser to examine the goods on offer; English proverb, mid 17th century.

Buy in the cheapest market and sell in the dearest.

sometimes with an implication of sharp practice; English proverb, late 16th century.

Let the buyer beware.

warning that it is up to a buyer to establish the nature and value of a purchase before completing the transaction; English proverb, early 16th century; the saying is also found in the form of the Latin tag *caveat emptor*.

Sell in May and go away (come back on St Leger's Day).

saying related to the cycle of activity on the London Stock Exchange. May, shortly after the start of the financial year, was traditionally a busy time, but during the summer months trading was slack as Londoners (including stockbrokers) took their holiday breaks away from the capital. The full form of the saying refers to the classic

Buying and Selling

St Leger horse race, taken as marking the end of the English summer social calendar.

You buy land, you buy stones; you buy meat, you buy bones.
every purchase has its drawbacks; English proverb, late 17th century.

Cats

See also DOGS

*Sayings about cats emphasize not only their
independence of humankind, but also their capacity
to survive:* A cat always lands on its feet.

A cat always lands on its feet.
a cat's natural agility typifies its ability to escape from
trouble; traditional saying.

A cat has nine lives.
traditional saying.

A cat may look at a king.
even someone in a lowly position has a right to observe
a person of power and influence; English proverb, mid
16th century.

Feed a dog for three days and he will remember your kindness for three years. Feed a cat for three years and she will forget your kindness in three days.
Japanese proverb.

It is better to feed one cat than many mice.
Norwegian proverb.

Touch not the cat but a glove.
but = without, and the cat referred to here is a wild cat;
Scottish proverb, early 19th century.

Causes and Consequences

Deliberate choice will have a result which may be unwelcome, as in After the feast comes the reckoning. *However, traditional wisdom also emphasizes that something of apparent unimportance may have significant consequences:* The mother of mischief is no bigger than a midge's wing.

After the feast comes the reckoning.

a period of pleasure or indulgence has to be paid for; English proverb, early 17th century, but now chiefly in modern North American use.

As you bake, so shall you brew.

as you begin, so shall you proceed; English proverb, late 16th century.

As you brew, so shall you bake.

your circumstances will be shaped by your own initial actions; English proverb, late 16th century.

As you make your bed, so you must lie upon it.

as you begin, so shall you proceed; English proverb, late 16th century.

As you sow, so you reap.

you will have to endure the consequences of your actions; English proverb, late 15th century; compare **They that sow the wind, shall reap the whirlwind** below.

Causes and Consequences

A fence between makes love more keen.

impediments between lovers are likely to increase fondness;
German proverb.

Good seed makes a bad crop.

something which has a sound basis will do well; English
proverb, mid 16th century.

Great oaks from little acorns grow.

great results may ensue from apparently small beginnings;
English proverb, late 14th century.

He who plants thorns must not expect to gather roses.

Arabic proverb.

**If you see a turtle on a fencepost, it didn't get there
by accident.**

regional American saying.

If you want to see heaven, you have to die yourself.

Indian proverb.

Kill the chicken to scare the monkey.

make an example of those in a weak position to frighten
possible stronger opponents; Chinese saying.

**The mother of mischief is no bigger than a
midge's wing.**

the origin of difficulties can be very small; English proverb,
early 17th century.

Caution

Sow much, reap much; sow little, reap little.
Chinese proverb.

There is reason in the roasting of eggs.
however odd an action may seem, there is a reason for it;
English proverb, mid 17th century.

They that sow the wind, shall reap the whirlwind.
those who have initiated a dangerous course must suffer the
consequences; English proverb, late 16th century; compare
As you sow, so you reap above.

**Who won't be ruled by the rudder must be ruled
by the rock.**
a ship which is not being steered on its course will run on to
a rock; English proverb, mid 17th century.

 # Caution

See also DANGER

*We may put ourselves at risk through lack of caution,
but someone who adheres too closely to the advice*
Better be safe than sorry *may miss out on possible
benefits, since* A cat in gloves catches no mice.

Be careful what you wish for, because you may get it.
modern saying, suggesting that the fulfilment of an unwise
objective may turn out to be unwelcome.

Caution

Better be safe than sorry.

urging the wisdom of taking precautions; English proverb,
mid 19th century.

A bird in the hand is worth two in the bush.

it is better to accept what one has than to try to get
more and risk losing everything; English proverb, mid
15th century.

Call on God, but row away from the rocks.

make an effort to avoid a dangerous situation;
Indian proverb.

A cat in gloves catches no mice.

deliberate restraint and caution (or 'pussyfooting') often
result in failure to achieve anything; English proverb,
late 16th century.

Caution is the parent of safety.

American proverb, early 18th century.

Cross the river by feeling the stones.

Chinese proverb, advising progress through wary
experimentation.

Delhi is far away.

warning that unexpected events may intervene in
apparently dangerous circumstances; Indian proverb,
deriving from the response of the 14th-century Sufi mystic
Nizamuddin Aulia to a threat from the Sultan of Delhi

Caution

(the Sultan in fact died before returning home); compare **God is high above, and the tsar is far away** and **The mountains are high, and the emperor is far away** at GOVERNMENT.

Discretion is the better part of valour.

often used to explain cautious action, and sometimes with allusion to Shakespeare's *1 Henry IV* (1597), 'The better part of valour is discretion'; English proverb, late 16th century.

Don't put all your eggs in one basket.

you should not chance everything on a single venture, but spread the risk; English proverb, mid 17th century.

Don't put up your umbrella before it rains.

do not take defensive action before it becomes necessary; modern saying.

Duck and cover.

US advice in the event of a missile attack, *c.*1950; associated particularly with the children's cartoon character 'Bert the Turtle'.

Full cup, steady hand.

used especially to caution against spoiling a comfortable or otherwise enviable situation by a careless action; English proverb, early 11th century.

He who fights and runs away, lives to fight another day.

English proverb, mid 16th century.

He who has been scalded by hot milk, blows even on cold lassi before drinking it.

lassi = an Indian drink, traditionally based on diluted buttermilk or yoghurt, and usually served chilled; Indian proverb; compare **Once bitten by a snake, a man will be afraid of a piece of rope for three years** below.

He who sups with the devil should have a long spoon.

one should be cautious when dealing with dangerous persons; English proverb, late 14th century.

If you can't be good, be careful.

often used as a humorous warning; English proverb, early 20th century; the same idea is found in 11th-century Latin, *si non caste tamen caute*.

Let sleeping dogs lie.

something which may be dangerous or difficult to handle is better left undisturbed; English proverb, late 14th century; compare **Poke a bush, a snake comes out** below.

Let well alone.

often used as a warning against raising problems which will then be difficult to resolve; English proverb, late 16th

Caution

century; compare **Never trouble trouble till trouble troubles you** below.

Look before you leap.
used to advise caution before committing oneself to a course of action; English proverb, mid 14th century.

The more you stir it [a turd] the worse it stinks.
disturbance of something naturally unpleasant will only make it more disagreeable; English proverb, mid 16th century.

Never trouble trouble till trouble troubles you.
another version of the advice that one should let well alone; English proverb, late 19th century.

Once bitten by a snake, a man will be afraid of a piece of rope for three years.
Chinese proverb; compare **He who has been scalded by hot milk, blows even on cold lassi before drinking it** above, and **Once bitten, twice shy** at EXPERIENCE.

Poke a bush, a snake comes out.
warning against unnecessary disturbance; Japanese proverb; compare **Let sleeping dogs lie** above.

Safe bind, safe find.
something kept securely will be readily found again; English proverb, mid 16th century.

Saw wood and say nothing.

warning against unnecessary disturbance; American proverb, late 19th century.

Second thoughts are best.

it is dangerous to act on one's first impulse without due thought; English proverb, late 16th century.

Steady as she goes!

injunction to hold carefully to the course set; nautical saying.

A stitch in time saves nine.

a small but timely intervention will ensure against the need for much more substantial repair later; English proverb, early 18th century.

Those who play at bowls must look out for rubbers.

one must beware of difficulties associated with a particular activity; *rubber* here is an alteration of *rub*, an obstacle or impediment to the course of a bowl; English proverb, mid 18th century.

Trust, but verify.

Russian proverb, used by President Ronald Reagan during negotiations with the Soviet Union and widely associated with him.

Certainty and Doubt

Trust in Allah, but tie up your camel.
Arab proverb; compare **Put your trust in God, and keep your powder dry** at PRACTICALITY.

We won't make a drama out of a crisis.
advertising slogan for Commercial Union insurance.

 # Certainty and Doubt

See also BELIEF, FAITH, INDECISION

We may be urged to be definite in our views, but proverbially Nothing is certain but death and taxes.

The eyes believe themselves; the ears believe other people.
others may persuade us not to believe the evidence of our own eyes; Greek proverb.

In matters of principle, stand like a rock; in matters of taste, swim with the current.
late 19th-century saying; from the mid 20th century associated with Thomas Jefferson, in the form 'In matters of style, swim with the current; in matters of principle, stand like a rock.'

Nothing is certain but death and taxes.
summarizing what in life is inevitable and inescapable; English proverb, early 18th century.

Chance and Luck

Against the view that Blind chance sweeps the world along, *there are suggestions that there are ways to make your own fortune:* Diligence is the mother of good luck. *Occasionally, too, the right patronage may be helpful:* The Devil looks after his own.

Accidents will happen (in the best regulated families).

the most orderly arrangements cannot prevent accidents from occurring; English proverb, mid 18th century.

Blind chance sweeps the world along.

American proverb, mid 20th century.

The devil looks after his own.

often used to comment on the good fortune of someone undeserving; English proverb, early 18th century.

The devil's children have the devil's luck.

commenting on the good fortune of someone undeserving; English proverb, late 17th century.

Diligence is the mother of good luck.

success results more from application and practice than from good fortune; English proverb, late 16th century.

Chance and Luck

Fools for luck.

a foolish person is traditionally fortunate; English proverb, mid 19th century.

A great fortune depends on luck; a smaller one on diligence.

for outstanding success we need good luck as well as the capacity for hard work; Chinese proverb.

The harder I work, the luckier I get.

modern saying, often as a response to having success attributed to good fortune.

If you want to live and thrive, let the spider run alive.

It was traditionally unlucky to harm a spider or a spider's web; English proverb, mid 19th century.

It is better to be born lucky than rich.

often with the implication that riches can be lost or spent, but that good luck gives one the capacity of improve one's fortunes; English proverb, mid 17th century.

Lightning never strikes the same place twice.

often used as an encouragement that a particular misfortune will not be repeated; English proverb, mid 19th century.

Lucky at cards, unlucky in love.

suggesting that good fortune in gambling is balanced by lack of success in love; English proverb, mid 19th century.

Moses took a chance.
used to urge someone to take a risk; American proverb, mid 20th century.

See a pin and pick it up, all the day you'll have good luck; see a pin and let it lie, bad luck you'll have all day.
extolling the virtues of thrift in small matters; English proverb, mid 19th century.

There is luck in odd numbers.
English proverb, late 16th century.

The third time is the charm.
modern saying; compare **Third time lucky** below.

Third time lucky.
reflecting the idea that three is a lucky number; often used to suggest making another effort after initial failure; English proverb, mid 19th century; compare **The third time is the charm** above.

Throw a lucky man into the sea, and he will come up with a fish in his mouth.
a fortunate person will have further luck; Arabic proverb.

You have two chances, Buckley's and none.
Australian proverb; in Australia, *Buckley's chance* means a slim chance or no chance at all, and is sometimes said to derive from the name of William Buckley (died 1856), who,

despite dire predictions as to his chances of survival, lived
with the Aboriginals for many years.

Change

See also BEGINNING, ENDING

Change may be refreshing (A change is as good as a
rest)*, or tiring* (Three removals are as bad as a fire).
*However, perhaps more importantly, there is an
awareness that some things cannot be changed:* No
matter how long a log floats in the river, it will never
become a crocodile.

Be sure you can better your condition before you make a change.
American proverb, mid 20th century.

A change is as good as a rest.
suggesting that a change of activity can be refreshing;
English proverb, late 19th century.

It is never too late to mend.
one can always try to improve; English proverb, late
16th century.

The leopard does not change his spots.
a person cannot change their essential nature, from the
Bible (Jeremiah 13:23), 'Can the Ethiopian change his skin,

or the leopard his spots?'; English proverb, mid 16th century; compare **By seeing one spot, you know the entire leopard** at CHARACTER.

Never say never.

used as a warning against over-confidence that circumstances cannot change; late 20th century saying; compare **Never is a long time** and TIME.

New brooms sweep clean.

often used in the context of someone newly appointed to a post who is making changes in personnel and procedures; English proverb, mid 16th century.

New lords, new laws.

new authorities are likely to change existing rules; English proverb, mid 16th century.

No matter how long a log floats in the river, it will never become a crocodile.

essential characteristics will not change; African proverb; compare **Feeding a snake with milk will not change its poisonous nature** at CHARACTER.

No more Mr Nice Guy.

said to assert that one will no longer be amiable or cooperative; mid 20th-century saying.

Nothing is for ever.

late 20th-century saying.

Change

Other times, other manners.
used in resignation or consolation; English proverb, late
16th century.

Out with the old, in with the new.
modern saying.

Semper eadem.
Latin, meaning 'Ever the same', the motto of Elizabeth I
(1533–1603).

There are no birds in last year's nest.
circumstances have changed, and former opportunities are
no longer there; English proverb, early 17th century.

Three removals are as bad as a fire.
moving house is so disruptive and unsettling, that the
effects of doing it three times are as devastating as a house
fire; English proverb, mid 18th century.

Times change and we with time.
we adapt in response to changes in the world around us;
English proverb, late 16th century.

**To change, and change for the better, are two
different things.**
German proverb.

Variety is the spice of life.

English proverb, late 18th century, originally with allusion
to William Cowper's *The Task* (1785), 'Variety's the very
spice of life,/That gives it all its flavour.'

When the music changes, so does the dance.

a reminder that we need to change with the times;
African proverb.

**When the wind of change blows, some build walls,
others build windmills.**

modern saying, sometimes claimed to be an old Chinese
proverb, but found only from the late 20th century.

You can't put new wine in old bottles.

often used in relation to the introduction of new ideas or
practices; English proverb, early 20th century, from the
Bible (Matthew 9:17), 'Neither do men put new wine into
old bottles: else the bottles break, and the wine runneth out,
and the bottles perish.'

Character

See also THE HUMAN RACE, REPUTATION

*A number of sayings reflect on essential characteristics
displayed through outward appearance:* By seeing one
spot, you know the entire leopard. *However, there is
some warning against making too ready assumptions*

Character

from outer circumstances: The man who is born in a stable is not a horse.

An ape's an ape, a varlet's a varlet, though they be clad in silk or scarlet.
inward nature cannot be overcome by outward show; English proverb, mid 16th century.

A bad penny always turns up.
referring to the inevitable return of an unwanted or disreputable person; English proverb, mid 18th century.

The bee sucks honey where the spider sucks poison.
we make the best or worst of things depending on our own nature; English proverb.

Better a good cow than a cow of a good kind.
good character is more important than distinguished lineage; English proverb, early 20th century.

By seeing one spot, you know the entire leopard.
Japanese proverb; compare **The leopard does not change his spots** at CHANGE.

Cet animal est très méchant: Quand on l'attaque, il se défend ['This animal is very vicious: when attacked, it defends itself'].
ironic recognition that a natural urge to defend yourself may be interpreted as aggression; French proverb.

Character is what we are; reputation is what others think we are.

American proverb, mid 20th century.

The child is the father of the man.

asserting the unity of character from childhood to adult life; English proverb, early 19th century; from Wordsworth's lines 'The Child is father of the Man; And I could wish my days to be Bound each to each by natural piety.'

Eagles don't catch flies.

great or important persons do not concern themselves with trifling matters; English proverb, mid 16th century.

Feeding a snake with milk will not change its poisonous nature.

kindness will not alter a bad character; Indian proverb; compare **No matter how long a log floats in the river, it will never become a crocodile** at CHANGE.

Iron sharpens iron.

friends of the same calibre can strengthen one another; modern saying, with biblical allusion to Proverbs 27:17, 'Iron sharpeneth iron; so a man sharpeneth the countenance of his friend.'

It takes all sorts to make a world.

often used in recognition that a particular group may encompass a wide range of character and background; English proverb, early 17th century.

Character

Like a fence, character cannot be strengthened by whitewash.
American proverb, mid 20th century.

The man who is born in a stable is not a horse.
sometimes attributed to the Duke of Wellington, who asserted that being born in Ireland did not make him Irish; English proverb, mid 19th century.

Once a —, always a —.
a particular way of life produces traits that cannot be eradicated; English proverb, early 17th century; compare **Once a priest, always a priest** at CLERGY.

The same fire that hardens the egg melts the butter.
different people will react in different ways to the same experiences; modern saying, but the idea is found in the early 17th century in the words of Francis Bacon (1561–1623), 'In one and the same fire, clay grows hard and wax melts.'

A sleeping fox counts hens in his dreams.
particular characteristics affect all we do; Russian proverb.

Still waters run deep.
now commonly used to assert that a placid exterior hides a passionate nature; English proverb, early 15th century; compare **Where the river is deepest, it makes the least noise** below.

A stream cannot rise above its source.

used to suggest that a person's natural level is set by their
ultimate origin; English proverb, mid 17th century.

The style is the man.

one's chosen style reflects one's essential characteristics;
English proverb, early 20th century, although a similar
thought is found earlier in French, in the Comte de Buffon's
words to the Académie Française on 25 August 1753,
'These things [subject matter] are external to the man;
style is the man.'

**There's many a good cock come out of a
tattered bag.**

something good may emerge from unpromising
surroundings (the reference is to cockfighting); English
proverb, late 19th century.

The tree is known by its fruit.

a person is judged by what they do and produce; English
proverb, early 16th century.

What can you expect from a pig but a grunt?

used rhetorically of coarse or boorish behaviour; English
proverb, mid 18th century.

What's bred in the bone will come out in the flesh.

inherent characteristics will in the end become apparent;
English proverb, late 15th century.

Charity

When the going gets tough, the tough get going.
pressure acts as a stimulus to the strong; English
proverb, mid 20th century, often used by Joseph Kennedy
(1888–1969) as an injunction to his children.

Where the river is deepest, it makes the least noise.
Italian proverb; compare **Still waters run deep** above.

**You cannot dream yourself into a character, you
must forge one out for yourself.**
American proverb, mid 20th century.

 Charity

See also GENEROSITY

Together with praise for the natural springs of charity,
The roots of charity are always green, *there may be
a note of self-interest:* Keep your own fish-guts for
your own sea-maws.

Charity begins at home.
you should look first to needs in your immediate vicinity;
English proverb, late 14th century.

**Charity is not a bone you throw to a dog but a bone
you share with a dog.**
the recipient of one's charity should not be treated as an
inferior; American proverb, mid 20th century.

Charity sees the need, not the cause.

true charity succours need regardless of whether the
needy person is responsible for their own situation;
German proverb.

**Give a man a fish, and you feed him for a day;
show him how to catch fish, and you feed him
for a lifetime.**

mid 20th century saying, perhaps deriving from a Chinese
saying; compare **Who teaches me for a day, is my father
for a lifetime** at TEACHING.

**If everyone gives a thread, the poor man will
have a shirt.**

a little from each person makes an effective whole;
Russian proverb.

Keep your own fish-guts for your own sea-maws.

any surplus product should be offered first to those in need
who are closest to you; Scottish proverb, early 18th century.

The roots of charity are always green.

true generosity constantly renews itself; American proverb,
mid 20th century.

Service is the rent we pay for our room on earth.

modern saying, deriving from the admission ceremony of
Toc H, a society, originally of ex-servicemen and women,
founded by Tubby Clayton (1885–1972) after the First

World War to promote Christian fellowship and
social service.

Children

See also THE FAMILY, PARENTS, YOUTH

*Changes in attitude have moved the focus on
child-rearing from the repressive* Children should be
seen and not heard *and* Spare the rod, and spoil the
child *to the duty of society to nurture as expressed by
the African saying,* It takes a village to raise a child.

**And the child that is born on the Sabbath day,
Is bonny, and blithe, and good and gay.**
line from a traditional rhyme (compare qualities associated
with birth on other days at entries under BEAUTY, GIFTS,
SORROW, TRAVEL, and WORK).

**The art of being a parent consists of sleeping when
the baby isn't looking.**
American proverb, mid 20th century.

Children: one is one, two is fun, three is a houseful.
American proverb, mid 20th century.

Children should be seen and not heard.
originally applied specifically to (young) women; English
proverb, early 15th century.

It takes a village to raise a child.

many in the community have a role in a child's
development; African proverb (Yoruba).

**Little children, little sorrows; big children,
great sorrows.**

even when grown up, children are likely to be a source of
concern to their parents; Danish proverb.

No moon, no man.

recording the traditional belief that a child born at the time
of the new moon or just before its appearance will not live
to grow up; English proverb, late 19th century.

Spare the rod and spoil the child.

the result of not disciplining a child is to spoil it; English
proverb, early 11th century, sometimes with allusion to
the Bible (Proverbs 13:24), 'He that spareth his rod hateth
his son.'

Choice

See also INDECISION

Choice may be inevitable, as in A door must be either
shut or open, *but it is noticeable how often the view is
that we find ourselves choosing between unpalatable
options:* Small choice in rotten apples.

Choice

Better red than dead.
slogan of nuclear disarmament campaigners, late 1950s.

Different strokes for different folks.
different ways of doing something are appropriate for
different people (the saying is of US origin, and *strokes*
here means 'comforting gestures of approval'); late
20th-century saying.

A door must be either shut or open.
said of two mutually exclusive alternatives; English proverb,
mid 18th century.

He that has a choice has trouble.
choosing between two things or persons may cause
difficulties; American proverb, mid 20th century.

No man can serve two masters.
English proverb, early 14th century.

The obvious choice is usually a quick regret.
selection on outward appearance alone soon disappoints;
American proverb, mid 20th century.

Of two evils choose the less.
English proverb, late 14th century.

Small choice in rotten apples.
if all options are unpalatable there is little choice to be had;
English proverb, late 16th century.

They offered death so you would be happy with a fever.

a worse possibility makes something inherently unwelcome acceptable; Persian proverb.

You pays your money and you takes your choice.

said when there is little or nothing to choose between two options; English proverb, mid 19th century.

The Christian Church

See also CLERGY, GOD, RELIGION

The essential strength of the Church is seen in its capacity to withstand persecution: The church is an anvil which has worn out many hammers.

The blood of the martyrs is the seed of the Church.

persecution causes the Church to grow; English proverb, mid 16th century, perhaps ultimately deriving from the *Apologeticus* of the Roman theologian Tertullian (*c.* AD 160–*c.*225), 'As often as we are mown down by you, the more we grow in numbers; the blood of Christians is the seed.

The Christian Church

Christ has no body now on earth but yours, no hands but yours, no feet but yours, yours are the eyes through which he looks compassion on this world, yours are the feet with which he is to go about doing good.

modern saying, often attributed to St Teresa of Ávila (1512–82), but not found in her writings.

The Christians to the lions!

saying reported by the Roman theologian Tertullian (*c.* AD 160–*c.*225) in his *Apologeticus*, 'If the Tiber rises, if the Nile does not rise, if the heavens give no rain, if there is an earthquake, famine, or pestilence, straightway the cry is…'

The church is an anvil which has worn out many hammers.

the passive strength of Christianity will outlast aggression; English proverb, mid 19th century.

A church is God between four walls.

American proverb, mid 20th century.

Meat and mass never hindered man.

indicating human need for physical and spiritual sustenance; English proverb, early 17th century.

The nearer the church, the farther from God.

sometimes used to indicate a lack of true spirituality where it is most likely to be found; English proverb, early 14th century.

You can't build a church with stumbling-blocks.

members of a church need to work together in fellowship;
American proverb, mid 20th century.

Christmas

*Sayings about Christmas give particular emphasis to
preparations for celebration, from the gifts appropriate
to the Twelve Days to the anticipated feasting:*
Christmas is coming, and the goose is getting fat.

**Christmas comes but once a year, and when it
comes it brings good cheer.**

traditional saying, going back to the 16th century.

Christmas is coming, and the goose is getting fat.

from a traditional rhyme, recorded from the 19th century
(goose was traditional Christmas fare).

**Christmas with the family, Easter with whomever
you want.**

Italian proverb, *Natale con i tuoi, Pasqua con chi vuoi.*

A green Yule makes a fat churchyard.

a mild winter is traditionally unhealthy (*Yule* is an archaic
term for Christmas); English proverb, mid 17th century.

Only — shopping days to Christmas.
the imminence of Christmas expressed in
commercial terms.

 # Circumstance and Situation

See also CHANGE

*It is as well to come to terms with circumstances, a
consensus expressed in the advice offered by the Indian
proverb,* If you live in the river, you should make
friends with the crocodile.

**Although the branch is broken off, the
trunk remains.**
damage, while unpleasant, is not necessarily disastrous;
Maori saying.

Circumstances alter cases.
a general principle may be modified in the light of
particular circumstances; English proverb, late
17th century.

**If you do not know where you have been, you
cannot know where you are going.**
understanding of your own situation is essential for
effective action; African proverb.

Circumstance and Situation

If you live in the river, you should make friends with the crocodile.
Indian proverb.

May you live in interesting times.
used ironically, as eventful times are often dangerous or unpleasant; modern saying, said to derive from a Chinese curse, but likely to be apocryphal.

New circumstances, new controls.
American proverb, mid 20th century.

No rose without a thorn.
even the pleasantest circumstances have their drawbacks; English proverb, mid 15th century.

One day honey, one day onions.
Arab proverb.

One man's loss is another man's gain.
often said by the gainer in self-congratulation; English proverb, early 16th century.

A rolling stone gathers no moss.
used to imply that someone who does not settle down will not prosper, or form lasting ties; English proverb, mid 14th century.

Cities

There's a time and place for everything.
often used as a warning against doing or saying something at a particular time or in a particular situation; English proverb, early 16th century.

There's no great loss without some gain.
said in consolation or resignation; English proverb, mid 17th century.

The wheel has come full circle.
the situation has returned to what it was in the past, as if completing a cycle, with reference to Shakespeare's *King Lear* 'The wheel is come full circle.'

 # Cities

See TOWNS AND CITIES

 # Clergy

See also THE CHRISTIAN CHURCH

Sayings relating to the clerical profession include the rather bleak assessment of the likely pressure on a cleric's family: Clergyman's sons always turn out badly. *However, there is no going back:* Once a priest, always a priest.

Clergymen's sons always turn out badly.

the implication is that the weight of expectation on clergymen's children is often itself damaging; English proverb, late 19th century.

Like people, like priest.

English proverb, late 16th century; from the Bible (Hosea 4:9), 'And there shall be like people, like priest.'

Nobody is born learned; bishops are made of men.

American proverb, mid 20th century.

Once a priest, always a priest.

English proverb, mid 19th century; compare **Once a —, always a —** at CHARACTER.

Computing

See also TECHNOLOGY

Sayings about the world of computing date from early days of the technology, when the instruction Do not fold, spindle or mutilate *was an important warning. However, some sayings are timeless:* Garbage in, garbage out *remains true through all developments.*

Do not fold, spindle or mutilate.

instruction on punched cards (1950s, and in differing forms from the 1930s).

Computing

Garbage in, garbage out.
in computing, incorrect or faulty input will always cause poor output; mid 20th century saying.

If you can't do it in Fortran, do it in assembly language. If you can't do it in assembly language, it's not worth doing.
saying on computer programming (*Fortran* = a high-level programming language used especially for scientific calculations).

It's not a bug, it's a feature.
bug = an error in a computer program or system; late 20th-century saying.

No manager ever got fired for buying IBM.
IBM advertising slogan.

There is no patch for stupid.
21st-century saying relating to cybersecurity, implying that the human element is the weakest part of any system.

To err is human but to really foul things up requires a computer.
late 20th-century saying; compare **to err is human (to forgive divine)** at MISTAKES.

Conscience

See also FORGIVENESS

Proverbial wisdom tends to dwell on the uncomfortable effects of a bad conscience. While A clean conscience is a good pillow, *permitting easy sleep, awareness of guilt makes the waking life unpleasant:* Evil doers are evil dreaders.

A clean conscience is a good pillow.

a clear conscience enables its possessor to sleep soundly; English proverb, early 18th century.

Conscience gets a lot of credit that belongs to cold feet.

American proverb, mid 20th century.

Do right and fear no man.

English proverb, mid 15th century.

Evil doers are evil dreaders.

someone engaged in wrongdoing is likely to be nervous and suspicious of others; English proverb, mid 16th century.

A guilty conscience needs no accuser.

awareness of one's own guilt has the same effect as an accusation; English proverb, late 14th century.

Let your conscience be your guide.

American proverb, mid 20th century.

Consequences

A quiet conscience sleeps in thunder.
someone with an untroubled conscience will sleep undisturbed whatever the noise; English proverb, late 16th century.

Consequences

See CAUSES AND CONSEQUENCES

Cooking

See also EATING, FOOD

Good equipment is important (A cook is no better than her stove), *but you cannot always judge by outward appearances:* All are not cooks who sport white caps and carry long knives.

All are not cooks who sport white caps and carry long knives.
American proverb, mid 20th century.

A cook is no better than her stove.
American proverb, mid 20th century.

Fish, to taste good, must swim three times—in water, in butter, and in wine.
the best way to cook fish; Polish proverb.

God sends meat, but the Devil sends cooks.

anything which is in itself good or useful may be spoiled or
perverted by the use to which it is put; English proverb, mid
16th century.

It is a poor cook that cannot lick his own fingers.

a good cook assesses their food with their own sense of
taste; English proverb.

Keep one eye on the frying-pan, and one on the cat.

Italian proverb.

Cooperation ❀

*Sayings about cooperation emphasize the positive side
of working with others, as in* When spider webs unite,
they can tie up a lion. *However, the dangers of not
cooperating are also considered:* If you don't believe in
cooperation, watch what happens to a wagon when
one wheel comes off.

All arts are brothers; each is a light to the other.

American proverb, mid 19th century.

A chain is no stronger than its weakest link.

often used when identifying a particular point of vulnerability;
English proverb, mid 19th century; compare **You are the
weakest link ... goodbye** at STRENGTH AND WEAKNESS.

Cooperation

Cross the river in a crowd, and the crocodile won't eat you.
Madagascar saying.

Dog does not eat dog.
people of the same profession should not attack each other;
English proverb, mid 16th century.

Each of us at a handle of the basket.
Maori proverb.

Every little helps.
English proverb, early 17th century.

Four eyes see more than two.
two people are more observant than one alone; English
proverb, late 16th century.

Hawks will not pick out hawks' eyes.
powerful people from the same group will not attack one
another; English proverb, late 16th century.

**He who travels fast, travels alone, and he who
travels far, travels in the company of others.**
African proverb.

**If you don't believe in cooperation, watch what
happens to a wagon when one wheel comes off.**
American proverb, mid 20th century.

If you think cooperation is unnecessary, just try running your car a while on three wheels.

American proverb, mid 20th century.

It takes two to make a bargain.

often used to imply that both parties must be prepared to give some ground; English proverb, late 16th century.

It takes two to tango.

meaning that a cooperative venture requires a contribution from both participants; mid 20th-century saying, from the 1952 song by Al Hoffman and Dick Manning.

Little birds that can sing and won't sing must be made to sing.

those who refuse to obey or cooperate will be forced to do so; English proverb, late 17th century.

Many hands make light work.

often used as an encouragement to join in with assistance; English proverb, mid 14th century.

One good turn deserves another.

English proverb, early 15th century.

One hand washes the other.

referring to cooperation between two closely linked persons or organizations; English proverb, late 16th century.

Cooperation

A single arrow is easily broken, but not ten in a bundle.
when people combine, they can resist attack;
Japanese proverb.

A single bracelet does not jingle.
to make an effect we need the help of others; African proverb.

There is honour among thieves.
sometimes used ironically; English proverb, early
19th century.

A trouble shared is a trouble halved.
discussing a problem will lessen its impact; English proverb,
mid 20th century.

Union is strength.
English proverb, mid 17th century; *unity* is a popular
alternative for *union*, especially when used as a
trade-union slogan.

United we stand, divided we fall.
a watchword of the American Revolution, English proverb,
late 18th century.

We live in each other's shadow.
Irish proverb.

When spider webs unite, they can tie up a lion.
African proverb.

When the lips are gone, the teeth are cold.
Chinese proverb.

**With your food basket, and with my food basket,
the guest will have enough.**
Maori proverb.

Corruption ✳

Sayings such as A golden key can open any door
*remind us that there is always likely to be someone who
is open to bribery—and that the practice may spread,
given that* The rotten apple injures its neighbour.

Corruption will find a dozen alibis for its evil deeds.
American proverb, mid 20th century.

Every man has his price.
everyone is susceptible to the right bribe; English proverb,
mid 18th century.

A golden key can open any door.
any access is guaranteed if enough money is offered; English
proverb, late 16th century.

If gold rusts, what will iron do?
if someone of admirable character succumbs to temptation,
what is likely to happen to a person of less upright
character; English proverb.

It's not what you know, it's who you know.

stressing the importance of personal influence; late 20th
century saying.

The rotten apple injures its neighbour.

often used to mean that one corrupt person in an organization
is likely to affect others; English proverb, mid 14th century.

When money speaks, the truth keeps silent.

Russian proverb.

Countries and Peoples

*Sayings about countries and peoples may reflect either
a cherished self-image (An Englishman's word is his
bond), or a less flattering opinion from someone who
does not belong to the people concerned:* Scratch a
Russian and you find a Tartar.

Advance Australia.

catchphrase used as a patriotic slogan or motto, mid 19th
century onwards; the national anthem of Australia (officially
adopted in 1984) includes the lines, 'In joyful strains then
let us sing Advance Australia fair.'

A mare usque ad mare.

Latin, meaning 'From sea unto sea'; motto of Canada,
taken from the Bible (Psalm 72), 'He shall have dominion

also from sea to sea, and from the river unto the ends of the earth.'

America is a tune. It must be sung together.
American proverb, mid 20th century.

Australians wouldn't give a XXXX for anything else.
advertising slogan for Castlemaine lager, 1986 onwards.

England is the paradise of women, the hell of horses, and the purgatory of servants.
English proverb, late 16th century.

England's difficulty is Ireland's opportunity.
associated with the aspirations of Irish nationalism; English proverb, mid 19th century.

An Englishman's word is his bond.
a promise given is regarded as having the force of a legal agreement; English proverb, early 16th century.

Every land has its own law.
Scottish proverb, early 17th century, used to emphasize the individuality of a nation or group.

Every Turk is born a soldier.
Turkish saying.

God made the world, but the Dutch made Holland.
traditional saying, recorded from the 19th century.

The Country and the Town

Good Americans when they die go to Paris.
coinage attributed to Thomas Gold Appleton (1812–84);
American proverb, mid 19th century.

It is a striking coincidence that the word American ends in *can*.
American proverb, mid 20th century.

A nation without a language is a nation without a heart.
Welsh proverb.

Scratch a Russian and you find a Tartar.
if a person is harmed their real national character will be
revealed; English proverb, early 19th century.

 # The Country and the Town

*The contrast between urban and rural life embodies
what is often seen as a key cultural division.*

An everyday story of country folk.
traditional summary of the BBC's long-running radio soap
opera *The Archers*.

God made the country and man made the town.
contrasting rural and urban life; English proverb, mid
17th century, in this form from William Cowper's poem
The Task (1785).

If you have not lived in the country, you do not know what hardship means.

contrasting rural and urban poverty; Chinese proverb.

You can take the boy out of the country but you can't take the country out of the boy.

even when a person moves away from the place they were brought up in, they retain its essential manners and customs; English proverb, mid 20th century.

Courage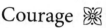

See also DANGER, FEAR

Courage may be admirable itself, but proverbial wisdom also stresses the practical advantages that it may bring: Fortune favours the brave.

Attack is the best form of defence.

English proverb, late 18th century; compare **The best defence is a good offence** below.

The best defence is a good offence.

late 20th-century American version of **Attack is the best form of defence** above.

A bully is always a coward.

English proverb, early 19th century.

Courage

Courage is fear that has said its prayers.

American proverb, mid 20th century.

Courage without conduct is like a ship without ballast.

American proverb, mid 20th century.

Don't cry before you're hurt.

sometimes used as a warning against appealing for sympathy on the assumption of an unpleasant outcome; English proverb, mid 16th century.

Faint heart never won fair lady.

often used as an encouragement to action; English proverb, mid 16th century.

For every Pharaoh there is a Moses.

a liberator will arise against every oppressor; Middle Eastern proverb.

Fortune favours the brave.

a person who acts bravely is likely to be successful; English proverb, late 14th century, originally often with allusion to *Phormio* by the Roman comic dramatist Terence, 'Fortune assists the brave', and Virgil *The Aeneid*, 'Fortune assists the bold.'

None but the brave deserve the fair.

English proverb, late 17th century, from Dryden's poem *Alexander's Feast* (1697), 'None but the brave deserves the fair.'

You never know what you can do till you try.
often used as encouragement to the reluctant; English
proverb, early 19th century.

Crime and Punishment

See also GUILT, JUSTICE, THE LAW, MURDER

From Ill gotten goods never thrive *in the 16th century,
to* Crime doesn't pay *in the 20th century, there is a
consensus that wrongdoing is unlikely benefit the
perpetrator—even if society does not follow the kind of
draconian practice enshrined in the recommendation,*
Hang a thief when he's young, and he'll no steal
when he's old.

A conservative is a liberal who's been mugged.
American saying, 1980s.

Crime doesn't pay.
American proverb, early 20th century; a slogan of the FBI
and the cartoon detective Dick Tracy.

Crime leaves a trail like a water beetle.
Malay proverb.

Crime must be concealed by crime.
American proverb, mid 20th century.

Crime and Punishment

Hang a thief when he's young, and he'll no steal when he's old.
Scottish proverbial saying, early 19th century.

If there were no receivers, there would be no thieves.
English proverb, late 14th century.

Ill gotten goods never thrive.
something which is acquired dishonestly is unlikely to be the basis of lasting prosperity; English proverb, early 16th century.

Little thieves are hanged, but great ones escape.
sufficient power and influence can ensure that a wrongdoer is not punished; English proverb, mid 17th century.

Opportunity makes a thief.
often used to imply that the carelessness of the person who is robbed has contributed to the crime; English proverb, early 13th century.

Three strikes and you're out.
referring to legislation which provides that an offender's third felony is punishable by life imprisonment or other severe sentence; deriving from the terminology of baseball, in which a batter who has had three strikes, or three fair opportunities of hitting the ball, is out; late 20th-century saying.

When thieves fall out, honest men come by their own.

meaning that it is through thieves quarrelling over their stolen goods that they are likely to be caught, and the goods recovered; English proverb, mid 16th century.

You'll die facing the monument.

warning of the end of a life of crime; in Glasgow, prisoners were hanged facing Nelson's Monument on Glasgow Green; Scottish proverb.

Crises

Sayings on this topic focus on how to meet a crisis, whether by 'keeping calm' or taking more active measures.

Any port in a storm.

when one is in trouble or difficulty, support or shelter from any source is welcome; English proverb, mid 18th century.

Keep calm and carry on.

poster designed by the Ministry of Information in 1939 but not used in the Second World War; rediscovered and popularized in the early 21st century.

Criticism

Never waste a good crisis.
modern saying in various forms, often linked with the
advice 'Never let a serious crisis go to waste' of
Rahm Emmanuel, Chief of Staff in Barack Obama's
first administration.

**When disaster strikes and all hope is gone, get
down on your knees and pray for Shackleton.**
paraphrase of Apsley Cherry-Garrard's tribute to the
Antarctic explorer Ernest Shackleton (1874–1922) by
British geologist Raymond Priestley (1886–1974) in a
lecture 'Twentieth Century Man against Antarctica' (1950).

 # Criticism

See also LIKES AND DISLIKES

*While self-examination can be a wholesome discipline,
we should not be too ready to criticize others:*
Don't judge a man till you've walked two moons in
his moccasins.

The best place for criticism is in front of your mirror.
judge yourself before others; American proverb, mid
20th century.

Criticism is something you can avoid by saying nothing, doing nothing, and being nothing.

abstaining from criticism will result in complete inaction; American proverb, mid 20th century.

Don't judge a man till you've walked two moons in his moccasins.

warning against judging without understanding circumstances; modern saying, said to be of Native American origin.

Custom and Habit

Sayings about custom tend towards the negative: there is a perception that enshrined practice is likely to lead to someone being less able to deal with changes: You can't teach an old dog new tricks.

A bad custom is like a good cake, better broken than kept.

we should use our judgement to decide whether a custom is worthy of respect; English proverb.

Custom is mummified by habit and glorified by law.

American proverb, mid 20th century.

Habits are cobwebs at first, and cables at last.

traditional saying, recorded from the 19th century.

Custom and Habit

Old habits die hard.
it is difficult to break long-established habits; English
proverb, mid 18th century.

Sow an act, and reap a habit.
recommending the development of good practice;
English proverb.

What is new cannot be true.
used to imply that innovation is less soundly based than
custom which has been proved by experience; English
proverb, mid 17th century.

You cannot shift an old tree without it dying.
often used to suggest the risk involved in moving an elderly
person who has lived in the same place for many years;
English proverb, early 16th century.

You can't teach an old dog new tricks.
someone who is already set in their ways is not able to
learn new ways of doing things; English proverb, mid
16th century.

Dance

Dancing may require some innate ability—You need more than dancing shoes to be a dancer—*but dancing is still seen as a natural form of expression:* We're fools whether we dance or not, so we might as well dance.

One who cannot dance blames the uneven floor.
Indian proverb; compare **A bad workman blames his tools** at APOLOGY AND EXCUSES.

We're fools whether we dance or not, so we might as well dance.
modern saying, claimed to be a Japanese proverb.

When you go to dance, take heed whom you take by the hand.
English proverb, early 17th century.

You need more than dancing shoes to be a dancer.
American proverb, mid 20th century.

Danger

See also CAUTION, COURAGE, FEAR

A risk may be taken rightly, since The post of honour is the post of danger, *but peril can result from overconfidence:* When the lion shows its teeth, don't assume that it is smiling.

Danger

Adventures are to the adventurous.
the person who wants exciting things to happen must take
the initiative; English proverb, mid 19th century.

A common danger causes common action.
American proverb, mid 20th century.

Heaven protects children, sailors, and drunken men.
often used (in a number of variant forms) to imply that
someone unable to look after themselves has been
undeservedly lucky; English proverb, mid 19th century.

He who rides a tiger is afraid to dismount.
once a dangerous or troublesome venture is begun, the
safest course is to carry it through to the end; English
proverb, late 19th century.

If you play with fire you get burnt.
if you involve yourself with something potentially
dangerous you are likely to be hurt; English proverb, late
19th century.

It is the calm and silent water that drowns the man.
the greatest danger may be concealed beneath an innocent
appearance; African proverb.

**Just when you thought it was safe to go back in
the water.**
advertising copy for the film *Jaws 2* (1978), featuring the
return of the great white shark to bathing beaches.

Light the blue touch paper and retire immediately.
traditional instruction for lighting fireworks.

More than one yew bow in Chester.
you may escape danger once, but not a second time (*Chester* representing the English, the traditional enemy for Wales); Welsh proverb.

The post of honour is the post of danger.
English proverb, mid 16th century.

Three things are not to be trusted; a cow's horn, a dog's tooth, and a horse's hoof.
one may be gored, bitten, or kicked, without warning; English proverb, late 14th century.

We have no friends but the mountains.
inhospitable terrain is more reliable than an ally as a source of safety; Kurdish proverb.

When the lion shows its teeth, don't assume that it is smiling.
a warning sign from a source of power should not be taken lightly; Arab proverb.

When you ask a bear to dance, you can't stop just because you are tired.
modern American saying.

Death

Who dares wins.
motto of the British Special Air Service regiment;
from 1942.

The wolves are well fed and the sheep are safe.
when a predator's immediate needs have been satisfied,
there is temporary safety for the prey; Russian proverb.

Women and children first.
order given on a ship in difficulty, indicating that women
and children should be allowed onto the lifeboats before
men; in allusive (and often humorous) use, warning of a
risky or unpleasant situation; from the mid 19th century.

 # Death

See also MOURNING

*The end of life may offer an escape from some pressures,
since Death pays all debts, but the main note is one
of resignation in the face of the inevitable:* There is a
remedy for everything except death.

As a tree falls, so shall it lie.
one should not alter one's long-established practices and
customs because of approaching death; English proverb,
mid 16th century, from the Bible (Ecclesiastes 11:3), 'In the
place where the tree falleth, there it shall be.'

Blessed are the dead that the rain rains on.

English proverb, early 17th century.

[Death is] Nature's way of telling you to slow down.

American life insurance saying, in *Newsweek* 25 April 1960.

Death is the great leveller.

all people will be equal in death, whatever their material
prosperity; English proverb, early 18th century.

Death pays all debts.

the death of a person cancels out their obligations; English
proverb, early 17th century.

Et in Arcadia ego.

Latin tomb inscription, 'And I too in Arcadia', of disputed
meaning, often depicted in classical paintings, notably
by Poussin in 1655.

One funeral makes many.

sometimes with the implication that attendance at a
deathbed or funeral may have fatal consequences; English
proverb, late 19th century.

Stone-dead hath no fellow.

traditionally used by advocates of the death penalty, to
suggest that only when a dangerous person is dead can one
be sure that they will pose no further threat; English
proverb, mid 17th century.

Debt and Borrowing

There is a remedy for everything except death.
English proverb, mid 15th century.

You can only die once.
used to encourage someone in a dangerous or difficult
enterprise; English proverb, mid 15th century.

Young men may die, but old men must die.
death is inevitable for all, and can at best be postponed until
old age; English proverb, mid 16th century.

 # Debt and Borrowing

See also THRIFT

*The idea that a national debt could be a national
blessing might sound upbeat, but more sayings stress the
dangers of getting into debt, summed up generally in
the 15th-century assertion* He that goes a-borrowing,
goes a-sorrowing.

Better to go to bed supperless than rise in debt.
English proverb, mid 17th-century saying.

A borrowed cloak does not keep you warm.
Arabic proverb, warning against relying on resources
borrowed from another.

Debt and Borrowing

Have a horse of your own, and you may borrow another's.

evidence that you have resources of your own makes it more likely that you will be lent something; English proverb.

He that goes a-borrowing, goes a-sorrowing.

involving oneself in debt is likely to lead to unhappiness; English proverb, late 15th century.

Lend your money and lose your friend.

debt puts a strain on friendship; English proverb, late 15th century.

A man in debt is caught in a net.

American proverb, mid 20th century.

A national debt, if it is not excessive, will be to us a national blessing.

American proverb; often attributed to the American politician Alexander Hamilton (c.1755–1804).

Neither a borrower, nor a lender be.

advising caution in financial dealings with others; English proverb, early 17th century, from the words of Polonius to his son Laertes in Shakespeare *Hamlet* (1601), 'Neither a borrower, nor a lender be, For loan oft loses both itself and friend.'

Deception

Out of debt, out of danger.
someone in debt is vulnerable and at risk from others;
English proverb, mid 17th century.

Short reckonings make long friends.
the prompt settlement of any debt between friends ensures
that their friendship will not be damaged; English proverb,
mid 16th century.

 Deception

See also LIES

*Deception may not benefit the perpetrator, since we are
told that* Cheats never prosper, *but there is also a
warning that we have some responsibility for ensuring
that we are not deceived:* Fool me once, shame on you;
fool me twice, shame on me.

Cheats never prosper.
English proverb, early 19th century.

Deceit is a lie, that wears a smile.
American proverb, mid 20th century.

**Fool me once, shame on you; fool me twice,
shame on me.**
if someone is deceived twice by the same person, their own
stupidity is to blame; late 20th-century saying.

The quickness of the hand deceives the eye.

saying associated with the art of conjuring; recorded from
the mid 19th century.

Deeds

See WORDS AND DEEDS

Defiance

See also DETERMINATION

Apart from the traditional reflection that You can take
a horse to water, but you can't make him drink,
*defiance is often expressed through a slogan, from the
17th-century* No surrender! *to the anti-Poll Tax cry*
Can't pay, won't pay *of the early 1990s.*

Burn, baby, burn.

black extremist slogan in use during the Los Angeles riots,
August 1965.

Can't pay, won't pay.

anti-Poll Tax slogan, *c.*1990.

Ils ne passeront pas.

French, 'They shall not pass', slogan used by the French
army at the defence of Verdun in 1916; variously attributed
to Marshal Pétain and to General Robert Nivelle, and

Defiance

subsequently taken up by Republicans in the Spanish Civil War in the form *No pasarán!*

Nemo me impune lacessit.
Latin, 'No one provokes me with impunity', motto of the Crown of Scotland and of all Scottish regiments.

No surrender!
Protestant Northern Irish slogan originating with the defenders of Derry against the Catholic forces of James II in 1689.

They haif said: Quhat say they? Lat thame say.
motto of the Earl Marischal of Scotland, inscribed at Marischal College, Aberdeen, 1593; a similarly defiant motto in Greek has been found engraved in remains from classical antiquity.

You can take a horse to the water, but you can't make him drink.
even if you create the right circumstances you cannot persuade someone to do something against their will; English proverb, late 12th century.

The wiser man gives in.
obstinate defiance is likely to be damaging to yourself; German proverb.

Delay

See HASTE AND DELAY

Determination

See also DEFIANCE

Refusal to be deterred by apparent failure can overcome both disappointment, as in the encouraging Fall seven times, stand up eight, *and difficult circumstances, since* A determined fellow can do more with a rusty monkey wrench than a lot of people can with a machine shop.

The best fish swim near the bottom.

patience and persistence are necessary for the best results; English proverb.

Beyond mountains there are more mountains.

overcoming the first obstacle is likely to bring you face to face with another; Haitian proverb.

Constant dropping wears away a stone.

primarily used to mean that persistence will achieve a difficult or unlikely object; English proverb, mid 13th century.

Determination

A determined fellow can do more with a rusty monkey wrench than a lot of people can with a machine shop.
American proverb, mid 20th century.

Fall seven times, stand up eight.
Japanese proverb; compare **If at first you don't succeed, try, try, try again** below.

He that will to Cupar maun to Cupar.
if someone is determined on an end they will not be dissuaded (*Cupar* is a town in Fife, Scotland); Scottish traditional saying, early 18th century.

He who wills the end, wills the means.
someone sufficiently determined upon an outcome will also be ready to accept whatever is necessary to achieve it; English proverb, late 17th century.

If at first you don't succeed, try, try, try again.
English proverb, mid 19th century; compare **Fall seven times, stand up eight** above.

It is idle to swallow the cow and choke on the tail.
when a serious matter has been accepted, there is no point in quibbling over a trifle; when a great task is almost completed, it is senseless to give up; English proverb, mid 17th century.

It's dogged as does it.

steady perseverance will bring success; English proverb, mid 19th century.

Just say no.

motto of the Nancy Reagan Drug Abuse Fund, founded 1985.

Little strokes fell great oaks.

a person of size and stature can be brought down by a series of small blows; English proverb, early 15th century.

Nil carborundum illegitimi.

cod Latin for 'Don't let the bastards grind you down', in circulation during the Second World War, though possibly of earlier origin.

Put a stout heart to a stey brae.

determination is needed to climb a steep ('stey') hillside; Scottish proverb, late 16th century.

Revenons à ces moutons.

an exhortation to stop digressing and get back to the subject in hand; French, literally 'Let us return to these sheep', with allusion to the confused court scene in the Old French *Farce de Maistre Pierre Pathelin* (*c*.1470).

The show must go on.

American proverb, mid 19th century.

Determination

Slow and steady wins the race.

from the story of the race between the hare and the tortoise, in Aesop's *Fables*, in which the winner was the slow but persistent tortoise and not the swift but easily distracted hare; mid 18th-century saying.

A stern chase is a long chase.

a *stern chase* is a chase in which the pursuing ship follows directly in the wake of the pursued; English proverb, early 19th century.

The third time pays for all.

success after initial failure makes up for earlier disappointment; English proverb, late 16th century.

We shall not be moved.

title of labour and civil rights song (1931), adapted from an earlier gospel hymn.

We shall overcome.

title of song, originating from before the American Civil War, adapted as a Baptist hymn ('I'll Overcome Some Day', 1901) by C. Albert Tindley; revived in 1946 as a protest song by black tobacco workers, and in 1963 during the black civil rights campaign.

Where there's a will there's a way.

anything can be done if one has sufficient determination; English proverb, mid 17th century.

A wilful man must have his way.

a person set on their own ends will disregard advice in pursuing their chosen course; English proverb, early 19th century.

Difference

See SIMILARITY AND DIFFERENCE

Discontent

See SATISFACTION AND DISCONTENT

Discoveries

See INVENTIONS AND DISCOVERIES

Dislikes

See LIKES AND DISLIKES

Dogs

See also CATS, HORSES

The idea of the dog as protector goes back to the Cave canem *of the classical world, and is reinforced by the Persian proverb,* The dog is a lion in his own house.

Doubt

Cave canem.
Latin, 'beware of the dog', deriving originally from the Roman satirist Petronius (d. 65), *'Canis ingens, catena vinctus, in pariete erat pictus superque quadrata littera scriptum "Cave Canem".'*

[A huge dog, tied by a chain, was painted on the wall and over it was written in capital letters "Beware of the dog."]

The dog is a lion in his own house.
Persian proverb.

A dog is for life, not just for Christmas.
slogan of the National Canine Defence League (now Dogs Trust), from 1978.

Love me, love my dog.
English proverb, early 16th century.

There is no good flock without a good shepherd, and no good shepherd without a good dog.
motto of the International Sheep Dog Society, said to derive from a Scottish proverb.

 # Doubt
See CERTAINTY AND DOUBT

Dreams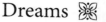

See also SLEEP

Apart from the warning from 19th-century America that Dreams retain the infirmities of our character, *dreams are traditionally seen as predictive, if they can be correctly interpreted.*

Dream of a funeral and you hear of a marriage.
English proverb, mid 17th century.

Dreams go by contraries.
English proverb, early 15th century.

Dreams retain the infirmities of our character.
American proverb, late 19th century.

Morning dreams come true.
English proverb, mid 16th century, recording a traditional superstition.

Those who lose dreaming are lost.
modern saying, said to be an Australian Aboriginal proverb.

To dream of the dead is a sign of rain.
traditional saying.

Dress

See also APPEARANCE

Dress may be important as protection from the elements (Ne'er cast a clout till May be out)*, or as allowing us to make a good impression:* If you want to get ahead, get a hat.

Blue and green should never be seen.
traditional warning against wearing the two colours together.

Clothes make the man.
what one wears is taken by others as an essential signal of status; English proverb, early 20th century.

Dress for the job you want, not for the job you have.
modern saying, used especially in the context of interviews.

Fine feathers make fine birds.
beautiful clothes confer beauty or style on the wearer; English proverb, late 16th century.

If you want to get ahead, get a hat.
advertising slogan for the British Hat Council, 1965.

It takes 40 dumb animals to make a fur coat, but only one to wear it.
slogan of an anti-fur campaign poster, 1980s; sometimes attributed to the English photographer David Bailey (1938–).

Ne'er cast a clout till May be out.

warning against leaving off old or warm clothes until the end of the month of May (the saying is sometimes mistakenly understood to refer to hawthorn blossom or *may*); English proverb, early 18th century.

Nine tailors make a man.

literally, a gentleman must select his attire from a number of sources (later also associated with bell-ringing, with the *nine tailors* or *tellers* indicating the nine knells traditionally rung at the death of a man); English proverb, early 17th century.

Drink

See also DRUNKENNESS, FOOD

Sayings about drink often emphasize the attractions or characteristics of a particular form of alcohol, whether it be beer, vodka, or whisky.

Alcohol will preserve anything but a secret.

American proverb, mid 20th century.

Don't ask a man to drink and drive.

British road safety slogan, from 1964.

Guinness is good for you.

reply universally given to researchers asking people why they drank Guinness; advertising slogan for Guinness, from *c.*1929.

Drunkenness

Heineken refreshes the parts other beers cannot reach.

slogan for Heineken lager, from 1975 onwards.

If you are cold, tea will warm you; if you are too heated, it will cool you; if you are depressed, it will cheer you; if you are excited, it will calm you.

modern saying, attributed to W. E. Gladstone (1809–98) since the mid 20th century.

I'm only here for the beer.

slogan for Double Diamond beer, 1971 onwards.

Today's rain is tomorrow's whisky.

modern Scottish saying.

Vodka is an aunt of wine.

Russian proverb.

 # Drunkenness

See also DRINK

Apart from the risks of becoming addicted (The drunkard's cure is to drink again), *there are other dangers in falling under the influence of alcohol:* When the wine is in, the wit is out.

The drunkard's cure is drink again.

American proverb, mid 20th century.

He that drinks beer, thinks beer.

warning against the effect of intoxication; English proverb, early 19th century.

There is truth in wine.

a person who is drunk is more likely to speak the truth; English proverb, mid 16th century (the saying is found earlier in Latin as *in vino veritas*).

When the wine is in, the wit is out.

when one is drunk one is likely to be indiscreet or to speak or act foolishly; English proverb, late 14th century.

Eating

See also COOKING, FOOD, HEALTH

In the 21st century, the saying You are what you eat *has gained a new prominence, but earlier proverbs may be more likely to reflect a world in which eating was not something to be taken for granted:* Hunger is the best sauce.

After dinner rest a while, after supper walk a mile.

the implication is that dinner is a heavy meal, while supper is a light one; English proverb, late 16th century.

After meat, mustard.

traditional comment on some essential ingredient which is brought too late to be of use; English proverb, late 16th century.

Breakfast like a king, lunch like a prince, and dine like a pauper.

modern saying, recommending lighter meals as you move through the day.

Eat to live, not live to eat.

distinguishing between necessity and indulgence; English proverb, late 14th century.

Fingers were made before forks.

commonly used as a polite excuse for eating with one's hands at table; English proverb, mid 18th century; the earlier variant 'God made hands before knives is found in the mid 16th century.

Go to work on an egg.

advertising slogan for the British Egg Marketing Board, from 1957; perhaps written by Fay Weldon or Mary Gowing.

Hunger is the best sauce.

food which is needed will be received most readily; English proverb, early 16th century.

The way one eats is the way one works.

Czech proverb; compare **You are what you eat** below.

We must eat a peck of dirt before we die.

often used as a consolatory remark in literal contexts; English proverb, mid 18th century.

You are what you eat.

English proverb, mid 20th century; in the early 19th century, the French jurist and gourmet Anthelme Brillat-Savarin (1755–1826) wrote, 'Tell me what you eat and I will tell you what you are'; compare **The way one eats is the way one works** above.

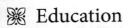 Education

See also KNOWLEDGE, TEACHING

The saying As the twig is bent, so is the tree inclined *reflects an awareness of the importance of early influences, but for late developers there is the encouragement,* It is never too late to learn.

As the twig is bent, so is the tree inclined.
early influences have a permanent effect; English proverb, early 18th century.

Education doesn't come by bumping your head against the school house.
American proverb, mid 20th century.

Genius without education is like silver in the mine.
American proverb, mid 18th century.

Give me a child for the first seven years, and you may do what you like with him afterwards.
traditionally regarded as a Jesuit maxim; recorded in Lean's *Collectanea* vol. 3 (1903).

The ink of a scholar is holier than the blood of a martyr.
modern saying, said to derive from an Arab proverb, but of uncertain origin.

It is never too late to learn.

English proverb, late 17th century.

Never let your education interfere with your intelligence.

American proverb, mid 20th century.

Never too old to learn.

English proverb, late 16th century.

Teachers open the door, but you must enter by yourself.

learning requires effort on the part of the student; Chinese proverb.

There is no royal road to learning.

English proverb, early 19th century, deriving from the words of the Greek mathematician Euclid (fl. *c*.300 BC) addressed to Ptolemy I of Egypt, 'There is no "royal road" to geometry.'

When the pupil is ready, the master arrives.

Indian proverb, deriving from Sanskrit.

Effort

See also ACHIEVEMENT

Proverbs such as He that would eat the fruit must climb the tree *and* No pain, no gain *emphasize how*

Effort

essential effort is to achievement. There is comparatively little concern that the effort might be expended ineffectually, although by implication we are warned to set our sights on an achievable goal: If the sky falls, we shall catch larks.

Easy come, easy go.

something which is acquired without effort will be lost without regret; English proverb, mid 17th century.

He that would eat the fruit must climb the tree.

someone who wishes to attain success must first make the necessary effort; English proverb, mid 17th century.

If a thing's worth doing, it's worth doing well.

if something is worth any effort at all, it should be taken seriously; English proverb, mid 18th century.

If the sky falls we shall catch larks.

used dismissively to indicate that something will be attainable only in the most unlikely circumstances; English proverb, mid 15th century.

Much cry and little wool.

referring to a disturbance without tangible result; in early usage, the image was that of shearing a pig, which would cry loudly but yield no wool; English proverb, late 15th century.

No pain, no gain.

nothing worth having can be achieved without effort;
English proverb, late 16th century.

One cannot become a good sailor sailing in a tranquil sea.

a person must be disciplined and educated to become a
useful citizen; Chinese proverb.

We're number two. We try harder.

advertising slogan for Avis car rentals.

Employment

See also MANAGEMENT

*One saying from the 18th century and one saying from
the 20th offer very different views of employment: the
belief that* The eye of a master does more work than
both his hands *contrasts with the cynical comment
from Soviet Russia:* We pretend to work, and they
pretend to pay us.

The eye of a master does more work than both his hands.

employees work harder when the person who is in charge is
present; English proverb, mid 18th century.

Ending

Jack of all trades and master of none.
a person who tries to master too many skills will learn none
of them properly; English proverb, early 17th century.

We pretend to work, and they pretend to pay us.
Russian saying of the Soviet era.

 Ending

See also BEGINNING, CHANGE

*Whether or not an ending is as successful as that
implied by* The end crowns the work, *it will inevitably
arrive. However, we should not assume too quickly that
something has been completed:* The opera isn't over till
the fat lady sings.

All good things must come to an end.
nothing lasts; although the addition of 'good' is a later
development; English proverb, mid 15th century.

All's well that ends well.
often used with the implication that difficulties have been
successfully negotiated; English proverb, late 14th century.

And they all lived happily ever after.
traditional ending for a fairy story.

Ending

Better an end with terror than terror without end.
20th-century German saying, associated with Philipp
Scheidermann (1865–1939), second head of government in
the Weimar Republic.

The end crowns the work.
the fulfilment of a process is its finest and most notable part;
English proverb, early 16th century.

End good, all good.
a good outcome means that the work has been worthwhile;
German proverb.

Everything has an end.
no condition lasts for ever; English proverb, late
14th century.

In my end is my beginning.
motto of Mary, Queen of Scots (1542–87).

The opera isn't over till the fat lady sings.
using an informal description of the culmination of a
traditional opera to indicate that a process is not yet
complete; late 20th century saying.

❀ Enemies

See also DANGER

While we should be cautious in our dealings with an enemy (Do not call a wolf to help you against the dogs), *shared enmity can be useful:* The enemy of my enemy is my friend.

Dead men don't bite.

killing an enemy puts an end to any threat they may pose; English proverb, mid 16th century.

Do not call a wolf to help you against the dogs.

advising against making alliance with someone likely to destroy you in your turn; Russian proverb.

The enemy of my enemy is my friend.

shared enmity provides common ground; American proverb, mid 20th century, often said to be 'an old Arab proverb'; compare **My brother and I against my cousin and my cousin and I against the stranger** at FAMILY.

Love your enemy—but don't put a gun in his hand.

indicating the practical limitations of charity; American proverb, mid 20th century.

Strike the serpent's head with your enemy's hand.

use one opponent to defeat another; English proverb.

There is no little enemy.

any enemy can be dangerous; English proverb, mid 17th century.

The Environment

In recent years political slogans such as Think globally, act locally *and sayings believed to derive from cultures in touch with a pre-industrial way of living such as* Touch the earth lightly *have combined to urge sensitivity and care in dealing with the natural world.*

The earth is man's only friend.

Bulgarian proverb.

The earth laughs at him who calls a place his own.

Indian proverb.

However high a bird may soar, it seeks its food on earth.

Danish proverb.

Save the whale.

environmental slogan associated with the alarm over the rapidly declining whale population which led in 1985 to a moratorium on commercial whaling.

The Environment

Take only photos, leave only footprints.

encouraging responsible behaviour when travelling in
wilderness areas; mid 20th-century saying, first found as
'Take nothing but pictures; leave nothing but footprints',
and often attributed to Chief Seattle (1786–1866) of the
Suquamish and Duwamish in the form 'Take only
memories, leave only footprints.'

Think globally, act locally.

Friends of the Earth slogan, c.1985.

Touch the earth lightly.

modern saying, said to derive from an Australian
Aboriginal proverb.

**We do not inherit the earth from our parents, we
borrow it from our children.**

modern saying, said to be of Native American origin.

**When the last tree is cut, the last river poisoned,
and the last fish dead, we will discover that we can't
eat money.**

Canadian saying, sometimes said to be of Native
American origin.

You have to be in the black to be in the green.

a landowner who is in debt is more likely to damage the
environment; modern New Zealand saying.

Envy

While being envied may sustain our pride, to feel envy is likely to make us discontented: The grass is always greener on the other side of the fence.

Better be envied than pitied.

even if one is unhappy it is preferable to be rich and powerful rather than poor and vulnerable; English proverb, mid 16th century.

Envy eats nothing but its own heart.

German proverb.

Envy feeds on the living; it ceases when they are dead.

American proverb, mid 20th century.

The grass is always greener on the other side of the fence.

something just out of reach always appears more desirable than what one already has; English proverb, mid 20th century.

If envy were a fever, all the world would be ill.

Envy is a common vice; Danish proverb.

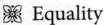

Equality

An idea expressed through several images.

After the game, the king and the pawn go into the same box.

rank is no protection against death; Italian proverb.

Diamond cuts diamond.

used of persons who are evenly matched in wit or cunning (only a diamond is hard enough to cut another diamond); English proverb, early 17th century.

Jack is as good as his master.

'Jack' is used variously as a familiar name for a sailor, a member of the common people, a serving man, and one who does odd jobs; English proverb, early 18th century.

Evil

See GOOD AND EVIL

Excellence

True excellence may be seldom encountered, since If something sounds too good to be true, it probably is.

Corruption of the best becomes the worst.

translation of the Latin saying *Corruptio optimi pessima*;
English proverb, early 19th century.

**If something sounds too good to be true,
it probably is.**

late 20th-century saying.

Excess

See also MODERATION

The idea that You can have too much of a good thing
*occurs in many cultures, from the medieval English
warning that* The pitcher will go to the well once too
often, *to the Chinese* Do not add legs to the snake after
you have finished drawing it.

**Do not add legs to the snake after you have
finished drawing it.**

advising against making superfluous and undesirable
additions; Chinese proverb.

Even nectar is a poison, if taken to excess.

too much of anything is inadvisable; Hindu proverb.

It is the last straw that breaks the camel's back.

the addition of one quite minor problem may prove
crushing to someone who is already overburdened; English
proverb, mid 17th century.

Excuses

The last drop makes the cup run over.
the addition of something in itself quite minor causes an excess; English proverb, mid 17th century.

The pitcher will go to the well once too often.
one should not repeat a risky action too often, or push one's luck too far; English proverb, mid 14th century.

You can have too much of a good thing.
excess even of something which is good in itself can be damaging; English proverb, late 15th century.

 ## Excuses
See APOLOGY AND EXCUSES

 ## Experience

While there is no doubt that experience is worth having (Experience is the father of wisdom), *it may be gained at the cost of some unpleasantness:* A burnt child dreads the fire.

Appetite comes with eating.
desire or facility increases as an activity proceeds; English proverb, mid 17th century.

A burnt child dreads the fire.

the memory of past hurt may act as a safeguard in the
future; English proverb, mid 13th century.

Experience is the best teacher.

sometimes used with the implication that learning by
experience may be painful; English proverb, mid
16th century.

**Experience is the comb which fate gives a man
when his hair is all gone.**

American proverb, mid 20th century.

Experience is the father of wisdom.

real understanding of something comes only from direct
experience of it; English proverb, mid 16th century.

Experience keeps a dear school.

lessons learned from experience can be painful; English
proverb, mid 18th century.

A fall into a ditch makes you wiser.

Chinese proverb.

Good soup is made in an old pot.

successful results are due to age and experience;
French proverb.

Experience

Live and learn.
often as a resigned or rueful comment on a disagreeable
experience; English proverb, early 17th century.

Once bitten, twice shy.
someone who has suffered an injury will in the future be
very cautious of the cause; English proverb, mid 19th
century; compare **Once bitten by a snake, a man will be
afraid of a piece of rope for three years** at CAUTION.

**Some folks speak from experience; others, from
experience, don't speak.**
American proverb, mid 20th century.

They that live longest, see most.
often used to comment on the experience of old age;
English proverb, early 17th century.

**Walking ten thousand miles is better than reading
ten thousand books.**
theoretical knowledge must be consolidated by practical
experience; Chinese proverb; compare **Walking
ten thousand miles; reading ten thousand books**
at KNOWLEDGE.

You cannot catch old birds with chaff.
the wise and experienced are not easily fooled; English
proverb, late 15th century.

You cannot put an old head on young shoulders.
you cannot expect someone who is young and
inexperienced to show the wisdom and maturity of an older
person; English proverb, late 16th century.

**You should make a point of trying every experience
once, excepting incest and folk-dancing.**
20th-century saying, repeated by Arnold Bax in *Farewell my
Youth* (1943), quoting 'a sympathetic Scot'.

Extravagance

See THRIFT AND EXTRAVAGANCE

Fact

 Fact

See HYPOTHESIS AND FACT

 Failure

See SUCCESS AND FAILURE

 Fame

See also REPUTATION

Lasting fame is not easily achieved, since even if it is well founded, without a written record it may be forgotten: Brave men lived before Agamemnon.

Brave men lived before Agamemnon.

to be remembered the exploits of a hero must be recorded; English proverb, early 19th century, from Horace (65–8 BC) *Odes*, 'Many brave men lived before Agamemnon's time, but they are all, unmourned and unknown, covered by the long night, because they lack their sacred poet.'

Common fame is seldom to blame.

reputation is generally founded on fact rather than rumour; English proverb, mid 17th century.

If any man seek for greatness, let him forget greatness and seek truth.

American proverb, mid 20th century.

136

More people know Tom Fool than Tom Fool knows.
English proverb, mid 17th century; *Tom Fool* was a name
given to the part of the fool in a play or morris dance.

A tall tree attracts the wind.
fame may make you the subject of hostile attention;
Chinese proverb.

Familiarity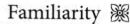

See also NEIGHBOURS

While it may be safer to stick with what you know
(Better the devil you know, than the devil you don't),
it may be difficult to recognize the virtues of the
familiar. Without the enchantment lent by distance,
Local ginger is not hot.

Better the devil you know than the devil you don't.
understanding of the nature of a danger may give one an
advantage, and is preferable to something which is
completely unknown, and which may well be worse; English
proverb, mid 19th century.

Better wed over the mixen than over the moor.
it is better to marry a neighbour than a stranger (a *mixen* is
a midden); English proverb, early 17th century.

Familiarity

Blue are the hills that are far away.
a distant view lends enchantment; English proverb, early
20th century.

Come live with me and you'll know me.
the implication is that only by living with a person will you
learn their real nature; English proverb, early 20th century.

Familiarity breeds contempt.
we value least the things which are most familiar; English
proverb, late 14th century.

If you lie down with dogs, you will get up with fleas.
asserting that human failings, such as dishonesty and
foolishness, are contagious; English proverb, late 16th
century (earlier in Latin).

Local ginger is not hot.
modern saying, said to derive from a Chinese proverb;
compare **A prophet is not without honour save in his own
country** below.

A man is known by the company he keeps.
originally used as a moral maxim or exhortation in the
context of preparation for marriage; English proverb, mid
16th century.

No man is a hero to his valet.
English proverb, mid 18th century, found earlier in French,
in a letter from the society hostess Mme Cornuel (1605–94).

A prophet is not without honour save in his own country.

English proverb, late 15th century, from the Bible (Matthew 13:57), 'A prophet is not without honour, save in his own country, and in his own house'; compare **Local ginger is not hot** above.

There is nothing new under the sun.

English proverb, late 16th century, from the Bible (Ecclesiastes 1:9), 'The thing that hath been, it is that which shall be; and that which is done is that which shall be done: and there is no new thing under the sun.'

The Family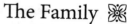

See also CHILDREN, PARENTS

Proverbial wisdom on the subject of the family finds a consensus in the view that Blood will tell. *The idea is expressed in detail in the Chinese saying,* Dragons beget dragons, phoenixes beget phoenixes, and burglars' children learn how to break into houses.

The apple never falls far from the tree.

family characteristics will assert themselves; English proverb, mid 19th century.

The Family

Blood is thicker than water.
in the end family ties will always count; English proverb,
mid 19th century.

Blood will tell.
family characteristics or heredity will in the end be
dominant; English proverb, mid 19th century.

The child of a frog is a frog.
Japanese proverb.

Children are certain cares, but uncertain comforts.
emphasizing the continuing responsibility and anxiety of
parenthood; English proverb, mid 17th century.

**Dragons beget dragons, phoenixes beget phoenixes,
and burglars' children learn how to break into houses.**
Chinese proverb; see **Like father, like son** below.

I belong by blood relationship; therefore I am.
on the importance of family ties in one's sense of identity;
African proverb.

A large family, quick help.
those related to you will provide ready help in time of need;
Serbian proverb.

Like father, like son.
often used to call attention to similarities in behaviour;
English proverb, mid 14th century.

Like mother, like daughter.
English proverb, early 14th century; the ultimate allusion is to the Bible (Ezekiel 16:44), 'As is the mother, so is her daughter.'

My brother and I against my cousin and my cousin and I against the stranger.
Arab proverb; compare **The enemy of my enemy is my friend** at ENEMIES.

The shoemaker's son always goes barefoot.
the family of a skilled or knowledgeable person are often the last to benefit from their expertise; English proverb, mid 16th century.

The son of a duck floats.
Arabic saying.

Fate

See also THE FUTURE

Views on fate see it as unlikely to be altered by human intervention: Man proposes, God disposes. *The only strongly contrary assessment is found in the modern American saying,* Fate can be taken by the horns, like a goat, and pushed in the right direction.

Fate

Every hog has its Martinmas.
everyone has their destiny; *Martinmas*, the feast of
St Martin, 11 November, was the season at which pigs
and other domestic animals were slaughtered before winter;
traditional saying.

**Fate can be taken by the horns, like a goat, and
pushed in the right direction.**
with sufficient determination one need not be a helpless
victim of fate; American proverb, mid 20th century.

Hanging and wiving go by destiny.
an expression of fatalism about the course of one's life;
English proverb, mid 16th century.

**If you're born to be hanged then you'll never
be drowned.**
used to qualify apparent good luck which may have an
unhappy outcome; English proverb, late 16th century.

Man proposes, God disposes.
often now said in consolation or resignation when plans
have been disrupted; English proverb, mid 15th century.

**The mills of God grind slowly, yet they grind
exceeding small.**
English proverb, mid 17th century; in its current form, it
derives from Henry Wadsworth Longfellow's translation of
Sinnegedichte by Friedrich von Logau, 'Though the mills of

God grind slowly, yet they grind exceeding small; Though with patience He stands waiting, with exactness grinds he all' (Von Logau's first line is itself a translation of an anonymous verse in Sextus Empiricus *Adversus Mathematicos*).

Sour, sweet, bitter, pungent, all must be tasted.
We have to experience both happiness and sadness in life; Chinese proverb.

What goes up must come down.
commonly associated with wartime bombing and anti-aircraft shrapnel, and often used with the implication that an exhilarating rise must be followed by a fall; early 20th-century saying.

What must be, must be.
used to acknowledge the force of circumstances; English proverb, late 14th century.

Fear

See also COURAGE, DANGER

A fearful person is likely to suffer from more than just the effects of the danger they fear: Cowards may die many times before their death.

Feelings

Cowards may die many times before their death.

English proverb, late 16th century; in this form, a
misquotation from Shakespeare *Julius Caesar* (1599)
'Cowards die many times before their deaths; /The valiant
never taste of death but once.'

Fear makes the wolf bigger than he is.

Fear exaggerates what we are afraid of; German proverb.

 # Feelings

See also LOVE

*Good feeling is seen as something without which there
can be little real enjoyment:* Better a dinner of herbs
than a stalled ox where hate is. *Beyond this, ill
will directed against another may rebound on the
perpetrator:* Curses, like chickens, come home
to roost.

**Better a dinner of herbs than a stalled ox
where hate is.**

simple food accompanied by goodwill and affection is
preferable to luxury in an atmosphere of ill will; English
proverb, mid 16th century, with allusion to the Bible
(Proverbs 15:17), 'Better a dinner of herbs where love is,
than a stalled ox with hatred therewith.'

Curses, like chickens, come home to roost.

ill will directed at another is likely to rebound on the originator; English proverb, late 14th century.

Out of the fullness of the heart the mouth speaks.

overwhelming feeling will express itself in speech; English proverb, late 14th century, originally with allusion to the Bible (Matthew 12:34), 'Out of the abundance of the heart the mouth speaketh.'

Sing before breakfast, cry before night.

warning against overconfidence in early happiness presaging a reversal of good fortune; English proverb, early 17th century.

Flattery

See PRAISE AND FLATTERY

Flowers

See also GARDENS

Flowers are a natural source of enjoyment, but they require nurturing and protection: It is not enough for a gardener to love flowers; he must also hate weeds.

Food

All the flowers of tomorrow are in the seeds of today.
Indian proverb; compare **A seed hidden in the heart of an apple is an orchard invisible** at TREES.

It is not enough for a gardener to love flowers; he must also hate weeds.
American proverb, mid 20th century.

Say it with flowers.
slogan for the Society of American Florists, from 1917.

 # Food

See also COOKING, DRINK, EATING

Some sayings focus on particular foodstuffs, as in the traditional warning Don't eat oysters unless there is an R in the month. *However, and more importantly, food is recognized as the most basic necessity:* No dinner without bread.

An apple pie without some cheese is like a kiss without a squeeze.
traditional saying, early 20th century.

Don't eat oysters unless there is an R in the month.
from the tradition that oysters were likely to be unsafe to eat in the warmer months between May and August.

Every pomegranate has one seed that has come from heaven.

Arabic proverb.

God never sends mouths but He sends meat.

used in resignation or consolation; English proverb, late 14th century.

A hungry man is an angry man.

someone deprived of a basic necessity will not be easily placated; English proverb, mid 17th century.

It's ill speaking between a full man and a fasting.

someone in need is never on good terms with someone who has all they want; English proverb, mid 17th century.

The more butter, the worse cheese.

the more cream used for butter, the less available for cheese; traditional saying.

No dinner without bread.

Russian proverb.

Of soup and love, the first is best.

Spanish proverb.

Twice-cooked cabbage is death.

Latin proverb.

Fools

Despite the hopeful note struck by the saying Fortune favours fools, *the consensus is that a foolish person is more likely to be unfortunate:* A fool and his money are soon parted.

Ask a silly question and you get a silly answer.

often used to indicate that the answer is so obvious that the question should not have been asked; English proverb, early 14th century.

Empty vessels make the most sound.

foolish and empty-headed people make the most noise; English proverb, mid 15th century.

A fool and his money are soon parted.

English proverb, late 16th century.

Fools build houses and wise men live in them.

a shrewd person chooses to save themselves trouble, and benefit from the effort expended by another; English proverb, late 17th century.

Fortune favours fools.

a foolish person is traditionally fortunate; English proverb, mid 16th century.

Never attribute to malice that which is adequately explained by stupidity.

modern saying, often known as 'Hanlon's razor'.

A wise man changes his mind, a fool never.

obstinacy is a mark of folly; Spanish proverb.

Foresight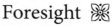

See also THE FUTURE

Foresight is seen as desirable (Prevention is better than cure), *but hard to achieve—while conversely,* It's easy to be wise after the event.

The afternoon knows what the morning never suspected.

Swedish proverb.

He who can see three days ahead will be rich for three thousand years.

even limited foresight is of great value; Japanese proverb.

If a man's foresight were as good as his hindsight, we would all get somewhere.

American proverb, mid 20th century.

Forgiveness

It is easy to be wise after the event.
the difficult thing is to make a correct judgement without
the benefit of hindsight; English proverb, early 17th century.

**It's too late to shut the stable door after the horse
has bolted.**
preventive measures taken after things have gone wrong are
of little effect; English proverb, mid 14th century.

Nothing is certain but the unforeseen.
warning against an overconfident belief in a future
occurrence; English proverb, late 19th century.

Prevention is better than cure.
English proverb, early 17th century.

To know the road ahead, ask those coming back.
Chinese proverb.

 # Forgiveness

See also CONSCIENCE, GUILT

Not only should we be ready to seek forgiveness (A fault
confessed is half redressed), *refusal to forgive is
associated with the likelihood that we have wronged
another:* Offenders never pardon.

Charity covers a multitude of sins.

charity as a virtue outweighs many faults; English proverb, early 17th century.

A fault confessed is half redressed.

by confessing what you have done wrong you have begun to make amends; English proverb, mid 16th century.

Forgiving the unrepentant is like drawing pictures on water.

forgiveness is meaningless unless there is true repentance on the part of the offender; Japanese proverb.

Good to forgive, best to forget.

it is even better to forget that you have been injured than to forgive the injury; North American proverb, mid 20th century.

Never let the sun go down on your anger.

recommending a swift reconciliation after a quarrel; from the Bible (Ephesians 4:26), 'Be ye angry and sin not: let not the sun go down upon your wrath.'

Offenders never pardon.

the experience of having wronged someone often fosters a continuing resentment of the victim; English proverb, mid 17th century.

Friendship

To know all is to forgive all.
English proverb, mid 20th century; the idea is found earlier
in French, in Mme de Stael *Corinne* (1807), '*Tout
comprendre rend très indulgent* [To be totally understanding
makes one very indulgent].'

 # Friendship

*Although the good intentions of our friends can
sometimes be a burden* (Save us from our friends),
we depend on having them: A friend in need is a
friend indeed.

**Be kind to your friends: if it weren't for them, you
would be a total stranger.**
American proverb, mid 20th century.

A friend in need is a friend indeed.
a *friend in need* is one who helps when someone is in need
or difficulty; English proverb, mid 11th century.

A friend to all is a friend to none.
traditional saying affirming the value of true friendship over
surface amiability.

Hold a true friend with both your hands.
real friendship is something to be cherished;
African proverb.

Life without a friend, is death without a witness.

friendship gives meaning to life; Spanish proverb.

The road to a friend's house is never long.

Danish proverb.

Save us from our friends.

the earnest help of friends can sometimes be
unintentionally damaging; English proverb, late
15th century.

Two is company, but three is none.

often used with the alternative ending 'three's a crowd';
English proverb, early 18th century.

Futility ❊

See also ACHIEVEMENT

*There are a number of ways of invoking the picture of a
futile course of action, from* Dogs bark, but the caravan
goes on *to* You can't make a silk purse out of a sow's ear.

Dogs bark, but the caravan goes on.

trivial criticism will not deflect the progress of something
important; English proverb, late 19th century.

Do not push the river, it will flow by itself.

typifying pointless activity; Polish proverb.

153

Futility

Hot water does not burn down the house.
typifying ineffective action; African proverb.

In vain the net is spread in the sight of the bird.
a person who has seen the process by which someone
intends to harm them is unlikely to be in danger; English
proverb, late 14th century.

Sue a beggar and catch a louse.
it is pointless to try to obtain restitution from someone
without resources; English proverb, mid 17th century.

You cannot carry two watermelons in one hand.
typifying an attempted action that is bound to fail; modern
saying, said to be an Arabic proverb.

You cannot get a quart into a pint pot.
used of any situation in which the prospective contents are
too large for the container; English proverb, late 19th century.

You cannot get blood from a stone.
often used, as a resigned admission, to mean that it is
hopeless to try to extort money or sympathy from those
who have none; English proverb, mid 17th century.

You cannot make bricks without straw.
nothing can be made or achieved if one does not have the
correct materials; English proverb, mid 17th century, with
allusion to the Bible (Exodus) in Pharaoh's decree to the
taskmasters set over the Israelites in Egypt, 'Ye shall no

more give the people straw to make brick, as heretofore: let them go and gather straw for themselves.'

You can put lipstick on a pig, but it will still be a pig.
superficial improvements will not alter the fundamental structure; modern saying.

You can put your boots in the oven but that doesn't make them biscuits.
modern American saying.

You can't make a silk purse out of a sow's ear.
inherent nature cannot be overcome by nurture; English proverb, early 16th century.

You can't unscramble scrambled eggs.
the results of some actions cannot be undone; modern saying.

The Future

See also FORESIGHT, THE PAST, THE PRESENT

The future may be bright, but too much focus on it may mean that we lose sight of what is actually happening:
There is no future like the present.

Coming events cast their shadow before.
some initial effects indicating the nature of an event may be felt before it takes place; English proverb, early 19th century.

The Future

He that follows freits, freits will follow him.
someone who looks for portents of the future will find
himself dogged by them (*freits* are omens); Scottish proverb,
early 18th century.

An inch ahead is darkness.
we have no knowledge of the future; Japanese proverb.

There is no future like the present.
American proverb, mid 20th century.

Today you; tomorrow me.
often used in the context of the inevitability of death to each
person; English proverb, mid 13th century.

Tomorrow is another day.
English proverb, early 16th century.

Tomorrow is often the busiest day of the year.
commenting on the tendency to put off necessary work;
Spanish proverb.

Tomorrow never comes.
used in the context of something which is constantly
predicted to be imminent, but which never comes; English
proverb, early 16th century.

You can have apricots tomorrow.
Arabic saying.

Games

See SPORTS AND GAMES

Gardens

See also FLOWERS

Gardening is seen as a source of joy, but also one that requires a good deal of attention, especially where keeping control of weeds is concerned: One year's seeding makes seven years' weeding.

The answer lies in the soil.

traditional gardening advice.

Dig for victory.

Second World War slogan, encouraging production of food in gardens and allotments.

A garden is never finished.

no true gardener ever feels their work is complete; modern saying.

If you would be happy for a week take a wife; if you would be happy for a month kill a pig; but if you would be happy all your life plant a garden.

the saying exists in a variety of forms, but marriage is nearly always given as one of the ephemeral forms of happiness; English proverb, mid 17th century.

Gardens

Life begins on the day you start a garden.
modern saying, claimed to be a Chinese proverb.

More things grow in the garden than the gardener sows.
some plants will appear as part of the natural process;
Spanish proverb.

One year's seeding makes seven years' weeding.
the allusion is to the danger of allowing weeds to grow and
seed themselves; English proverb, late 19th century.

Parsley seed goes nine times to the Devil.
parsley is often slow to germinate, and there was a
superstition that it belonged to the Devil, and had to be
sown nine times before it would come up; English proverb,
mid 17th century.

Select a proper site for your garden and half your work is done.
Chinese proverb.

Sow corn in clay, and plant vines in sand.
Spanish traditional saying.

Sow dry and set wet.
seeds should be sown in dry ground and then given water;
English proverb, mid 17th century.

Walnuts and pears you plant for your heirs.
both trees are tradionally slow growing, so that the benefit
will be felt by future generations; English proverb, mid
17th century.

Generosity 🎕

See also GRATITUDE

Generosity is seen as an obligation (It is better to give
than to receive), *and one which should be readily
fulfilled:* He gives twice who gives quickly.

Be kind. Everyone you meet is fighting a hard battle.
modern saying (sometimes misattributed to Plato).

A bird never flew on one wing.
frequently used to justify a further gift, especially
another drink; early 18th-century proverb, mainly
Scottish and Irish.

Friday's child is loving and giving.
English proverb, mid 19th century, from a traditional rhyme
(compare qualities associated with birth on other days at
entries under BEAUTY, SORROW, TRAVEL, and WORK).

**Give a thing, and take a thing, to wear the devil's
gold ring.**
a school children's rhyme, chanted when a person gives
something and then asks for it back; English proverb, late
16th century.

God

He gives twice who gives quickly.
associating readiness to give with generosity; English
proverb, mid 16th century.

It is better to give than to receive.
English proverb, late 14th century, ultimately with allusion
to the Bible (Acts 20:35), 'It is more blessed to give
than to receive.'

**It is easy to be generous with other
people's property.**
traditional saying, of classical origin.

 # God

While God may be omnipotent (All things are possible
with God), *we are expected to make some efforts on
our own behalf*: God helps them that help themselves.

All things are possible with God.
English proverb, late 17th century, from the Bible (Matthew
19:26), 'With men this is impossible; but with God all
things are possible.'

God helps them that help themselves.
often used in urging someone to action; English proverb.

God writes straight with crooked lines.
God can use any instrument to achieve His ends;
Portuguese proverb.

The nature of God is a circle of which the centre is everywhere and the circumference is nowhere.

medieval saying, said to have been traced to a lost treatise of Empedocles; quoted in the *Roman de la Rose*, and by St Bonaventura in *Itinerarius Mentis in Deum*.

There's probably no God. Now stop worrying and enjoy your life.

slogan for a secular poster campaign on London buses, January 2009.

Good and Evil

See also VIRTUE

Although some goodness is unassailable (The sun loses nothing by shining into a puddle), *there is an insistence on the corrupting effects of evil:* He that touches pitch shall be defiled.

The greater the sinner, the greater the saint.

a sinner who has reformed is likely to be more virtuous that someone who is morally neutral; English proverb, late 18th century.

He that touches pitch shall be defiled.

a person who chooses to put themselves in contact with wrongdoing will be marked by it; English proverb, early

Good and Evil

14th century, with allusion to the Bible (Ecclesiasticus 13:1), 'He that toucheth pitch shall be defiled therewith.'

Honi soit qui mal y pense.
French, 'Evil be to him who evil thinks', the motto of the Order of the Garter, originated by Edward III, probably on 23 April of 1348 or 1349.

Ill weeds grow apace.
used to comment on the apparent success enjoyed by an ill-doer; English proverb, late 15th century.

Satan rebuking sin.
originally meaning that the worst possible stage has been reached; in later use, an ironic comment on the nature of the person delivering the rebuke; English proverb, early 17th century.

The sun loses nothing by shining into a puddle.
something which is naturally clear and radiant cannot be tainted or diminished by association; English proverb, early 14th century, of classical origin.

Two blacks don't make a white.
one injury or instance of wrongdoing does not justify another; English proverb, early 18th century.

Two wrongs don't make a right.
a first injury does not justify a second in retaliation; English proverb, late 18th century.

What is got under the Devil's back is spent under his belly.

what is gained improperly will be spent on folly and debauchery; English proverb, late 16th century.

Where God builds a church, the Devil will build a chapel.

the establishment of something which is itself good may also create the opening for something evil; English proverb, mid 16th century.

Gossip

While gossip may be seen as a natural part of human relations (Gossip is the lifeblood of society), it is more generally seen as likely to be damaging: according to the wartime security slogan, Careless talk costs lives.

Careless talk costs lives.

Second World War security slogan.

A dog that will fetch a bone will carry a bone.

someone given to gossip carries talk both ways; English proverb, early 19th century.

Give a dog a bad name and hang him.

once a person's reputation has been blackened his plight is hopeless; English proverb, early 18th century.

Gossip

Gossip is the lifeblood of society.
American proverb, mid 20th century.

Gossip is vice enjoyed vicariously.
American proverb, early 20th century.

The greater the truth, the greater the libel.
English proverb, late 18th century.

Loose lips sink ships.
American Second World War security slogan.

A tale never loses in the telling.
implying that a story is often exaggerated when it is
repeated; English proverb, mid 16th century.

**Those who live in glass houses shouldn't
throw stones.**
it is unwise to criticize or slander another if you are
vulnerable to retaliation; English proverb, mid 17th century.

What the soldier said isn't evidence.
hearsay evidence alone cannot be relied on; English
proverb, mid 19th century, originally from Charles Dickens
Pickwick Papers (1837), 'You must not tell us what the
soldier, or any other man, said … it's not evidence.'

Whoever gossips to you will gossip about you.
a warning against enjoyment of gossip; Spanish proverb.

Government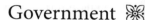

See also POLITICS, SOCIETY

*From the point of view of the subject, government is
seen not only as powerful but also often as out of reach:*
God is high above, and the tsar is far away.

The cat, the rat, and Lovell the dog, rule all England under the hog.

contemporary rhyme referring to William *Catesby*, Richard
Ratcliffe, and Francis *Lovell*, favourites of Richard III, whose
personal emblem was a white boar.

Divide and rule.

government control is more easily exercised if possible
opponents are separated into factions; English proverb,
early 17th century.

God is high above, and the tsar is far away.

the source of central power is out of the reach of local
interests; Russian proverb; compare **The mountains are
high, and the emperor is far away** below, and **Delhi is far
away** at CAUTION.

The mountains are high, and the emperor is far away.

the source of central power is out of the reach of local
interests; Chinese proverb; compare **God is high above,**

and the tsar is far away above, and **Delhi is far away**
at CAUTION.

No fist is big enough to hide the sky.
there are limits to the powers of even the most repressive
regime; African saying.

 # Gratitude

See also GENEROSITY

*The ungrateful person may discover too late the value of
what they have received:* You never miss the water till
the well runs dry.

The Devil was sick, the Devil a saint would be.
promises made in adversity may not be kept in prosperity;
English proverb, early 17th century.

Don't overload gratitude, if you do, she'll kick.
American proverb, mid 18th century.

Never look a gift horse in the mouth.
warning against questioning the quality or use of a lucky
chance or gift; referring to the fact that it is by a horse's teeth
that its age is judged; English proverb, early 16th century.

The river that forgets its source will dry up.
ingratitude brings its own punishment; African proverb.

When you drink water, remember who dug the well.

a warning against taking the efforts of others for granted; modern saying, said to be a Chinese proverb.

You never miss the water till the well runs dry.

applied to situations in which it is only when a source of support or sustenance has been withdrawn that its importance is understood; English proverb, early 17th century.

Greed

See also MONEY

When we give in to greed we are likely to find the appetite insatiable: Much would have more.

The more you get the more you want.
English proverb, mid 14th century.

Much would have more.
the ownership of substantial possessions creates in the owner the desire for still more; English proverb, mid 14th century.

Need makes greed.
Scottish proverb.

Guilt

Pigs get fat, but hogs get slaughtered.
used as a warning against greed; modern saying.

The sea refuses no river.
the sea's capacity is so great that anyone who chooses may
find a place there; English proverb, early 17th century.

**Where the carcase is, there shall the eagles be
gathered together.**
English proverb, mid 16th century, from the Bible (Matthew
24:28), 'Wheresoever the carcase is, there will the eagles be
gathered together.'

Guilt

See also CRIME AND PUNISHMENT

The experience of guilt is likely to be intolerable (The
guilty one always runs); *we may as well* Confess
and be hanged.

Confess and be hanged.
guilt must be confessed and the due punishment accepted
for true repentance; English proverb, late 16th century.

The guilty flee when no man pursueth.
saying, with biblical allusion to Proverbs 28:1, 'The wicked
flee when no man pursueth; but the righteous are bold
as a lion.'

The guilty one always runs.

American proverb, mid 20th century.

Not guilty, but don't do it again.

comment on what is taken as a lucky escape from
conviction; informal legal saying.

We are all guilty.

supposedly typical of the liberal view that all members of
society bear responsibility for its wrongs; used particularly
as a catchphrase by the psychiatrist 'Dr Heinz Kiosk', created
by the satirist Peter Simple (pseudonym of Michael
Wharton, 1913–2006).

We name the guilty men.

supposedly now a cliché of investigative journalism; *Guilty
Men* was the title of a tract by Michael Foot, Frank Owen,
and Peter Howard, published under the pseudonym of
'Cato', which attacked the supporters of the Munich
agreement and the appeasement policy of Neville
Chamberlain.

Habit

See CUSTOM AND HABIT

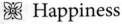 Happiness

See also HOPE

The unwise person will recognize happiness only when it is lost (Blessings brighten as they take their flight). *An alternative way is to find reasons for happiness in unpromising circumstances:* It is a poor heart that never rejoices.

Blessings brighten as they take their flight.

it is only when something is lost that one realizes its value; English proverb, mid 18th century.

Call no man happy till he dies.

traditionally attributed to the Athenian statesman and poet Solon (*c.*640–after 556 BC) in the form 'Call no man happy before he dies, he is at best but fortunate'; English proverb, mid 16th century.

A good time was had by all.

title of a collection of poems published in 1937 by Stevie Smith (1902–71), taken from the characteristic conclusion of accounts of social events in parish magazines.

**Happiness is the only thing we can give
without having.**

modern saying.

Happiness is what you make of it.

American proverb, mid 19th century.

Hell is where heaven is not.

English proverb, late 16th century.

**If I keep a green bough in my heart a singing bird
will come.**

we have some role in creating our own happiness;
Chinese proverb.

It is a poor heart that never rejoices.

often used to explain a celebratory action, and implying that
circumstances are not in general unrelievedly bad; English
proverb, mid 19th century.

Time flies when you are having fun.

modern saying, often in ironical usage.

Haste and Delay

*While the hurried action associated with lack of
thought is likely to be ineffectual* (More haste, less
speed), *procrastination in itself is not an answer:*
Delays are dangerous.

Haste and Delay

Always in a hurry, always behind.
North American proverb, mid 20th century.

Delays are dangerous.
used as a warning against procrastination; English proverb, late 16th century.

Don't hurry—start early.
American proverb, mid 20th century.

Haste is from the Devil.
often used to mean that undue haste results in work being done badly or carelessly; English proverb, mid 17th century.

Haste makes waste.
hurried work is likely to be wasteful; English proverb, late 14th century.

Make haste slowly.
advising a course of careful preparation; English proverb, late 16th century; the idea is found in the classical world in the words of the Roman Emperor Augustus (63 BC–AD 14), 'Festina lente [Make haste slowly].'

More haste, less speed.
speed here meant originally 'success' rather than 'swiftness', and the meaning is that hurried work is likely to be less successful; English proverb, mid 14th century.

Never put off till tomorrow what you can do today.

English proverb, late 14th century.

Procrastination is the thief of time.

someone who continually puts things off ultimately achieves little; English proverb, mid 18th century, from Edward Young *Night Thoughts* (1742–5).

Health

See also EATING, MEDICINE, SICKNESS

The preservation of health is seen as lying in our own hands, though the medium of adopting a sensible lifestyle: Early to bed and early to rise, makes a man healthy, wealthy, and wise.

An apple a day keeps the doctor away.

eating an apple each day keeps one healthy; English proverb, mid 19th century; compare **Eat leeks in March and ramsons in May, and all the year after physicians may play** below.

Don't die of ignorance.

Aids publicity campaign, 1987.

Early to bed and early to rise, makes a man healthy, wealthy, and wise.

linking a healthy and sober lifestyle with material success; English proverb, late 15th century.

Health

Eat leeks in March and ramsons in May, and all the year after physicians may play.
ramsons = wild garlic; Welsh proverb; compare **An apple a day keeps the doctor away** above.

Eat till you're cold, live to grow old.
traditional saying.

Even your closest friends won't tell you.
advertising slogan for Listerine mouthwash, US, 1923.

Every good quality is contained in ginger.
Indian proverb.

Health is wealth.
traditional saying.

He who has health has hope; and he who has hope has everything.
Arabic proverb.

More die of food than famine.
American proverb, mid 20th century.

Slip, slop, slap.
sun protection slogan, meaning slip on a T-shirt, slop on some suncream, slap on a hat; Australian health education programme, 1980s.

Those who do not find time for exercise will have to find time for illness.

traditional saying.

Your food is your medicine.

Indian proverb.

History ✤

To make a mark on history is not necessarily something to be sought: Happy is the country which has no history. *Beyond this, the objectivity of history is seen rather sceptically:* Until the lions produce their own historian, the story of the hunt will gratify the hunter.

Happy is the country which has no history.

memorable events are likely to be unhappy and disruptive; English proverb, early 19th century; compare a comment attributed to the French political philosopher Montesquieu (1689–1755) by Thomas Carlyle, 'Happy the people whose annals are blank in history-books!'

History is a fable agreed upon.

American proverb, mid 20th century.

History is fiction with the truth left out.

American proverb, mid 20th century.

The Home

History is written by the victors.
modern saying.

History repeats itself.
English proverb, mid 19th century.

Until the lions produce their own historian, the story of the hunt will glorify the hunter.
African proverb.

 # The Home

See also HOUSEWORK

There are various ways of expressing the importance of having a home, from East, west, home's best, *to the Chinese assertion that* Falling leaves have to return to their roots.

East, west, home's best.
English proverb, mid 19th century.

An Englishman's home is his castle.
a person has the right to refuse entry to his home; reflecting a legal principle, as formulated by the English jurist Edward Coke (1552–1634), 'For a man's house is his castle, *et domus sua cuique est tutissimum refugium* [and each man's home is his safest refuge]'; English proverb, late 16th century.

Every cock will crow upon his own dunghill.

everyone is confident and at ease on their home; English
proverb, mid 13th century.

Falling leaves have to return to their roots.

everything must ultimately return to its origins;
Chinese proverb.

Home is home though it's never so homely.

no place can compare with one's own home; English
proverb, mid 16th century.

Home is where the heart is.

one's true home is wherever the person one loves most is;
English proverb, late 19th century.

Home is where the mortgage is.

American proverb, mid 20th century.

Lang may yer lum reek!

long may your chimney smoke, often used as a toast;
Scottish saying.

There's no place like home.

English proverb, late 16th century; the saying is found
earlier in Greek, in the work of the Greek poet Hesiod
(*c.*700 BC).

✳ Honesty

See also CORRUPTION, DECEPTION, LIES, TRUTH

Honesty is essential in even the smallest actions (It's a
sin to steal a pin), *although it is not always realistically
to be expected* (Honesty is more praised than
practised). *However, apart from moral duty there may
be pragmatic reasons for adopting it:* Honesty is the
best policy.

Children and fools tell the truth.

implying that they lack the cunning to see possible danger;
tradition sometimes adds drunkards; English proverb, mid
16th century.

Confession is good for the soul.

confession is essential to repentance and forgiveness;
English proverb, mid 17th century.

He who steals an egg will steal a camel.

someone who is guilty of petty dishonesty is likely to be
guilty of more serious theft; modern saying, said to be an
Arabic proverb.

Honesty is more praised than practised.

it is easier to advise another person to be honest than to be
honest oneself; American proverb, mid 20th century.

Honesty is the best policy.

as well as being right, to be honest may also achieve a more successful outcome; English proverb, early 17th century.

A howlin' coyote ain't stealin' no chickens.

American proverb, mid 20th century.

It's a sin to steal a pin.

even if what is stolen is of little value, the action is still wrong; English proverb, late 19th century.

Nothing is stolen without hands.

if money or goods are missing, someone has stolen them; English proverb, early 17th century.

Sell honestly, but not honesty.

a play on words meaning that honesty is the essential virtue in commerce; American proverb, mid 20th century.

Hope

See also HAPPINESS, OPTIMISM AND PESSIMISM

Hope may make difficult circumstances bearable (If it were not for hope, the heart would break), but over-indulgence in its promises will not lead to happiness: He that lives in hope dances to an ill tune.

Hope

Blessed is he who expects nothing, for he shall never be disappointed.

English proverb, early 18th century, originally with allusion to Alexander Pope (1688–1744), '"Blessed is the man who expects nothing, for he shall never be disappointed" was the ninth beatitude.'

A drowning man will clutch at a straw.

when hope is slipping away one grasps at the slightest chance; English proverb, mid 16th century.

He that lives in hope dances to an ill tune.

hoping for something better may constrain one's freedom of action; English proverb, late 16th century.

Hope deferred makes the heart sick.

implying that it is worse to have had one's hopes raised and then dashed, than to have been resigned to not having something; English proverb, late 14th century, from the Bible (Proverbs 13:12), 'Hope deferred maketh the heart sick: but when the desire cometh, it is a tree of life.'

Hope is a good breakfast but a bad supper.

while it is pleasant to begin something in a hopeful mood, the hopes need to have been fulfilled by the time it ends; English proverb, mid 17th century.

Hope is the pillar of the world.

African proverb.

Hope springs eternal.

English proverb, mid 18th century, from Alexander Pope
(1688–1744) *An Essay on Man* (1733), 'Hope springs eternal
in the human breast: /Man never Is, but always To be blest.'

If it were not for hope, the heart would break.

referring to the role of hope in warding off complete
despair; English proverb, mid 13th century.

In the kingdom of hope, there is no winter.

Russian proverb.

It is better to travel hopefully than to arrive.

often with the implication that something long sought may
be disappointing when achieved; English proverb, late 19th
century; from Robert Louis Stevenson *Virginibus Puerisque*
(1881), 'To travel hopefully is a better thing than to arrive,
and the true success is to labour.'

While there's life there's hope.

often used as encouragement not to despair in an
unpromising situation; English proverb, mid 16th century.

Horses

See also CATS, DOGS

*Sayings about horses reflect interests in choosing, and
keeping, a horse, with an emphasis on personal*

Horses

judgement and management: Care, and not fine
stables, makes a good horse.

Care, and not fine stables, makes a good horse.
Danish proverb.

No foot, no horse.
relating to horse care, and recorded in North America as 'no
hoof, no horse'; English proverb, mid 18th century.

**One white foot, buy him; two white feet, try him;
three white feet, look well about him; four white
feet, go without him.**
on horse-dealing, categorizing features in a horse which are
believed to be unlucky; English proverb, recorded in various
forms from the 15th century.

Pace makes the race.
from horse racing, relating to the setting of odds;
modern saying.

**There is nothing so good for the inside of a man as
the outside of a horse.**
recommending the healthful effects of horse-riding; English
proverb, early 20th century.

**The wind of heaven is that which blows between a
horse's ears.**
saying, said to be an Arabic proverb.

Hospitality ✵

Hospitality is a natural source of enjoyment (It is merry in hall when beards wag all), *but guests can overstay their welcome. An African proverb recommends a way of dealing with this:* Treat your guest as a guest for two days; on the third day give him a hoe.

Always leave the party when you are still having a good time.

implying that pleasure of this kind is transient; American proverb, mid 20th century.

The company makes the feast.

the success of a social occasion depends on those present rather than on the food and drink provided; English proverb, mid 17th century.

The first day a guest, the second day a guest, the third day a calamity.

Indian proverb.

Fish and guests stink after three days.

one should not outstay one's welcome; English proverb, late 16th century.

Food without hospitality is medicine.

American proverb, mid 20th century.

Housework

A guest is like the morning dew.
a good guest does not stay very long; African proverb.

Hospitality and medicine must be confined to three days.
Indian proverb.

It is merry in hall when beards wag all.
when conversation is in full flow; English proverb, early 14th century.

The pot boils; friendship lives.
some friendships will not outlast the provision of hospitality; proverb of classical origin.

There isn't much to talk about at some parties until after one or two couples leave.
American proverb, mid 20th century.

Treat your guest as a guest for two days; on the third day give him a hoe.
African proverb.

 # Housework

See also THE HOME

Apart from slogans promoting cleaning devices such as Hoover's It beats as it sweeps as it cleans, *sayings about housework tend to focus on it as the traditional sphere of activity for women:* A woman's work is never done.

He that will thrive must first ask his wife.
the husband's material welfare depends on the way in which his wife manages the household; English proverb, late 15th century.

It beats as it sweeps as it cleans.
advertising slogan for Hoover vacuum cleaners, 1919.

Persil washes whiter—and it shows.
advertising slogan for Persil washing powder, 1970s.

They that wash on Monday
Have all the week to dry;
They that wash on Tuesday
Are not so much awry;
They that wash on Wednesday
Are not so much to blame;
They that wash on Thursday
Wash for very shame;
They that wash on Friday
Wash in sorry need;
And they that wash on Saturday,
Are lazy folk indeed.
traditional rhyme.

The Human Race

A woman's work is never done.
reflecting the traditional responsibilities of the housewife;
English proverb, late 16th century.

The Human Race

The view that Man is the measure of all things *can be
traced back to the classical world, but later sayings
suggest more of a limitation:* The best of men are but
men at best, *or even the dialect summary,* There's nowt
so queer as folk.

**All mankind is divided into three classes: those that
are immovable, those that are movable, and those
that move.**
modern saying, said to be an Arabic proverb.

Am I not a man and a brother?
motto on the seal of the British and Foreign Anti-Slavery
Society, 1787, depicting a kneeling slave in chains
uttering these words (subsequently a popular
Wedgwood cameo).

The best of men are but men at best.
even someone of great moral worth is still human and
fallible; English proverb, late 17th century.

God sleeps in the stone, dreams in the plant, stirs in the animal, and awakens in man.

traditional saying, frequently said to be of Indian origin; the wording varies in different languages.

Man is a wolf to man.

English proverb, mid 16th century, from the Roman comic dramatist Plautus (c.250–184 BC), 'A man is a wolf rather than a man to another man, when he hasn't yet found out what he's like.'

Man is the measure of all things.

everything could be understood in terms of humankind; English proverb, mid 16th century; found earlier in the classical world in the words of the Greek sophist Protagoras (b. c.485 BC), 'That man is the measure of all things.'

There's nowt so queer as folk.

English proverb, early 20th century.

What is the most important thing in life? It is people, people, people.

Maori proverb.

Young saint, old devil.

unnaturally good and moral behaviour at an early age is likely to change in later life; English proverb, early 15th century.

Hypothesis and Fact

See also SCIENCE, THINKING

While Facts are stubborn things, *they will not always be reached through speculation: the question* How many angels can dance on the head of a pin? *has become a type of fruitless hypothesis.*

The exception proves the rule.

originally this meant that the recognition of something as an exception proved the existence of a rule, but it is now more often used or understood as justifying divergence from a rule (compare **There is an exception to every rule** below); English proverb, mid 17th century.

Facts are stubborn things.

used to indicate a core of reality that cannot be adjusted to people's wishes; English proverb, early 18th century.

How many angels can dance on the head of a pin?

regarded satirically as a characteristic speculation of scholastic philosophy, particularly as exemplified by 'Doctor Scholasticus' (Anselm of Laon, d. 1117) and as used in medieval comedies.

Nullius in verba.

Latin, 'in the word of none', motto of the Royal Society, emphasizing reliance on experiment rather than authority; adapted from the Roman poet Horace *Epistles*, 'Not bound to swear allegiance to any master, wherever the wind takes me I travel as a visitor.'

One story is good till another is told.

doubt may be cast on an apparently convincing account by a second told from a different angle; English proverb, late 16th century.

The proof of the pudding is in the eating.

the truth of an assertion will be demonstrated by how things actually turn out; proof here means test'; English proverb, early 14th century.

There is an exception to every rule.

English proverb, late 16th century; compare **The exception proves the rule** above.

 Idleness

See also ACTION AND INACTION, WORDS AND DEEDS

Idleness is not only seen as damaging and dangerous in itself (An idle brain is the devil's workshop), *it is not even necessarily enjoyable for the person who gives way to it:* Idle people have the least leisure.

As good be an addled egg as an idle bird.

an idle person will produce nothing; English proverb, late 16th century.

Better be idle than ill doing.

Scottish proverb.

Better to wear out than to rust out.

it is better to remain active than to succumb to idleness; in this form frequently attributed to Richard Cumberland, Bishop of Peterborough (1631–1718); English proverb, mid 16th century.

A day without work is a day without food.

modern saying, associated with Zen Buddhism.

The devil finds work for idle hands to do.

someone who has no work to do will get into mischief; English proverb, early 18th century.

Doing nothing is doing ill.
failing to do anything is effectively wrong-doing;
traditional saying.

An idle brain is the devil's workshop.
those who do not apply themselves to their work are most
likely to get into trouble; English proverb, early
17th century.

Idleness is never enjoyable unless there is plenty to do.
American proverb, mid 20th century; the idea is found in
the Jerome K. Jerome *Idle Thoughts of an Idle Fellow* (1886),
'It is impossible to enjoy idling thoroughly unless one has
plenty of work to do.'

Idleness is the root of all evil.
English proverb, early 15th century; the idea has been
attributed to the French theologian, monastic reformer, and
abbot St Bernard of Clairvaux (1090–1153); compare
Money is the root of all evil at MONEY.

Idle people have the least leisure.
lazy people are the least able to manage their time
efficiently; English proverb, late 17th century.

If you won't work you shan't eat.
essential sustenance is seen as a reward for industry; English
proverb, mid 16th century, from the Bible (II Thessalonians
3:10), 'If any would not work, neither should he eat.'

Ignorance

Who is more busy than he who has the least to do?
English proverb, early 17th century.

Ignorance

Ignorance is not necessarily seen as an unhappy state:
Ignorance is bliss *from the 18th century finds an echo
from a Russian saying of the Soviet era,* The less you
know, the better you sleep.

The husband is always the last to know.
relating to marital infidelity; English proverb, early
17th century.

Ignorance is bliss.
English proverb, mid 18th century, from Thomas Gray *Ode
on a Prospect of Eton College* (1747), 'Where ignorance is
bliss, 'Tis folly to be wise.'

Ignorance is voluntary misfortune.
one has chosen not to remedy the condition; American
proverb, mid 20th century.

It is dark at the foot of the lighthouse.
we often miss what is closest to us; Japanese proverb.

Ignorance

The last one to know about the sea is the fish.
the person with most reason to know about something
often knows least; modern saying, claimed to be a
Chinese proverb.

The less you know, the better you sleep.
Russian saying of the Soviet era.

Man is the enemy of that of which he is ignorant.
fear is a common response to the unknown; Arab proverb.

Nothing so bold as a blind mare.
those who know least about a situation are least likely to be
deterred by it; English proverb, early 17th century.

A slice off a cut loaf isn't missed.
if someone has already been diminished or damaged,
further damage may go unnoticed; English proverb, late
16th century (first recorded in Shakespeare's *Titus
Andronicus*, 1592).

**What the eye doesn't see, the heart doesn't
grieve over.**
now sometimes used with the implication that information
is being withheld to prevent difficulties; English proverb,
mid 16th century.

What you don't know can't hurt you.
English proverb, late 16th century.

Inaction

When the blind lead the blind, both shall fall into the ditch.
when a person is guided by someone equally inexperienced, both are likely to come to grief; English proverb, late 9th century, from the Bible (Matthew 15:14), 'They be blind leaders of the blind. And if the blind lead the blind, both shall fall into the ditch.'

Inaction

See ACTION AND INACTION

Indecision

See also CERTAINTY AND DOUBT

The consensus on indecision is that the person who cannot make a choice is likely to lose by it: Between two stools one falls to the ground.

Between two stools one falls to the ground.
inability to choose between, or accommodate oneself to, alternative viewpoints or courses of action may end in disaster; English proverb, late 14th century.

The cat would eat fish, but would not wet her feet.
commenting on a situation in which desire for something is checked by unwillingness to risk discomfort in acquiring it; English proverb, early 13th century.

Councils of war never fight.

people discussing matters in a group never reach the decision to fight, which an individual would make; English proverb, mid 19th century.

First thoughts are best.

advice to trust an instinctive reaction, often used as a warning against indecision; English proverb, early 20th century.

He who hesitates is lost.

often used to urge decisive action on someone; English proverb, early 18th century; early usages refer specifically to women, as in Joseph Addison *Cato* (1713), 'The woman that deliberates is lost.'

If you run after two hares you will catch neither.

one must decide on one's goal; English proverb, early 16th century.

Indecision is fatal, so make up your mind.

American proverb, mid 20th century.

Inventions and Discoveries

A theme which stresses the challenge of the new.

Inventions and Discoveries

Always something new out of Africa.
English proverb, mid 16th century; from the words of Pliny
the Elder (AD 23–79), *'Semper aliquid novi Africam adferre*
[Africa always brings [us] something new]', originally
referring to the hybridization of African animals.

**Do not follow where the path may lead. Go instead
where there is no path and leave a trail.**
late 20th-century saying, often attributed to Ralph Waldo
Emerson (1803–82), but not found in his works.

Here be dragons.
alluding to a traditional indication of early map-makers
that a region was unexplored and potentially dangerous.

**If you don't make mistakes you don't
make anything.**
English proverb, late 19th century; the idea is found in a
speech made at the Mansion House in London by the
American lawyer and diplomat Edward John Phelps
(1822–1900) on 24 January 1889: 'The man who makes
no mistakes does not usually make anything.'

**There is one thing stronger than all the armies
in the world; and that is an idea whose time
has come.**
mid 20th-century saying; the idea is found in Victor Hugo
Histoire d'un Crime (written 1851–2, published 1877),

'A stand can be made against invasion by an army; no stand can be made against invasion by an idea.'

Turkeys, heresy, hops, and beer came into England all in one year.

perhaps referring to 1521. The *turkey*, found domesticated in Mexico in 1518, was soon afterwards introduced into Europe; in 1521, the Pope conferred on Henry VIII the title Defender of the Faith, in recognition of his opposition to the Lutheran *heresy;* the *hop* plant is believed to have been introduced into the south of England from Flanders between 1520 and 1524; and *beer* as the name of hopped malt liquor became common only in the 16th century; English proverb, late 16th century.

Journalism

See NEWS AND JOURNALISM

Justice

See also CRIME AND PUNISHMENT, THE LAW

Fairness and honest dealing are desirable in themselves (Fair play's a jewel), *but beyond this there are serious consequences in making it difficult for anyone to obtain justice:* Justice delayed is justice denied.

All's fair in love and war.

in certain conditions rules do not apply, and any measures are acceptable; English proverb, early 17th century.

Be just before you're generous.

often used in the context of advising that one should settle any obligations before indulging in generosity; English proverb, mid 18th century.

A fair exchange is no robbery.

sometimes used of an action regarded as cancelling out an obligation which has been incurred; English proverb, mid 16th century.

Fair play's a jewel.

applauding the value of honest dealing; English proverb, early 19th century.

The fox should not be on the jury at the goose's trial.

a member of a jury must be unbiased; English proverb.

Give and take is fair play.

English proverb, late 18th century.

Give the Devil his due.

one should acknowledge the strengths and capabilities of even the most unpleasant person; English proverb, late 16th century.

Justice delayed is justice denied.

English proverb, late 20th century; compare a clause from Magna Carta (1215), 'To no man will we sell, or deny, or delay, right or justice.'

One law for the rich and another for the poor.

English proverb, mid 19th century.

There are two sides to every question.

a problem can be seen from more than one angle; English proverb, early 19th century.

Turn about is fair play.

recommending equality of opportunity; English proverb, mid 18th century.

We all love justice—at our neighbour's expense.

American proverb, mid 20th century.

Justice

What goes around comes around.
often used as a comment on someone becoming subject
to what they have visited on others; late 20th century,
of US origin.

What's sauce for the goose is sauce for the gander.
originally meaning that what is suitable for a woman is
also suitable for a man, but now sometimes used in wider
contexts; English proverb, late 17th century.

Knowledge ❈

While knowledge is to be sought (The larger the
shoreline of knowledge, the longer the shoreline of
wonder, *and more simply* Knowledge is power), *we
may be betrayed by over-confidence in our prowess:*
A little knowledge is a dangerous thing.

The cobbler to his last and the gunner to his linstock.

the gunner's *linstock* was a long pole used to hold a match
for firing a cannon, and the saying is a fanciful extension
of **let the cobbler stick to his last** below; English proverb,
mid 18th century.

Every picture tells a story.

advertisement for Doan's Backache Kidney Pills
(early 1900s).

The good Christian should beware of mathematicians, and all those who make empty prophecies. The danger already exists that mathematicians have made a covenant with the Devil to darken the spirit and to confine man in the bonds of Hell.

mistranslation of St Augustine's *De Genesi ad Litteram*,
'Hence, a devout Christian must avoid astrologers and all
impious soothsayers, especially when they tell the truth, for
fear of leading his soul into error by consorting with

Knowledge

demons and entangling himself with the bonds of such
association' (the Latin word *mathematicus* means both
'mathematician' and 'astrologer').

I pointed out to you the stars and all you saw was the tip of my finger.
African proverb.

Knowledge and timber shouldn't be much used until they are seasoned.
American proverb, mid 19th century.

Knowledge is power.
English proverb, late 16th century, often with allusion to
Francis Bacon *Meditationes Sacrae* (1597), 'Knowledge
itself is power.'

The larger the shoreline of knowledge, the longer the shoreline of wonder.
North American proverb, mid 20th century.

Learning is a treasure that follows its owner everywhere.
reflecting on the advantage knowledge has over material
possessions; Chinese proverb.

Learning is better than house and land.
reflecting on the difference between knowledge and
material, and therefore ephemeral, possessions; English
proverb, late 18th century.

Let the cobbler stick to his last.

people should concern themselves only with things they know something about (the cobbler's *last* is a shoemaker's model for shaping or repairing a shoe or boot); English proverb, mid 16th century; compare **The cobbler to his last and the gunner to his linstock** above.

A little knowledge is a dangerous thing.

English proverb, early 18th century; alteration of Alexander Pope *An Essay on Criticism* (1711), 'A little learning is a dangerous thing; Drink deep, or taste not the Pierian spring.'

One half of the world does not know how the other half lives.

often used to comment on a lack of communication between neighbouring groups; English proverb, early 17th century.

The sea of learning has no end.

Chinese proverb.

Straws tell which way the wind blows.

English proverb, mid 17th century.

There will be trouble if the cobbler starts making pies.

a warning against stepping outside one's area of expertise; modern saying, said to be a Russian proverb.

Knowledge

Walking ten thousand miles; reading ten thousand books.

theoretical knowledge and practical experience are of equal value; Chinese proverb, compare **Walking ten thousand miles is better than reading ten thousand books** at EXPERIENCE.

What's hit is history, what's missed is mystery.

on the importance of securing a dead specimen of a new species; late 19th century saying.

When a pine needle falls in the forest, the eagle sees it, the deer hears it, and the bear smells it.

modern saying, said to be of Native American origin.

When house and land are gone and spent, then learning is most excellent.

contrasting the value of learning with the ephemeral nature of material possessions; English proverb, mid 18th century.

The Law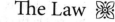

See also CRIME AND PUNISHMENT, JUSTICE

The legal world is often seen as a perilous one (The more laws, the more thieves and bandits), *although not every saying goes as far as the Scottish proverb:* Home is home, as the Devil said when he found himself in the Court of Session.

The devil makes his Christmas pies of lawyers' tongues and clerks' fingers.

the lawyers' tongues and clerks' fingers stand for the words and actions of the legal profession as welcomed by the Devil; English proverb, late 16th century.

Gray's Inn for walks, Lincoln's Inn for a wall, The Inner Temple for a garden, And the Middle Temple for a hall.

on the four Inns of Court; traditional rhyme, mid 17th century.

Hard cases make bad law.

difficult cases cause the clarity of the law to be obscured by exceptions and strained interpretations; the saying may now also be used to imply that a law framed in response to a particularly distressing case may not be well thought out or well based; English proverb, mid 19th century.

The Law

Home is home, as the Devil said when he found himself in the Court of Session.
The *Court of Session* is the supreme civil tribunal of Scotland, established in 1532; Scottish proverbial saying, mid 19th century.

Ignorance of the law is no excuse for breaking it.
English proverb, early 15th century.

A man who is his own lawyer has a fool for his client.
English proverb, early 19th century.

The more laws, the more thieves and bandits.
a rigid and over-detailed code of law is likely to foster rather than prevent lawbreaking; English proverb, late 16th century; the idea is found in the *Tao-te Ching* of Lao Tzu (*c.*604–531 BC), 'The more laws and orders are made prominent, The more thieves and bandits there will be.'

No one should be judge in his own cause.
it is impossible to be impartial where your own interest is involved; English proverb, mid 15th century.

Possession is nine points of the law.
although it does not reflect any specific legal ruling, in early use the satisfaction of ten (sometimes twelve) points was commonly asserted to attest to full entitlement or ownership; possession, represented by nine (or eleven)

points is therefore the closest substitute for this; English
proverb, early 17th century.

Rules are made to be broken.
English proverb, mid 20th century; the idea expressed by
Christopher North in *Blackwood's Magazine* for May 1830,
'Laws were made to be broken.'

Where the law is uncertain, there is no law.
legal saying, late 18th century; earliest found in Latin *Ubi
jus incertum, ibi jus nullum.*

Leadership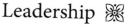

See also MANAGEMENT

*While the health of an organization can be judged by
that of its leadership (The fish always stinks from the
head downwards), there is also an awareness that
a successful leader can also at need give loyalty
and support to another: A good leader is
also a good follower.*

As one fern frond dies, another is born to take its place.
Maori proverb, applied particularly to chiefs.

Equality is difficult, but superiority is painful.
on the difficulties of leadership; African proverb.

Leisure

The fish always stinks from the head downwards.
as the freshness of a dead fish can be judged from the condition of its head, any corruption in a country or organization will be manifested first in its leaders; English proverb, late 16th century.

A good leader is also a good follower.
American proverb, mid 20th century.

He that cannot obey cannot command.
the experience of being under orders teaches one how they should be given; English proverb, late 15th century.

He who would lead must be a bridge.
Welsh saying.

If the people will lead, then the leaders must follow.
modern saying.

If you are not the lead dog the view never changes.
Canadian saying.

One mountain cannot accommodate two tigers.
there cannot be two leaders; Chinese proverb.

 # Leisure

See also IDLENESS, WORK

Leisure is more than idleness in that it provides essential refreshment: All work and no play makes Jack a dull boy.

All work and no play makes Jack a dull boy.

warning against a lifestyle without any form of relaxation;
English proverb, mid 17th century.

The busiest men have the most leisure.

someone who is habitually busy is likely to make best use
of their time; English proverb, late 19th century.

Take time to smell the roses.

it is important to spend some time in leisure;
modern saying.

The gods do not subtract from a man's allotted span the time spent fishing.

modern saying, sometimes claimed to have originated in an
Assyrian tablet.

Letters

Letters can be a key form of human communication:
A love letter sometimes costs more than a
three-cent stamp.

Do not close a letter without reading it.

American proverb, mid 20th century.

A love letter sometimes costs more than a three-cent stamp.

American proverb, mid 20th century.

Lies

Someone, somewhere, wants a letter from you.
advertising slogan for the British Post Office, 1960s.

 # Lies

See also DECEPTION, HONESTY, TRUTH

Lies have their own power (A lie can go round the world and back again while the truth is lacing up its boots)*, but in the end a falsehood will be exposed:* The liar's candle lasts till evening.

An abomination unto the Lord, but a very present help in time of trouble.
definition of a lie, an amalgamation of lines from the Bible (Proverbs 12:22, 'Lying lips are abomination to the Lord', and Psalms 46:1, 'God is our hope and strength: a very present help in trouble'), often attributed to the American politician Adlai Stevenson (1900–62).

Even a liar tells the truth sometimes.
modern saying.

Half the truth is often a whole lie.
something which is partially true can still convey a completely false impression; English proverb, mid 18th century.

A liar ought to have a good memory.

implying that one lie is likely to lead to the need for another; English proverb, mid 16th century, 1st century AD in Latin.

The liar's candle lasts till evening.

a lie will be exposed sooner or later; Turkish proverb.

A lie can go around the world and back again while the truth is lacing up its boots.

American proverb, late 19th century; a variant is recorded in the words of C. H. Spurgeon in *Gems from Spurgeon* (1859), 'It is well said in the old proverb, "a lie will go round the world while truth is pulling its boots on."'

One seldom meets a lonely lie.

implying that one is likely to lead to the need for another; American proverb, mid 20th century.

To tell a falsehood is like the cut of a sabre, for though the wound may heal the scar will remain.

Persian proverb.

Life

See also LIFESTYLES

While not necessarily easy (Life isn't all beer and skittles), *the ultimate verdict is positive, if somewhat bleak:* A live dog is better than a dead lion.

Life

Art is long and life is short.
originally from the Greek physician Hippocrates (*c*.460–357 BC), comparing the difficulties encountered in learning the art of medicine or healing with the shortness of human life ('Art' is now commonly understood in the proverb in a less specific sense); often quoted in the Latin version *Ars longa, vita brevis* from the rendering by the Roman philosopher and poet Seneca; English proverb, late 14th century.

Be happy while y'er leevin, For y'er a lang time deid.
Scottish motto for a house.

Life is a sexually transmitted disease.
graffito found on the London Underground.

Life is harder than crossing a field.
Russian proverb.

Life isn't all beer and skittles.
life is not unalloyed pleasure or relaxation; English proverb, mid 19th century.

Life is the best gift; the rest is extra.
African proverb (Swahili).

Life's a bitch, and then you die.
modern saying, late 20th century.

A live dog is better than a dead lion.

often used in the context of a lesser person taking the place of a greater one who has died; English proverb, late 14th century, from the Bible (Ecclesiastes 9:4), 'A living dog is better than a dead lion.'

Man cannot live by bread alone.

a person needs spiritual as well as physical sustenance; English proverb, late 19th century, after the Bible (Matthew 4:4), 'Man shall not live by bread alone, but by every word that proceedeth out of the mouth of God.'

Tout passe, tout casse, tout lasse.

French, meaning 'everything passes, everything perishes, everything palls'.

Lifestyles

See also LIFE

Common wisdom enshrines suggestions for essential principles by which to order our lives, from the simple Do as you would be done by, *to the Middle Eastern advice* If you have two coins, use one to buy bread, the other to buy hyacinths.

Lifestyles

Anyone can carry his burden, however heavy, until nightfall. Anyone can do his work, however hard, for a day. Anyone can live sweetly, patiently, lovingly, purely, till the sun goes down. And this is all that life really means.

traditional saying, late 19th century; associated with the writer Robert Louis Stevenson (1850–94) from the early 20th century.

Before enlightenment, chop wood, carry water. After enlightenment, chop wood, carry water.

Zen saying.

Do as you would be done by.

English proverb, late 16th century; in Charles Kingsley's *The Water Babies* (1863), Mrs *Doasyouwouldbedoneby* is the motherly and benevolent figure who is contrasted with her stern sister, Mrs *Bedonebyasyoudid*.

Do unto others as you would they should do unto you.

English proverb, early 10th century; from the Bible (Matthew), 'Therefore all things whatsoever ye would that men should do to you, do ye even so to them: for this is the law and the prophets.'

Eat, drink and be merry, for tomorrow we die.

a conflation of two biblical sayings, Ecclesiastes 8:15, 'A man hath no better thing under the sun, than to eat, and to drink, and to be merry', and Isaiah 22:13, 'Let us eat and drink; for tomorrow we shall die'; English proverb, late 19th century.

Fear less, hope more; Eat less, chew more; Whine less, breathe more; Talk less, say more; Love more, and all good things will be yours.
Swedish saying.

If you have two coins, use one to buy bread, the other to buy hyacinths.
both the mind and the body should be fed; Middle Eastern proverb (sometimes roses or lilies are suggested instead).

Make love not war.
student slogan, 1960s.

Likes and Dislikes

See also CRITICISM

From One man's meat is another man's poison *to* Tastes differ, *there is an acceptance that there is no consensus of personal preference.*

Every man to his taste.
often used to comment on someone else's choice; English proverb, late 16th century.

Losing

One man's meat is another man's poison.

pointing out that what may be necessary to one person is
injurious to another; English proverb, late 16th century.

One man's trash is another man's treasure.

modern saying.

Tastes differ.

different people will like or approve of different things;
English proverb, early 19th century.

There is no accounting for tastes.

often used in recognition of a difference in choice between
two people; English proverb, late 18th century.

You can't please everyone.

English proverb, late 15th century.

 Losing

See WINNING AND LOSING

 Love

See also MARRIAGE, RELATIONSHIPS

Love may be a powerful force (Love makes the world
go round), *but it does not necessarily bring ease:* The
course of true love never did run smooth.

The course of true love never did run smooth.
English proverb, late 16th century; originally from
Shakespeare *A Midsummer Night's Dream* (1595–6).

It is best to be off with the old love before you are on with the new.
English proverb, early 19th century.

Jove but laughs at lovers' perjury.
English proverb, mid 16th century; from the Roman poet
Tibullus (c.50–19 BC) and ultimately from the Greek poet
Hesiod (c.700 BC).

Kissing goes by favour.
a kiss is often given as a reward for something done; English
proverb, early 17th century.

Love and a cough cannot be hid.
love can no more be concealed than a cough can be
suppressed; English proverb, early 14th century.

Love begets love.
English proverb, early 16th century.

Love is blind.
Cupid, the god of love, was traditionally portrayed as blind,
shooting his arrows at random, but the saying is generally
used to mean that a person is often unable to see faults in the
one they love; English proverb, late 14th century; compare
L'amour est aveugle; l'amitié ferme les yeux at RELATIONSHIPS.

Love

Love laughs at locksmiths.
love is too strong a force to be denied by ordinary barriers;
English proverb, early 19th century, from the title of a play
by George Colman the Younger (1762–1836).

Love makes the world go round.
English proverb, mid 19th century, from a traditional
French song.

Love makes time pass, and time makes love pass.
French proverb.

Love will find a way.
love is a force which cannot be stemmed or denied; English
proverb, early 17th century.

One cannot love and be wise.
English proverb, early 16th century; the statement 'to love
and be wise is scarcely allowed to God' is found in Latin in
the writings of the 1st-century Roman writer Publilius Syrus.

The quarrel of lovers is the renewal of love.
love can be renewed through reconciliation; English
proverb, early 16th century.

There are as good fish in the sea as ever came
out of it.
now often used as a consolation to rejected lovers in the
form 'there are plenty more fish in the sea'; English proverb,
late 16th century.

'Tis better to have loved and lost, than never to have loved at all.

English proverb, early 18th century.

When the furze is in bloom, my love's in tune.

with the implication that some furze can always be found in bloom; English proverb, mid 18th century; compare **When the gorse is out of bloom, kissing's out of fashion below.**

When the gorse is out of bloom, kissing's out of fashion.

the idea behind the saying is that gorse is always in flower somewhere (compare **When the furze is in bloom, my love's in tune** above).

Loyalty

Loyalty is a key virtue (It's an ill bird that fouls its own nest) *that is best demonstrated over a long period:* Quickly come, quickly go.

It's an ill bird that fouls its own nest.

a condemnation of a person who brings his own family, home, or country into disrepute by his words; English proverb, mid 13th century.

Luck

Love me little, love me long.
love of great intensity is unlikely to last; English proverb,
early 16th century.

Quickly come, quickly go.
English proverb, late 16th century.

Luck

See CHANCE AND LUCK

Management ❀

See also EMPLOYMENT, LEADERSHIP

One traditional saying can be seen as an endorsement of the principle of delegation: Why keep a dog and bark yourself?

A committee is a group of the unwilling, chosen from the unfit, to do the unnecessary.
20th-century saying.

Hire slow, fire fast.
modern saying.

The nail that sticks up is certain to be hammered down.
Japanese proverb.

We trained hard ... but it seemed that every time we were beginning to form up into teams we would be reorganized. I was to learn later in life that we tend to meet any new situation by reorganizing; and a wonderful method it can be for creating the illusion of progress while producing confusion, inefficiency, and demoralization.
late 20th-century saying, frequently (and wrongly) attributed to the Roman satirist Petronius Arbiter (d. AD 65).

Manners

Why keep a dog and bark yourself?
often used to advise against carrying out work which can
be done for you by somebody else; English proverb, late
16th century.

**You cannot control the winds, but you can adjust
the sails.**
you may not be able to control matters, but you can respond
deftly to them; modern saying.

You can only manage what you can measure.
modern saying.

 # Manners

See also BEHAVIOUR

While courtesy is seen as an obligation (Manners
maketh man), *there is also a note of pragmatism:*
There is nothing lost by civility.

Civility costs nothing.
one should behave with at least minimal courtesy; English
proverb, early 18th century.

A civil question deserves a civil answer.
English proverb, mid 19th century.

Everyone speaks well of the bridge which carries him over.

someone is naturally well disposed towards a source of help, whether or not it has been beneficial to others; English proverb, late 17th century.

Manners maketh man.

motto of William of Wykeham (1324–1404), bishop of Winchester and founder of Winchester College; English proverb, mid 14th century.

Striking manners are bad manners.

American proverb, mid 20th century.

The test of good manners is being able to put up pleasantly with bad ones.

American proverb, mid 20th century.

There is nothing lost by civility.

English proverb, late 19th century.

Marriage

See also LOVE, MEN AND WOMEN, WEDDINGS

Despite the assertion that Marriages are made in heaven, *much proverbial wisdom takes a sceptical view of the happiness offered by the wedded state:* Needles and pins, needles and pins, when a man marries his trouble begins.

Marriage

Better be an old man's darling than a young man's slave.
English proverb, mid 16th century.

Better one house spoiled than two.
said of two wicked or foolish people joined in marriage;
English proverb, late 16th century.

Change the name and not the letter, change for the worse and not the better.
it is unlucky for a woman to marry a man whose surname
begins with the same letter as her own; English proverb,
mid 19th century.

A deaf husband and a blind wife are always a happy couple.
each will remain unaware of drawbacks in the other (the
saying is sometimes reversed to a blind husband and a deaf
wife); English proverb, late 16th century.

The grey mare is the better horse.
the wife rules, or is more competent than, the husband;
English proverb, mid 16th century.

Marriage is a lottery.
referring either to one's choice of partner, or more generally
to the element of chance involved in how a marriage will
turn out; English proverb, mid 17th century.

Marriages are made in heaven.

often used ironically; English proverb, mid 16th century.

Marry in haste and repent at leisure.

the formula is also applied to rash steps taken in other
circumstances; English proverb, mid 16th century; the idea
is found in William Congreve's play *The Old Bachelor*
(1693), 'Thus grief still treads upon the heels of pleasure: /
Married in haste, we may repent at leisure.'

**Needles and pins, needles and pins, when a man
marries his trouble begins.**

traditional saying (originally a nursery rhyme), perhaps
reflecting on the pressures of domestic life; English proverb,
mid 19th century.

Never marry for money, but marry where money is.

distinguishing between monetary gain as a primary object
and a side benefit; English proverb, late 19th century.

**There goes more to marriage than four bare legs
in a bed.**

physical compatibility is not enough for a successful
marriage; English proverb, mid 16th century.

Wedlock is a padlock.

English proverb, late 17th century.

A widow is a rudderless boat.

Chinese proverb.

Means

You do not marry the person you love, you love the person you marry.
Indian proverb.

A young man married is a young man marred.
often used as an argument against marrying too young;
English proverb, late 16th century.

 # Means
See WAYS AND MEANS

 # Medicine
See also SICKNESS

What drugs can do may be limited (The best doctors
are Dr Diet, Dr Quiet, and Dr Merryman), *and some
remedies may be in our own hands:* Laughter is the
best medicine.

**The best doctors are Dr Diet, Dr Quiet, and
Dr Merryman.**
outline of an appropriate regime for someone who is ill;
English proverb, mid 16th century.

Good ethics start with good facts.
modern saying in medical ethics.

Good medicine always has a bitter taste.

modern saying, sometimes claimed to be a Japanese proverb.

Keep taking the tablets.

supposedly traditional advice from a doctor, especially when little change in the patient's condition is envisaged.

Laughter is the best medicine.

late 20th-century saying; the idea is an ancient one, as in the Bible (Proverbs 17:22), 'A merry heart doeth good like medicine.'

Medicine can prolong life, but death will seize the doctor, too.

American proverb, mid 20th century.

Similia similibus curantur.

Latin, 'Like cures like,' motto of homeopathic medicine attributed to S. Hahnemann (1755–1843), although not found in this form in Hahnemann's writings.

Meeting and Parting

See also ABSENCE

While parting may be seen as a regrettable inevitability (The best of friends must part), *meeting is not necessarily welcome:* Talk of the Devil, and he is bound to appear.

Men

The best of friends must part.
no friendship is so close that separation is impossible;
English proverb, early 17th century.

Nice to see you—to see you, nice.
catchphrase used by Bruce Forsyth in 'The Generation
Game' on BBC Television, 1973 onwards.

Talk of the Devil, and he is bound to appear.
to speak of the Devil may be to invite his presence; often
abbreviated to 'Talk of the Devil', and used when a person
just spoken of is seen; English proverb, mid 17th century.

 # Men

See also MEN AND WOMEN

*Proverbial wisdom about men seems to be summed up
in the succinct,* Boys will be boys.

Boys will be boys.
English proverb, early 17th century, often used ironically.

I married my husband for life, not for lunch.
20th-century saying, origin unknown.

The way to a man's heart is through his stomach.
English proverb, early 19th century.

Men and Women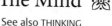

See also MARRIAGE, MEN, WOMEN

A loving partnership between men and women is seen as the natural pattern of life: Every Jack has his Jill.

Every Jack has his Jill.

all lovers have found a mate; English proverb, early 17th century.

A good Jack makes a good Jill.

used of the effect of a husband on his wife; English proverb, early 17th century.

A man is as old as he feels, and a woman as old as she looks.

both parts of the proverb are sometimes used on their own; English proverb, late 19th century.

The Mind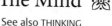

See also THINKING

The mind is seen as essential to independent life: Whom the gods would destroy, they first make mad.

A mind enlightened is like heaven; a mind in darkness is hell.

Chinese proverb.

Misfortunes

Mind has no sex.

modern saying, ultimately an alteration of the thought of
Mary Wollstonecraft (1759–97) in her *A Vindication of the
Rights of Women* (1792), 'To give a sex to mind was not very
consistent with the principles of a man [Rousseau] who
argued so warmly, and so well, for the immortality of the soul.'

A mind is a terrible thing to waste.

motto of the United Negro College Fund.

Our memory is always at fault, never our judgement.

American proverb, mid 20th century.

Whom the gods would destroy, they first make mad.

often used to comment on a foolish action seen as self-
destructive in its effect; English proverb, early 17th century;
the idea is found in the medieval period, in a scholiastic
annotation to Sophocles's *Antigone*, 'Whenever God
prepares evil for a man, He first damages his mind, with
which he deliberates.'

 # Misfortunes

See also ADVERSITY, CHANCE AND LUCK

Misfortunes are inevitable (The bread never falls but
on its buttered side), *but we should not allow ourselves*

to be overwhelmed by a sense of our own bad luck:
I cried because I had no shoes, until I met a man
who had no feet.

Bad things come in threes.

the belief that an accident or misfortune is likely to be
accompanied by two more is traditional, although in this
form it is only recorded from the late 20th century.

The bread never falls but on its buttered side.

if something goes wrong, the outcome is likely to be as bad
as possible; English proverb, mid 19th century.

Help you to salt, help you to sorrow.

in which salt is regarded as a sign of bad luck (especially if
spilt at table); English proverb, mid 17th century.

I cried because I had no shoes, until I met a man who had no feet.

modern saying derived from a Persian original; compare
the words of the Persian poet Sadi (*c*.1213–91) in *The
Rose Garden*, 'I never complained at the vicissitudes of
fortune...excepting once, when my feet were bare, and
I had not the means of procuring myself shoes. I entered
the great mosque at Cufah with a heavy heart when I beheld
a man who had no feet. I offered up praise and thanks
giving to God for his bounty, and bore with patience the
want of shoes.'

Mistakes

If anything can go wrong, it will.

modern saying reflecting a supposed law of nature, said
to have been coined as a maxim in 1949 by George Nichols,
as the development of a remark made by a colleague,
Captain E. Murphy; the rule is popularly known as
'Murphy's Law'.

It is no use crying over spilt milk.

it is pointless to repine when it is too late to prevent the
misfortune; English proverb, mid 17th century.

It never rains but it pours.

if one thing has gone wrong, worse will follow; English
proverb, early 18th century.

Misfortunes never come singly.

English proverb, early 14th century.

Mistakes

*Not even the greatest expert can avoid making some
mistakes: we are warned that* Homer sometimes nods,
and Even monkeys sometimes fall off a tree.

Even monkeys sometimes fall off a tree.

even the most adept can be careless and make errors;
Japanese proverb.

Mistakes

He is always right who suspects that he makes mistakes.

warning against overconfidence; Spanish proverb.

He who slaps his own face should not cry out.

there is no point in complaining about trouble caused by your own error; Arabic proverb.

Homer sometimes nods.

even the greatest expert may make a mistake (nods here means 'becomes drowsy', implying a momentary lack of attention); English proverb, late 14th century, ultimately with allusion to the Roman poet Horace (65–8 BC), 'I'm aggrieved when sometimes even excellent Homer nods.'

A miss is as good as a mile.

if you miss the target, it hardly matters by how much; the syntax has been distorted by abridgement, and the original form was 'an inch in a miss is as good as an ell' (an *ell* being a former measure of length equal to about 1.1 metres); English proverb, early 17th century.

There's many a slip 'twixt cup and lip.

much can go wrong between the initiation of a process and its completion, often used as a warning; English proverb, mid 16th century.

Moderation

To err is human (to forgive divine).
English proverb, late 16th century (in its given form, from
Alexander Pope's *An Essay on Criticism* (1711), 'To err is
human: to forgive, divine'; compare **To err is human but to
really foul things up requires a computer** at COMPUTERS.

Wink at sma' fauts, ye hae great anes yoursel.
avoid criticizing the mistakes of others, as you yourself have
great ones; Scottish proverb; the idea is found in the Bible
(Matthew 7:3), 'Why beholdest thou the mote that is in thy
brother's eye, but considerest not the beam that is in thine
own eye?'

 # Moderation
See also EXCESS, GREED

*Moderation is not only a sensible precaution against
overindulgence* (Enough is as good as a feast)*, it can be
positively beneficial in making an effect:* Less is more.

Enough is as good as a feast.
used as a warning against overindulgence, or overdoing
something; English proverb, late 14th century.

Enough is enough.
originally used as an expression of content or satisfaction,
but now more usually employed as a reprimand, warning

someone against persisting in an inappropriate or excessive course of action; English proverb, mid 16th century.

The half is better than the whole.

advising economy or restraint; English proverb, mid 16th century, from the Greek poet Hesiod (fl. *c.*700 BC) *Works and Days,* 'the half is greater than the whole.'

Keep no more cats than will catch mice.

recommending efficiency and the ethic of steady work to justify one's place; English proverb, late 17th century.

Less is more.

something simple often has more effect; English proverb, mid 19th century.

Moderation in all things.

English proverb, mid 19th century, from the Greek poet Hesiod (fl. *c.*700 BC) *Works and Days,* 'Observe due measure; moderation is best in all things'; compare **There is measure in all things** below.

There is measure in all things.

English proverb, late 14th century; compare **Moderation in all things** above.

Money

See also THRIFT, WEALTH

It is natural to want money (Get the money honestly if you can), *but its power is in the end limited:* Money can't buy happiness.

Bad money drives out good.

money of lower intrinsic value tends to circulate more freely than money of higher intrinsic and equal nominal value, though what is recognized as money of higher value being hoarded; English proverb, early 20th century; known as 'Gresham's law' from Thomas Gresham (d. 1579), English financier and founder of the Royal Exchange.

The best things in life are free.

English proverb, early 20th century, originally from the title of a song (1927) by Buddy De Sylva and Lew Brown.

Cash is king.

modern saying, summarizing the position in a recession.

Get the money honestly if you can.

American proverb, early 19th century; the idea is found in the classical world, in the poetry of Horace (65–8 BC), 'If possible honestly, if not, somehow, make money.'

He that cannot pay, let him pray.

if you have no material resources, prayer is your only resort;
English proverb, early 17th century.

Money can't buy happiness.

English proverb, mid 19th century.

Money has no smell.

English proverb, early 20th century in this form, but
originally deriving from a comment made by the Roman
Emperor Vespasian (AD 9–79), in response to an objection
to a tax on public lavatories; compare **Where there's muck
there's brass** below.

Money is like sea water. The more you drink, the thirstier you become.

possession of wealth creates an addiction to money;
modern saying.

Money isn't everything.

often said in consolation or resignation; English proverb,
early 20th century.

Money is power.

English proverb, mid 18th century.

Money is the root of all evil.

English proverb, mid 15th century, deriving from the Bible
(I Timothy 6:10), 'The love of money is the root of all evil';
compare **Idleness is the root of all evil** at IDLENESS.

Money

Money, like manure, does no good till it is spread.
English proverb, early 19th century; the idea is found earlier in the *Essays* of Francis Bacon (1561–1626), 'Money is like muck, not good except it be spread.'

Money makes the dog dance.
Spanish proverb.

Money makes the mare to go.
referring to money as a source of power; English proverb, late 15th century.

Money talks.
money has influence; English proverb, mid 17th century.

Shrouds have no pockets.
worldly wealth cannot be kept and used after death; English proverb, mid 19th century.

Time is money.
often used to mean that time spent fruitlessly on something represents a real loss of money which could have been earned in that time; English proverb, late 16th century.

Where there's muck there's brass.
dirty or unpleasant activities are also lucrative (brass here means 'money'); English proverb, late 17th century; compare **Money has no smell** above.

You cannot serve God and Mammon.

now generally used of wealth regarded as an evil influence; English proverb, mid 16th century, ultimately from the Bible (Matthew 6:24), 'No man can serve two masters...Ye cannot serve God and mammon.'

Mourning

See also DEATH, SORROW

Mourning is inevitable and natural (Grief is the price we pay for love), *but overindulgence in it is not a sign of sincere feeling:* A bellowing cow soon forgets her calf.

A bellowing cow soon forgets her calf.

the person who laments most loudly is the one who is soonest comforted; English proverb, late 19th century.

Grief is the price we pay for love.

late 20th-century saying.

Let the dead bury the dead.

often used to mean that the past should be left undisturbed; English proverb, early 19th century (see Matthew 8:22).

No flowers by request.

an intimation that no flowers are desired at a funeral.

Murder

**You can shed tears that she is gone or you can smile
because she has lived.**
preface to the Order of Service at the funeral of Queen
Elizabeth the Queen Mother, 2002.

Murder

*Traditional sayings emphasize not only that murder
cannot be concealed* (Murder will out), *but also that it
is likely to breed further killing:* Blood will have blood.

Blood will have blood.
killing will provoke further killing; English proverb, mid
15th century; in this form from Shakespeare *Macbeth*
(1606), It will have blood, they say blood will have blood.'

Guns don't kill people; people kill people.
National Rifle Association slogan.

Killing no murder.
English proverb, mid 17th century, originally from the title
of a pamphlet by Edward Sexby (d. 1658), 'Killing no
murder briefly discourst in three questions', an apology
for tyrannicide.

Murder will out.
the crime of murder can never be successfully concealed;
English proverb, early 14th century.

Music

The world of music may offer great enjoyment, but it is not a shield from reality: we are told from the 17th century that Music helps not the toothache.

It takes seven years to make a piper.
Scottish proverb.

Music helps not the toothache.
English proverb, mid 17th century.

Why should the devil have all the best tunes?
commonly attributed to the English evangelist Rowland
Hill (1744–1833); many hymns are sung to popular secular
melodies, and this practice was especially favoured by
the Methodists.

Names

Names enshrine the essence of individual identity: If the cap fits, wear it.

The beginning of wisdom is to call things by their right names.
modern saying claimed to be a Chinese proverb.

By Tre, Pol, and Pen, you shall know the Cornish men.
traditional saying, referring to the frequency of these elements in Cornish names; English proverb, mid 16th century.

If the cap fits, wear it.
used with reference to the assumed suitability of a name or description to a person's behaviour; English proverb, mid 18th century.

If the shoe fits, wear it.
one has to accept it when a particular comment is shown to apply to oneself; found mainly in the US; English proverb, late 18th century.

It is not what you call me. It is what I answer to.
African proverb.

Only the camel knows the hundredth name of God.
saying from Arab folklore; in Islam there are ninety-nine names for Allah (referred to as the ninety-nine names of God'), in the main taken or derived from the Koran.

Nature

See also THE ENVIRONMENT

Nature is seen as a powerful force beyond our control:
You can drive out nature with a pitchfork, but she keeps on coming back.

Nature abhors a vacuum.
English proverb, mid 16th century.

One for the mouse, one for the crow, one to rot, one to grow.
traditionally used when sowing seed, and enumerating the ways in which some of the crop will be lost, leaving the residue to germinate; English proverb, mid 19th century.

You can drive out nature with a pitchfork but she keeps on coming back.
English proverb, mid 16th century, from the Roman poet Horace (65–8 BC) *Epistles*, 'You may drive out nature with a pitchfork, but she will always return.'

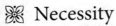 Necessity

Necessity may accustom us to difficult choices
(Desperate diseases must have desperate remedies),
but it may also have possible benefits: Necessity
sharpens industry.

Beggars can't be choosers.

someone who is destitute is in no position to criticize what
may be offered; English proverb, mid 16th century.

Desperate diseases must have desperate remedies.

in a difficult or dangerous situation it may be necessary to
take extreme or risky measures; English proverb, mid 16th
century; compare **Exceptional times require exceptional
measures** below.

Even a worm will turn.

even a meek person will resist or retaliate if pushed too far;
English proverb, mid 16th century.

Exceptional times require exceptional measures.

modern saying; compare **Desperate diseases must have
desperate remedies** above.

Hunger drives the wolf out of the wood.

even the fiercest animal will be driven from shelter by acute
need; English proverb, late 15th century.

If the mountain will not come to Mahomet, Mahomet must go to the mountain.

used in the context of an apparently insoluble situation. The saying refers to a story of Muhammad recounted by Francis Bacon in his *Essays*, in which the Prophet called a hill to him, and when it did not move, made this remark; English proverb, early 17th century.

Make a virtue of necessity.

one should do with a good grace what is unavoidable; English proverb, late 14th century.

Necessity is the mother of invention.

need is often a spur to the creative process; English proverb, mid 16th century.

Necessity knows no law.

someone in extreme need will disregard rules or prohibitions; English proverb, late 14th century.

Necessity sharpens industry.

American proverb, mid 20th century.

Needs must when the devil drives.

used in recognition of overwhelming force of circumstance; English proverb, mid 15th century.

When all fruit fails, welcome haws.

often used of someone taking of necessity an older or otherwise unsuitable lover (*haws*, the red fruit of the

Neighbours

hawthorn, are contrasted with fruits generally eaten as food); English proverb, early 18th century.

Who says A must say B.
only recorded in English from North American sources, and meaning that if a first step is taken; the second will inevitably follow; English proverb, mid 19th century.

Neighbours

See also FAMILIARITY, FRIENDSHIP

Common wisdom advises care in not overstepping limits with one's neighbours, both in terms of territory (Good fences make good neighbours) *and personal intimacy* (You should know a man seven years before you stir his fire).

Good fences make good neighbours.
this reduces the possibility of disputes over adjoining land; English proverb, mid 17th century.

A hedge between keeps friendship green.
it is wise to have a clear boundary between neighbours; English proverb.

Love your neighbour, but don't pull down your hedge.
do not let feelings of friendship lead you to act unwisely; English proverb.

A wall between both best preserves friendship.

it is wise to have a clear boundary between neighbours;
Spanish proverb.

What a neighbour gets is not lost.

one is likely to benefit from the gain of a neighbour or
friend; English proverb, mid 16th century.

You should know a man seven years before you stir his fire.

used as a caution against over-familiarity on slight
acquaintance; English proverb, early 19th century.

News and Journalism

The traditional view that Bad news travels fast *is
countered by an African saying:* One who sees
something good must tell of it.

All the news that's fit to print.

motto of the *New York Times,* from 1896; coined by Adolph
S. Ochs (1858–1935).

Bad news travels fast.

bad news is more likely to be talked about; English proverb,
late 16th century.

Light for all.

slogan of the *Baltimore Sun.*

News and Journalism

No news is good news.
often used in consolation or resignation; English proverb,
early 17th century.

One who sees something good must tell of it.
African proverb.

Watch this space!
further developments are expected and more information
will be given later; *space* = an area of a newspaper for a
specific purpose, especially for advertising.

Opinion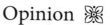

See also ARGUMENT, THINKING

Independent ideas may be approved (Thought is free), *but too great an affection for one's own views can degenerate into obstinacy:* Those who never retract their opinions, love themselves more than they love truth.

He that complies against his will is of his own opinion still.

English proverb, late 17th century, from Samuel Butler *Hudibras* pt 3 (1680), 'He that complies against his will, Is of his own opinion still.'

So many men, so many opinions.

the greater the number of people involved, the greater the number of different opinions there will be; English proverb, late 14th century, from Terence (c.190–159 BC) *Phormio*, 'There are as many opinions as there are people: each has his own correct way.'

Those who never retract their opinions, love themselves more than they love truth.

American proverb, mid 20th century.

Thought is free.

while speech and action can be limited, one's powers of imagination and speculation cannot be regulated; English proverb, late 14th century.

Opportunity

Where there are two Jews, there are three opinions.
Jewish saying.

The wish is father to the thought.
one's opinions are influenced by one's wishes; English
proverb, late 16th century, from Shakespeare *2 Henry IV*
(1597), 'Thy wish was father, Harry, to that thought.'

 # Opportunity

While we may have many opportunities (The world is
one's oyster), *we are warned that an opportunity
missed will not come again:* He that will not when he
may, when he will he shall have nay.

All is fish that comes to the net.
everything can be used to advantage; English proverb, early
16th century.

All is grist that comes to the mill.
all experience or knowledge is useful (*grist* is corn that is
ground to make flour); English proverb, mid 17th century.

A bleating sheep loses a bite.
opportunities may be lost through idle chatter; English
proverb, late 16th century.

Every crisis provides an opportunity.

often used as encouragement in facing difficult circumstances; modern saying.

Every dog has his day.

everyone, however insignificant, has a moment of strength and power; English proverb, mid 16th century.

He that will not when he may, when he will he shall have nay.

if an opportunity is not taken when offered, it may well not occur again; English proverb, late 10th century.

If the camel once gets his nose in the tent, his body will soon follow.

an apparently insignificant opening is likely to lead to more serious developments; Arabic proverb.

If you snooze, you lose.

it is advisable to stay alert to opportunities; modern saying.

It is good fishing in troubled waters.

a difficult situation offers opportunities to those prepared to exploit it; English proverb, late 16th century.

It's not what you know, but whom you know.

American proverb, mid 20th century.

Opportunity

Make hay while the sun shines.
one should take advantage of favourable circumstances
which may not last; English proverb, mid 16th century.

The mill cannot grind with the water that is past.
an opportunity that has been missed cannot then be used;
English proverb, early 17th century.

No time like the present.
often used to urge swift and immediate action; English
proverb, mid 16th century.

**Opportunities look for you when you are
worth finding.**
North American proverb, mid 20th century; compare
**Opportunity never knocks for persons not worth a
rap** below.

**Opportunity never knocks for persons not
worth a rap.**
American proverb, mid 20th century.

Opportunity never knocks twice at any man's door.
a chance once missed will not occur again; English proverb,
mid 16th century.

**A person who misses his chance, and the monkey
who misses his branch, can't be saved.**
Indian proverb.

A postern door makes a thief.

referring to the opportunity offered by a back or side
entrance; English proverb, mid 15th century.

Strike while the iron is hot.

one should take advantage of opportunity; the allusion was
originally to the work of a blacksmith; English proverb, late
14th century.

Take the goods the gods provide.

one should accept and be grateful for unearned benefits;
English proverb, late 17th century.

Time and tide wait for no man.

often used as an exhortation to act, in the knowledge that a
favourable moment will not last for ever; English proverb,
late 14th century.

When one door shuts, another opens.

as one possible course of action is closed off, another
opportunity offers; English proverb, late 16th century.

When the cat's away, the mice will play.

many will take advantage of a situation in which rules are
not enforced or authority is lacking; English proverb,
early 17th century.

A wise man turns chance into good fortune.

traditional saying.

Optimism and Pessimism

The world is one's oyster.

opportunities are unlimited; an *oyster* is seen as both a delicacy and a source of pearls. Perhaps originally with allusion to Shakespeare's *The Merry Wives of Windsor* (1597), 'The world's mine oyster, which I, with sword will open'; English proverb, early 17th century.

Optimism and Pessimism

See also HOPE

Adopting a positive attitude may be recommended (Turn your face to the sun, and the shadows fall behind you), *but we should beware of overconfidence:* Don't halloo till you are out of the wood.

All's for the best in the best of all possible worlds.

English proverb, early 20th century, from Voltaire *Candide* (1759), 'In this best of possible worlds...all is for the best.'

Another day, another dollar.

a world-weary comment on routine toil to earn a living, originally referring to the custom of paying sailors by the day, so that the longer the voyage, the greater the financial reward; American proverb, mid 20th century.

Optimism and Pessimism

The darkest hour is just before dawn.
suggesting that the experience of complete despair may mean that matters have reached the lowest point and may shortly improve; English proverb, mid 17th century.

Don't bargain for fish that are still in the water.
Indian proverb; compare **Don't sell the skin till you have caught the bear** below.

Don't count your chickens before they are hatched.
one should not make, or act upon, an assumption (usually favourable) which may turn out to be ill-founded; English proverb, late 16th century; compare **Chickens are counted in the autumn** at AUTUMN.

Don't halloo till you are out of the wood.
you should not exult until danger and difficulty are past (halloo means 'shout in order to attract attention'); English proverb, late 18th century.

Don't sell the skin till you have caught the bear.
do not act upon an assumption of success which may turn out to be ill-founded; English proverb, late 16th century (early versions have *lion* or *beast* in place of *bear*); compare **Don't bargain for fish that are still in the water** above.

Every cloud has a silver lining.
even the gloomiest circumstance has some hopeful element in it; English proverb, mid 19th century.

Optimism and Pessimism

God's in his heaven; all's right with the world.
English proverb, from early 16th century in the form 'God
is where he was'; now largely replaced by this poem from
Robert Browning *Pippa Passes* (1841), 'God's in his
heaven—All's right with the world!'

**If ifs and ands were pots and pans, there'd be no
work for tinkers' hands.**
traditional response to an over-optimistic conditional
expression, in which *ands* is the plural form of *and* = 'if';
English proverb, mid 19th century.

If wishes were horses, beggars would ride.
what one wishes for is often far from reality; English
proverb, early 17th century.

If you had teeth of iron, you could eat iron coconuts.
saying from Senegal.

It's an ill wind that blows nobody any good.
good luck may arise from the source of another's
misfortune; English proverb, early 17th century.

The sharper the storm, the sooner it's over.
the more intense something is, the shorter time it is likely to
last; English proverb, late 19th century.

Optimism and Pessimism

Turn your face to the sun, and the shadows fall behind you.

recommending a positive attitude; modern saying, said to derive from a Maori proverb.

When the axe came into the forest, the trees said 'The handle is one of us!'

relying for safety on a supposed link with a potential aggressor may offer a false hope; Russian proverb.

When things are at their worst they begin to mend.

when a bad situation has reached its worst possible point, the next change must reflect at least a small improvement; English proverb, mid 18th century.

Parents

See also CHILDREN, THE FAMILY

Pride and affection in one's child (Praise the child, and you make love to the mother) *may be associated with ambitions for the child's worldly success:* Parents want their children to become dragons.

A father is a banker provided by nature.
French proverb.

He who takes the child by the hand takes the mother by the heart.
Danish proverb.

It is a wise child that knows its own father.
a child's legal paternity might not reflect an actual blood link; English proverb, late 16th century.

A mother understands what a child does not say.
Jewish proverb.

My son is my son till he gets him a wife, but my daughter's my daughter all the days of her life.
while a man who establishes his own family relegates former blood ties to second place, a woman's filial role is not affected by her marriage; English proverb, late 17th century.

Parents want their children to become dragons.
parents want their children to be successful;
Chinese proverb.

Praise the child, and you make love to the mother.
English proverb, early 19th century.

Send the beloved child on a journey.
Japanese proverb.

To understand your parents' love, you must raise children yourself.
Chinese proverb.

When drinking water, remember the source.
advocating filial piety; Chinese proverb.

Parting

See MEETING AND PARTING

The Past

See also THE FUTURE, HISTORY, THE PRESENT

The past may represent something that cannot now be changed (The past at least is secure), *or which still has the power to affect the future:* The past is always ahead of us.

The Past

Old sins cast long shadows.
current usage is likely to refer to the wrong done by
one generation affecting its descendants; English proverb,
early 20th century.

The past always looks better than it was; it's only pleasant because it isn't here.
American proverb, late 19th century.

The past at least is secure.
American proverb, early 19th century.

The past is always ahead of us.
the past is a reminder of what has been and what may be;
Maori proverb.

Things past cannot be recalled.
what has already happened cannot be changed; English
proverb, late 15th century.

What's done cannot be undone.
English proverb, mid 15th century.

You have drunk from wells you did not dig, and been warmed by fires you did not build.
the present generation depends on those who have
gone before; modern saying, said to be of Native
American origin.

Patience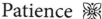

See also DETERMINATION, HASTE AND DELAY

Not only is patience recommended as in itself the right way to behave (Bear and forbear)*, it promises ultimate satisfaction:* If you sit by the river long enough, you will see the body of your enemy float by.

All commend patience, but none can endure to suffer.
American proverb, mid 20th century.

All things come to those who wait.
often used as an adjuration to patience; English proverb, early 16th century.

Bear and forbear.
recommending patience and tolerance; English proverb, late 16th century.

Don't put the cart before the horse.
don't reverse the proper order of things; English proverb, early 16th century.

First thing first.
English proverb, late 19th century.

Hurry no man's cattle.
sometimes used as an injunction to be patient with someone; English proverb, early 19th century.

Patience

If you sit by the river long enough, you will see the body of your enemy float by.
advocating patience in the face of wrongs; modern saying, said to derive from a Japanese proverb.

I sit on the shore, and wait for the wind.
what is expected will arrive sooner or later; Russian proverb.

It is a long lane that has no turning.
commonly used as an assertion that an unfavourable situation will eventually change for the better; English proverb, mid 19th century.

The longest way home is the shortest way home.
not trying to take a short cut is often the most effective way; English proverb, mid 17th century.

The man who removes a mountain begins by carrying away small stones.
a major enterprise begins with small but essential tasks; modern saying, claimed to be a Chinese proverb.

Nothing should be done in haste but gripping a flea.
used as a warning against rash action; English proverb, mid 17th century.

One step at a time.
recommending cautious progression along a desired route; English proverb, mid 19th century.

Patience is a virtue.

often used as an exhortation; English proverb, late
14th century.

Rome was not built in a day.

used to warn against trying to achieve too much at once;
English proverb, mid 16th century.

Slow but sure.

sure here means 'sure-footed, deliberate'; English proverb,
late 17th century.

Softly, softly, catchee monkey.

advocating caution or guile as the best way to achieve an
end; English proverb, early 20th century.

There is luck in leisure.

it is often advisable to wait before acting; English proverb,
mid 19th century.

Time brings roses.

patience is likely to be rewarded; German proverb.

A watched pot never boils.

to pay too close an attention to the development of a desired
event appears to inhibit the result; English proverb, mid
19th century.

Peace

We must learn to walk before we can run.
a solid foundation is necessary for faster progress; English
proverb, mid 14th century.

What can't be cured must be endured.
there is no point in complaining about what is unavoidable;
English proverb, late 16th century.

Where water flows, a channel is formed.
success will come when conditions are right; Chinese proverb.

**With time and patience the mulberry leaf
becomes satin.**
allowing time for a process to complete itself will be
rewarded (silkworms feed chiefly on mulberry leaves);
English proverb, late 17th century.

Peace
See also WARFARE

*Peace may be desirable, but is perhaps only fully
appreciated in contrast to strife:* After a storm
comes a calm.

After a storm comes a calm.
often used with the implication that a calm situation is
only achieved after stress and turmoil; English proverb, late
14th century.

Ban the bomb.
US anti-nuclear slogan, 1953 onwards, adopted by the
Campaign for Nuclear Disarmament.

Nothing can bring you peace but yourself.
American proverb, mid 19th century.

Peace is the dream of the wise; war is the history of man.
saying, recorded from the 19th century.

Pessimism ✾

See OPTIMISM AND PESSIMISM

Politics ✾

See also GOVERNMENT

*Sayings about politics can bring together a wide range
of views, perhaps exemplified in the words,* Politics
makes strange bedfellows.

Are you now or have you ever been a member of the Communist Party?
formal question put to those appearing before the
Committee on UnAmerican Activities during the McCarthy
campaign of 1950–4 against alleged Communists in the

Politics

US government and other institutions; the allusive form *are you now or have you ever been?* derives from this.

As Maine goes, so goes the nation.
American political saying relating to presidential elections, *c.*1840.

Democracy is better than tyranny.
an imperfect system is better than a bad one; American proverb.

I am a Marxist—of the Groucho tendency.
slogan found at Nanterre in Paris, 1968.

In politics a man must learn to rise above principle.
American proverb, mid 20th century.

It'll play in Peoria.
catchphrase of the Nixon administration (early 1970s) meaning 'it will be acceptable to middle America', but originating in a standard music hall joke of the 1930s.

Lean liberty is better than fat slavery.
asserting that freedom matters more than any material comfort; English proverb, early 17th century.

Liberté! Égalité! Fraternité!
French, 'Freedom! Equality! Brotherhood!', motto of the French Revolution, 1789, but of earlier origin.

Politics

Not to be a republican at twenty is proof of want of heart; to be one at thirty is proof of want of head.
often used in the form 'Not to be a socialist…'; saying attributed to Georges Clemenceau (1841–1929) and to François Guizot (1787–1874).

The passion for freedom never dies.
saying, claimed to be a Greek proverb.

The personal is political.
1970s feminist slogan, coined by Carol Hanisch.

A politician is an animal who can sit on a fence and yet keep both ears to the ground.
American saying, mid 20th century.

Politics makes strange bedfellows.
political alliances in a common cause may bring together those of widely differing views; English proverb, mid 19th century.

Power to the people.
slogan of the Black Panther movement, from c.1968 onwards.

A straw vote only shows which way the hot air blows.
American proverb, early 20th century.

267

Possessions

Three acres and a cow.
regarded as the requirement for self-sufficiency; late
19th-century political slogan.

The voice of the people is the voice of God.
English version of the Latin *vox populi, vox dei*; English
proverb, early 15th century; the Latin form is found in the
writings of the English scholar and theologian Alcuin
(*c*.735–804), 'And those people should not be listened to
who keep saying the voice of the people is the voice of
God, since the riotousness of the crowd is always very
close to madness.'

Vote early and vote often.
American election slogan, already current when quoted by
William Porcher Miles in the House of Representatives,
31 March 1858.

Possessions

*There is considerable emphasis on the idea of ensuring
that you keep what you have (What you have, hold),
even if you do not immediately feel that it has a
purpose:* Keep a thing seven years and you'll always
find a use for it.

Finders keepers (losers weepers).
English proverb, early 19th century.

Findings keepings.

English proverb, mid 19th century.

If you have nothing, you have nothing to lose.

modern saying, claimed to be an Arabic proverb.

Keep a thing seven years and you'll always find a use for it.

recommending caution and thrift; English proverb, early 17th century.

Light come, light go.

something gained without effort can be lost without much regret; English proverb, late 14th century.

What you have, hold.

with reference to an uncompromising position based on a refusal to make any concession; English proverb, mid 15th century.

What you spend, you have.

the only real possessions one has are those of which one can dispose; English proverb, early 14th century.

You cannot lose what you never had.

used in consolation or resignation; English proverb, late 16th century.

Poverty

See also MONEY, WEALTH

Poverty can be destructive, both in sapping
independence (Empty sacks will never stand upright)
and destroying relationships: When poverty comes in
at the door, love flies out of the window.

Both poverty and prosperity come from spending money—prosperity from spending it wisely.

American proverb, mid 20th century.

Empty sacks will never stand upright.

those in an extremity of need cannot survive; English
proverb, mid 17th century.

Make poverty history.

slogan of a campaign launched in 2005 by a coalition of
charities and other groups to pressure governments to take
action to reduce poverty.

A moneyless man goes fast through the market.

someone without resources is unable to pause to buy
anything (or, in a modern variant, rushes to wherever
what they lack may be found); English proverb, early
18th century.

Poverty comes from God, but not dirt.

American proverb, mid 20th century.

Poverty is a blessing hated by all men.

poverty may shield you from worldly temptations, but it is unpleasant to experience; Italian proverb.

Poverty is no disgrace, but it's a great inconvenience.

English proverb, late 16th century.

Poverty is not a crime.

English proverb, late 16th century.

When poverty comes in at the door, love flies out of the window.

the strains of living in poverty often destroy a loving relationship; English proverb, mid 17th century.

Power

The exercise of power may make someone predatory (Big fish eat little fish), *but we should remember that even an apparently weak person can be effective:* A mouse may help a lion.

Better be the head of a dog than the tail of a lion.

it is preferable to be at the head of a small organization than in a lowly position in a large one; English proverb, late 16th century.

Power

Big fish eat little fish.

the rich and powerful are likely to prey on those who are less strong, often used with the implication that each predator is in turn victim to a stronger one; English proverb, early 13th century.

He who pays the piper calls the tune.

the person financially responsible for something can control what is done; English proverb, late 19th century.

Kings have long arms.

a king's power reaches a long way; English proverb, mid 16th century.

Might is right.

English proverb, early 14th century.

A mouse may help a lion.

alluding to Aesop's fable of the lion and the rat, in which a rat saved a lion which had been trapped in a net by gnawing through the cords which bound it; English proverb, mid 16th century.

Power corrupts.

English proverb, late 19th century.

Power is like an egg; if you hold it too tightly, it breaks, and if you hold it too loosely, it drops and breaks.

power should be exercised with proper attention, but without repression; African proverb.

Set a beggar on horseback, and he'll ride to the Devil.

a person unused to power will make unwise use of it;
English proverb, late 16th century.

They that dance must pay the fiddler.

you must be prepared to make recompense for the provision
of an essential service; English proverb, mid 17th century.

When elephants fight, it is the grass that gets hurt.

the weak are likely to suffer as a result of the conflicts of the
strong and powerful; African proverb (Swahili).

When whales fight, the shrimp's back is broken.

Korean proverb.

Where the needle goes, the thread must follow.

Polish saying.

Practicality

See also CIRCUMSTANCE AND SITUATION

*We should be ready to accept the limitations imposed
by circumstances:* Cut your coat according to
your cloth.

A big fish is caught with a big bait.

African saying.

Praise and Flattery

Cut your coat according to your cloth.

actions taken should suit one's circumstances or resources;
English proverb, mid 16th century.

He who wants a rose must respect the thorn.

someone wanting a desirable object needs to be aware of the
dangers it brings with it; Persian proverb; compare **No rose
without a thorn** at CIRCUMSTANCE AND SITUATION and **Do not
grieve that rose trees have thorns, rather rejoice that
thorny bushes bear roses** at SATISFACTION.

The only part of a pig that can't be used is its squeak.

traditional saying.

Put your trust in God, and keep your powder dry.

often attributed to Oliver Cromwell (1599–1658); English
proverb, mid 19th century; compare **Trust in Allah, but tie
up your camel** at CAUTION.

You cannot make an omelette without breaking eggs.

often used in the context of a regrettable political necessity
which is said to be justified because it will benefit the
majority; English proverb, mid 19th century.

 # Praise and Flattery

Praise that is well based is worth having (Praise from Sir
Hubert is praise indeed), *but flattery is worthless:*
Flattery, like perfume, should be smelled, not swallowed.

Praise and Flattery

The cuckoo praises the rooster because the rooster praises the cuckoo.

Russian saying, based on Ivan Krylov's fable 'The Cuckoo and the Rooster' (1834).

Flattery is soft soap, and soft soap is ninety per cent lye.

distinguishing between soundly based compliment and insincere congratulation (*lye* is a strongly alkaline solution, especially of potassium hydroxide, used for washing or cleansing); American proverb, mid 19th century.

Flattery, like perfume, should be smelled, not swallowed.

American proverb, mid 19th century.

Give credit where credit is due.

English proverb, late 18th century.

Imitation is the sincerest form of flattery.

English proverb, early 19th century, from Charles Caleb Colton *Lacon* (1820).

Praise from Sir Hubert is praise indeed.

popular saying, a misquotation of a line from Thomas Morton *A Cure for the Headache* (1797), 'Approbation from Sir Hubert Stanley is praise indeed.'

Prejudice and Tolerance

While we should accept the views of others (Live and let live), *real prejudice is both unwelcome and difficult to eradicate:* No tree takes so deep a root as prejudice.

Judge not, that ye be not judged.

used as a warning against overhasty criticism of someone; English proverb, late 15th century, from the Bible (Matthew 7:1).

Live and let live.

often used in the context of coexistence between deeply divided groups; English proverb, early 17th century.

No tree takes so deep a root as prejudice.

emphasizing how difficult it is to eradicate prejudice; American proverb, mid 20th century.

There's none so blind as those who will not see.

used in reference to someone who is unwilling to recognize unwelcome facts; English proverb, mid 16th century.

There's none so deaf as those who will not hear.

used to refer to someone who chooses not to listen to unwelcome information; English proverb, mid 16th century.

Preparation and Readiness

Forethought is endorsed (The early bird catches the worm), *but we should not expend too much attention on circumstances that have not yet arisen:* Don't cross the bridge till you come to it.

Be prepared.

motto of the Scout and Guide organizations, deriving from the initials of Robert Baden-Powell (1857–1941), the founder.

Dig the well before you are thirsty.

make necessary preparations before you are in need; Japanese proverb.

Don't cross the bridge till you come to it.

warning that you should not concern yourself with possible difficulties unless and until they arise; English proverb, mid 19th century.

Don't throw away the old bucket, until you know whether the new one holds water.

do not get rid of a useful resource until you are sure that its replacement functions properly; Swedish proverb.

The early bird catches the worm.

someone who is energetic and efficient is most likely to be successful; English proverb, mid 17th century; compare **It's the second mouse that gets the cheese** below.

Preparation and Readiness

The early man never borrows from the late man.
someone who has made their preparations has no need to turn to someone less efficient; English proverb, mid 17th century.

Forewarned is forearmed.
if one has been warned in advance about a problem one can make preparations for dealing with it; English proverb, early 16th century.

For want of a nail the shoe was lost; for want of a shoe the horse was lost; and for want of a horse the man was lost.
often quoted allusively to imply that one apparently small circumstance can result in a large-scale disaster; English proverb, early 17th century (late 15th century in French).

Have an umbrella ready before it rains.
be sure you are prepared for difficult times; modern saying.

Hope for the best and prepare for the worst.
recommending a balance between optimism and realism; English proverb, mid 16th century.

If you want peace, you must prepare for war.
a country in a state of military preparedness is unlikely to be attacked; English proverb, mid 16th century; the idea is found in the classical world in the *Nicomachaean Ethics* of Aristotle, 'We make war that we may live in peace.'

Preparation and Readiness

It's the second mouse that gets the cheese.

modern addition to **The early bird catches the worm** above, suggesting the dangers of being the first to make a venture, and the possible benefits of following directly behind a pioneer; compare **The only free cheese is in a mousetrap** at TEMPTATION.

Measure seven times, cut once.

care taken in preparation will prevent errors (originally referring to carpentry and needlework); Russian proverb.

No one was ever lost on a straight road.

if you know where you are going you will not make mistakes; Indian proverb.

Pick your battles.

modern saying.

No plan survives first contact with the enemy.

modern saying, from the German soldier and statesman Helmuth von Moltke (1800–91), 'No plan of operations reaches with any certainly beyond the first encounter with the enemy's main force.'

Prayer to God, and service to the tsar, are never wasted.

Russian proverb.

To fail to prepare is to prepare to fail.

modern saying.

The Present

See also THE FUTURE, THE PAST

Although it may seem that what we want never arrives (Jam tomorrow and jam yesterday, but never jam today), we should not lose sight of the fact that the present is what we have: Yesterday has gone, tomorrow is yet to be. Today is the miracle.

Better an egg today than a hen tomorrow.
take advantage of what is available now, rather than waiting for possible advantages later; English proverb.

Enjoy the present moment and don't grieve for the future.
American proverb, mid 20th century.

Jam tomorrow and jam yesterday, but never jam today.
English proverb, late 19th century, from Lewis Carroll *Through the Looking-Glass* (1872), 'The rule is, jam to-morrow and jam yesterday—but never jam today!'

Yesterday has gone, tomorrow is yet to be. Today is the miracle.
modern saying.

Yesterday is ashes; tomorrow is wood. Only today does the fire burn brightly.
emphasizing the importance of enjoying and valuing the present rather than dwelling in the past, which cannot be changed, or the future, which has not yet happened; Canadian saying, said to be of Inuit origin.

Pride

See also SELF-ESTEEM AND SELF-ASSERTION

Pride may shield us from distress (Pride feels no pain), *but the shelter is not likely to last:* Pride goes before a fall.

He that will not stoop for a pin [a penny] will never be worth a point [a pound].
if pride prevents you from taking a small benefit, you will not make further gains; English proverb.

Pride feels no pain.
implying that inordinate self-esteem will not allow the admission that one might be suffering; English proverb, early 17th century.

Pride goes before a fall.
often with the implication that proud and haughty behaviour will contribute to its own downfall; English proverb, late 14th century, often with allusion to the Bible

(Proverbs 16:18), 'Pride goeth before destruction, and an haughty spirit before a fall.'

Stupidity and pride grow on the same tree.
pride is likely to blind us to a wise course of action;
German proverb.

 # Problems and Solutions

See also WAYS AND MEANS

A particular situation or course of action is likely to
affect what you then do: If you lead your mule to the
top of the minaret, then you must lead him
down again.

**If you lead your mule to the top of the minaret, then
you must lead him down again.**
if you get yourself into a difficult position, you will have to
extricate yourself; Arab proverb.

**Never bid the Devil good morrow until you
meet him.**
a warning against trying to deal with problems or
difficulties before they have actually occurred; English
proverb, late 19th century, said to be an old Irish saying.

When all you have is a hammer, everything looks like a nail.

often used to comment on the wholesale application of one solution or method to the solution of any problem; English proverb, late 20th century (chiefly North America).

Why did the chicken cross the road?

traditional puzzle question, to which the answer is, 'to get to the other side'; mid 19th century.

Punctuality ✿

See also TIME

Punctuality shows a proper courtesy (Punctuality is the politeness of princes), *and also has practical advantages:* First come, first served.

Better late than never.

even if one has missed the first chance of doing something, it is better to attempt it than not to do it at all; English proverb, early 14th century.

First come, first served.

English proverb, late 14th century.

Punctuality is the art of guessing correctly how late the other party is going to be.

American proverb, mid 20th century.

Punishment

Punctuality is the politeness of princes.
English proverb, mid 19th century; the idea is found earlier in French, in a comment by Louis XVIII (1755–1824), 'Punctuality is the politeness of kings.'

Punctuality is the soul of business.
English proverb, mid 19th century.

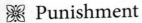 # Punishment
See CRIME AND PUNISHMENT

Quantities and Qualities

From Little fish are sweet *to* One spoonful of tar spoils a barrel of honey, *there is a consensus that a small quantity of something can be potent.*

All that glitters is not gold.

an attractive appearance is not necessarily evidence of intrinsic value; English proverb, early 13th century.

Drops that gather one by one finally become a sea.

Persian proverb.

How long is a piece of string?

traditional saying, used to indicate that something cannot be given a finite measurement.

Little fish are sweet.

small gifts are always acceptable; English proverb, early 19th century.

Many a little makes a mickle.

the proper form of the proverb **Many a mickle makes a muckle** below (*mickle* in Scottish usage means 'a large quantity or amount'); English proverb, mid 13th century.

Many a mickle makes a muckle.

an alteration of the proverb **Many a little makes a mickle** above; the result is actually nonsensical, since *muckle* is a

Quantities and Qualities

variant of *mickle*, and both mean 'a large quantity or amount'.

The more the merrier.
English proverb, late 14th century.

The nearer the bone, the sweeter the meat.
the juiciest meat lies next to the bone, or the meat closest to the bone is particularly precious because it may represent one's last scrap of food; English proverb, late 14th century.

Never mind the quality, feel the width.
used as the title of a television comedy series (1967–9) about a tailoring business in the East End of London, ultimately probably an inversion of a cloth trade saying.

One spoonful of tar spoils a barrel of honey.
Russian proverb.

Small is beautiful.
title of a book by E. F. Schumacher, 1973.

There is safety in numbers.
now with the implication that a number of people will be unscathed where an individual might be in danger; English proverb, late 17th century.

Where's the beef?
advertising slogan for Wendy's Hamburgers in a campaign launched 9 January 1984, and subsequently taken up by the

Quantities and Qualities

American politician Walter Mondale in a televised debate
with Gary Hart during the campaign for the US presidential
campaign, 11 March 1984: 'When I hear your new ideas I'm
reminded of that ad, "Where's the beef?" '

The whole is more than the sum of the parts.
traditional saying, probably deriving from Aristotle
Metaphysica, 'Whenever anything which has several parts is
such that the whole is something over and above its parts,
and not just the sum of them, like a heap, then it always has
some cause.'

**You can count the apples on one tree, but not the
trees in one apple.**
African proverb.

Rank

The implicit acceptance of the desirability of social rank in It takes three generations to make a gentleman *is questioned by the traditional rhyme from the time of the Peasants' Revolt:* When Adam delved and Eve span, who was then the gentleman?

Everybody loves a lord.
English proverb, mid 19th century.

If two ride on a horse, one must ride behind.
of two people engaged on the same task, one must take a subordinate role; English proverb, late 16th century.

It takes three generations to make a gentleman.
English proverb, early 19th century; the idea that it took three generations before the possession of wealth conferred the status of gentleman occurs from the late 16th century.

When Adam delved and Eve span, who was then the gentleman?
traditional rhyme taken in this form by John Ball as the text of his revolutionary sermon on the outbreak of the Peasants' Revolt, 1381; it appears in the writings of Richard Rolle of Hampole (1290–1349) as, 'When Adam dalfe and Eve spane /Go spire if thou may spede, /Where was than the pride of man /That now merres his mede?'

Where Macgregor sits is the head of the table.

sometimes attributed to 'Rob Roy' MacGregor (other names
are used as well as Macgregor); English proverb, mid
19th century.

You may know a gentleman by his horse, his hawk, and his greyhound.

traditional accoutrements of leisure for those of rank;
Welsh proverb.

Readiness

See PREPARATION AND READINESS

Reading

See also BOOKS

Reading is not only a valuable activity (The man who
reads is the man who leads), *it can provide a bond*: It
is a tie between men to have read the same book.

He that runs may read.

meaning very clear and readable; English proverb, late
16th century, originally with allusion to the Bible (Habakkuk
2:2), 'Write the vision, and make it plain upon tables, that
he may run that readeth it', reinforced by John Keble's
'Septuagesima' (1827), 'There is a book, who runs may read.'

Rebellion

It is a tie between men to have read the same book.
American proverb, mid 19th century.

The man who reads is the man who leads.
American proverb, mid 20th century.

Rebellion

See REVOLUTION AND REBELLION

Relationships

See also FEELINGS, FRIENDSHIP, LOVE

*Proverbial wisdom reflects both on relationships
between individuals* (There is always one who kisses,
and one who turns the cheek), *and the wider link
between the individual and society* (I am because we
are; we are because I am).

I am because we are; we are because I am.
whatever affects the individual affects the whole community
and whatever affects the whole community affects the
individual; African proverb.

It is easy to kindle a fire on a familiar hearth.
a relationship which has once existed can be revived;
Welsh proverb.

L'amour est aveugle; l'amitié ferme les yeux.

French proverb, meaning that love is blind, while friendship closes its eyes; compare **Love is blind** at LOVE.

There is always one who kisses, and one who turns (or offers) the cheek.

traditional saying, said to be of French origin.

Treat a man as he is, and that is what he remains. Treat a man as he can be, and that is what he becomes.

modern saying, from Goethe *Wilhelm Meisters Lehrjare* (1795–6), 'When we take people, thou wouldst say, merely as they are, we make them worse; when we treat them as if they were what they should be, we improve them as far as they can be improved.'

Religion

See also THE CHRISTIAN CHURCH, THE CLERGY, GOD

Religious practice is seen as a way of life: Laborare est orare [To work is to pray].

The family that prays together stays together.

motto devised by Al Scalpone for the Roman Catholic Family Rosary Crusade, 1947.

Reputation

Laborare est orare.
Latin, 'To work is to pray,' a traditional motto of the
Benedictine order, also found in the form '*Ora, lege, et
labora* [Pray, read, and work].'

Man's extremity is God's opportunity.
great distress or danger may prompt a person to turn to
God for help; English proverb, early 17th century.

When you pray, move your feet.
advocating works as well as faith; saying, said to be of
Quaker origin.

 # Reputation
See also FAME

Not only is a good reputation a positive advantage
(When a tiger dies it leaves its skin. When a man dies
he leaves his name), *to acquire a bad reputation can be
dangerous, since there is ready belief in the idea that
there is* No smoke without fire.

De mortuis nil nisi bonum.
Latin, literally the injunction 'Of the dead, speak kindly or
not at all'; compare **Never speak ill of the dead** below.

The devil is not so black as he is painted.
someone may not be as bad as their reputation; English
proverb, mid 16th century.

Reputation

A good name is better than a golden girdle.
French proverb.

A good reputation stands still; a bad one runs.
American proverb, mid 20th century.

He that has an ill name is half hanged.
someone with a bad reputation is already half way to being
condemned on any charge brought against them; English
proverb, late 14th century; compare **Give a dog a bad name
and hang him** at GOSSIP.

**A man's best reputation for his future is his record
of the past.**
American proverb, mid 20th century.

Never speak ill of the dead.
English proverb, mid 16th century; see *De mortuis nil nisi
bonum* above.

No smoke without fire.
rumour is generally founded on fact; English proverb, late
14th century, earlier in French and Latin.

**One may steal a horse, while another may not look
over a hedge.**
while one person is endlessly indulged, another is treated
with suspicion on the slightest evidence; English proverb,
mid 16th century.

Responsibility

Speak as you find.

English proverb, late 16th century.

Throw dirt enough, and some will stick.

persistent slander will in the end be believed; English
proverb, mid 17th century.

**When a tiger dies it leaves its skin. When a man dies
he leaves his name.**

a person leaves behind more than a body; Japanese proverb.

 # Responsibility

*It is as well to be ready to take responsibility for
ourselves, since* Don't care was made to care; *however,
there is an awareness that there may be a price to be
paid:* Take what you want, and pay for it, says God.

Don't care was made to care.

traditional rebuke to someone who has asserted their lack of
concern; from the first words of a children's rhyme, 'Don't
care was made to care, don't care was hung'; English saying,
mid 20th century.

Everybody's business is nobody's business.

when something is of some interest to everyone, no single
person takes full responsibility for it; English proverb, early
17th century.

Every herring must hang by its own gill.

everyone is accountable for their own actions; English proverb, early 17th century.

Take what you want, and pay for it, says God.

traditional saying, sometimes said to be of Spanish origin.

Those who eat salty fish will have to accept being thirsty.

everyone is responsible for the consequences of their own actions; Chinese proverb.

Revenge

It is tempting to seek revenge (Revenge is sweet), *but the unforgiving person may achieve more than they intend:* An eye for an eye makes the whole world blind.

Don't cut off your nose to spite your face.

warning against spiteful revenge which is likely to result in your own hurt or loss; English proverb, mid 16th century.

Don't get mad, get even.

late 20th-century saying.

An eye for an eye makes the whole world blind.

modern saying, often attributed to Mahatma Gandhi (1869–1948); often with allusion to the Bible (Exodus 21:23), 'Life for life, /Eye for eye, tooth for tooth.'

Revolution and Rebellion

He laughs last who laughs best.
the most successful person is the one who is finally
triumphant; English proverb, early 17th century.

He who laughs last, laughs longest.
early 20th-century saying.

If you want revenge, dig two graves.
pursuit of revenge is likely to be destructive to the pursuer
as well as to their object; saying, claimed to be of Chinese or
Japanese origin.

Living well is the best revenge.
traditional saying.

Revenge is a dish that can be eaten cold.
vengeance need not be exacted immediately; English
proverb, late 19th century.

Revenge is sweet.
English proverb, mid 16th century.

 # Revolution and Rebellion

A revolution may begin with an idea (Every
revolution was first a thought in one's man's mind),
but it will end in violence: Revolutions are not made
with rosewater.

Every revolution was first a thought in one man's mind.

American proverb, mid 19th century.

Revolutions are not made by men in spectacles.

American proverb, late 19th century.

Revolutions are not made with rosewater.

revolutions involve violence and ruthless behaviour; English proverb, early 19th century.

Whosoever draws his sword against the prince must throw away the scabbard.

anyone who tries to assassinate or depose a monarch must remain constantly on the defence; English proverb, early 17th century.

Rivers

Rivers may have their own identity, but in the end they come to same place: All rivers run into the sea.

All rivers run into the sea.

English proverb, early 16th century; originally with allusion to the Bible (Ecclesiastes 1:7), 'All the rivers run into the sea; yet the sea is not full; unto the place from whence the rivers come, thither they return again.'

Royalty

Says Tweed to Till—'What gars ye rin sae still?' Says
Till to Tweed—'Though ye rin with speed And I rin
slaw, For ae man that ye droon I droon twa.'
traditional Scottish rhyme.

Royalty

The royalty of a sovereign confers a special quality (The
king can do no wrong), *but in lesser figures may not
be greatly regarded:* Camels, fleas, and princes exist
everywhere.

Camels, fleas, and princes exist everywhere.
referring to the large numbers of offspring of some rulers;
Persian proverb.

The king can do no wrong.
something cannot be wrong if it is done by someone of
sovereign power, who alone is not subject to the law of the
land; translation of the Latin legal maxim *rex non potest
peccare*; English proverb, mid 17th century.

A king's chaff is worth more than other men's corn.
even minor benefits available to those attending on a
sovereign are more substantial than the best that can be
offered by those of lesser status; English proverb, early
17th century.

Satisfaction and Discontent

Satisfaction is most likely to be found by making the best of what is available: Half a loaf is better than no bread.

Acorns were good till bread was found.

until something better is found, what one has will be judged satisfactory; English proverb, late 16th century.

The answer is a lemon.

a *lemon* as the type of something unsatisfactory, perhaps referring to the least valuable symbol in a fruit machine; English proverb, early 20th century.

Better are small fish than an empty dish.

a little is preferable to nothing at all; English proverb, late 17th century.

Do not grieve that rose trees have thorns, rather rejoice that thorny bushes bear roses.

advocating an emphasis on positive aspects; Arab proverb; compare **No rose without a thorn** at CIRCUMSTANCE AND SITUATION, and **He who wants a rose must respect the thorn** at PRACTICALITY.

Go further and fare worse.

it is often wise to take what is on offer; English proverb, mid 16th century.

Sayings

Half a loaf is better than no bread.
to have part of something is better than having nothing at all; English proverb, mid 16th century.

Something is better than nothing.
even a possession of intrinsically little value is preferable to being empty-handed; English proverb, mid 16th century.

What you've never had you've never missed.
English proverb, early 20th century.

 Sayings

See also WORDS

Common wisdom is often enshrined in popular sayings:
Proverbs are the coins of the people.

The devil can quote Scripture for his own ends.
it is possible for someone engaged in wrongdoing to quote selectively from the Bible in apparent support of their position, and alluding to the temptation of Christ by the Devil in the Bible (Matthew); English proverb, late 16th century.

Proverbs are the coins of the people.
Russian proverb.

There is no proverb without a grain of truth.
Russian proverb.

To understand the people acquaint yourself with their proverbs.

Arab proverb.

Traduttore traditore.

Italian, meaning 'Translators, traitors.'

Science

A saying such as Science has no enemy but the ignorant *will hold whether 'science' has its original meaning of 'knowledge', or the more specific modern sense.*

Laws of Thermodynamics:
1) You cannot win, you can only break even.
2) You can only break even at absolute zero.
3) You cannot reach absolute zero.

folklore among physicists.

Much science, much sorrow.

suggesting that learning may increase one's awareness of difficult questions; English proverb, early 17th century.

Science has no enemy but the ignorant.

English proverb, mid 16th century, from Latin *Scientia non habet inimicum nisi ignorantem.*

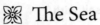

The Sea

Recommendations about seamanship are alive to the dangers of the sea: He that would go to sea for pleasure would go to hell for a pastime.

The good seaman is known in bad weather.
American proverb, mid 18th century.

He that would go to sea for pleasure would go to hell for a pastime.
with reference to the dangers involved in going to sea; English proverb, late 19th century.

If the Bermudas let you pass, you must beware of Hatteras.
traditional saying on the dangers of sailing in the Atlantic, and especially of the waters around Cape Hatteras in North Carolina.

One hand for oneself and one for the ship.
literally, hold on with one hand, and work the ship with the other; English proverb, late 18th century.

The sea wants to be visited.
referring to those who make their living from the sea; Scottish saying.

Secrecy ✹

*While it may be desirable to keep information
confidential* (Don't ask, don't tell, One does not wash
one's dirty linen in public), *it is likely to be difficult:*
Fields have eyes and woods have ears.

The day has eyes, the night has ears.

there is always someone watching or listening;
traditional saying.

Dead men tell no tales.

often used to imply that a person's knowledge of a secret will
die with them; English proverb, mid 17th century.

Don't ask, don't tell.

summary of the Clinton administration's compromise
policy on homosexuals serving in the armed forces, as
described by Sam Nunn (1938–) in May 1993.

Fields have eyes and woods have ears.

one may always be spied on by unseen watchers or listeners;
English proverb, early 13th century.

Listeners never hear good of themselves.

English proverb, mid 17th century.

Little pitchers have large ears.

children overhear what is not meant for them (a pitcher's
ears are its handles); English proverb, mid 16th century.

303

Secrecy

Never tell tales out of school.
a warning against indiscretion; English proverb, mid
16th century.

No names, no pack drill.
if nobody is named as being responsible, nobody can be
blamed or punished *(pack drill* = a military punishment of
walking up and down carrying full equipment); English
proverb, early 20th century; the expression is now used
generally to express an unwillingness to provide
detailed information.

One does not wash one's dirty linen in public.
discreditable matters should be dealt with privately; English
proverb, early 19th century.

A secret is either too good to keep or too bad not to tell.
American proverb, mid 20th century.

See all your best work go unnoticed.
advertisement for staff for MI5, 2005.

Those who hide can find.
those who have concealed something know where it is to be
found; English proverb, early 15th century.

Three may keep a secret, if two of them are dead.
the only way to keep a secret is to tell no one else; English
proverb, mid 16th century.

Walls have ears.

care should be taken for possible eavesdroppers; English
proverb, late 16th century.

What is done by night appears by day.

secrets are likely to be revealed; English proverb.

Will the real — please stand up?

catchphrase from an American TV game show (1955–66) in
which a panel was asked to identify the 'real' one of three
candidates all claiming to be a particular person; after the
guesses were made, the compère would request the 'real'
candidate to stand up.

You can't hide an awl in a sack.

some things are too conspicuous to hide; Russian proverb.

Self-Esteem and Self-Assertion

See also PRIDE

A saying such as The bigger the hat, the smaller the
property *suggests self-assertion, but more traditional
sayings warn against boasting of one's attributes:* Clever
hawks conceal their claws.

The bigger the hat, the smaller the property.
Australian saying.

Self-Esteem and Self-Assertion

Clever hawks conceal their claws.
it is not necessary to boast of one's abilities;
Japanese proverb.

Deny self for self's sake.
the result of self-denial is likely to be self-improvement;
American proverb, mid 18th century.

A frog in a well knows nothing of the ocean.
one should be aware of the limitations of one's own
experience; Japanese proverb.

Here's tae us; wha's like us?
Gey few, and they're a' deid.
Scottish toast, probably of 19th century origin.

Know thyself.
English proverb, late 14th century; inscribed in Greek on
the temple of Apollo at Delphi; Plato, in *Protagoras,* ascribes
the saying to the Seven Wise Men of the 6th century BC.

The kumara does not speak of its own sweetness.
one should not praise oneself (a *kumara* is a sweet potato);
Maori proverb.

**The peacock is always happy because it never looks
at its ugly feet.**
a person does not see their own faults; Persian proverb.

Self-praise is no recommendation.

a person's own favourable account of themselves is of dubious worth; English proverb, early 19th century.

Self-Interest

Pragmatic advice on watching your own interests (Self-preservation is the first law of nature) *may be set against reflections on fulfilling one's one responsibilities:* If every man would sweep his own doorstep the city would soon be clean.

Every man for himself and God for us all.

ultimately God is concerned for humankind while individuals are concerned only for themselves; English proverb, mid 16th century.

Every man for himself, and the Devil take the hindmost.

each person must look out for their own interests, and the weakest is likely to come to disaster; English proverb, early 16th century.

Every man is the architect of his own fortune.

each person is ultimately responsible for what happens to them; English proverb, mid 16th century.

Self-Interest

Hear all, see all, say nowt, tak' all, keep all, gie nowt, and if tha ever does owt for nowt do it for thysen.

now associated with Yorkshire, and caricaturing supposedly traditional Yorkshire attributes, in the picture of someone who is shrewd, taciturn, grasping, and selfish; English proverb, early 15th century.

If every man would sweep his own doorstep the city would soon be clean.

if everyone fulfils their own responsibilities, what is necessary will be done; English proverb, early 17th century.

If you want a thing done well, do it yourself.

no one else has so much interest in your own welfare; English proverb, mid 17th century.

If you would be well served, serve yourself.

no one else has so much interest in your own welfare; English proverb, mid 17th century.

Near is my kirtle, but nearer my smock.

used as a justification for putting one's own interests first (a *kirtle* is a woman's skirt or gown, and a *smock* is an undergarment); English proverb, mid 15th century.

Near is my shirt, but nearer my skin.

a justification of self-interest; English proverb, late 16th century.

A satisfied person does not know the hungry person.
African proverb.

Self-interest is the rule, self-sacrifice the exception.
American proverb, mid 20th century.

Self-preservation is the first law of nature.
the instinct for self-preservation is inbuilt and instinctive;
English proverb, mid 17th century.

Selling

See BUYING AND SELLING

Sex

See also LOVE, MARRIAGE

A question such as Did the earth move for you?
*suggests a less bleak view of sex than the dismissive
view that* Dirty water will quench fire.

Did the earth move for you?
supposedly said to one's partner after sexual intercourse,
after Ernest Hemingway *For Whom the Bell Tolls* (1940),
'But did thee feel the earth move.'

Sickness

Dirty water will quench fire.

mainly used to mean that a man's sexual needs can be
satisfied by any woman, however ugly or immoral; English
proverb, mid 16th century.

Post coitum omne animal triste.

Latin, 'After coition every animal is sad.'

Why buy a cow when milk is so cheap?

putting forward an argument for choosing the least
troublesome alternative; frequently used as an argument
against marriage; English proverb, mid 17th century.

 Sickness

See also HEALTH, MEDICINE

*While sickness should be avoided, ailments are not
necessarily fatal: A creaking door hangs longest.*

Coughs and sneezes spread diseases. Trap the germs in your handkerchief.

Second World War health slogan (1942).

A creaking door hangs longest.

someone who is apparently in poor health may well outlive
the ostensibly stronger; English proverb, late 17th century.

Diseases come on horseback but go away on foot.

sickness may occur swiftly, but recovery is likely to be slow;
English proverb, late 16th century.

Feed a cold and starve a fever.

probably intended as two separate admonitions, but sometimes interpreted to mean that if you feed a cold you will have to starve a fever later; English proverb, mid 19th century.

From the bitterness of disease, man learns the sweetness of health.

Catalan proverb.

An imaginary ailment is worse than a disease.

Yiddish proverb.

Silence

See also SPEECH

Silence can be impressive in itself (Silence is a still noise) *as well as a guard against idle talk:* A shut mouth catches no flies.

A shut mouth catches no flies.

a warning against the dangers of idle talk; English proverb, late 16th century.

Silence is a still noise.

American proverb, late 19th century.

Silence means consent.

English proverb, late 14th century; translation of a Latin tag, '*Qui tacet consentire videtur* [He who is silent seems to

311

consent]', said to have been spoken by Thomas More (1478–1535) when asked at his trial why he was silent on being asked to acknowledge the king's supremacy over the Church. The principle is not accepted in modern English law.

Speech is silver, but silence is golden.
discretion can be more valuable than the most eloquent words; English proverb, mid 19th century; compare **Who knows most, speaks least** at SPEECH.

Speech sows, silence reaps.
once an argument has been put, it is wise to give time for the words to have an effect; saying, said to be a Persian proverb.

A still tongue makes a wise head.
a person who is not given to idle talk, and who listens to others, is likely to be wise; English proverb, mid 16th century.

Similarity and Difference

Similarity may be a bond (Birds of a feather flock together), *or may promote rivalry:* Two swords cannot fit in one scabbard.

All cats are grey in the dark.
darkness obscures inessential differences; English proverb, mid 16th century.

Similarity and Difference

Birds of a feather flock together.

people of the same (usually unscrupulous) character tend to associate; English proverb, mid 16th century.

Comparisons are odious.

often used to suggest that to compare two different things or persons is unhelpful or misleading; English proverb, mid 15th century.

East is east, and west is west.

an assertion of ineradicable racial and cultural differences; English proverb, late 19th century, from Kipling 'The Ballad of East and West' (1892), 'Oh, East is East, and West is West, and never the twain shall meet, Till Earth and Sky stand presently at God's great Judgement Seat; But there is neither East nor West, Border, nor Breed, nor Birth, When two strong men stand face to face, tho' they come from the ends of the earth!'

Extremes meet.

opposite extremes have much in common; English proverb, mid 18th century.

From the sweetest wine, the tartest vinegar.

the strongest hate comes from former love; English proverb, late 16th century.

Like breeds like.

a particular kind of event may well be the genesis of a similar occurrence; English proverb, mid 16th century.

Situation

Like will to like.
those of similar nature and inclination are drawn together;
English proverb, late 14th century.

One nail drives out another.
like will counter like; English proverb, mid 13th century.

Two of a trade never agree.
close association with someone makes disagreement over policy
and principles more likely; English proverb, early 17th century.

Two swords do not fit in one scabbard.
Indian proverb.

When Greek meets Greek, then comes the tug of war.
when two people of a similar kind are opposed, there is a
struggle for supremacy; English proverb, late 17th century,
from Nathaniel Lee *The Rival Queens* (1677), 'When Greeks
joined Greeks, then was the tug of war!'

 # Situation

See CIRCUMSTANCE AND SITUATION

 # Sleep

See also DREAMS

Sleep is a source of essential refreshment (One hour's
sleep before midnight is worth two after), *but*

overindulgence in it is a bad sign: Some sleep five hours; nature requires seven, laziness nine, and wickedness eleven.

The beginning of health is sleep.
Irish proverb.

The morning knows more than the evening.
the mind is clearer after sleep; Russian proverb.

One hour's sleep before midnight is worth two after.
English proverb, mid 17th century.

Six hours' sleep for a man, seven for a woman, and eight for a fool.
implying that the more sleep a person needs, the less vigorous and effective they are likely to be; English proverb, early 17th century.

Some sleep five hours; nature requires seven, laziness nine, and wickedness eleven.
American proverb, mid 20th century.

We never sleep.
motto of the American detective agency founded by Allan Pinkerton (c.1855).

✖ Smoking

Sayings about smoking trace a changing attitude to the habit, culminating in the warning Smoking can seriously damage your health.

Coffee without tobacco is like a Jew without a rabbi.
Moroccan proverb.

Happiness is a cigar called Hamlet.
advertising slogan for Hamlet cigars, UK.

More doctors recommend Camels than any other cigarette.
advertising slogan for Camel cigarettes.

Smoking can seriously damage your health.
government health warning now required by British law to be printed on cigarette packets; in the form 'Smoking can damage your health' from early 1970s.

You're never alone with a Strand.
advertising slogan for Strand cigarettes, 1960; the image of loneliness was so strongly conveyed by the solitary smoker that sales were adversely affected.

Solitude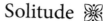

While you may be hampered by companionship (He travels the fastest who travels alone), *there are risks in solitude:* The lone sheep is in danger of the wolf.

Better alone than in bad company.

American proverb, late 17th century.

He travels the fastest who travels alone.

implying that single-minded pursuit of an objective is more easily achieved by someone without family commitments; English proverb, late 19th century; from Kipling 'The Winners' (1890), 'Down to Gehenna or up to the Throne, He travels the fastest who travels alone.'

The lone sheep is in danger of the wolf.

stressing the importance of mutual support; English proverb, late 16th century.

No man is an island.

every person has some connection with and responsibility for others; saying from John Donne's 'Meditation XVII' from 'Devotions upon Emergent Occasions' (1624).

Solutions

See PROBLEMS AND SOLUTIONS

❀ Sorrow

See also MOURNING, SUFFERING

*Grief is inevitable, but we may find ways of dealing
with it—perhaps by seeking the support of others:*
Misery loves company.

He that conceals his grief, finds no remedy for it.

trying to hide distress means that you do not recover from
it; proverb, said to be of Turkish origin.

Misery loves company.

English proverb, late 16th century, now predominantly
current in the United States.

Wednesday's child is full of woe.

traditional rhyme, mid 19th century (compare qualities
associated with birth on other days at entries under BEAUTY,
GIFTS, TRAVEL, and WORK).

You cannot prevent the birds of sorrow from flying overhead, but you can prevent them from building nests in your hair.

sorrow may be unavoidable, but one can respond to it in
different ways; Chinese proverb.

Speech

While conversation is endorsed by the slogan It's good to talk, *there is a traditional consensus that concision in speech is desirable:* Length begets loathing.

Brevity is the soul of wit.

English proverb, early 17th century, from Shakespeare *Henry IV, Part 2* (1597).

If I listen, I have the advantage; if I speak, others have it.

a warning against rushing into speech; Arabic proverb.

It's good to talk.

advertising slogan for British Telecom from 1994.

Length begets loathing.

in reference to verbosity; English proverb, mid 18th century.

Listen a thousand times, and speak once.

warning against making a hasty response; Turkish proverb.

Who knows most, speaks least.

English proverb, mid 17th century.

Sports and Games

The saying Nice guys finish last *might be applied to the results of a number of games.*

Spring

Chess is a sea where a gnat may drink and an elephant may bathe.

the game may be played at many levels; modern saying, said to derive from an Indian proverb.

Drive for show, and putt for dough.

Golf saying meaning that matches are won in the final strokes on the green, and not by the opening drive from the tee.

Nice guys finish last.

modern saying, from a casual remark by the American coach Leo Durocher (1906–91), 'I called off his players' names as they came marching up the steps behind him ... All nice guys. They'll finish last. Nice guys. Finish last.'

Spring

See also AUTUMN, SUMMER, WINTER

Individual months have their own character (March comes in like a lion, and goes out like a lamb), *but spring as a season depends on progression:* April showers bring forth May flowers.

April and May are the keys to the whole year.

good weather in April and May lays an essential foundation for the rest of the year; German proverb.

April showers bring forth May flowers.
English proverb.

A cold April the barn will fill.
cold weather in April is likely to mean a good harvest later
in the year; traditional saying.

A cold May and windy, a full barn will find ye.
Cold and windy weather in May is a predictor of a good
harvest; traditional saying; in its original form, 'a full barn
and findy [an obsolete word meaning "weighty, plentiful"]'.

**March borrowed from April three days, and they
were ill.**
English proverb.

March comes in like a lion, and goes out like a lamb.
English proverb.

May chickens come cheeping.
English proverb.

On the first of March, the crows begin to search.
English proverb.

A peck of March dust is worth a king's ransom.
English proverb.

Rain in spring is as precious as oil.
Chinese proverb.

Strength and Weakness

So many mists in March, so many frosts in May.
English proverb.

Spring is sooner recognized by plants than by men.
Chinese proverb.

 # Strength and Weakness

Individuals may be specially gifted with strength (Only an elephant can bear an elephant's load), *but there may be an interrelationship between the strong and the weak:* The caribou feeds the wolf, but it is the wolf that keeps the caribou strong.

The caribou feeds the wolf, but it is the wolf that keeps the caribou strong.
stressing the interrelationship between predator and prey;
Inuit proverb.

An elephant does not die of one broken rib.
a strong person will not be brought down by a minor injury;
African proverb.

Every tub must stand on its own bottom.
it is necessary to support oneself by one's own efforts;
English proverb, mid 16th century.

If you are afraid of wolves, don't go into the forest.
Russian proverb.

If you don't like the heat, get out of the kitchen.

if you choose to work in a particular sphere you must also deal with its pressures; English proverb, mid 20th century, from a comment associated with the American statesman Harry S. Truman (though attributed by him to his 'military jester' Harry Vaughan, 1893–1981), 'If you can't stand the heat, get out of the kitchen.'

It is the pace that kills.

used as a warning against working under extreme pressure; English proverb, mid 19th century.

Only an elephant can bear an elephant's load.

heavy responsibilities require significant strength; Indian proverb (Marathi).

Only the eagle can gaze at the sun.

only a strong person can undertake a demanding task; English proverb; late 16th century.

A reed before the wind lives on, while mighty oaks fall.

something which bends to the force of the wind is less likely to be broken than something which tries to withstand it; English proverb, late 14th century.

Strength through joy.

German Labour Front slogan from 1933, coined by Robert Ley (1890–1945).

Success and Failure

The weakest go to the wall.
usually said to derive from the installation of seating
(around the walls) in the churches of the late Middle Ages;
English proverb, early 16th century.

What does not kill you makes you stronger.
an encouragement in difficult circumstances;
modern saying.

You are the weakest link . . . goodbye.
catchphrase used by Anne Robinson on the television game
show *The Weakest Link* (2000–); compare **A chain is no
stronger than its weakest link** at COOPERATION.

 # Success and Failure

See also WINNING AND LOSING

Success and failure are both part of life (You win a few,
you lose a few)*, and it is wise to remember that notable
and sudden success is likely to be transient:* Up like a
rocket, down like a stick.

The bigger they are, the harder they fall.
English proverb, early 20th century, commonly attributed in
its current form to the boxer Robert Fitzsimmons, prior to a
fight, *c*.1900.

Do not laugh at the fallen; there may be slippery places ahead.

it is wise to remember when seeing someone in trouble that you too may have difficulties; African proverb.

From clogs to clogs is only three generations.

the *clog*, a shoe with a thick wooden sole, was worn by manual workers in the north of England. The implication is that the energy and ability required to raise a person's material status from poverty is often not continued to the third generation, and that the success is therefore not sustained; English proverb, late 19th century, said to be a Lancashire proverb.

From shirtsleeves to shirtsleeves in three generations.

wealth gained in one generation will be lost by the third; English proverb, early 20th century. The saying is often attributed to the Scottish-born American industrialist and philanthropist Andrew Carnegie (1835–1919) but is not found in his writings.

From the sublime to the ridiculous is only one step.

English proverb, late 19th century; the idea is found earlier in the writings of Thomas Paine *The Age of Reason* pt 2 (1795), 'The sublime and the ridiculous are often so nearly related, that it is difficult to class them separately. One step above the sublime, makes the ridiculous; and one step above the ridiculous, makes the sublime again.' A similar

Success and Failure

comment is found in a comment of Napoleon's after the
1812 retreat from Moscow, 'There is only one step from the
sublime to the ridiculous.'

He who fails to plan, plans to fail.
modern saying.

He who leaves succeeds.
moving away from home territory leads to success;
Italian proverb.

Let them laugh that win.
triumphant laughter should be withheld until success is
assured; English proverb, mid 16th century.

Nothing succeeds like success.
someone already regarded as successful is likely to attract
more support; English proverb, mid 19th century.

The only place where success comes before work is in a dictionary.
modern saying.

The race is not to the swift, nor the battle to the strong.
the person with the most apparent advantages will not
necessarily be successful; English proverb, mid 17th
century; often with allusion to the Bible (Ecclesiastes 9:11).

Success and Failure

A rising tide lifts all boats.

usually taken to mean that a prosperous society benefits
everybody; in America the expression was particularly
associated with John Fitzgerald Kennedy (1917–63); English
proverb, mid 20th century.

Rooster today, feather duster tomorrow.

one who is currently successful may subsequently find that
circumstances change dramatically; Australian saying.

Success has many fathers, while failure is an orphan.

once something is seen to succeed many people will claim
to have initiated it, while responsibility for failure is likely to
be disclaimed; English proverb, mid 20th century; the idea
is found in the diary (for 9 September 1942) of Mussolini's
son-in-law Count Galeazzo Ciano (1903–44), 'Victory has
a hundred fathers, but no one wants to recognise defeat
as his own.'

Up like a rocket, down like a stick.

sudden marked success is likely to be followed by equally
sudden failure; English proverb, late 19th century; the
simile is found earlier in Thomas Paine's (1737–1809)
comment on Edmund Burke's losing the parliamentary
debate on the French Revolution to Charles James Fox, 'As
he rose like a rocket, he fell like the stick.'

Suffering

When an elephant is in trouble, even a frog can kick him.

the weak can attack the strong when they are in difficulty; Indian proverb.

You win a few, you lose a few.

one has to accept failure as well as success, and used as an expression of consolation or resignation; English proverb, mid 20th century.

Suffering

See also MOURNING, SORROW, SYMPATHY

Suffering may ennoble (Crosses are ladders that lead to heaven), *but the slogan* Beauty without cruelty *reminds us that we have no right to inflict it to satisfy our own wants.*

Beauty without cruelty.

slogan for Animal Rights.

Crosses are ladders that lead to heaven.

the way to heaven is through suffering; crosses refers either to the crucifix, or more generally to troubles or misfortunes; English proverb, early 17th century.

No cross, no crown.

cross is here used punningly, as in **Crosses are ladders that lead to heaven** above; English proverb, early 17th century.

Summer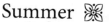

See also AUTUMN, SPRING, WINTER

Summer may see the longest days of the year (Barnaby bright, Barnaby bright, the longest day and the shortest night), *but it does not necessarily imply good weather:* A dripping June sets all in tune.

Barnaby bright, Barnaby bright, the longest day and the shortest night.

in the Old Style calendar St Barnabas' Day, 11 June, was reckoned the longest day of the year; English proverb, mid 17th century.

A cherry year, a merry year; a plum year, a dumb year.

recording the tradition that a good crop of cherries is a promising sign for the year; English proverb, late 17th century.

A dripping June sets all in tune.

English proverb.

One swallow does not make a summer.

English proverb.

Surprise

Saint Swithin's day, if thou be fair, for forty days it will remain; Saint Swithin's day, if thou bring rain, for forty days it will remain.

Saint Swithin's day is 15 July, and the tradition may have its origin in the heavy rain said to have occurred when his relics were to be transferred to a shrine in Winchester Cathedral; English proverb, early 17th century.

Summer is the mother of the poor.

for someone living in poverty, summer is easier than cold weather; Italian proverb.

A swarm in May is worth a load of hay; a swarm in June is worth a silver spoon; but a swarm in July is not worth a fly.

traditional beekeepers' saying, meaning that the later in the summer it is, the less time there will be for bees to collect pollen from flowers in blossom; English proverb, mid 17th century.

 # Surprise

A saying such as You could have knocked me down with a feather *suggests a lack of awareness that* The unexpected always happens.

The age of miracles is past.

often used ironically, or as a comment on failure; English proverb, late 16th century.

Nobody expects the Spanish Inquisition.

from the script of an episode of *Monty Python's Flying Circus* (BBC TV programme, 1970), 'Nobody expects the Spanish Inquisition! Our chief weapon is surprise—surprise and fear...fear and surprise...our two weapons are fear and surprise—and ruthless efficiency....'

The unexpected always happens.

warning against an overconfident belief that something cannot occur; English proverb, late 19th century.

Wonders will never cease.

often used ironically to comment on an unusual circumstance; English proverb, late 18th century.

You could have knocked me down with a feather.

expressing great surprise; English saying, mid 19th century.

Sympathy

While we cannot necessarily depend on unstinting sympathy (Laugh and the world laughs with you, weep and you weep alone), *to seek for it is natural:* One kind word warms three winter months.

God makes the back to the burden.

an assertion that nothing is truly insupportable used in resignation or consolation; English proverb, early 19th century.

Sympathy

God tempers the wind to the shorn lamb.
God so arranges it that bad luck does not unduly plague the
weak or unfortunate; English proverb, mid 17th century.

**Laugh and the world laughs with you, weep and you
weep alone.**
English proverb, late 19th century; in this form from the
poem 'Solitude' by the American poet Ella Wheeler Wilcox
(1855–1919), 'Laugh and the world laughs with you; Weep,
and you weep alone'; ultimately echoing the Bible (Romans
16:15), 'Rejoice with them that do rejoice, and weep with
them that weep', and Horace (c.65–8) *Ars Poetica*, 'Men's
faces laugh on those who laugh, and correspondingly weep
on those who weep.'

Nothing so bad but it might have been worse.
used in resignation or consolation; English proverb, late
19th century.

One kind word warms three winter months.
Japanese proverb.

Pity is akin to love.
English proverb, early 17th century.

**The rock in the water does not know the pain of the
rock in the sun.**
awareness of your own suffering prevents you from
understanding the pain of those in different circumstances;
Hawaiian proverb.

Sympathy

Shared joy is double joy, and shared sorrow is double sorrow.

proverb, said to be of German origin.

The tears of the stranger are only water.

sympathy for grief may be limited to those whom we already know; Russian proverb.

❀ Teaching

See also EDUCATION

Teaching is important (Who teaches me for a day is my father for a lifetime), *but it may have its limitations:* Tell me and I'll forget. Show me and I'll remember. Involve me and I'll be changed forever.

He teaches ill who teaches all.

English proverb, early 17th century.

He that teaches himself has a fool for a master.

English proverb, early 17th century.

Nobody forgets a good teacher.

Teacher Training Agency slogan, late 20th century.

Tell me and I'll forget. Show me and I'll remember. Involve me and I'll be changed forever.

Japanese proverb.

Who teaches me for a day is my father for a lifetime.

Chinese proverb; compare **Give a man a fish, and you feed him for a day; show him how to catch fish, and you feed him for a lifetime** at CHARITY.

Technology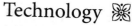

See also CHANGE, COMPUTING, SCIENCE

Technology may provide us with solutions (You press the button, we do the rest), *but it can also constrict us:* Science finds, industry applies, man conforms.

The camera never lies.
20th-century saying.

Let your fingers do the walking.
1960s advertisement for the Bell System Telephone Directory Yellow Pages.

Science finds, industry applies, man conforms.
subtitle of guidebook to 1933 Chicago World's Fair.

Vorsprung durch Technik.
German, 'Progress through technology', advertising slogan for Audi motors, from 1986.

You press the button, we do the rest.
advertising slogan to launch the Kodak camera 1888, coined by George Eastman (1854–1932).

✻ Temptation

What is forbidden is particularly attractive (Naughty but nice)*; however, the attraction is likely to conceal danger:* The only free cheese is in a mousetrap.

The bleating of the lamb excites the tiger.
of a prey staked out to attract a predator; Indian proverb; used by Kipling in *Stalky & Co.* (1899) in the form 'the bleating of the kid…'

Fish follow the bait.
English proverb, 17th century.

The fish will soon be caught that nibbles at every bait.
English proverb, 16th century.

Naughty but nice.
advertising slogan for cream cakes in the first half of the 1980s; earlier, the title of a 1939 film.

The only free cheese is in a mousetrap.
Russian proverb; compare **It's the second mouse that gets the cheese** at PREPARATION AND READINESS.

Stolen fruit are sweet.
The knowledge that something is forbidden makes it more attractive; English proverb, early 17th century.

Stolen waters are sweet.

something which has been obtained secretly or illicitly
seems particularly attractive; English proverb, late
14th century.

There's no such thing as a free lunch.

colloquial axiom in American economics from the mid
20th century, much associated with the economist Milton
Friedman (1912–2006), but not coined by him.

Thinking

See also HYPOTHESIS AND FACT, OPINION

*Thought may or may not be original (Great minds
think alike), but we should exercise the faculty:* To
question and ask is a moment's shame, but to
question and not ask is a lifetime's shame.

Elementary, my dear Watson.

remark attributed to Sherlock Holmes, but not found in
this form in any book by Arthur Conan Doyle; first found
in P. G. Wodehouse *Psmith Journalist* (1915).

Great minds think alike.

English proverb, early 17th century, now often
used ironically.

Thoroughness

To question and ask is a moment's shame, but to question and not ask is a lifetime's shame.
Japanese proverb.

Two heads are better than one.
it is advisable to discuss a problem with another person;
English proverb, late 14th century.

 # Thoroughness

See also DETERMINATION

Even if you are putting yourself at risk, thoroughness is to be recommended: Might as well be hanged for a sheep as for a lamb.

Do not spoil the ship for a ha'porth of tar.
used generally to warn against risking loss or failure through unwillingness to allow relatively trivial expenditure; *ship* is a dialectal pronunciation of *sheep,* and the original literal sense was 'do not allow sheep to die for the lack of a trifling amount of tar', *tar* being used to protect sores and wounds on sheep from flies; English proverb, early 17th century.

In for a penny, in for a pound.
If one is to be involved at all, it may as well be fully; English proverb, late 17th century.

Nothing venture, nothing gain.

a later variant of **Nothing venture, nothing have** below;
English proverb, early 17th century.

Nothing venture, nothing have.

one must be prepared to take some risks to gain a desired
end; English proverb, late 14th century.

One might as well be hanged for a sheep as a lamb.

if one is going to incur a severe penalty it may as well be for
something substantial; English proverb, late 17th century.

Thrift and Extravagance

See also DEBT AND BORROWING, MONEY, POVERTY, WEALTH

*Thrift is not only desirable itself, but is likely to be
rewarded* (A penny saved is a penny earned); *however,
it may be easier to admire than to practise it:* Most
people consider thrift a fine virtue in ancestors.

Bang goes sixpence.

ironic commentary on regretted expenditure, deriving from
a cartoon in *Punch* of 5 December 1868, featuring a miserly
Scotsman. The caption read, 'a had na' been the-erre abune
Twa Hoours when—Bang—went Saxpence!'

Make do and mend.

wartime slogan, 1940s.

Thrift and Extravagance

Most people consider thrift a fine virtue in ancestors.
American proverb, mid 20th century.

A penny saved is a penny earned.
used as an exhortation to thrift; English proverb, mid
17th century.

Penny wise and pound foolish.
too much concern with saving small sums may result in
larger loss if necessary expenditure on maintenance and
safety has been withheld; English proverb, early 17th century.

Spare at the spigot, and let out the bunghole.
referring to the practice of being overcareful on the one
hand, and carelessly generous on the other. A *spigot* is a peg
or pin used to regulate the flow of liquid through a tap on a
cask, and a *bunghole* is a hole through which a cask is filled
or emptied, and which is closed by a bung; English proverb,
mid 17th century.

Spare well and have to spend.
the person who is thrifty and careful with their resources
can use them lavishly when the occasion offers; English
proverb, mid 16th century.

**Stretch your arm no further than your sleeve
will reach.**
you should not spend more than you can afford; English
proverb, mid 16th century.

Take care of the pence and the pounds will take care of themselves.

thrift and small savings will grow to substantial wealth; English proverb, mid 18th century.

Thrift is a great revenue.

care with expenditure is one of the best ways of providing an income for oneself; English proverb, mid 17th century.

Wilful waste makes woeful want.

deliberate misuse of resources is likely to lead to severe shortage; English proverb, early 18th century.

Time

See also TRANSIENCE

Time is seen not only as a powerful force (Time works wonders), *but as one which is beyond any control:* An inch of gold cannot buy time.

Be the day weary or be the day long, at last it ringeth to evensong.

even the most difficult time will come to an end; English proverb, early 16th century.

Even a stopped clock is right twice a day.

modern humorous saying.

Time

An inch of gold cannot buy time.
time cannot be bought with money; Chinese proverb.

Man fears Time, but Time fears the Pyramids.
Egyptian proverb.

The morning daylight appears plainer when you put out your candle.
American proverb.

Never is a long time.
often used to indicate that circumstances may ultimately change; English proverb, late 14th century.

Spring forward, fall back.
a reminder that clocks are moved *forward* in the spring, and *back* in the fall (autumn).

There is a time for everything.
there is always a suitable time to do something; English proverb, late 14th century, from the Bible (Ecclesiastes 3:1), 'To every thing there is a season, and a time to every purpose under heaven.'

Time is a great healer.
initial pain is felt less keenly with the passage of time; English proverb, late 14th century.

Time will tell.

the true nature of something is likely to emerge over a period of time, and conversely it is only after time has passed that something can be regarded as settled; English proverb, mid 16th century.

Time works wonders.

often used to suggest that with the passage of time something initially unknown and unwelcome will become familiar and acceptable; English proverb, late 16th century.

You have the watches, but we have the time.

early 21st-century saying, said to be an Afghan saying addressed to ISAF/NATO forces.

Tolerance

SEE PREJUDICE AND TOLERANCE

Town

SEE THE COUNTRY AND THE TOWN

Towns and Cities

SEE also BRITISH TOWNS AND REGIONS

Individual cities may be seen as a spiritual as well as geographical centre: All roads lead to Rome.

Transience

All roads lead to Rome.
English proverb, late 14th century, earlier in Latin.

From Madrid to heaven, and in heaven a little window from which to look down on Madrid.
Spanish saying.

Isfahan is half the world.
Isfahan was the capital of Persia from 1598 until 1722; Persian proverb.

Next year in Jerusalem!
traditionally the concluding words of the Jewish Passover service, expressing the hope of the Diaspora that Jews dispersed throughout the world would once more be reunited.

See Naples and die.
implying that after seeing Naples, one could have nothing left on earth to wish for; Goethe noted it as an Italian proverb in his diary in 1787.

Transience

See also OPPORTUNITY, TIME

Awareness of transience may be used as a comfort (And this, too, shall pass away) *or as a warning: Sic transit gloria mundi.*

And this, too, shall pass away.

traditional saying said to be true for all times and situations;
the story is told by Edward Fitzgerald in *Polonius* (1852),
'The Sultan asked for a signet motto, that should hold good
for Adversity or Prosperity, Solomon gave him—"This also
shall pass away." '

Sic transit gloria mundi.

Latin, 'Thus passes the glory of the world', said during the
coronation of a new Pope, while flax is burned (used at the
coronation of Alexander V in Pisa, 7 July 1409, but earlier
in origin).

Time flies.

English proverb, late 14th century, from Virgil (70–19 BC)
Georgics, '*Sedfugit interea, fugit inreparabile tempus* [But
meanwhile it is flying, irretrievable time is flying].'

Travel

See also COUNTRIES AND PEOPLES

Travel may provide us with many different experiences
(Every two miles the water changes, every twelve
miles the speech), *but we are also warned:* Go abroad
and you'll hear news of home.

Travel

Been there, done that, got the T-shirt.
evoking a jaded tourist as the image of someone who is
bored by too much sightseeing.

Clunk, click, every trip.
road safety campaign promoting the use of seatbelts, 1971.

**Every two miles the water changes, every twelve
miles the speech.**
commenting on the changes experienced by travellers
(the number of miles varies); Indian proverb.

Go abroad and you'll hear news of home.
information about one's imnmediate vicinity may have
become more widely publicized; English proverb, late
17th century.

Have gun, will travel.
supposedly characteristic statement of a hired gunman in a
western; popularized as the title of an American television
series (1957–64).

**The heaviest baggage for the traveller is an
empty purse.**
travelling is difficult without the money to pay for it;
German proverb.

If it's Tuesday, this must be Belgium.
late 20th-century saying, from the title of a 1969 film
written by David Shaw.

If you don't know where you are going, any road will do.

modern saying, originally with allusion to Lewis Carroll.

Is your journey really necessary?

1939 slogan, coined to discourage Civil Servants from going home for Christmas.

Let the train take the strain.

British Rail slogan, 1970 onwards.

Roads are made by walking.

Spanish proverb.

Thursday's child has far to go.

line from a traditional rhyme (compare qualities associated with birth on other days at entries under BEAUTY, GIFTS, SORROW, and WORK).

Travel broadens the mind.

English proverb, early 20th century.

The traveller discards his sense of shame.

people will behave in a strange country as they will not behave in their own; Japanese proverb.

Travelling is learning.

African proverb.

Treachery

**Travelling is one way of lengthening life, at least
in appearance.**
American proverb, mid 20th century.

**A wise man will climb Mount Fuji once, but only a
fool will climb it twice.**
Japanese proverb.

 Treachery

See TRUST AND TREACHERY

 Trees

*The oak, the ash, and the elm may have particular
attributes, but any tree can link the past with the
future:* Trees planted by the ancestors provide shade
for their descendants.

**The best time to plant a tree was twenty years ago.
The second best is now.**
even if you regret not having already planted a tree, it is still
worth doing so; modern saying.

Beware of an oak, it draws the stroke; avoid an ash, it counts the flash; creep under the thorn, it can save you from harm.

recording traditional beliefs on where to shelter from lightning during a thunderstorm; English proverb, late 19th century.

Every elm has its man.

perhaps referring to the readiness of the tree to drop its branches on the unwary (elm wood was also traditionally used for coffins); English proverb, early 20th century.

In the woods it rains twice.

after a rainstorm, water continues to drip from overhead branches; German proverb.

One generation plants the trees; another sits in their shade.

Chinese proverb.

To plant a tree is to plant hope.

modern saying.

A seed hidden in the heart of an apple is an orchard invisible.

Welsh proverb; compare **All the flowers of tomorrow are in the seeds of today** at GARDENS.

Trust and Treachery

Trees planted by the ancestors provide shade for their descendants.

Chinese proverb; a comparable idea is found in the western classical world, in the writings of Caecilius Statius (d. after 166 BC) *Synephebi*, 'He plants the trees to serve another age.'

When the oak is before the ash, then you will only get a splash; When the ash is before the oak, then you will get a soak.

a traditional way of predicting whether the summer will be wet or dry on the basis of whether the oak or the ash is first to come into leaf in the spring; English proverb, mid 19th century.

 Trust and Treachery

The traditional warning Promises, like piecrust, are made to be broken, *current since the 17th century, emphasizes the shrewdness of the Russian proverb,* Test before you trust.

Confidence is a plant of slow growth.

English proverb.

Fear the Greeks bearing gifts.

English proverb, late 19th century; originally from Virgil (70–19 BC) *Aeneid*, '*Equo ne credite, Teucri, Quidquid id est, timeo Danaos et dona ferentes* [Do not trust the horse,

Trojans. Whatever it is, I fear the Greeks even when they bring gifts.]'

Please to remember the Fifth of November, Gunpowder Treason and Plot. We know no reason why gunpowder treason Should ever be forgot.

traditional rhyme on the Gunpowder Plot (1605).

Promises, like piecrust, are made to be broken.

English proverb, late 17th century.

Test before you trust.

Russian proverb.

Would you buy a used car from this man?

campaign slogan directed against Richard Nixon.

You cannot run with the hare and hunt with the hounds.

you must take one of two opposing sides; English proverb, mid 15th century.

Truth

See also HONESTY, LIES

Telling the truth is an obligation (Tell the truth and shame the devil), *but an admixture of tact may be*

Truth

advisable: When you shoot an arrow of truth, dip its point in honey.

Believe it or not.
title of syndicated newspaper feature (from 1918), written by Robert L. Ripley.

Fact is stranger than fiction.
English proverb, mid 19th century; compare **Truth is stranger than fiction** below.

Many a true word is spoken in jest.
an apparent joke may often include a shrewd comment, or what is spoken of as unlikely or improbable may in the future turn out to be true; English proverb, late 14th century.

An old error is always more popular than a new truth.
German proverb.

Se non è vero, è molto ben trovato.
Italian, 'If it is not true, it is a happy invention'; common saying from the 16th century.

Tell the truth and shame the devil.
by telling the truth one is taking the right course however embarrassing or difficult it may be; English proverb, mid 16th century; compare **Truth makes the Devil blush** below.

Truth is stranger than fiction.

implying that no invention can be as remarkable as what may actually happen; English proverb, early 19th century, from Byron *Don Juan* (1819–24), ''Tis strange—but true; for truth is always strange; Stranger than fiction'; compare **Fact is stranger than fiction** above.

Truth lies at the bottom of a well.

sometimes used to imply that the truth of a situation can be hard to find; English proverb, mid 16th century.

Truth makes the Devil blush.

English proverb, mid 20th century; compare **Tell the truth and shame the devil** above.

Truth will out.

in the end what has really happened will become apparent; English proverb, mid 15th century.

What everybody says must be true.

sometimes used ironically to assert that popular gossip is often inaccurate; English proverb, late 14th century.

When you shoot an arrow of truth, dip its point in honey.

advocating tact; Arab proverb.

Value

A sense of values is worth having: If you pay peanuts, you get monkeys, *and conversely* Gold may be bought too dear.

Everything has a price, but jade is priceless.
modern saying said to derive from a Chinese proverb extolling the value of jade.

Gold may be bought too dear.
wealth may be acquired at too great a price; English proverb, mid 16th century.

I am not rich enough to buy cheap goods.
a warning against practising false economies; modern saying.

If you pay peanuts, you get monkeys.
a poor rate of pay will attract only poorly qualified and incompetent staff (*peanuts* here means 'a small sum of money'); English proverb, mid 20th century.

It is a poor dog that's not worth whistling for.
a dog is of no value if the owner will not even go to the trouble of whistling for it; English proverb, mid 16th century.

Little things please little minds.
English proverb, late 16th century.

Nothing comes from nothing.
English proverb, late 14th century.

Nothing for nothing.
summarizing the attitude that nothing will be offered unless a return is assured; English proverb, early 18th century.

What can a monkey know of the taste of ginger?
ginger as the type of a rare and expensive delicacy; Indian proverb.

The worth of a thing is what it will bring.
the real value of something can only be measured by what another person is willing to pay for it; English proverb, mid 16th century.

Virtue

See also GOOD AND EVIL

Virtue should be pursued for its own sake (Virtue is its own reward), *although it will not necessarily evoke gratitude in others:* No good deed goes unpunished.

The good die young.
English proverb, late 17th century, often used ironically; compare **Whom the gods love die young** at YOUTH.

Good men are scarce.
English proverb, early 17th century.

Virtue

He lives long who lives well.
the reputation derived from living a good and moral life
will mean that one's name will last; English proverb, mid
16th century.

No good deed goes unpunished.
modern humorous saying, sometimes attributed to Oscar
Wilde but not traced in his writings.

See no evil, hear no evil, speak no evil.
conventionally represented by 'the three wise monkeys'
covering their eyes, ears, and mouth respectively with their
hands, and used particularly to imply a deliberate refusal to
notice something that is wrong; English proverb, early
20th century.

Virtue is its own reward.
the satisfaction of knowing that one has observed
appropriate moral standards should be all that is sought;
English proverb, early 16th century.

Warfare

See also THE ARMED FORCES, PEACE

War is seen as likely to cause more than physical injury and death: When war is declared, Truth is the first casualty.

A bayonet is a weapon with a worker at each end.
British pacifist slogan, 1940.

A bigger bang for a bigger buck.
Charles E. Wilson's defence policy, in *Newsweek* 22 March 1954.

Remember the Alamo!
Texan battle-cry at the battle of San Jacinto, 1836, referring to the defence of a Franciscan mission in the Texan War of Independence, in which all of the defenders were killed.

War is God's way of teaching Americans geography.
modern saying, widely attributed to the American writer Ambrose Bierce (1842–c.1914), but not found before the 1950s.

War will cease when men refuse to fight.
pacifist slogan, from c.1936, often in the form 'Wars will cease when...'

Ways and Means

When war is declared, Truth is the first casualty.
epigraph to Arthur Ponsonby's *Falsehood in Wartime*
(1928), perhaps deriving from Samuel Johnson in *The Idler*
11 November 1758, 'Among the calamities of war may be
jointly numbered the diminution of the love of truth, by the
falsehoods which interest dictates and credulity encourages';
attributed also to Hiram Johnson, speaking in the US
Senate, 1918, but not recorded in his speech.

Ways and Means

When choosing the right tool (Honey catches more
flies than vinegar)*, it is as well to be aware of what is
really essential:* It hardly matters if it is a white cat or a
black cat that catches the mice.

Catching's before hanging.
an essential step must be taken before the consequences can
ensue; English proverb, early 19th century.

Eat the mangoes. Do not count the trees.
concentrate on the task in hand; Indian proverb.

The end justifies the means.
English proverb, late 16th century.

Even if the sky falls down, there is a hole to escape.
there is often a way out of disaster; modern saying, said to
be a Korean proverb.

Fight fire with fire.

one should counter like with like; English proverb, mid
19th century.

Fire is a good servant, but a bad master.

acknowledging that fire is both essential for living and
potentially destructive; English proverb, early 17th century.

First catch your hare.

referring to the first essential step that must be taken before
a process can begin; English proverb, early 19th century,
often attributed to the English cook Hannah Glasse (fl. 1747),
but her directions for making hare soup are, 'Take your hare
when it is cased' (*cased* here meaning 'skinned').

Give a man enough rope, and he will hang himself.

often used to mean that someone given enough licence or
freedom will defeat themselves through their own mistakes;
English proverb, mid 17th century.

The hammer shatters glass, but forges steel.

modern saying, said to be of Russian origin.

Honey catches more flies than vinegar.

soft or ingratiating words achieve more than sharpness;
English proverb, mid 17th century.

If you can't beat them, join them.

often used in consolation or resignation; English proverb,
mid 20th century.

Ways and Means

It hardly matters if it is a white cat or a black cat that catches the mice.
Chinese proverb.

It is good to make a bridge of gold to a flying enemy.
it is wiser to give passage to an enemy in flight, who may be desperate, than to bring them to bay; English proverb, late 16th century.

An old poacher makes the best gamekeeper.
someone who has formerly taken part in wrongdoing knows best how to counter it in others; English proverb, late 14th century.

One size does not fit all.
an assertion of individual requirements; earlier versions are based on the metaphor of different size shoes for different feet; English proverb, early 17th century.

The paths are many, but the goal is the same.
Indian proverb, deriving from Sanskrit.

The pen is mightier than the sword.
written words may often have more lasting force than military strength; English proverb, mid 17th century; compare **What is written with a pen cannot be cut out with an axe** at WRITING.

Set a thief to catch a thief.

used to imply that the person best placed to catch someone
out in dishonest practices is one whose own nature tends
that way; English proverb, mid 17th century.

A short cut is often a wrong cut.

a warning against trying to cut corners; Danish proverb.

There are more ways of killing a cat than choking it with cream.

there are more ways of achieving an end than giving an
opponent a glut of what they most want; English proverb,
mid 19th century.

There are more ways of killing a dog than choking it with butter.

there are more ways of achieving an end than giving an
opponent a glut of what they most want; English proverb,
mid 19th century.

There are more ways of killing a dog than hanging it.

there are more ways than one of achieving an end; English
proverb, late 17th century.

There is more than one way to skin a cat.

English proverb, mid 19th century.

Weakness

There is nothing like leather.
referring to the toughness and durability of leather (the saying comes from one of Aesop's fables, in which a leatherworker contributed this opinion to a discussion on how to fortify a city); English proverb, late 17th century.

What matters is what works.
late 20th-century saying.

 # Weakness

See STRENGTH AND WEAKNESS

 # Wealth

See also MONEY, THRIFT

Possession of wealth confers status (Money makes a man), *and may be self-renewing:* Money makes money.

A diamond is forever.
advertising slogan for De Beers Consolidated Mines, 1940s onwards.

Few have too much, and fewer too little.
too much wealth is not necessarily a good thing; Danish proverb.

If you really want to make a million, found a new religion.

previously attributed to L. Ron Hubbard (1911–86) in
B. Corydon and L. Ron Hubbard Jr. *L. Ron Hubbard* (1987),
but attribution subsequently rejected by L. Ron Hubbard Jr.,
who also dissociated himself from this book.

Money makes a man.

possession of wealth confers status; English proverb, early
16th century.

Money makes money.

implying that those who are already wealthy are likely to
become more so; English proverb, late 16th century.

Never ask about the first million.

modern saying, popularly associated with the very rich in
former Soviet bloc countries.

The rich man gets his ice in the summer, and the poor man gets his in the winter.

contrasting luxury with hardship through apparent equality;
English proverb, early 20th century.

The Weather

*Traditional sayings about weather are likely to be
predictive* (North wind doth blow, we shall have snow,
Rain before seven, fine before eleven), *but a more*

The Weather

modern saying focuses on how to respond to such changes: There is no such thing as bad weather, only the wrong clothes.

As the day lengthens, so the cold strengthens.
recording the tradition that the coldest weather arrives when days begin to grow lighter; English proverb, early 17th century.

Clear moon, frost soon.
a clear night sky in winter may be a precursor of frost; traditional rhyme recorded from the 19th century.

Green Christmas, white Easter.
mild weather at Christmas may mean snow at Easter; German proverb.

Long foretold, long last; short notice, soon past.
if there is a long gap between the signs that the weather will change and the change itself, then the predicted weather will last a long time. If the intervening period is a short one, then the predicted weather will be of correspondingly short duration; English proverb, mid 19th century.

Nine months of winter and three months of hell.
on the long cold winters and hot summers supposedly typical of the Castilian climate; Spanish saying.

North wind doth blow, we shall have snow.
traditional weather rhyme, deriving from a nursery rhyme
of the early 19th century.

Rain before seven, fine before eleven.
English proverb, mid 19th century.

Rain, rain, go away, come again another day.
traditional rhyme, mid 17th century.

**Red sky at night, shepherd's delight, Red sky in the
morning, shepherd's warning.**
good and bad weather respectively is presaged by a red sky
at sunset and dawn; English proverb, late 14th century.

**Robin Hood could brave all weathers but a
thaw wind.**
a *thaw wind* is a cold wind which accompanies the breaking
up of frost; English proverb, mid 19th century.

**So much sun as shines on Shrove Tuesday, so it
shines all Lent.**
traditional prediction.

**There is no such thing as bad weather, only the
wrong clothes.**
late 20th-century saying.

Weddings

A warm January, a cold May.
mild weather in January means there will be cold weather in May; Welsh proverb.

When the stars begin to huddle, the earth will soon become a puddle.
when cloud cover begins to thicken (threatening rain), groups of stars still visible appear to huddle together; traditional rhyme recorded from the 19th century.

When the wind is in the east, 'tis good for neither man nor beast.
referring to the traditional bitterness of the east wind; English proverb, early 17th century.

Winter thunder, summer hunger.
thunderstorms in winter are taken as presage of a poor harvest; English proverb.

 # Weddings

See also MARRIAGE

The day chosen for one's wedding may turn out to be important: Marry in May, rue for aye, *but* Happy is the bride the sun shines on.

Always a bridesmaid, never a bride.

recording the belief that to be a bridesmaid too often is unlucky for one's own chances of marriage; English proverb, late 19th century.

Happy is the bride the sun shines on.

English proverb, mid 17th century.

Marry in May, rue for aye.

English proverb, late 17th century.

Now you will feel no rain, for each of you will be shelter for the other. Now you will feel no cold, for each of you will be warmth for the other.

from the saying known as the 'Apache Blessing'.

One wedding brings another.

English proverb, mid 17th century.

Winning and Losing

See also SUCCESS AND FAILURE

There is a consensus that winning and losing are both a part of the pattern of life: What you lose on the swings, you gain on the roundabouts.

Heads I win, tails you lose.

I win in any event; *heads* and *tails* the obverse and reverse images on a coin; English proverb, late 17th century.

Winter

What you lose on the swings, you gain on the roundabouts.
One's losses and gains tend to cancel one another out; English proverb, early 20th century.

A winner never quits, and a quitter never wins.
American proverb, early 20th century.

You can't win them all.
used as an expression of consolation or resignation; English proverb, mid 20th century.

 # Winter

See also AUTUMN, SPRING, SUMMER, THE WEATHER

Sayings about winter reflect both weather lore (February fill dyke, be it black or white), *and traditional activities for the season:* On Saint Thomas the Divine, kill all turkeys, geese and swine.

Candlemas day, put beans in the clay, put candles and candlesticks away.
recording the tradition that the feast of Candlemas, on 2 February, was the time for planting beans; English proverb, late 17th century.

February fill dyke, be it black or white.
February is a month likely to bring rain (black) or snow
(white); English proverb, mid 16th century.

The fire is winter's fruit.
Arabic proverb.

**If Candlemas day be sunny and bright, winter will
have another flight; if Candlemas day be cloudy
with rain, winter is gone and won't come again.**
English proverb, late 17th century.

**If in February there be no rain, 'tis neither good for
hay nor grain.**
a drought in February will be damaging to crops later in the
year; English proverb, early 18th century.

**If Saint Paul's day be fair and clear, it will betide a
happy year.**
the feast of the conversion of St Paul is 25 January; English
proverb, late 16th century.

**On Saint Thomas the Divine kill all turkeys, geese
and swine.**
21 December, the traditional feast-day in the Western
Church of St Thomas the Apostle, taken as marking the
season at which domestic animals not kept through the
winter were to be slaughtered; English proverb, mid
18th century.

Wisdom

The winter does not go without looking backward.
there is likely to be bad weather towards the end of winter; Finnish proverb.

Winter either bites with its teeth or lashes with its tail.
bad weather is expected at either the beginning or the end of winter; Montenegrin proverb.

Winter is summer's heir.
the warmth of summer naturally gives way to the cold of winter; English proverb.

Winter never rots in the sky.
the arrival of winter is not delayed; English proverb, early 17th century.

Wisdom

Wisdom may be found in unexpected places.

Fools ask questions that wise men cannot answer.
a foolish person may put a question to which there is no simple or easily given answer; English proverb, mid 17th century.

A little nonsense now and then, is relished by the wisest men.
American proverb, early 20th century.

Out of the mouths of babes —.

young children may sometimes speak with disconcerting wisdom; English proverb, late 19th century, with allusion to the Bible (Psalms), 'Out of the mouth of very babes and sucklings hast thou ordained strength, because of thine enemies.'

Women

See also MEN AND WOMEN

Traditional views on what is appropriate for women (A whistling woman and a crowing hen, is good for neither God nor men) *contrast with more radical assessments of a woman's place in the world:* Women hold up half the sky.

Burn your bra.

feminist slogan, 1970s.

Far-fetched and dear-bought is good for ladies.

expensive or exotic articles are suitable for women; English proverb, mid 14th century.

The female of the species is more deadly than the male.

English proverb, early 20th century, from the title of a poem (1919) by Rudyard Kipling.

Women

The hand that rocks the cradle rules the world.

referring to the strength of a woman's indirect influence on the male world; English proverb, mid 19th century.

Hell hath no fury like a woman scorned.

a woman whose love has turned to hate is the most savage of creatures; a fury here may be either one of the avenging deities of classical mythology, or more generally someone in a state of frenzied rage; English proverb, late 17th century.

Long and lazy, little and loud; fat and fulsome, pretty and proud.

categorizing supposed physical and temperamental characteristics in women; English proverb, late 16th century.

Silence is a woman's best garment.

often used as recommending a traditionally submissive and discreet role for women; English proverb, mid 16th century.

Votes for women.

slogan of the women's suffrage movement, adopted when it proved impossible to use a banner with the longer slogan 'Will the Liberal Party Give Votes for Women?' made by Emmeline Pankhurst, Christabel Pankhurst, and Annie Kenney.

A whistling woman and a crowing hen are neither fit for God nor men.

both the woman and the hen are considered unnatural, and therefore unlucky; English proverb, early 18th century.

A woman, a dog, and a walnut tree, the more you beat them the better they be.

the walnut tree was beaten firstly to bring down the fruit, and then to break down long shoots and encourage short fruit-bearing ones; English proverb, late 16th century.

A woman and a ship ever want mending.

both women and ships require constant attention and expenditure; English proverb, late 16th century.

A woman's place is in the home.

reflecting the traditional view of a woman's role; English proverb, mid 19th century.

Women hold up half the sky.

women should be considered equal in status to men; Chinese proverb.

Words

See also NAMES, SAYINGS, SPEECH, WORDS AND DEEDS, WRITING

There are contrasting views on the power of a word: we are told that The swiftest horse cannot overtake the

Words

word once spoken, *but on the other hand,* Hard words
break no bones.

All words are pegs to hang ideas on.
American proverb, late 19th century.

Elephants are contagious.
Surrealist 'proverb'.

Hard words break no bones.
the damage done by verbal attack is limited; English
proverb, late 17th century.

I before e, except after c.
traditional spelling rule, 19th century.

If you take hyphens seriously you will go mad.
said to be from a style book in use with Oxford University
Press, New York; perhaps apocryphal.

The quick brown fox jumps over the lazy dog.
traditional sentence used by keyboarders to ensure that all
letters of the alphabet are functioning.

**Sticks and stones may break my bones, but words
will never hurt me.**
verbal attack does no real injury; English proverb, late
19th century.

The swiftest horse cannot overtake the word once spoken.

Chinese proverb; compare Horace (65–8) *Epistles*, 'And once sent out, a word takes wing beyond recall.'

Words and Deeds

See also ACTION AND INACTION, WORDS

There is a consensus in favour of action (Example is better than precept), but we are warned that it is also wise to keep a guard on the tongue: Don't add insult to injury.

Actions speak louder than words.

real feeling is expressed not by what someone says but by what they do; English proverb, early 17th century.

Brag is a good dog, but Holdfast is better.

perseverance is a better quality than ostentation; English proverb, early 18th century.

Don't add insult to injury.

recommendation not to treat a person one has hurt with contempt as well; American proverb, mid 18th century.

Example is better than precept.

English proverb, early 15th century.

Words and Deeds

Fine words butter no parsnips.
nothing is ever achieved by fine words alone (*butter* was
the traditional garnish for parsnips); English proverb,
mid 17th century.

**It is not the same thing to talk of bulls as to be in
the bullring.**
Spanish saying.

One picture is worth ten thousand words.
English proverb, early 20th century.

An ounce of practice is worth a pound of precept.
a small amount of practical assistance is worth more than a
great deal of advice; English proverb, late 16th century.

Philosophy bakes no bread.
traditional criticism of philosophy as lacking practical
application, recorded from the 19th century.

Practise what you preach.
you should follow the advice you give to others; English
proverb, late 14th century.

Stabs heal, but bad words never.
words can inflict more lasting wounds than any physical
hurt; Spanish proverb.

Talk is cheap.

it is easier to say than to do something; English proverb, mid 19th century.

Talk will not cook rice.

modern saying, said to be a Chinese proverb.

Threatened men live long.

threats are often not put into effect, and those who express resentment are actually much less dangerous than those who conceal animosity; English proverb, mid 16th century.

The tongue is like a sharp knife, it can kill without drawing blood.

Chinese saying.

Vision without action is a daydream, Action without vision is a nightmare.

recommending a balance between idealism and reality; modern saying, said to derive from a Japanese proverb.

Words are sweet, but they never take the place of food.

African proverb.

Work

See also EMPLOYMENT, IDLENESS, LEISURE

Industry is traditionally commended (Practice makes perfect), *but it should be properly rewarded:* The labourer is worthy of his hire.

Arbeit macht frei.

German, 'Work liberates', words inscribed on the gates of Dachau concentration camp, 1933, and subsequently on those of Auschwitz.

The better the day, the better the deed.

frequently used to justify working on a Sunday or Holy Day; English proverb, early 17th century.

Every man to his trade.

one should operate within one's own area of expertise; English proverb, late 16th century.

Fools and bairns should never see half-done work.

the unwise and the inexperienced may judge the quality of a finished article from its rough unfinished state; English proverb, early 18th century.

From beavers, bees should learn to mend their ways. A bee works; a beaver works and plays.

American proverb, mid 20th century.

Work

The labourer is worthy of his hire.

someone should be properly recompensed for effort;
English proverb, late 14th century, from the Bible
(Luke 10:7).

Like master, like man.

English proverb, mid 16th century; *man* here
means 'servant'.

One volunteer is worth two pressed men.

a *pressed man* was someone forcibly enlisted by the press
gang, a body of men which in the 18th and 19th centuries
was employed to enlist men forcibly into service in the army
or navy; English proverb, early 18th century.

Practice makes perfect.

often used as an encouragement; English proverb, mid
16th century.

Root, hog, or die.

advocating hard work and independence; *root* (of an
animal), turn up the ground with its snout in search of food;
American proverb, early 19th century.

Saturday's child works hard for a living.

first line of a traditional rhyme, mid 19th century (compare
qualities associated with birth on other days at entries under
BEAUTY, GIFTS, SORROW, and TRAVEL).

Work

A short horse is soon curried.

a slight task is soon completed (literally, that it does not take long to rub down a short horse with a curry-comb); English proverb, mid 14th century.

Too many cooks spoil the broth.

the involvement of too many people is likely to mean that something is done badly; English proverb, late 16th century.

Trifles make perfection, but perfection is no trifle.

American proverb, mid 20th century, from a comment attributed to the painter Michelangelo (1475–1564).

Two boys are half a boy, and three boys are no boy at all.

the more boys there are present, the less work will be done; English proverb, mid 20th century.

Where bees are, there is honey.

industrious work is necessary to create riches; English proverb, early 17th century.

Work expands so as to fill the time available.

English proverb, mid 20th century, from C. Northcote Parkinson *Parkinson's Law* (1958), 'Work expands so as to fill the time available for its completion.'

Worry

Worry is not only exhausting (Care killed the cat,
It is not work that kills, but worry), *but ultimately
pointless:* Worry is like a rocking chair: both give you
something to do, but neither get you anywhere.

Care killed the cat.
the meaning of *care* has shifted somewhat from 'worry,
grief' to 'care, caution'; English proverb, late 16th century.

Do not meet troubles half way.
warning against anxiety about something that has not yet
happened; English proverb, late 19th century.

It is not work that kills, but worry.
direct effort is less stressful than constant concern; English
proverb, late 19th century.

Sufficient unto the day is the evil thereof.
dealing with unpleasant matters should be left until it
becomes necessary; English proverb, mid 18th century, with
allusion to the Bible (Matthew 6:34).

Worry is interest paid on trouble before it falls due.
American proverb, early 20th century.

Worry is like a rocking chair: both give you something to do, but neither gets you anywhere.
American proverb, mid 20th century.

Writing

Worry often gives a small thing a big shadow.
Swedish proverb.

 # Writing

See also BOOKS, WORDS

Not only is writing powerful (What is written with a pen cannot be cut out with an axe), *it is likely to reveal the essential nature of the writer:* Writing is a picture of the writer's heart.

The art of writing is the art of applying the seat of the pants to the seat of the chair.
American proverb, mid 20th century.

For most of history, Anonymous was a woman.
modern saying, mid 20th century, often associated with the English writer Virginia Woolf (1882–1941).

He who would write and can't write can surely review.
American proverb, mid 19th century.

Paper bleeds little.
Spanish proverb.

Paper is patient.
paper allows the writer to put down what they choose; German proverb.

What is written with a pen cannot be cut out with an axe.

words are more powerful than violence; Russian proverb; compare **The pen is mightier than the sword** at
WAYS AND MEANS.

Writing is a picture of the writer's heart.

Chinese proverb.

Youth

See also AGE, CHILDREN

To be young is often to overestimate one's powers
(Young folks think old folks to be fools, but old folks
know young folks to be fools), *but even the
irresponsible young may grow up to more serious ways:*
Wanton kittens make sober cats.

All dancing girls are nineteen years old.

Japanese proverb.

Never send a boy to do a man's job.

someone who is young and inexperienced should not be
given too much responsibility; English proverb, mid
20th century.

**The old net is cast aside while the new net
goes fishing.**

the future belongs to the young; Maori proverb.

Soon ripe, soon rotten.

a warning against precocity, meaning that notably early
achievement is unlikely to be long-lasting; English proverb,
late 14th century (earlier in Latin).

Wanton kittens make sober cats.

someone who in youth is light-minded and lascivious
may be soberly behaved in later life; English proverb,
early 18th century.

Whom the gods love die young.

the happiest fate is to die before health and strength are lost;
English proverb, mid 16th century; the idea is found in the
classical world in Menander (342–c.292 BC) *Dis Exapaton*,
'Whom the gods love dies young'; compare also **The good
die young** at VIRTUE.

**Young folks think old folks to be fools, but old folks
know young folks to be fools.**

asserting the value of the experience of life which comes
with age over youth and inexperience; English proverb, late
16th century.

Youth must be served.

Some indulgence should be given to the wishes and
enthusiasms of youth; English proverb, early 19th century.

Keyword Index 🏵

Each context line represents the opening words of a proverb (initial 'a' and 'the' being omitted). The proverb will be found in alphabetical sequence in the given section.

Aberdeen Take away Aberdeen and twelve BRITISH TOWNS AND REGIONS

abhors Nature abhors a vacuum NATURE

abide He that cannot abide a bad market BUSINESS

able Behind an able man ACHIEVEMENT

abomination abomination unto the Lord, but LIES

abroad Go abroad and you'll hear news of home TRAVEL

absence Absence is the mother of disillusion ABSENCE
Absence makes the heart grow fonder ABSENCE
Absence of evidence ABSENCE
little absence does much ABSENCE

absent absent get farther away ABSENCE
He who is absent ABSENCE

accidents Accidents will happen CHANCE AND LUCK

accounting There is no accounting for tastes LIKES AND DISLIKES

accuser guilty conscience needs no accuser CONSCIENCE

accuses He who excuses himself, accuses APOLOGY AND EXCUSES

achieving Still achieving, still pursuing ACHIEVEMENT

acorns Acorns were good till bread was found SATISFACTION AND DISCONTENT
Great oaks from little acorns CAUSES AND CONSEQUENCES

acres Three acres and a cow POLITICS

act Sow an act, and reap CUSTOM AND HABIT
Think globally, act locally ENVIRONMENT

action Action is worry's worst enemy ACTION AND INACTION
Action this day ACTION AND INACTION
Action without thought ACTION AND INACTION
Common danger causes common action DANGER
Vision without action is a daydream WORDS AND DEEDS

actions Actions speak louder than words WORDS AND DEEDS

Adam When Adam delved and Eve span RANK

addled As good be an addled egg IDLENESS

advance Advance Australia COUNTRIES AND PEOPLES

advantage If I listen, I have the advantage SPEECH

adventures Adventures are to the adventurous DANGER

Keyword Index

adventurous Adventures are to the adventurous DANGER

adversity Adversity introduces a man ADVERSITY
Adversity is the foundation of virtue ADVERSITY
Adversity makes strange ADVERSITY
dose of adversity is often ADVERSITY

advertise Don't advertise what you can't ADVERTISING
It pays to advertise ADVERTISING

advice Ask advice, but use ADVICE
Never give advice ADVICE

Africa Always something new out of Africa INVENTIONS AND DISCOVERIES

after After dinner rest a while EATING
After meat, mustard EATING
And they all lived happily ever after ENDING

afternoon afternoon knows what the morning never suspected FORESIGHT

again Not guilty, but don't do it again GUILT

Agamemnon Brave men lived before Agamemnon FAME

age Age is just a number AGE
age of miracles is past SURPRISE
For the unlearned, old age is winter AGE
gets better with age AGE

agree Birds in their little nests agree ARGUMENT
Two of a trade never agree SIMILARITY AND DIFFERENCE

ahead He who can see three days ahead FORESIGHT
If you want to get ahead DRESS
past is always ahead of us PAST

ailment imaginary ailment is worse than a disease SICKNESS

Alamo Remember the Alamo WARFARE

alcohol Alcohol will preserve anything DRINK

alibis Corruption will find a dozen alibis CORRUPTION

alike Great minds think alike THINKING

all All cats are grey in the dark SIMILARITY AND DIFFERENCE
All is fish that comes to the net OPPORTUNITY
All roads lead to Rome TOWNS AND CITIES
All's for the best OPTIMISM AND PESSIMISM
All that glitters is not gold QUANTITIES AND QUALITIES
All things are possible with God GOD
All things come to those who wait PATIENCE
Hear all, see all, say nowt SELF-INTEREST
He teaches ill who teaches all TEACHING
Light for all NEWS AND JOURNALISM
Moderation in all things MODERATION
One size does not fit all WAYS AND MEANS
There is measure in all things MODERATION

Allah Trust in Allah, but tie up your camel CAUTION

388

alone Better alone than in bad
company SOLITUDE
He travels the fastest who
travels alone SOLITUDE
He who travels fast, travels
alone COOPERATION
live by bread alone LIFE
You're never alone with a
Strand SMOKING

always always a priest CLERGY
Always in a hurry, always
behind HASTE AND DELAY
Once a —, always
a — CHARACTER

am I am because we
are RELATIONSHIPS

America America is a
tune COUNTRIES AND PEOPLES

Americans Good Americans
when they die COUNTRIES AND
PEOPLES
War is God's way of teaching
Americans geography
WARFARE

amour L'amour est
aveugle RELATIONSHIPS

ancestors Trees planted by the
ancestors TREES

angels How many angels can
dance on HYPOTHESIS
AND FACT

anger Anger improves
nothing ANGER

angry He that will be
angry ANGER
hungry man is an angry
man FOOD
When angry count a
hundred ANGER

animal Cet animal est très
méchant CHARACTER
politician is an animal
who can sit POLITICS

animals It takes forty dumb
animals DRESS

anonymous For most of history,
Anonymous was a
woman WRITING

another Another day, another
dollar OPTIMISM AND PESSIMISM
One wedding brings
another WEDDINGS
Tomorrow is another
day FUTURE

answer answer is a
lemon SATISFACTION AND
DISCONTENT
answer lies in the soil GARDENS
civil question deserves a civil
answer MANNERS
soft answer turneth away
wrath ANGER

anvil church is an
anvil CHRISTIAN CHURCH

ape ape's an ape, a varlet's a
varlet CHARACTER

apology Apology is only
egoism APOLOGY AND EXCUSES

appearance Merit in
appearance APPEARANCE

appearances Appearances are
deceptive APPEARANCE

appetite Appetite comes with
eating EXPERIENCE

apple apple a day keeps the
doctor away HEALTH
apple never falls far from the
tree FAMILY
apple pie without some
cheese FOOD
rotten apple injures its
neighbour CORRUPTION
seed hidden in the heart of an
apple TREES

apples Small choice in rotten
apples CHOICE

Keyword Index

You can count the apples on one tree QUANTITIES AND QUALITIES

apricots You can have apricots tomorrow FUTURE

April April and May are keys to the whole year SPRING
April showers bring forth May flowers SPRING
cold April the barn will fill SPRING
cuckoo comes in April BIRDS
March borrowed from April three days SPRING

Arbeit Arbeit macht frei WORK

Arcadia Et in Arcadia ego DEATH

arch arch never sleeps ARCHITECTURE

architect Every man is the architect of his own SELF-INTEREST

ardua Per ardua ad astra ACHIEVEMENT

are Are you now or have you ever been POLITICS
I am because we are RELATIONSHIPS

argue Do not argue against the sun ARGUMENT

argument only thing a heated argument ever ARGUMENT

arguments more arguments you win, the less ARGUMENT

arm Stretch your arm no further than THRIFT

arms Kings have long arms POWER

army army knows how to gain a victory ARMED FORCES
army of stags led by a lion ARMED FORCES
singing army and a ARMED FORCES

around What goes around comes around JUSTICE

arrow single arrow is easily broken COOPERATION
When you shoot an arrow of truth TRUTH

art Art is long and life is short LIFE
art of being a parent CHILDREN
art of writing is the art of applying WRITING

arts All arts are brothers COOPERATION

ash When the oak is before the ash TREES

ashes Yesterday is ashes; tomorrow is wood PRESENT

ask Ask advice, but use ADVICE
Ask a silly question and you get FOOLS
Don't ask, don't tell SECRECY
Never ask about the first million WEALTH
To question and ask is a moment's shame THINKING

asked Never give advice unless asked ADVICE

asleep shrimp that falls asleep ACTION AND INACTION

assistant Assistant heads must roll BROADCASTING

attack Attack is the best form of defence COURAGE

aunt Vodka is an aunt of wine DRINK

Australia Advance Australia COUNTRIES AND PEOPLES

Australians Australians wouldn't give COUNTRIES AND PEOPLES

autumn Chickens are counted in the autumn AUTUMN

autumns All autumns do not fill granaries AUTUMN

away Rain, rain, go
away WEATHER

awl You can't hide an awl in a
sack SECRECY

axe When the axe came into the
forest OPTIMISM AND PESSIMISM

B Who says A must
say B NECESSITY

babes Out of the mouths of
babes — WISDOM

baby Burn, baby, burn DEFIANCE

back God makes the back to the
burden SYMPATHY

Spring forward, fall back TIME

What is got under the Devil's
back GOOD AND EVIL

bad bad custom is like a good
cake CUSTOM AND HABIT

bad excuse is better
than APOLOGY AND EXCUSES

Bad money drives out
good MONEY

Bad news travels fast NEWS
AND JOURNALISM

bad penny always turns
up CHARACTER

Bad things come in
threes MISFORTUNES

bad workman blames his
tools APOLOGY AND EXCUSES

Better alone than in bad
company SOLITUDE

Give a dog a bad name and
hang GOSSIP

good seaman is known in bad
weather SEA

Hard cases make bad law LAW

He that cannot abide a bad
market BUSINESS

Nothing so bad but it might
have been SYMPATHY

Stabs heal, but bad words
never WORDS AND DEEDS

Striking manners are bad
manners MANNERS

There is no such thing as bad
weather WEATHER

baggage heaviest baggage for the
traveller TRAVEL

bairns Fools and bairns should
never see WORK

bait big fish is caught with a big
bait PRACTICALITY

Fish follow the
bait TEMPTATION

bake As you bake, so shall you
brew CAUSES AND
CONSEQUENCES

ban Ban the bomb PEACE

bandits more laws, the more
thieves and bandits LAW

bang Bang goes sixpence THRIFT

bigger bang for a bigger
buck WARFARE

banker father is a banker
provided by nature PARENTS

bargain Don't bargain for fish
that are still OPTIMISM AND
PESSIMISM

It takes two to make a
bargain COOPERATION

bark Dogs bark, but the caravan
goes FUTILITY

Do not judge a tree by its
bark APPEARANCE

Why keep a dog and bark
yourself MANAGEMENT

barking barking dog never
bites ACTION AND INACTION

barn cold April the barn will
fill SPRING

Barnaby Barnaby bright, Barnaby
bright SUMMER

barrel One spoonful of tar spoils
a barrel QUANTITIES AND
QUALITIES

Keyword Index

basket Don't put all your eggs in one basket CAUTION
Each of us at a handle of the basket COOPERATION
with your food basket COOPERATION

battle Be kind. Everyone you meet is fighting a hard battle GENEROSITY
race is not to the swift, nor the battle SUCCESS AND FAILURE

battles Pick your battles PREPARATION AND READINESS

bayonet bayonet is a weapon with a worker WARFARE

be Be what you would seem BEHAVIOUR
What must be, must be FATE

beans Candlemas day, put beans in the clay WINTER

bear Bear and forbear PATIENCE
When you ask a bear to dance DANGER

beards It is merry in hall when beards wag all HOSPITALITY

bears bulls make money, the bears make BUYING AND SELLING

beat If you can't beat them, join them WAYS AND MEANS

beats It beats as it sweeps as it cleans HOUSEWORK

beautiful Black is beautiful BEAUTY
It is the beautiful bird BEAUTY
Small is beautiful QUANTITIES AND QUALITIES

beauty Beauty draws with a single hair BEAUTY
Beauty is a good letter BEAUTY
Beauty is in the eye of the beholder BEAUTY
Beauty is only skin deep BEAUTY
Beauty is power BEAUTY
Beauty without cruelty SUFFERING

beavers From beavers, bees should learn WORK

bed As you make your bed CAUSES AND CONSEQUENCES
Early to bed and early to rise HEALTH

bedfellows Adversity makes strange bedfellows ADVERSITY
Politics makes strange bedfellows POLITICS

bee bee sucks honey where the spider CHARACTER

beef Where's the beef QUANTITIES AND QUALITIES

been Been there, done that, got the T-shirt TRAVEL

beer He that drinks beer, thinks beer DRUNKENNESS
I'm only here for the beer DRINK
Life isn't all beer and skittles LIFE
Turkeys, heresy, hops, and beer INVENTIONS AND DISCOVERIES

bees From beavers, bees should learn WORK
Where bees are, there is honey WORK

before Dig the well before you are thirsty PREPARATION AND READINESS
Have an umbrella ready before it rains PREPARATION AND READINESS
I before e, except after c WORDS

beforehand Pay beforehand was never well BUSINESS

Keyword Index

begets Love begets love   LOVE

beggar Set a beggar on
horseback   POWER
Sue a beggar and catch a
louse   FUTILITY

beggars Beggars can't be
choosers   NECESSITY
If wishes were horses,
beggars   OPTIMISM AND
PESSIMISM

beginning Beginning is
easy   BEGINNING
beginning of health is
sleep   SLEEP
beginning of wisdom is
to call things   NAMES
good beginning makes a
good   BEGINNING
In my end is my
beginning   ENDING

begins longest journey begins
with a single   BEGINNING

begun sooner begun, the sooner
done   BEGINNING
Well begun is half
done   BEGINNING

behaviour Good behaviour is the
last   BEHAVIOUR

behind Always in a hurry, always
behind   HASTE AND DELAY
Behind an able
man   ACHIEVEMENT

beholder Beauty is in the eye of
the beholder   BEAUTY

Belgium If it's Tuesday, this must
be Belgium   TRAVEL

believe Believe it or not   TRUTH
Believe nothing of what you
hear   BELIEF
eyes believe themselves
CERTAINTY AND DOUBT

believer believer is a songless
bird   BELIEF

believing Believing has a core of
unbelieving   BELIEF
Seeing is believing   BELIEF

bellowing bellowing cow soon
forgets her calf   MOURNING

belong I belong by blood
relationship   FAMILY

ben Se non e vero, e molto ben
trovato   TRUTH

bent As the twig is
bent   EDUCATION

Bermudas If the Bermudas let
you pass   SEA

best All's for the best   OPTIMISM
AND PESSIMISM
best doctors are Dr Quiet,
Dr Diet   MEDICINE
best fish swim near the
bottom   DETERMINATION
best of friends must
part   MEETING AND PARTING
best of men are but men at
best   HUMAN RACE
best place for
criticism   CRITICISM
best things in life are
free   MONEY
best time to plant a tree
was   TREES
corruption of the
best   EXCELLENCE
East, west, home's best   HOME
Experience is the best
teacher   EXPERIENCE
Good to forgive, best to
forget   FORGIVENESS
Honesty is the best
policy   HONESTY
Hope for the best and prepare
for   PREPARATION AND READINESS
Laughter is the best
medicine   MEDICINE
Life is the best gift   LIFE

Keyword Index

Of soup and love, the first is
best FOOD

See all your best work go
unnoticed SECRECY

Why should the devil have all
the best MUSIC

better Be sure you can better
your condition CHANGE

Better a dinner of
herbs FEELINGS

Better an egg today than a hen
tomorrow PRESENT

Better an end with
terror ENDING

Better be an old man's
darling MARRIAGE

Better be envied than
pitied ENVY

Better be idle than ill
doing IDLENESS

Better be safe than
sorry CAUTION

Better be the head of a
dog POWER

Better late than
never PUNCTUALITY

Better one house spoiled than
two MARRIAGE

better the day, the better the
deed WORK

Better the devil you
know FAMILIARITY

Better to go to bed
supperless DEBT AND
BORROWING

Better to light one
candle ACTION AND INACTION

Better to wear out than to
rust IDLENESS

Better wed over the
mixen FAMILIARITY

Democracy is better than
tyranny POLITICS

Example is better than
precept WORDS AND DEEDS

Half a loaf is better than no
bread SATISFACTION AND
DISCONTENT

half is better than the
whole MODERATION

It is better to give than to
receive GENEROSITY

It is better to travel
hopefully HOPE

less you know, the better you
sleep IGNORANCE

past always looks better PAST

Prevention is better than
cure FORESIGHT

Something is better than
nothing SATISFACTION AND
DISCONTENT

'Tis better to have loved and
lost LOVE

To change, and change for the
better CHANGE

Two heads are better than
one THINKING

between Between two stools one
falls INDECISION

hedge between keeps friendship
green NEIGHBOURS

wall between both best
preserves NEIGHBOURS

beware Beware of an oak, it
draws the stroke TREES

Beware of the man of one
book BOOKS

beyond Beyond mountains there
are more DETERMINATION

big Big fish eat little
fish POWER

big fish is caught with a big
bait PRACTICALITY

No fist is big enough to hide the
sky GOVERNMENT

bigger bigger bang for a bigger buck WARFARE
bigger the hat SELF-ESTEEM AND SELF-ASSERTION
bigger they are, the harder they fall SUCCESS AND FAILURE
Fear makes the wolf bigger FEAR

bill swan brings snow on its bill BIRDS

bind Safe bind, safe find CAUTION

bird believer is a songless bird BELIEF
bird in the hand is worth two CAUTION
bird never flew on one wing GENEROSITY
early bird catches the worm PREPARATION AND READINESS
However high a bird may soar ENVIRONMENT
It is the beautiful bird that BEAUTY
It's an ill bird that fouls its own nest LOYALTY

birds Birds in their little nests ARGUMENT
Birds of a feather flock together SIMILARITY AND DIFFERENCE
Birds of prey do not sing BIRDS
Fine feathers make fine birds DRESS
Inside the forest there are many birds ABILITY
Little birds that can sing COOPERATION
There are no birds in last year's nest CHANGE
You cannot catch old

birds EXPERIENCE
You cannot prevent the birds of sorrow SORROW

bishops bishops are made men CLERGY

bitch Life's a bitch, and then you die LIFE

bite bleating sheep loses a bite OPPORTUNITY
Dead men don't bite ENEMIES

bites barking dog never bites ACTION AND INACTION

bitten Once bitten by a snake CAUTION
Once bitten, twice shy EXPERIENCE

bitter Good medicine always has a bitter taste MEDICINE
Sour, sweet, bitter, pungent FATE

black Black is beautiful BEAUTY
devil is not so black as he is painted REPUTATION
February fill dyke, be it black or white WINTER
You have to be in the black to be in the green ENVIRONMENT

blacks Two blacks don't make a white GOOD AND EVIL

blame Common fame is seldom to blame FAME

blames One who cannot dance blames DANCE

bleating bleating of the lamb excites the tiger TEMPTATION
bleating sheep loses a bite OPPORTUNITY

bleeds Paper bleeds little WRITING

blessed Blessed are the dead that the rain DEATH
Blessed is he who expects nothing HOPE

Keyword Index

blessing Poverty is a blessing
hated by all   POVERTY

blessings Blessings brighten as
they take   HAPPINESS

blind Blind chance
sweeps   CHANCE AND LUCK
blind man's wife needs no
paint   APPEARANCE
deaf husband and a blind
wife   MARRIAGE
Love is blind   LOVE
Nothing so bold as a blind
mare   IGNORANCE
There's none so blind as
those   PREJUDICE AND
TOLERANCE
When the blind lead the
blind   IGNORANCE

blood Blood is thicker than
water   FAMILY
blood of the martyrs is the
seed   CHRISTIAN CHURCH
Blood will have blood   MURDER
Blood will tell   FAMILY
I belong by blood
relationship   FAMILY
You cannot get blood from a
stone   FUTILITY

bloody bloody war and a sickly
season   ARMED FORCES

bloom When the furze is in
bloom   LOVE
When the gorse is out of
bloom   LOVE

blow Blow your own horn, even
if   ADVERTISING
North wind doth
blow   WEATHER

blows It's an ill wind that blows
nobody   OPTIMISM AND
PESSIMISM
Straws tell which way the wind
blows   KNOWLEDGE

blue Blue and green should
never be   DRESS
Blue are the hills that are
far   FAMILIARITY
Light the blue touch
paper   DANGER

blush Truth makes the Devil
blush   TRUTH

boat widow is a rudderless
boat   MARRIAGE

boats rising tide lifts all
boats   SUCCESS AND FAILURE

body Christ has no body now on
earth   CHRISTIAN CHURCH
larger the body, the bigger the
heart   BODY

boils pot boils, friendship
lives   HOSPITALITY
watched pot never
boils   PATIENCE

bold Nothing so bold as a blind
mare   IGNORANCE

bomb Ban the bomb   PEACE

bond Englishman's word is his
bond   COUNTRIES AND PEOPLES

bone Charity is not
a bone   CHARITY
dog that will fetch a bone   GOSSIP
nearer the bone, the sweeter the
meat   QUANTITIES AND QUALITIES
What's bred in the
bone   CHARACTER
While two dogs are fighting for
a bone   ARGUMENT

bones Hard words break no
bones   WORDS
Sticks and stones may break my
bones   WORDS

bonum De mortuis nil nisi
bonum   REPUTATION

book Beware of the man of one
book   BOOKS
book is like a garden   BOOKS

Keyword Index

great book is a great
evil   BOOKS
You can't tell a book by its
cover   APPEARANCE
boots You can put your boots in
the oven   FUTILITY
born child that is born on the
Sabbath   CHILDREN
Every Turk is born a
soldier   COUNTRIES AND PEOPLES
If you're born to be
hanged   FATE
It is better to be born
lucky   CHANCE AND LUCK
man who is born in a
stable   CHARACTER
Nobody is born learned   CLERGY
Yorkshire born and Yorkshire
bred   BRITISH TOWNS AND
REGIONS
borrowed borrowed cloak does
not keep you warm   DEBT AND
BORROWING
March borrowed from April
three days   SPRING
borrower Neither a borrower, nor
a lender be   DEBT AND
BORROWING
borrowing He that goes
a-borrowing   DEBT AND
BORROWING
borrows early man never borrows
from the late   PREPARATION AND
READINESS
bottles You can't put new wine in
old bottles   CHANGE
bottom best fish swim near the
bottom   DETERMINATION
Every tub must stand on its
own bottom   STRENGTH AND
WEAKNESS
Truth lies at the bottom of a
well   TRUTH

bough If I keep a green bough in
my heart   HAPPINESS
bought Gold may be bought too
dear   VALUE
bow More than one yew bow in
Chester   DANGER
bowls Those who play at
bowls   CAUTION
boy Never send a boy to do a
man's job   YOUTH
You can take the boy out of the
country   COUNTRY AND THE
TOWN
boys Boys will be boys   MEN
Two boys are half a boy   WORK
bra Burn your bra   WOMEN
bracelet single bracelet does not
jingle   COOPERATION
brae Put a stout heart to a stey
brae   DETERMINATION
brag Brag is a good dog, but
Holdfast   WORDS AND DEEDS
brain idle brain is the devil's
workshop   IDLENESS
branch Although the branch is
broken off   CIRCUMSTANCE AND
SITUATION
brass Where there's muck there's
brass   MONEY
brave Brave men lived before
Agamemnon   FAME
Fortune favours the
brave   COURAGE
None but the brave deserve the
fair   COURAGE
Robin Hood could brave all
weathers   WEATHER
bread Acorns were good till
bread was found   SATISFACTION
AND DISCONTENT
bread never falls but on its
buttered side   MISFORTUNES
Half a loaf is better than

397

Keyword Index

no bread SATISFACTION AND
DISCONTENT
No dinner without
bread FOOD
Philosophy bakes no
bread WORDS AND DEEDS
break Hard words break no
bones WORDS
If it were not for hope, the
heart HOPE
Sticks and stones may break my
bones WORDS
breakfast Breakfast like a king,
lunch like EATING
Hope is a good breakfast HOPE
Sing before breakfast,
cry FEELINGS
bred What's bred in the
bone CHARACTER
Yorkshire born and Yorkshire
bred BRITISH TOWNS AND
REGIONS
breeds Like breeds
like SIMILARITY AND DIFFERENCE
brevity Brevity is the soul of
wit SPEECH
brew As you brew, so shall you
bake CAUSES AND
CONSEQUENCES
bricks You cannot make bricks
without straw FUTILITY
bride Always a bridesmaid, never
a bride WEDDINGS
Happy is the bride the sun
shines on WEDDINGS
bridesmaid Always a bridesmaid,
never a bride WEDDINGS
bridge Don't cross the bridge till
you come to it PREPARATION
AND READINESS
Everyone speaks well of the
bridge MANNERS
He who would lead must be a

bridge LEADERSHIP
It is good to make a bridge of
gold WAYS AND MEANS
bridges September dries up wells
and breaks down
bridges AUTUMN
bright Barnaby bright, Barnaby
bright SUMMER
brighten Blessings brighten as
they take HAPPINESS
bring worth of a thing is what it
will bring VALUE
broadens Travel broadens the
mind TRAVEL
broke If it ain't broke ACTION
AND INACTION
broken Although the branch is
broken off CIRCUMSTANCE AND
SITUATION
elephant does not die of one
broken rib STRENGTH AND
WEAKNESS
Rules are made to be
broken LAW
single arrow is easily
broken COOPERATION
brooms New brooms sweep
clean CHANGE
broth Too many cooks spoil the
broth WORK
brother Am I not a man and a
brother HUMAN RACE
My brother and I against my
cousin FAMILY
brothers All arts are
brothers COOPERATION
brown quick brown fox jumps
over the lazy dog WORDS
buck bigger bang for a bigger
buck WARFARE
bucket Don't throw away the old
bucket PREPARATION AND
READINESS

bug It's not a bug, it's a feature COMPUTING

build Fools build houses and wise men FOOLS

It is easier to build two ARCHITECTURE

building Building and marrying of children ARCHITECTURE

In settling an island, the first building ARCHITECTURE

No good building without ARCHITECTURE

built Rome was not built in a day PATIENCE

bull Bull markets climb a wall of worry BUSINESS

bullring It is not the same thing to talk of bulls, as to be in the bullring WORDS AND DEEDS

bulls bulls make money, the bears make BUYING AND SELLING

It is not the same thing to talk of bulls, as to be in the bullring WORDS AND DEEDS

bully bully is always a coward COURAGE

bumping Education doesn't come by bumping EDUCATION

burden Anyone can carry his burden, however heavy, until nightfall LIFESTYLES

God makes the back to the burden SYMPATHY

burn Burn, baby, burn DEFIANCE

Burn your bra WOMEN

Hot water does not burn down FUTILITY

burnt burnt child dreads the fire EXPERIENCE

If you play with fire you get burnt DANGER

bury Let the dead bury their dead MOURNING

bush Good wine needs no bush ADVERTISING

Poke a bush, a snake comes CAUTION

busiest busiest men have the most leisure LEISURE

Tomorrow is often the busiest day FUTURE

business Business before pleasure BUSINESS

Business goes where it is invited BUSINESS

Business is like a car BUSINESS

Business is war BUSINESS

Business neglected BUSINESS

Everybody's business is nobody's RESPONSIBILITY

Punctuality is the soul of business PUNCTUALITY

busy Who is more busy than he who has least to do? IDLENESS

butter Fine words butter no parsnips WORDS AND DEEDS

more butter, the worse cheese FOOD

buttered bread never falls but on its buttered side MISFORTUNES

button You press the button, we do the rest TECHNOLOGY

buy Buy in the cheapest market BUYING AND SELLING

inch of gold cannot buy time TIME

One white foot, buy him HORSES

Why buy a cow when milk is so cheap SEX

Would you buy a used car from this man? TRUST AND TREACHERY

You buy land, you buy stones BUYING AND SELLING

buyer buyer has need of a hundred eyes BUYING AND SELLING

Keyword Index

Let the buyer beware BUYING AND SELLING

cabbage Twice-cooked cabbage is death FOOD

Caesar *Aut Caesar, aut nihil* AMBITION

cake bad custom is like a good cake CUSTOM AND HABIT

You cannot have your cake ACHIEVEMENT

calf bellowing cow soon forgets her calf MOURNING

call beginning of wisdom is to call things NAMES

Call on God, but row away CAUTION

Do not call a wolf to help you ENEMIES

It is not what you call me NAMES

calls He who pays the piper calls the tune POWER

calm After a storm comes a calm PEACE

In a calm sea every man ACHIEVEMENT

It is the calm and silent water DANGER

Keep calm and carry on CRISES

camel He who steals an egg will steal a camel HONESTY

Only the camel knows the hundredth NAMES

Trust in Allah, but tie up your camel CAUTION

camels Camels, fleas, and princes ROYALTY

More doctors recommend Camels SMOKING

camera camera never lies TECHNOLOGY

candle Better to light one candle ACTION AND INACTION

liar's candle lasts till evening LIES

Candlemas Candlemas day, beans in the clay WINTER

If Candlemas day be sunny and bright WINTER

canem *Cave canem* DOGS

cap If the cap fits, wear it NAMES

car Business is like a car BUSINESS

Would you buy a used car from this man TRUST AND TREACHERY

caravan Dogs bark, but the caravan goes FUTILITY

carborundum *Nil carborundum illegitimi* DETERMINATION

carcase Where the carcase is GREED

cards Lucky at cards, unlucky in love CHANCE AND LUCK

care Care, and not fine stables HORSES

Care killed the cat WORRY

Don't care was made to care RESPONSIBILITY

Take care of the pence and the pounds THRIFT

careful Be careful what you wish for CAUTION

If you can't be good, be careful CAUTION

careless Careless talk costs lives GOSSIP

cares Children are certain cares FAMILY

caribou caribou feeds the wolf STRENGTH AND WEAKNESS

carpenter carpenter is known by his chips APPEARANCE

carry Anyone can carry his burden, however heavy, until nightfall LIFESTYLES

You cannot carry two watermelons   FUTILITY

cart Don't put the cart before the horse   PATIENCE

cases Circumstances alter cases   CIRCUMSTANCE AND SITUATION

Hard cases make bad law   LAW

cash Cash is king   MONEY

castle Englishman's home is his castle   HOME

cat Care killed the cat   WORRY

cat always lands on its feet   CATS

cat has nine lives   CATS

cat in gloves catches no mice   CAUTION

cat may look at a king   CATS

cat would eat fish   INDECISION

cat, the rat, and Lovell the dog   GOVERNMENT

It hardly matters if it is a white cat or   WAYS AND MEANS

It is better to feed one cat   CATS

There are more ways of killing a cat   WAYS AND MEANS

There is more than one way to skin a cat   WAYS AND MEANS

Touch not the cat but a glove   CATS

When the cat's away, the mice will   OPPORTUNITY

catch First catch your hare   WAYS AND MEANS

Never try to catch a falling knife   BUSINESS

Set a thief to catch a thief   WAYS AND MEANS

Sue a beggar and catch a louse   FUTILITY

catchee Softlee, softlee, catchee monkey   PATIENCE

catches Honey catches more flies than vinegar   WAYS AND MEANS

catching Catching's before hanging   WAYS AND MEANS

cats All cats are grey in the dark   SIMILARITY AND DIFFERENCE

Keep no more cats than will catch mice   MODERATION

Wanton kittens make sober cats   YOUTH

cattle Hurry no man's cattle   PATIENCE

caught fish will soon be caught that nibbles   TEMPTATION

cause need, not the cause   CHARITY

caution Caution is the parent of safety   CAUTION

cave Cave canem   DOGS

cease War will cease when men refuse to fight   WARFARE

certain Nothing is certain but death   CERTAINTY AND DOUBT

Nothing is certain but the unforeseen   FORESIGHT

chaff king's chaff is worth more   ROYALTY

chain chain is no stronger than its weakest   COOPERATION

chance Blind chance sweeps   CHANCE AND LUCK

Moses took a chance   CHANCE AND LUCK

person who misses his chance   OPPORTUNITY

wise man turns chance into good fortune   OPPORTUNITY

chances You have two chances   CHANCE AND LUCK

change change is as good as a rest   CHANGE

Change the name and not the letter   MARRIAGE

leopard does not change his

Keyword Index

spots CHANGE
Times change and we with
time CHANGE
To change, and change for the
better CHANGE
changes Every two miles the
water changes TRAVEL
When the music
changes CHANGE
wise man changes his
mind FOOLS
channel Where water flows, a
channel PATIENCE
character Character is what we
are CHARACTER
Like a fence, character
cannot CHARACTER
charity Charity begins at
home CHARITY
Charity covers a multitude of
sins FORGIVENESS
Charity is not a bone CHARITY
Charity sees the need CHARITY
roots of charity are always
green CHARITY
charm third time is the
charm CHANCE AND LUCK
chase stern chase is a long
chase DETERMINATION
cheap It is as cheap
sitting ACTION AND INACTION
Pile it high, sell it
cheap BUSINESS
Talk is cheap WORDS AND
DEEDS
Why buy a cow when milk is
so cheap SEX
cheapest Buy in the cheapest
market BUYING AND SELLING
cheats Cheats never
prosper DECEPTION
cheeping May chickens come
cheeping SPRING

cheese apple pie without some
cheese FOOD
more butter, the worse
cheese FOOD
only free cheese is in a
mousetrap TEMPTATION
cherries He who likes
cherries ACHIEVEMENT
cherry cherry year, a merry
year SUMMER
chess Chess is a sea where a gnat
may drink SPORTS AND GAMES
Chester More than one yew bow
in Chester DANGER
chicken Kill the chicken to
scare CAUSES AND
CONSEQUENCES
Why did the chicken cross
the road PROBLEMS AND
SOLUTIONS
chickens Chickens are counted in
the autumn AUTUMN
Curses, like chickens, come
home FEELINGS
Don't count your chickens
before OPTIMISM AND PESSIMISM
howlin' coyote ain't stealin' no
chickens HONESTY
May chickens come
cheeping SPRING
child burnt child dreads the
fire EXPERIENCE
child is the father of the
man CHARACTER
child of a frog is a frog FAMILY
child that is born on the
Sabbath CHILDREN
Friday's child is loving and
giving GENEROSITY
Give me a child for the first
seven EDUCATION
He who takes the child by the
hand PARENTS

It is a wise child that knows   PARENTS

It takes a village to raise a child   CHILDREN

Monday's child is fair of face   BEAUTY

mother understands what the child   PARENTS

Praise the child, and you make love to   PARENTS

Saturday's child works hard for a living   WORK

Send the beloved child on a journey   PARENTS

Thursday's child has far to go   TRAVEL

Wednesday's child is full of woe   SORROW

children Building and marrying of children   ARCHITECTURE

Children and fools tell the truth   HONESTY

Children are certain cares   FAMILY

Children: one is one   CHILDREN

Children should be seen and not   CHILDREN

Heaven protects children, sailors   DANGER

Little children, little sorrows   CHILDREN

Parents want their children to become   PARENTS

Women and children first   DANGER

chimneys It is easier to build two chimneys   ARCHITECTURE

chips carpenter is known by his chips   APPEARANCE

choice He that has a choice   CHOICE

obvious choice is usually   CHOICE

choose Never choose your women or linen   APPEARANCE

Of two evils choose the less   CHOICE

choosers Beggars can't be choosers   NECESSITY

chop Before enlightenment, chop wood, carry water   LIFESTYLES

Christ Christ has no body now on earth   CHRISTIAN CHURCH

Christian good Christian should beware   KNOWLEDGE

Christians Christians to the lions   CHRISTIAN CHURCH

Christmas Christmas comes but once a year   CHRISTMAS

Christmas is coming, and the goose   CHRISTMAS

Christmas with the family   CHRISTMAS

devil makes his Christmas pies   LAW

dog is for life, not just for Christmas   DOGS

Green Christmas, white Easter   WEATHER

Only — shopping days to Christmas   CHRISTMAS

church church is an anvil   CHRISTIAN CHURCH

church is God between four walls   CHRISTIAN CHURCH

He is a good dog who goes to church   BEHAVIOUR

nearer the church   CHRISTIAN CHURCH

Where God builds a church   GOOD AND EVIL

You can't build a church with   CHRISTIAN CHURCH

churchyard green Yule makes a fat churchyard   CHRISTMAS

Keyword Index

cigar Happiness is a cigar called Hamlet SMOKING

circle nature of God is a circle GOD

wheel has come full circle CIRCUMSTANCE AND SITUATION

circumspice *Si monumentum requiris, circumspice* ARCHITECTURE

circumstances Circumstances alter cases CIRCUMSTANCE AND SITUATION

New circumstances, new controls CIRCUMSTANCE AND SITUATION

civil civil question deserves a civil answer MANNERS

civility Civility costs nothing MANNERS

There is nothing lost by civility MANNERS

claws conceal their claws SELF-ESTEEM AND SELF-ASSERTION

clay Candlemas day, put beans in the clay WINTER

Sow corn in clay GARDENS

clean clean conscience is a good pillow CONSCIENCE

New brooms sweep clean CHANGE

cleanliness Cleanliness is next to godliness BEHAVIOUR

cleans It beats as it sweeps as it cleans HOUSEWORK

clear Clear moon, frost soon WEATHER

clergymen Clergymen's sons always CLERGY

clever Clever hawks conceal their claws SELF-ESTEEM AND SELF-ASSERTION

click Clunk, click, every trip TRAVEL

climbers Hasty climbers have sudden falls AMBITION

climbs higher the monkey climbs AMBITION

cloak borrowed cloak does not keep you warm DEBT AND BORROWING

clock Even a stopped clock is right twice a day TIME

clogs From clogs to clogs is only three SUCCESS AND FAILURE

close Do not close a letter without reading it LETTERS

closest Even your closest friends won't HEALTH

cloth Cut your coat according to your cloth PRACTICALITY

clothes Clothes make the man DRESS

cloud Every cloud has a silver lining OPTIMISM AND PESSIMISM

clout Ne'er cast a clout till May be out DRESS

clunk Clunk, click, every trip TRAVEL

clutch drowning man will clutch at a straw HOPE

coat Cut your coat according to your cloth PRACTICALITY

cobbler cobbler to his last and the gunner KNOWLEDGE

Let the cobbler stick to his last KNOWLEDGE

There will be trouble if the cobbler KNOWLEDGE

cobwebs Habits are cobwebs at first CUSTOM AND HABIT

cock Every cock will crow upon his own HOME

There's many a good cock CHARACTER

coconuts If you had teeth of steel, you could eat iron coconuts OPTIMISM AND PESSIMISM

coffee Coffee without tobacco SMOKING

coincidence It is a striking coincidence that COUNTRIES AND PEOPLES

coins If you have two coins LIFESTYLES
Proverbs are the coins of the people SAYINGS

coitum Post coitum omne animal triste SEX

cold As the day lengthens, so the cold WEATHER
cold April the barn will fill SPRING
Cold hands, warm heart BODY
cold May and windy SPRING
Eat till you're cold HEALTH
Feed a cold and starve a fever SICKNESS
If you are cold, tea will warm you DRINK
warm January, a cold May WEATHER

colour good horse cannot be of a bad colour APPEARANCE

comb Experience is the comb EXPERIENCE

come Easy come, easy go EFFORT
Light come, light go POSSESSIONS
Quickly come, quickly go LOYALTY

comes Tomorrow never comes FUTURE
What goes around comes around JUSTICE

coming Coming events cast their shadow FUTURE

command He that cannot obey cannot command LEADERSHIP

committee committee is a group of the unwilling MANAGEMENT

common common danger causes common action DANGER
Common fame is seldom to blame FAME

communications Evil communications corrupt BEHAVIOUR

company Better alone than in bad company SOLITUDE
company makes the feast HOSPITALITY
man is known by the company he FAMILIARITY
Misery loves company SORROW
Two is company, but three is none FRIENDSHIP

comparisons Comparisons are odious SIMILARITY AND DIFFERENCE

complies He that complies against his will OPINION

concealed Crime must be concealed CRIME AND PUNISHMENT

conceals He that conceals his grief SORROW

condition Be sure you can better your condition CHANGE

conduct Courage without conduct COURAGE

confess Confess and be hanged GUILT

confessed fault confessed is half redressed FORGIVENESS

confession Confession is good for the soul HONESTY

confidence Confidence is a plant of slowth growth TRUST AND TREACHERY

Keyword Index

conscience clean conscience is a good pillow   CONSCIENCE
Conscience gets a lot of credit   CONSCIENCE
guilty conscience needs no accuser   CONSCIENCE
Let your conscience be your guide   CONSCIENCE
quiet conscience sleeps in thunder   CONSCIENCE

consent Silence means consent   SILENCE

conservative conservative is a liberal who's   CRIME AND PUNISHMENT

constant Constant dropping wears away   DETERMINATION

contact No plan survives first contact   PREPARATION AND READINESS

contagious Elephants are contagious   WORDS

contempt Familiarity breeds contempt   FAMILIARITY

contraries Dreams go by contraries   DREAMS

control You cannot control the winds   MANAGEMENT

controls New circumstances, new controls   CIRCUMSTANCE AND SITUATION

cook cook is no better than her stove   COOKING
It is a poor cook that cannot lick   COOKING
Talk will not cook rice   WORDS AND DEEDS

cooks All are not cooks who   COOKING
Too many cooks spoil the broth   WORK

cooperation If you don't believe in cooperation   COOPERATION

If you think cooperation is   COOPERATION

core Believing has a core of unbelieving   BELIEF

corn Sow corn in clay   GARDENS

Cornwall There are more saints in Cornwall   BRITISH TOWNS AND REGIONS

corrupt Evil communications corrupt   BEHAVIOUR

corruption Corruption of the best   EXCELLENCE
Corruption will find a dozen alibis   CORRUPTION

corrupts Power corrupts   POWER

costs Careless talk costs lives   GOSSIP
Civility costs nothing   MANNERS
love letter sometimes costs more   LETTERS

cough Love and a cough   LOVE

coughs Coughs and sneezes spread diseases   SICKNESS

councils Councils of war never fight   INDECISION

counsel fool may give a wise man counsel   ADVICE
Night brings counsel   ADVICE

count Don't count your chickens before   OPTIMISM AND PESSIMISM
Eat the mangoes. Do not count the trees   WAYS AND MEANS
When angry count a hundred   ANGER
You can count the apples on one tree   QUANTITIES AND QUALITIES

counted Chickens are counted in the autumn   AUTUMN

country everyday story of country folk   COUNTRY AND THE TOWN

God made the
country   COUNTRY AND THE
TOWN
Happy is the country   HISTORY
If you have not lived in the
country   COUNTRY AND THE
TOWN
You can take the boy out of the
country   COUNTRY AND THE
TOWN
Your King and country need
you   ARMED FORCES

courage Courage is fear
that   COURAGE
Courage without
conduct   COURAGE

course course of true love never
did run smooth   LOVE

courses Horses for
courses   ABILITY

cousin My brother and I against
my cousin   FAMILY

cover Duck and cover   CAUTION
You can't tell a book by its
cover   APPEARANCE

cow bellowing cow soon forgets
her calf   MOURNING
Better a good cow   CHARACTER
It is idle to swallow the
cow   DETERMINATION
Three acres and a cow   POLITICS
Why buy a cow when milk
is so cheap   SEX

coward bully is always a
coward   COURAGE

cowards Cowards may die many
times   FEAR

cowl cowl does not make the
monk   APPEARANCE

coyote howlin' coyote ain't stealin'
no chickens   HONESTY

cradle hand that rocks the cradle
rules   WOMEN

creaking creaking door hangs
longest   SICKNESS

credit Conscience gets a lot of
credit   CONSCIENCE
Give credit where credit
is due   PRAISE AND FLATTERY

Crediton Kirton was a borough
town   BRITISH TOWNS AND
REGIONS

cried I cried because I had no
shoes   MISFORTUNES

crime Crime doesn't pay   CRIME
AND PUNISHMENT
Crime leaves a trail like   CRIME
AND PUNISHMENT
Crime must be
concealed   CRIME AND
PUNISHMENT
Poverty is not a
crime   POVERTY

crisis Every crisis provides an
opportunity   OPPORTUNITY
Never waste a good
crisis   CRISES

criticism best place for
criticism   CRITICISM
Criticism is
something   CRITICISM

crooked God writes straight with
crooked lines   GOD

crop Good seed makes a bad
crop   CAUSES AND
CONSEQUENCES

cross Cross the river by
feeling   CAUTION
Cross the river in a
crowd   COOPERATION
Don't cross the bridge till
you come to it   PREPARATION
AND READINESS
No cross, no crown   SUFFERING
Why did the chicken cross the
road   PROBLEMS AND SOLUTIONS

Keyword Index

crosses Crosses are ladders that lead to heaven   SUFFERING

crossing Life is harder than crossing a field   LIFE

crow Every cock will crow upon his own   HOME
One for the mouse, one for the crow   NATURE

crowd Cross the river in a crowd   COOPERATION

crowing whistling woman and a crowing hen   WOMEN

crown No cross, no crown   SUFFERING

crowns end crowns the work   ENDING

crows On the first of March, crows begin   SPRING

cruelty Beauty without cruelty   SUFFERING

cry Don't cry before you're hurt   COURAGE
Much cry and little wool   EFFORT
Sing before breakfast, cry   FEELINGS

crying It is no use crying over spilt milk   MISFORTUNES

cuckoo cuckoo comes in April   BIRDS
cuckoo praises the rooster   PRAISE AND FLATTERY

culture man without culture is like   APPEARANCE

cup Full cup, steady hand   CAUTION
last drop makes the cup run over   EXCESS
There's many a slip 'twixt cup and lip   MISTAKES

Cupar He that will to Cupar   DETERMINATION

curantur *Similia similibus curantur*   MEDICINE

cure drunkard's cure is drink again   DRUNKENNESS
No cure, no pay   BUSINESS
Prevention is better than cure   FORESIGHT

cured What can't be cured must be endured   PATIENCE

curried short horse is soon curried   WORK

curses Curses, like chickens, come home   FEELINGS

custom bad custom is like a good cake   CUSTOM AND HABIT
Custom is mummified by habit   CUSTOM AND HABIT

customer customer is always right   BUSINESS

cut Cut your coat according to your cloth   PRACTICALITY
Don't cut off your nose to spite   REVENGE
Measure seven times, cut once   PREPARATION AND READINESS
short cut is often a wrong cut   WAYS AND MEANS
slice off a cut loaf isn't missed   IGNORANCE

dance Money makes the dog dance   MONEY
One who cannot dance blames   DANCE
They that dance must pay the fiddler   POWER
We're fools whether we dance or   DANCE
When you ask a bear to dance   DANGER
When you go to dance, take heed   DANCE

dances He that lives in hope dances to an ill tune   HOPE

Keyword Index

dancing All dancing girls are nineteen YOUTH
You need more than dancing shoes DANCE

danger common danger causes common action DANGER
lone sheep is in danger from the wolf SOLITUDE
Out of debt, out of danger DEBT AND BORROWING
post of honour is the post of danger DANGER

dangerous Delays are dangerous HASTE AND DELAY
little knowledge is a dangerous thing KNOWLEDGE

dares Who dares wins DANGER

dark All cats are grey in the dark SIMILARITY AND DIFFERENCE
It is dark at the foot of the lighthouse IGNORANCE

darkest darkest hour is just before dawn OPTIMISM AND PESSIMISM

darkness An inch ahead is darkness FUTURE

darling Better be an old man's darling MARRIAGE

daughter Like mother, like daughter FAMILY

dawn darkest hour is just before dawn OPTIMISM AND PESSIMISM

day Action this day ACTION AND INACTION
Another day, another dollar OPTIMISM AND PESSIMISM
apple a day keeps the doctor away HEALTH
As the day lengthens, so the cold WEATHER
Be the day weary or be the day long TIME

better the day, the better the deed WORK
day has eyes, the night has ears SECRECY
day without work is a day without food IDLENESS
Every dog has his day OPPORTUNITY
Not a day without a line ART
Rome was not built in a day PATIENCE
Sufficient unto the day is the evil WORRY
Tomorrow is another day FUTURE
Tomorrow is often the busiest day FUTURE
What is done by night appears by day SECRECY
Who teaches me for a day is my father TEACHING

daydream Vision without action is a daydream WORDS AND DEEDS

daylight morning daylight appears plainer TIME

days He who can see three days ahead FORESIGHT
March borrowed from April three days SPRING
Treat your guest as a guest for two days HOSPITALITY

dead Better red than dead CHOICE
Blessed are the dead that the rain DEATH
Dead men don't bite ENEMIES
Dead men tell no tales SECRECY
It's ill waiting for dead men's shoes AMBITION
Let the dead bury their dead MOURNING

Keyword Index

live dog is better than a dead
lion   LIFE

Never speak ill of the
dead   REPUTATION

Stone-dead hath no
fellow   DEATH

To dream of the dead is a sign
of rain   DREAMS

deadly female of the species is
more deadly   WOMEN

deaf deaf husband and a blind
wife   MARRIAGE

There's none so deaf as
those   PREJUDICE AND
TOLERANCE

dear Experience keeps a dear
school   EXPERIENCE

Far-fetched and dear-
bought   WOMEN

Gold may be bought too
dear   VALUE

death Death is nature's
way   DEATH

Death is the great
leveller   DEATH

Death pays all debts   DEATH

Life without a friend, is
death   FRIENDSHIP

Nothing is certain but
death   CERTAINTY AND DOUBT

They offered death   CHOICE

Twice-cooked cabbage is
death   FOOD

debt man in debt is caught in a
net   DEBT AND BORROWING

national debt, if it is not
excessive   DEBT AND
BORROWING

Out of debt, out of
danger   DEBT AND BORROWING

debts Death pays all
debts   DEATH

deceit Deceit is a lie   DECEPTION

deceptive Appearances are
deceptive   APPEARANCE

declared When war is declared,
Truth is the first   WARFARE

deed better the day, the better
the deed   WORK

No good deed goes
unpunished   VIRTUE

deep Still waters run
deep   CHARACTER

deepest Where the river is
deepest   CHARACTER

defence Attack is the best form
of defence   COURAGE

deferred Hope deferred makes
the heart sick   HOPE

defiled He that touches pitch
shall be defiled   GOOD AND EVIL

delayed Justice delayed is justice
denied   JUSTICE

delays Delays are
dangerous   HASTE AND DELAY

Delhi Delhi is far away   CAUTION

delight Red sky at night,
shepherd's delight   WEATHER

delved When Adam delved and
Eve span   RANK

democracy Democracy is better
than tyranny   POLITICS

denied Justice delayed is justice
denied   JUSTICE

deny Deny self for self's
sake   SELF-ESTEEM AND
SELF-ASSERTION

deserve None but the brave
deserve the fair   COURAGE

desperate Desperate diseases
must have   NECESSITY

destroy Whom the gods would
destroy   MIND

determined determined
fellow can do more
with   DETERMINATION

410

Devil Better the Devil you know FAMILIARITY

Devil can quote Scripture SAYINGS

Devil finds work for idle hands IDLENESS

Devil is not so black as he is painted REPUTATION

Devil looks after his own CHANCE AND LUCK

Devil makes his Christmas pies LAW

Devil's children have the Devil's luck CHANCE AND LUCK

Devil was sick, the Devil a saint GRATITUDE

Every man for himself, and the Devil SELF-INTEREST

Give the Devil his due JUSTICE

God sends meat, but the Devil COOKING

good painter can draw a devil ART

Haste is from the Devil HASTE AND DELAY

He who sups with the Devil CAUTION

Home is home, as the Devil said LAW

idle brain is the Devil's workshop IDLENESS

It is easier to raise the Devil BEGINNING

Needs must when the devil drives NECESSITY

Never bid the Devil good morrow PROBLEMS AND SOLUTIONS

Talk of the Devil MEETING AND PARTING

Tell the truth and shame the Devil TRUTH

Truth makes the Devil blush TRUTH

What is got under the Devil's back GOOD AND EVIL

Why should the Devil have all the best MUSIC

Young saint, old devil HUMAN RACE

dew guest is like the morning dew HOSPITALITY

diamond Diamond cuts diamond EQUALITY

diamond is forever WEALTH

die Cowards may die many times FEAR

Don't die of ignorance HEALTH

Eat, drink and be merry, for tomorrow we die LIFESTYLES

elephant does not die of one broken rib STRENGTH AND WEAKNESS

Good Americans when they die COUNTRIES AND PEOPLES

good die young VIRTUE

Life's a bitch, and then you die LIFE

More die of food than famine HEALTH

Old habits die hard CUSTOM AND HABIT

Old soldiers never die ARMED FORCES

Root, hog, or die WORK

See Naples and die TOWNS AND CITIES

Whom the gods love die young YOUTH

You can only die once DEATH

You'll die facing the monument CRIME AND PUNISHMENT

Young men may die, but old men DEATH

Keyword Index

dies Call no man happy
till he dies HAPPINESS
When an elder dies, it
is as if AGE
When a tiger dies it leaves
its skin REPUTATION

diet best doctors are Dr Quiet,
Dr Diet MEDICINE

differ Tastes differ LIKES AND
DISLIKES

different Different strokes for
different folks CHOICE

difficult difficult is done
at once ACHIEVEMENT
Equality is difficult, but
superiority LEADERSHIP

difficulty England's difficulty is
Ireland's COUNTRIES AND
PEOPLES

dig Dig for victory GARDENS
Dig the well before you are
thirsty PREPARATION AND
READINESS
If you want revenge, dig two
graves REVENGE

digging When you are in a hole,
stop digging APOLOGY AND
EXCUSES

diligence Diligence is the mother
of CHANCE AND LUCK

dinner After dinner rest a
while EATING
better the salad, the worse the
dinner COOKING
No dinner without bread FOOD

dirt Throw dirt enough, and some
will stick REPUTATION
We must eat a peck of
dirt EATING

dirty Dirty water will
quench fire SEX
One does not wash one's
dirty linen SECRECY

disaster When disaster
strikes CRISES

discretion Discretion is the
better part CAUTION

disease From the bitterness of
disease, man learns the
sweetness of health SICKNESS
imaginary ailment is worse than
a disease SICKNESS
Life is a sexually transmitted
disease LIFE

diseases Coughs and sneezes
spread diseases SICKNESS
Desperate diseases must
have NECESSITY
Diseases come on
horseback but go away
on foot SICKNESS

disgrace Poverty is no
disgrace POVERTY

dish Better are small fish than an
empty dish SATISFACTION AND
DISCONTENT
Revenge is a dish that can be
eaten REVENGE

disillusion Absence is the mother
of disillusion ABSENCE

disposes Man proposes, God
disposes FATE

distance Distance lends
enchantment APPEARANCE

ditch fall into a ditch makes you
wiser EXPERIENCE

divide Divide and
rule GOVERNMENT

divided United we stand, divided
we COOPERATION

divine To err is human (to forgive
divine) MISTAKES

do Do as I say, not as
I do BEHAVIOUR
Do as you would be
done by LIFESTYLES

Do unto others as you would they LIFESTYLES
Make do and mend THRIFT
Not guilty, but don't do it again GUILT
You never know what you can do COURAGE
doctor apple a day keeps the doctor away HEALTH
doctors best doctors are Dr Quiet, Dr Diet MEDICINE
More doctors recommend Camels SMOKING
doers Evil doers are evil dreaders CONSCIENCE
dog barking dog never bites ACTION AND INACTION
Better be the head of a dog POWER
Brag is a good dog, but Holdfast WORDS AND DEEDS
cat, the rat, and Lovell the dog GOVERNMENT
Dog does not eat dog COOPERATION
dog is a lion in his own house DOGS
dog is for life, not just for Christmas DOGS
dog that will fetch a bone GOSSIP
Every dog has his day OPPORTUNITY
Feed a dog for three days CATS
Give a dog a bad name and hang GOSSIP
He is a good dog who goes to church BEHAVIOUR
If you are not the lead dog LEADERSHIP
It is a poor dog that's not worth VALUE

It is easy to find a stick to beat a dog APOLOGY AND EXCUSES
live dog is better than a dead lion LIFE
Love me, love my dog DOGS
Money makes the dog dance MONEY
quick brown fox jumps over the lazy dog WORDS
There are more ways of killing a dog WAYS AND MEANS
Why keep a dog and bark yourself MANAGEMENT
woman, a dog, and a walnut tree WOMEN
You can't teach an old dog new tricks CUSTOM AND HABIT
dogged It's dogged as does it DETERMINATION
dogs Dogs bark, but the caravan goes FUTILITY
If you lie down with dogs FAMILIARITY
Let sleeping dogs lie CAUTION
While two dogs are fighting ARGUMENT
dollar Another day, another dollar OPTIMISM AND PESSIMISM
done Do as you would be done by LIFESTYLES
If you want a thing done well SELF-INTEREST
If you want something done ACTION AND INACTION
Whatever man has done ACHIEVEMENT
What's done cannot be undone PAST
don't Don't ask, don't tell SECRECY
Don't care was made to care RESPONSIBILITY

Keyword Index

door creaking door hangs
longest   SICKNESS
door must be either shut or
open   CHOICE
golden key can open any
door   CORRUPTION
postern door makes a
thief   OPPORTUNITY
Teachers open the
door   EDUCATION
When one door shuts, another
opens   OPPORTUNITY
When poverty comes in at
the door   POVERTY

dose dose of adversity is
often   ADVERSITY

double Shared joy is double
joy   SYMPATHY

doubt When in doubt, do
nowt   ACTION AND INACTION

dough Drive for show, and
putt for dough   SPORTS
AND GAMES

down Up like a rocket, down like
a stick   SUCCESS AND FAILURE
What goes up must come
down   FATE

dragons Dragons beget
dragons   FAMILY
Here be dragons   INVENTIONS
AND DISCOVERIES

drama We won't make a drama
out of   CAUTION

draw good painter can draw a
devil   ART

draws Whosoever draws his
sword against   REVOLUTION AND
REBELLION

dreaders Evil doers are evil
dreaders   CONSCIENCE

dream Dream of a
funeral   DREAMS
peace is the dream of the

wise   PEACE
To dream of the dead is a sign
of rain   DREAMS
You cannot dream yourself
into   CHARACTER

dreaming Those who lose
dreaming   DREAMS

dreams Dreams go by
contraries   DREAMS
Dreams retain the infirmities
of   DREAMS
God sleeps in the stone,
dreams   HUMAN RACE
Morning dreams come
true   DREAMS

dress Dress for the job you
want   DRESS

drink Don't ask a man to drink
and drive   DRINK
drunkard's cure is drink
again   DRUNKENNESS
Eat, drink and be merry, for
tomorrow   LIFESTYLES
When you drink water,
remember   GRATITUDE

drinking When drinking water,
remember the   PARENTS

drinks He that drinks beer, thinks
beer   DRUNKENNESS

dripping dripping June sets all in
tune   SUMMER

drive Don't ask a man to drink
and drive   DRINK
Drive for show, and putt for
dough   SPORTS AND GAMES

drives Needs must when the devil
drives   NECESSITY
One nail drives out another
SIMILARITY AND DIFFERENCE

drop last drop makes the cup run
over   EXCESS

dropping Constant dropping
wears away   DETERMINATION

414

drops Drops that gather one by one QUANTITIES AND QUALITIES

drowning drowning man will clutch at a straw HOPE

drunk You have drunk from wells you did not PAST

drunkard drunkard's cure is drink again DRUNKENNESS

druv Sussex won't be druv BRITISH TOWNS AND REGIONS

dry Sow dry and set wet GARDENS

duck Duck and cover CAUTION
son of a duck floats FAMILY

due Give credit where credit is due PRAISE AND FLATTERY
Give the Devil his due JUSTICE

dumb It takes forty dumb animals DRESS

duster Rooster today, feather duster tomorrow SUCCESS AND FAILURE

Dutch God made the world, but the Dutch made Holland COUNTRIES AND PEOPLES

duty first duty of a soldier ARMED FORCES

dyke February fill dyke, be it black or white WINTER

eagle Only the eagle can gaze at the sun STRENGTH AND WEAKNESS

eagles Eagles don't catch flies CHARACTER

early Don't hurry—start early HASTE AND DELAY
early bird catches the worm PREPARATION AND READINESS
early man never borrows from the late PREPARATION AND READINESS

Early to bed and early to rise HEALTH
Vote early and vote often POLITICS

earned penny saved is a penny earned THRIFT

ears day has eyes, the night has ears SECRECY
Fields have eyes and woods have ears SECRECY
Little pitchers have large ears SECRECY
Walls have ears SECRECY

earth Did the earth move for you SEX
earth is man's only friend ENVIRONMENT
earth laughs at him who ENVIRONMENT
Touch the earth lightly ENVIRONMENT
We do not inherit the earth ENVIRONMENT

easier It is easier to build two chimneys ARCHITECTURE
It is easier to raise the Devil BEGINNING

east East is east, and west is west SIMILARITY AND DIFFERENCE
East, west, home's best HOME
When the wind is in the east WEATHER

Easter Christmas with the family, Easter with whomever CHRISTMAS
Green Christmas, white Easter WEATHER

easy Beginning is easy BEGINNING
Easy come, easy go EFFORT
It is easy to be generous with GENEROSITY
It is easy to be wise after the event FORESIGHT

Keyword Index

It is easy to find a stick to beat a dog   APOLOGY AND EXCUSES

eat Dog does not eat dog   COOPERATION

Eat, drink and be merry, for tomorrow   LIFESTYLES

Eat leeks in March and ramsons in May   HEALTH

Eat the mangoes. Do not count the trees   WAYS AND MEANS

Eat till you're cold   HEALTH

Eat to live, not live to eat   EATING

Fear less, hope more; Eat less   LIFESTYLES

If you won't work you shan't eat   IDLENESS

We must eat a peck of dirt   EATING

You are what you eat   EATING

eaten Revenge is a dish that can be eaten   REVENGE

eating Appetite comes with eating   EXPERIENCE

proof of the pudding is in the eating   HYPOTHESIS AND FACT

eats way one eats is the way one works   EATING

educate inform, educate, and entertain   BROADCASTING

education Education doesn't come by bumping   EDUCATION

Genius without education   EDUCATION

Never let your education   EDUCATION

egg As good be an addled egg   IDLENESS

Better an egg today than a hen tomorrow   PRESENT

Go to work on an egg   EATING

He who steals an egg will steal a camel   HONESTY

Power is like an egg   POWER

same fire that hardens the egg   CHARACTER

eggs Don't put all your eggs in one basket   CAUTION

There is reason in the roasting of eggs   CAUSES AND CONSEQUENCES

You can't unscramble scrambled eggs   FUTILITY

egoism Apology is only egoism   APOLOGY AND EXCUSES

elder When an elder dies, it is as if   AGE

elementary Elementary, my dear Watson   THINKING

elephant elephant does not die of one broken rib   STRENGTH AND WEAKNESS

When an elephant is in trouble   SUCCESS AND FAILURE

elephants Elephants are contagious   WORDS

When elephants fight, it is the grass   POWER

eleven Rain before seven, fine before eleven   WEATHER

elm Every elm has its man   TREES

emperor mountains are high, and the emperor   GOVERNMENT

empty Better are small fish than an empty dish   SATISFACTION AND DISCONTENT

Empty sacks will never stand upright   POVERTY

Empty vessels make the most sound   FOOLS

enchantment Distance lends enchantment   APPEARANCE

end All good things must come to an end   ENDING

Better an end with terror   ENDING

end crowns the work ENDING
End good, all good ENDING
end justifies the means WAYS AND MEANS
Everything has an end ENDING
He who wills the end DETERMINATION
In my end is my beginning ENDING
sea of learning has no end KNOWLEDGE
endured What can't be cured must be endured PATIENCE
enemy Action is worry's worst enemy ACTION AND INACTION
enemy of my enemy is my friend ENEMIES
Love your enemy ENEMIES
Man is the enemy of IGNORANCE
Science has no enemy but the ignorant SCIENCE
There is no little enemy ENEMIES
England England is the paradise of women COUNTRIES AND PEOPLES
England's difficulty is Ireland's COUNTRIES AND PEOPLES
Englishman Englishman's home is his castle HOME
Englishman's word is his bond COUNTRIES AND PEOPLES
enjoy Enjoy the present moment PRESENT
enjoyable Idleness is never enjoyable IDLENESS
enlightened mind enlightened is like heaven MIND
enlightenment Before enlightenment, chop wood, carry water LIFESTYLES

enough Enough is as good as a feast MODERATION
Enough is enough MODERATION
entertain inform, educate, and entertain BROADCASTING
envied Better be envied than pitied ENVY
envy Envy eats nothing but its own heart ENVY
Envy feeds on the living ENVY
If envy were a fever ENVY
equality Equality is difficult, but superiority LEADERSHIP
err To err is human but to really COMPUTING
To err is human (to forgive divine) MISTAKES
error old error is always more popular TRUTH Essex
Essex Essex stiles, Kentish miles BRITISH TOWNS AND REGIONS
eternal Hope springs eternal HOPE
ethics Good ethics start with good facts MEDICINE
Eve When Adam delved and Eve span RANK
even Don't get mad, get even REVENGE
evening liar's candle lasts till evening LIES
morning knows no more than the evening SLEEP
event It is easy to be wise after the event FORESIGHT
events Coming events cast their shadow FUTURE
ever Are you now or have you ever been POLITICS
Nothing is for ever CHANGE
every Every man to his taste LIKES AND DISLIKES

Keyword Index

Every painter paints himself   ART

everybody Everybody's business is nobody's   RESPONSIBILITY

What everybody says must be true   TRUTH

everyday everyday story of country folk   COUNTRY AND THE TOWN

everything Everything has an end   ENDING

Money isn't everything   MONEY

There is a time for everything   TIME

evidence Absence of evidence   ABSENCE

What the soldier said isn't evidence   GOSSIP

evil Evil communications corrupt   BEHAVIOUR

Evil doers are evil dreaders   CONSCIENCE

great book is a great evil   BOOKS

Money is the root of all evil   MONEY

Never do evil that good may come   BEHAVIOUR

See no evil, hear no evil, speak no evil   VIRTUE

Sufficient unto the day is the evil   WORRY

evils Of two evils choose the less   CHOICE

example Example is better than precept   WORDS AND DEEDS

exception exception proves the rule   HYPOTHESIS AND FACT

There is an exception to every rule   HYPOTHESIS AND FACT

exceptional Exceptional times require   NECESSITY

excessive national debt, if it is not excessive   DEBT AND BORROWING

exchange fair exchange is no robbery   JUSTICE

excuse bad excuse is better than   APOLOGY AND EXCUSES

Ignorance of the law is no excuse   LAW

excuses Don't make excuses   APOLOGY AND EXCUSES

He who excuses himself, accuses   APOLOGY AND EXCUSES

exercise Those who do not find time for exercise   HEALTH

expands Work expands so as to fill the time   WORK

expect What can you expect from a pig   CHARACTER

expects Blessed is he who expects nothing   HOPE

experience Experience is the best teacher   EXPERIENCE

Experience is the comb   EXPERIENCE

Experience is the father   EXPERIENCE

Experience keeps a dear school   EXPERIENCE

Some folks speak from experience   EXPERIENCE

extremes Extremes meet   SIMILARITY AND DIFFERENCE

extremity Man's extremity is God's opportunity   RELIGION

eye Beauty is in the eye of the beholder   BEAUTY

eye for an eye makes   REVENGE

eye of a master does more work   EMPLOYMENT

Keep one eye on the frying-pan   COOKING

Please your eye and plague BEAUTY

quickness of the hand deceives the eye DECEPTION

What the eye doesn't see, the heart IGNORANCE

eyes buyer has need of a hundred eyes BUYING AND SELLING

day has eyes, the night has ears SECRECY

eyes are the window of the soul BODY

eyes believe themselves CERTAINTY AND DOUBT

Fields have eyes and woods have ears SECRECY

Four eyes see more than two COOPERATION

Hawks will not pick out hawks' eyes COOPERATION

fable History is a fable HISTORY

face He who slaps his own face MISTAKES

Monday's child is fair of face BEAUTY

Turn your face to the sun OPTIMISM AND PESSIMISM

fact Fact is stranger than fiction TRUTH

facts Facts are stubborn things HYPOTHESIS AND FACT

Good ethics start with good facts MEDICINE

fail He who fails to plan, plans to fail SUCCESS AND FAILURE

To fail to prepare is to prepare to fail PREPARATION AND READINESS

fails He who fails to plan, plans to fail SUCCESS AND FAILURE

When all fruit fails, welcome haws NECESSITY

failure Success has many fathers, while failure SUCCESS AND FAILURE

faint Faint heart never won fair lady COURAGE

fair All's fair in love and war JUSTICE

Faint heart never won fair lady COURAGE

Fair exchange is no robbery JUSTICE

Fair play's a jewel JUSTICE

fair skin hides seven defects APPEARANCE

Give and take is fair play JUSTICE

Monday's child is fair of face BEAUTY

None but the brave deserve the fair COURAGE

Saint Swithin's day, if thou be fair SUMMER

Turn about is fair play JUSTICE

faith Faith will move mountains BELIEF

fake Fake it 'til you make it BEHAVIOUR

fall bigger they are, the harder they fall SUCCESS AND FAILURE

Even monkeys sometimes fall off a tree MISTAKES

fall into a ditch makes you wiser EXPERIENCE

Fall seven times, stand up eight DETERMINATION

Pride goes before a fall PRIDE

Spring forward, fall back TIME

fallen Do not laugh at the fallen SUCCESS AND FAILURE

falling Falling leaves have to return HOME

Never try to catch a falling knife BUSINESS

Keyword Index

falls apple never falls far from the tree FAMILY
As a tree falls, so shall it lie DEATH
Between two stools one falls INDECISION
Hasty climbers have sudden falls AMBITION
If the sky falls we shall catch larks EFFORT

falsehood To tell a falsehood is like the cut of LIES

fame Common fame is seldom to blame FAME

familiarity Familiarity breeds contempt FAMILIARITY

family Christmas with the family CHRISTMAS
family that prays together stays RELIGION
large family, quick help FAMILY

famine More die of food than famine HEALTH

far Delhi is far away CAUTION
Far-fetched and dear-bought WOMEN
God is high above, and the tsar GOVERNMENT
Thursday's child has far to go TRAVEL

fast Bad news travels fast NEWS AND JOURNALISM
He who travels fast, travels alone COOPERATION
moneyless man goes fast through POVERTY

fastest He travels the fastest who travels alone SOLITUDE

fat green Yule makes a fat churchyard CHRISTMAS
opera isn't over till the fat lady sings ENDING

Pigs get fat, but hogs get GREED

fatal Indecision is fatal INDECISION

fate Fate can be taken by the horns FATE

father child is the father of the man CHARACTER
father is a banker provided by nature PARENTS
Like father, like son FAMILY
Who teaches me for a day is my father TEACHING
wish is father to the thought OPINION

fathers Success has many fathers, while failure SUCCESS AND FAILURE

fault fault confessed is half redressed FORGIVENESS
Our memory is always at fault MIND

faults Wink at sma' fauts, ye hae great anes MISTAKES

favour Kissing goes by favour LOVE

fear Courage is fear that COURAGE
Do right and fear no man CONSCIENCE
Fear less, hope more; Eat less LIFESTYLES
Fear makes the wolf bigger FEAR
Fear the Greeks bearing gifts TRUST AND TREACHERY

feast After the feast, comes the reckoning CAUSES AND CONSEQUENCES
company makes the feast HOSPITALITY
Enough is as good as a feast MODERATION

420

feather Birds of a feather flock together SIMILARITY AND DIFFERENCE
Rooster today, feather duster tomorrow SUCCESS AND FAILURE

feathers Fine feathers make fine birds DRESS

feature It's not a bug, it's a feature COMPUTING

February February fill dyke, be it black or white WINTER

fed wolves are well fed and the sheep DANGER

feed Feed a cold and starve a fever SICKNESS
Feed a dog for three days CATS
Give a man fish, and you feed CHARITY

feeding Feeding a snake with milk CHARACTER

feeds Envy feeds on the living ENVY

feel Never mind the quality, feel the width QUANTITIES AND QUALITIES

feet cat always lands on its feet CATS
When you pray, move your feet RELIGION

fellow Stone-dead hath no fellow DEATH

female female of the species is more deadly WOMEN

fence fence between makes love more CAUSES AND CONSEQUENCES
Like a fence, character cannot CHARACTER

fencepost see a turtle on a fencepost CAUSES AND CONSEQUENCES

fences Good fences make good neighbours NEIGHBOURS

fern As one fern frond dies, another LEADERSHIP

fever Feed a cold and starve a fever SICKNESS
If envy were a fever ENVY

few Few have too much, and fewer too little WEALTH
You win a few, you lose a few SUCCESS AND FAILURE

fiction Fact is stranger than fiction TRUTH
History is fiction HISTORY
Truth is stranger than fiction TRUTH

fiddler They that dance must pay the fiddler POWER

field Life is harder than crossing a field LIFE

fields Fields have eyes and woods have ears SECRECY

fifth Please to remember the Fifth TRUST AND TREACHERY

fight Councils of war never fight INDECISION
Fight fire with fire WAYS AND MEANS
war will cease when men refuse to fight WARFARE
When elephants fight POWER

fighting While two dogs are fighting ARGUMENT

fights He who fights and runs away CAUTION

fill Work expands so as to fill the time WORK

find Safe bind, safe find CAUTION
Seek and ye shall find ACTION AND INACTION
Speak as you find REPUTATION
Those who hide can find SECRECY

finders Finders keepers (losers weepers) POSSESSIONS

421

Keyword Index

Seekers are finders
ACHIEVEMENT

findings Findings
keepings POSSESSIONS

fine Fine feathers make fine
birds DRESS

Fine words butter no
parsnips WORDS AND DEEDS

Rain before seven, fine before
eleven WEATHER

fingers Fingers were made before
forks EATING

Let your fingers do the
walking TECHNOLOGY

fire burnt child dreads the
fire EXPERIENCE

Dirty water will quench
fire SEX

Fight fire with fire WAYS AND
MEANS

Fire is a good servant, but a bad
master WAYS AND MEANS

fire is winter's fruit WINTER

Hire slow, fire
fast MANAGEMENT

If you play with fire you get
burnt DANGER

It is easy to kindle a
fire RELATIONSHIPS

No smoke without
fire REPUTATION

same fire that
hardens CHARACTER

fired No manager ever got
fired COMPUTING

first First catch your hare WAYS
AND MEANS

first day a guest, the second
day HOSPITALITY

First impressions are BEGINNING

First things first PATIENCE

First thoughts are
best INDECISION

Give me a child for the first
seven EDUCATION

If at first you don't
succeed DETERMINATION

In settling an island, the first
building ARC HITECTURE

It is the first step BEGINNING

No plan survives first
contact PREPARATION AND
READINESS

On the first of March, crows
begin SPRING

There is always a first
time BEGINNING

Women and children
first DANGER

fish All is fish that comes to
the net OPPORTUNITY

best fish swim near the
bottom DETERMINATION

Better are small fish than an
empty dish SATISFACTION AND
DISCONTENT

Big fish eat little fish POWER

big fish is caught with a big
bait PRACTICALITY

cat would eat fish INDECISION

Don't bargain for fish that are
still OPTIMISM AND PESSIMISM

fish always stinks from the
head LEADERSHIP

Fish and guests stink after three
days HOSPITALITY

Fish follow the
bait TEMPTATION

fish will soon be caught that
nibbles TEMPTATION

Fish, to taste good, must
swim COOKING

Give a man a fish, and you
feed CHARITY

Keep your own fish-
guts CHARITY

Little fish are sweet QUANTITIES AND QUALITIES

There are as good fish in the sea LOVE

Those who eat salty fish RESPONSIBILITY

fishing It is good fishing in troubled waters OPPORTUNITY

fist No fist is big enough to hide the sky GOVERNMENT

fit One size does not fit all WAYS AND MEANS

fits If the cap fits, wear it NAMES

If the shoe fits, wear it NAMES

fix If it ain't broke, don't fix it ACTION AND INACTION

flag Trade follows the flag BUSINESS

flagpole Let's run it up the flagpole ADVERTISING

flattery Flattery is soft soap PRAISE AND FLATTERY

Flattery, like perfume PRAISE AND FLATTERY

Imitation is the sincerest form of flattery PRAISE AND FLATTERY

fleas fleas, and princes ROYALTY

flee guilty flee when no man pursueth GUILT

flew bird never flew on one wing GENEROSITY

flies Eagles don't catch flies CHARACTER

Honey catches more flies than vinegar WAYS AND MEANS

shut mouth catches no flies SILENCE

Time flies TRANSIENCE

Time flies when you're having fun HAPPINESS

flight While heron is a bird of a single flight BIRDS

floats No matter how long a log floats CHANGE

son of a duck floats FAMILY

flock Birds of a feather flock together SIMILARITY AND DIFFERENCE

There is no good flock without DOGS

flow Do not push the river, it will flow FUTILITY

flowers All the flowers of tomorrow FLOWERS

April showers bring forth May flowers SPRING

No flowers by request MOURNING

Say it with flowers FLOWERS

flows Where water flows, a channel PATIENCE

fly Pigs may fly BELIEF

foe willing foe and sea room ARMED FORCES

fold Do not fold, spindle or COMPUTING

folk everyday story of country folk COUNTRY AND THE TOWN

There's nowt so queer as folk HUMAN RACE

folks Different strokes for different folks CHOICE

Young folks think old folks to be fools YOUTH

follow Do not follow where the path may lead INVENTIONS AND DISCOVERIES

Fish follow the bait TEMPTATION

follower good leader is also a good follower LEADERSHIP

follows He that follows freits FUTURE

Learning is a treasure that follows KNOWLEDGE

423

Keyword Index

fonder Absence makes the heart grow fonder ABSENCE

food day without work is a day without food IDLENESS
Food without hospitality is medicine HOSPITALITY
More die of food than famine HEALTH
with your food basket COOPERATION
Your food is your medicine HEALTH

fool fool and his money are soon parted FOOLS
fool at forty is a fool indeed AGE
fool may give a wise man ADVICE
Fool me once, shame on you DECEPTION
He that teaches himself has a fool for TEACHING
man who is his own lawyer has a fool LAW
There's no fool like an old fool AGE

foolish Penny wise and pound foolish THRIFT

fools Children and fools tell the truth HONESTY
Fools and bairns should never see WORK
Fools ask questions that wise men KNOWLEDGE
Fools build houses and wise men FOOLS
Fools for luck CHANCE AND LUCK
Fortune favours fools FOOLS
We're fools whether we dance or DANCE
Young folks think old folks to be fools YOUTH

foot Diseases come on horseback but go away on foot SICKNESS
It is dark at the foot of the lighthouse IGNORANCE
No foot, no horse HORSES
One white foot, buy him HORSES

footprints Take only photos, leave only footprints ENVIRONMENT

forbear Bear and forbear PATIENCE

forearmed Forewarned is forearmed PREPARATION AND READINESS

foresight If a man's foresight were as good FORESIGHT

forest If you are afraid of wolves, don't go into the forest STRENGTH AND WEAKNESS
Inside the forest there are many birds ABILITY
When a pine needle falls in the forest KNOWLEDGE
When the axe came into the forest OPTIMISM AND PESSIMISM

foretold Long foretold, long last WEATHER

forever diamond is forever WEALTH

forewarned Forewarned is forearmed PREPARATION AND READINESS

forget Good to forgive, best to forget FORGIVENESS
Tell me and I'll forget. Show me and TEACHING

forgets bellowing cow soon forgets her calf MOURNING
Nobody forgets a good teacher TEACHING
river that forgets its source GRATITUDE

424

Keyword Index

forgive Good to forgive, best to forget FORGIVENESS
To err is human (to forgive divine) MISTAKES
To know all is to forgive all FORGIVENESS

forgiving Forgiving the unrepentant FORGIVENESS

forks Fingers were made before forks EATING

Fortran If you can't do it in Fortran COMPUTING

fortune Fortune favours fools FOOLS
Fortune favours the brave COURAGE
great fortune depends on luck CHANCE AND LUCK
wise man turns chance into good fortune OPPORTUNITY

forty fool at forty is a fool indeed AGE
It takes forty dumb animals DRESS
Life begins at forty AGE

forward Spring forward, fall back TIME

fouls It's an ill bird that fouls its own nest LOYALTY

foundation Adversity is the foundation ADVERSITY

four Four eyes see more than two COOPERATION

fox fox may grow grey, but never AGE
fox should not be on the jury JUSTICE
quick brown fox jumps over the lazy dog WORDS
sleeping fox counts hens CHARACTER

free best things in life are free MONEY
only free cheese is in a mousetrap TEMPTATION
There's no such thing as a free lunch TEMPTATION
Thought is free OPINION

freedom passion for freedom never dies POLITICS

freits He that follows freits FUTURE

Friday Friday's child is loving and giving GENEROSITY

friend earth is man's only friend ENVIRONMENT
enemy of my enemy is my friend ENEMIES
friend in need is a friend indeed FRIENDSHIP
friend to all is a friend to none FRIENDSHIP
Hold a true friend with both your hands FRIENDSHIP
Lend your money, and lose your friend DEBT AND BORROWING
Life without a friend, is death FRIENDSHIP
road to a friend's house is never long FRIENDSHIP

friends Be kind to your friends FRIENDSHIP
best of friends must part MEETING AND PARTING
Even your closest friends won't HEALTH
Save us from our friends FRIENDSHIP
Short reckonings make long friends DEBT AND BORROWING
We have no friends but the mountains DANGER

friendship hedge between keeps friendship green NEIGHBOURS

Keyword Index

pot boils, friendship
lives HOSPITALITY
frog child of a frog is a
frog FAMILY
frog in a well knows
nothing of SELF-ESTEEM AND
SELF-ASSERTION
frond As one fern frond dies,
another LEADERSHIP
frost Clear moon, frost
soon WEATHER
frosts So many mists in March, so
many frosts SPRING
fruit fire is winter's fruit WINTER
He that would eat fruit EFFORT
September blow soft till the
fruit's AUTUMN
stolen fruit are
sweet TEMPTATION
tree is known by its
fruit CHARACTER
When all fruit fails, welcome
haws NECESSITY
frying Keep one eye on the
frying-pan COOKING
Fuji wise man will climb Mount
Fuji once TRAVEL
full Full cup, steady
hand CAUTION
It's ill speaking between a
full man FOOD
fullness Out of the fullness of
the heart FEELINGS
fun Time flies when you're
having fun HAPPINESS
funeral Dream of a
funeral DREAMS
One funeral makes
many DEATH
furrow old horse does not spoil
the furrow AGE
further Go further and fare worse
SATISFACTION AND DISCONTENT

fury Hell hath no fury like a
woman scorned WOMEN
furze When the furze is in
bloom LOVE
future man's best reputation for
his future REPUTATION
There's no future like the
present FUTURE
gain No pain, no gain EFFORT
Nothing venture, nothing
gain THOROUGHNESS
One man's loss is another
man's gain CIRCUMSTANCE
AND SITUATION
There's no great loss without
some gain CIRCUMSTANCE AND
SITUATION
game After the game, the king
and the pawn EQUALITY
Lookers-on see most of the
game ACTION AND INACTION
gamekeeper old poacher makes
the best gamekeeper WAYS
AND MEANS
garbage Garbage in, garbage
out COMPUTING
garden book is like a
garden BOOKS
garden is never
finished GARDENS
More things grow in the
garden GARDENS
Select a proper site for your
garden GARDENS
gardener It is not enough for a
gardener FLOWERS
garment Silence is a woman's best
garment WOMEN
gather Drops that gather one by
one QUANTITIES AND QUALITIES
gaze Only the eagle can gaze at
the sun STRENGTH AND
WEAKNESS

Keyword Index

generation One generation plants
the trees TREES
generations It takes three
generations to make RANK
generous Be just before you're
generous JUSTICE
It is easy to be generous
with GENEROSITY
genius Genius is an infinite
capacity ABILITY
gentleman You may know a
gentleman by RANK
geography War is God's way of
teaching Americans
geography WARFARE
get more you get the more
you want GREED
gift Life is the best gift LIFE
Never look a gift horse in the
mouth GRATITUDE
gifts Fear the Greeks bearing
gifts TRUST AND TREACHERY
gill Every herring must hang by
its own gill RESPONSIBILITY
ginger Every good quality is
contained in ginger HEALTH
Local ginger is not
hot FAMILIARITY
older the ginger, the more
pungent AGE
girdle good name is better than a
golden girdle REPUTATION
girl prettiest girl in the
world BEAUTY
girls All dancing girls are
nineteen YOUTH
give Give a man a fish, and you
feed CHARITY
Give and take is fair play JUSTICE
Give a thing, and take a
thing GENEROSITY
He gives twice who gives
quickly GENEROSITY

giving Friday's child is loving and
giving GENEROSITY
Glasgow Glasgow's miles
better BRITISH TOWNS
AND REGIONS
glass hammer shatters glass, but
forges steel WAYS AND MEANS
Those who live in glass
houses GOSSIP
glitters All that glitters is not
gold QUANTITIES AND QUALITIES
globally Think globally, act
locally ENVIRONMENT
gloria Sic transit gloria
mundi TRANSIENCE
glove Touch not the cat but a
glove CATS
gloves cat in gloves catches no
mice CAUTION
gnat Chess is a sea where a gnat
may drink SPORTS AND GAMES
Don't strain at a gnat, and
swallow BELIEF
go Go further and fare
worse SATISFACTION AND
DISCONTENT
Light come, light
go POSSESSIONS
Quickly come, quickly
go LOYALTY
goal paths are many, but the
goal is the same WAYS AND
MEANS
God All things are possible with
God GOD
Call on God, but row
away CAUTION
church is God between four
walls CHRISTIAN CHURCH
Every man for himself and God
for us all SELF-INTEREST
God helps them that help
themselves GOD

Keyword Index

God is high above, and the tsar   GOVERNMENT

God made the country   COUNTRY AND THE TOWN

God made the world, but the Dutch made Holland   COUNTRIES AND PEOPLES

God makes the back to the burden   SYMPATHY

God never sends mouths   FOOD

God sends meat, but the Devil   COOKING

God's in his heaven; all's right   OPTIMISM AND PESSIMISM

God sleeps in the stone, dreams   HUMAN RACE

God tempers the wind to the shorn lamb   SYMPATHY

God writes straight with crooked lines   GOD

Man proposes, God disposes   FATE

Man's extremity is God's opportunity   RELIGION

May God in his mercy look down   BRITISH TOWNS AND REGIONS

mills of God grind slowly   FATE

nature of God is a circle   GOD

nearer the church, the farther from God   CHRISTIAN CHURCH

Poverty comes from God   POVERTY

prayer to God, and service to the tsar   PREPARATION AND READINESS

Put your trust in God, and keep   PRACTICALITY

robin and the wren are God's   BIRDS

There's probably no God   GOD

voice of the people is the voice of God   POLITICS

War is God's way of teaching Americans geography   WARFARE

Where God builds a church   GOOD AND EVIL

You cannot serve God and Mammon   MONEY

Your soul may belong to God   ARMED FORCES

godliness Cleanliness is next to godliness   BEHAVIOUR

gods gods do not subtract   LEISURE

gods send nuts to those   AGE

Take the goods the gods provide   OPPORTUNITY

Whom the gods love die young   YOUTH

Whom the gods would destroy   MIND

goes As Maine goes, so goes the nation   POLITICS

Steady as she goes   CAUTION

What goes around comes around   JUSTICE

going If you don't know where you are going   TRAVEL

When the going gets tough   CHARACTER

gold All that glitters is not gold   QUANTITIES AND QUALITIES

Gold may be bought too dear   VALUE

If gold rusts, what will iron do   CORRUPTION

inch of gold cannot buy time   TIME

It is good to make a bridge of gold   WAYS AND MEANS

golden golden key can open any door   CORRUPTION
golden rule of life is   BEGINNING
good name is better than a golden girdle   REPUTATION
Speech is silver, but silence is golden   SILENCE

good All good things must come to an end   ENDING
Any publicity is good   ADVERTISING
Bad money drives out good   MONEY
Better a good cow   CHARACTER
change is as good as a rest   CHANGE
confession is good for the soul   HONESTY
End good, all good   ENDING
Every good quality is contained in ginger   HEALTH
good beginning makes a good   BEGINNING
Good behaviour is the last   BEHAVIOUR
good die young   VIRTUE
Good ethics start with good facts   MEDICINE
Good fences make good neighbours   NEIGHBOURS
good horse cannot be of a bad colour   APPEARANCE
good leader is also a good follower   LEADERSHIP
Good medicine always has a bitter taste   MEDICINE
Good men are scarce   VIRTUE
good name is better than a golden girdle   REPUTATION
good reputation stands still   REPUTATION
good seaman is known in bad weather   SEA

Good seed makes a bad crop   CAUSES AND CONSEQUENCES
Good soup is made in an old pot   EXPERIENCE
good time was had by all   HAPPINESS
Good to forgive, best to forget   FORGIVENESS
Good wine needs no bush   ADVERTISING
Guinness is good for you   DRINK
He is a good dog who goes to church   BEHAVIOUR
Hope is a good breakfast   HOPE
If something sounds too good to be true   EXCELLENCE
If you can't be good, be careful   CAUTION
It is good fishing in troubled waters   OPPORTUNITY
It's good to talk   SPEECH
liar ought to have a good memory   LIES
Never bid the Devil good morrow   PROBLEMS AND SOLUTIONS
Never do evil that good may come   BEHAVIOUR
No good deed goes unpunished   VIRTUE
No news is good news   NEWS AND JOURNALISM
One good turn deserves another   COOPERATION
One who sees something good   NEWS AND JOURNALISM
secret is either too good to keep   SECRECY
test of good manners is   MANNERS

Keyword Index

There are as good fish
in the sea LOVE
There is no good flock
without DOGS
There is nothing so good for the
inside HORSES
You can have too much of a
good thing EXCESS
goods Ill gotten goods never
thrive CRIME AND PUNISHMENT
Take the goods the gods
provide OPPORTUNITY
goose Christmas is coming, and
the goose CHRISTMAS
What's sauce for the
goose JUSTICE
gorse When the gorse is out of
bloom LOVE
gossip Gossip is the lifeblood of
society GOSSIP
Gossip is vice GOSSIP
gossips Whoever gossips to
you GOSSIP
grain There is no proverb without
a grain SAYINGS
granaries All autumns do not fill
granaries AUTUMN
grandmother Don't teach your
grandmother ADVICE
grass grass is always
greener ENVY
When elephants fight, it is the
grass POWER
While the grass grows, the
steed ACHIEVEMENT
gratitude Don't overload
gratitude GRATITUDE
graves If you want revenge, dig
two graves REVENGE
Gray Gray's Inn for
walks LAW
great Death is the great
leveller DEATH

great book is a great
evil BOOKS
Great minds think
alike THINKING
Great oaks from little
acorns CAUSES AND
CONSEQUENCES
soldier of the Great War, known
unto ARMED FORCES
Wink at sma' fauts, ye hae great
anes MISTAKES
greater greater the sinner,
the greater the saint GOOD
AND EVIL
greater the truth, the greater
the libel GOSSIP
greatness If any man seek for
greatness FAME
greed Need makes greed GREED
Greek When Greek meets
Greek SIMILARITY AND
DIFFERENCE
Greeks Fear the Greeks bearing
gifts TRUST AND TREACHERY
green Blue and green should
never be DRESS
Green Christmas, white
Easter WEATHER
green Yule makes a fat
churchyard CHRISTMAS
hedge between keeps friendship
green NEIGHBOURS
If I keep a green bough in my
heart HAPPINESS
roots of charity are always
green CHARITY
You have to be in the black to
be in the green ENVIRONMENT
greener grass is always
greener ENVY
grey All cats are grey in the
dark SIMILARITY AND
DIFFERENCE

430

fox may grow grey   AGE
grey mare is the better
horse   MARRIAGE
grief Grief is the price we pay for
love   MOURNING
He that conceals his
grief   SORROW
grieve Do not grieve that rose
trees have thorns   SATISFACTION
AND DISCONTENT
grind mill cannot grind with the
water that   OPPORTUNITY
mills of God grind slowly fate
grist All is grist that comes to the
mill   OPPORTUNITY
Groucho I am a Marxist—of the
Groucho   POLITICS
grow Ill weeds grow
apace   GOOD AND EVIL
More things grow in the
garden   GARDENS
guessing Punctuality is the art of
guessing   PUNCTUALITY
guest first day a guest, the second
day   HOSPITALITY
guest is like the morning
dew   HOSPITALITY
Treat your guest as a guest for
two days   HOSPITALITY
guests Fish and guests stink after
three days   HOSPITALITY
guide Let your conscience be
your guide   CONSCIENCE
guilty guilty conscience needs no
accuser   CONSCIENCE
guilty flee when no man
pursueth   GUILT
guilty one always runs   GUILT
Not guilty, but don't do it
again   GUILT
We are all guilty   GUILT
We name the guilty
men   GUILT

Guinness Guinness is good for
you   DRINK
gun Have gun, will travel   TRAVEL
gunner cobbler to his last and the
gunner   KNOWLEDGE
guns Guns don't kill
people   MURDER
guy No more Mr Nice
Guy   CHANGE
guys Nice guys finish
last   SPORTS AND GAMES
habit Custom is mummified by
habit   CUSTOM AND HABIT
habits Habits are cobwebs at
first   CUSTOM AND HABIT
Old habits die hard   CUSTOM
AND HABIT
had What you've never
had   SATISFACTION AND
DISCONTENT
You cannot lose what you never
had   POSSESSIONS
hair Beauty draws with a single
hair   BEAUTY
half Do not meet troubles half
way   WORRY
Half a loaf is better than no
bread   SATISFACTION AND
DISCONTENT
half is better than the
whole   MODERATION
Half the truth is often a whole
lie   LIES
One half of the world does not
know   KNOWLEDGE
Two boys are half a boy   WORK
Well begun is half
done   BEGINNING
Halifax From Hell, Hull, and
Halifax   BRITISH TOWNS AND
REGIONS
hall It is merry in hall when
beards wag all   HOSPITALITY

431

Keyword Index

halloo Don't halloo till you are
out of the wood OPTIMISM AND
PESSIMISM

halved trouble shared is a trouble
halved COOPERATION

Hamlet Happiness is a cigar
called Hamlet SMOKING

hammer hammer shatters
glass, but forges steel WAYS
AND MEANS
When all you have is a hammer
PROBLEMS AND SOLUTIONS

hand bird in the hand is
worth two CAUTION
Full cup, steady hand CAUTION
hand that rocks the cradle
rules WOMEN
hand will not reach what the
heart ACHIEVEMENT
He who takes the child by the
hand PARENTS
One hand for oneself and one
for the ship SEA
One hand washes the
other COOPERATION
quickness of the hand deceives
the eye DECEPTION

handle Each of us at a
handle COOPERATION

hands Cold hands, warm
heart BODY
devil finds work for idle
hands IDLENESS
Hold a true friend with both
your hands FRIENDSHIP
Many hands make light
work COOPERATION
no hands but yours
CHRISTIAN CHURCH
Nothing is stolen without
hands HONESTY

handsome Handsome is as
handsome BEHAVIOUR

hang Every herring must hang by
its own gill RESPONSIBILITY
Give a dog a bad name and
hang GOSSIP
Hang a thief when he's
young CRIME AND PUNISHMENT

hanged Confess and be
hanged GUILT
If you're born to be hanged FATE
Little thieves are
hanged CRIME AND PUNISHMENT
One might as well be hanged
for a sheep THOROUGHNESS

hanging Catching's before
hanging WAYS AND MEANS
Hanging and wiving go by
destiny FATE

hangs creaking door hangs
longest SICKNESS

happens unexpected always
happens SURPRISE

happily all lived happily
ever after ENDING

happiness Happiness is a cigar
called Hamlet SMOKING
Happiness is the only
thing HAPPINESS
Happiness is what you
make HAPPINESS
Money can't buy
happiness MONEY

happy Be happy while y'er
leevin LIFE
Call no man happy till he
dies HAPPINESS
Happy is the bride the sun
shines on WEDDINGS
Happy is the country HISTORY
If you would be happy for a
week GARDENS
peacock is always happy
because SELF-ESTEEM AND
SELF-ASSERTION

hard Hard cases make bad
law LAW
Hard words break no
bones WORDS

harder bigger they are, the harder
they fall SUCCESS AND FAILURE
harder I work, the
luckier CHANCE AND LUCK
Life is harder than crossing a
field LIFE
We're number two. We try
harder EFFORT

hardship After hardship comes
relief ADVERSITY

hare First catch your hare WAYS
AND MEANS
You cannot run with
the hare TRUST AND
TREACHERY

hares If you run after two
hares INDECISION

haste Haste is from the
Devil HASTE AND DELAY
Haste makes waste HASTE
AND DELAY
Make haste slowly HASTE AND
DELAY
Marry in haste and repent at
leisure MARRIAGE
More haste, less speed HASTE
AND DELAY
Nothing should be done in
haste PATIENCE

hat bigger the hat SELF-ESTEEM
AND SELF-ASSERTION

hated Poverty is a blessing hated
by all POVERTY

have Nothing venture, nothing
have THOROUGHNESS
What you have, hold
POSSESSIONS
What you spend, you
have POSSESSIONS

You cannot have your
cake ACHIEVEMENT

hawks Clever hawks conceal
their claws SELF-ESTEEM AND
SELF-ASSERTION
Hawks will not pick out hawks'
eyes COOPERATION

haws When all fruit fails,
welcome haws NECESSITY

hay Make hay while the sun
shines OPPORTUNITY
swarm in May is worth a load
of hay SUMMER

head Better be the head
of a dog POWER
fish always stinks from the
head LEADERSHIP
Strike the serpent's
head ENEMIES
Where Macgregor sits is the
head RANK
You cannot put an old
head EXPERIENCE

heads Assistant heads must
roll BROADCASTING
Heads I win, tails you
lose WINNING AND LOSING
Two heads are better than
one THINKING

heal Stabs heal, but bad
words never WORDS
AND DEEDS

healer Time is a great
healer TIME

health beginning of health is
sleep SLEEP
From the bitterness of disease,
man learns the sweetness of
health SICKNESS
He who has health has
hope HEALTH

hear Believe nothing of what you
hear BELIEF

Keyword Index

Hear all, see all, say nowt
SELF-INTEREST
Listeners never hear
good SECRECY
See no evil, hear no evil, speak
no evil VIRTUE
heart Absence makes the heart
grow fonder ABSENCE
Cold hands, warm heart BODY
Envy eats nothing but its own
heart ENVY
Faint heart never won fair
lady COURAGE
hand will not reach what the
heart ACHIEVEMENT
Home is where the heart
is HOME
Hope deferred makes the heart
sick HOPE
If it were not for hope,
the heart HOPE
It is a poor heart that never
rejoices HAPPINESS
larger the body, the bigger the
heart BODY
Out of the fullness of the
heart FEELINGS
Put a stout heart to a stey
brae DETERMINATION
way to a man's heart is
through MEN
What the eye doesn't see, the
heart IGNORANCE
Writing is a picture of the
writer's heart WRITING
heat If you don't like the heat,
get out STRENGTH AND
WEAKNESS
heated only thing a heated
argument ever ARGUMENT
heaven Crosses are ladders that
lead to heaven SUFFERING
From Madrid to

heaven TOWNS AND CITIES
God's in his heaven; all's
right OPTIMISM AND PESSIMISM
Heaven protects children,
sailors DANGER
Hell is where heaven is
not HAPPINESS
If you want to see
heaven CAUSES AND
CONSEQUENCES
Marriages are made in
heaven MARRIAGE
mind enlightened is like
heaven MIND
wind of heaven is that which
blows between a horse's
ears HORSES
heaviest heaviest baggage for the
traveller TRAVEL
hedge hedge between keeps
friendship green NEIGHBOURS
Heineken Heineken refreshes the
parts DRINK
heir Winter is summer's
heir WINTER
hell From Hell, Hull, and Halifax
BRITISH TOWNS AND REGIONS
Hell hath no fury like a woman
scorned WOMEN
Hell is where heaven is
not HAPPINESS
road to hell is paved
with ACTION AND INACTION
help Do not call a wolf to help
you ENEMIES
God helps them that help
themselves GOD
Help you to salt, help you to
sorrow MISFORTUNES
large family, quick help FAMILY
mouse may help a lion POWER
helps Every little
helps COOPERATION

434

Keyword Index

God helps them that help themselves GOD

hen Better an egg today than a hen tomorrow PRESENT
whistling woman and a crowing hen WOMEN

hens sleeping fox counts hens CHARACTER

herbs Better a dinner of herbs FEELINGS

here Here be dragons INVENTIONS AND DISCOVERIES
Here's tae us; wha's like us SELF-ESTEEM AND SELF-ASSERTION

heresy Turkeys, heresy, hops, and beer INVENTIONS AND DISCOVERIES

hero No man is a hero to his valet FAMILIARITY

heron white heron is a bird of BIRDS

herring Every herring must hang by its own gill RESPONSIBILITY

hesitates He who hesitates is lost INDECISION

hide No fist is big enough to hide the sky GOVERNMENT
Those who hide can find SECRECY
You can't hide an awl in a sack SECRECY

high God is high above, and the tsar GOVERNMENT
mountains are high, and the emperor GOVERNMENT

higher higher the monkey climbs AMBITION

hills Blue are the hills that are far FAMILIARITY

himself Every man for himself and God for us all SELF-INTEREST

Every man for himself, and the Devil SELF-INTEREST

hire Hire slow, fire fast MANAGEMENT
labourer is worthy of his hire WORK

history History is a fable HISTORY
History is fiction HISTORY
History is written by the victors HISTORY
History repeats itself HISTORY
Make poverty history POVERTY
What's hit is history KNOWLEDGE

hit What's hit is history KNOWLEDGE

hog Every hog has his Martinmas FATE
Root, hog, or die WORK

hogs Pigs get fat, but hogs get GREED

hold Hold a true friend with both your hands FRIENDSHIP
What you have, hold POSSESSIONS

Holdfast Brag is a good dog, but Holdfast WORDS AND DEEDS

hole When you are in a hole, stop digging APOLOGY AND EXCUSES

Holland God made the world, but the Dutch made Holland COUNTRIES AND PEOPLES

home Charity begins at home CHARITY
East, west, home's best HOME
Englishman's home is his castle HOME
Go abroad and you'll hear news of home TRAVEL
Home is home HOME

435

Keyword Index

Home is home, as the Devil said   LAW

Home is where the heart is   HOME

Home is where the mortgage is   HOME

There's no place like home   HOME

Who goes home?   POLITICS

woman's place is in the home   WOMEN

Homer Homer sometimes nods   MISTAKES

honestly Get the money honestly if you can   MONEY

Sell honestly, but not honesty   HONESTY

honesty Honesty is more praised than practiced   HONESTY

Honesty is the best policy   HONESTY

Sell honestly, but not honesty   HONESTY

honey bee sucks honey where the spider   CHARACTER

Honey catches more flies than vinegar   WAYS AND MEANS

One day honey, one day onions   CIRCUMSTANCE AND SITUATION

Where bees are, there is honey   WORK

honi Honi soit qui mal y pense   GOOD AND EVIL

honour post of honour is the post of danger   DANGER

prophet is not without honour   FAMILIARITY

There is honour among thieves   COOPERATION

hope Fear less, hope more; Eat less   LIFESTYLES

He that lives in hope dances to

an ill tune   HOPE

He who has health has hope   HEALTH

Hope deferred makes the heart sick   HOPE

Hope for the best and prepare for   PREPARATION AND READINESS

Hope is a good breakfast   HOPE

Hope is the pillar of the world   HOPE

Hope springs eternal   HOPE

If it were not for hope, the heart   HOPE

In the kingdom of hope   HOPE

To plant a tree is to plant hope   TREES

While there's life there's hope   HOPE

hopefully It is better to travel hopefully   HOPE

hopes smaller the lizard, the greater its hopes   AMBITION

hops Turkeys, heresy, hops, and beer   INVENTIONS AND DISCOVERIES

horn Blow your own horn, even if   ADVERTISING

horns Fate can be taken by the horns   FATE

horse Don't put the cart before the horse   PATIENCE

good horse cannot be of a bad colour   APPEARANCE

grey mare is the better horse   MARRIAGE

If two ride on a horse   RANK

If you have a horse of your own   DEBT AND BORROWING

Never look a gift horse in the mouth   GRATITUDE

No foot, no horse   HORSES

old horse does not spoil the furrow   AGE

One may steal a
horse   REPUTATION
short horse is soon
curried   WORK
swiftest horse cannot overtake
the word   WORDS
wind of heaven is that which
blows between a horse's
ears   HORSES
You can take a horse to the
water   DEFIANCE
horseback Diseases come on
horseback but go away on
foot   SICKNESS
Set a beggar on
horseback   POWER
horses Horses for
courses   ABILITY
If wishes were horses,
beggars   OPTIMISM AND
PESSIMISM
hospitality Food without
hospitality is
medicine   HOSPITALITY
Hospitality and medicine must
be   HOSPITALITY
hot Hot water does not burn
down   FUTILITY
little pot is soon hot   ANGER
Local ginger is not
hot   FAMILIARITY
Strike while the iron is
hot   OPPORTUNITY
hour darkest hour is just before
dawn   OPTIMISM AND PESSIMISM
One hour's sleep before
midnight   SLEEP
hours Six hours' sleep for a
man   SLEEP
Some sleep five hours; nature
requires   SLEEP
house Better one house spoiled
than two   MARRIAGE

dog is a lion in his own
house   DOGS
Learning is better than house
and land   KNOWLEDGE
When house and land are
gone   KNOWLEDGE
houses Fools build houses and
wise men   FOOLS
howling howlin' coyote ain't
stealin' no chickens   HONESTY
Hubert Praise from Sir
Hubert   PRAISE AND FLATTERY
huddle When the stars begin to
huddle, the earth will soon
become a puddle   WEATHER
Hull From Hell, Hull, and Halifax
BRITISH TOWNS AND REGIONS
human To err is human but to
really   COMPUTING
To err is human (to forgive
divine)   MISTAKES
hundred buyer has need of a
hundred eyes   BUYING AND
SELLING
When angry count a
hundred   ANGER
hundredth Only the camel knows
the hundredth   NAMES
hunger Hunger drives the
wolf out of the wood   NECESSITY
Hunger is the best
sauce   EATING
Winter thunder, summer
hunger   WEATHER
hungry hungry man is an angry
man   FOOD
satisfied person does not know
the hungry   SELF-INTEREST
hurry Always in a hurry, always
behind   HASTE AND DELAY
Don't hurry—start
early   HASTE AND DELAY
Hurry no man's cattle   PATIENCE

Keyword Index

hurt Don't cry before you're
hurt   COURAGE
What you don't know can't hurt
you   IGNORANCE

husband husband is always the
last to know   IGNORANCE
I married my husband for
life   MEN

hyphens If you take hyphens
seriously   WORDS

I I before e, except after c   WORDS

ice rich man gets his ice in
summer   WEALTH

ideas All words are pegs to hang
ideas on   WORDS

idle Better be idle than ill
doing   IDLENESS
devil finds work for idle
hands   IDLENESS
idle brain is the devil's
workshop   IDLENESS
Idle people have the least
leisure   IDLENESS

idleness Idleness is the root of all
evil   IDLENESS

ifs If ifs and ans were pots and
pans   OPTIMISM AND PESSIMISM

ignorance Ignorance is
bliss   IGNORANCE
Ignorance is voluntary
misfortune   IGNORANCE
Ignorance of the law is no
excuse   LAW

ignorant Science has no enemy
but the ignorant   SCIENCE

ill Better be idle than ill
doing   IDLENESS
Doing nothing is ill   IDLENESS
He that has an ill
name   REPUTATION
He that lives in hope dances to
an ill tune   HOPE
Ill gotten goods never

thrive   CRIME AND PUNISHMENT
Ill weeds grow apace   GOOD
AND EVIL
It's an ill bird that fouls its own
nest   LOYALTY
It's an ill wind that blows
nobody   OPTIMISM AND
PESSIMISM
It's ill speaking between a full
man   FOOD
It's ill waiting for dead men's
shoes   AMBITION
Never speak ill of the
dead   REPUTATION

imaginary imaginary ailment is
worse than a disease   SICKNESS

imitation Imitation is the
sincerest form of
flattery   PRAISE AND FLATTERY

important What is the most
important thing   HUMAN RACE

impressions First impressions
are   BEGINNING

impune Nemo me impune
lacessit   DEFIANCE

inch inch ahead is darkness
FUTURE
inch of gold cannot buy
time   TIME

indecision Indecision is
fatal   INDECISION

indeed friend in need is a friend
indeed   FRIENDSHIP

industry Necessity sharpens
industry   NECESSITY
Science finds, industry
applies   TECHNOLOGY

infinite Genius is an infinite
capacity   ABILITY

infirmities Dreams retain the
infirmities of   DREAMS

inform inform, educate, and
entertain   BROADCASTING

inherit We do not inherit the earth   ENVIRONMENT

injury Don't add insult to injury   WORDS AND DEEDS

ink ink of a scholar is holier than   EDUCATION

inn Gray's Inn for walks   LAW

inquisition Nobody expects the Spanish Inquisition   SURPRISE

inside There is nothing so good for the inside   HORSES

insult Don't add insult to injury   WORDS AND DEEDS

interest Worry is interest paid on trouble   WORRY

interesting May you live in interesting times   CIRCUMSTANCE AND SITUATION

introduces Adversity introduces a man   ADVERSITY

invention Necessity is the mother of invention   NECESSITY

invited Business goes where it is invited   BUSINESS

Ireland England's difficulty is Ireland's   COUNTRIES AND PEOPLES

iron If gold rusts, what will iron do   CORRUPTION
If you had teeth of steel, you could eat iron coconuts   OPTIMISM AND PESSIMISM
Iron sharpens iron   CHARACTER
Strike while the iron is hot   OPPORTUNITY

Isfahan Isfahan is half the world   TOWNS AND CITIES

island No man is an island   SOLITUDE

Jack All work and no play makes Jack   LEISURE
Every Jack has his Jill   MEN AND WOMEN
good Jack makes a good Jill   MEN AND WOMEN
Jack is as good as his master   EQUALITY
Jack of all trades and master of none   EMPLOYMENT

jade Everything has a price, but jade is   VALUE

jam Jam tomorrow and jam yesterday   PRESENT

January warm January, a cold May   WEATHER

Jerusalem Next year in Jerusalem   TOWNS AND CITIES

jest Many a true word is spoken in jest   TRUTH

jewel Fair play's a jewel   JUSTICE

Jews Where there are two Jews, there are three opinions   OPINION

Jill Every Jack has his Jill   MEN AND WOMEN
good Jack makes a good Jill   MEN AND WOMEN

jingle single bracelet does not jingle   COOPERATION

job Dress for the job you want   DRESS
Never send a boy to do a man's job   YOUTH

join If you can't beat them, join them   WAYS AND MEANS

journey Is your journey really necessary   TRAVEL
longest journey begins with a single   BEGINNING
Send the beloved child on a journey   PARENTS

Jove Jove but laughs at lovers' perjury   LOVE

Keyword Index

joy Shared joy is double
  joy   SYMPATHY
  Strength through
  joy   STRENGTH AND WEAKNESS
judge Do not judge a tree by its
  bark   APPEARANCE
  Don't judge a man
  until   CRITICISM
  Judge not, that ye be not judged
  PREJUDICE AND TOLERANCE
  No one should be judge in his
  own   LAW
judged Judge not, that ye be not
  judged   PREJUDICE AND
  TOLERANCE
June dripping June sets all in
  tune   SUMMER
jury fox should not be on the
  jury   JUSTICE
just Be just before you're
  generous   JUSTICE
  Just say no   DETERMINATION
  Just when you thought it was
  safe   DANGER
justice Justice delayed is justice
  denied   JUSTICE
  We all love justice   JUSTICE
justifies end justifies the
  means   WAYS AND MEANS
keep It is one thing to keep your
  morals   BEHAVIOUR
  Keep a thing seven
  years   POSSESSIONS
  Keep calm and carry on   CRISES
  Keep one eye on the
  frying-pan   COOKING
  Keep your own shop   BUSINESS
  secret is either too good to
  keep   SECRECY
  Three may keep a
  secret   SECRECY
Kent Some places of Kent
  BRITISH TOWNS AND REGIONS

Kentish Essex stiles, Kentish miles
  BRITISH TOWNS AND REGIONS
key golden key can open any
  door   CORRUPTION
keys April and May are keys to
  the whole year   SPRING
kill Guns don't kill
  people   MURDER
  Kill the chicken to
  scare   CAUSES AND
  CONSEQUENCES
  What does not kill you makes
  you   STRENGTH AND WEAKNESS
killed Care killed the cat   WORRY
killing Killing no
  murder   MURDER
  There are more ways of killing a
  cat   WAYS AND MEANS
  There are more ways of killing a
  dog   WAYS AND MEANS
kills It is not work that kills, but
  worry   WORRY
  It is the pace that
  kills   STRENGTH AND WEAKNESS
kind Be kind. Everyone you meet
  is fighting a hard
  battle   GENEROSITY
  Be kind to your
  friends   FRIENDSHIP
  One kind word warms three
  winter   SYMPATHY
kindle It is easy to kindle a
  fire   RELATIONSHIPS
kindness By a sweet tongue and
  kindness   BEHAVIOUR
king After the game, the king and
  the pawn   EQUALITY
  Breakfast like a king, lunch
  like   EATING
  Cash is king   MONEY
  king can do no wrong   ROYALTY
  king's chaff is worth
  more   ROYALTY

440

may look at a king CATS

peck of March dust is worth a king's SPRING

Your King and Country need you ARMED FORCES

kingdom In the kingdom of hope HOPE

kings Kings have long arms POWER

kirtle Near is my kirtle, but nearer my smock SELF-INTEREST

Kirton Kirton was a borough town BRITISH TOWNS AND REGIONS

kisses There is always one who kisses RELATIONSHIPS

kissing Kissing goes by favour LOVE

kittens Wanton kittens make sober cats YOUTH

knife never try to catch a falling knife BUSINESS

Tongue is like a sharp knife WORDS AND DEEDS

knocked You could have knocked me down SURPRISE

knocks Opportunity never knocks for OPPORTUNITY

Opportunity never knocks twice OPPORTUNITY

know Better the devil you know FAMILIARITY

Come live with me and you'll know FAMILIARITY

husband is always the last to know IGNORANCE

If you do not know where CIRCUMSTANCE AND SITUATION

If you don't know where you are going TRAVEL

It's not what you know CORRUPTION

It's not what you know OPPORTUNITY

last one to know about the sea IGNORANCE

less you know, the better you sleep IGNORANCE

One half of the world does not know KNOWLEDGE

satisfied person does not know the hungry SELF-INTEREST

To know all is to forgive all FORGIVENESS

To know the road ahead, ask those coming back FORESIGHT

What you don't know can't hurt you IGNORANCE

You never know what you can do COURAGE

You should know a man seven years NEIGHBOURS

knowledge Knowledge and timber KNOWLEDGE

Knowledge is power KNOWLEDGE

larger the shoreline of knowledge KNOWLEDGE

little knowledge is a dangerous thing KNOWLEDGE

known man is known by the company he FAMILIARITY

soldier of the Great War, known unto ARMED FORCES

knows frog in a well knows nothing of SELF-ESTEEM AND SELF-ASSERTION

Necessity knows no law NECESSITY

Only the camel knows the hundredth NAMES

Who knows most, speaks least SPEECH

Keyword Index

kumara kumara does not speak
of its own SELF-ESTEEM AND
SELF-ASSERTION
laborare Laborare est
orare RELIGION
labourer labourer is worthy of his
hire WORK
ladders Crosses are
ladders that lead to
heaven SUFFERING
lady Faint heart never won fair
lady COURAGE
opera isn't over till the fat lady
sings ENDING
lamb bleating of the lamb excites
the tiger TEMPTATION
God tempers the wind to the
shorn lamb SYMPATHY
land Every land has its own
law COUNTRIES AND PEOPLES
Learning is better than house
and land KNOWLEDGE
When house and land are
gone KNOWLEDGE
You buy land, you buy
stones BUYING AND SELLING
lands cat always lands on its
feet CATS
lane It is a long lane that has no
turning PATIENCE
lang Lang may yer lum
reek HOME
language nation without a
language is COUNTRIES AND
PEOPLES
large large family, quick
help FAMILY
Little pitchers have large
ears SECRECY
larger larger the body, the bigger
the heart BODY
larger the shoreline of
knowledge KNOWLEDGE

larks If the sky falls we shall catch
larks EFFORT
last cobbler to his last and the
gunner KNOWLEDGE
He laughs last, laughs
longest REVENGE
husband is always the last to
know IGNORANCE
It is the last straw EXCESS
last drop makes the cup run
over EXCESS
last one to know about the
sea IGNORANCE
Let the cobbler stick to his
last KNOWLEDGE
Nice guys finish last SPORTS
AND GAMES
When the last tree is
cut ENVIRONMENT
late Better late than
never PUNCTUALITY
early man never borrows from
the late PREPARATION AND
READINESS
It is never too late to
learn EDUCATION
It is never too late to
mend CHANGE
It's too late to shut the
stable door FORESIGHT
laugh Do not laugh at the
fallen SUCCESS AND FAILURE
Laugh and the world laughs
with you SYMPATHY
Let them laugh that
win SUCCESS
AND FAILURE
laughs earth laughs at him
who ENVIRONMENT
He who laughs last, laughs
longest REVENGE
Jove but laughs at lovers'
perjury LOVE

442

Laugh and the world laughs
with you   SYMPATHY
Love laughs at
locksmiths   LOVE
laughter Laughter is the best
medicine   MEDICINE
law Every land has its own
law   COUNTRIES AND PEOPLES
Hard cases make bad law   LAW
Ignorance of the law is no
excuse   LAW
Necessity knows no
law   NECESSITY
One law for the rich   JUSTICE
Possession is nine points of the
law   LAW
Self-preservation is the first law
of nature   SELF-INTEREST
Where the law is uncertain,
there is no law   LAW
laws Laws of
Thermodynamics   SCIENCE
more laws, the more thieves
and bandits   LAW
New lords, new laws   CHANGE
lawyer man who is his own
lawyer has a fool   LAW
lazy Long and lazy, little and
loud   WOMEN
quick brown fox jumps over
the lazy dog   WORDS
lead He who would lead must
be a bridge   LEADERSHIP
If the people will
lead   LEADERSHIP
If you are not the lead
dog   LEADERSHIP
leader good leader is also a good
follower   LEADERSHIP
leads man who reads is the man
who leads   READING
leap Look before you
leap   CAUTION

learn It is never too late to
learn   EDUCATION
Live and learn   EXPERIENCE
Never too old to
learn   EDUCATION
We must learn to walk
before   PATIENCE
learned Nobody is born
learned   CLERGY
learning Learning is a treasure
that follows   KNOWLEDGE
Learning is better than house
and land .   KNOWLEDGE
sea of learning has no
end   KNOWLEDGE
There is no royal road to
learning   EDUCATION
Travelling is learning   TRAVEL
leather There is nothing like
leather   WAYS AND MEANS
leave Always leave the party
when   HOSPITALITY
leaves Falling leaves have to
return   HOME
He who leaves
succeeds   SUCCESS AND FAILURE
led army of stags led by a
lion   ARMED FORCES
leeks Eat leeks in March and
ramsons in May   HEALTH
legs Do not add legs to the
snake   EXCESS
leisure busiest men have the most
leisure   LEISURE
Idle people have the least
leisure   IDLENESS
Marry in haste and repent at
leisure   MARRIAGE
There is luck in
leisure   PATIENCE
lemon answer is a
lemon   SATISFACTION AND
DISCONTENT

443

Keyword Index

lemons If life hands you
lemons   ADVERSITY

lend Lend your money, and lose
your friend   DEBT AND
BORROWING

lender Neither a borrower, nor a
lender be   DEBT AND
BORROWING

length Length begets
loathing   SPEECH

lengthening Travelling is one way
of lengthening life   TRAVEL

lengthens As the day lengthens,
so the cold   WEATHER

leopard leopard does not change
his spots   CHANGE

less Fear less, hope more; Eat
less   LIFESTYLES
Less is more   MODERATION
less you know, the better you
sleep   IGNORANCE
Of two evils choose the
less   CHOICE

let Let sleeping dogs lie   CAUTION
Let well alone   CAUTION
Let your conscience be your
guide   CONSCIENCE
Live and let live   PREJUDICE AND
TOLERANCE

letter Beauty is a good
letter   BEAUTY
Change the name and not the
letter   MARRIAGE
Do not close a letter without
reading it   LETTERS
love letter sometimes costs
more   LETTERS
Someone, somewhere, wants a
letter   LETTERS

leveller Death is the great
leveller   DEATH

liar liar ought to have a good
memory   LIES

liar's candle lasts till
evening   LIES

libel greater the truth, the greater
the libel   GOSSIP

liberal conservative is a liberal
who's   CRIME AND PUNISHMENT

*liberté Liberté! Égalité!
Fraternité!*   POLITICS

library library is a repository of
medicine   BOOKS

lick It is a poor cook that cannot
lick   COOKING

lie As a tree falls, so shall it
lie   DEATH
Deceit is a lie   DECEPTION
Half the truth is often a whole
lie   LIES
If you lie down with
dogs   FAMILIARITY
lie can go around the
world   LIES
One seldom meets a lonely
lie   LIES

lies camera never
lies   TECHNOLOGY

life Art is long and life is
short   LIFE
best things in life are
free   MONEY
dog is for life, not just for
Christmas   DOGS
golden rule of life is   BEGINNING
If life hands you
lemons   ADVERSITY
I married my husband for
life   MEN
Life begins at forty   AGE
Life begins on the day you
start   GARDENS
Life is a sexually transmitted
disease   LIFE
Life is harder than crossing a
field   LIFE

Life isn't all beer and skittles LIFE
Life is the best gift LIFE
Life's a bitch, and then you die LIFE
Life without a friend, is death FRIENDSHIP
Medicine can prolong life, but MEDICINE
Travelling is one way of lengthening life TRAVEL
Variety is the spice of life CHANGE
While there's life there's hope HOPE
lifeblood Gossip is the lifeblood of society GOSSIP
light Light come, light go POSSESSIONS
Light for all NEWS AND JOURNALISM
Light the blue touch paper DANGER
Many hands make light work COOPERATION
lighthouse It is dark at the foot of the lighthouse IGNORANCE
lightly Touch the earth lightly ENVIRONMENT
lightning Lightning never strikes twice CHANCE AND LUCK
like Here's tae us; wha's like us SELF-ESTEEM AND SELF-ASSERTION
If you don't like the heat, get out STRENGTH AND WEAKNESS
Like breeds like SIMILARITY AND DIFFERENCE
Like father, like son FAMILY
Like master, like man WORK
Like mother, like daughter FAMILY
Like people, like priest CLERGY

Like will to like SIMILARITY AND DIFFERENCE
Lincoln Lincoln was, London is BRITISH TOWNS AND REGIONS
line Not a day without a line ART
linen Never choose your women or linen APPEARANCE
One does not wash one's dirty linen SECRECY
lining Every cloud has a silver lining OPTIMISM AND PESSIMISM
link You are the weakest link STRENGTH AND WEAKNESS
lion army of stags led by a lion ARMED FORCES
dog is a lion in his own house DOGS
live dog is better than a dead lion LIFE
March comes in like a lion SPRING
mouse may help a lion POWER
When the lion shows its teeth DANGER
lions Christians to the lions CHRISTIAN CHURCH
Until the lions produce their own HISTORY
lip There's many a slip 'twixt cup and lip MISTAKES
lips Loose lips sink ships GOSSIP
When the lips are gone, the teeth are cold COOPERATION
lipstick You can put lipstick on a pig FUTILITY
listen If I listen, I have the advantage SPEECH
Listen a thousand times, and speak once SPEECH
listeners Listeners never hear good SECRECY

Keyword Index

little Big fish eat little
fish POWER
Every little helps COOPERATION
Few have too much, and fewer
too little WEALTH
little absence does much
good ABSENCE
Little children, little
sorrows CHILDREN
Little fish are sweet QUANTITIES
AND QUALITIES
little knowledge is a dangerous
thing KNOWLEDGE
Little pitchers have large
ears SECRECY
little pot is soon hot ANGER
Little strokes fell great
oaks DETERMINATION
Little things please little
minds VALUE
Love me little, love me
long LOYALTY
Many a little makes a mickle
QUANTITIES AND QUALITIES
There is no little
enemy ENEMIES
live Come live with me and you'll
know FAMILIARITY
Eat to live, not live to
eat EATING
If you want to live and
thrive CHANCE AND LUCK
Live and learn EXPERIENCE
Live and let live PREJUDICE AND
TOLERANCE
live dog is better than a dead
lion LIFE
Man cannot live by bread
alone LIFE
They that live longest, see
most EXPERIENCE
Threatened men live
long WORDS AND DEEDS

lived And they all lived happily
ever after ENDING
lives Careless talk costs
lives GOSSIP
cat has nine lives CATS
He lives long who lives
well VIRTUE
He that lives in hope dances to
an ill tune HOPE
living Be happy while y'er
leevin LIFE
Envy feeds on the living ENVY
Living well is the best
revenge REVENGE
Saturday's child works hard for
a living WORK
lizard smaller the lizard, the
greater its hopes AMBITION
loaf Half a loaf is better than no
bread SATISFACTION AND
DISCONTENT
slice off a cut loaf isn't
missed IGNORANCE
loathing Length begets
loathing SPEECH
local Local ginger is not
hot FAMILIARITY
locally Think globally, act
locally ENVIRONMENT
locksmiths Love laughs at
locksmiths LOVE
loft September blow soft till the
fruit's in the loft AUTUMN
log No matter how long a log
floats CHANGE
London Lincoln was, London is
BRITISH TOWNS AND REGIONS
lone lone sheep is in danger from
the wolf SOLITUDE
lonely One seldom meets a lonely
lie LIES
long Art is long and life is
short LIFE

Be the day weary or be the day long TIME

He lives long who lives well VIRTUE

How long is a piece of string QUANTITIES AND QUALITIES

It is a long lane that has no turning PATIENCE

Kings have long arms POWER

Lang may yer lum reek HOME

Long and lazy, little and loud WOMEN

Long foretold, long last WEATHER

Love me little, love me long LOYALTY

Never is a long time TIME

stern chase is a long chase DETERMINATION

Threatened men live long WORDS AND DEEDS

longest He who laughs last, laughs longest REVENGE

longest journey begins with a single BEGINNING

longest way home is the shortest PATIENCE

They that live longest, see most EXPERIENCE

look Look before you leap CAUTION

lookers Lookers-on see most of the game ACTION AND INACTION

loose Loose lips sink ships GOSSIP

lord abomination unto the Lord, but LIES

Everybody loves a lord RANK

lords New lords, new laws CHANGE

lose Heads I win, tails you lose WINNING AND LOSING

If you snooze, you lose OPPORTUNITY

Lend your money, and lose your friend DEBT AND BORROWING

Those who lose dreaming DREAMS

What you lose on the swings WINNING AND LOSING

You cannot lose what you never had POSSESSIONS

You win a few, you lose a few SUCCESS AND FAILURE

losers Finders keepers (losers weepers) POSSESSIONS

loses tale never loses in the telling GOSSIP

loss One man's loss is another man's gain CIRCUMSTANCE AND SITUATION

There's no great loss without CIRCUMSTANCE AND SITUATION

lost For want of a nail the shoe was lost PREPARATION AND READINESS

He who hesitates is lost INDECISION

No one was ever lost on a straight road PREPARATION AND READINESS

There is nothing lost by civility MANNERS

'Tis better to have loved and lost LOVE

What a neighbour gets is not lost NEIGHBOURS

lottery Marriage is a lottery MARRIAGE

louder Actions speak louder than words WORDS AND DEEDS

louse Sue a beggar and catch a louse FUTILITY

Keyword Index

lousy Lousy but loyal   LOYALTY

love All's fair in love and
war   JUSTICE
course of true love never did
run smooth   LOVE
fence between makes love
more   CAUSES AND
CONSEQUENCES
Grief is the price we pay for
love   MOURNING
It is best to be off with the old
love   LOVE
Love and a cough   LOVE
Love begets love   LOVE
Love is blind   LOVE
Love laughs at
locksmiths   LOVE
love letter sometimes costs
more   LETTERS
Love makes the world go
round   LOVE
Love makes time pass   LOVE
Love me, love my dog   DOGS
Love will find a way   LOVE
Love your enemy   ENEMIES
Love your neighbour, but
don't   NEIGHBOURS
Lucky at cards, unlucky in
love   CHANCE AND LUCK
Make love not war   LIFESTYLES
Of soup and love, the first is
best   FOOD
One cannot love and be
wise   LOVE
Pity is akin to love   SYMPATHY
To understand your parents'
love   PARENTS
We all love justice   JUSTICE
Whom the gods love die
young   YOUTH
You do not marry the person
you love   MARRIAGE

loved better to have loved   LOVE

Lovell cat, the rat, and Lovell the
dog   GOVERNMENT

lovers Jove but laughs at lovers'
perjury   LOVE
quarrel of lovers is the
renewal   LOVE

loves Everybody loves a
lord   RANK
Misery loves
company   SORROW

loving Friday's child is loving and
giving   GENEROSITY

loyal Lousy but loyal   LOYALTY

luck devil's children have the
devil's luck   CHANCE AND LUCK
Fools for luck   CHANCE
AND LUCK
great fortune depends on
luck   CHANCE AND LUCK
There is luck in
leisure   PATIENCE
There is luck in odd
numbers   CHANCE AND LUCK

luckier harder I work, the
luckier   CHANCE AND LUCK

lucky It is better to be born
lucky   CHANCE AND LUCK
Lucky at cards, unlucky in
love   CHANCE AND LUCK
Third time lucky   CHANCE
AND LUCK
Throw a lucky man into
the sea   CHANCE AND LUCK

lum Lang may yer lum
reek   HOME

lunch Breakfast like a king, lunch
like   EATING
There's no such thing as a free
lunch   TEMPTATION

Macgregor Where Macgregor sits
is the head   RANK

mad Don't get mad, get
even   REVENGE

Madrid From Madrid to heaven TOWNS AND CITIES

Mahomet If the mountain will not come to Mahomet NECESSITY

Maine As Maine goes, so goes the nation POLITICS

make Fake it 'til you make it BEHAVIOUR

Happiness is what you make HAPPINESS

If you don't make mistakes INVENTIONS AND DISCOVERIES

Make do and mend THRIFT

Make love not war LIFESTYLES

maketh Manners maketh man MANNERS

mal Honi soit qui mal y pense GOOD AND EVIL

malice Never attribute to malice what is adequately explained by stupidity FOOLS

Mammon You cannot serve God and Mammon MONEY

man Am I not a man and a brother HUMAN RACE

child is the father of the man CHARACTER

Clothes make the man DRESS

earth is man's only friend ENVIRONMENT

Every elm has its man TREES

Like master, like man WORK

Man cannot live by bread alone LIFE

Man fears Time, but Time fears TIME

man is as old as he feels MEN AND WOMEN

Man is a wolf to man HUMAN RACE

man is known by the company he FAMILIARITY

Man is the enemy of IGNORANCE

Man is the measure HUMAN RACE

Manners maketh man MANNERS

Man proposes, God disposes FATE

man who is born in a stable CHARACTER

Never send a boy to do a man's job YOUTH

Nine tailors make a man DRESS

No moon, no man CHILDREN

Six hours' sleep for a man SLEEP

way to a man's heart is through MEN

Whatever man has done ACHIEVEMENT

manage You can only manage what you can MANAGEMENT

manager No manager ever got fired COMPUTING

Manchester What Manchester says today BRITISH TOWNS AND REGIONS

mangoes Eat the mangoes. Do not count the trees WAYS AND MEANS

mankind All mankind is divided into three HUMAN RACE

manners Other times, other manners CHANGE

Striking manners are bad manners MANNERS

test of good manners is MANNERS

manure Money, like manure, does no good MONEY

Keyword Index

many Many a little makes a
  mickle   QUANTITIES AND
  QUALITIES
  Many a mickle makes a
  muckle   QUANTITIES AND
  QUALITIES
  Many hands make light
  work   COOPERATION
  So many men, so many
  opinions   OPINION
March Eat leeks in March and
  ramsons in May   HEALTH
  March borrowed from April
  three days   SPRING
  March comes in like a
  lion   SPRING
  On the first of March, crows
  begin   SPRING
  peck of March dust is worth a
  king's   SPRING
  So many mists in March, so
  many frosts   SPRING
mare A mare usque ad
  mare   COUNTRIES
  AND PEOPLES
mare grey mare is the better
  horse   MARRIAGE
  Money makes the mare to
  go   MONEY
  Nothing so bold as a blind
  mare   IGNORANCE
market He that cannot abide a
  bad market   BUSINESS
markets Bull markets climb a
  wall of worry   BUSINESS
marriage Marriage is a
  lottery   MARRIAGE
  There goes more to
  marriage   MARRIAGE
marriages Marriages are made in
  heaven   MARRIAGE
married I married my husband
  for life   MEN

young man married
  is a   MARRIAGE
marry Marry in haste and repent
  at leisure   MARRIAGE
  Marry in May, rue for
  aye   WEDDINGS
  Never marry for money,
  but   MARRIAGE
marrying Building and
  marrying of children
  ARCHITECTURE
Martinmas Every hog has his
  Martinmas   FATE
martyrs blood of the
  martyrs   CHRISTIAN CHURCH
Marxist I am a Marxist—of the
  Groucho   POLITICS
mass Meat and mass   CHRISTIAN
  CHURCH
master eye of a master does more
  work   EMPLOYMENT
  Fire is a good servant, but a bad
  master   WAYS AND MEANS
  Jack is as good as his
  master   EQUALITY
  Jack of all trades and master of
  none   EMPLOYMENT
  Like master, like man   WORK
  When the pupil is ready, the
  master   EDUCATION
masters No man can serve two
  masters   CHOICE
matters What matters is what
  works   WAYS AND MEANS
May April and May are keys to
  the whole year   SPRING
  April showers bring forth May
  flowers   SPRING
  cold May and windy   SPRING
  Eat leeks in March and ramsons
  in May   HEALTH
  He that will not when he
  may   OPPORTUNITY

Keyword Index

Marry in May, rue for
aye WEDDINGS
May chickens come
cheeping SPRING
Ne'er cast a clout till May be
out DRESS
Sell in May and go
away BUYING AND SELLING
swarm in May is worth a load
of hay SUMMER
warm January, a cold
May WEATHER
means end justifies the
means WAYS AND MEANS
measure Man is the measure of
all things HUMAN RACE
Measure seven times, cut
once PREPARATION AND
READINESS
There is measure in all
things MODERATION
measures Exceptional times
require exceptional
measures NECESSITY
meat After meat,
mustard EATING
God sends meat, but the
Devil COOKING
Meat and mass CHRISTIAN
CHURCH
nearer the bone, the sweeter the
meat QUANTITIES AND QUALITIES
One man's meat is another
man's poison LIKES AND
DISLIKES
medicine Food without hospitality
is medicine HOSPITALITY
Good medicine always has a
bitter taste MEDICINE
Hospitality and medicine
must be HOSPITALITY
Laughter is the best
medicine MEDICINE

library is a repository of
medicine BOOKS
Medicine can prolong life,
but MEDICINE
Your food is your
medicine HEALTH
meet Do not meet troubles
half way WORRY
Extremes meet SIMILARITY
AND DIFFERENCE
meets When Greek meets
Greek SIMILARITY AND
DIFFERENCE
memory liar ought to have a
good memory LIES
Our memory is always at
fault MIND
men best of men are but men at
best HUMAN RACE
mend It is never too late to
mend CHANGE
Make do and
mend THRIFT
mending woman and a ship ever
want mending WOMEN
mercy May God in his mercy
look down BRITISH TOWNS
AND REGIONS
merit Merit in appearance
is APPEARANCE
merrier more the
merrier QUANTITIES AND
QUALITIES
merry cherry year, a merry
year SUMMER
Eat, drink and be merry, for
tomorrow LIFESTYLES
It is merry in hall when beards
wag all HOSPITALITY
mice cat in gloves catches no
mice CAUTION
It is better to feed one cat than
many mice CATS

451

Keyword Index

Keep no more cats than will catch mice   MODERATION

When the cat's away, the mice will   OPPORTUNITY

mickle Many a little makes a mickle   QUANTITIES AND QUALITIES

Many a mickle makes a muckle   QUANTITIES AND QUALITIES

midnight One hour's sleep before midnight   SLEEP

might Might is right   POWER

mightier pen is mightier than the sword   WAYS AND MEANS

mile miss is as good as a mile   MISTAKES

miles Essex stiles, Kentish miles   BRITISH TOWNS AND REGIONS

Every two miles the water changes   TRAVEL

Glasgow's miles better   BRITISH TOWNS AND REGIONS

Walking ten thousand miles   EXPERIENCE

Walking ten thousand miles   KNOWLEDGE

milk Feeding a snake with milk   CHARACTER

It is no use crying over spilt milk   MISFORTUNES

Why buy a cow when milk is so cheap   SEX

mill All is grist that comes to the mill   OPPORTUNITY

mill cannot grind with the water that   OPPORTUNITY

million If you really want to make a million   WEALTH

Never ask about the first million   WEALTH

mills mills of God grind slowly   FATE

mind mind enlightened is like heaven   MIND

Mind has no sex   MIND

mind is a terrible thing to waste   MIND

Out of sight, out of mind   ABSENCE

Travel broadens the mind   TRAVEL

wise man changes his mind   FOOLS

minds Great minds think alike   THINKING

Little things please little minds   VALUE

miracles age of miracles is past   SURPRISE

mischief mother of mischief is no bigger   CAUSES AND CONSEQUENCES

misery Misery loves company   SORROW

misfortune Ignorance is voluntary misfortune   IGNORANCE

misfortunes Misfortunes never come singly   MISFORTUNES

miss miss is as good as a mile   MISTAKES

You never miss the water till the well   GRATITUDE

missed slice off a cut loaf isn't missed   IGNORANCE

misses person who misses his chance   OPPORTUNITY

mistakes If you don't make mistakes   INVENTIONS AND DISCOVERIES

mists So many mists in March, so many frosts   SPRING

mixen Better wed over the mixen   FAMILIARITY

mockingbird mockingbird has no voice BIRDS

moderation Moderation in all things MODERATION

moment Enjoy the present moment PRESENT

To question and ask is a moment's shame THINKING

Monday Monday's child is fair of face BEAUTY

They that wash on Monday HOUSEWORK

money bulls make money, the bears make BUYING AND SELLING

fool and his money are soon parted FOOLS

Get the money honestly if you can MONEY

Lend your money, and lose your friend DEBT AND BORROWING

Money can't buy happiness MONEY

Money has no smell MONEY

Money is like sea water MONEY

Money isn't everything MONEY

Money is power MONEY

Money is the root of all evil MONEY

Money like manure, does no good MONEY

Money makes a man WEALTH

Money makes money WEALTH

Money makes the dog dance MONEY

Money makes the mare to go MONEY

Money talks MONEY

Never marry for money, but MARRIAGE

Time is money MONEY

When money speaks, the truth CORRUPTION

You pays your money CHOICE

moneyless moneyless man goes fast through POVERTY

monk cowl does not make the monk APPEARANCE

monkey higher the monkey climbs AMBITION

rusty monkey wrench DETERMINATION

Softlee, softlee, catchee monkey PATIENCE

What can a monkey know of the taste VALUE

monkeys Even monkeys sometimes fall off a tree MISTAKES

If you pay peanuts, you get monkeys VALUE

months Nine months of winter WEATHER

monument You'll die facing the monument CRIME AND PUNISHMENT

monumentum *Si monumentum requiris, circumspice* ARCHITECTURE

moon Clear moon, frost soon WEATHER

No moon, no man CHILDREN

morals It is one thing to keep your morals BEHAVIOUR

more Fear less, hope more; Eat less LIFESTYLES

Less is more MODERATION

more arguments you win, the less ARGUMENT

more butter, the worse cheese FOOD

More haste, less speed HASTE AND DELAY

Keyword Index

more laws, the more thieves and bandits   LAW

more the merrier   QUANTITIES AND QUALITIES

More things grow in the garden   GARDENS

more you get the more you want   GREED

Much would have more   GREED

whole is more than the sum   QUANTITIES AND QUALITIES

morning afternoon knows what the morning never suspected   FORESIGHT

guest is like the morning dew   HOSPITALITY

morning daylight appears plainer   TIME

Morning dreams come true   DREAMS

morning knows no more than the evening   SLEEP

morrow Never bid the Devil good morrow   PROBLEMS AND SOLUTIONS

mortgage Home is where the mortgage is   HOME

mortuis De mortuis nil nisi bonum   REPUTATION

Moses For every Pharaoh there is a Moses   COURAGE

Moses took a chance   CHANCE AND LUCK

moss rolling stone gathers no moss   CIRCUMSTANCE AND SITUATION

most Who knows most, speaks least   SPEECH

mother Absence is the mother of disillusion   ABSENCE

Diligence is the mother of   CHANCE AND LUCK

Like mother, like daughter   FAMILY

mother of mischief is no bigger   CAUSES AND CONSEQUENCES

mother understands what the child   PARENTS

Necessity is the mother of invention   NECESSITY

Summer is the mother of the poor   SUMMER

mount wise man will climb Mount Fuji once   TRAVEL

mountain If the mountain will not come to Mahomet   NECESSITY

man who removes a mountain   PATIENCE

One mountain cannot accommodate two   LEADERSHIP

mountains Beyond mountains there are more   DETERMINATION

Faith will move mountains   BELIEF

mountains are high, and the emperor   GOVERNMENT

We have no friends but the mountains   DANGER

mouse It's the second mouse that gets   PREPARATION AND READINESS

mouse may help a lion   POWER

One for the mouse, one for the crow   NATURE

mousetrap only free cheese is in a mousetrap   TEMPTATION

mouth Never look a gift horse in the mouth   GRATITUDE

shut mouth catches no flies   SILENCE

mouths God never sends mouths but   FOOD

Out of the mouths of babes — WISDOM

moutons *Revenons à ces moutons* DETERMINATION

move Did the earth move for you SEX

When you pray, move your feet RELIGION

moved shall not be moved DETERMINATION

moves If it moves, salute it ARMED FORCES

much Few have too much, and fewer too little WEALTH

Much would have more GREED

Sow much, reap much CAUSES AND CONSEQUENCES

You can have too much of a good thing EXCESS

muck Where there's muck there's brass MONEY

muckle Many a mickle makes a muckle QUANTITIES AND QUALITIES

mulberry With time and patience the mulberry leaf PATIENCE

mule If you lead your mule to the top PROBLEMS AND SOLUTIONS

multitude Charity covers a multitude of sins FORGIVENESS

mummified Custom is mummified by habit CUSTOM AND HABIT

murder Killing no murder MURDER

Murder will out MURDER

music Music helps not the toothache MUSIC

When the music changes CHANGE

must What must be, must be FATE

mustard After meat, mustard EATING

nail For want of a nail the shoe was lost PREPARATION AND READINESS

nail that sticks up is certain to MANAGEMENT

One nail drives out another SIMILARITY AND DIFFERENCE

name Change the name and not the letter MARRIAGE

Give a dog a bad name and hang GOSSIP

good name is better than a golden girdle REPUTATION

He that has an ill name REPUTATION

We name the guilty men GUILT

names No names, no pack drill SECRECY

Naples See Naples and die TOWNS AND CITIES

nation As Maine goes, so goes the nation POLITICS

Nation shall speak peace unto BROADCASTING

nation without a language COUNTRIES AND PEOPLES

national national debt, if it is not excessive DEBT AND BORROWING

nature Death is nature's way DEATH

father is a banker provided by nature PARENTS

Nature abhors a vacuum NATURE

Self-preservation is the first law of nature SELF-INTEREST

Some sleep five hours; nature requires SLEEP

You can drive out nature with a pitchfork NATURE

Keyword Index

naughty Naughty but
  nice TEMPTATION
near Near is my kirtle, but nearer
  my smock SELF-INTEREST
  Near is my shirt, but nearer my
  skin SELF-INTEREST
nearer nearer the bone, the
  sweeter the meat QUANTITIES
  AND QUALITIES
  nearer the church, the
  farther from God CHRISTIAN
  CHURCH
necessary Is your journey really
  necessary TRAVEL
necessity Make a virtue of
  necessity NECESSITY
  Necessity is the mother of
  invention NECESSITY
  Necessity knows no
  law NECESSITY
  Necessity sharpens
  industry NECESSITY
nectar Even nectar is a
  poison EXCESS
need Charity sees the
  need CHARITY
  friend in need is a friend
  indeed FRIENDSHIP
  Need makes greed GREED
  Your King and Country need
  you ARMED FORCES
needle When a pine needle falls
  in the forest KNOWLEDGE
  Where the needle goes the
  thread must follow POWER
needles Needles and pins, needles
  and pins MARRIAGE
needs Needs must when the devil
  drives NECESSITY
neglected Business neglected
  BUSINESS
neighbour Love your neighbour,
  but don't NEIGHBOURS

rotten apple injures its
  neighbour CORRUPTION
  What a neighbour gets is not
  lost NEIGHBOURS
neighbours Good fences make
  good neighbours NEIGHBOURS
nemo Nemo me impune
  lacessit DEFIANCE
nest It's an ill bird that fouls its
  own nest LOYALTY
  There are no birds in last year's
  nest CHANGE
nests Birds in their little
  nests ARGUMENT
net All is fish that comes to the
  net OPPORTUNITY
  In vain the net is
  spread FUTILITY
  man in debt is caught in a
  net DEBT AND BORROWING
  old net is cast aside while the
  new net YOUTH
never Better late than
  never PUNCTUALITY
  It is never too late to
  learn EDUCATION
  Never is a long time TIME
  Never let the sun go down
  on FORGIVENESS
  Never say never CHANGE
  Never too old to
  learn EDUCATION
  Opportunity never knocks
  for OPPORTUNITY
  Opportunity never knocks
  twice OPPORTUNITY
new Always something new out
  of Africa INVENTIONS AND
  DISCOVERIES
  New brooms sweep
  clean CHANGE
  New circumstances, new controls
  CIRCUMSTANCE AND SITUATION

456

New lords, new laws CHANGE
old net is cast aside while the
new net YOUTH
Out with the old, in with the
new CHANGE
There is nothing new under the
sun FAMILIARITY
What is new cannot be
true CUSTOM AND HABIT
You can't put new wine in old
bottles CHANGE
You can't teach an old dog new
tricks CUSTOM AND HABIT
news All the news that's fit to
print NEWS AND JOURNALISM
Bad news travels fast NEWS
AND JOURNALISM
Go abroad and you'll hear news
of home TRAVEL
No news is good news NEWS
AND JOURNALISM
next Next year in
Jerusalem TOWNS AND CITIES
nibbles fish will soon be caught
that nibbles TEMPTATION
nice Naughty but
nice TEMPTATION
Nice guys finish last SPORTS
AND GAMES
Nice to see you MEETING AND
PARTING
No more Mr Nice
Guy CHANGE
night day has eyes, the night has
ears SECRECY
Night brings counsel ADVICE
Red sky at night, shepherd's
delight WEATHER
nil Nil carborundum
illegitimi DETERMINATION
nine cat has nine lives CATS
Nine months of
winter WEATHER

Nine tailors make a
man DRESS
Parsley seed goes nine
times GARDENS
Possession is nine points of the
law LAW
stitch in time saves
nine CAUTION
nineteen All dancing girls are
nineteen YOUTH
no Just say no DETERMINATION
No cross, no crown SUFFERING
No foot, no horse HORSES
No man is an island SOLITUDE
No names, no
pack drill SECRECY
No surrender DEFIANCE
There's no such thing as a free
lunch TEMPTATION
nobody Everybody's business is
nobody's RESPONSIBILITY
Nobody expects the Spanish
Inquisition SURPRISE
nod nod's as good as a
wink ADVICE
nods Homer sometimes
nods MISTAKES
noise Silence is a still
noise SILENCE
nonsense little nonsense now and
then, is relished by the wisest
men WISDOM
north North wind doth
blow WEATHER
Northamptonshire
Northamptonshire for
squires BRITISH TOWNS AND
REGIONS
nose Don't cut off your nose to
spite REVENGE
not Not a day without a line ART
Not guilty, but don't do it
again GUILT

Keyword Index

nothing Doing nothing
is ill   IDLENESS
If you have nothing
POSSESSIONS
Nothing can bring you
peace but   PEACE
Nothing comes from
nothing   VALUE
Nothing for nothing   VALUE
Nothing is certain but
death   CERTAINTY AND DOUBT
Nothing is certain but the
unforeseen   FORESIGHT
Nothing is for ever   CHANGE
Nothing is stolen without
hands   HONESTY
Nothing so bad but it might
have been   SYMPATHY
Nothing succeeds like
success   SUCCESS AND FAILURE
Nothing venture, nothing
gain   THOROUGHNESS
Nothing venture, nothing
have   THOROUGHNESS
Something is better than
nothing   SATISFACTION AND
DISCONTENT
There is nothing like
leather   WAYS AND MEANS
now And now for
something   CHANGE
nowt Hear all, see all, say
nowt   SELF-INTEREST
There's nowt so queer as
folk   HUMAN RACE
When in doubt, do
nowt   ACTION AND INACTION
nullius Nullius in
verba   HYPOTHESIS AND FACT
number Age is just a
number   AGE
numbers There is luck in odd
numbers   CHANCE AND LUCK

There is safety in numbers
QUANTITIES AND QUALITIES
nuts gods send nuts to
those   AGE
oak When the oak is before the
ash   TREES
oaks Great oaks from little
acorns   CAUSES AND
CONSEQUENCES
Little strokes fell great
oaks   DETERMINATION
obedience first duty of a soldier is
obedience   ARMED FORCES
obey He that cannot obey cannot
command   LEADERSHIP
obvious obvious choice is
usually   CHOICE
odd There is luck in odd
numbers   CHANCE AND LUCK
odious Comparisons are
odious   SIMILARITY AND
DIFFERENCE
offenders Offenders never
pardon   FORGIVENESS
offered They offered
death   CHOICE
old Better be an old man's
darling   MARRIAGE
Don't throw away the old
bucket   PREPARATION AND
READINESS
For the unlearned, old age is
winter   AGE
Good soup is made in an old
pot   EXPERIENCE
man is as old as he feels   MEN
AND WOMEN
Never too old to
learn   EDUCATION
old error is always more
popular   TRUTH
Old habits die hard   CUSTOM
AND HABIT

old horse does not spoil the furrow AGE

old net is cast aside while the new net YOUTH

old poacher makes the best gamekeeper WAYS AND MEANS

Old sins cast long shadows PAST

Old soldiers never die ARMED FORCES

Out with the old CHANGE

There's no fool like an old fool AGE

You cannot catch old birds EXPERIENCE

You cannot put an old head EXPERIENCE

You cannot shift an old tree CUSTOM AND HABIT

You can't put new wine in old bottles CHANGE

You can't teach an old dog new tricks CUSTOM AND HABIT

Young folks think old folks to be fools YOUTH

Young men may die, but old men DEATH

Young saint, old devil HUMAN RACE

older older the ginger, the more pungent AGE

omelette You cannot make an omelette PRACTICALITY

once Christmas comes but once a year CHRISTMAS

Once a —, always a — CHARACTER

Once a priest, always CLERGY

one Beware of the man of one book BOOKS

Children: one is one CHILDREN

One for sorrow, two for mirth BIRDS

One good turn deserves another COOPERATION

One mountain cannot accommodate two LEADERSHIP

One step at a time PATIENCE

onions One day honey, one day onions CIRCUMSTANCE AND SITUATION

only Only — shopping days to Christmas CHRISTMAS

open door must be either shut or open CHOICE

Teachers open the door EDUCATION

opens When one door shuts, another opens OPPORTUNITY

opera opera isn't over till the fat lady sings ENDING

opinions So many men, so many opinions OPINION

Those who never retract their opinions OPINION

Where there are two Jews, there are three opinions OPINION

opportunities Opportunities look for you OPPORTUNITY

opportunity Every crisis provides an opportunity OPPORTUNITY

Man's extremity is God's opportunity RELIGION

Opportunity makes a thief CRIME AND PUNISHMENT

Opportunity never knocks for OPPORTUNITY

Opportunity never knocks twice OPPORTUNITY

orare Laborare est orare RELIGION

other Other times, other manners CHANGE

others Do unto others as you would they LIFESTYLES

ounce ounce of practice is worth a pound of WORDS AND DEEDS

Keyword Index

out Don't halloo till you are out
of the wood   OPTIMISM AND
PESSIMISM
Out of debt, out of
danger   DEBT AND BORROWING
Out of sight, out of
mind   ABSENCE
Out with the old   CHANGE

oven You can put your boots in
the oven   FUTILITY

overcome We shall
overcome   DETERMINATION

overload Don't overload
gratitude   GRATITUDE

own He who slaps his own
face   MISTAKES

oyster world is one's
oyster   OPPORTUNITY

oysters Don't eat oysters
unless   FOOD

pace It is the pace that
kills   STRENGTH AND WEAKNESS
Pace makes the race   HORSES

pack drill No names, no
pack drill   SECRECY

padlock Wedlock is a
padlock   MARRIAGE

pain No pain, no gain   EFFORT
Pride feels no pain   PRIDE
rock in the water does not
know the pain   SYMPATHY

paint blind man's wife needs no
paint   APPEARANCE

painted black as he is
painted   REPUTATION

painter Every painter paints
himself   ART
good painter can draw a
devil   ART

paints Every painter paints
himself   ART

palmam Palmam qui
meruit   ACHIEVEMENT

pans If ifs and ands were pots and
pans   OPTIMISM AND PESSIMISM

paper Paper bleeds
little   WRITING
Paper is patient   WRITING

paradise England is the paradise
of women   COUNTRIES AND
PEOPLES

pardon Offenders never
pardon   FORGIVENESS

parent art of being a
parent   CHILDREN
Caution is the parent of
safety   CAUTION

parents Parents want their
children to become   PARENTS
To understand your parents'
love   PARENTS

parsley Parsley seed goes nine
times   GARDENS

parsnips Fine words butter no
parsnips   WORDS AND DEEDS

part best of friends must
part   MEETING AND PARTING

parted fool and his money are
soon parted   FOOLS

parts Heineken refreshes the
parts   DRINK

party Always leave the party
when   HOSPITALITY

pass And this, too, shall pass
away   TRANSIENCE
If the Bermudas let you
pass   SEA
Love makes time pass   LOVE

passe Tout passe, tout casse   LIFE

passeront Ils ne passeront
pas   DEFIANCE

passion passion for freedom
never dies   POLITICS

past age of miracles is
past   SURPRISE
past always looks better   PAST

Keyword Index

past is always ahead of us PAST
Things past cannot be
recalled PAST

patch There is no patch for
stupid COMPUTERS

paternoster No penny, no
paternoster BUSINESS

path Do not follow where the
path may lead INVENTIONS AND
DISCOVERIES

paths paths are many, but the
goal is the same WAYS AND
MEANS

patience All commend
patience PATIENCE
Patience is a virtue PATIENCE
With time and patience the
mulberry leaf PATIENCE

patient Paper is patient WRITING

Paul If Saint Paul's day be fair and
clear WINTER

pawn After the game, the king
and the pawn EQUALITY

pay Can't pay, won't
pay DEFIANCE
Crime doesn't pay CRIME AND
PUNISHMENT
He that cannot pay, let him
pray MONEY
If you pay peanuts, you get
monkeys VALUE
No cure, no pay BUSINESS
Pay beforehand was never
well BUSINESS
price we pay for
love MOURNING
Service is the rent we
pay CHARITY
Take what you want, and pay
for it RESPONSIBILITY
They that dance must pay the
fiddler POWER

pays Death pays all debts DEATH
He who pays the piper calls the
tune POWER
It pays to advertise
ADVERTISING
third time pays for
all DETERMINATION
You pays your money CHOICE

peace If you want peace, you
must prepare PREPARATION
AND READINESS
Nation shall speak peace
unto BROADCASTING
Nothing can bring you peace
but PEACE
Peace is the dream of the
wise PEACE

peacock peacock is always happy
because SELF-ESTEEM AND
SELF-ASSERTION

peanuts If you pay peanuts, you
get monkeys VALUE

pears Walnuts and pears you
plant for GARDENS

peck peck of March dust is worth
a king's SPRING
We must eat a peck of
dirt EATING

Peebles Peebles for
pleasure BRITISH TOWNS AND
REGIONS

pegs All words are pegs to hang
ideas on WORDS

pen pen is mightier than the
sword WAYS AND MEANS
What is written with a
pen WRITING

pence Take care of the
pence THRIFT

penny bad penny always turns
up CHARACTER
In for a penny, in for a
pound THOROUGHNESS

461

Keyword Index

No penny, no paternoster BUSINESS
penny saved is a penny earned THRIFT
Penny wise and pound foolish THRIFT

pense Honi soit qui mal y pense GOOD AND EVIL

people Guns don't kill people MURDER
If the people will lead LEADERSHIP
Like people, like priest CLERGY
Power to the people POLITICS
Proverbs are the coins of the people SAYINGS
To understand the people SAYINGS
voice of the people is the voice of God POLITICS

Peoria It'll play in Peoria POLITICS

perfect Practice makes perfect WORK

perfection Trifles make perfection WORK

perfume Flattery, like perfume PRAISE AND FLATTERY

perjury Jove but laughs at lovers' perjury LOVE

Persil Persil washes whiter HOUSEWORK

personal personal is political POLITICS

Pharaoh For every Pharaoh there is a Moses COURAGE

philosophy Philosophy bakes no bread WORDS AND DEEDS

photos Take only photos ENVIRONMENT

pick Pick your battles PREPARATION AND READINESS

See a pin and pick it up CHANCE AND LUCK

picture Every picture tells a story KNOWLEDGE
One picture is worth ten thousand words WORDS AND DEEDS
Writing is a picture of the writer's heart WRITING

pie apple pie without some cheese FOOD
Promises, like piecrust, are made TRUST AND TREACHERY

pies devil makes his Christmas pies LAW

pig only part of a pig that can't be used PRACTICALITY
What can you expect from a pig CHARACTER
You can put lipstick on a pig FUTILITY

pigs Pigs get fat, but hogs get GREED
Pigs may fly BELIEF

pile Pile it high, sell it cheap BUSINESS

pillar Hope is the pillar of the world HOPE

pillow clean conscience is a good pillow CONSCIENCE

pilot In a calm sea, every man is a pilot ACHIEVEMENT

pin He that will not stoop for a pin PRIDE
It's a sin to steal a pin HONESTY
See a pin and pick it up CHANCE AND LUCK

pine When a pine needle falls in the forest KNOWLEDGE

pins Needles and pins, needles and pins MARRIAGE

pint You cannot get a quart into a pint FUTILITY

462

piper He who pays the piper calls the tune POWER
It takes seven years to make a piper MUSIC

pitch He that touches pitch shall be defiled GOOD AND EVIL

pitcher pitcher will go to the well EXCESS

pitchers Little pitchers have large ears SECRECY

pitchfork You can drive out nature with a pitchfork NATURE

pitied Better be envied than pitied ENVY

pity Pity is akin to love SYMPATHY

place There's a time and a place CIRCUMSTANCE AND SITUATION
There's no place like home HOME

plague Please your eye and plague BEAUTY

plan He who fails to plan, plans to fail SUCCESS AND FAILURE
No plan survives first contact PREPARATION AND READINESS

plans He who fails to plan, plans to fail SUCCESS AND FAILURE

plant best time to plant a tree was TREES
Confidence is a plant of slowth growth TRUST AND TREACHERY
To plant a tree is to plant hope TREES
Walnuts and pears you plant for GARDENS

planted Trees planted by the ancestors TREES

plants One generation plants the trees TREES

play All work and no play makes Jack LEISURE
Fair play's a jewel JUSTICE
Give and take is fair play JUSTICE
If you play with fire you get burnt DANGER
It'll play in Peoria POLITICS
Turn about is fair play JUSTICE

please Little things please little minds VALUE
Please to remember the Fifth TRUST AND TREACHERY
Please your eye and plague BEAUTY
You can't please everyone LIKES AND DISLIKES

pleasure Business before pleasure BUSINESS
He that would go to sea for pleasure SEA
Peebles for pleasure BRITISH TOWNS AND REGIONS

poacher old poacher makes the best gamekeeper WAYS AND MEANS

pockets Shrouds have no pockets MONEY

pointed I pointed out to you the stars KNOWLEDGE

poison Even nectar is a poison EXCESS
One man's meat is another man's poison LIKES AND DISLIKES

poke Poke a bush, a snake comes CAUTION

policy Honesty is the best policy HONESTY

politeness Punctuality is the politeness of princes PUNCTUALITY

Keyword Index

political personal is
political   POLITICS
politics In politics, a man must
learn to rise   POLITICS
Politics makes strange
bedfellows   POLITICS
pomegranate Every pomegranate
has one seed   FOOD
poor It is a poor cook   COOKING
It is a poor dog that's not
worth   VALUE
It is a poor heart that never
rejoices   HAPPINESS
Summer is the mother of the
poor   SUMMER
port Any port in a storm   CRISES
possession Possession is nine
points   LAW
possible All things are possible
with God   GOD
post Post coitum omne animal
triste   SEX
post post of honour is the post of
danger   DANGER
postern postern door makes a
thief   OPPORTUNITY
pot Good soup is made in an old
pot   EXPERIENCE
little pot is soon hot   ANGER
pot boils, friendship
lives   HOSPITALITY
watched pot never
boils   PATIENCE
pots If ifs and ands were pots and
pans   OPTIMISM AND PESSIMISM
pound In for a penny, in for a
pound   THOROUGHNESS
ounce of practice is worth a
pound of   WORDS AND DEEDS
Penny wise and pound
foolish   THRIFT
pounds Take care of the pence
and the pounds   THRIFT

pours It never rains but it
pours   MISFORTUNES
poverty Both poverty and
prosperity   POVERTY
Make poverty history   POVERTY
Poverty comes from
God   POVERTY
Poverty is a blessing   POVERTY
Poverty is no
disgrace   POVERTY
Poverty is not a
crime   POVERTY
power Beauty is power   BEAUTY
Knowledge is
power   KNOWLEDGE
Money is power   MONEY
Power corrupts   POWER
Power is like an egg   POWER
Power to the
people   POLITICS
practice ounce of practice is
worth a pound of   WORDS AND
DEEDS
Practice makes perfect   WORK
practise practise what you
preach   WORDS AND DEEDS
practised Honesty is
more praised than
practised   HONESTY
praise Praise the child, and you
make love to   PARENTS
Self-praise is no
recommendation   SELF-ESTEEM
AND SELF-ASSERTION
praised Honesty is more praised
than practised   HONESTY
pray He that cannot pay, let him
pray   MONEY
When you pray, move your
feet   RELIGION
prayer Prayer to God, and service
to the tsar   PREPARATION AND
READINESS

Keyword Index

prays family that prays together stays RELIGION

preach Practise what you preach WORDS AND DEEDS

precept Example is better than precept WORDS AND DEEDS

prepare Hope for the best and prepare for PREPARATION AND READINESS

If you want peace, you must prepare PREPARATION AND READINESS

To fail to prepare is to prepare to fail PREPARATION AND READINESS

prepared Be prepared PREPARATION AND READINESS

present Enjoy the present moment PRESENT

No time like the present OPPORTUNITY

There's no future like the present FUTURE

preservation Self-preservation is the first law of nature SELF-INTEREST

press You press the button, we do the rest TECHNOLOGY

pressed One volunteer is worth two pressed men WORK

pretend We pretend to work EMPLOYMENT

prettiest prettiest girl in the world BEAUTY

pretty Pretty is as pretty does BEHAVIOUR

prevention Prevention is better than cure FORESIGHT

prey Birds of prey do not sing BIRDS

price Every man has his price CORRUPTION

Everything has a price, but jade is VALUE

Grief is the price we pay for love MOURNING

pride Pride feels no pain PRIDE

Pride goes before a fall PRIDE

Stupidity and pride grow PRIDE

priest Like people, like priest CLERGY

Once a priest, always CLERGY

princes Camels, fleas, and princes ROYALTY

Punctuality is the politeness of princes PUNCTUALITY

principle In matters of principle, stand CERTAINTY

print All the news that's fit to print NEWS AND JOURNALISM

probably There's probably no God GOD

procrastination Procrastination is the thief of time HASTE AND DELAY

promises Promises, like piecrust, are made TRUST AND TREACHERY

proof proof of the pudding is in the eating HYPOTHESIS AND FACT

prophet prophet is not without honour FAMILIARITY

prophets Is Saul also among the prophets ABILITY

proposes Man proposes, God disposes FATE

prosper Cheats never prosper DECEPTION

prosperity Both poverty and prosperity POVERTY

proverb There is no proverb without a grain SAYINGS

465

Keyword Index

proverbs Proverbs are the coins of the people   SAYINGS

providence Providence is always on the side of   ARMED FORCES

public One does not wash one's dirty linen   SECRECY

publicity Any publicity is good publicity   ADVERTISING

pudding proof of the pudding is in the eating   HYPOTHESIS AND FACT

puddle sun loses nothing by shining into a puddle   GOOD AND EVIL

When the stars begin to huddle, the earth will soon become a puddle   WEATHER

punctuality Punctuality is the art of guessing   PUNCTUALITY

Punctuality is the politeness of princes   PUNCTUALITY

Punctuality is the soul of business   PUNCTUALITY

pungent older the ginger, the more pungent   AGE

Sour, sweet, bitter, pungent   FATE

pupil When the pupil is ready, the master   EDUCATION

purse You can't make a silk purse   FUTILITY

pursueth guilty flee when no man pursueth   GUILT

push Do not push the river, it will flow   FUTILITY

put Never put off till tomorrow   HASTE AND DELAY

putt Drive for show, and putt for dough   SPORTS AND GAMES

quality Every good quality is contained in ginger   HEALTH

Never mind the quality, feel the width   QUANTITIES AND QUALITIES

quarrel It takes two to make a quarrel   ARGUMENT

quarrel of lovers is the renewal   LOVE

quart You cannot get a quart into a pint   FUTILITY

queer There's nowt so queer as folk   HUMAN RACE

question Ask a silly question and you get   FOOLS

civil question deserves a civil answer   MANNERS

Fools ask questions that wise men   WISDOM

There are two sides to every question   JUSTICE

To question and ask is a moment's shame   THINKING

quick quick brown fox jumps over the lazy dog   WORDS

quickly He gives twice who gives quickly   GENEROSITY

Quickly come, quickly go   LOYALTY

quickness quickness of the hand deceives the eye   DECEPTION

quiet best doctors are Dr Quiet, Dr Diet   MEDICINE

quiet conscience sleeps in thunder   CONSCIENCE

quits winner never quits, and a quitter never wins   WINNING AND LOSING

quitter winner never quits, and a quitter never wins   WINNING AND LOSING

quote devil can quote Scripture   SAYINGS

race Pace makes the race   HORSES

466

race is not to the swift, nor the battle SUCCESS AND FAILURE

Slow and steady wins the race DETERMINATION

radio Always turn the radio on before BROADCASTING

rain Blessed are the dead that the rain DEATH

Now you will feel no rain WEDDINGS

Rain before seven, fine before eleven WEATHER

Rain, rain, go away WEATHER

Today's rain is tomorrow's whisky DRINK

To dream of the dead is a sign of rain DREAMS

rains Have an umbrella ready before it rains PREPARATION AND READINESS

In the woods it rains twice TREES

It never rains but it pours MISFORTUNES

raise It is easier to raise the Devil BEGINNING

ramsons Eat leeks in March and ramsons in May HEALTH

rat cat, the rat, and Lovell the dog GOVERNMENT

read He that runs may read READING

reading Do not close a letter without reading it LETTERS

reads man who reads is the man who leads READING

real Will the real — please stand up SECRECY

reap As you sow, so you reap CAUSES AND CONSEQUENCES

Sow an act, and reap CUSTOM AND HABIT

Sow much, reap much CAUSES AND CONSEQUENCES

reaps Speech sows, silence reaps SILENCE

reason There is reason in the roasting of eggs CAUSES AND CONSEQUENCES

recalled Things past cannot be recalled PAST

receive He gives twice who gives quickly GENEROSITY

receivers If there were no receivers CRIME AND PUNISHMENT

reckonings Short reckonings make long friends DEBT AND BORROWING

recommendation Self-praise is no recommendation SELF-ESTEEM AND SELF-ASSERTION

red Better red than dead CHOICE

Red sky at night, shepherd's delight WEATHER

redressed fault confessed is half redressed FORGIVENESS

reed reed before the wind lives on STRENGTH AND WEAKNESS

reek Lang may yer lum reek HOME

rejoices It is a poor heart that never rejoices HAPPINESS

relationship I belong by blood relationship FAMILY

remedy There is a remedy for everything DEATH

remember Please to remember the Fifth TRUST AND TREACHERY

Remember the Alamo WARFARE

When you drink water, remember GRATITUDE

removals Three removals are as bad CHANGE

Keyword Index

renewal quarrel of lovers is the renewal LOVE

rent Service is the rent we pay CHARITY

repeats History repeats itself HISTORY

repent Marry in haste and repent at leisure MARRIAGE

republican Not to be a republican at twenty POLITICS

reputation good reputation stands still REPUTATION
man's best reputation for his future REPUTATION

request No flowers by request MOURNING

rest After dinner rest a while EATING
change is as good as a rest CHANGE
You press the button, we do the rest TECHNOLOGY

revenge If you want revenge, dig two graves REVENGE
Living well is the best revenge REVENGE
Revenge is a dish that can be eaten REVENGE
Revenge is sweet REVENGE

revenons *Revenons à ces moutons* DETERMINATION

revenue Thrift is a great revenue THRIFT

revolution Every revolution was first a thought REVOLUTION AND REBELLION

revolutions Revolutions are not made by REVOLUTION AND REBELLION
Revolutions are not made with REVOLUTION AND REBELLION

reward Virtue is its own reward VIRTUE

rib elephant does not die of one broken rib STRENGTH AND WEAKNESS

rice Talk will not cook rice WORDS AND DEEDS

rich One law for the rich JUSTICE
rich man gets his ice in summer WEALTH

ride If wishes were horses, beggars would ride OPTIMISM AND PESSIMISM

rides He who rides a tiger DANGER

ridiculous From the sublime to the ridiculous SUCCESS AND FAILURE

right customer is always right BUSINESS
Do right and fear no man CONSCIENCE
Even a stopped clock is right twice a day TIME
God's in his heaven; all's right OPTIMISM AND PESSIMISM
He is always right who suspects MISTAKES
Might is right POWER
Two wrongs don't make a right GOOD AND EVIL

ripe Soon ripe, soon rotten YOUTH

rise Early to bed and early to rise HEALTH
In politics, a man must learn to rise POLITICS
stream cannot rise above its source CHARACTER

rising rising tide lifts all boats SUCCESS AND FAILURE

river Cross the river by feeling CAUTION
Cross the river in a crowd COOPERATION

Do not push the river, it will flow   FUTILITY

If you sit by the river long enough   PATIENCE

live in the river   CIRCUMSTANCE AND SITUATION

river that forgets its source   GRATITUDE

sea refuses no river   GREED

Where the river is deepest   CHARACTER

rivers All rivers run into the sea   RIVERS

road No one was ever lost on a straight road   PREPARATION AND READINESS

road to a friend's house is never long   FRIENDSHIP

road to hell is paved with   ACTION AND INACTION

There is no royal road to learning   EDUCATION

To know the road ahead, ask those coming back   FORESIGHT

Why did the chicken cross the road   PROBLEMS AND SOLUTIONS

roads All roads lead to Rome   TOWNS AND CITIES

Roads are made by walking   TRAVEL

roasting There is reason in the roasting of eggs   CAUSES AND CONSEQUENCES

robbery Fair exchange is no robbery   JUSTICE

robin robin and the wren are God's   BIRDS

Robin Hood could brave all weathers   WEATHER

rock In matters of principle, stand like a rock   CERTAINTY

rock in the water does not know the pain   SYMPATHY

rocket Up like a rocket, down like a stick   SUCCESS AND FAILURE

rocking Worry is like a rocking chair   WORRY

rocks hand that rocks the cradle rules   WOMEN

rod Spare the rod and spoil   CHILDREN

roll Assistant heads must roll   BROADCASTING

rolling rolling stone gathers no moss   CIRCUMSTANCE AND SITUATION

Romans When in Rome, do as the Romans do   BEHAVIOUR

Rome All roads lead to Rome   TOWNS AND CITIES

Rome was not built in a day   PATIENCE

When in Rome, do as the Romans do   BEHAVIOUR

room There's always room at the top   AMBITION

rooster cuckoo praises the rooster   PRAISE AND FLATTERY

Rooster today, feather duster tomorrow   SUCCESS AND FAILURE

root Money is the root of all evil   MONEY

No tree takes so deep a root   PREJUDICE AND TOLERANCE

Root, hog, or die   WORK

roots roots of charity are always green   CHARITY

rope Give a man enough rope   WAYS AND MEANS

rose Do not grieve that rose trees have thorns   SATISFACTION AND DISCONTENT

He who wants a rose   PRACTICALITY

No rose without a thorn   CIRCUMSTANCE AND SITUATION

Keyword Index

roses Take time to smell the
roses   LEISURE
Time brings roses   PATIENCE

rots Winter never rots in the
sky   WINTER

rotten rotten apple injures its
neighbour   CORRUPTION
Small choice in rotten
apples   CHOICE
Soon ripe, soon rotten   YOUTH

round Love makes the world go
round   LOVE

row Call on God, but row
away   CAUTION

royal There is no royal road to
learning   EDUCATION

rudder Who won't be ruled by the
rudder   CAUSES AND
CONSEQUENCES

rudderless widow is a rudderless
boat   MARRIAGE

rue Marry in May, rue for
aye   WEDDINGS

rule Divide and
rule   GOVERNMENT
exception proves the
rule   HYPOTHESIS AND FACT
golden rule of life is   BEGINNING
Self-interest is the rule
SELF-INTEREST
There is an exception to every
rule   HYPOTHESIS AND FACT

ruled Who won't be ruled by the
rudder   CAUSES AND
CONSEQUENCES

rules hand that rocks the cradle
rules   WOMEN
Rules are made to be
broken   LAW

run All rivers run into the
sea   RIVERS
You cannot run with the
hare   TRUST AND TREACHERY

runs guilty one always
runs   GUILT
He that runs may
read   READING
He who fights and runs
away   CAUTION

Russian Scratch a Russian
and you find   COUNTRIES
AND PEOPLES

rust Better to wear out than to
rust   IDLENESS

rusts If gold rusts, what will iron
do   CORRUPTION

Sabbath child that is born on the
Sabbath   CHILDREN

sack You can't hide an awl in a
sack   SECRECY

sacks Empty sacks will never
stand upright   POVERTY

safe Better be safe than
sorry   CAUTION
Just when you thought it was
safe   DANGER
Safe bind, safe find   CAUTION

safety Caution is the parent of
safety   CAUTION
There is safety in
numbers   QUANTITIES AND
QUALITIES

said They haif said: Quhat say
they   DEFIANCE
What the soldier said isn't
evidence   GOSSIP

sailor One cannot become a good
sailor   EFFORT

sailors Heaven protects children,
sailors   DANGER

saint Devil was sick, the Devil a
saint   GRATITUDE
greater the sinner, the greater
the saint   GOOD AND EVIL
If Saint Paul's day be fair and
clear   WINTER

on Saint Thomas the
Divine WINTER
Young saint, old devil
HUMAN RACE

saints There are more saints in
Cornwall BRITISH TOWNS AND
REGIONS

salt Help you to salt, help you to
sorrow MISFORTUNES

salty Those who eat salty
fish RESPONSIBILITY

salute If it moves, salute it
ARMED FORCES

Satan Satan rebuking sin GOOD
AND EVIL

satisfied satisfied person does not
know the hungry
SELF-INTEREST

Saturday Saturday's child works
hard for a living WORK

sauce Hunger is the best
sauce EATING
What's sauce for the
goose JUSTICE

Saul Is Saul also among the
prophets ABILITY

save Save the
whale ENVIRONMENT
Save us from our
friends FRIENDSHIP

saved penny saved is a penny
earned THRIFT

saw Saw wood and say
nothing CAUTION

say Do as I say, not as
I do BEHAVIOUR
Hear all, see all, say nowt
SELF-INTEREST
Saw wood and say
nothing CAUTION
Say it with flowers FLOWERS
They haif said: Quhat say
they DEFIANCE

says What everybody says must
be true TRUTH
What Manchester says
today BRITISH TOWNS AND
REGIONS
Who says A must say
B NECESSITY

scabbard Two swords do not fit
in one scabbard SIMILARITY
AND DIFFERENCE

scalded He who has been
scalded CAUTION

scarce Good men are
scarce VIRTUE

scare Kill the chicken to
scare CAUSES AND
CONSEQUENCES

scholar ink of a scholar is holier
than EDUCATION

school Experience keeps a dear
school EXPERIENCE
Never tell tales out of
school SECRECY

science Much science, much
sorrow SCIENCE
Science finds, industry
applies TECHNOLOGY
Science has no enemy but the
ignorant SCIENCE

scorned Hell hath no fury like a
woman scorned WOMEN

scrambled You can't unscramble
scrambled eggs FUTILITY

scratch Scratch a Russian and you
find COUNTRIES AND PEOPLES

scripture devil can quote
Scripture SAYINGS

sea All rivers run into the
sea RIVERS
Chess is a sea where a gnat may
drink SPORTS AND GAMES
He that would go to sea for
pleasure SEA

Keyword Index

In a calm sea, every man is a pilot ACHIEVEMENT

last one to know about the sea IGNORANCE

Money is like sea water MONEY

sea of learning has no end KNOWLEDGE

sea refuses no river GREED

sea wants to be visited SEA

There are as good fish in the sea LOVE

Throw a lucky man into the sea CHANCE AND LUCK

willing foe and sea room ARMED FORCES

seaman good seaman is known in bad weather SEA

second It's the second mouse that gets PREPARATION AND READINESS

Second thoughts are best CAUTION

secret secret is either too good to keep SECRECY

Three may keep a secret SECRECY

secure past at least is secure PAST

see He who can see three days ahead FORESIGHT

Lookers-on see most of the game ACTION AND INACTION

Nice to see you MEETING AND PARTING

See all your best work go unnoticed SECRECY

See Naples and die TOWNS AND CITIES

See no evil, hear no evil, speak no evil VIRTUE

They that live longest, see most EXPERIENCE

What the eye doesn't see, the heart IGNORANCE

What you see is what you get APPEARANCE

seed blood of the martyrs is the seed CHRISTIAN CHURCH

Every pomegranate has one seed FOOD

Good seed makes a bad crop CAUSES AND CONSEQUENCES

seed hidden in the heart of an apple TREES

seeding One year's seeding makes seven GARDENS

seeing By seeing one spot CHARACTER

Seeing is believing BELIEF

seek Seek and ye shall find ACTION AND INACTION

seekers Seekers are finders ACHIEVEMENT

seem Be what you would seem BEHAVIOUR

seen Children should be seen and not CHILDREN

sees One who sees something good NEWS AND JOURNALISM

self Deny self for self's sake SELF-ESTEEM AND SELF-ASSERTION

self-praise Self-praise is no recommendation SELF-ESTEEM AND SELF-ASSERTION

sell Don't sell the skin till you have caught OPTIMISM AND PESSIMISM

Pile it high, sell it cheap BUSINESS

Sell honestly, but not honesty HONESTY

Sell in May and go away BUYING AND SELLING

semper Semper eadem CHANGE

send Never send a boy to do a man's job   YOUTH

September September blow soft till the fruit's   AUTUMN
September dries up wells   AUTUMN

seriously Seriously, though, he's   ACHIEVEMENT

serpent Strike the serpent's head   ENEMIES

servant Fire is a good servant, but a bad master   WAYS AND MEANS

serve You cannot serve God and Mammon   MONEY

served Youth must be served   YOUTH

service Prayer to God, and service to the tsar   PREPARATION AND READINESS
Service is the rent we pay   CHARITY

set Sow dry and set wet   GARDENS

settling In settling an island, the first building   ARCHITECTURE

seven Fall seven times, stand up eight   DETERMINATION
Give me a child for the first seven   EDUCATION
It takes seven years to make a piper   MUSIC
Keep a thing seven years   POSSESSIONS
Measure seven times, cut once   PREPARATION AND READINESS
One year's seeding makes seven   GARDENS
Rain before seven, fine before eleven   WEATHER
You should know a man seven years   NEIGHBOURS

sex Mind has no sex   MIND

sexually Life is a sexually transmitted disease   LIFE

Shackleton When disaster strikes...pray for Shackleton   CRISES

shadow Coming events cast their shadow   FUTURE
We live in each other's shadow   COOPERATION
Worry often gives a small thing a big shadow   WORRY

shadows Old sins cast long shadows   PAST

shame Fool me once, shame on you   DECEPTION
Tell the truth and shame the devil   TRUTH
To question and ask is a moment's shame   THINKING

shared Shared joy is double joy   SYMPATHY
trouble shared is a trouble halved   COOPERATION

sharpens Iron sharpens iron   CHARACTER

sharper sharper the storm, the sooner it's over   OPTIMISM AND PESSIMISM

shed You can shed tears that she is gone   MOURNING

sheep bleating sheep loses a bite   OPPORTUNITY
lone sheep is in danger from the wolf   SOLITUDE
One might as well be hanged for a sheep   THOROUGHNESS
wolves are well fed and the sheep   DANGER

shepherd Red sky at night, shepherd's delight   WEATHER

shines Make hay while the sun shines   OPPORTUNITY

Keyword Index

So much sun as shines
on WEATHER

shining sun loses nothing by
shining into a puddle GOOD
AND EVIL

ship Do not spoil the ship for a
ha'porth of tar THOROUGHNESS
One hand for oneself and one
for the ship SEA
woman and a ship ever want
mending WOMEN

ships Loose lips sink
ships GOSSIP

shirt Near is my shirt, but nearer
my skin SELF-INTEREST

shirtsleeves From shirtsleeves to
shirtsleeves SUCCESS AND
FAILURE

shoe For want of a nail the shoe
was lost PREPARATION AND
READINESS
If the shoe fits,
wear it NAMES

shoemaker shoemaker's son
always goes FAMILY

shoes I cried because I had no
shoes MISFORTUNES
It's ill waiting for dead men's
shoes AMBITION
You need more than dancing
shoes DANCE

shoot When you shoot an arrow
of truth TRUTH

shop Keep your own
shop BUSINESS

shopping Only — shopping days
to Christmas CHRISTMAS

shore I sit on the shore, and wait
for the wind PATIENCE

shoreline larger the shoreline of
knowledge KNOWLEDGE

shorn God tempers the wind to
the shorn lamb SYMPATHY

short Art is long and life is
short LIFE
short cut is often a wrong
cut WAYS AND MEANS
short horse is soon
curried WORK
Short reckonings make
long friends DEBT AND
BORROWING

shortest longest way home is the
shortest PATIENCE

show Drive for show, and putt for
dough SPORTS AND GAMES
show must go
on DETERMINATION
Tell me and I'll forget. Show me
and TEACHING

showers April showers bring
forth May flowers SPRING

shrimp shrimp that falls
asleep ACTION AND INACTION
When whales fight, the shrimp's
back is broken POWER

shrouds Shrouds have no
pockets MONEY

shut door must be either shut or
open CHOICE
It's too late to shut the
stable door FORESIGHT
shut mouth catches no
flies SILENCE

shuts When one door shuts,
another opens OPPORTUNITY

shy Once bitten, twice
shy EXPERIENCE

sick Devil was sick, the Devil a
saint GRATITUDE
Hope deferred makes the heart
sick HOPE

sickly bloody war and a sickly
season ARMED FORCES

side bread never falls but on its
buttered side MISFORTUNES

Providence is always on the side of   ARMED FORCES

sides There are two sides to every question   JUSTICE

sight Out of sight, out of mind   ABSENCE

silence Silence is a still noise   SILENCE
Silence is a woman's best garment   WOMEN
Silence means consent   SILENCE
Speech is silver, but silence is golden   SILENCE
Speech sows, silence reaps   SILENCE

silent It is the calm and silent water   DANGER

silk You can't make a silk purse   FUTILITY

silly Ask a silly question and you get   FOOLS

silver Every cloud has a silver lining   OPTIMISM AND PESSIMISM
Speech is silver, but silence is golden   SILENCE

similia Similia similibus curantur   MEDICINE

sin It's a sin to steal a pin   HONESTY
Satan rebuking sin   GOOD AND EVIL

sincerest Imitation is the sincerest form of flattery   PRAISE AND FLATTERY

sing Birds of prey do not sing   BIRDS
Little birds that can sing   COOPERATION
Sing before breakfast, cry   FEELINGS

singing singing army and a   ARMED FORCES

single Beauty draws with a single hair   BEAUTY

longest journey begins with a single   BEGINNING

single arrow is easily broken   COOPERATION

single bracelet does not jingle   COOPERATION

singly Misfortunes never come singly   MISFORTUNES

sings opera isn't over till the fat lady sings   ENDING

sinner greater the sinner, the greater the saint   GOOD AND EVIL

sins Charity covers a multitude of sins   FORGIVENESS
Old sins cast long shadows   PAST

sir Praise from Sir Hubert   PRAISE AND FLATTERY

site Select a proper site for your garden   GARDENS

sitting It is as cheap sitting as standing   ACTION AND INACTION

sixpence Bang goes sixpence   THRIFT

size One size does not fit all   WAYS AND MEANS

skin Beauty is only skin deep   BEAUTY
Don't sell the skin till you have caught   OPTIMISM AND PESSIMISM
fair skin hides seven defects   APPEARANCE
Near is my shirt, but nearer my skin   SELF-INTEREST
There is more than one way to skin a cat   WAYS AND MEANS
When a tiger dies it leaves its skin   REPUTATION

skittles Life isn't all beer and skittles   LIFE

sky If the sky falls we shall catch larks   EFFORT

Keyword Index

No fist is big enough to hide the sky   GOVERNMENT

Red sky at night, shepherd's delight   WEATHER

Winter never rots in the sky   WINTER

Women hold up half the sky   WOMEN

slap Slip, slop, slap   HEALTH

slaps He who slaps his own face   MISTAKES

sleep beginning of health is sleep   SLEEP

less you know, the better you sleep   IGNORANCE

One hour's sleep before midnight   SLEEP

Six hours' sleep for a man   SLEEP

Some sleep five hours; nature requires   SLEEP

We never sleep   SLEEP

sleeping Let sleeping dogs lie   CAUTION

sleeping fox counts hens   CHARACTER

sleeps quiet conscience sleeps in thunder   CONSCIENCE

slice slice off a cut loaf isn't missed   IGNORANCE

slip Slip, slop, slap   HEALTH

There's many a slip 'twixt cup and lip   MISTAKES

slop Slip, slop, slap   HEALTH

slow Confidence is a plant of slow growth   TRUST AND TREACHERY

Slow and steady wins the race   DETERMINATION

Slow but sure   PATIENCE

slowly Make haste slowly   HASTE AND DELAY

small Better are small fish than an empty dish   SATISFACTION AND DISCONTENT

Small choice in rotten apples   CHOICE

Small is beautiful   QUANTITIES AND QUALITIES

Wink at sma' fauts, ye hae great anes   MISTAKES

smaller bigger the hat, the smaller the property   SELF-ESTEEM AND SELF-ASSERTION

smaller the lizard, the greater its hopes   AMBITION

smell Money has no smell   MONEY

Take time to smell the roses   LEISURE

smock Near is my kirtle, but nearer my smock   SELF-INTEREST

smoke No smoke without fire   REPUTATION

smoking Smoking can seriously damage   SMOKING

smooth course of true love never did run smooth   LOVE

snake Do not add legs to the snake   EXCESS

Feeding a snake with milk   CHARACTER

Once bitten by a snake   CAUTION

Poke a bush, a snake comes   CAUTION

sneezes Coughs and sneezes spread diseases   SICKNESS

snooze If you snooze, you lose   OPPORTUNITY

snow swan brings snow on its bill   BIRDS

soap Flattery is soft soap   PRAISE AND FLATTERY

soar However high a bird may soar   ENVIRONMENT

sober Wanton kittens make sober cats   YOUTH

476

Keyword Index

society Gossip is the lifeblood of society GOSSIP

soft Flattery is soft soap PRAISE AND FLATTERY

soft answer turneth away wrath ANGER

softly Softlee, softlee, catchee monkey PATIENCE

soil answer lies in the soil GARDENS

soldier Every Turk is born a soldier COUNTRIES AND PEOPLES

first duty of a soldier ARMED FORCES

soldier of the Great War, known unto ARMED FORCES

What the soldier said isn't evidence GOSSIP

soldiers Old soldiers never die ARMED FORCES

someone Someone, somewhere, wants a letter LETTERS

something And now for something CHANGE

Something is better than nothing SATISFACTION AND DISCONTENT

son Like father, like son FAMILY

My son is my son till he gets him PARENTS

shoemaker's son always goes FAMILY

son of a duck floats FAMILY

songless believer is a songless bird BELIEF

sons Clergymen's sons always CLERGY

soon Soon ripe, soon rotten YOUTH

sooner sooner begun, the sooner done BEGINNING

sorrow Help you to salt, help you to sorrow MISFORTUNES

Much science, much sorrow SCIENCE

One for sorrow, two for mirth BIRDS

sorrows Little children, little sorrows CHILDREN

sorry Better be safe than sorry CAUTION

sorts It takes all sorts CHARACTER

soul Brevity is the soul of wit SPEECH

Confession is good for the soul HONESTY

eyes are the window of the soul BODY

Punctuality is the soul of business PUNCTUALITY

Your soul may belong to God ARMED FORCES

sound Empty vessels make the most sound FOOLS

soup Good soup is made in an old pot EXPERIENCE

Of soup and love, the first is best FOOD

sour Sour, sweet, bitter, pungent FATE

source river that forgets its source GRATITUDE

stream cannot rise above its source CHARACTER

sow As you sow, so you reap CAUSES AND CONSEQUENCES

If you do not sow in the spring AUTUMN

Sow an act, and reap CUSTOM AND HABIT

Sow corn in clay GARDENS

Sow dry and set wet GARDENS

sow may whistle, though it has ABILITY

Keyword Index

Sow much, reap much   CAUSES
AND CONSEQUENCES
They that sow the
wind   CAUSES AND
CONSEQUENCES

sows Speech sows, silence
reaps   SILENCE

space Watch this space   NEWS
AND JOURNALISM

Spanish Nobody expects the
Spanish Inquisition   SURPRISE

spare Spare at the spigot   THRIFT
Spare the rod and
spoil   CHILDREN
Spare well and have to
spend   THRIFT

speak kumara does not speak
of its own   SELF-ESTEEM AND
SELF-ASSERTION
Listen a thousand times, and
speak once   SPEECH
Never speak ill of the
dead   REPUTATION
See no evil, hear no evil, speak
no evil   VIRTUE
Some folks speak from
experience   EXPERIENCE
Speak as you
find   REPUTATION

speaks Everyone speaks well of
the bridge   MANNERS
Who knows most, speaks
least   SPEECH

species female of the species is
more deadly   WOMEN

speculate If you don't
speculate   BUSINESS

speech Speech is silver, but
silence is golden   SILENCE
Speech sows, silence
reaps   SILENCE

speed More haste, less
speed   HASTE AND DELAY

spend Spare well and have to
spend   THRIFT
What you spend, you
have   POSSESSIONS

spice Variety is the spice of
life   CHANGE

spider bee sucks honey where the
spider   CHARACTER
When spider webs
unite   COOPERATION

spigot Spare at the spigot   THRIFT

spilt It is no use crying over
spilt milk   MISFORTUNES

spindle Do not fold,
spindle or   COMPUTING

spite Don't cut off your nose to
spite   REVENGE

spoil Do not spoil the ship for a
ha'porth of tar   THOROUGHNESS
Spare the rod and
spoil   CHILDREN
Too many cooks spoil the
broth   WORK

spoiled Better one house spoiled
than two   MARRIAGE

spoils One spoonful of tar spoils a
barrel   QUANTITIES AND
QUALITIES

spoonful One spoonful of tar
spoils a barrel   QUANTITIES AND
QUALITIES

spot By seeing one
spot   CHARACTER

spots leopard does not change his
spots   CHANGE

spring If you do not sow in the
spring   AUTUMN
Spring forward, fall back   TIME

springs Hope springs
eternal   HOPE

squeak only part of a pig that
can't be used is its
squeak   PRACTICALITY

Keyword Index

squires Northamptonshire for squires BRITISH TOWNS AND REGIONS

stable It's too late to shut the stable door FORESIGHT
man who is born in a stable CHARACTER

stables Care, and not fine stables HORSES

stabs Stabs heal, but bad words never WORDS AND DEEDS

stags army of stags led by a lion ARMED FORCES

stand Empty sacks will never stand upright POVERTY
Fall seven times, stand up eight DETERMINATION
Will the real — please stand up SECRECY

standing It is as cheap sitting as standing ACTION AND INACTION

stars I pointed out to you the stars KNOWLEDGE
When the stars begin to huddle WEATHER

start Don't hurry—start early HASTE AND DELAY
Life begins on the day you start GARDENS

starve Feed a cold and starve a fever SICKNESS

stays family that prays together stays RELIGION

steady Slow and steady wins the race DETERMINATION
Steady as she goes CAUTION

steal It's a sin to steal a pin HONESTY
One may steal a horse REPUTATION

stealin' howlin' coyote ain't stealin' no chickens HONESTY

steals He who steals an egg will steal a camel HONESTY

steed While the grass grows, the steed ACHIEVEMENT

steel hammer shatters glass, but forges steel WAYS AND MEANS

step It is the first step BEGINNING
One step at a time PATIENCE

stern stern chase is a long chase DETERMINATION

stey Put a stout heart to a stey brae DETERMINATION

stick It is easy to find a stick to beat a dog APOLOGY AND EXCUSES
Let the cobbler stick to his last KNOWLEDGE
Throw dirt enough, and some will stick REPUTATION
Up like a rocket, down like a stick SUCCESS AND FAILURE

sticks nail that sticks up is certain to MANAGEMENT
Sticks and stones may break my bones WORDS

stiles Essex stiles, Kentish miles BRITISH TOWNS AND REGIONS

still Silence is a still noise SILENCE
Still achieving, still pursuing ACHIEVEMENT
still tongue makes a wise head SILENCE
Still waters run deep CHARACTER

stink Fish and guests stink after three days HOSPITALITY

stinks fish always stinks from the head LEADERSHIP

stir more you stir it CAUTION

stitch stitch in time saves nine CAUTION

Keyword Index

stolen Nothing is stolen without
hands   HONESTY
Stolen fruit are
sweet   TEMPTATION
Stolen waters are
sweet   TEMPTATION

stone God sleeps in the stone,
dreams   HUMAN RACE
Stone-dead hath no
fellow   DEATH
You cannot get blood from a
stone   FUTILITY

stones Cross the river by feeling
the stones   CAUTION
Sticks and stones may break my
bones   WORDS
You buy land, you buy
stones   BUYING AND SELLING

stools Between two stools one
falls   INDECISION

stoop He that will not stoop for a
pin   PRIDE

stopped Even a stopped clock is
right twice a day   TIME

storm After a storm comes a
calm   PEACE
Any port in a storm   CRISES
sharper the storm, the sooner
it's over   OPTIMISM AND
PESSIMISM

story everyday story of country
folk   COUNTRY AND THE TOWN
Every picture tells a
story   KNOWLEDGE
One story is good till
another is told   HYPOTHESIS
AND FACT

stout Put a stout heart to a stey
brae   DETERMINATION

stove cook is no better than her
stove   COOKING

straight God writes straight with
crooked lines   GOD

No one was ever lost on a
straight road   PREPARATION AND
READINESS

strain Don't strain at a gnat, and
swallow   BELIEF
Let the train take the
strain   TRAVEL

Strand You're never alone with a
Strand   SMOKING

strange Politics makes strange
bedfellows   POLITICS

stranger Fact is stranger than
fiction   TRUTH
tears of the stranger are only
water   SYMPATHY
Truth is stranger than
fiction   TRUTH

straw drowning man will clutch
at a straw   HOPE
It is the last straw   EXCESS
straw vote only shows which
way   POLITICS
You cannot make bricks
without straw   FUTILITY

straws Straws tell which way the
wind blows   KNOWLEDGE

stream stream cannot rise above
its source   CHARACTER

strength Strength through
joy   STRENGTH AND WEAKNESS
Union is strength
COOPERATION

stretch Stretch your arm no
further than   THRIFT

strike Strike while the iron is
hot   OPPORTUNITY

strikes Lightning never strikes
twice   CHANCE AND LUCK
Three strikes and you're
out   CRIME AND PUNISHMENT

striking It is a striking
coincidence that   COUNTRIES
AND PEOPLES

480

Striking manners are bad manners   MANNERS

string How long is a piece of string   QUANTITIES AND QUALITIES

strokes Different strokes for different folks   CHOICE

Little strokes fell great oaks   DETERMINATION

stronger There is one thing stronger than   INVENTIONS AND DISCOVERIES

stubborn Facts are stubborn things   HYPOTHESIS AND FACT

stupid There is no patch for stupid   COMPUTERS

stupidity Never attribute to malice what is adequately explained by stupidity   FOOLS

Stupidity and pride grow   PRIDE

style style is the man   CHARACTER

sublime From the sublime to the ridiculous   SUCCESS AND FAILURE

succeed If at first you don't succeed   DETERMINATION

succeeds He who leaves succeeds   SUCCESS AND FAILURE

Nothing succeeds like success   SUCCESS AND FAILURE

success Nothing succeeds like success   SUCCESS AND FAILURE

only place where success comes before   SUCCESS AND FAILURE

Success has many fathers, while failure   SUCCESS AND FAILURE

sue Sue a beggar and catch a louse   FUTILITY

sufficient Sufficient unto the day is the evil   WORRY

sum whole is more than the sum   QUANTITIES AND QUALITIES

summer One swallow does not make a summer   SUMMER

rich man gets his ice in summer   WEALTH

Summer is the mother of the poor   SUMMER

Winter is summer's heir   WINTER

Winter thunder, summer hunger   WEATHER

sun Do not argue against the sun   ARGUMENT

Happy is the bride the sun shines on   WEDDINGS

Make hay while the sun shines   OPPORTUNITY

Never let the sun go down on   FORGIVENESS

Only the eagle can gaze at the sun   STRENGTH AND WEAKNESS

So much sun as shines on   WEATHER

sun loses nothing by shining into a puddle   GOOD AND EVIL

There is nothing new under the sun   FAMILIARITY

Turn your face to the sun   OPTIMISM AND PESSIMISM

sunny If Candlemas day be sunny and bright   WINTER

superiority Equality is difficult, but superiority   LEADERSHIP

supperless Better to go to bed supperless   DEBT AND BORROWING

sups He who sups with the devil   CAUTION

sure Slow but sure   PATIENCE

surrender No surrender   DEFIANCE

suspects He is always right who suspects   MISTAKES

Keyword Index

Sussex Sussex won't be druv   BRITISH TOWNS AND REGIONS

swallow Don't strain at a gnat, and swallow   BELIEF
It is idle to swallow the cow   DETERMINATION
One swallow does not make a summer   SUMMER

swan swan brings snow on its bill   BIRDS

swarm swarm in May is worth a load of hay   SUMMER

sweep If every one would sweep his own   SELF-INTEREST

sweeps It beats as it sweeps as it cleans   HOUSEWORK

sweet By a sweet tongue and kindness   BEHAVIOUR
Little fish are sweet   QUANTITIES AND QUALITIES
Revenge is sweet   REVENGE
Sour, sweet, bitter, pungent   FATE
Stolen fruit are sweet   TEMPTATION
Stolen waters are sweet   TEMPTATION
Words are sweet, but they never take   WORDS AND DEEDS

sweeter nearer the bone, the sweeter the meat   QUANTITIES AND QUALITIES

sweetest From the sweetest wine, the tartest   SIMILARITY AND DIFFERENCE

swift race is not to the swift, nor the battle   SUCCESS AND FAILURE

swiftest swiftest horse cannot overtake the word   WORDS

swim Fish, to taste good, must swim   COOKING

swings What you lose on the swings   WINNING AND LOSING

Swithin Saint Swithin's day, if thou be fair   SUMMER

sword pen is mightier than the sword   WAYS AND MEANS
Whosoever draws his sword against   REVOLUTION AND REBELLION

swords Two swords do not fit in one scabbard   SIMILARITY AND DIFFERENCE

tablets Keep taking the tablets   MEDICINE

tailors Nine tailors make a man   DRESS

tails Heads I win, tails you lose   WINNING AND LOSING

take Give a thing, and take a thing   GENEROSITY
Take away Aberdeen and twelve   BRITISH TOWNS AND REGIONS
Take the goods the gods provide   OPPORTUNITY
Take what you want, and pay for it   RESPONSIBILITY

takes It takes all sorts   CHARACTER
It takes two to make a bargain   COOPERATION
It takes two to tango   COOPERATION

taking Keep taking the tablets   MEDICINE

tale tale never loses in the telling   GOSSIP

tales Dead men tell no tales   SECRECY
Never tell tales out of school   SECRECY

talk Careless talk costs lives   GOSSIP

If you can talk, you can sing   ABILITY

It's good to talk   SPEECH

Talk is cheap   WORDS AND DEEDS

Talk of the Devil   MEETING AND PARTING

Talk will not cook rice   WORDS AND DEEDS

There isn't much to talk about   HOSPITALITY

talks Money talks   MONEY

tall tall tree attracts the wind   FAME

tango It takes two to tango   COOPERATION

tar Do not spoil the ship for a ha'porth of tar   THOROUGHNESS

One spoonful of tar spoils a barrel   QUANTITIES AND QUALITIES

tartest From the sweetest wine, the tartest   SIMILARITY AND DIFFERENCE

taste Every man to his taste   LIKES AND DISLIKES

Fish, to taste good, must swim   COOKING

Good medicine always has a bitter taste   MEDICINE

What can a monkey know of the taste   VALUE

tastes Tastes differ   LIKES AND DISLIKES

There is no accounting for tastes   LIKES AND DISLIKES

tea If you are cold, tea will warm you   DRINK

teach Don't teach your grandmother   ADVICE

You can't teach an old dog new tricks   CUSTOM AND HABIT

teacher Experience is the best teacher   EXPERIENCE

teachers Teachers open the door   EDUCATION

teaches He teaches ill who teaches all   TEACHING

He that teaches himself has a fool for   TEACHING

Who teaches me for a day is my father   TEACHING

tears tears of the stranger are only water   SYMPATHY

You can shed tears that she is gone   MOURNING

teeth If you had teeth of steel, you could eat iron coconuts   OPTIMISM AND PESSIMISM

When the lion shows its teeth   DANGER

When the lips are gone, the teeth are cold   COOPERATION

Winter either bites with its teeth   WINTER

wolf may lose his teeth, but never   AGE

tell Dead men tell no tales   SECRECY

Don't ask, don't tell   SECRECY

Never tell tales out of school   SECRECY

Tell me and I'll forget. Show me and   TEACHING

Tell the truth and shame the devil   TRUTH

Time will tell   TIME

telling tale never loses in the telling   GOSSIP

tempers God tempers the wind to the shorn lamb   SYMPATHY

terror Better an end with terror   ENDING

test Test before you trust   TRUST AND TREACHERY

Keyword Index

test of good manners
is   MANNERS

that Been there, done that, got
the T-shirt   TRAVEL

thermodynamics Laws of
Thermodynamics   SCIENCE

thicker Blood is thicker than
water   FAMILY

thief Hang a thief when he's
young   CRIME AND PUNISHMENT
Opportunity makes a
thief   CRIME AND PUNISHMENT
postern door makes a
thief   OPPORTUNITY
Procrastination is the thief of
time   HASTE AND DELAY
Set a thief to catch a
thief   WAYS AND MEANS

thieves Little thieves are
hanged   CRIME AND PUNISHMENT
more laws, the more thieves
and bandits   LAW
There is honour among
thieves   COOPERATION
When thieves fall out   CRIME
AND PUNISHMENT

thing If a thing's worth
doing   EFFORT
You can have too much of a
good thing   EXCESS

think Think globally, act
locally   ENVIRONMENT

third third time is the
charm   CHANCE AND LUCK
Third time lucky   CHANCE AND
LUCK
third time pays for
all   DETERMINATION

thirsty Dig the well before you
are thirsty   PREPARATION AND
READINESS

Thomas On Saint Thomas the
Divine   WINTER

thorn No rose without a
thorn   CIRCUMSTANCE AND
SITUATION

thorns Do not grieve that rose
trees have thorns   SATISFACTION
AND DISCONTENT
He who plants thorns   CAUSES
AND CONSEQUENCES

thought Action without
thought   ACTION AND INACTION
Every revolution was first a
thought   REVOLUTION AND
REBELLION
Thought is free   OPINION
wish is father to the
thought   OPINION

thoughts First thoughts are
best   INDECISION
Second thoughts are
best   CAUTION

thread If everyone gives a
thread   CHARITY
Where the needle goes the
thread must follow   POWER

threatened Threatened men live
long   WORDS AND DEEDS

three All mankind is divided into
three   HUMAN RACE
Fish and guests stink after three
days   HOSPITALITY
From clogs to clogs is only
three   SUCCESS AND FAILURE
He who can see three days
ahead   FORESIGHT
It takes three generations to
make   RANK
Three acres and a cow   POLITICS
Three may keep a
secret   SECRECY
Three removals are as
bad   CHANGE
Three strikes and you're
out   CRIME AND PUNISHMENT

Three things are not to be trusted   DANGER

Two is company, but three is none   FRIENDSHIP

threes Bad things come in threes   MISFORTUNES

thrift Most people consider thrift a fine virtue   THRIFT

Thrift is a great revenue   THRIFT

thrive He that will thrive must first ask   HOUSEWORK

If you want to live and thrive   CHANCE AND LUCK

Ill gotten goods never thrive   CRIME AND PUNISHMENT

throw Throw a lucky man into the sea   CHANCE AND LUCK

Throw dirt enough, and some will stick   REPUTATION

thunder quiet conscience sleeps in thunder   CONSCIENCE

Winter thunder, summer hunger   WEATHER

Thursday Thursday's child has far to go   TRAVEL

tide rising tide lifts all boats   SUCCESS AND FAILURE

Time and tide wait for no man   OPPORTUNITY

tie It is a tie between men   READING

tiger bleating of the lamb excites the tiger   TEMPTATION

He who rides a tiger   DANGER

When a tiger dies it leaves its skin   REPUTATION

Till Says Tweed to Till   RIVERS

timber Knowledge and timber   KNOWLEDGE

time good time was had by all   HAPPINESS

Love makes time pass   LOVE

Man fears Time, but Time fears   TIME

Never is a long time   TIME

No time like the present   OPPORTUNITY

Procrastination is the thief of time   HASTE AND DELAY

stitch in time saves nine   CAUTION

Take time to smell the roses   LEISURE

There is always a first time   BEGINNING

There is a time for everything   TIME

There's a time and a place   CIRCUMSTANCE AND SITUATION

third time is the charm   CHANCE AND LUCK

Those who do not find time for exercise   HEALTH

Time and tide wait for no man   OPPORTUNITY

Time brings roses   PATIENCE

Time flies   TRANSIENCE

Time flies when you're having fun   HAPPINESS

Time is a great healer   TIME

Time is money   MONEY

Time will tell   TIME

Time works wonders   TIME

With time and patience the mulberry leaf   PATIENCE

Work expands so as to fill the time   WORK

You have the watches, but we have the time   TIME

times Exceptional times require   NECESSITY

May you live in interesting times   CIRCUMSTANCE AND SITUATION

Keyword Index

Other times, other manners CHANGE

Times change and we with time CHANGE

tobacco Coffee without tobacco SMOKING

today Better an egg today than a hen tomorrow PRESENT

Today's rain is tomorrow's whisky DRINK

Today you; tomorrow me FUTURE

told One story is good till another is told HYPOTHESIS AND FACT

tomorrow All the flowers of tomorrow FLOWERS

Better an egg today than a hen tomorrow PRESENT

Eat, drink and be merry, for tomorrow LIFESTYLES

Jam tomorrow and jam yesterday PRESENT

Never put off till tomorrow HASTE AND DELAY

Today's rain is tomorrow's whisky DRINK

Today you; tomorrow me FUTURE

Tomorrow is another day FUTURE

Tomorrow is often the busiest day FUTURE

Tomorrow never comes FUTURE

Yesterday has gone, tomorrow is yet PRESENT

Yesterday is ashes; tomorrow is wood PRESENT

You can have apricots tomorrow FUTURE

tongue By a sweet tongue and kindness BEHAVIOUR

still tongue makes a wise head SILENCE

Tongue is like a sharp knife WORDS AND DEEDS

too Too many cooks spoil the broth WORK

tools bad workman blames his tools APOLOGY AND EXCUSES

toothache Music helps not the toothache MUSIC

top If you lead your mule to the top PROBLEMS AND SOLUTIONS

There's always room at the top AMBITION

touch Light the blue touch paper DANGER

Touch the earth lightly ENVIRONMENT

touches He that touches pitch shall be defiled GOOD AND EVIL

tout Tout passe, tout casse LIFE

trade Every man to his trade WORK

There are tricks in every trade BUSINESS

Trade follows the flag BUSINESS

Two of a trade never agree SIMILARITY AND DIFFERENCE

trades Jack of all trades and master of none EMPLOYMENT

traduttore Traduttore traditore SAYINGS

trail Crime leaves a trail CRIME AND PUNISHMENT

train Let the train take the strain TRAVEL

trained We trained hard MANAGEMENT

transit Sic transit gloria mundi TRANSIENCE

trash One man's trash is another man's treasure LIKES AND DISLIKES

travel better to travel hopefully HOPE

Keyword Index

Have gun, will travel   TRAVEL
Travel broadens the
mind   TRAVEL
traveller heaviest baggage for the
traveller   TRAVEL
travelling Travelling is
learning   TRAVEL
Travelling is one way of
lengthening life   TRAVEL
travels He travels the fastest who
travels alone   SOLITUDE
He who travels fast, travels
alone   COOPERATION
Tre By Tre, Pol, and Pen   NAMES
treasure Learning is a treasure
that follows   KNOWLEDGE
One man's trash is another man's
treasure   LIKES AND DISLIKES
treat Treat a man as he is, and
that   RELATIONSHIPS
tree As a tree falls, so shall it
lie   DEATH
best time to plant a tree
was   TREES
Do not judge a tree by its
bark   APPEARANCE
Even monkeys sometimes fall
off a tree   MISTAKES
falls far from the tree   FAMILY
No tree takes so deep a
root   PREJUDICE AND TOLERANCE
tall tree attracts the wind   FAME
To plant a tree is to plant
hope   TREES
tree is known by its
fruit   CHARACTER
When the last tree is
cut   ENVIRONMENT
woman, a dog, and a walnut
tree   WOMEN
You can count the apples on
one tree   QUANTITIES AND
QUALITIES

You cannot shift an old
tree   CUSTOM AND HABIT
trees Eat the mangoes. Do not
count the trees   WAYS AND
MEANS
One generation plants the
trees   TREES
Trees planted by the
ancestors   TREES
tricks There are tricks in every
trade   BUSINESS
You can't teach an old
dog new tricks   CUSTOM AND
HABIT
trifles Trifles make
perfection   WORK
trip Clunk, click, every
trip   TRAVEL
trouble Never trouble
trouble   CAUTION
There will be trouble if the
cobbler   KNOWLEDGE
trouble shared is a trouble
halved   COOPERATION
When an elephant is in
trouble   SUCCESS AND FAILURE
Worry is interest paid on
trouble   WORRY
troubled It is good fishing in
troubled waters
OPPORTUNITY
troubles Do not meet troubles
half way   WORRY
true course of true love never did
run smooth   LOVE
If something sounds too good
to be true   EXCELLENCE
Many a true word is spoken in
jest   TRUTH
Morning dreams come
true   DREAMS
What everybody says must be
true   TRUTH

Keyword Index

What is new cannot be
true   CUSTOM AND HABIT

trust Put your trust in God, and
keep   PRACTICALITY

Test before you trust   TRUST
AND TREACHERY

Trust but verify   CAUTION

Trust in Allah, but tie up your
camel   CAUTION

trusted Three things are not to be
trusted   DANGER

truth Children and fools tell the
truth   HONESTY

greater the truth, the greater the
libel   GOSSIP

Half the truth is often a whole
lie   LIES

Tell the truth and shame the
devil   TRUTH

There is truth in
wine   DRUNKENNESS

Truth is stranger than
fiction   TRUTH

Truth lies at the bottom of a
well   TRUTH

Truth makes the Devil
blush   TRUTH

Truth will out   TRUTH

When money speaks, the
truth   CORRUPTION

When war is declared, Truth is
the first   WARFARE

When you shoot an arrow of
truth   TRUTH

try We're number two. We try
harder   EFFORT

trying You should make a point
of trying   EXPERIENCE

tsar God is high above, and the
tsar   GOVERNMENT

Prayer to God, and service to
the tsar   PREPARATION AND
READINESS

tub Every tub must stand on its
own bottom   STRENGTH AND
WEAKNESS

Tuesday If it's Tuesday, this must
be Belgium   TRAVEL

tune America is a
tune   COUNTRIES AND PEOPLES

dripping June sets all in
tune   SUMMER

He that lives in hope dances to
an ill tune   HOPE

He who pays the piper calls the
tune   POWER

There's many a good tune   AGE

Turk Every Turk is born a
soldier   COUNTRIES AND PEOPLES

turkeys Turkeys, heresy, hops,
and beer   INVENTIONS AND
DISCOVERIES

turn Even a worm will
turn   NECESSITY

One good turn deserves
another   COOPERATION

Turn about is fair play   JUSTICE

Turn your face to the
sun   OPTIMISM AND PESSIMISM

turning It is a long lane that has
no turning   PATIENCE

turtle see a turtle on a
fencepost   CAUSES AND
CONSEQUENCES

Tweed Says Tweed to Till   RIVERS

twelve Take away Aberdeen and
twelve   BRITISH TOWNS AND
REGIONS

twice Even a stopped clock is
right twice a day   TIME

He gives twice who gives
quickly   GENEROSITY

In the woods it rains
twice   TREES

Lightning never strikes
twice   CHANCE AND LUCK

Twice-cooked cabbage is death FOOD

twig As the twig is bent EDUCATION

two Between two stools one falls INDECISION

bird in the hand is worth two CAUTION

If two ride on a horse RANK

If you have two coins LIFESTYLES

If you run after two hares INDECISION

If you want revenge, dig two graves REVENGE

It takes two to make a bargain COOPERATION

It takes two to make a quarrel ARGUMENT

It takes two to tango COOPERATION

No man can serve two masters CHOICE

One for sorrow, two for mirth BIRDS

One mountain cannot accommodate two LEADERSHIP

There are two sides to every question JUSTICE

Treat your guest as a guest for two days HOSPITALITY

Two blacks don't make a white GOOD AND EVIL

Two boys are half a boy WORK

Two heads are better than one THINKING

Two is company, but three is none FRIENDSHIP

Two of a trade never agree SIMILARITY AND DIFFERENCE

Two swords do not fit in one scabbard SIMILARITY AND DIFFERENCE

Two wrongs don't make a right GOOD AND EVIL

We're number two. We try harder EFFORT

While two dogs are fighting ARGUMENT

You cannot carry two watermelons FUTILITY

You have two chances CHANCE AND LUCK

tyranny Democracy is better than tyranny POLITICS

umbrella Don't put up your umbrella before CAUTION

Have an umbrella ready before it rains PREPARATION AND READINESS

unbelieving Believing has a core of unbelieving BELIEF

understand To understand the people SAYINGS

understands mother understands what the child PARENTS

undone What's done cannot be undone PAST

unexpected unexpected always happens SURPRISE

unforeseen Nothing is certain but the unforeseen FORESIGHT

union Union is strength COOPERATION

united United we stand, divided we COOPERATION

When spider webs unite COOPERATION

unlearned For the unlearned, old age is winter AGE

unlucky Lucky at cards, unlucky in love CHANCE AND LUCK

unnoticed See all your best work go unnoticed SECRECY

unpunished No good deed goes unpunished VIRTUE

Keyword Index

unrepentant Forgiving the unrepentant FORGIVENESS
unscramble You can't unscramble scrambled eggs FUTILITY
unwilling committee is a group of the unwilling MANAGEMENT
up Up like a rocket, down like a stick SUCCESS AND FAILURE
  What goes up must come down FATE
us Here's tae us; wha's like us SELF-ESTEEM AND SELF-ASSERTION
used Would you buy a used car from this man TRUST AND TREACHERY
vacuum Nature abhors a vacuum NATURE
vain In vain the net is spread FUTILITY
valet No man is a hero to his valet FAMILIARITY
variety Variety is the spice of life CHANGE
varlet ape's an ape, a varlet's a varlet CHARACTER
venture Nothing venture, nothing gain THOROUGHNESS
  Nothing venture, nothing have THOROUGHNESS
verba Nullius in verba HYPOTHESIS AND FACT
verify Trust but verify CAUTION
vero Se non è vero, è molto ben trovato TRUTH
vessels Empty vessels make the most sound FOOLS
vice Gossip is vice GOSSIP
victors History is written by the victors HISTORY
victory army knows how to gain a victory ARMED FORCES
  Dig for victory GARDENS

view Distance lends enchantment to the view APPEARANCE
village It takes a village to raise a child CHILDREN
virtue Adversity is the foundation of virtue ADVERSITY
  Make a virtue of necessity NECESSITY
  Most people consider thrift a fine virtue THRIFT
  Patience is a virtue PATIENCE
  Virtue is its own reward VIRTUE
vision Vision without action is a daydream WORDS AND DEEDS
visited sea wants to be visited SEA
vodka Vodka is an aunt of wine DRINK
voice mockingbird has no voice BIRDS
  voice of the people is the voice of God POLITICS
voluntary Ignorance is voluntary misfortune IGNORANCE
volunteer One volunteer is worth two pressed men WORK
Vorsprung Vorsprung durch Technik TECHNOLOGY
vote straw vote only shows which way POLITICS
  Vote early and vote often POLITICS
votes Votes for women WOMEN
wait All things come to those who wait PATIENCE
  I sit on the shore, and wait for the wind PATIENCE
  Time and tide wait for no man OPPORTUNITY
waiting It's ill waiting for dead men's shoes AMBITION

490

walk If you can walk, you can dance   ABILITY
We must learn to walk before   PATIENCE

walking Let your fingers do the walking   TECHNOLOGY
Roads are made by walking   TRAVEL
Walking ten thousand miles   EXPERIENCE
Walking ten thousand miles   KNOWLEDGE

walks Gray's Inn for walks   LAW

wall Bull markets climb a wall of worry   BUSINESS
wall between both best preserves   NEIGHBOURS
weakest go to the wall   STRENGTH AND WEAKNESS

walls Walls have ears   SECRECY
When the wind of change blows, some build walls   CHANGE

walnut woman, a dog, and a walnut tree   WOMEN

walnuts Walnuts and pears you plant for   GARDENS

want Dress for the job you want   DRESS
For want of a nail the shoe was lost   PREPARATION AND READINESS
If you want peace, you must prepare   PREPARATION AND READINESS
If you want something done   ACTION AND INACTION
more you get the more you want   GREED
Wilful waste makes woeful want   THRIFT

wanton Wanton kittens make sober cats   YOUTH

wants Someone, somewhere, wants a letter   LETTERS

war All's fair in love and war   JUSTICE
bloody war and a sickly season   ARMED FORCES
Business is war   BUSINESS
Councils of war never fight   INDECISION
Make love not war   LIFESTYLES
soldier of the Great War, known unto   ARMED FORCES
War is God's way of teaching Americans geography   WARFARE
War will cease when men refuse to fight   WARFARE
When war is declared, Truth is the first   WARFARE

warm warm January, a cold May   WEATHER

wash One does not wash one's dirty linen   SECRECY
They that wash on Monday   HOUSEWORK

washes One hand washes the other   COOPERATION
Persil washes whiter   HOUSEWORK

waste Haste makes waste   HASTE AND DELAY
mind is a terrible thing to waste   MIND
Wilful waste makes woeful want   THRIFT

watch Watch this space   NEWS AND JOURNALISM

watched watched pot never boils   PATIENCE

watches You have the watches, but we have the time   TIME

water Before enlightenment, chop wood, carry water   LIFESTYLES

Keyword Index

Blood is thicker than
water   FAMILY
Dirty water will quench
fire   SEX
Every two miles the water
changes   TRAVEL
Hot water does not burn
down   FUTILITY
It is the calm and silent
water   DANGER
mill cannot grind with the
water that   OPPORTUNITY
rock in the water does not
know the pain   SYMPATHY
tears of the stranger are only
water   SYMPATHY
When drinking water,
remember the   PARENTS
When you drink water,
remember   GRATITUDE
Where water flows, a
channel   PATIENCE
You can take a horse to the
water   DEFIANCE
You never miss the water till the
well   GRATITUDE
watermelons You cannot carry
two watermelons   FUTILITY
waters It is good fishing in
troubled waters   OPPORTUNITY
Still waters run
deep   CHARACTER
Stolen waters are
sweet   TEMPTATION
Watson Elementary, my dear
Watson   THINKING
way Love will find a way   LOVE
Straws tell which way the wind
blows   KNOWLEDGE
straw vote only shows which
way   POLITICS
There is more than one way to
skin a cat   WAYS AND MEANS

way one eats is the way one
works   EATING
wilful man must have his
way   DETERMINATION
ways There are more ways of
killing a cat   WAYS AND MEANS
There are more ways of killing a
dog   WAYS AND MEANS
weakest chain is no stronger than
its weakest   COOPERATION
weakest go to the
wall   STRENGTH AND WEAKNESS
You are the weakest
link   STRENGTH AND
WEAKNESS
weapon bayonet is a weapon with
a worker   WARFARE
wear Better to wear out than to
rust   IDLENESS
If the cap fits, wear it   NAMES
If the shoe fits, wear it   NAMES
weary Be the day weary or be the
day long   TIME
weather sea wants to be
visited   SEA
There is no such thing as bad
weather   WEATHER
weathers Robin Hood could
brave all weathers   WEATHER
webs When spider webs
unite   COOPERATION
wed Better wed over the
mixen   FAMILIARITY
wedding One wedding brings
another   WEDDINGS
wedlock Wedlock is a
padlock   MARRIAGE
Wednesday Wednesday's child is
full of woe   SORROW
weeds Ill weeds grow
apace   GOOD AND EVIL
weepers Finders keepers (losers
weepers)   POSSESSIONS

well Dig the well before you are
thirsty   PREPARATION AND
READINESS
frog in a well knows nothing
of   SELF-ESTEEM AND
SELF-ASSERTION
He lives long who lives
well   VIRTUE
If you want a thing done
well   SELF-INTEREST
Let well alone   CAUTION
pitcher will go to the
well   EXCESS
Truth lies at the bottom of a
well   TRUTH
Well begun is half
done   BEGINNING

wells September dries up
wells   AUTUMN
You have drunk from wells you
did not   PAST

west East is east, and west
is west   SIMILARITY
AND DIFFERENCE
East, west, home's
best   HOME

wet Sow dry and set
wet   GARDENS

whale Save the
whale   ENVIRONMENT

whales When whales fight, the
shrimp's back is
broken   POWER

what It's not what you
know   OPPORTUNITY
What you see is what you
get   APPEARANCE

wheel wheel has come full
circle   CIRCUMSTANCE AND
SITUATION

where If you do not know where
you have been   CIRCUMSTANCE
AND SITUATION

If you don't know where you are
going   TRAVEL
Where's the beef   QUANTITIES
AND QUALITIES
Where were you in
'62?   ABSENCE

whisky Today's rain is tomorrow's
whisky   DRINK

whistle sow may whistle, though
it has   ABILITY

whistling whistling woman and a
crowing hen   WOMEN

white February fill dyke, be it
black or white   WINTER
Green Christmas, white
Easter   WEATHER
It hardly matters if it is a white
cat or   WAYS AND MEANS
One white foot, buy
him   HORSES
Two blacks don't make a
white   GOOD AND EVIL
white heron is a bird of   BIRDS

whiter Persil washes
whiter   HOUSEWORK

whole half is better than the
whole   MODERATION
whole is more than
the sum   QUANTITIES AND
QUALITIES

widow widow is a rudderless
boat   MARRIAGE

width Never mind the quality,
feel the width   QUANTITIES AND
QUALITIES

wife blind man's wife needs no
paint   APPEARANCE
deaf husband and a blind
wife   MARRIAGE

wilful wilful man must have his
way   DETERMINATION
Wilful waste makes woeful
want   THRIFT

Keyword Index

will He that complies against his will OPINION

He that will not when he may OPPORTUNITY

He that will to Cupar DETERMINATION

Where there's a will DETERMINATION

willing willing foe and sea room ARMED FORCES

wills He who wills the end DETERMINATION

win Heads I win, tails you lose WINNING AND LOSING

Let them laugh that win SUCCESS AND FAILURE

You can't win them all WINNING AND LOSING

You win a few, you lose a few SUCCESS AND FAILURE

wind God tempers the wind to the shorn lamb SYMPATHY

I sit on the shore, and wait for the wind PATIENCE

It's an ill wind that blows nobody OPTIMISM AND PESSIMISM

North wind doth blow WEATHER

reed before the wind lives on STRENGTH AND WEAKNESS

Straws tell which way the wind blows KNOWLEDGE

tall tree attracts the wind FAME

They that sow the wind CAUSES AND CONSEQUENCES

When the wind is in the east WEATHER

When the wind of change blows, some build walls CHANGE

wind of heaven is that which blows between a horse's ears HORSES

windmills When the wind of change blows, some build...windmills CHANGE

window eyes are the window of the soul BODY

winds You cannot control the winds MANAGEMENT

windy cold May and windy SPRING

wine From the sweetest wine, the tartest SIMILARITY AND DIFFERENCE

Good wine needs no bush ADVERTISING

Like fine wine AGE

There is truth in wine DRUNKENNESS

Vodka is an aunt of wine DRINK

When the wine is in, the wit DRUNKENNESS

You can't put new wine in old bottles CHANGE

wing bird never flew on one wing GENEROSITY

wink Wink at sma' fauts, ye hae great anes MISTAKES

wins Who dares wins DANGER

winner never quits, and a quitter never wins WINNING AND LOSING

winner winner never quits, and a quitter never wins WINNING AND LOSING

winter fire is winter's fruit WINTER

For the unlearned, old age is winter AGE

Nine months of winter WEATHER

One kind word warms three winter SYMPATHY

winter does not go
without   WINTER

Winter either bites with its
teeth   WINTER

Winter is summer's heir   WINTER

Winter never rots in the
sky   WINTER

Winter thunder, summer
hunger   WEATHER

wisdom beginning of wisdom is
to call things   NAMES

wise fool may give a wise
man   ADVICE

Fools ask questions that wise
men   KNOWLEDGE

Fools build houses and wise
men   FOOLS

It is a wise child that
knows   PARENTS

It is easy to be wise after the
event   FORESIGHT

One cannot love and be
wise   LOVE

Peace is the dream of the
wise   PEACE

Penny wise and pound
foolish   THRIFT

still tongue makes a wise
head   SILENCE

wise man changes his
mind   FOOLS

wise man turns chance into
good fortune   OPPORTUNITY

wise man will climb Mount Fuji
once   TRAVEL

word to the wise is
enough   ADVICE

wiser fall into a ditch makes you
wiser   EXPERIENCE

wiser man gives in   DEFIANCE

wisest little nonsense now and
then, is relished by the wisest
men   WISDOM

wish Be careful what you wish
for   CAUTION

wish is father to the
thought   OPINION

wishes If wishes were horses,
beggars   OPTIMISM AND
PESSIMISM

wit Brevity is the soul of
wit   SPEECH

When the wine is in, the
wit   DRUNKENNESS

wiving Hanging and wiving go by
destiny   FATE

woe Wednesday's child is full of
woe   SORROW

wolf caribou feeds the
wolf   STRENGTH AND WEAKNESS

Do not call a wolf to help
you   ENEMIES

Fear makes the wolf
bigger   FEAR

Hunger drives the wolf out of
the wood   NECESSITY

lone sheep is in danger from the
wolf   SOLITUDE

Man is a wolf to man   HUMAN
RACE

wolf may lose his teeth, but
never   AGE

wolves If you are afraid of wolves,
don't go into the
forest   STRENGTH AND WEAKNESS

wolves are well fed and the
sheep   DANGER

woman For most of history,
Anonymous was a
woman   WRITING

Hell hath no fury like a woman
scorned   WOMEN

Silence is a woman's best
garment   WOMEN

whistling woman and a crowing
hen   WOMEN

Keyword Index

woman, a dog, and a walnut tree WOMEN

woman and a ship ever want mending WOMEN

woman's place is in the home WOMEN

woman's work is never done HOUSEWORK

women England is the paradise of women COUNTRIES AND PEOPLES

Never choose your women or linen APPEARANCE

Votes for women WOMEN

Women and children first DANGER

Women hold up half the sky WOMEN

wonders Time works wonders TIME

Wonders will never cease SURPRISE

wood Before enlightenment, chop wood, carry water LIFESTYLES

Don't halloo till you are out of the wood OPTIMISM AND PESSIMISM

Hunger drives the wolf out of the wood NECESSITY

Saw wood and say nothing CAUTION

woods Fields have eyes and woods have ears SECRECY

In the woods it rains twice TREES

wool Many go out for wool AMBITION

Much cry and little wool EFFORT

word Englishman's word is his bond COUNTRIES AND PEOPLES

Many a true word is spoken in jest TRUTH

One kind word warms three winter SYMPATHY

swiftest horse cannot overtake the word WORDS

word to the wise is enough ADVICE

words Actions speak louder than words WORDS AND DEEDS

All words are pegs to hang ideas on WORDS

Fine words butter no parsnips WORDS AND DEEDS

Hard words break no bones WORDS

One picture is worth ten thousand words WORDS AND DEEDS

Stabs heal, but bad words never WORDS AND DEEDS

Words are sweet, but they never take WORDS AND DEEDS

work All work and no play makes Jack LEISURE

day without work is a day without food IDLENESS

devil finds work for idle hands IDLENESS

end crowns the work ENDING

eye of a master does more work EMPLOYMENT

Go to work on an egg EATING

harder I work, the luckier CHANCE AND LUCK

If you won't work you shan't eat IDLENESS

It is not work that kills, but worry WORRY

Many hands make light work COOPERATION

See all your best work go unnoticed SECRECY

We pretend to work EMPLOYMENT

woman's work is never
done   HOUSEWORK

Work expands so as to fill the
time   WORK

worker bayonet is a weapon with
a worker   WARFARE

workman bad workman
blames his tools   APOLOGY
AND EXCUSES

works Saturday's child works
hard for a living   WORK

way one eats is the way one
works   EATING

What matters is what
works   WAYS AND MEANS

workshop idle brain is the devil's
workshop   IDLENESS

world Hope is the pillar of the
world   HOPE

Isfahan is half the
world   TOWNS AND CITIES

lie can go around the
world   LIES

Love makes the world go
round   LOVE

One half of the world does not
know   KNOWLEDGE

world is one's
oyster   OPPORTUNITY

worm early bird catches the
worm
PREPARATION AND READINESS

Even a worm will
turn   NECESSITY

worry Action is worry's worst
enemy   ACTION AND INACTION

Bull markets climb a wall of
worry   BUSINESS

It is not work that kills, but
worry   WORRY

Worry is interest paid   WORRY

Worry is like a rocking
chair   WORRY

Worry often gives a small thing
a big shadow   WORRY

worse Go further and fare
worse   SATISFACTION AND
DISCONTENT

worst When things are at their
worst   OPTIMISM AND PESSIMISM

worth If a thing's worth
doing   EFFORT

It is a poor dog that's not
worth   VALUE

One picture is worth ten
thousand words   WORDS AND
DEEDS

worth of a thing is what it will
bring   VALUE

worthy labourer is worthy of his
hire   WORK

would Do as you would be done
by   LIFESTYLES

wrath soft answer turneth away
wrath   ANGER

wren robin and the wren are
God's   BIRDS

write He who would write and
can't   WRITING

writer Writing is a picture of the
writer's heart   WRITING

writes God writes straight with
crooked lines   GOD

writing art of writing is the art of
applying   WRITING

Writing is a picture of the
writer's heart   WRITING

written What is written with a
pen   WRITING

wrong If anything can go wrong,
it will   MISFORTUNES

king can do no wrong   ROYALTY

short cut is often a wrong
cut   WAYS AND MEANS

wrongs Two wrongs don't make a
right   GOOD AND EVIL

Keyword Index

year April and May are keys to
the whole year   SPRING
cherry year, a merry
year   SUMMER
Christmas comes but once a
year   CHRISTMAS
Next year in Jerusalem   TOWNS
AND CITIES
One year's seeding makes
seven   GARDENS
years It takes seven years to make
a piper   MUSIC
Keep a thing seven
years   POSSESSIONS
You should know a man seven
years   NEIGHBOURS
yesterday Yesterday has gone,
tomorrow is yet   PRESENT
Yesterday is ashes; tomorrow is
wood   PRESENT

yew More than one yew bow in
Chester   DANGER
Yorkshire Yorkshire born and
Yorkshire bred   BRITISH TOWNS
AND REGIONS
young good die young   VIRTUE
Whom the gods love die
young   YOUTH
Young folks think old folks to
be fools   YOUTH
young man married is
a   MARRIAGE
Young men may die, but old
men   DEATH
Young saint, old devil
HUMAN RACE
youth Youth must be
served   YOUTH
Yule green Yule makes a fat
churchyard   CHRISTMAS

Little Oxford Dictionary of
Quotations

Little Oxford Dictionary of

Quotations

FIFTH EDITION

Edited by
Susan Ratcliffe

OXFORD
UNIVERSITY PRESS

OXFORD
UNIVERSITY PRESS

Great Clarendon Street, Oxford, OX2 6DP,
United Kingdom

Oxford University Press is a department of the University of Oxford.
It furthers the University's objective of excellence in research, scholarship,
and education by publishing worldwide. Oxford is a registered trade mark of
Oxford University Press in the UK and in certain other countries

First Edition published in 1994
Second Edition published in 2001
Third edition published in 2005
Fourth edition published in 2008
Fifth edition published in 2012

Impression: 6

British Library Cataloguing in Publication Data

Data available

Library of Congress Cataloging in Publication Data

Data available

ISBN 978–0–19–965450–5

Printed in India by Replika Press Pvt Ltd

❊ Contents

Foreword   vii

List of Subjects   ix

Little Oxford Dictionary of Quotations   1

Index of Authors   449

Foreword ✳

An English proverb has it that 'The best things come in small packages', and if that is true then this is the best dictionary of quotations. While the comprehensive *Oxford Dictionary of Quotations* includes over 20,000 quotations, here the essence of that volume is distilled into 4,000 of the most famous and most useful sayings in the English language. The words of the great and the good, or sometimes the bad but witty, are gathered together to enable the user to add colour to a speech or offer support for a point of view.

The quotations are arranged by subject, so that a variety of angles on the same topic can be found together: on **Weather**, you can choose to quote Jerome K. Jerome: 'The weather is like the Government, always in the wrong' or St Teresa of Ávila: 'There is no such thing as bad weather. All weather is good because it is God's'. Some themes encompass special events such as **Birthdays** ('But after all, what *are* birthdays? Here today and gone tomorrow' A. A. Milne), some cover interests such as **Music** ('Music is a higher revelation than all wisdom and philosophy' Beethoven), while others are more abstract such as **Happiness** ('Happiness is a how, not a what; a talent, not an object' Hermann Hesse) or **Old Age** ('Age is whatever you think it is. You are as old as you think you are' Muhammad Ali). New themes in this edition include **Facts**, **India**, **Kissing**, and **Wisdom** ('The fool wonders, the wise man asks', said Disraeli).

Within each theme the quotations are arranged in alphabetical order of author's name, and a brief description is given for each author. Where a little more background information is necessary to understand the quotation, this

Foreword

is supplied after the author details. An index is provided to help readers seeking a quotation from a particular author.

Oxford continues to collect and authenticate new quotations as it has for over seventy years. Some of these quotations are by current authors, such as the writer Maya Angelou: 'You may not control all the events that happen to you but you can decide not to be reduced by them' or, on a more modern topic, the novelist Terry Pratchett: 'One of the universal rules of happiness is: always be wary of any helpful item that weighs less than its operating manual'. Others may go back more than two thousand years, but still resonate today: it was the Greek philosopher Plato who said: 'Of all animals the boy is the most unmanageable'. Perhaps that was what Willa Cather had in mind when she said 'The dead might as well try to speak to the living as the old to the young'. But the dead do speak to us: why else would we continue to quote the inventor Thomas Alva Edison 'The value of an idea lies in the using of it'. Perhaps the French moralist Montaigne has the answer: 'I quote others only the better to express myself'.

St Ambrose wrote more than 1500 years ago that 'No duty is more urgent than that of returning thanks'. It is not a duty but a pleasure to thank the many people who have contributed to this book, in particular Joanna Harris, Commissioning Editor for Quotations, Susanne Charlett, Jean Harker, and Verity Mason for their contributions to the Quotations Reading Programme, Ralph Bates for library research, and Kim Allen for proofreading. And it is perhaps appropriate to conclude with the words of E. F. Schumacher and Mies van der Rohe: 'Small is beautiful' and 'Less is more'.

SUSAN RATCLIFFE

Oxford 2012

List of Subjects ✻

A

Ability
Absence
Achievement
Acting
Action
Advertising
Advice
Africa
Ambition
America
Anger
Animals
Anxiety
Apology
Appearance
Architecture
Argument
Armed Forces
Art
Australia
Autumn

B

Babies
Baseball
Beauty
Beginning
Behaviour
Belief
Bereavement
Biography
Birds

Birth
Birthdays
Boats
The Body
Books
Boredom
Boxing
Brevity
Britain
Bureaucracy
Business

C

Canada
Careers
Cars
Cats
Censorship
Certainty
Chance
Change
Character
Charity
Charm
Children
Choice
Christmas
The Church
The Cinema
Civilization
Class
Clothes
Computers
Conscience

Conversation
Cookery
Cooperation
The Country
Courage
Creativity
Cricket
Crime
Crises
Criticism
Cruelty
Custom
Cynicism

D

Dance
Danger
Day
Death
Debt
Deceit
Democracy
Despair
Determination
Diaries
Diplomacy
Discontent
Discovery see
   Invention and
   Discovery
Dogs
Doubt
Drawing
Dreams

List of Subjects

Drink
Drugs

E

The Earth
Eating
Economics
Education
Effort
Elections
Ending
Enemies
England
The Environment
Envy and Jealousy
Equality
Europe
Evil
Examinations
Exercise
Experience

F

Facts
Failure
Fame
The Family
Fashion
Fate
Fathers
Fear
Festivals
Fishing
Flight
Flowers
Food
Foolishness

Football
Forgiveness
France
Friendship
The Future

G

Gardens
The Generation
  Gap
Genius
Gifts
God
Golf
Good Looks
Goodness
Gossip
Government
Greatness

H

Habit
Happiness
Hatred
Health
The Heart
Heaven
Hell
Heroes
History
Home
Honesty
Honour
Honours
Hope
Hospitality
Houses

Housework
The Human Race
Human Rights
Humour
Hypocrisy

I

Idealism
Ideas
Idleness
Ignorance
Imagination
India
Indifference
Individuality
Insight
Intelligence
Invention and
  Discovery
Ireland

J

Jealousy *see* Envy
  and Jealousy
Journalism
Justice

K

Kissing
Knowledge

L

Language
Languages

List of Subjects

The Law
Leadership
Leisure
Letters
Liberty
Libraries
Lies
Life
Life Sciences
Lifestyles
Literature
London
Love
Lovers
Luck

M

Madness
Management
Manners
Marriage
Mathematics
Meaning
Medicine
Meeting
Memory
Men
Men and Women
Middle Age
The Mind
Misfortune
Mistakes
Moderation
Money
Morality
Mothers
Mountains

Murder
Music

N

Names
Nature
News
Night

O

Old Age
Opinion
Optimism
Originality

P

Painting
Parents
Parties
Parting
The Past
Patience
Patriotism
Peace
Perfection
Persistence
Pessimism
Philosophy
Photography
Planning
Pleasure
Poetry
Politicians
Politics

Pollution
Poverty
Power
Practicality
Praise
Prayer
Prejudice
The Present
The Presidency
Pride
Progress
Promises
Protest
Punctuality
Punishment

Q

Quotations

R

Race
Railways
Reading
Reality
Relationships
Religion
Retirement
Revenge
Revolution
Royalty

S

Satisfaction
Science

List of Subjects

Scotland
Sculpture
The Sea
Secrecy
The Self
Self-Knowledge
Sex
Sickness
Silence
Singing
The Skies
Sleep
Society
Solitude
Sorrow
Speechmaking
Sport
Spring
Statistics
Strength
Style
Success
Suffering
Summer
The Supernatural
Sympathy

T

Taxes
Teaching
Technology
Television
Temptation
Tennis
Thanks
The Theatre
Thinking
Time
Toasts
The Town
Transience
Travel
Trust and Treachery
Truth

U

The Universe

V

Violence

W

Wales
War
Wealth
Weather
Weddings
Winning
Winter
Wisdom
Wit
Woman's Role
Women
Words
Work
Writing

Y

Youth

Ability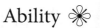

Natural abilities are like natural plants, that need pruning by study.
Francis Bacon 1561–1626 English courtier

If a man write a better book, preach a better sermon, or make a better mouse-trap than his neighbour, tho' he build his house in the woods, the world will make a beaten path to his door.
Ralph Waldo Emerson 1803–82 American writer

DUMBLEDORE: It is our choices, Harry, that show what we truly are, far more than our abilities.
J. K. Rowling 1965–   English novelist

MARLON BRANDO: I could have had class. I could have been a contender.
Budd Schulberg 1914–2009 American writer, *in the film* On the Waterfront

Non omnia possumus omnes.
We can't all do everything.
Virgil 70–19 BC Roman poet

Intelligence is quickness to apprehend as distinct from ability, which is capacity to act wisely on the thing apprehended.
Alfred North Whitehead 1861–1947 English philosopher

Absence

The Lord watch between me and thee, when we are absent one from another.
Bible

The heart may think it knows better: the senses know that absence blots people out. We have really no absent friends.
Elizabeth Bowen 1899–1973 Anglo-Irish novelist

Achievement

The absent are always in the wrong.
Philippe Néricault Destouches 1680–1754 French dramatist

Absence diminishes commonplace passions and increases great ones, as the wind extinguishes candles and kindles fire.
Duc de la Rochefoucauld 1613–80 French moralist

Absence makes the heart grow fonder.
Proverb

Most of what matters in your life takes place in your absence.
Salman Rushdie 1947– Indian-born British novelist

 # Achievement see also **Ambition**, **Effort**

That's one small step for a man, one giant leap for mankind.
Neil Armstrong 1930–2012 American astronaut, *stepping onto the moon*

We can lift ourselves out of ignorance, we can find ourselves as creatures of excellence and intelligence and skill.
Richard Bach 1936– American novelist

The desire accomplished is sweet to the soul.
Bible

Give us the tools and we will finish the job.
Winston Churchill 1874–1965 British statesman

None climbs so high as he who knows not whither he is going.
Oliver Cromwell 1599–1658 English statesman

The distance is nothing; it is only the first step that is difficult.
Mme Du Deffand 1697–1780 French literary hostess, *commenting on the legend that St Denis, carrying his head in his hands, walked two leagues*

The reward of a thing well done, is to have done it.
Ralph Waldo Emerson 1803–82 American writer

Those who believe that they are exclusively in the right are generally those who achieve something.
Aldous Huxley 1894–1963 English novelist

Being the richest man in the cemetery doesn't matter to me…Going to bed at night saying we've done something wonderful…that's what matters to me.
Steve Jobs 1955–2011 American computer executive

He has, indeed, done it very well; but it is a foolish thing well done.
Samuel Johnson 1709–84 English lexicographer

It is sobering to consider that when Mozart was my age he had already been dead for a year.
Tom Lehrer 1928– American humorist

He who does *something* at the head of one regiment, will eclipse him who does *nothing* at the head of a hundred.
Abraham Lincoln 1809–65 American statesman

Fame is an accident; merit a thing absolute.
Herman Melville 1819–91 American novelist

So little done, so much to do.
Cecil Rhodes 1853–1902 South African statesman

Acting see also **Cinema**, **Theatre**

To grasp the full significance of life is the actor's duty, to interpret it is his problem, and to express it his dedication.
Marlon Brando 1924–2004 American actor

Just say the lines and don't trip over the furniture.
Noël Coward 1899–1973 English dramatist

Action

Actors are cattle.
Alfred Hitchcock 1899–1980 British-born film director

Acting is a masochistic form of exhibitionism. It is not quite the occupation of an adult.
Laurence Olivier 1907–89 English actor

She ran the whole gamut of the emotions from A to B.
Dorothy Parker 1893–1967 American critic

Acting is merely the art of keeping a large group of people from coughing.
Ralph Richardson 1902–83 English actor

Suit the action to the word, the word to the action.
William Shakespeare 1564–1616 English dramatist

They say an actor is only as good as his parts. Well, my parts have done me pretty well, darling.
Barbara Windsor 1937– English actress

Action

But men must know, that in this theatre of man's life it is reserved only for God and angels to be lookers on.
Francis Bacon 1561–1626 English courtier

Vision without action is merely a dream. Action without vision just passes the time. Vision with action can change the world.
Joel Arthur Barker American futurist

Let's roll.
Todd Beamer 1968–2001, *as Beamer and other passengers were planning to storm the cockpit of the hijacked United Airlines Flight 93, 11 September 2001*

Better to light a candle than curse the darkness.
Peter Benenson 1921–2005 English lawyer

The world can only be grasped by action, not by
contemplation…The hand is the cutting edge of the mind.
Jacob Bronowski 1908–74 Polish-born scientist

Action is consolatory. It is the enemy of thought and the
friend of flattering illusions.
Joseph Conrad 1857–1924 Polish-born English novelist

Think nothing done while aught remains to do.
Samuel Rogers 1763–1855 English poet

If it were done when 'tis done, then 'twere well
It were done quickly.
William Shakespeare 1564–1616 English dramatist

Advertising

Word of mouth is the best medium of all.
Bill Bernbach 1911–82 American advertising executive

Advertising is the most fun you can have with your
clothes on.
Jerry Della Femina 1936– American advertising executive

Promise, large promise, is the soul of an advertisement.
Samuel Johnson 1709–84 English lexicographer

Society drives people crazy with lust and calls it
advertising.
John Lahr 1941– American critic

Advertising may be described as the science of arresting
human intelligence long enough to get money from it.
Stephen Leacock 1869–1944 Canadian humorist

Half the money I spend on advertising is wasted, and the
trouble is I don't know which half.
Lord Leverhulme 1851–1925 English industrialist

Advice

The consumer isn't a moron; she is your wife.
   David Ogilvy 1911–99 British-born advertising executive

Advertising is the rattling of a stick inside a swill bucket.
   George Orwell 1903–50 English novelist

Good wine needs no bush.
   Proverb

Advice

Books will speak plain when counsellors blanch.
   Francis Bacon 1561–1626 English courtier

Well, if you knows of a better 'ole, go to it.
   Bruce Bairnsfather 1888–1959 British cartoonist

A word spoken in due season, how good is it!
   Bible

Advice is seldom welcome; and those who want it the most always like it the least.
   Lord Chesterfield 1694–1773 English writer

Fools need advice most, but wise men only are the better for it.
   Benjamin Franklin 1706–90 American statesman and scientist

Get the advice of everybody whose advice is worth having—they are very few—and then do what you think best yourself.
   Charles Stewart Parnell 1846–91 Irish nationalist leader

After all, when you seek advice from someone it's certainly not because you want them to give it. You just want them to be there while you talk to yourself.
   Terry Pratchett 1948–2015 English novelist

Look for what's missing. Many advisers can tell a president how to improve what's proposed, or what's gone amiss. Few are able to see what isn't there.
> **Donald Rumsfeld** 1932– American politician

I always pass on good advice. It is the only thing to do with it. It is never of any use to oneself.
> **Oscar Wilde** 1854–1900 Irish dramatist

Africa ✳

The state of Africa is a scar on the conscience of the world.
> **Tony Blair** 1953– British Labour statesman

We have Africa in our blood and Africa has our bones. We are all Africans.
> **Richard Dawkins** 1941– English biologist

We are…a nation of dancers, singers and poets.
> **Olaudah Equiano** c.1745–c.97 African writer and former slave, *of the Ibo people*

The shape of Africa resembles a revolver, and the Congo is the trigger.
> **Frantz Fanon** 1925–61 French West Indian psychoanalyst

In Africa a thing is true at first light and a lie by noon.
> **Ernest Hemingway** 1899–1961 American novelist

The wind of change is blowing through this continent.
> **Harold Macmillan** 1894–1986 British Conservative statesman

I have dedicated my life to this struggle of the African people. I have fought against white domination, and I have fought against black domination. I have cherished the ideal of a democratic and free society in which all persons live together in harmony with equal opportunities.
> **Nelson Mandela** 1918–2013 South African statesman

Ambition

Semper aliquid novi Africam adferre.
Africa always brings [us] something new.
Pliny the Elder AD 23-79 Roman senator

 Ambition see also **Achievement**, **Effort**

No bird soars too high, if he soars with his own wings.
William Blake 1757-1827 English poet

Aut Caesar, aut nihil.
Caesar or nothing.
Cesare Borgia 1476-1507 Italian statesman

Ah, but a man's reach should exceed his grasp,
Or what's a heaven for?
Robert Browning 1812-89 English poet

Well is it known that ambition can creep as well as soar.
Edmund Burke 1729-97 Irish-born politician

[I] had rather be first in a village than second at Rome.
Julius Caesar 100-44 BC Roman statesman

Ambition leads me not only farther than any other man
has been before me, but as far as I think it possible for man
to go.
James Cook 1728-79 English explorer

At the age of six I wanted to be a cook. At seven I wanted to
be Napoleon. And my ambition has been growing steadily
ever since.
Salvador Dali 1904-89 Spanish painter

Hitch your wagon to a star.
Ralph Waldo Emerson 1803-82 American writer

Better to reign in hell, than serve in heaven.
John Milton 1608-74 English poet

Fain would I climb, yet fear I to fall.
> **Walter Ralegh** c.1552–1618 English courtier, *line written on a window-pane; Queen Elizabeth I (1533–1603) replied 'If thy heart fails thee, climb not at all'*

When that the poor have cried, Caesar hath wept;
Ambition should be made of sterner stuff.
> **William Shakespeare** 1564–1616 English dramatist

The world continues to offer glittering prizes to those who have stout hearts and sharp swords.
> **F. E. Smith** 1872–1930 British lawyer

There is always room at the top.
> **Daniel Webster** 1782–1852 American politician

America ✳

Good Americans, when they die, go to Paris.
> **Thomas Gold Appleton** 1812–84 American epigrammatist

America! America!
God shed His grace on thee
And crown thy good with brotherhood
From sea to shining sea!
> **Katherine Lee Bates** 1859–1929 American writer

God bless America,
Land that I love,
Stand beside her and guide her
Thru the night with a light from above.
> **Irving Berlin** 1888–1989 American songwriter

We are a nation of communities…a brilliant diversity spread like stars, like a thousand points of light in a broad and peaceful sky.
> **George Bush** 1924– American statesman

America

There is nothing wrong with America that cannot be fixed
by what is right with America.
>**Bill Clinton** 1946– American statesman

Isn't this a billion dollar country?
>**Charles Foster** 1828–1904 American politician, *responding to a
Democratic gibe about a 'million dollar Congress'*

Yes, America is gigantic, but a gigantic mistake.
>**Sigmund Freud** 1856–1939 Austrian psychoanalyst

Go West, young man, and grow up with the country.
>**Horace Greeley** 1811–72 American journalist

America is not a lie, it is a disappointment. But it can be a
disappointment only because it is also a hope.
>**Samuel Huntington** 1927–2008 American political scientist

Give me your tired, your poor,
Your huddled masses yearning to breathe free.
>**Emma Lazarus** 1849–87 American poet

There is not a black America and a white America and
Latino America and Asian America; there's the United
States of America.
>**Barack Obama** 1961– American statesman

I like to be in America!
OK by me in America!
Ev'rything free in America
For a small fee in America!
>**Stephen Sondheim** 1930– American songwriter

Overpaid, overfed, oversexed, and over here.
>**Tommy Trinder** 1909–89 British comedian, *of American troops
in Britain during the Second World War*

America is a vast conspiracy to make you happy.
>**John Updike** 1932–2009 American writer

The United States themselves are essentially the greatest poem.
Walt Whitman 1819–92 American poet

America is God's Crucible, the great Melting-Pot where all the races of Europe are melting and re-forming!
Israel Zangwill 1864–1926 Jewish writer

Anger

An angry look on the face is wholly against nature.
Marcus Aurelius AD 121–180 Roman emperor

Anger makes dull men witty, but it keeps them poor.
Francis Bacon 1561–1626 English courtier

A soft answer turneth away wrath.
Bible

Anger is never without an argument, but seldom with a good one.
Lord Halifax 1633–95 English politician

Anger is a short madness.
Horace 65–8 BC Roman poet

When angry, count ten before you speak; if very angry a hundred.
Thomas Jefferson 1743–1826 American statesman

Usually, when people are sad, they don't do anything. They just cry over their condition. But when they get angry, they bring about a change.
Malcolm X 1925–65 American civil rights campaigner

Never let the sun go down on your anger.
Proverb

Animals

When angry, count four; when very angry, swear.
Mark Twain 1835–1910 American writer

 # Animals see also **Cats**, **Dogs**

All things bright and beautiful,
All creatures great and small,
All things wise and wonderful,
The Lord God made them all.
Cecil Frances Alexander 1818–95 Irish poet

The question is not, Can they reason? nor, Can they talk?
but, Can they suffer?
Jeremy Bentham 1748–1832 English philosopher

A righteous man regardeth the life of his beast: but the
tender mercies of the wicked are cruel.
Bible

Tiger Tiger, burning bright,
In the forests of the night;
What immortal hand or eye,
Could frame thy fearful symmetry?
William Blake 1757–1827 English poet

A four-legged friend, a four-legged friend,
He'll never let you down.
J. Brooks

Wee, sleekit, cow'rin', tim'rous beastie,
O what a panic's in thy breastie!
Robert Burns 1759–96 Scottish poet, *on a mouse*

Wherever there is animal worship, there is human
sacrifice.
G. K. Chesterton 1874–1936 English writer

I am fond of pigs. Dogs look up to us. Cats look down on us. Pigs treat us as equals.
   Winston Churchill 1874–1965 British statesman

Animals, whom we have made our slaves, we do not like to consider our equal.
   Charles Darwin 1809–82 English naturalist

Where in this wide world can man find nobility without pride,
Friendship without envy, or beauty without vanity?
   Ronald Duncan 1914–82 English dramatist, *on the horse*

Animals are such agreeable friends—they ask no questions, they pass no criticism.
   George Eliot 1819–80 English novelist

I hate a word like 'pets': it sounds so much
Like something with no living of its own.
   Elizabeth Jennings 1926–2001 English poet

Anxiety ✳

What's the use of worrying?
It never was worth while,
So, pack up your troubles in your old kit-bag,
And smile, smile, smile.
   George Asaf 1880–1951 British songwriter

A ruffled mind makes a restless pillow.
   Charlotte Brontë 1816–55 English novelist

In trouble to be troubled
Is to have your trouble doubled.
   Daniel Defoe 1660–1731 English novelist

Apology

Anxiety is love's greatest killer.
Anaïs Nin 1903–77 American writer

O polished perturbation! golden care!
William Shakespeare 1564–1616 English dramatist

What though care killed a cat, thou hast mettle enough in thee to kill care.
William Shakespeare 1564–1616 English dramatist

Neurosis is the way of avoiding non-being by avoiding being.
Paul Tillich 1886–1965 German-born theologian

 Apology

If you have to eat crow, eat it while it's hot.
Alben W. Barkley 1877–1956 American politician

Very sorry can't come. Lie follows by post.
Lord Charles Beresford 1846–1919 British politician,
telegraphed message to the Prince of Wales, on being summoned to dine at the eleventh hour

Never make a defence or apology before you be accused.
Charles I 1600–49 British monarch

Never complain and never explain.
Benjamin Disraeli 1804–81 British statesman

Several excuses are always less convincing than one.
Aldous Huxley 1894–1963 English novelist

It is a good rule in life never to apologize. The right sort of people do not want apologies, and the wrong sort take a mean advantage of them.
P. G. Wodehouse 1881–1975 English writer

Appearance see also **Body**

For the Lord seeth not as man seeth: for man looketh on the outward appearance, but the Lord looketh on the heart.
   Bible

Even I don't wake up looking like Cindy Crawford.
   Cindy Crawford 1966– American model

If everyone were cast in the same mould, there would be no such thing as beauty.
   Charles Darwin 1809–82 English naturalist

I am the family face;
Flesh perishes, I live on.
   Thomas Hardy 1840–1928 English novelist

At 50, everyone has the face he deserves.
   George Orwell 1903–50 English novelist

Men seldom make passes
At girls who wear glasses.
   Dorothy Parker 1893–1967 American critic

It costs a lot of money to look this cheap.
   Dolly Parton 1946– American singer

Had Cleopatra's nose been shorter, the whole face of the world would have changed.
   Blaise Pascal 1623–62 French scientist and philosopher

There's no art
To find the mind's construction in the face.
   William Shakespeare 1564–1616 English dramatist

It is only shallow people who do not judge by appearances.
   Oscar Wilde 1854–1900 Irish dramatist

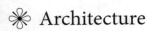 Architecture

A monstrous carbuncle on the face of a much-loved and elegant friend.
> **Charles, Prince of Wales** 1948– , *on the proposed extension to the National Gallery, London*

We shape our buildings, and afterwards our buildings shape us.
> **Winston Churchill** 1874–1965 British statesman

Light (God's eldest daughter) is a principal beauty in a building.
> **Thomas Fuller** 1608–61 English preacher

Less is more.
> **Ludwig Mies van der Rohe** 1886–1969 German-born architect

God is in the details.
> **Ludwig Mies van der Rohe** 1886–1969 German-born architect

When we build, let us think that we build for ever.
> **John Ruskin** 1819–1900 English critic

Architecture in general is frozen music.
> **Friedrich von Schelling** 1775–1854 German philosopher

Form follows function.
> **Louis Henri Sullivan** 1856–1924 American architect

Well building hath three conditions. Commodity, firmness, and delight.
> **Henry Wotton** 1568–1639 English diplomat

The physician can bury his mistakes, but the architect can only advise his client to plant vines—so they should go as far as possible from home to build their first buildings.
> **Frank Lloyd Wright** 1867–1959 American architect

Argument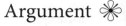

It takes in reality only one to make a quarrel. It is useless for the sheep to pass resolutions in favour of vegetarianism, while the wolf remains of a different opinion.
Dean Inge 1860–1954 English writer

There is no good in arguing with the inevitable. The only argument available with an east wind is to put on your overcoat.
James Russell Lowell 1819–91 American poet

The Catholic and the Communist are alike in assuming that an opponent cannot be both honest and intelligent.
George Orwell 1903–50 English novelist

Who can refute a sneer?
William Paley 1743–1805 English theologian

The argument of the broken window pane is the most valuable argument in modern politics.
Emmeline Pankhurst 1858–1928 English suffragette leader

I am not arguing with you—I am telling you.
James McNeill Whistler 1834–1903 American-born painter

Armed Forces see also **War**

Lions led by donkeys.
Anonymous, *associated with British forces during the First World War, but of earlier origin*

The sergeant is the army.
Dwight D. Eisenhower 1890–1969 American statesman

Armed Forces

Old soldiers never die,
They simply fade away.
J. Foley 1906–70 British songwriter

The courage of a soldier is found to be the cheapest, and most common, quality of human nature.
Edward Gibbon 1737–94 English historian

How do you ask a man to be the last man to die in Vietnam?
How do you ask a man to be the last man to die for a mistake?
John Kerry 1943– American politician

O it's Tommy this, an' Tommy that, an' 'Tommy, go away';
But it's 'Thank you, Mister Atkins,' when the band begins
to play.
Rudyard Kipling 1865–1936 English writer

Remember that there is not one of you who does not carry in his cartridge-pouch the marshal's baton of the duke of Reggio; it is up to you to bring it forth.
Louis XVIII 1755–1824 French monarch, *to military cadets*

An army without culture is a dull-witted army, and a dull-witted army cannot defeat the enemy.
Mao Zedong 1893–1976 Chinese statesman

When I was in the military, they gave me a medal for killing two men and a discharge for loving one.
Leonard Matlovich 1943–88 American soldier

An army marches on its stomach.
Napoleon I 1769–1821 French emperor

What passing-bells for these who die as cattle?
Only the monstrous anger of the guns.
Wilfred Owen 1893–1918 English poet

Wars may be fought with weapons, but they are won by men.
George S. Patton 1885–1945 American general

A man who is good enough to shed his blood for the country is good enough to be given a square deal afterwards.
Theodore Roosevelt 1858–1919 American statesman

When the military man approaches, the world locks up its spoons and packs off its womankind.
George Bernard Shaw 1856–1950 Irish dramatist

Theirs not to make reply,
Theirs not to reason why,
Theirs but to do and die:
Into the valley of Death
Rode the six hundred.
Alfred, Lord Tennyson 1809–92 English poet, *on the charge of the Light Brigade*

Discipline is the soul of an army. It makes small numbers formidable; procures success to the weak and esteem to all.
George Washington 1732–99 American statesman

I don't know what effect these men will have upon the enemy, but, by God, they frighten me.
Duke of Wellington 1769–1852 British general, *popular version of Wellington's remark: 'As Lord Chesterfield said of the generals of his day, "I only hope that when the enemy reads the list of their names, he trembles as I do"'*

Art see also **Painting**, **Sculpture**

You don't have to like everything.
Alan Bennett 1934– English writer, *proposing a notice for the National Gallery*

Art is meant to disturb, science reassures.
Georges Braque 1882–1963 French painter

Art

A product of the untalented, sold by the unprincipled to the utterly bewildered.
Al Capp 1907–79 American cartoonist, *on abstract art*

Without tradition art is a flock of sheep without a shepherd. Without innovation it is a corpse.
Winston Churchill 1874–1965 British statesman

An artist cannot speak about his art any more than a plant can discuss horticulture.
Jean Cocteau 1889–1963 French film director

Art for art's sake, with no purpose, for any purpose perverts art. But art achieves a purpose which is not its own.
Benjamin Constant 1767–1834 French novelist

I always said God was against art and I still believe it.
Edward Elgar 1857–1934 English composer

All art is autobiographical; the pearl is the oyster's autobiography.
Federico Fellini 1920–93 Italian film director

The artist must be in his work as God is in creation, invisible and all-powerful; one must sense him everywhere but never see him.
Gustave Flaubert 1821–80 French novelist

In art one is either a plagiarist or a revolutionary.
Paul Gauguin 1848–1903 French painter, *usually quoted as 'Art is either plagiarism or revolution'*

In art the best is good enough.
Johann Wolfgang von Goethe 1749–1832 German writer

The proletarian state must bring up thousands of excellent 'mechanics of culture', 'engineers of the soul'.
Maxim Gorky 1868–1936 Russian writer

Life is short, the art long.
> **Hippocrates** c.460–357 BC Greek physician, *often quoted in Latin as 'Ars longa, vita brevis [Art is long, life is short]'*

It's clever, but is it Art?
> **Rudyard Kipling** 1865–1936 English writer

We all know that Art is not truth. Art is a lie that makes us realize truth.
> **Pablo Picasso** 1881–1973 Spanish painter

Life without industry is guilt, and industry without art is brutality.
> **John Ruskin** 1819–1900 English critic

Art is not a handicraft, it is the transmission of feeling the artist has experienced.
> **Leo Tolstoy** 1828–1910 Russian novelist

Australia

Who knows but that England may revive in New South Wales when it has sunk in Europe.
> **Joseph Banks** 1743–1820 English botanist

A nation for a continent and a continent for a nation.
> **Edmund Barton** 1849–1920 Australian statesman, *on Australian federation*

True patriots we; for be it understood,
We left our country for our country's good.
> **Henry Carter** d. 1806, *written for the opening of the Playhouse, Sydney, New South Wales, when the actors were principally convicts*

Australia is a lucky country run mainly by second-rate people who share its luck.
> **Donald Richmond Horne** 1921– Australian writer

Autumn

Australia has a marvellous sky and air and blue clarity, and a hoary sort of land beneath it, like a Sleeping Princess on whom the dust of ages has settled.
D. H. Lawrence 1885–1930 English writer

In joyful strains then let us sing
Advance Australia fair.
P. D. McCormick c.1834–1916 Australian musician

What Great Britain calls the Far East is to us the near north.
Robert Gordon Menzies 1894–1978 Australian statesman

The crimson thread of kinship runs through us all.
Henry Parkes 1815–95 Australian statesman, *on Australian federation*

Above our writers—and other artists—looms the intimidating mass of Anglo-Saxon culture. Such a situation almost inevitably produces the characteristic Australian Cultural Cringe.
Arthur Angell Phillips 1900–85 Australian critic

 Autumn

Early autumn—
rice field, ocean,
one green.
Matsuo Basho 1644–94 Japanese poet

Now is the time for the burning of the leaves.
Laurence Binyon 1869–1943 English poet

'What is autumn?' 'A second spring, where every leaf is a flower.'
Albert Camus 1913–60 French writer

/>

It was one of those perfect English autumnal days which
occur more frequently in memory than in life.
   P. D. James 1920–2014 English writer

Season of mists and mellow fruitfulness,
Close bosom-friend of the maturing sun;
Conspiring with him how to load and bless
With fruit the vines that round the thatch-eaves run.
   John Keats 1795–1821 English poet

I want to go south, where there is no autumn, where the
cold doesn't crouch over one like a snow-leopard waiting
to pounce.
   D. H. Lawrence 1885–1930 English writer

O wild West Wind, thou breath of Autumn's being,
Thou, from whose unseen presence the leaves dead
Are driven, like ghosts from an enchanter fleeing.
   Percy Bysshe Shelley 1792–1822 English poet

For man, autumn is a time of harvest, of gathering together.
For nature, it is a time of sowing, of scattering abroad.
   Edwin Way Teale 1899–1980 American journalist

In…the fall, the whole country goes to glory.
   Frances Trollope 1780–1863 English writer, *of North America*

Babies see also Birth

There is no finer investment for any community than
putting milk into babies.
   Winston Churchill 1874–1965 British statesman

So for the mother's sake the child was dear,
And dearer was the mother for the child.
   Samuel Taylor Coleridge 1772–1834 English poet

Baseball

It is a pleasant thing to reflect upon, and furnishes a complete answer to those who contend for the general degeneration of the human species, that every baby born into the world is a finer one than the last.
Charles Dickens 1812–70 English novelist

There never was a child so lovely but his mother was glad to get him asleep.
Ralph Waldo Emerson 1803–82 American writer

Having a baby is like getting a tattoo on your face. You really need to be certain it's what you want before you commit.
Elizabeth Gilbert 1969– American writer

A loud noise at one end and no sense of responsibility at the other.
Ronald Knox 1888–1957 English writer, *definition of a baby*

Diaper backward spells repaid. Think about it.
Marshall McLuhan 1911–80 Canadian communications scholar

A baby is God's opinion that life should go on.
Carl Sandburg 1878–1967 American poet

You know more than you think you do.
Benjamin Spock 1903–98 American paediatrician, *opening words of* Baby and Child Care

 # Baseball

Think! How the hell are you gonna think and hit at the same time?
Yogi Berra 1925–2015 American baseball player

A ball player's got to be kept hungry to become a big leaguer. That's why no boy from a rich family ever made the big leagues.
Joe DiMaggio 1914–99 American baseball player

Baseball is very big with my people. It figures. It's the only way we can get to shake a bat at a white man without starting a riot.

Dick Gregory 1932–   American comedian

Take me out to the ball game,
Take me out with the crowd.
Buy me some peanuts and cracker-jack—
I don't care if I never get back.

Jack Norworth 1879–1959 American songwriter

All you have to do is keep the five players who hate your guts away from the five who are undecided.

Casey Stengel 1891–1975 American baseball player

Baseball, it is said, is only a game. True. And the Grand Canyon is only a hole in Arizona. Not all holes, or games, are created equal.

George F. Will 1941–   American columnist

Beauty see also **Good Looks**

Being thought of as a beautiful woman has spared me nothing in life. No heartache, no trouble. Beauty is essentially meaningless.

Halle Berry 1968–   American actress

Consider the lilies of the field, how they grow; they toil not, neither do they spin:
And yet I say unto you, That even Solomon in all his glory was not arrayed like one of these.

Bible

If you get simple beauty and naught else,
You get about the best thing God invents.

Robert Browning 1812–89 English poet

Beauty

I never saw an ugly thing in my life: for let the form of an
object be what it may,—light, shade, and perspective will
always make it beautiful.
   John Constable 1776–1837 English painter

Beauty is mysterious as well as terrible. God and devil are
fighting there, and the battlefield is the heart of man.
   Fedor Dostoevsky 1821–81 Russian novelist

Beauty will save the world.
   Fedor Dostoevsky 1821–81 Russian novelist

He was afflicted by the thought that where Beauty was,
nothing ever ran quite straight, which, no doubt, was why
so many people looked on it as immoral.
   John Galsworthy 1867–1933 English novelist

All things counter, original, spare, strange;
Whatever is fickle, freckled (who knows how?)
With swift, slow; sweet, sour; adazzle, dim;
He fathers-forth whose beauty is past change:
   Praise him.
   Gerard Manley Hopkins 1844–89 English poet

'Beauty is truth, truth beauty,'—that is all
Ye know on earth, and all ye need to know.
   John Keats 1795–1821 English poet

A thing of beauty is a joy for ever:
Its loveliness increases; it will never
Pass into nothingness.
   John Keats 1795–1821 English poet

At some point in life the world's beauty becomes enough.
You don't need to photograph, paint or even remember it.
It is enough.
   Toni Morrison 1931– American novelist

Remember that the most beautiful things in the world are the most useless; peacocks and lilies for instance.
John Ruskin 1819–1900 English critic

Beauty is all very well at first sight; but who ever looks at it when it has been in the house three days?
George Bernard Shaw 1856–1950 Irish dramatist

Beauty is no more than a promise of happiness.
Stendhal 1783–1842 French novelist

It is amazing how complete is the delusion that beauty is goodness.
Leo Tolstoy 1828–1910 Russian novelist

Beginning see also Ending

In the beginning God created the heaven and the earth. And the earth was without form, and void; and darkness was upon the face of the deep.
Bible

'Begin at the beginning,' the King said, gravely, 'and go on till you come to the end: then stop.'
Lewis Carroll 1832–98 English writer

What we call the beginning is often the end
And to make an end is to make a beginning.
The end is where we start from.
T. S. Eliot 1888–1965 American-born British poet

All this will not be finished in the first 100 days. Nor will it be finished in the first 1,000 days, nor in the life of this Administration, nor even perhaps in our lifetime on this planet. But let us begin.
John F. Kennedy 1917–63 American statesman

Behaviour

Are you sitting comfortably? Then I'll begin.
   Julia Lang 1921– British radio presenter

A tower of nine storeys begins with a heap of earth.
The journey of a thousand *li* starts from where one stands.
   Lao Tzu c.604–c.531 BC Chinese philosopher

I've started so I'll finish.
   Magnus Magnusson 1929–2007 Icelandic broadcaster, *said
   when a contestant's time ran out while a question was being put
   on* Mastermind

If we wait for the moment when everything, absolutely
everything, is ready, we shall never begin.
   Ivan Turgenev 1818–83 Russian novelist

 Behaviour see also **Manners**

When I go to Rome, I fast on Saturday, but here [Milan]
I do not. Do you also follow the custom of whatever church
you attend, if you do not want to give or receive scandal.
   St Ambrose c.339–397 French-born bishop of Milan, *usually
   quoted as 'When in Rome, do as the Romans do'*

Private faces in public places
Are wiser and nicer
Than public faces in private places.
   W. H. Auden 1907–73 English poet

In necessary things, unity; in doubtful things, liberty; in all
things, charity.
   Richard Baxter 1615–91 English divine

When people are on their best behaviour they aren't always
at their best.
   Alan Bennett 1934– English writer

Caesar's wife must be above suspicion.
Julius Caesar 100–44 BC Roman statesman

He only does it to annoy,
Because he knows it teases.
Lewis Carroll 1832–98 English writer

He was a verray, parfit gentil knyght.
Geoffrey Chaucer c.1343–1400 English poet

Take the tone of the company that you are in.
Lord Chesterfield 1694–1773 English writer

O tempora, O mores!
Oh, the times! Oh, the manners!
Cicero 106–43 BC Roman statesman

I get too hungry for dinner at eight.
I like the theatre, but never come late.
I never bother with people I hate.
That's why the lady is a tramp.
Lorenz Hart 1895–1943 American songwriter

Be a good animal, true to your instincts.
D. H. Lawrence 1885–1930 English writer

Go directly—see what she's doing, and tell her she mustn't.
Punch 1841–1992 English humorous periodical

Belief

For what a man would like to be true, that he more readily
believes.
Francis Bacon 1561–1626 English courtier

Every time a child says 'I don't believe in fairies' there is a
little fairy somewhere that falls down dead.
J. M. Barrie 1860–1937 Scottish writer

Belief

Lord, I believe; help thou mine unbelief.
Bible

Faith is the substance of things hoped for, the evidence of things not seen.
Bible

Of course not, but I am told it works even if you don't believe in it.
Niels Bohr 1885–1962 Danish physicist, *when asked whether he really believed a horseshoe hanging over his door would bring him luck*

Why, sometimes I've believed as many as six impossible things before breakfast.
Lewis Carroll 1832–98 English writer

It is wrong, always, everywhere and for any one, to believe anything upon insufficient evidence.
William Clifford 1845–79 English mathematician and philosopher

I do not believe…I know.
Carl Gustav Jung 1875–1961 Swiss psychologist

Credulity is the man's weakness, but the child's strength.
Charles Lamb 1775–1834 English writer

Nothing is so firmly believed as that which we least know.
Montaigne 1533–92 French moralist

We can believe what we choose. We are answerable for what we choose to believe.
John Henry Newman 1801–90 English theologian

What is wanted is not the will to believe, but the wish to find out, which is its exact opposite.
Bertrand Russell 1872–1970 British philosopher

There lives more faith in honest doubt,
Believe me, than in half the creeds.
Alfred, Lord Tennyson 1809–92 English poet

Certum est quia impossibile est.

It is certain because it is impossible.
Tertullian c.AD 160–c.225 Roman theologian, *often quoted as*
'Credo quia impossibile [I believe because it is impossible]'

Bereavement see also **Sorrow**

You can shed tears that she is gone or you can smile because
she has lived.
Anonymous, *preface to the Order of Service at the funeral of
Queen Elizabeth the Queen Mother, 2002*

He was my North, my South, my East and West,
My working week and my Sunday rest,
My noon, my midnight, my talk, my song;
I thought that love would last for ever: I was wrong.
W. H. Auden 1907–73 English poet

Blessed are they that mourn: for they shall be comforted.
Bible

Do not stand at my grave and weep:
I am not there. I do not sleep.
I am a thousand winds that blow.
I am the diamond glints on snow…
Do not stand at my grave and cry;
I am not there, I did not die.
Mary E. Frye 1905–2004 American poet, *quoted in letter left by
British soldier Stephen Cummins when killed by the IRA*

Bereavement

Bereavement is a universal and integral part of our experience of love. It follows marriage as normally as marriage follows courtship or as autumn follows summer.
    C. S. Lewis 1898–1963 English literary scholar

A man's dying is more the survivors' affair than his own.
    Thomas Mann 1875–1955 German novelist

Time does not bring relief; you all have lied
Who told me time would ease me of my pain!
    Edna St Vincent Millay 1892–1950 American poet

I can't think of a more wonderful thanksgiving for the life I have had than that everyone should be jolly at my funeral.
    Lord Mountbatten 1900–79 British statesman

The spring has gone out of the year.
    Pericles c.495–429 BC Greek statesman, *funeral oration*

I come to bury Caesar, not to praise him.
The evil that men do lives after them,
The good is oft interrèd with their bones.
    William Shakespeare 1564–1616 English dramatist

Moderate lamentation is the right of the dead, excessive grief the enemy to the living.
    William Shakespeare 1564–1616 English dramatist

The bitterest tears shed over graves are for words left unsaid and deeds left undone.
    Harriet Beecher Stowe 1811–96 American novelist

Even memory is not necessary for love. There is a land of the living and a land of the dead and the bridge is love, the only survival, the only meaning.
    Thornton Wilder 1897–1975 American writer

But how could I forget thee? Through what power,
Even for the least division of an hour,

Have I been so beguiled as to be blind
To my most grievous loss?
William Wordsworth 1770–1850 English poet

He first deceased; she for a little tried
To live without him: liked it not, and died.
Henry Wotton 1568–1639 English diplomat

Biography ✳

A well-written Life is almost as rare as a well-spent one.
Thomas Carlyle 1795–1881 Scottish historian

An autobiography is an obituary in serial form with the last
instalment missing.
Quentin Crisp 1908–99 English writer

There is properly no history; only biography.
Ralph Waldo Emerson 1803–82 American writer

Nobody can write the life of a man, but those who have eat
and drunk and lived in social intercourse with him.
Samuel Johnson 1709–84 English lexicographer

Lives of great men all remind us
We can make our lives sublime,
And, departing, leave behind us
Footprints on the sands of time.
Henry Wadsworth Longfellow 1807–82 American poet

To write one's memoirs is to speak ill of everybody except
oneself.
Marshal Pétain 1856–1951 French statesman

Discretion is not the better part of biography.
Lytton Strachey 1880–1932 English biographer

Birds

Every great man nowadays has his disciples, and it is always
Judas who writes the biography.
    Oscar Wilde 1854–1900 Irish dramatist

Birds

That's the wise thrush; he sings each song twice over,
Lest you should think he never could recapture
The first fine careless rapture!
    Robert Browning 1812–89 English poet

The bisy larke, messager of day.
    Geoffrey Chaucer c.1343–1400 English poet

It was the Rainbow gave thee birth,
And left thee all her lovely hues.
    W. H. Davies 1871–1940 Welsh poet, *of the kingfisher*

I caught this morning morning's minion, kingdom of
    daylight's dauphin, dapple-dawn-drawn Falcon.
    Gerard Manley Hopkins 1844–89 English poet

Oh, a wondrous bird is the pelican!
His bill will hold more than his belican.
He can take in his beak
Enough food for a week
But I'm damned if I see how the helican.
    Dixon Lanier Merritt 1879–1972 American editor

Alone and warming his five wits,
The white owl in the belfry sits.
    Alfred, Lord Tennyson 1809–92 English poet

I once had a sparrow alight upon my shoulder for a moment
while I was hoeing in a village garden, and I felt that I was

more distinguished by that circumstance than I should have been by any epaulette I could have worn.
Henry David Thoreau 1817–62 American writer

Birth see also **Babies**

It doesn't matter about being born in a duckyard, as long as you're hatched from a swan's egg!
Hans Christian Andersen 1805–75 Danish writer

In sorrow thou shalt bring forth children.
Bible

No phallic hero, no matter what he does to himself or to another to prove his courage, ever matches the solitary, existential courage of the woman who gives birth.
Andrea Dworkin 1946–2005 American feminist

I am not yet born; O fill me
With strength against those who would freeze my humanity.
Louis MacNeice 1907–63 British poet

Death and taxes and childbirth! There's never any convenient time for any of them.
Margaret Mitchell 1900–49 American novelist

Men should be bewailed at their birth, and not at their death.
Montesquieu 1689–1755 French political philosopher

Good work, Mary. We all knew you had it in you.
Dorothy Parker 1893–1967 American critic, *telegram to Mrs Sherwood on the arrival of her baby*

Love set you going like a fat gold watch.
The midwife slapped your footsoles, and your bald cry

Birthdays

Took its place among the elements.
Sylvia Plath 1932–63 American poet

What you say of the pride of giving life to an immortal soul is very fine, dear, but I own I can not enter into that; I think much more of our being like a cow or a dog at such moments; when our poor nature becomes so very animal and unecstatic.
Queen Victoria 1819–1901 British monarch

Our birth is but a sleep and a forgetting…
Not in entire forgetfulness,
And not in utter nakedness,
But trailing clouds of glory do we come.
William Wordsworth 1770–1850 English poet

 # Birthdays

A diplomat is a man who always remembers a woman's birthday but never remembers her age.
Robert Frost 1874–1963 American poet

You know you're getting old when the candles cost more than the cake.
Bob Hope 1903–2003 American comedian

Do you count your birthdays thankfully?
Horace 65–8 BC Roman poet

One of the sadder things, I think,
Is how our birthdays slowly sink:
Presents and parties disappear,
The cards grow fewer year by year.
Philip Larkin 1922–85 English poet

Believing, hear, what you deserve to hear:
Your birthday as my own to me is dear…

But yours gives most; for mine did only lend
Me to the world; yours gave to me a friend.
    Martial c.AD 40–c.104 Roman epigrammatist

EEYORE: But after all, what *are* birthdays? Here today and
gone tomorrow.
    A. A. Milne 1882–1956 English writer

Our birthdays are feathers in the broad wing of time.
    Jean Paul Richter 1763–1825 German novelist

Boats

Jolly boating weather,
And a hay harvest breeze,
Blade on the feather,
Shade off the trees
Swing, swing together
With your body between your knees.
    William Cory 1823–92 English poet

A wet sheet and a flowing sea,
A wind that follows fast
And fills the white and rustling sail
And bends the gallant mast.
    Allan Cunningham 1784–1842 Scottish poet

There is *nothing*—absolutely nothing—half so much worth
doing as simply messing about in boats.
    Kenneth Grahame 1859–1932 Scottish-born writer

Quinquireme of Nineveh from distant Ophir
Rowing home to haven in sunny Palestine,
With a cargo of ivory,
And apes and peacocks,
Sandalwood, cedarwood, and sweet white wine.
    John Masefield 1878–1967 English poet

The Body see also **Appearance**

I will give thanks unto thee, for I am fearfully and
wonderfully made.
Bible

A woman watches her body uneasily, as though it were an
unreliable ally in the battle for love.
Leonard Cohen 1934–2016 Canadian singer

i like my body when it is with your
body. It is so quite new a thing.
Muscles better and nerves more.
e. e. cummings 1894–1962 American poet

The leg, a source of much delight,
which carries weight and governs height.
Ian Dury 1942–2000 British rock singer

Anatomy is destiny.
Sigmund Freud 1856–1939 Austrian psychoanalyst

The body says what words cannot.
Martha Graham 1894–1991 American dancer

For some inexplicable reason the sense of smell does not
hold the high position it deserves among its sisters. There is
something of the fallen angel about it.
Helen Keller 1880–1968 American writer

Nothing tastes as good as skinny feels.
Kate Moss 1974– English model, *when asked for her motto*

I'm fat, but I'm thin inside. Has it ever struck you that there's
a thin man inside every fat man, just as they say there's a
statue inside every block of stone?
George Orwell 1903–50 English novelist

Our bodies are our gardens, to which our wills are gardeners.
William Shakespeare 1564–1616 English dramatist

You can never be too rich or too thin.
Wallis Simpson (Duchess of Windsor) 1896–1986

Every man is the builder of a temple, called his body.
Henry David Thoreau 1817–62 American writer

Our body is a machine for living. It is organized for that, it is its nature. Let life go on in it unhindered and let it defend itself.
Leo Tolstoy 1828–1910 Russian novelist

I sing the body electric.
Walt Whitman 1819–92 American poet

The human body is the best picture of the human soul.
Ludwig Wittgenstein 1889–1951 Austrian-born philosopher

Books see also **Libraries**, **Literature**, **Reading**

Some books are undeservedly forgotten; none are undeservedly remembered.
W. H. Auden 1907–73 English poet

Some books are to be tasted, others to be swallowed, and some few to be chewed and digested.
Francis Bacon 1561–1626 English courtier

Books say: she did this because. Life says: she did this. Books are where things are explained to you; life is where things aren't.
Julian Barnes 1946– English novelist

Of making many books there is no end; and much study is a weariness of the flesh.
Bible

Books

A great book is like great evil.
Callimachus c.305–c.240 BC Greek poet

A classic is a book that has never finished saying what it has to say.
Italo Calvino 1923–85 Italian writer

'What is the use of a book', thought Alice, 'without pictures or conversations?'
Lewis Carroll 1832–98 English writer

I don't trust books. They're all fact, no heart.
Stephen Colbert 1964– American satirist

There is more treasure in books than in all the pirates' loot on Treasure Island.
Walt Disney 1901–66 American film producer

Another damned, thick, square book! Always scribble, scribble, scribble! Eh! Mr Gibbon?
Duke of Gloucester 1743–1805

A book must be the axe for the frozen sea within us.
Franz Kafka 1883–1924 Czech novelist

To produce a mighty book, you must choose a mighty theme.
Herman Melville 1819–91 American novelist

A good book is the precious life-blood of a master spirit.
John Milton 1608–74 English poet

There is no book so bad that some good cannot be got out of it.
Pliny the Elder AD 23–79 Roman senator

The principle of procrastinated rape is said to be the ruling one in all the great best-sellers.
V. S. Pritchett 1900–97 English writer

I hate books; they only teach us to talk about things we know nothing about.
Jean-Jacques Rousseau 1712–78 French philosopher

All books are divisible into two classes, the books of the hour, and the books of all time.
John Ruskin 1819–1900 English critic

No furniture so charming as books.
Sydney Smith 1771–1845 English essayist

A good book is the best of friends, the same to-day and for ever.
Martin Tupper 1810–89 English writer

'*Classic.*' A book which people praise and don't read.
Mark Twain 1835–1910 American writer

Publish and be damned.
Duke of Wellington 1769–1852 British general, *replying to a blackmail threat*

Boredom

Nothing happens, nobody comes, nobody goes, it's awful!
Samuel Beckett 1906–89 Irish writer

Life, friends, is boring. We must not say so…
And moreover my mother told me as a boy
(repeatedly) 'Ever to confess you're bored
means you have no
Inner Resources.'
John Berryman 1914–72 American poet

Everyone is a bore to someone. That is unimportant.
The thing to avoid is being a bore to oneself.
Gerald Brenan 1894–1987 British writer

Boxing

What's wrong with being a boring kind of guy?
George Bush 1924- American statesman

Millions long for immortality who don't know what to do with themselves on a rainy Sunday afternoon.
Susan Ertz 1894–1985 American writer

Nothing, like something, happens anywhere.
Philip Larkin 1922–85 English poet

We often forgive those who bore us, but we cannot forgive those whom we bore.
Duc de la Rochefoucauld 1613–80 French moralist

Boredom is…a vital problem for the moralist, since half the sins of mankind are caused by the fear of it.
Bertrand Russell 1872–1970 British philosopher

A healthy male adult bore consumes *each year* one and a half times his own weight in other people's patience.
John Updike 1932–2009 American writer

The secret of being a bore…is to tell everything.
Voltaire 1694–1778 French writer

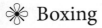 # Boxing

Float like a butterfly, sting like a bee.
Muhammad Ali 1942–2016 American boxer, *summary of his boxing strategy*

I'm the greatest.
Muhammad Ali 1942–2016 American boxer

Boxing's just showbusiness with blood.
Frank Bruno 1961- English boxer

Brevity

Honey, I just forgot to duck.

>**Jack Dempsey** 1895–1983 American boxer, *to his wife, on losing the World Heavyweight title*

The bigger they are, the further they have to fall.

>**Robert Fitzsimmons** 1862–1917 New Zealand boxer, *prior to a boxing match*

We was robbed!

>**Joe Jacobs** 1896–1940 American boxing manager, *after Jack Sharkey beat Max Schmeling (of whom Jacobs was manager) in a heavyweight title fight*

He can run. But he can't hide.

>**Joe Louis** 1914–81 American boxer, *of Billy Conn, his opponent*

Brevity

It is a foolish thing to make a long prologue, and to be short in the story itself.

>**Bible**

The beauty of concision…is that you can only repeat conventional thoughts.

>**Noam Chomsky** 1928– American linguist

I strive to be brief, and I become obscure.

>**Horace** 65–8 BC Roman poet

I have made this [letter] longer than usual, only because I have not had the time to make it shorter.

>**Blaise Pascal** 1623–62 French scientist and philosopher

Words are like leaves; and where they most abound,
Much fruit of sense beneath is rarely found.

>**Alexander Pope** 1688–1744 English poet

Britain

If there is anywhere a thing said in two sentences that could have been as clearly and as engagingly said in one, then it's amateur work.
   Robert Louis Stevenson 1850–94 Scottish novelist

Britain

Great Britain has lost an empire and has not yet found a role.
   Dean Acheson 1893–1971 American politician

The land of embarrassment and breakfast.
   Julian Barnes 1946– English novelist, *of Britain*

You cannot trust people who have such bad cuisine. It is the country with the worst food after Finland.
   Jacques Chirac 1932– French statesman, *on the British*

The British nation is unique in this respect. They are the only people who like to be told how bad things are, who like to be told the worst.
   Winston Churchill 1874–1965 British statesman

What is our task? To make Britain a fit country for heroes to live in.
   David Lloyd George 1863–1945 British statesman

Fifty years on from now, Britain will still be the country of long shadows on county [cricket] grounds, warm beer, invincible green suburbs, dog lovers, and—as George Orwell said—old maids bicycling to Holy Communion through the morning mist.
   John Major 1943– British statesman

No sex, please—we're British.
   Anthony Marriott 1931–2014 and **Alistair Foot** British dramatists

44

Rule, Britannia, rule the waves;
Britons never will be slaves.
    James Thomson 1700–48 Scottish poet

Other nations use 'force'; we Britons alone use 'Might'.
    Evelyn Waugh 1903–66 English novelist

Bureaucracy see also Management

A memorandum is written not to inform the reader but to
protect the writer.
    Dean Acheson 1893–1971 American politician

It is an inevitable defect, that bureaucrats will care more for
routine than for results.
    Walter Bagehot 1826–77 English economist

Guidelines for bureaucrats: (1) When in charge, ponder.
(2) When in trouble, delegate. (3) When in doubt, mumble.
    James H. Boren 1925– American bureaucrat

The Civil Service is profoundly deferential—'Yes, Minister!
No, Minister! If you wish it, Minister!'
    Richard Crossman 1907–74 British politician

A desk is a dangerous place from which to watch the world.
    John le Carré 1931– English novelist

The man who is denied the opportunity of taking decisions
of importance begins to regard as important the decisions
he is allowed to take.
    C. Northcote Parkinson 1909–93 English writer

Back in the East you can't do much without the right papers,
but *with* the right papers you can do *anything*. They *believe*
in papers. Papers are power.
    Tom Stoppard 1937– British dramatist

45

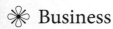 # Business

There is nothing more requisite in business than dispatch.
Joseph Addison 1672–1719 English writer

A merchant shall hardly keep himself from doing wrong.
Bible (Apocrypha)

Rule No 1: never lose money. Rule No 2: never forget rule No 1.
Warren Buffett 1930– American businessman

They [corporations] cannot commit treason, nor be outlawed, nor excommunicate, for they have no souls.
Edward Coke 1552–1634 English jurist

Here's the rule for bargains: 'Do other men, for they would do you.' That's the true business precept.
Charles Dickens 1812–70 English novelist

Remember that time is money.
Benjamin Franklin 1706–90 American statesman and scientist

Necessity never made a good bargain.
Benjamin Franklin 1706–90 American statesman and scientist

If business always made the right decisions, business wouldn't be business.
J. Paul Getty 1892–1976 American industrialist

Only the paranoid survive.
Andrew Grove 1936–2016 American businessman

The best of all monopoly profits is a quiet life.
J. R. Hicks 1904–89 British economist

Only a fool holds out for the top dollar.
Joseph P. Kennedy 1888–1969 American financier, *selling stock before the Wall Street crash of 1929*

Never invest in any idea you can't illustrate with a crayon.
  Peter Lynch 1944-   American investor

A salesman is got to dream, boy. It comes with the territory.
  Arthur Miller 1915-2005 American dramatist

After a certain point money is meaningless. It ceases to be the goal. The game is what counts.
  Aristotle Onassis 1906-75 Greek businessman

The customer is never wrong.
  César Ritz 1850-1918 Swiss hotel proprietor

I think that business practices would improve immeasurably if they were guided by 'feminine' principles—qualities like love and care and intuition.
  Anita Roddick 1942-2007 English businesswoman

People of the same trade seldom meet together, even for merriment and diversion, but the conversation ends in a conspiracy against the public, or in some contrivance to raise prices.
  Adam Smith 1723-90 Scottish economist

Deals are my art form. Other people paint beautifully on canvas or write wonderful poetry. I like making deals, preferably big deals. That's how I get my kicks.
  Donald Trump 1946-   American businessman

The public be damned! I'm working for my stockholders.
  William H. Vanderbilt 1821-85 American railway magnate

[Commercialism is] doing well that which should not be done at all.
  Gore Vidal 1925-2012 American writer

There is only one boss. The customer. And he can fire everybody in the company from the chairman on down, simply by spending his money somewhere else.
  Sam Walton 1919-92 American businessman

Canada

You cannot be a success in any business without believing
that it is the greatest business in the world…You have to put
your heart in the business and the business in your heart.
Thomas Watson Snr. 1874–1956 American businessman

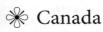 # Canada

Americans are benevolently ignorant about Canada, while
Canadians are malevolently well-informed about the United
States.
John Bartlet Brebner 1895–1957 Canadian historian

Dusty, cobweb-covered, maimed, and set at naught,
Beauty crieth in an attic, and no man regardeth.
O God! O Montreal!
Samuel Butler 1835–1902 English novelist

I am rather inclined to believe that this is the land God gave
to Cain.
Jacques Cartier 1491–1557 French explorer

Some say that no one ever leaves Montreal, for that city, like
Canada itself, is designed to preserve the past, a past that
happened somewhere else.
Leonard Cohen 1934–2016 Canadian singer

I see Canada as a country torn between a very northern,
rather extraordinary, mystical spirit which it fears and its
desire to present itself to the world as a Scotch banker.
Robertson Davies 1913–95 Canadian novelist

Vive Le Québec Libre.

Long Live Free Quebec.
Charles de Gaulle 1890–1970 French statesman

If some countries have too much history, we have too much
geography.
William Lyon Mackenzie King 1874–1950 Canadian statesman

That's ours—lock, stock and iceberg.
> **Brian Mulroney** 1939– Canadian statesman, *asked about Canadian sovereignty over the Arctic*

To be Prime Minister of Canada, you need the hide of a rhinoceros, the morals of St. Francis, the patience of Job, the wisdom of Solomon, the strength of Hercules, the leadership of Napoleon, the magnetism of a Beatle and the subtlety of Machiavelli.
> **Lester Pearson** 1897–1972 Canadian statesman

Mon pays ce n'est pas un pays, c'est l'hiver.

My country is not a country, it is winter.
> **Gilles Vigneault** 1928– Canadian singer

These two nations have been at war over a few acres of snow near Canada, and…they are spending on this fine struggle more than Canada itself is worth.
> **Voltaire** 1694–1778 French writer

O Canada! Our home and native land!
True patriot love in all thy sons command.
With glowing hearts we see thee rise,
The True North strong and free!
> **Robert Stanley Weir** 1856–1926 Canadian lawyer

Careers see also **Work**

I will undoubtedly have to seek what is happily known as gainful employment, which I am glad to say does not describe holding public office.
> **Dean Acheson** 1893–1971 American politician

For promotion cometh neither from the east, nor from the west: nor yet from the south.
> **Bible**

Cars

McJob: A low-pay, low-prestige, low-dignity, low benefit, no-future job in the service sector.
Douglas Coupland 1961– Canadian writer

To do nothing and get something, formed a boy's ideal of a manly career.
Benjamin Disraeli 1804–81 British statesman

By working faithfully eight hours a day, you may eventually get to be a boss and work twelve hours a day.
Robert Frost 1874–1963 American poet

It is wonderful, when a calculation is made, how little the mind is actually employed in the discharge of any profession.
Samuel Johnson 1709–84 English lexicographer

I didn't get where I am today without....
David Nobbs 1935–2015 British novelist, *catchphrase used by Reginald Perrin's manager C. J.*

Thou art not for the fashion of these times,
Where none will sweat but for promotion.
William Shakespeare 1564–1616 English dramatist

It is difficult to get a man to understand something when his salary depends on his not understanding it.
Upton Sinclair 1878–1968 American novelist

The test of a vocation is the love of the drudgery it involves.
Logan Pearsall Smith 1865–1946 American writer

 ## Cars

Take it easy driving—the life you save may be mine.
James Dean 1931–55 American actor

[There are] only two classes of pedestrians in these days of reckless motor traffic—the quick, and the dead.
Lord Dewar 1864–1930 British industrialist

The horseless vehicle is the coming wonder.

Thomas Alva Edison 1847–1931 American inventor, *in 1895*

The poetry of motion! The *real* way to travel! The *only* way to travel! Here today—in next week tomorrow!

Kenneth Grahame 1859–1932 Scottish-born writer

O bliss! O poop-poop! O my!

Kenneth Grahame 1859–1932 Scottish-born writer

What good is speed if the brain has oozed out on the way?

Karl Kraus 1874–1936 Austrian satirist

The car has become an article of dress without which we feel uncertain, unclad and incomplete in the urban compound.

Marshall McLuhan 1911–80 Canadian communications scholar

Beneath this slab
John Brown is stowed.
He watched the ads,
And not the road.

Ogden Nash 1902–71 American humorist

Cats

Macavity, Macavity, there's no one like Macavity,
There never was a Cat of such deceitfulness and suavity.
He always has an alibi, and one or two to spare:
At whatever time the deed took place — MACAVITY WASN'T THERE!

T. S. Eliot 1888–1965 American-born British poet

Cats, I always think, only jump into your lap to check if you are cold enough, yet, to eat.

Anne Enright 1962– Irish writer

He walked by himself, and all places were alike to him.

Rudyard Kipling 1865–1936 English writer

Censorship

Cats seem to go on the principle that it never does any harm to ask for what you want.
Joseph Wood Krutch 1893–1970 American critic and naturalist

If a fish is the movement of water embodied, given shape, then cat is a diagram and pattern of subtle air.
Doris Lessing 1919–2013 English writer

When I play with my cat, who knows whether she isn't amusing herself with me more than I am with her?
Montaigne 1533–92 French moralist

The trouble with a kitten is
THAT
Eventually it becomes a
CAT.
Ogden Nash 1902–71 American humorist

For I will consider my Cat Jeoffry…
For he counteracts the powers of darkness by his electrical
    skin and glaring eyes.
For he counteracts the Devil, who is death, by brisking
    about the life.
Christopher Smart 1722–71 English poet

 # Censorship

Is it a book you would even wish your wife or your servants to read?
Mervyn Griffith-Jones 1909–79 British lawyer,
of D. H. Lawrence's Lady Chatterley's Lover

Wherever books will be burned, men also, in the end, are burned.
Heinrich Heine 1797–1856 German poet

One has to multiply thoughts to the point where there aren't enough policemen to control them.
Stanislaw Lec 1909–66 Polish writer

The power of the press is very great, but not so great as the power of suppress.
Lord Northcliffe 1865–1922 British newspaper proprietor

If these writings of the Greeks agree with the book of God, they are useless and need not be preserved; if they disagree, they are pernicious and ought to be destroyed.
Caliph Omar c.581–644, *on burning the library of Alexandria*

Don't you see that the whole aim of Newspeak is to narrow the range of thought? In the end we shall make thoughtcrime literally impossible, because there will be no words in which to express it.
George Orwell 1903–50 English novelist

It is obvious that 'obscenity' is not a term capable of exact legal definition; in the practice of the Courts, it means 'anything that shocks the magistrate'.
Bertrand Russell 1872–1970 British philosopher

If decade after decade the truth cannot be told, each person's mind begins to roam irretrievably. One's fellow countrymen become harder to understand than Martians.
Alexander Solzhenitsyn 1918–2008 Russian novelist

The state has no place in the nation's bedrooms.
Pierre Trudeau 1919–2000 Canadian statesman

I disapprove of what you say, but I will defend to the death your right to say it.
Voltaire 1694–1778 French writer, *a later summary of his attitude towards Helvétius following the burning of the latter's* De l'esprit

Certainty see also **Doubt**

My mind is not a bed to be made and re-made.
James Agate 1877–1947 British writer

If a man will begin with certainties, he shall end in doubts;
but if he will be content to begin with doubts, he shall end
in certainties.
Francis Bacon 1561–1626 English courtier

We often call a certainty a hope, to bring it luck.
Elizabeth Bibesco 1897–1945 British writer

The archbishop is usually to be found nailing his colours to
the fence.
Frank Field 1942– British politician, *of Archbishop Runcie*

What, never?
No, never!
What, *never*?
Hardly ever!
W. S. Gilbert 1836–1911 English writer

I'll give you a definite maybe.
Sam Goldwyn 1882–1974 American film producer

The answers we have found have only served to raise a
whole set of new questions. In some ways we feel that we
are as confused as ever, but we think we are confused on a
higher level, and about more important things.
Earl C. Kelley 1895–1970 American educationist

It's one thing to be certain, but you can be certain and you
can be wrong.
John Kerry 1943– American politician

I wish I was as cocksure of anything as Tom Macaulay is of
everything.
Lord Melbourne 1779–1848 British statesman

Ah, what a dusty answer gets the soul
When hot for certainties in this our life!
George Meredith 1828–1909 English writer

The only certainty is that nothing is certain.
Pliny the Elder AD 23–79 Roman senator

Minds like beds always made up,
(more stony than a shore)
unwilling or unable.
William Carlos Williams 1883–1963 American poet

Chance see also **Luck**

Cast thy bread upon the waters: for thou shalt find it after
many days.
Bible

But for the grace of God there goes John Bradford.
John Bradford c.1510–55 English martyr, *on seeing a group of*
criminals being led to their execution; usually quoted as 'There but
for the grace of God go I'

The best laid schemes o' mice an' men
Gang aft a-gley.
Robert Burns 1759–96 Scottish poet

The chapter of knowledge is a very short, but the chapter of
accidents is a very long one.
Lord Chesterfield 1694–1773 English writer

If there were no coincidence, it would be the greatest
coincidence of all.
G. K. Chesterton 1874–1936 English writer

At this moment he was unfortunately called out by a person
on business from Porlock.
Samuel Taylor Coleridge 1772–1834 English poet, *preliminary*
note to 'Kubla Khan', explaining why the poem remained unfinished

Change

Accidents will occur in the best-regulated families.
Charles Dickens 1812–70 English novelist

If an army of monkeys were strumming on typewriters they *might* write all the books in the British Museum.
Arthur Eddington 1882–1944 British astrophysicist

I am convinced that *He* [God] does not play dice.
Albert Einstein 1879–1955 German-born theoretical physicist

Mr Bond, they have a saying in Chicago: 'Once is happenstance. Twice is coincidence. The third time it's enemy action.'
Ian Fleming 1908–64 English writer, *Goldfinger* to James Bond

Predictability: Does the flap of a butterfly's wings in Brazil set off a tornado in Texas?
Edward N. Lorenz 1917–2008 American meteorologist

O! many a shaft, at random sent,
Finds mark the archer little meant!
And many a word, at random spoken,
May soothe or wound a heart that's broken.
Sir Walter Scott 1771–1832 Scottish novelist

There is a tide in the affairs of men,
Which, taken at the flood, leads on to fortune.
William Shakespeare 1564–1616 English dramatist

 Change see also **Beginning, Ending**

He that will not apply new remedies must expect new evils; for time is the greatest innovator.
Francis Bacon 1561–1626 English courtier

Can the Ethiopian change his skin, or the leopard his spots?
Bible

Change

Variety's the very spice of life,
That gives it all its flavour.
   William Cowper 1731–1800 English poet

       He not busy being born
Is busy dying.
   Bob Dylan 1941– American singer

When it is not necessary to change, it is necessary not to change.
   Lucius Cary, Viscount Falkland 1610–43 English politician

Most of the change we think we see in life
Is due to truths being in and out of favour.
   Robert Frost 1874–1963 American poet

We must be the change we wish to see in the world.
   Mahatma Gandhi 1869–1948 Indian statesman

You can't step twice into the same river.
   Heraclitus c.540–c.480 BC Greek philosopher

Consistency is contrary to nature, contrary to life. The only completely consistent people are the dead.
   Aldous Huxley 1894–1963 English novelist

Change is not made without inconvenience, even from worse to better.
   Samuel Johnson 1709–84 English lexicographer

Plus ça change, plus c'est la même chose.

The more things change, the more they are the same.
   Alphonse Karr 1808–90 French writer

If we want things to stay as they are, things will have to change.
   Giuseppe di Lampedusa 1896–1957 Italian writer

Change

JUDY GARLAND: Toto, I've a feeling we're not in Kansas any more.
Noel Langley 1911–80 American screenwriter, *in the film* The Wizard of Oz

It is best not to swap horses when crossing streams.
Abraham Lincoln 1809–65 American statesman

Change and decay in all around I see;
O Thou, who changest not, abide with me.
Henry Francis Lyte 1793–1847 English hymn-writer

Tomorrow to fresh woods, and pastures new.
John Milton 1608–74 English poet

And now for something completely different.
Monty Python's Flying Circus 1969–74 British television programme

Growth [is] the only evidence of life.
John Henry Newman 1801–90 English theologian

God, give us the serenity to accept what cannot be changed;
Give us the courage to change what should be changed;
Give us the wisdom to distinguish one from the other.
Reinhold Niebuhr 1892–1971 American theologian

        Forward, forward let us range,
Let the great world spin for ever down the ringing grooves of change.
Alfred, Lord Tennyson 1809–92 English poet

If we do not find anything pleasant, at least we shall find something new.
Voltaire 1694–1778 French writer

All changed, changed utterly:
A terrible beauty is born.
W. B. Yeats 1865–1939 Irish poet

Character

It is not in the still calm of life, or the repose of a pacific station, that great characters are formed…Great necessities call out great virtues.
Abigail Adams 1744–1818 American letter writer

A thick skin is a gift from God.
Konrad Adenauer 1876–1967 German statesman

You will never make a crab walk straight.
Aristophanes c.450–c.385 BC Greek comic dramatist

In one and the same fire, clay grows hard and wax melts.
Francis Bacon 1561–1626 English courtier

Talent develops in quiet places, character in the full current of human life.
Johann Wolfgang von Goethe 1749–1832 German writer

Those who stand for nothing fall for anything.
Alex Hamilton 1936–

A man's character is his fate.
Heraclitus c.540–c.480 BC Greek philosopher

A propensity to hope and joy is real riches: one to fear and sorrow, real poverty.
David Hume 1711–76 Scottish philosopher

Nothing gives one person so great advantage over another, as to remain always cool and unruffled under all circumstances.
Thomas Jefferson 1743–1826 American statesman

If you can fill the unforgiving minute
With sixty seconds' worth of distance run,
Yours is the Earth and everything that's in it,

Charity

And—which is more—you'll be a Man, my son!
Rudyard Kipling 1865–1936 English writer

I see the better things, and approve; I follow the worse.
Ovid 43 BC–c.AD 17 Roman poet

You can tell a lot about a fellow's character by his way of eating jellybeans.
Ronald Reagan 1911–2004 American statesman

My nature is subdued
To what it works in, like the dyer's hand.
William Shakespeare 1564–1616 English dramatist

If you can't stand the heat, get out of the kitchen.
Harry Vaughan 1893–1981 American military aide, *associated with Harry S. Truman*

We are what we pretend to be.
Kurt Vonnegut 1922–2007 American writer

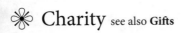 Charity see also **Gifts**

God loveth a cheerful giver.
Bible

CHAIRMAN: What is service?
CANDIDATE: The rent we pay for our room on earth.
Tubby Clayton 1885–1972 British clergyman, *admission ceremony of Toc H*

The best form of charity I know is the art of meeting a payroll.
J. Paul Getty 1892–1976 American industrialist

Charity

You cannot feed the hungry on statistics.
David Lloyd George 1863–1945 British statesman

People often feed the hungry so that nothing may disturb their own enjoyment of a good meal.
W. Somerset Maugham 1874–1965 English novelist

Do good by stealth, and blush to find it fame.
Alexander Pope 1688–1744 English poet

He gives the poor man twice as much good who gives quickly.
Publilius Syrus fl. 1st century BC Roman writer

'Tis not enough to help the feeble up,
But to support him after.
William Shakespeare 1564–1616 English dramatist

Thy necessity is yet greater than mine.
Philip Sidney 1554–86 English writer, *on giving his water-bottle to a dying soldier on the battle-field of Zutphen; commonly quoted as 'thy need is greater than mine'*

Charity begins today. Today somebody is suffering, today somebody is in the street, today somebody is hungry.
Mother Teresa 1910–97 Roman Catholic nun

No one would remember the Good Samaritan if he'd only had good intentions. He had money as well.
Margaret Thatcher 1925–2013 British stateswoman

Friends, I have lost a day.
Titus AD 39–81 Roman emperor, *on reflecting that he had done nothing to help anybody all day*

Behold, I do not give lectures or a little charity,
When I give I give myself.
Walt Whitman 1819–92 American poet

Charm

Charm…it's a sort of bloom on a woman. If you have it, you don't need to have anything else; and if you don't have it, it doesn't much matter what else you have.
J. M. Barrie 1860–1937 Scottish writer

You know what charm is: a way of getting the answer yes without having asked any clear question.
Albert Camus 1913–60 French writer

All charming people have something to conceal, usually their total dependence on the appreciation of others.
Cyril Connolly 1903–74 English writer

Oozing charm from every pore,
He oiled his way around the floor.
Alan Jay Lerner 1918–86 American songwriter

 # Children see also **Babies, Family, Youth**

Children sweeten labours, but they make misfortunes more bitter.
Francis Bacon 1561–1626 English courtier

Quality time? There's always another load of washing.
Julian Barnes 1946– English novelist

Childhood is measured out by sounds and smells
And sights, before the dark of reason grows.
John Betjeman 1906–84 English poet

Suffer the little children to come unto me, and forbid them not: for of such is the kingdom of God.
Bible

When I was a child, I spake as a child, I understood as a child, I thought as a child: but when I became a man, I put away childish things.
Bible

There is no such thing as other people's children.
Hillary Rodham Clinton 1947- American lawyer

Our greatest natural resource is the minds of our children.
Walt Disney 1901–66 American film producer

Alas, regardless of their doom,
The little victims play!
No sense have they of ills to come,
Nor care beyond to-day.
Thomas Gray 1716–71 English poet

Allow them [children] to be happy their own way, for what better way will they ever find?
Samuel Johnson 1709–84 English lexicographer

If there is anything that we wish to change in the child, we should first examine it and see whether it is not something that could better be changed in ourselves.
Carl Gustav Jung 1875–1961 Swiss psychologist

A child is owed the greatest respect; if you ever have something disgraceful in mind, don't ignore your son's tender years.
Juvenal c.AD 60–c.140 Roman satirist

Literature is mostly about having sex and not much about having children. Life is the other way round.
David Lodge 1935- English novelist

It should be noted that children at play are not playing about; their games should be seen as their most serious-minded activity.
Montaigne 1533–92 French moralist

Choice

The affection you get back from children is sixpence given
as change for a sovereign.
Edith Nesbit 1858–1924 English writer

Of all animals the boy is the most unmanageable.
Plato 429–347 BC Greek philosopher

Behold the child, by Nature's kindly law
Pleased with a rattle, tickled with a straw.
Alexander Pope 1688–1744 English poet

A child is not a vase to be filled, but a fire to be lit.
François Rabelais c.1494–c.1553 French humanist

Any man who hates dogs and babies can't be all bad.
Leo Rosten 1908–97 American writer, *of W. C. Fields, and often
attributed to him*

Grown-ups never understand anything for themselves,
and it is tiresome for children to be always and forever
explaining things to them.
Antoine de Saint-Exupéry 1900–44 French novelist

The Child is father of the Man.
William Wordsworth 1770–1850 English poet

 # Choice

White shall not neutralize the black, nor good
Compensate bad in man, absolve him so:
Life's business being just the terrible choice.
Robert Browning 1812–89 English poet

The die is cast.
Julius Caesar 100–44 BC Roman statesman, *at the crossing of
the Rubicon*

Any customer can have a car painted any colour that he wants so long as it is black.
> **Henry Ford** 1863–1947 American car manufacturer, *of the Model T Ford*

Two roads diverged in a wood, and I—
I took the one less travelled by,
And that has made all the difference.
> **Robert Frost** 1874–1963 American poet

How happy could I be with either,
Were t'other dear charmer away!
> **John Gay** 1685–1732 English writer

Which do you want? A whipping and no turnips or turnips and no whipping?
> **Toni Morrison** 1931– American novelist

You pays your money and you takes your choice.
> **Punch** 1841–1992 English humorous periodical

I'll make him an offer he can't refuse.
> **Mario Puzo** 1920–99 American novelist

To be, or not to be: that is the question.
> **William Shakespeare** 1564–1616 English dramatist

Take care to get what you like or you will be forced to like what you get.
> **George Bernard Shaw** 1856–1950 Irish dramatist

There is no real alternative.
> **Margaret Thatcher** 1925–2013 British stateswoman

Between two evils, I always pick the one I never tried before.
> **Mae West** 1892–1980 American film actress

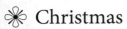 # Christmas

Christmas won't be Christmas without any presents.
> **Louisa May Alcott** 1832–88 American novelist

I'm dreaming of a white Christmas,
Just like the ones I used to know.
> **Irving Berlin** 1888–1989 American songwriter

And girls in slacks remember Dad,
And oafish louts remember Mum,
And sleepless children's hearts are glad,
And Christmas-morning bells say 'Come!'
> **John Betjeman** 1906–84 English poet

She brought forth her firstborn son, and wrapped him in
swaddling clothes, and laid him in a manger; because there
was no room for them in the inn.
> **Bible**

Yes, Virginia, there is a Santa Claus.
> **Francis Pharcellus Church** 1839–1906 American editor,
> *newspaper editorial replying to a letter from eight-year-old*
> *Virginia O'Hanlon*

Christmas is the Disneyfication of Christianity.
> **Don Cupitt** 1934– British theologian

'Bah,' said Scrooge. 'Humbug!'
> **Charles Dickens** 1812–70 English novelist, *responding to the*
> *greeting 'Merry Christmas'*

A lovely thing about Christmas is that it's compulsory, like a
thunderstorm, and we all go through it together.
> **Garrison Keillor** 1942– American writer

'Twas the night before Christmas, when all through the house
Not a creature was stirring, not even a mouse.
> **Clement C. Moore** 1779–1863 American writer

Be nice to yu turkeys dis Christmas
Cos' turkeys just wanna hav fun.
Benjamin Zephaniah 1958–   British poet

The Church see also **Religion**

The nearer the Church the further from God.
Bishop Lancelot Andrewes 1555–1626 English preacher

He cannot have God for his father who has not the church
for his mother.
St Cyprian C.AD 200–258 Roman writer and martyr

A church is God between four walls.
Victor Hugo 1802–85 French writer

I want to throw open the windows of the Church so that we
can see out and the people can see in.
John XXIII 1881–1963 Italian pope

We are an Easter people and Alleluia is our song.
John Paul II 1920–2005 Polish pope

'The Church is an anvil which has worn out many hammers',
and the story of the first collision is, in essentials, the story
of all.
Alexander Maclaren 1826–1910 Scottish divine

The Church [of England] should go forward along the path
of progress and be no longer satisfied only to represent the
Conservative Party at prayer.
Maude Royden 1876–1956 English writer

I never saw, heard, nor read, that the clergy were beloved
in any nation where Christianity was the religion of the
country. Nothing can render them popular, but some degree
of persecution.
Jonathan Swift 1667–1745 Irish poet and satirist

The Cinema

As often as we are mown down by you, the more we grow in numbers; the blood of Christians is the seed.
> **Tertullian** c.AD 160–c.225 Roman theologian, *traditionally* '*The blood of the martyrs is the seed of the Church*'

I look upon all the world as my parish.
> **John Wesley** 1703–91 English preacher

 # The Cinema see also **Acting**

WILLIAM HOLDEN: You used to be in pictures. You used to be big.
GLORIA SWANSON: I am big. It's the pictures that got small.
> **Charles Brackett** 1892–1969 and **Billy Wilder** 1906–2002 American screenwriters, *in the film* Sunset Boulevard

There are no rules in film-making. Only sins. And the cardinal sin is dullness.
> **Frank Capra** 1897–1991 American film director

All I need to make a comedy is a park, a policeman and a pretty girl.
> **Charlie Chaplin** 1889–1977 English film actor

GEORGES FRANJU: Movies should have a beginning, a middle and an end.
GODARD: Certainly, but not necessarily in that order.
> **Jean-Luc Godard** 1930– French film director

Photography is truth. The cinema is truth 24 times per second.
> **Jean-Luc Godard** 1930– French film director

Nobody knows anything.
> **William Goldman** 1931– American writer, *on the film industry*

Pictures are for entertainment, messages should be delivered by Western Union.

Sam Goldwyn 1882–1974 American film producer

Why should people go out and pay to see bad movies when they can stay at home and see bad television for nothing?

Sam Goldwyn 1882–1974 American film producer

If I made Cinderella, the audience would immediately be looking for a body in the coach.

Alfred Hitchcock 1899–1980 British-born film director

We've got more stars than there are in the heavens, all of them except for that damned Mouse over at Disney.

Louis B. Mayer 1885–1957 American film executive

The trouble, Mr Goldwyn, is that you are only interested in art and I am only interested in money.

George Bernard Shaw 1856–1950 Irish dramatist, *telegraphed version of the outcome of a conversation between Shaw and Sam Goldwyn*

This is the biggest electric train a boy ever had!

Orson Welles 1915–85 American film director, *of the RKO studios*

It is like writing history with lightning. And my only regret is that it is all so terribly true.

Woodrow Wilson 1856–1924 American statesman, *on seeing D. W. Griffith's film* The Birth of a Nation

Civilization

The three great elements of modern civilization, Gunpowder, Printing, and the Protestant Religion.

Thomas Carlyle 1795–1881 Scottish historian

Civilization and profits go hand in hand.

Calvin Coolidge 1872–1933 American statesman

Civilization

JOURNALIST: Mr Gandhi, what do you think of modern civilization?
GANDHI: That would be a good idea.
   Mahatma Gandhi 1869–1948 Indian statesman

If a nation expects to be ignorant and free, in a state of civilization, it expects what never was and never will be.
   Thomas Jefferson 1743–1826 American statesman

Whenever I hear the word culture…I release the safety-catch of my Browning!
   Hanns Johst 1890–1978 German dramatist, *often attributed to Hermann Goering, and quoted as 'Whenever I hear the word culture, I reach for my pistol!'*

If civilization had been left in female hands, we would still be living in grass huts.
   Camille Paglia 1947–   American writer

You can't say civilization don't advance, however, for in every war they kill you in a new way.
   Will Rogers 1879–1935 American actor

Civilization has made the peasantry its pack animal. The bourgeoisie in the long run only changed the form of the pack.
   Leon Trotsky 1879–1940 Russian revolutionary

In Italy for thirty years under the Borgias they had warfare, terror, murder, bloodshed—they produced Michelangelo, Leonardo da Vinci and the Renaissance. In Switzerland they had brotherly love, five hundred years of democracy and peace and what did that produce…? The cuckoo clock.
   Orson Welles 1915–85 American film director

Class

The rich man in his castle,
The poor man at his gate,
God made them, high or lowly,
And ordered their estate.
    Cecil Frances Alexander 1818–95 Irish poet

Il faut épater le bourgeois.
One must astonish the bourgeois.
    Charles Baudelaire 1821–67 French poet

Like many of the Upper Class
He liked the Sound of Broken Glass.
    Hilaire Belloc 1870–1953 British writer

The Stately Homes of England,
How beautiful they stand,
To prove the upper classes
Have still the upper hand.
    Noël Coward 1899–1973 English dramatist

O let us love our occupations,
Bless the squire and his relations,
Live upon our daily rations,
And always know our proper stations.
    Charles Dickens 1812–70 English novelist

The proletarians have nothing to lose but their chains. They
have a world to win. WORKING MEN OF ALL COUNTRIES,
UNITE!
    Karl Marx 1818–83 and **Friedrich Engels** 1820–95 German
    philosopher and German socialist, *commonly rendered
    'Workers of the world, unite!'*

71

Clothes

When Adam dalfe and Eve spane…
Where was than the pride of man?
> **Richard Rolle de Hampole** c.1290–1349 English mystic, *taken in the form 'When Adam delved and Eve span, who was then the gentleman?' by John Ball as the text of his revolutionary sermon on the outbreak of the Peasants' Revolt, 1381*

The State is an instrument in the hands of the ruling class, used to break the resistance of the adversaries of that class.
> **Joseph Stalin** 1879–1953 Soviet dictator

The French want no-one to be their *superior*. The English want *inferiors*. The Frenchman constantly raises his eyes above him with anxiety. The Englishman lowers his beneath him with satisfaction.
> **Alexis de Tocqueville** 1805–59 French historian

Clothes

It is totally impossible to be well dressed in cheap shoes.
> **Hardy Amies** 1909–2003 English couturier

From the cradle to the grave, underwear first, last and all the time.
> **Bertolt Brecht** 1898–1956 German dramatist

No perfumes, but very fine linen, plenty of it, and country washing.
> **Beau Brummell** 1778–1840 English dandy

Look for the woman in the dress. If there is no woman, there is no dress.
> **Coco Chanel** 1883–1971 French couturière

The sense of being well-dressed gives a feeling of inward tranquillity which religion is powerless to bestow.
> **Miss C. F. Forbes** 1817–1911 English writer

A sweet disorder in the dress
Kindles in clothes a wantonness.
> **Robert Herrick** 1591–1674 English poet

Dress cute wherever you go. Life is too short to blend in.
> **Paris Hilton** 1981– American heiress

You should never have your best trousers on when you go
out to fight for freedom and truth.
> **Henrik Ibsen** 1828–1906 Norwegian dramatist

A tie is a noose, and inverted though it is, it will hang a man
nonetheless if he's not careful.
> **Yann Martel** 1963– Canadian writer

I have often said that I wish I had invented blue jeans.
> **Yves Saint Laurent** 1936–2008 French couturier

His socks compelled one's attention without losing one's
respect.
> **Saki** 1870–1916 Scottish writer

The apparel oft proclaims the man.
> **William Shakespeare** 1564–1616 English dramatist

Beware of all enterprises that require new clothes.
> **Henry David Thoreau** 1817–62 American writer

Computers

To err is human but to really foul things up requires a
computer.
> **Anonymous**

Google is white bread for the mind.
> **Tara Brabazon** 1969– Australian academic

I like to think
(it has to be!)

Computers

of a cybernetic ecology
where we are free of our labours
and joined back to nature,
returned to our mammal
brothers and sisters,
and all watched over
by machines of loving grace.
>   **Richard Brautigan** 1935–84 American writer

The email of the species is deadlier than the mail.
>   **Stephen Fry** 1957– English comedian

I think computer viruses should count as life. Maybe it says
something about human nature, that the only form of life
we have created so far is purely destructive.
>   **Stephen Hawking** 1942– English theoretical physicist

The PC is the LSD of the '90s.
>   **Timothy Leary** 1920–96 American psychologist

Computer says No.
>   **Matt Lucas** 1974– and **David Walliams** 1971– British
>   comedians

You have zero privacy anyway. Get over it.
>   **Scott McNealy** 1954– American businessman, *on the
>   introduction of Jini networking technology*

If you have a child, you'll notice they'll have two states,
asleep or online.
>   **Eric Schmidt** 1955– American computer executive

On the Internet, nobody knows you're a dog.
>   **Peter Steiner** 1940– American cartoonist

We used to have lots of questions to which there were no
answers. Now with the computer there are lots of answers
to which we haven't thought up the questions.
>   **Peter Ustinov** 1921–2004 British actor

We've all heard that a million monkeys banging on a million typewriters will eventually reproduce the entire works of Shakespeare. Now, thanks to the Internet, we know this is not true.

Robert Wilensky 1951– American academic

Conscience

We have erred, and strayed from thy ways like lost sheep. We have followed too much the devices and desires of our own hearts.

Book of Common Prayer 1662

Conscience is thoroughly well-bred and soon leaves off talking to those who do not wish to hear it.

Samuel Butler 1835–1902 English novelist

O dignitosa coscienza e netta,
Come t'è picciol fallo amaro morso!

O pure and noble conscience, how bitter a sting to thee is a little fault!

Dante Alighieri 1265–1321 Italian poet

In many walks of life, a conscience is a more expensive encumbrance than a wife or a carriage.

Thomas De Quincey 1785–1859 English essayist

A good conscience is a continual Christmas.

Benjamin Franklin 1706–90 American statesman and scientist

I cannot and will not cut my conscience to fit this year's fashions.

Lillian Hellman 1905–84 American dramatist

Conversation

Cowardice asks the question, 'Is it safe?' Expediency asks the question, 'Is it politic?' Vanity asks the question, 'Is it popular?' But Conscience asks the question, 'Is it right?'
    Martin Luther King 1929–68 American civil rights leader

The one thing that doesn't abide by majority rule is a person's conscience.
    Harper Lee 1926–2016 American novelist

Conscience: the inner voice which warns us that someone may be looking.
    H. L. Mencken 1880–1956 American journalist

Thus conscience doth make cowards of us all.
    William Shakespeare 1564–1616 English dramatist

Corporations have neither bodies to be punished, nor souls to be condemned, they therefore do as they like.
    Edward, 1st Baron Thurlow 1731–1806 English jurist,
    usually quoted as 'Did you ever expect a corporation to have a conscience, when it has no soul to be damned, and no body to be kicked?'

 # Conversation see also **Speechmaking**

On every formal visit a child ought to be of the party, by way of provision for discourse.
    Jane Austen 1775–1817 English novelist

Although there exist many thousand subjects for elegant conversation, there are persons who cannot meet a cripple without talking about feet.
    Ernest Bramah 1868–1942 English writer

'The time has come,' the Walrus said,
'To talk of many things:

Of shoes—and ships—and sealing wax—
Of cabbages—and kings.'
Lewis Carroll 1832–98 English writer

Religion is by no means a proper subject of conversation in a mixed company.
Lord Chesterfield 1694–1773 English writer

Too much agreement kills a chat.
Eldridge Cleaver 1935–98 American political activist

Someone to tell it to is one of the fundamental needs of human beings.
Miles Franklin 1879–1954 Australian writer

And, when you stick on conversation's burrs,
Don't strew your pathway with those dreadful *urs*.
Oliver Wendell Holmes 1809–94 American physician

A…sharp tongue is the only edged tool that grows keener with constant use.
Washington Irving 1783–1859 American writer

Questioning is not the mode of conversation among gentlemen. It is assuming a superiority.
Samuel Johnson 1709–84 English lexicographer

Must I always be a mere listener?
Juvenal c.AD 60–c.140 Roman satirist

The opposite of talking isn't listening. The opposite of talking is waiting.
Fran Lebowitz 1950– American writer

With thee conversing I forget all time.
John Milton 1608–74 English poet

A good listener is not only popular everywhere, but after a while he knows something.
Wilson Mizner 1876–1933 American dramatist

Cookery

The feast of reason and the flow of soul.
Alexander Pope 1688–1744 English poet

I am not bound to please thee with my answer.
William Shakespeare 1564–1616 English dramatist

 # Cookery see also **Eating**, **Food**

Anyone who tells a lie has not a pure heart, and cannot make a good soup.
Ludwig van Beethoven 1770–1827 German composer

Be content to remember that those who can make omelettes properly can do nothing else.
Hilaire Belloc 1870–1953 British writer

Cooking is the most ancient of the arts, for Adam was born hungry.
Anthelme Brillat-Savarin 1755–1826 French gourmet

Good food is always a trouble and its preparation should be regarded as a labour of love.
Elizabeth David 1913–92 British cook

Heaven sends us good meat, but the Devil sends cooks.
David Garrick 1717–79 English actor-manager

Kissing don't last: cookery do!
George Meredith 1828–1909 English writer

I never see any home cooking. All I get is fancy stuff.
Philip, Duke of Edinburgh 1921– Greek-born husband of Elizabeth II

The cook was a good cook, as cooks go; and as cooks go, she went.
Saki 1870–1916 Scottish writer

Cooperation

If a house be divided against itself, that house cannot stand.
Bible

Bear ye one another's burdens.
Bible

When bad men combine, the good must associate; else they will fall, one by one, an unpitied sacrifice in a contemptible struggle.
Edmund Burke 1729–97 Irish-born politician

All for one, one for all.
Alexandre Dumas 1802–70 French novelist

We must indeed all hang together, or, most assuredly, we shall all hang separately.
Benjamin Franklin 1706–90 American statesman and scientist

If someone claps his hand a sound arises. Listen to the sound of the single hand!
Hakuin 1686–1769 Japanese monk

If we cannot end now our differences, at least we can help make the world safe for diversity.
John F. Kennedy 1917–63 American statesman

We must learn to live together as brothers or perish together as fools.
Martin Luther King 1929–68 American civil rights leader

When Hitler attacked the Jews I was not a Jew, therefore, I was not concerned. And when Hitler attacked the Catholics, I was not a Catholic, and therefore, I was not concerned. And when Hitler attacked the unions and the industrialists, I was not a member of the unions and

The Country

I was not concerned. Then, Hitler attacked me and the Protestant church—and there was nobody left to be concerned.

    Martin Niemöller 1892–1984 German theologian

Government and cooperation are in all things the laws of life; anarchy and competition the laws of death.

    John Ruskin 1819–1900 English critic

 # The Country see also **Environment**

'Tis distance lends enchantment to the view,
And robes the mountain in its azure hue.

    Thomas Campbell 1777–1844 Scottish poet

God made the country, and man made the town.

    William Cowper 1731–1800 English poet

It is my belief, Watson, founded upon my experience, that the lowest and vilest alleys in London do not present a more dreadful record of sin than does the smiling and beautiful countryside.

    Arthur Conan Doyle 1859–1930 Scottish-born writer

Green belts should be the start of the countryside, not a ditch between Subtopias.

    Hugh Gaitskell 1906–63 British politician

Our salvation can only come through the farmer. Neither the lawyers, nor the doctors, nor the rich landlords are going to secure it.

    Mahatma Gandhi 1869–1948 Indian statesman

Agriculture is the foundation of manufactures; since the productions of nature are the materials of art.

    Edward Gibbon 1737–94 English historian

Courage

There is nothing good to be had in the country, or if there is, they will not let you have it.
William Hazlitt 1778–1830 English essayist

The Farmer will never be happy again;
He carries his heart in his boots;
For either the rain is destroying his grain
Or the drought is destroying his roots.
A. P. Herbert 1890–1971 English writer

Oh, give me land, lots of land under starry skies above,
Don't fence me in.
Cole Porter 1891–1964 American songwriter

I have no relish for the country; it is a kind of healthy grave.
Sydney Smith 1771–1845 English essayist

Anybody can be good in the country.
Oscar Wilde 1854–1900 Irish dramatist

Courage ✳

No coward soul is mine,
No trembler in the world's storm-troubled sphere:
I see Heaven's glories shine,
And faith shines equal, arming me from fear.
Emily Brontë 1818–48 English writer

Courage is rightly esteemed the first of human qualities
because as has been said, it is the quality which guarantees
all others.
Winston Churchill 1874–1965 British statesman

Boldness, and again boldness, and always boldness!
Georges Jacques Danton 1759–94 French revolutionary

Courage is the price that Life exacts for granting peace,
The soul that knows it not, knows no release

Courage

From little things.
Amelia Earhart 1898–1937 American aviator

What counts is not necessarily the size of the dog in the
fight — it's the size of the fight in the dog.
Dwight D. Eisenhower 1890–1969 American statesman

Grace under pressure.
Ernest Hemingway 1899–1961 American novelist, *when asked
what he meant by 'guts'*

Tender-handed stroke a nettle,
And it stings you for your pains;
Grasp it like a man of mettle,
And it soft as silk remains.
Aaron Hill 1685–1750 English writer

When you know you're licked before you begin but you
begin anyway and you see it through no matter what.
You rarely win, but sometimes you do.
Harper Lee 1926–2016 American novelist, *on 'real courage'*

Courage is not simply *one* of the virtues but the form of
every virtue at the testing point.
C. S. Lewis 1898–1963 English literary scholar

As to moral courage, I have very rarely met with two o'clock
in the morning courage: I mean instantaneous courage.
Napoleon I 1769–1821 French emperor

Life shrinks or expands in proportion to one's courage.
Anaïs Nin 1903–77 American writer

Cowards die many times before their deaths;
The valiant never taste of death but once.
William Shakespeare 1564–1616 English dramatist

Fortune assists the bold.
Virgil 70–19 BC Roman poet, *often quoted as 'Fortune favours
the brave'*

Creativity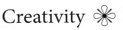

The more you reason, the less you create.
Raymond Chandler 1888–1959 American writer

Think before you speak is criticism's motto; speak before you think creation's.
E. M. Forster 1879–1970 English novelist

That which is creative must create itself.
John Keats 1795–1821 English poet

Poems are made by fools like me,
But only God can make a tree.
Joyce Kilmer 1886–1918 American poet

Nothing can be created out of nothing.
Lucretius c.94–55 BC Roman poet

The worst crime is to leave a man's hands empty.
Men are born makers, with that primal simplicity
In every maker since Adam.
Derek Walcott 1930–2017 West Indian writer

Urge and urge and urge,
Always the procreant urge of the world.
Walt Whitman 1819–92 American poet

Cricket

Bowl fast, bowl faster. When you play Test cricket you don't give Englishmen an inch. Play it tough, all the way. Grind them into the dust.
Don Bradman 1908–2001 Australian cricketer

Never read print, it spoils one's eye for the ball.
W. G. Grace 1848–1915 English cricketer, *habitual advice to his players*

Crime

It's more than a game. It's an institution.
Thomas Hughes 1822–96 English lawyer and writer

What do they know of cricket who only cricket know?
Cyril Lionel Robert James 1901–89 Trinidadian writer

Cricket—a game which the English, not being a spiritual people, have invented in order to give themselves some conception of eternity.
Lord Mancroft 1914–87 British politician

Cricket civilizes people and creates good gentlemen. I want everyone to play cricket in Zimbabwe; I want ours to be a nation of gentlemen.
Robert Mugabe 1924– African stateman

There's a breathless hush in the Close to-night—
Ten to make and the match to win—
A bumping pitch and a blinding light,
An hour to play and the last man in.
Henry Newbolt 1862–1938 English writer

Personally, I have always looked on cricket as organized loafing.
William Temple 1881–1944 English theologian

 # Crime see also **Justice, Murder, Punishment**

Labour is the party of law and order in Britain today. Tough on crime and tough on the causes of crime.
Tony Blair 1953– British statesman

Once in the racket you're always in it.
Al Capone 1899–1947 American gangster

Crime isn't a disease, it's a symptom. Cops are like a doctor that gives you aspirin for a brain tumour.
Raymond Chandler 1888–1959 American writer

Thieves respect property. They merely wish the property to become their property that they may more perfectly respect it.

G. K. Chesterton 1874–1936 English writer

The mood and temper of the public in regard to the treatment of crime and criminals is one of the most unfailing tests of the civilization of any country.

Winston Churchill 1874–1965 British statesman

Thou shalt not steal; an empty feat,
When it's so lucrative to cheat.

Arthur Hugh Clough 1819–61 English poet

Singularity is almost invariably a clue. The more featureless and commonplace a crime is, the more difficult is it to bring it home.

Arthur Conan Doyle 1859–1930 Scottish-born writer

For de little stealin' dey gits you in jail soon or late. For de big stealin' dey makes you Emperor and puts you in de Hall o' Fame when you croaks.

Eugene O'Neill 1888–1953 American dramatist

Crime doesn't pay.

Proverb

Crises

Don't panic.

Douglas Adams 1952–2001 English writer, *on the cover of* The Hitch Hiker's Guide to the Galaxy

Comin' in on a wing and a pray'r.

Harold Adamson 1906–80 American songwriter

Crises

Crisis? What Crisis?
> **Anonymous**, *Sun headline, summarizing James Callaghan on the winter of discontent: 'I don't think other people in the world would share the view* [that] *there is mounting chaos'*

Keep calm and carry on.
> **Anonymous**, *poster designed by the Ministry of Information in 1939 but not used in World War II; re-discovered and popularized in the early 21st century*

You never want a serious crisis to go to waste.
> **Rahm Emanuel** 1959– American politician, *often quoted as 'Never waste a good crisis'*

The illustrious bishop of Cambrai was of more worth than his chambermaid, and there are few of us that would hesitate to pronounce, if his palace were in flames, and the life of only one of them could be preserved, which of the two ought to be preferred.
> **William Godwin** 1756–1836 English philosopher

For it is your business, when the wall next door catches fire.
> **Horace** 65–8 BC Roman poet

My friends, as I have discovered myself, there are no disasters, only opportunities. And, indeed, opportunities for fresh disasters.
> **Boris Johnson** 1964– British politician

If you can keep your head when all about you
Are losing theirs and blaming it on you.
> **Rudyard Kipling** 1865–1936 English writer

A trifle consoles us because a trifle upsets us.
> **Blaise Pascal** 1623–62 French scientist and philosopher

We're eyeball to eyeball, and I think the other fellow just blinked.
> **Dean Rusk** 1909– American politician

I myself have always deprecated…in crisis after crisis, appeals to the Dunkirk spirit as an answer to our problems.
Harold Wilson 1916–95 British statesman

I'm at my best in a messy, middle-of-the-road muddle.
Harold Wilson 1916–95 British statesman

Criticism

A man must serve his time to every trade
Save censure—critics all are ready made.
Lord Byron 1788–1824 English poet

Everything must be like something, so what is this like?
E. M. Forster 1879–1970 English novelist

No theoretician, no writer on art, however interesting he or she might be, could be as interesting as Picasso. A good writer on art may give you an insight to Picasso, but, after all, Picasso was there first.
David Hockney 1937– British artist

Parodies and caricatures are the most penetrating of criticisms.
Aldous Huxley 1894–1963 English novelist

I don't care anything about reasons, but I know what I like.
Henry James 1843–1916 American novelist

This will never do.
Francis, Lord Jeffrey 1773–1850 Scottish critic, *on Wordsworth's* The Excursion

You *may* abuse a tragedy, though you cannot write one. You may scold a carpenter who has made you a bad table, though you cannot make a table. It is not your trade to make tables.
Samuel Johnson 1709–84 English lexicographer, *on literary criticism*

Criticism

I cry all the way to the bank.
Liberace 1919–87 American showman, *on bad reviews*

People who like this sort of thing will find this the sort of thing they like.
Abraham Lincoln 1809–65 American statesman, *judgement of a book*

One should look long and carefully at oneself before one considers judging others.
Molière 1622–73 French comic dramatist

I am sitting in the smallest room of my house. I have your review before me. In a moment it will be behind me.
Max Reger 1873–1916 German composer, *responding to a savage review*

If you are not criticized, you may not be doing much.
Donald Rumsfeld 1932– American politician

Remember, a statue has never been set up in honour of a critic!
Jean Sibelius 1865–1957 Finnish composer

I never read a book before reviewing it; it prejudices a man so.
Sydney Smith 1771–1845 English essayist

As learned commentators view
In Homer more than Homer knew.
Jonathan Swift 1667–1745 Irish poet and satirist

A critic is a man who knows the way but can't drive the car.
Kenneth Tynan 1927–80 English critic

I maintain that two and two would continue to make four, in spite of the whine of the amateur for three, or the cry of the critic for five.
James McNeill Whistler 1834–1903 American-born painter

Cruelty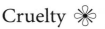

Boys throw stones at frogs for fun, but the frogs don't die for 'fun', but in sober earnest.
Bion c.325–c.255 BC Greek philosopher

A robin red breast in a cage
Puts all Heaven in a rage.
William Blake 1757–1827 English poet

Man's inhumanity to man
Makes countless thousands mourn!
Robert Burns 1759–96 Scottish poet

Cruelty, like every other vice, requires no motive outside itself—it only requires opportunity.
George Eliot 1819–80 English novelist

The healthy man does not torture others—generally it is the tortured who turn into torturers.
Carl Gustav Jung 1875–1961 Swiss psychologist

Our language lacks words to express this offence, the demolition of a man.
Primo Levi 1919–87 Italian writer, *of a year spent in Auschwitz*

I must be cruel only to be kind.
William Shakespeare 1564–1616 English dramatist

This was the most unkindest cut of all.
William Shakespeare 1564–1616 English dramatist

All cruel people describe themselves as paragons of frankness.
Tennessee Williams 1911–83 American dramatist

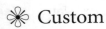 Custom

One can't carry one's father's corpse about everywhere.
Guillaume Apollinaire 1880–1918 French poet, *on tradition*

Custom reconciles us to everything.
Edmund Burke 1729–97 Irish-born politician

Tradition means giving votes to the most obscure of all classes, our ancestors. It is the democracy of the dead.
G. K. Chesterton 1874–1936 English writer

I confess myself to be a great admirer of tradition. The longer you can look back, the farther you can look forward.
Winston Churchill 1874–1965 British statesman

Actions receive their tincture from the times,
And as they change are virtues made or crimes.
Daniel Defoe 1660–1731 English novelist

Custom, then, is the great guide of human life.
David Hume 1711–76 Scottish philosopher

The tradition of all the dead generations weighs like a nightmare on the brain of the living.
Karl Marx 1818–83 German philosopher

Everyone calls barbarism what is not customary to him.
Molière 1622–73 French comic dramatist

But to my mind,—though I am native here,
And to the manner born,—it is a custom
More honoured in the breach than the observance.
William Shakespeare 1564–1616 English dramatist

Laws are sand, customs are rock. Laws can be evaded and punishment escaped, but an openly transgressed custom brings sure punishment.
Mark Twain 1835–1910 American writer

Cynicism

Kill them all; God will recognize his own.
Arnald-Amaury d. 1225 French abbot, *when asked how the true Catholics could be distinguished from the heretics at the massacre of Béziers*

Nothing matters very much and very few things matter at all.
Arthur James Balfour 1848–1930 British statesman

Never glad confident morning again!
Robert Browning 1812–89 English poet

What makes all doctrines plain and clear?
About two hundred pounds a year.
And that which was proved true before,
Prove false again? Two hundred more.
Samuel Butler 1612–80 English poet

To get practice in being refused.
Diogenes c.400–c.325 BC Greek philosopher, *reply when asked why he was begging for alms from a statue*

Pathos, piety, courage—they exist, but are identical, and so is filth. Everything exists, nothing has value.
E. M. Forster 1879–1970 English novelist

Cynicism is an unpleasant way of saying the truth.
Lillian Hellman 1905–84 American dramatist

Paris is well worth a mass.
Henri IV 1553–1610 French monarch

Cynicism is our shared common language, the Esperanto that actually caught on.
Nick Hornby 1957– British writer

Dance

SIR HUMPHREY APPLEBY: A cynic is what an idealist calls a realist.
Jonathan Lynn 1943– and **Antony Jay** 1930–2016 English writers, *in* Yes Minister

A man who knows the price of everything and the value of nothing.
Oscar Wilde 1854–1900 Irish dramatist, *definition of a cynic*

 # Dance

A dance is a measured pace, as a verse is a measured speech.
Francis Bacon 1561–1626 English courtier

There may be trouble ahead,
But while there's moonlight and music and love and romance,
Let's face the music and dance.
Irving Berlin 1888–1989 American songwriter

On with the dance! let joy be unconfined;
No sleep till morn, when Youth and Pleasure meet
To chase the glowing Hours with flying feet.
Lord Byron 1788–1824 English poet

This wondrous miracle did Love devise,
For dancing is love's proper exercise.
John Davies 1569–1626 English poet

The truest expression of a people is in its dances and its music. Bodies never lie.
Agnes de Mille 1908–93 American dancer

Dance is the hidden language of the soul.
Martha Graham 1894–1991 American dancer

Come, and trip it as ye go
On the light fantastic toe.
John Milton 1608–74 English poet

[Dancing is] a perpendicular expression of a horizontal desire.
        George Bernard Shaw 1856–1950 Irish dramatist

Danger

Risk comes from not knowing what you're doing.
        Warren Buffett 1930–   American businessman

Dangers by being despised grow great.
        Edmund Burke 1729–97 Irish-born politician

Nothing in life is so exhilarating as to be shot at without result.
        Winston Churchill 1874–1965 British statesman

When there is no peril in the fight, there is no glory in the triumph.
        Pierre Corneille 1606–84 French dramatist

In skating over thin ice, our safety is in our speed.
        Ralph Waldo Emerson 1803–82 American writer

Out of this nettle, danger, we pluck this flower, safety.
        William Shakespeare 1564–1616 English dramatist

Considering how dangerous everything is nothing is really very frightening.
        Gertrude Stein 1874–1946 American writer

Day see also **Night**

This is the day which the Lord hath made: we will rejoice and be glad in it.
        Bible

Morning has broken
Like the first morning.
        Eleanor Farjeon 1881–1965 English writer

Death

Awake! for Morning in the bowl of night
Has flung the stone that puts the stars to flight.
     Edward Fitzgerald 1809–83 English poet

What are days for?
Days are where we live.
     Philip Larkin 1922–85 English poet

I have a horror of sunsets, they're so romantic, so operatic.
     Marcel Proust 1871–1922 French novelist

Night's candles are burnt out, and jocund day
Stands tiptoe on the misty mountain tops.
     William Shakespeare 1564–1616 English dramatist

 Death see also **Bereavement**

It's not that I'm afraid to die. I just don't want to be there
when it happens.
     Woody Allen 1935–   American film director

Death is only an horizon, and an horizon is only the limit of
our sight.
     Anonymous, *traditional saying, sometimes attributed to William
     Penn (1644–1718)*

To die will be an awfully big adventure.
     J. M. Barrie 1860–1937 Scottish writer

For dust thou art, and unto dust shalt thou return.
     Bible

O death, where is thy sting? O grave, where is thy victory?
     Bible

In the midst of life we are in death.
     Book of Common Prayer 1662

Forasmuch as it hath pleased Almighty God of his great mercy to take unto himself the soul of our dear brother here departed, we therefore commit his body to the ground; earth to earth, ashes to ashes, dust to dust; in sure and certain hope of the Resurrection to eternal life.
Book of Common Prayer 1662

If I should die, think only this of me:
That there's some corner of a foreign field
That is for ever England.
Rupert Brooke 1887–1915 English poet

However many ways there may be of being alive, it is certain that there are vastly more ways of being dead.
Richard Dawkins 1941– English biologist

Any man's death diminishes me, because I am involved in Mankind; And therefore never send to know for whom the bell tolls; it tolls for thee.
John Donne 1572–1631 English poet

Death be not proud, though some have called thee
Mighty and dreadful, for thou art not so.
John Donne 1572–1631 English poet

The bodies of those that made such a noise and tumult when alive, when dead, lie as quietly among the graves of their neighbours as any others.
Jonathan Edwards 1703–58 American theologian

Death, therefore, the most awful of evils, is nothing to us, seeing that, when we are death is not come, and when death is come, we are not.
Epicurus 341–271 BC Greek philosopher

Death is nothing if one can approach it as such. I was just a tiny night-light, suffocated in its own wax, and on the point of expiring.
E. M. Forster 1879–1970 English novelist

Death

Death is nothing at all; it does not count. I have only slipped
away into the next room.

Henry Scott Holland 1847–1918 English theologian

I would rather be tied to the soil as another man's serf, even
a poor man's, who hadn't much to live on himself, than be
King of all these the dead and destroyed.

Homer fl. 8th century BC Greek poet

Non omnis moriar.

I shall not altogether die.

Horace 65–8 BC Roman poet

Remembering that you are going to die is the best way to
avoid the trap of thinking you have something to lose.

Steve Jobs 1955–2011 American computer executive

Depend upon it, Sir, when a man knows he is to be hanged
in a fortnight, it concentrates his mind wonderfully.

Samuel Johnson 1709–84 English lexicographer

Now more than ever seems it rich to die,
To cease upon the midnight with no pain.

John Keats 1795–1821 English poet

This parrot is no more! It has ceased to be! It's expired
and gone to meet its maker! This is a late parrot! It's a
stiff! Bereft of life it rests in peace—if you hadn't nailed it
to the perch it would be pushing up the daisies! It's rung
down the curtain and joined the choir invisible! THIS IS AN
EX–PARROT!

Monty Python's Flying Circus 1969–74 British television
programme

And all our calm is in that balm—
Not lost but gone before.

Caroline Norton 1808–77 English poet

Die, my dear Doctor, that's the last thing I shall do!
Lord Palmerston 1784–1865 British statesman

Guns aren't lawful;
Nooses give;
Gas smells awful;
You might as well live.
Dorothy Parker 1893–1967 American critic

We shall die alone.
Blaise Pascal 1623–62 French scientist and philosopher

Abiit ad plures.
He's gone to join the majority [the dead].
Petronius d. AD 65 Roman satirist

Anyone can stop a man's life, but no one his death;
a thousand doors open on to it.
Seneca ('the Younger') c.4 BC–AD 65 Roman philosopher

Nothing in his life
Became him like the leaving it.
William Shakespeare 1564–1616 English dramatist

To die, to sleep;
To sleep: perchance to dream: ay, there's the rub;
For in that sleep of death what dreams may come
When we have shuffled off this mortal coil,
Must give us pause.
William Shakespeare 1564–1616 English dramatist

If there wasn't death, I think you couldn't go on.
Stevie Smith 1902–71 English poet

Death must be distinguished from dying, with which it is
often confused.
Sydney Smith 1771–1845 English essayist

Debt

One death is a tragedy, a million deaths a statistic.
Joseph Stalin 1879–1953 Soviet dictator

For though from out our bourne of time and place
The flood may bear me far,
I hope to see my pilot face to face
When I have crossed the bar.
Alfred, Lord Tennyson 1809–92 English poet

Though lovers be lost love shall not;
And death shall have no dominion.
Dylan Thomas 1914–53 Welsh poet

So it goes.
Kurt Vonnegut 1922–2007 American novelist

I know death hath ten thousand several doors
For men to take their exits.
John Webster c.1580–c.1625 English dramatist

       The good die first,
And they whose hearts are dry as summer dust
Burn to the socket.
William Wordsworth 1770–1850 English poet

Nor dread nor hope attend
A dying animal;
A man awaits his end
Dreading and hoping all.
W. B. Yeats 1865–1939 Irish poet

 Debt

Be not made a beggar by banqueting upon borrowing.
Bible

Rather go to bed supperless than rise in debt.
Benjamin Franklin 1706–90 American statesman and scientist

Deceit

The human species, according to the best theory I can form of it, is composed of two distinct races, *the men who borrow*, and *the men who lend*.
   Charles Lamb 1775–1834 English writer

Should we really let our people starve so we can pay our debts?
   Julius Nyerere 1922–99 Tanzanian statesman

You can't put your VISA bill on your American Express card.
   P. J. O'Rourke 1947– American writer

A small debt makes a man your debtor; a large one, an enemy.
   Seneca ('the Younger') c.4 BC–AD 65 Roman philosopher

Neither a borrower, nor a lender be.
   William Shakespeare 1564–1616 English dramatist

Deceit see also **Honesty**, **Lies**

I count false words the foulest plague of all.
   Aeschylus c.525–456 BC Greek tragedian

Propaganda is a soft weapon: hold it in your hands too long, and it will move about like a snake, and strike the other way.
   Jean Anouilh 1910–87 French dramatist

An open foe may prove a curse,
But a pretended friend is worse.
   John Gay 1685–1732 English writer

It was beautiful and simple as all truly great swindles are.
   O. Henry 1862–1910 American short-story writer

Democracy

Do not be too straight or too soft; straight trees are cut down, but crooked trees remain standing.
Kautilya (Chanakya) fl. c.300 BC Hindu statesman

You may fool all the people some of the time; you can even fool some of the people all the time; but you can't fool all of the people all the time.
Abraham Lincoln 1809–65 American statesman

A deception that elevates us is dearer than a host of low truths.
Alexander Pushkin 1799–1837 Russian poet

O what a tangled web we weave,
When first we practise to deceive!
Sir Walter Scott 1771–1832 Scottish novelist

 # Democracy see also **Elections**, **Politics**

The cure for the ills of Democracy is more Democracy.
John Adams 1735–1826 American statesman

The basis of a democratic state is liberty.
Aristotle 384–322 BC Greek philosopher

Democracy means government by discussion, but it is only effective if you can stop people talking.
Clement Attlee 1883–1967 British statesman

Democracy is the best revenge.
Benazir Bhutto 1953–2007 Pakistani stateswoman

One man shall have one vote.
John Cartwright 1740–1824 English political reformer

Democracy is the worst form of Government except all those other forms that have been tried from time to time.
Winston Churchill 1874–1965 British statesman

As for our majority…one is enough.
Benjamin Disraeli 1804-81 British statesman

So Two cheers for Democracy: one because it admits variety and two because it permits criticism. Two cheers are quite enough: there is no occasion to give three. Only Love the Beloved Republic deserves that.
E. M. Forster 1879–1970 English novelist

All the world over, I will back the masses against the classes.
W. E. Gladstone 1809-98 British statesman

We here highly resolve that the dead shall not have died in vain, that this nation, under God, shall have a new birth of freedom; and that government of the people, by the people, and for the people, shall not perish from the earth.
Abraham Lincoln 1809-65 American statesman

I never could believe that Providence had sent a few men into the world, ready booted and spurred to ride, and millions ready saddled and bridled to be ridden.
Richard Rumbold c.1622-85 English republican conspirator

Democracy substitutes election by the incompetent many for appointment by the corrupt few.
George Bernard Shaw 1856-1950 Irish dramatist

Democracy is not worth a brass farthing if it is being installed by bayonets.
Alexander Solzhenitsyn 1918–2008 Russian novelist

If one must serve, I hold it better to serve a well-bred lion, who is naturally stronger than I am, than two hundred rats of my own breed.
Voltaire 1694–1778 French writer

The world must be made safe for democracy.
Woodrow Wilson 1856-1924 American statesman

Despair see also **Hope**, **Pessimism**

My God, my God, look upon me; why hast thou
forsaken me?
> **Bible**

There is no despair so absolute as that which comes with the
first moments of our first great sorrow, when we have not
yet known what it is to have suffered and be healed, to have
despaired and have recovered hope.
> **George Eliot** 1819–80 English novelist

In a real dark night of the soul it is always three o'clock in
the morning.
> **F. Scott Fitzgerald** 1896–1940 American novelist

Not, I'll not, carrion comfort, Despair, not feast on thee;
Not untwist—slack they may be—these last strands of man
In me or, most weary, cry *I can no more.* I can;
Can something, hope, wish day come, not choose not to be.
> **Gerard Manley Hopkins** 1844–89 English poet

Don't despair, not even over the fact that you don't despair.
> **Franz Kafka** 1883–1924 Czech novelist

Human life begins on the far side of despair.
> **Jean-Paul Sartre** 1905–80 French philosopher

 # Determination see also **Persistence**

Ils ne passeront pas.
They shall not pass.
> **Anonymous**, *slogan of the French army at the defence of Verdun,*
> *1916*

Determination

Nil carborundum illegitimi.
Don't let the bastards grind you down.
Anonymous, *cod Latin saying, in circulation during the Second World War, though possibly of earlier origin*

Thought shall be the harder, heart the keener, courage the greater, as our might lessens.
The Battle of Maldon 1000

I can only go one way. I've not got a reverse gear.
Tony Blair 1953– British statesman

Never give in. Never give in, *never, never, never, never*—in nothing, great or small, large or petty—never give in, except to convictions of honour and good sense. Never yield to force: never yield to the apparently overwhelming might of the enemy.
Winston Churchill 1874–1965 British statesman

Say not the struggle naught availeth,
The labour and the wounds are vain,
The enemy faints not, nor faileth,
And as things have been, things remain.
Arthur Hugh Clough 1819–61 English poet

The best way out is always through.
Robert Frost 1874–1963 American poet

I will either find a way, or make one.
Hannibal 247–182 BC Carthaginian general, *on crossing the Alps*

Under the bludgeonings of chance
My head is bloody, but unbowed.
W. E. Henley 1849–1903 English poet

When the going gets tough, the tough get going.
Joseph P. Kennedy 1888–1969 American financier

Determination

With malice toward none; with charity for all; with firmness in the right, as God gives us to see the right, let us strive on to finish the work we are in.
Abraham Lincoln 1809–65 American statesman

Yes we can.
Barack Obama 1961– American statesman

What's the difference between a hockey mom and a pitbull? Lipstick.
Sarah Palin 1964– American politician

Difficulties are just things to overcome after all.
Ernest Shackleton 1874–1922 British explorer

One man that has a mind and knows it can always beat ten men who haven't and don't.
George Bernard Shaw 1856–1950 Irish dramatist

Do not underestimate the determination of a quiet man.
Iain Duncan Smith 1954– British politician

That which we are, we are;
One equal temper of heroic hearts,
Made weak by time and fate, but strong in will
To strive, to seek, to find, and not to yield.
Alfred, Lord Tennyson 1809–92 English poet

We shall not be diverted from our course. To those waiting with bated breath for that favourite media catch-phrase, the U-turn, I have only this to say. 'You turn if you want to; the lady's not for turning.'
Margaret Thatcher 1925–2013 British stateswoman

Children, if you are tired, keep going; if you are scared, keep going; if you are hungry, keep going; if you want to taste freedom, keep going.
Harriet Tubman c.1820–1913 American abolitionist, *apparently a modern paraphrase of her views*

Diaries

What is more dull than a discreet diary? One might just as well have a discreet soul.

Henry 'Chips' Channon 1897–1958 British politician

To be a good diarist one must have a little snouty, sneaky mind.

Harold Nicolson 1886–1968 English diplomat

One need not write in a diary what one is to remember for ever.

Sylvia Townsend Warner 1893–1978 English writer

I always say, keep a diary and some day it'll keep you.

Mae West 1892–1980 American film actress

I never travel without my diary. One should always have something sensational to read in the train.

Oscar Wilde 1854–1900 Irish dramatist

Diplomacy

To jaw-jaw is always better than to war-war.

Winston Churchill 1874–1965 British statesman

There is only one thing worse than fighting with allies, and that is fighting without them!

Winston Churchill 1874–1965 British statesman

Euphemisms are unpleasant truths wearing diplomatic cologne.

Quentin Crisp 1908–99 English writer

Treaties, you see, are like girls and roses: they last while they last.

Charles de Gaulle 1890–1970 French statesman

Diplomacy

I feel happier now that we have no allies to be polite to and to pamper.
George VI 1895–1952 British monarch

Let us never negotiate out of fear. But let us never fear to negotiate.
John F. Kennedy 1917–63 American statesman

One of the things I learnt when I was negotiating was that until I changed myself I could not change others.
Nelson Mandela 1918–2013 South African statesman

We will extend a hand if you are willing to unclench your fist.
Barack Obama 1961– American statesman

We are prepared to go to the gates of Hell—but no further.
Pius VII 1742–1823 Italian pope, *attempting to reach an agreement with Napoleon*

I'm afraid you've got a bad egg, Mr Jones.
Oh no, my Lord, I assure you! Parts of it are excellent!
Punch 1841–1992 English humorous periodical

Speak softly and carry a big stick; you will go far.
Theodore Roosevelt 1858–1919 American statesman

You can no more make an agreement with those leaders of Colombia than you can nail currant jelly to the wall. And the failure to nail currant jelly to the wall is not due to the nail. It's due to the currant jelly.
Theodore Roosevelt 1858–1919 American statesman

By indirections find directions out.
William Shakespeare 1564–1616 English dramatist

An ambassador is an honest man sent to lie abroad for the good of his country.
Henry Wotton 1568–1639 English diplomat

Discontent see also **Satisfaction**

When you don't have any money, the problem is food.
When you have money, it's sex. When you have both
it's health.
     J. P. Donleavy 1926– Irish-American novelist

We loathe our manna, and we long for quails.
     John Dryden 1631–1700 English poet

It is an uneasy lot at best, to be what we call highly taught
and yet not to enjoy: to be present at this great spectacle
of life and never to be liberated from a small hungry
shivering self.
     George Eliot 1819–80 English novelist

If I can think of it, it isn't what I want.
     Randall Jarrell 1914–65 American poet

          It is a flaw
In happiness, to see beyond our bourn—
It forces us in summer skies to mourn:
It spoils the singing of the nightingale.
     John Keats 1795–1821 English poet

It is better to be a human being dissatisfied than a pig
satisfied; better to be Socrates dissatisfied than a fool
satisfied.
     John Stuart Mill 1806–73 English philosopher

Whoever is dissatisfied with himself is continually ready for
revenge, and we others will be his victims.
     Friedrich Nietzsche 1844–1900 German philosopher

Were there none who were discontented with what they
have, the world would never reach anything better.
     Florence Nightingale 1820–1910 English nurse

Discovery

'Tis just like a summer birdcage in a garden; the birds that are without despair to get in, and the birds that are within despair, and are in a consumption, for fear they shall never get out.

John Webster c.1580–c.1625 English dramatist

He spoke with a certain what-is-it in his voice, and I could see that, if not actually disgruntled, he was far from being gruntled.

P. G. Wodehouse 1881–1975 English writer

 ## Discovery see Invention

 ## Dogs

In the whole history of the world there is but one thing that money cannot buy, to wit: the wag of a dog's tail.

Josh Billings 1818–85 American humorist, *sometimes quoted as 'Money will buy you a pretty good dog, but it won't buy the wag of his tail'*

The great pleasure of a dog is that you may make a fool of yourself with him and not only will he not scold you, but he will make a fool of himself too.

Samuel Butler 1835–1902 English novelist

Near this spot are deposited the remains of one who possessed beauty without vanity, strength without insolence, courage without ferocity, and all the virtues of Man, without his vices.

Lord Byron 1788–1824 English poet, *epitaph on his Newfoundland dog*

To his dog, every man is Napoleon: hence the constant popularity of dogs.

Aldous Huxley 1894–1963 English novelist

Brothers and Sisters, I bid you beware
Of giving your heart to a dog to tear.
Rudyard Kipling 1865–1936 English writer

A door is what a dog is perpetually on the wrong side of.
Ogden Nash 1902–71 American humorist

I am his Highness' dog at Kew;
Pray, tell me sir, whose dog are you?
Alexander Pope 1688–1744 English poet, *engraved on the collar of a dog*

The more one gets to know of men, the more one values dogs.
A. Toussenel 1803–85 French writer, *attributed to Mme Roland in the form 'The more I see of men, the more I like dogs'*

The dog is a gentleman; I hope to go to his heaven, not man's.
Mark Twain 1835–1910 American writer

Doubt see also Certainty

Oh! let us never, never doubt
What nobody is sure about!
Hilaire Belloc 1870–1953 British writer

How long halt ye between two opinions?
Bible

I'm a man of no convictions. At least, I think I am.
Christopher Hampton 1946– English dramatist

I am too much of a sceptic to deny the possibility of anything.
T. H. Huxley 1825–95 English biologist

I respect faith but doubt is what gets you an education.
Wilson Mizner 1876–1933 American dramatist

Ten thousand difficulties do not make one doubt.
John Henry Newman 1801–90 English theologian

Drawing

Now, the melancholy god protect thee, and the tailor make thy doublet of changeable taffeta, for thy mind is a very opal.
William Shakespeare 1564–1616 English dramatist

I must have a prodigious quantity of mind; it takes me as much as a week, sometimes, to make it up.
Mark Twain 1835–1910 American writer

Life is doubt,
And faith without doubt is nothing but death.
Miguel de Unamuno 1864–1937 Spanish philosopher

Doubt is not a pleasant condition. But certainty is an absurd one.
Voltaire 1694–1778 French writer

 # Drawing

Not a day without a line.
Apelles Greek painter of the 4th century BC, *proverbial summary of his philosophy*

A picture equals a movement in space.
Emily Carr 1871–1945 Canadian artist

Treat nature in terms of the cylinder, the sphere, the cone, all in perspective.
Paul Cézanne 1839–1906 French painter

I rarely draw what I see—I draw what I feel in my body.
Barbara Hepworth 1903–75 English sculptor

Drawing is the true test of art.
J. A. D. Ingres 1780–1867 French painter

An active line on a walk, moving freely without a goal. A walk for walk's sake.
Paul Klee 1879–1940 German-Swiss painter

Dreams

Have you noticed…there is never any third act in a nightmare? They bring you to a climax of terror and then leave you there. They are the work of poor dramatists.
Max Beerbohm 1872–1956 English critic

The armoured cars of dreams, contrived to let us do so many a dangerous thing.
Elizabeth Bishop 1911–79 American poet

All the things one has forgotten scream for help in dreams.
Elias Canetti 1905–94 Bulgarian-born writer

When we dream that we are dreaming, the moment of awakening is at hand.
J. M. Coetzee 1940–   South African novelist

The interpretation of dreams is the royal road to a knowledge of the unconscious activities of the mind.
Sigmund Freud 1856–1939 Austrian psychoanalyst

The dream of reason produces monsters.
Goya 1746–1828 Spanish painter

Was it a vision, or a waking dream?
Fled is that music:—do I wake or sleep?
John Keats 1795–1821 English poet

They who dream by day are cognizant of many things which escape those who dream only by night.
Edgar Allan Poe 1809–49 American writer

O God! I could be bounded in a nut-shell, and count myself a king of infinite space, were it not that I have bad dreams.
William Shakespeare 1564–1616 English dramatist

The quick Dreams,
The passion-wingèd Ministers of thought.
Percy Bysshe Shelley 1792–1822 English poet

Drink

One reason why I don't drink is because I wish to know when I am having a good time.
Nancy Astor 1879–1964 British politician

When the wine is in, the wit is out.
Thomas Becon 1512–67 English clergyman

Wine is a mocker, strong drink is raging.
Bible

Freedom and Whisky gang thegither!
Robert Burns 1759–96 Scottish poet

I have taken more out of alcohol than alcohol has taken out of me.
Winston Churchill 1874–1965 British statesman

A man shouldn't fool with booze until he's fifty; then he's a damn fool if he doesn't.
William Faulkner 1897–1962 American novelist

I often wonder what the Vintners buy
One half so precious as the Goods they sell.
Edward Fitzgerald 1809–83 English poet

Drink not the third glass.
George Herbert 1593–1633 English poet

And malt does more than Milton can
To justify God's ways to man.
A. E. Housman 1859–1936 English poet

You're not drunk if you can lie on the floor without holding on.
Dean Martin 1917–95 American actor

Candy
Is dandy
But liquor
Is quicker.
Ogden Nash 1902–71 American humorist

I'm only a beer teetotaller, not a champagne teetotaller.
George Bernard Shaw 1856–1950 Irish dramatist

First the man takes a drink,
Then the drink takes a drink,
Then the drink takes the man!
Edward Rowland Sill 1841–87 American educator, *frequently quoted as a Japanese proverb*

I'm not so think as you drunk I am.
J. C. Squire 1884–1958 English man of letters

Wine is bottled poetry.
Robert Louis Stevenson 1850–94 Scottish novelist

The lips that touch liquor must never touch mine.
George W. Young 1846–1919

Drugs

I'll die young, but it's like kissing God.
Lenny Bruce 1925–66 American comedian, *on his drug addiction*

Junk is the ideal product…the ultimate merchandise. No sales talk necessary. The client will crawl through a sewer and beg to buy.
William S. Burroughs 1914–97 American novelist

I experimented with marijuana a time or two. And I didn't like it, and I didn't inhale.
Bill Clinton 1946– American statesman

The Earth

Thou hast the keys of Paradise, oh just, subtle, and mighty opium!
Thomas De Quincey 1785–1859 English essayist

In this country, don't forget, a habit is no damn private hell. There's no solitary confinement outside of jail. A habit is hell for those you love.
Billie Holiday 1915–59 American singer

Every form of addiction is bad, no matter whether the narcotic be alcohol or morphine or idealism.
Carl Gustav Jung 1875–1961 Swiss psychologist

A drug is neither moral or immoral—it's a chemical compound.
Frank Zappa 1940–93 American rock musician

 # The Earth

The earth is what we all have in common.
Wendell Berry 1934– American poet

The earth is the Lord's, and all that therein is: the compass of the world, and they that dwell therein.
Bible

Topography displays no favourites; North's as near as West. More delicate than the historians' are the map-makers' colours.
Elizabeth Bishop 1911–79 American poet

In every outthrust headland, in every curving beach, in every grain of sand there is a story of the earth.
Rachel Carson 1907–64 American zoologist

How inappropriate to call this planet Earth when it is clearly Ocean.
Arthur C. Clarke 1917–2008 English science fiction writer

Now there is one outstandingly important fact regarding Spaceship Earth, and that is that no instruction book came with it.

R. Buckminster Fuller 1895–1983 American designer

In my view, climate change is the most severe problem we are facing today—more serious even than the threat of terrorism.

David King 1939– British scientist

To me, it underscores our responsibility to deal more kindly with one another, and to preserve and cherish the pale blue dot, the only home we've ever known.

Carl Sagan 1934–96 American astronomer, *of Earth as photographed by Voyager 1*

Need for a knowledge of geography is greater than the need of gardens for water after the stars have failed to fulfil their promise of rain.

Yāqūt d. 1229 Arab geographer

Eating see also **Cookery**, **Food**

Tell me what you eat and I will tell you what you are.

Anthelme Brillat-Savarin 1755–1826 French gourmet

Some hae meat and canna eat,
And some wad eat that want it:
But we hae meat and we can eat,
And sae the Lord be thankit.

Robert Burns 1759–96 Scottish poet

Hunger is the best sauce in the world.

Cervantes 1547–1616 Spanish novelist

It's a very odd thing—
As odd as can be—

Eating

That whatever Miss T eats
Turns into Miss T.
Walter de la Mare 1873–1956 English poet

Gluttony is an emotional escape, a sign something is
eating us.
Peter De Vries 1910–93 American novelist

One can say everything best over a meal.
George Eliot 1819–80 English novelist

ANTHONY HOPKINS: I do wish we could chat longer, but I'm
having an old friend for dinner.
Thomas Harris 1940– and **Ted Tally** 1952– American writer
and American screenwriter, *in the film* The Silence of the
Lambs

I don't eat anything with a face.
Linda McCartney 1941–98 American photographer

Time for a little something.
A. A. Milne 1882–1956 English writer

One should eat to live, and not live to eat.
Molière 1622–73 French comic dramatist

The appetite grows by eating.
François Rabelais c.1494–c.1553 French humanist

Now good digestion wait on appetite,
And health on both!
William Shakespeare 1564–1616 English dramatist

We each day dig our graves with our teeth.
Samuel Smiles 1812–1904 English writer

He sows hurry and reaps indigestion.
Robert Louis Stevenson 1850–94 Scottish novelist

I'll fill hup the chinks wi' cheese.
> **R. S. Surtees** 1805–64 English novelist

MICHAEL DOUGLAS: Lunch is for wimps.
> **Stanley Weiser** and **Oliver Stone** 1946– American
> screenwriters, *in the film* Wall Street

One cannot think well, love well, sleep well, if one has not
dined well.
> **Virginia Woolf** 1882–1941 English novelist

Economics

It's the economy, stupid.
> **Anonymous**, *slogan of Bill Clinton's first presidential campaign*

There's no such thing as a free lunch.
> **Anonymous**

There is enough in the world for everyone's need, but not
enough for everyone's greed.
> **Frank Buchman** 1878–1961 American evangelist

Capitalism is using its money; we socialists throw it away.
> **Fidel Castro** 1927–2016 Cuban statesman

Inflation is the one form of taxation that can be imposed
without legislation.
> **Milton Friedman** 1912–2006 American economist

The safest way to double your money is to fold it over and
put it in your pocket.
> **Frank McKinney ('Kin') Hubbard** 1868–1930 American
> humorist

Gross national product…measures everything, in short,
except that which makes life worthwhile.
> **Robert Kennedy** 1925–68 American politician

Economics

The green shoots of economic spring are appearing once again.
Norman Lamont 1942– British politician, *often quoted as 'the green shoots of recovery'*

If the policy isn't hurting, it isn't working.
John Major 1943– British statesman, *on controlling inflation*

Government's view of the economy could be summed up in a few short phrases: If it moves, tax it. If it keeps moving, regulate it. And if it stops moving, subsidize it.
Ronald Reagan 1911–2004 American statesman

We have always known that heedless self-interest was bad morals; we know now that it is bad economics.
Franklin D. Roosevelt 1882–1945 American statesman

Wall Street indexes predicted nine out of the last five recessions.
Paul A. Samuelson 1915–2009 American economist

Call a thing immoral or ugly, soul-destroying or a degradation of man, a peril to the peace of the world or to the well-being of future generations: as long as you have not shown it to be 'uneconomic' you have not really questioned its right to exist, grow, and prosper.
E. F. Schumacher 1911–77 German-born economist

It's a recession when your neighbour loses his job; it's a depression when you lose yours.
Harry S. Truman 1884–1972 American statesman

What a country calls its vital economic interests are not the things which enable its citizens to live, but the things which enable it to make war.
Simone Weil 1909–43 French philosopher

MICHAEL DOUGLAS: Greed—for lack of a better word—is good. Greed is right. Greed works.
> **Stanley Weiser** and **Oliver Stone** 1946– American screenwriters American screenwriters, *in the film* Wall Street

It is not that pearls fetch a high price *because* men have dived for them; but on the contrary, men dive for them because they fetch a high price.
> **Richard Whately** 1787–1863 English philosopher

Education see also **Examinations**, **Teaching**

What one knows is, in youth, of little moment; they know enough who know how to learn.
> **Henry Brooks Adams** 1838–1918 American historian

What sculpture is to a block of marble, education is to a human soul.
> **Joseph Addison** 1672–1719 English writer

Give me a child for the first seven years, and you may do what you like with him afterwards.
> **Anonymous**, *attributed as a Jesuit maxim*

The roots of education are bitter, but the fruit is sweet.
> **Aristotle** 384–322 BC Greek philosopher

I said…how, and why, young children, were sooner allured by love, than driven by beating, to attain good learning.
> **Roger Ascham** 1515–68 English scholar

Studies serve for delight, for ornament, and for ability.
> **Francis Bacon** 1561–1626 English courtier

The dread of beatings! Dread of being late!
And, greatest dread of all, the dread of games!
> **John Betjeman** 1906–84 English poet

Education

Ask me my three main priorities for Government, and I tell you: education, education and education.
   Tony Blair 1953–   British statesman

That lyf so short, the craft so long to lerne.
   Geoffrey Chaucer c.1343–1400 English poet

In education there should be no class distinction.
   Confucius 551–479 BC Chinese philosopher

C-l-e-a-n, clean, verb active, to make bright, to scour. W-i-n, win, d-e-r, der, winder, a casement. When the boy knows this out of the book, he goes and does it.
   Charles Dickens 1812–70 English novelist

A University should be a place of light, of liberty, and of learning.
   Benjamin Disraeli 1804–81 British statesman

Study as if you were to live for ever; live as if you were to die tomorrow.
   St Edmund of Abingdon c.1175–1240 English scholar

The value of an education in a liberal arts college is not the learning of many facts but the training of the mind to think something that cannot be learned from textbooks.
   Albert Einstein 1879–1955 German-born theoretical physicist

You send your child to the schoolmaster, but 'tis the schoolboys who educate him.
   Ralph Waldo Emerson 1803–82 American writer

The proper study of mankind is books.
   Aldous Huxley 1894–1963 English novelist

Education is the most powerful weapon which you can use to change the world.
   Nelson Mandela 1918–2013 South African statesman

Effort

If you educate a man you educate one person, but if you educate a woman you educate a family.
Ruby Manikan Indian church leader

My spelling is Wobbly. It's good spelling but it Wobbles, and the letters get in the wrong places.
A. A. Milne 1882–1956 English writer

Education costs money, but then so does ignorance.
Claus Moser 1922–2015 British statistician

Know then thyself, presume not God to scan;
The proper study of mankind is man.
Alexander Pope 1688–1744 English poet

I would I had bestowed that time in the tongues that I have in fencing, dancing, and bear-baiting. O! had I but followed the arts!
William Shakespeare 1564–1616 English dramatist

Education is what survives when what has been learned has been forgotten.
B. F. Skinner 1904–90 American psychologist

What does education often do? It makes a straight-cut ditch of a free, meandering brook.
Henry David Thoreau 1817–62 American writer

The best thing for being sad…is to learn something.
T. H. White 1906–64 English novelist

Effort

We're number two. We try harder.
Anonymous, *advertising slogan for Avis car rentals*

Madam, if a thing is possible, consider it done; the impossible? that will be done.
Charles Alexandre de Calonne 1734–1802 French statesman

Elections

Now, *here*, you see, it takes all the running *you* can do, to keep in the same place. If you want to get somewhere else, you must run at least twice as fast as that!
Lewis Carroll 1832–98 English writer

Oh, how I am tired of the struggle!
Johann Wolfgang von Goethe 1749–1832 German writer

HOMER SIMPSON: Kids, you tried your best, and you failed miserably. The lesson is, never try.
Matt Groening 1954– American humorist

Between us and excellence, the gods have placed the sweat of our brows.
Hesiod fl. 700 BC Greek poet

Mountains will go into labour, and a silly little mouse will be born.
Horace 65–8 BC Roman poet

I had done all that I could; and no man is well pleased to have his all neglected, be it ever so little.
Samuel Johnson 1709–84 English lexicographer

Superhuman effort isn't worth a damn unless it achieves results.
Ernest Shackleton 1874–1922 British explorer

Things won are done; joy's soul lies in the doing.
William Shakespeare 1564–1616 English dramatist

 # Elections see also **Democracy**

Vote early and vote often.
Anonymous, *US election slogan, already current by 1858*

Vote for the man who promises least; he'll be the least disappointing.
Bernard Baruch 1870–1965 American financier

One man shall have one vote.
> **John Cartwright** 1740–1824 English political reformer

Hell, I never vote *for* anybody. I always vote *against*.
> **W. C. Fields** 1880–1946 American humorist

I always voted at my party's call,
And I never thought of thinking for myself at all.
> **W. S. Gilbert** 1836–1911 English writer

To give victory to the right, not bloody bullets, but peaceful
ballots only, are necessary.
> **Abraham Lincoln** 1809–65 American statesman, *usually quoted
as 'The ballot is stronger than the bullet'*

If voting changed anything, they'd abolish it.
> **Ken Livingstone** 1945– British politician

One of the nuisances of the ballot is that when the oracle
has spoken you never know what it means.
> **Lord Salisbury** 1830–1903 British statesman

It's not the voting that's democracy, it's the counting.
> **Tom Stoppard** 1937– British dramatist

Ending ✻

It ain't over till it's over.
> **Yogi Berra** 1925–2015 American baseball player

Better is the end of a thing than the beginning thereof.
> **Bible**

Now this is not the end. It is not even the beginning of the
end. But it is, perhaps, the end of the beginning.
> **Winston Churchill** 1874–1965 British statesman, *on the Battle
of Egypt*

Enemies

The party's over, it's time to call it a day.
Betty Comden 1917–2006 and **Adolph Green** 1915–2002
American songwriters

This is the way the world ends
Not with a bang but a whimper.
T. S. Eliot 1888–1965 American-born British poet

In my end is my beginning.
Mary, Queen of Scots 1542–87

The opera ain't over 'til the fat lady sings.
Proverb

The rest is silence.
William Shakespeare 1564–1616 English dramatist

This is the beginning of the end.
Charles-Maurice de Talleyrand 1754–1838 French statesman,
on the announcement of Napoleon's Pyrrhic victory at Borodino,
1812

They think it's all over—it is now.
Kenneth Wolstenholme 1920–2002 English sports
commentator

 # Enemies

He who has a thousand friends has not a friend to spare,
And he who has one enemy will meet him everywhere.
Ali ibn-Abi-Talib c.602–661 Arab ruler

Not while I'm alive 'e ain't!
Ernest Bevin 1881–1951 British politician, *reply to the observation*
that Nye Bevan was sometimes his own worst enemy

Love your enemies, do good to them which hate you.
Bible

Enemies

An injury is much sooner forgotten than an insult.
Lord Chesterfield 1694–1773 English writer

You can calculate the worth of a man by the number of his enemies, and the importance of a work of art by the harm that is spoken of it.
Gustave Flaubert 1821–80 French novelist

Better to have him inside the tent pissing out, than outside pissing in.
Lyndon Baines Johnson 1908–73 American statesman,
of J. Edgar Hoover

People wish their enemies dead—but I do not; I say give them the gout, give them the stone!
Lady Mary Wortley Montagu 1689–1762 English writer

I have none. I had them all shot.
Ramón María Narváez 1800–68 Spanish statesman, *asked on his deathbed if he forgave his enemies*

The enemies of my enemies are my friends.
Proverb

AL PACINO: Keep your friends close, but your enemies closer.
Mario Puzo 1920–99 and **Francis Ford Coppola** 1939–
American novelist and American film director, *in the film*
The Godfather: Part II, *often wrongly attributed to Sun Tzu*

There is nothing in the whole world so painful as feeling that one is not liked. It always seems to me that people who hate me must be suffering from some strange form of lunacy.
Sei Shōnagon c.966–c.1013 Japanese diarist

I have always made one prayer to God, a very short one. Here it is, 'My God, make our enemies very ridiculous!'
Voltaire 1694–1778 French writer

England see also **Britain**, **London**

I will not cease from mental fight,
Nor shall my sword sleep in my hand,
Till we have built Jerusalem,
In England's green and pleasant land.
> **William Blake** 1757–1827 English poet

Oh, to be in England
Now that April's there.
> **Robert Browning** 1812–89 English poet

The Thames is liquid history.
> **John Burns** 1858–1943 British politician, *to an American, who had compared the Thames disparagingly with the Mississippi*

In England there are sixty different religions, and only one sauce.
> **Francesco Caracciolo** 1752–99 Neapolitan diplomat

Mad dogs and Englishmen
Go out in the midday sun.
> **Noël Coward** 1899–1973 English dramatist

What should they know of England who only England know?
> **Rudyard Kipling** 1865–1936 English writer

England is a nation of shopkeepers.
> **Napoleon I** 1769–1821 French emperor

England expects that every man will do his duty.
> **Horatio, Lord Nelson** 1758–1805 British admiral, *at the battle of Trafalgar*

There'll always be an England.
> **Ross Parker** 1914–74 and **Hugh Charles** 1907–95 British songwriters

Ask any man what nationality he would prefer to be, and ninety-nine out of a hundred will tell you that they would prefer to be Englishmen.
Cecil Rhodes 1853–1902 South African statesman

This royal throne of kings, this sceptred isle,
This earth of majesty, this seat of Mars…
This blessèd plot, this earth, this realm, this England.
William Shakespeare 1564–1616 English dramatist

The froth at top, dregs at bottom, but the middle excellent.
Voltaire 1694–1778 French writer, *comparing the English to their own beer*

You never find an Englishman among the under-dogs—except in England, of course.
Evelyn Waugh 1903–66 English novelist

The English country gentleman galloping after a fox—the unspeakable in full pursuit of the uneatable.
Oscar Wilde 1854–1900 Irish dramatist

We must be free or die, who speak the tongue
That Shakespeare spake; the faith and morals hold
Which Milton held.
William Wordsworth 1770–1850 English poet

The Environment see also **Country**, **Pollution**

Think globally, act locally.
Anonymous, *Friends of the Earth slogan*

Come, friendly bombs, and fall on Slough!
It isn't fit for humans now,
There isn't grass to graze a cow.
Swarm over, Death!
John Betjeman 1906–84 English poet

The Environment

Woe unto them that join house to house, that lay field to field, till there be no place.
Bible

And was Jerusalem builded here
Among these dark Satanic mills?
William Blake 1757–1827 English poet

O all ye Green Things upon the Earth, bless ye the Lord.
Book of Common Prayer 1662

I do not know of any environmental group in any country that does not view its government as an adversary.
Gro Harlem Brundtland 1939– Norwegian stateswoman

What would the world be, once bereft
Of wet and wildness? Let them be left,
O let them be left, wildness and wet;
Long live the weeds and the wilderness yet.
Gerard Manley Hopkins 1844–89 English poet

I am I plus my surroundings and if I do not preserve the latter, I do not preserve myself.
José Ortega y Gasset 1883–1955 Spanish writer

The parks are the lungs of London.
William Pitt 1708–78 British statesman

Consult the genius of the place in all.
Alexander Pope 1688–1744 English poet

It's not that easy being green.
Joe Raposo 1937–89 American songwriter, *sung by the Muppet Kermit the frog*

Small is beautiful.
E. F. Schumacher 1911–77 German-born economist

Climate change is the greatest market failure the world has ever seen.
Nicholas Stern 1946– British economist

In wildness is the preservation of the world.
Henry David Thoreau 1817–62 American writer

Envy and Jealousy

Thou shalt not covet thy neighbour's house, thou shalt not covet thy neighbour's wife.
Bible

Jealousy is no more than feeling alone against smiling enemies.
Elizabeth Bowen 1899–1973 Anglo-Irish novelist

The danger chiefly lies in acting well;
No crime's so great as daring to excel.
Charles Churchill 1731–64 English poet

Thou shalt not covet; but tradition
Approves all forms of competition.
Arthur Hugh Clough 1819–61 English poet

Some folks rail against other folks, because other folks have what some folks would be glad of.
Henry Fielding 1707–54 English novelist

Envy can scarcely hold back her tears, when she sees nothing to cry about.
Ovid 43 BC–c.AD 17 Roman poet

To jealousy, nothing is more frightful than laughter.
Françoise Sagan 1935–2004 French novelist

        O! beware, my lord, of jealousy;
It is the green-eyed monster which doth mock
The meat it feeds on.
William Shakespeare 1564–1616 English dramatist

Equality see also **Human Rights**

Equality may perhaps be a right, but no power on earth can ever turn it into a fact.
Honoré de Balzac 1799–1850 French novelist

He maketh his sun to rise on the evil and on the good, and sendeth rain on the just and on the unjust.
Bible

A man's a man for a' that.
Robert Burns 1759–96 Scottish poet

When every one is somebodee,
Then no one's anybody.
W. S. Gilbert 1836–1911 English writer

Your levellers wish to level *down* as far as themselves; but they cannot bear levelling *up* to themselves.
Samuel Johnson 1709–84 English lexicographer

I have a dream that one day on the red hills of Georgia the sons of former slaves and the sons of former slave owners will be able to sit down together at the table of brotherhood.
Martin Luther King 1929–68 American civil rights leader

All animals are equal but some animals are more equal than others.
George Orwell 1903–50 English novelist

Hath not a Jew eyes? hath not a Jew hands, organs, dimensions, senses, affections, passions?…If you prick us, do we not bleed? if you tickle us, do we not laugh? if you poison us, do we not die? and if you wrong us, shall we not revenge?
William Shakespeare 1564–1616 English dramatist

Make all men equal today, and God has so created them
that they shall all be unequal tomorrow.
Anthony Trollope 1815–82 English novelist

Europe ✽

Whoever speaks of Europe is wrong, [it is] a geographical
concept.
Otto von Bismarck 1815–98 German statesman

Fog in Channel—Continent isolated.
Russell Brockbank 1913–79 British cartoonist, *newspaper
placard in cartoon*

From Stettin in the Baltic to Trieste in the Adriatic an iron
curtain has descended across the Continent.
Winston Churchill 1874–1965 British statesman

Each time we have to choose between Europe and the open
sea, we shall always choose the open sea.
Winston Churchill 1874–1965 British statesman

Without Britain Europe would remain only a torso.
Ludwig Erhard 1897–1977 German statesman

It means the end of a thousand years of history.
Hugh Gaitskell 1906–63 British politician, *on a European
federation*

If I want to talk to Europe who do I call?
Henry Kissinger 1923– American politician

The policy of European integration is in reality a question of
war and peace in the 21st century.
Helmut Kohl 1930– German statesman

Evil

I want the whole of Europe to have one currency; it will
make trading much easier.
Napoleon I 1769–1821 French emperor

You're thinking of Europe as Germany and France. I don't.
I think that's old Europe. If you look at the entire Nato
Europe today, the centre of gravity is shifting to the east.
Donald Rumsfeld 1932– American politician

Better fifty years of Europe than a cycle of Cathay.
Alfred, Lord Tennyson 1809–92 English poet

 # Evil see also **Goodness**

The fearsome, word-and-thought-defying *banality of evil*.
Hannah Arendt 1906–75 American philosopher

I and the public know
What all schoolchildren learn,
Those to whom evil is done
Do evil in return.
W. H. Auden 1907–73 English poet

With love for mankind and hatred of sins.
St Augustine of Hippo AD 354–430 Roman theologian, *often
quoted as 'Love the sinner but hate the sin'*

There is no peace, saith the Lord, unto the wicked.
Bible

It is necessary only for the good man to do nothing for evil
to triumph.
Edmund Burke 1729–97 Irish-born politician

The face of 'evil' is always the face of total need.
William S. Burroughs 1914–97 American novelist

As soon as men decide that all means are permitted to fight an evil, then their good becomes indistinguishable from the evil that they set out to destroy.
Christopher Dawson 1889–1970 English historian

What we call evil is simply ignorance bumping its head in the dark.
Henry Ford 1863–1947 American car manufacturer

All things truly wicked start from an innocence.
Ernest Hemingway 1899–1961 American novelist

But if he does really think that there is no distinction between virtue and vice, why, Sir, when he leaves our houses, let us count our spoons.
Samuel Johnson 1709–84 English lexicographer

No one ever suddenly became depraved.
Juvenal c.AD 60–c.140 Roman satirist

Farewell remorse! All good to me is lost;
Evil, be thou my good.
John Milton 1608–74 English poet

An orgy looks particularly alluring seen through the mists of righteous indignation.
Malcolm Muggeridge 1903–90 British journalist

By the pricking of my thumbs,
Something wicked this way comes.
William Shakespeare 1564–1616 English dramatist

The line dividing good and evil cuts through the heart of every human being. And who is willing to destroy a piece of his own heart?
Alexander Solzhenitsyn 1918–2008 Russian novelist

Examinations

There are a thousand hacking at the branches of evil to one who is striking at the root.
Henry David Thoreau 1817–62 American writer

 Examinations

Truth is no more at issue in an examination than thirst at a wine-tasting or fashion at a striptease.
Alan Bennett 1934– English writer

Examinations are formidable even to the best prepared, for the greatest fool may ask more than the wisest man can answer.
Charles Caleb Colton c.1780–1832 English clergyman

Life isn't like coursework, baby. It's one damn essay crisis after another.
Boris Johnson 1964– British politician

I evidently knew more about economics than my examiners.
John Maynard Keynes 1883–1946 English economist,
explaining why he performed badly in the Civil Service examinations

In examinations those who do not wish to know ask questions of those who cannot tell.
Walter Raleigh 1861–1922 English critic

Do not on any account attempt to write on both sides of the paper at once.
W. C. Sellar 1898–1951 and **R. J. Yeatman** 1898–1968 British writers

Had silicon been a gas, I would have been a major-general by now.
James McNeill Whistler 1834–1903 American-born painter,
having been found 'deficient in chemistry' in a West Point examination

Exercise see also **Health**

If you walk hard enough, you probably don't need any other God.
> **Bruce Chatwin** 1940–89 English travel writer

The wise, for cure, on exercise depend;
God never made his work for man to mend.
> **John Dryden** 1631–1700 English poet

Exercise is the yuppie version of bulimia.
> **Barbara Ehrenreich** 1941– American sociologist

Exercise is bunk. If you are healthy, you don't need it: if you are sick you shouldn't take it.
> **Henry Ford** 1863–1947 American car manufacturer

The sovereign invigorator of the body is exercise, and of all the exercises, walking is best.
> **Thomas Jefferson** 1743–1826 American statesman

A bear, however hard he tries,
Grows tubby without exercise.
> **A. A. Milne** 1882–1956 English writer

The only exercise I take is walking behind the coffins of friends who took exercise.
> **Peter O'Toole** 1932–2013 Irish-born British actor

Avoid running at all times.
> **Leroy ('Satchel') Paige** 1906–82 American baseball player

Those who do not find time for exercise will have to find time for illness.
> **Proverb**

All you need to run is good shoes.
> **Paula Radcliffe** 1973– British long-distance runner

Experience

There's no easy way out [of exercise]. If there were, I would
have bought it. And believe me, it would be one of my
favourite things!

Oprah Winfrey 1954–   American talk show hostess

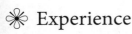 # Experience

All experience is an arch to build upon.

Henry Brooks Adams 1838–1918 American historian

You may not control all the events that happen to you but
you can decide not to be reduced by them.

Maya Angelou 1928–2014 American writer

You should make a point of trying every experience once,
excepting incest and folk-dancing.

Anonymous

Experience isn't interesting till it begins to repeat itself—in
fact, till it does that, it hardly *is* experience.

Elizabeth Bowen 1899–1973 Anglo-Irish novelist

Everyone knows I'm all in favour of apprenticeships, but let
me tell you this is no time for a novice.

Gordon Brown 1951–   British statesman

Experience is the best of schoolmasters, only the school fees
are heavy.

Thomas Carlyle 1795–1881 Scottish historian

The courtiers who surround him [Louis XVIII] have
forgotten nothing and learnt nothing.

Charles Dumouriez 1739–1823 French general

We had the experience but missed the meaning.

T. S. Eliot 1888–1965 American-born British poet

Everything has been said before. But since nobody listens we have to keep going back and beginning all over again.
André Gide 1869–1951 French novelist

Experience is not what happens to a man; it is what a man does with what happens to him.
Aldous Huxley 1894–1963 English novelist

HARRISON FORD: It's not the years, honey, it's the mileage.
George Lucas 1944– American film director, *in the film* Raiders of the Lost Ark

We took risks, we knew we took them; things have come out against us, and therefore we have no cause for complaint.
Robert Falcon Scott 1868–1912 English explorer

Education is when you read the fine print; experience is what you get when you don't.
Pete Seeger 1919–2014 American folk singer

Experience is the name everyone gives to their mistakes.
Oscar Wilde 1854–1900 Irish dramatist

Facts see also **Knowledge**

In fact the *a priori* reasoning is so entirely satisfactory to me that if the facts won't fit in, why so much the worse for the facts is my feeling.
Erasmus Darwin 1804–81 English physician, *to his brother Charles, after reading his book,* The Origin of Species

MR GRADGRIND: Now, what I want is, Facts…Facts alone are wanted in life.
Charles Dickens 1812–70 English novelist

SHERLOCK HOLMES: Data! data! data!…I can't make bricks without clay.
Arthur Conan Doyle 1859–1930 Scottish-born writer

Failure

What can be asserted without evidence can also be
dismissed without evidence.
    Christopher Hitchens 1949–2011 English-born American writer

Facts do not cease to exist because they are ignored.
    Aldous Huxley 1894–1963 English novelist

When the facts change, I change my mind.
    John Maynard Keynes 1883–1946 English economist

Get your facts first, and then you can distort 'em as much as
you please.
    Mark Twain 1835–1910 American writer

 Failure see also **Success**

History to the defeated
May say Alas but cannot help or pardon.
    W. H. Auden 1907–73 English poet

Ever tried. Ever failed. No matter. Try again. Fail again.
Fail better.
    Samuel Beckett 1906–89 Irish writer

She knows there's no success like failure
And that failure's no success at all.
    Bob Dylan 1941– American singer

Man is not made for defeat. A man can be destroyed but not
defeated.
    Ernest Hemingway 1899–1961 American novelist

Failure is not an option.
    Gene Kranz 1933– American space flight director, *summarized
version of announcement to ground crew in Houston as Apollo 13
approached the critical earth-to-moon decision loop*

Vae victis.

Down with the defeated!

Livy 59 BC–AD 17 Roman historian

Show me a good loser and I'll show you a loser.

Vince Lombardi 1913–70 American football coach

There are some defeats more triumphant than victories.

Montaigne 1533–92 French moralist

There is only one step from the sublime to the ridiculous.

Napoleon I 1769–1821 French emperor

We fail!
But screw your courage to the sticking-place,
And we'll not fail.

William Shakespeare 1564–1616 English dramatist

Our business in this world is not to succeed, but to continue to fail, in good spirits.

Robert Louis Stevenson 1850–94 Scottish novelist

Failure is not fatal, but failure to change might be.

John Wooden 1910–2010 American basketball player

Fame

Seven wealthy towns contend for HOMER dead
Through which the living HOMER begged his bread.

Anonymous

There's no such thing as bad publicity except your own obituary.

Brendan Behan 1923–64 Irish dramatist

Let us now praise famous men, and our fathers that begat us.

Bible

Fame

A prophet is not without honour, save in his own country,
and in his own house.
   Bible

I awoke one morning and found myself famous.
   Lord Byron 1788–1824 English poet

Fame is a fickle food
Upon a shifting plate.
   Emily Dickinson 1830–86 American poet

The deed is all, the glory nothing.
   Johann Wolfgang von Goethe 1749–1832 German writer

Popularity? It is glory's small change.
   Victor Hugo 1802–85 French writer

No path of flowers leads to glory.
   Jean de la Fontaine 1621–95 French poet

We're more popular than Jesus now; I don't know which will
go first—rock 'n' roll or Christianity.
   John Lennon 1940–80 English pop singer, *of the Beatles*

Fame is the spur that the clear spirit doth raise
(That last infirmity of noble mind)
To scorn delights, and live laborious days.
   John Milton 1608–74 English poet

Famous men have the whole earth as their memorial.
   Pericles c.495–429 BC Greek statesman

So long as men can breathe, or eyes can see,
So long lives this, and this gives life to thee.
   William Shakespeare 1564–1616 English dramatist

You always hide just in the middle of the limelight.
   George Bernard Shaw 1856–1950 Irish dramatist, *to
   T. E. Lawrence, who had complained of Press attention*

Celebrity is a mask that eats into the face.
John Updike 1932–2009 American writer

In the future everybody will be world famous for fifteen minutes.
Andy Warhol 1927–87 American artist

The Family see also **Children**, **Parents**

He that hath wife and children hath given hostages to fortune; for they are impediments to great enterprises, either of virtue or mischief.
Francis Bacon 1561–1626 English courtier

Thy wife shall be as the fruitful vine: upon the walls of thine house.
Thy children like the olive-branches: round about thy table.
Bible

As I leave the second most important job I could ever hold, I cherish even more the first—as a husband and father.
Gordon Brown 1951–   British statesman, *on resigning as Prime Minister*

We begin our public affections in our families. No cold relation is a zealous citizen.
Edmund Burke 1729–97 Irish-born politician

[It is] time to turn our attention to pressing challenges like…how to make American families more like the Waltons and a little bit less like the Simpsons.
George Bush 1924–   American statesman

Believe me, family solidarity is after all the only good thing. I have been deprived of it, so I know.
Marie Curie 1867–1934 Polish-born French physicist

Fashion

One would be in less danger
From the wiles of the stranger
If one's own kin and kith
Were more fun to be with.
Ogden Nash 1902–71 American humorist

A little more than kin, and less than kind.
William Shakespeare 1564–1616 English dramatist

If a man's character is to be abused, say what you will,
there's nobody like a relation to do the business.
William Makepeace Thackeray 1811–63 English novelist

All happy families resemble one another, but each unhappy
family is unhappy in its own way.
Leo Tolstoy 1828–1910 Russian novelist

It is no use telling me that there are bad aunts and good
aunts. At the core, they are all alike. Sooner or later, out
pops the cloven hoof.
P. G. Wodehouse 1881–1975 English writer

 # Fashion

A little of what you call frippery is very necessary towards
looking like the rest of the world.
Abigail Adams 1744–1818 American letter writer

Fashion often starts off beautiful and becomes ugly, whereas
art starts off ugly sometimes and becomes beautiful.
David Bailey 1938– English photographer

Fashion is made to become unfashionable.
Coco Chanel 1883–1971 French couturière

One had as good be out of the world, as out of the fashion.
Colley Cibber 1671–1757 English dramatist

Haute Couture should be fun, foolish and almost unwearable.
Christian Lacroix 1951– French couturier

I don't design clothes, I design dreams.
Ralph Lauren 1939– American fashion designer

Hip is the sophistication of the wise primitive in a giant jungle.
Norman Mailer 1923–2007 American writer

Fashion is more usually a gentle progression of revisited ideas.
Bruce Oldfield 1950– English fashion designer

Every generation laughs at the old fashions, but follows religiously the new.
Henry David Thoreau 1817–62 American writer

It is charming to totter into vogue.
Horace Walpole 1717–97 English connoisseur

A fashion…is usually a form of ugliness so intolerable that we have to alter it every six months.
Oscar Wilde 1854–1900 Irish dramatist

Fate

Must it be? It must be.
Ludwig van Beethoven 1770–1827 German composer

Canst thou bind the sweet influences of Pleiades, or loose the bands of Orion?
Bible

Fate is not an eagle, it creeps like a rat.
Elizabeth Bowen 1899–1973 Anglo-Irish novelist

Nothing have I found stronger than Necessity.
Euripides c.485–c.406 BC Greek dramatist

Fathers

There once was a man who said, 'Damn!
It is borne in upon me I am
An engine that moves
In predestinate grooves,
I'm not even a bus, I'm a tram.'
Maurice Evan Hare 1886–1967 English limerick writer

What we call fate does not come into us from the outside,
but emerges from us.
Rainer Maria Rilke 1875–1926 German poet

If it be now, 'tis not to come; if it be not to come, it will be
now; if it be not now, yet it will come: the readiness is all.
William Shakespeare 1564–1616 English dramatist

We are merely the stars' tennis-balls, struck and bandied
Which way please them.
John Webster c.1580–c.1625 English dramatist

Every bullet has its billet.
William III 1650–1702 British monarch

 # Fathers

One father is more than a hundred schoolmasters.
George Herbert 1593–1633 English poet

Being a father
Is quite a bother,
But I like it, rather.
Ogden Nash 1902–71 American humorist

I can do one of two things. I can be president of the United
States or I can control Alice. I cannot possibly do both.
Theodore Roosevelt 1858–1919 American statesman, *on his
daughter*

The fundamental defect of fathers, in our competitive society, is that they want their children to be a credit to them.
Bertrand Russell 1872–1970 British philosopher

It doesn't matter who my father was; it matters who I remember he was.
Anne Sexton 1928–74 American poet

It is a wise father that knows his own child.
William Shakespeare 1564–1616 English dramatist

If men do not keep on speaking terms with children, they cease to be men, and become merely machines for eating and for earning money.
John Updike 1932–2009 American writer

Fear

We must travel in the direction of our fear.
John Berryman 1914–72 American poet

No passion so effectually robs the mind of all its powers of acting and reasoning as fear.
Edmund Burke 1729–97 Irish-born politician

If hopes were dupes, fears may be liars.
Arthur Hugh Clough 1819–61 English poet

Be afraid. Be very afraid.
David Cronenberg 1943– Canadian film director

Nothing in life is to be feared, it is only to be understood.
Marie Curie 1867–1934 Polish-born French physicist

I will show you fear in a handful of dust.
T. S. Eliot 1888–1965 American-born British poet

There is no terror in a bang, only in the anticipation of it.
Alfred Hitchcock 1899–1980 British-born film director

Festivals

Fear is, of all passions, that which weakens the judgment most.
Cardinal de Retz 1613–79 French cardinal

The only thing we have to fear is fear itself.
Franklin D. Roosevelt 1882–1945 American statesman

Only the unknown frightens men. But once a man has faced the unknown, that terror becomes the known.
Antoine de Saint-Exupéry 1900–44 French novelist

       Present fears
Are less than horrible imaginings.
William Shakespeare 1564–1616 English dramatist

In time we hate that which we often fear.
William Shakespeare 1564–1616 English dramatist

Our deepest fear is not that we are inadequate. Our deepest fear is that we are powerful beyond measure. It is our light, not our darkness, that most frightens us.
Marianne Williamson 1953– American writer

 Festivals see also **Christmas**

Hogmanay, like all festivals, being but a bank from which we can only draw what we put in.
J. M. Barrie 1860–1937 Scottish writer

Hurrah for the fun!
Is the pudding done?
Hurrah for the pumpkin pie!
Lydia Maria Child 1802–80 American abolitionist, *on Thanksgiving Day*

The true essentials of a feast are only fun and feed.
Oliver Wendell Holmes 1809–94 American physician

The holiest of all holidays are those
Kept by ourselves in silence and apart;
The secret anniversaries of the heart.
　　Henry Wadsworth Longfellow 1807–82 American poet

Time has no divisions to mark its passage, there is never
a thunderstorm or blare of trumpets to announce the
beginning of a new month or year. Even when a new
century begins it is only we mortals who ring bells and fire
off pistols.
　　Thomas Mann 1875–1955 German novelist

Tonight's December thirty-first,
Something is about to burst…
Hark, it's midnight, children dear.
Duck! Here comes another year!
　　Ogden Nash 1902–71 American humorist

Ring out the old, ring in the new,
Ring, happy bells, across the snow:
The year is going, let him go;
Ring out the false, ring in the true.
　　Alfred, Lord Tennyson 1809–92 English poet

April 1. This is the day upon which we are reminded of what
we are on the other three hundred and sixty-four.
　　Mark Twain 1835–1910 American writer

Fishing

If fishing is a religion, fly fishing is high church.
　　Tom Brokaw 1940– American journalist

I love fishing. It's like transcendental meditation with a
punch-line.
　　Billy Connolly 1942– Scottish comedian

Flight

Fishing is unquestionably a form of madness but, happily,
for the once-bitten there is no cure.
Lord Home 1903–95 British statesman

All men are equal before fish.
Herbert Hoover 1874–1964 American statesman

Fly fishing may be a very pleasant amusement; but angling
or float fishing I can only compare to a stick and a string,
with a worm at one end and a fool at the other.
Samuel Johnson 1709–84 English lexicographer

It has always been my private conviction that any man
who pits his intelligence against a fish and loses has it
coming.
John Steinbeck 1902–68 American novelist

As no man is born an artist, so no man is born an angler.
Izaak Walton 1593–1683 English writer

 # Flight

Every flyer who ventures across oceans to distant lands is
a potential explorer; in his or her breast burns the same
fire that urged the adventurers of old to set forth in their
sailing-ships for foreign lands.
Jean Batten 1909–82 New Zealand aviator

Had I been a man I might have explored the Poles,
or climbed Mount Everest, but as it was, my spirit found
outlet in the air.
Amy Johnson 1903–41 English aviator

I feel about airplanes the way I feel about diets. It seems to
me that they are wonderful things for other people to go on.
Jean Kerr 1923–2003 American writer

I was astonished at the effect my successful landing in
France had on the nations of the world. To me, it was like a
match lighting a bonfire.
   Charles Lindbergh 1902–74 American aviator

Oh! I have slipped the surly bonds of earth
And danced the skies on laughter-silvered wings;…
And, while with silent lifting mind I've trod
The high, untrespassed sanctity of space,
Put out my hand and touched the face of God.
   John Gillespie Magee 1922–41 American airman

I did not fully understand the dread term 'terminal illness'
until I saw Heathrow for myself.
   Dennis Potter 1935–94 English dramatist

There are only two emotions in a plane: boredom and terror.
   Orson Welles 1915–85 American film director

Flowers

Unkempt about those hedges blows
An English unofficial rose.
   Rupert Brooke 1887–1915 English poet

Flowers…are a proud assertion that a ray of beauty
outvalues all the utilities of the world.
   Ralph Waldo Emerson 1803–82 American writer

I sometimes think that never blows so red
The rose as where some buried Caesar bled.
   Edward Fitzgerald 1809–83 English poet

People from a planet without flowers would think we
must be mad with joy the whole time to have such things
about us.
   Iris Murdoch 1919–99 English novelist

Food

RICHARD GRIFFITHS: Flowers are essentially tarts; prostitutes
for the bees.
> **Bruce Robinson** 1946– English screenwriter, *in the film*
> Withnail and I

> Daffodils,
> That come before the swallow dares, and take
> The winds of March with beauty.
> **William Shakespeare** 1564–1616 English dramatist

I wandered lonely as a cloud
That floats on high o'er vales and hills,
When all at once I saw a crowd,
A host, of golden daffodils;
Beside the lake, beneath the trees,
Fluttering and dancing in the breeze.
> **William Wordsworth** 1770–1850 English poet

To me the meanest flower that blows can give
Thoughts that do often lie too deep for tears.
> **William Wordsworth** 1770–1850 English poet

 # Food see also **Cookery**, **Eating**

Shake and shake
The catsup bottle.
None will come,
And then a lot'll.
> **Richard Armour** 1906–89 American poet

I'm President of the United States, and I'm not going to eat
any more broccoli!
> **George Bush** 1924– American statesman

Doubtless God could have made a better berry, but
doubtless God never did.
> **William Butler** 1535–1618 English physician, *on the strawberry*

Take away that pudding—it has no theme.
Winston Churchill 1874–1965 British statesman

OLIVER TWIST: Please, sir, I want some more.
Charles Dickens 1812–70 English novelist

Cheese, milk's leap toward immortality.
Clifton Fadiman 1904–99 American critic

A cucumber should be well sliced, and dressed with pepper and vinegar, and then thrown out, as good for nothing.
Samuel Johnson 1709–84 English lexicographer

I am a great eater of beef, and I believe that does harm to my wit.
William Shakespeare 1564–1616 English dramatist

There is no love sincerer than the love of food.
George Bernard Shaw 1856–1950 Irish dramatist

A hen's egg is, quite simply, a work of art, a masterpiece of design and construction with, it has to be said, brilliant packaging.
Delia Smith English cook

Serenely full, the epicure would say,
Fate cannot harm me, I have dined to-day.
Sydney Smith 1771–1845 English essayist

Many's the long night I've dreamed of cheese—toasted, mostly.
Robert Louis Stevenson 1850–94 Scottish novelist

Cauliflower is nothing but cabbage with a college education.
Mark Twain 1835–1910 American writer

What moistens the lip and what brightens the eye?
What calls back the past, like the rich pumpkin pie?
John Greenleaf Whittier 1807–92 American poet

✳ Foolishness

The world is full of fools, and he who would not see it should live alone and smash his mirror.
Anonymous

There's a sucker born every minute.
Phineas T. Barnum 1810–91 American showman

For ye suffer fools gladly, seeing ye yourselves are wise.
Bible

Never give a sucker an even break.
W. C. Fields 1880–1946 American humorist

I won't say she was silly, but I think one of us was silly, and it wasn't me.
Elizabeth Gaskell 1810–65 English novelist

Mix a little foolishness with your prudence: it's good to be silly at the right moment.
Horace 65–8 BC Roman poet

A knowledgeable fool is a greater fool than an ignorant fool.
Molière 1622–73 French comic dramatist

Fools rush in where angels fear to tread.
Alexander Pope 1688–1744 English poet

The follies which a man regrets most, in his life, are those which he didn't commit when he had the opportunity.
Helen Rowland 1875–1950 American writer

The ultimate result of shielding men from the effects of folly, is to fill the world with fools.
Herbert Spencer 1820–1903 English philosopher

Let us be thankful for the fools. But for them the rest of us could not succeed.
Mark Twain 1835–1910 American writer

Be wise with speed;
A fool at forty is a fool indeed.
Edward Young 1683–1765 English poet

Football ✳

The great fallacy is that the game is first and last about winning. It is nothing of the kind. The game is about glory, it is about doing things in style and with a flourish, about going out and beating the lot, not waiting for them to die of boredom.
Danny Blanchflower 1926–93 Northern Irish footballer

Football, wherein is nothing but beastly fury, and extreme violence, whereof proceedeth hurt, and consequently rancour and malice do remain with them that be wounded.
Thomas Elyot 1499–1546 English diplomat

Football is an art more central to our culture than anything the Arts Council deigns to recognize.
Germaine Greer 1939– Australian feminist

The natural state of the football fan is bitter disappointment, no matter what the score.
Nick Hornby 1957– British writer

Football is a simple game; 22 men chase a ball for 90 minutes and at the end, the Germans win.
Gary Lineker 1960– English footballer

Oh, he's football crazy, he's football mad
And the football it has robbed him o' the wee bit sense he had.
Jimmie McGregor 1932– Scottish singer

The goal was scored a little bit by the hand of God, another bit by head of Maradona.
Diego Maradona 1960– Argentinian footballer, *on his controversial goal against England in the 1986 World Cup*

Forgiveness

Football? It's the beautiful game.
Pelé 1940- Brazilian footballer

To say that these men paid their shillings to watch twenty-two hirelings kick a ball is merely to say that a violin is wood and catgut, that *Hamlet* is so much paper and ink. For a shilling the Bruddersford United AFC offered you Conflict and Art.
J. B. Priestley 1894–1984 English writer

Some people think football is a matter of life and death…I can assure them it is much more serious than that.
Bill Shankly 1913–81 Scottish footballer

Football and cookery are the two most important subjects in the country.
Delia Smith English cook

 # Forgiveness

Her sins, which are many, are forgiven; for she loved much.
Bible

It is easier to forgive an enemy than to forgive a friend.
William Blake 1757–1827 English poet

I shall be an autocrat: that's my trade. And the good Lord will forgive me: that's his.
Catherine the Great 1729–96 Russian empress

After such knowledge, what forgiveness?
T. S. Eliot 1888–1965 American-born British poet

God may pardon you, but I never can.
Elizabeth I 1533–1603 English monarch

Forgive but never forget.
John F. Kennedy 1917–63 American statesman

Every one says forgiveness is a lovely idea, until they have something to forgive.
C. S. Lewis 1898–1963 English literary scholar

True reconciliation does not consist in merely forgetting the past.
Nelson Mandela 1918–2013 South African statesman

We read that we ought to forgive our enemies; but we do not read that we ought to forgive our friends.
Cosimo de' Medici 1389–1464 Italian statesman

When a deep injury is done to us, we never recover until we forgive.
Alan Paton 1903–88 South African writer

To err is human; to forgive, divine.
Alexander Pope 1688–1744 English poet

Youth, which is forgiven everything, forgives itself nothing: age, which forgives itself everything, is forgiven nothing.
George Bernard Shaw 1856–1950 Irish dramatist

The stupid neither forgive nor forget; the naïve forgive and forget; the wise forgive but do not forget.
Thomas Szasz 1920–2012 Hungarian-born psychiatrist

France

Everything ends this way in France. Weddings, christenings, duels, burials, swindlings, affairs of state—everything is a pretext for a good dinner.
Jean Anouilh 1910–87 French dramatist

France was long a despotism tempered by epigrams.
Thomas Carlyle 1795–1881 Scottish historian

Friendship

How can you govern a country which has 246 varieties of cheese?
  Charles de Gaulle 1890–1970 French statesman

France, mother of arts, of warfare, and of laws.
  Joachim Du Bellay 1522–60 French poet

Vive la différence, mais vive l'entente cordiale.
Long live the difference, but long live the Entente Cordiale.
  Elizabeth II 1926– British monarch

GROUNDSKEEPER WILLIE AS FRENCH TEACHER: Bonjourr, you cheese-eating surrender monkeys.
  Matt Groening 1954– American humorist

The French soul is stronger than the French mind, and Voltaire shatters against Joan of Arc.
  Victor Hugo 1802–85 French writer

They order, said I, this matter better in France.
  Laurence Sterne 1713–68 English novelist

If the French noblesse had been capable of playing cricket with their peasants, their chateaux would never have been burnt.
  G. M. Trevelyan 1876–1962 English historian

Friendship

Champagne for my real friends, real pain for my sham friends.
  Francis Bacon 1909–92 Irish painter

We must take our friends as they are.
  James Boswell 1740–95 Scottish lawyer

There is no man so friendless but what he can find a friend sincere enough to tell him disagreeable truths.
  Edward Bulwer-Lytton 1803–73 British novelist

Should auld acquaintance be forgot
And never brought to mind?

Robert Burns 1759–96 Scottish poet

Friendship is like money, easier made than kept.

Samuel Butler 1835–1902 English novelist

Give me the avowed, erect and manly foe;
Firm I can meet, perhaps return the blow;
But of all plagues, good Heaven, thy wrath can send,
Save me, oh, save me, from the candid friend.

George Canning 1770–1827 British statesman

A woman can become a man's friend only in the following
stages—first an acquaintance, next a mistress, and only then
a friend.

Anton Chekhov 1860–1904 Russian writer

Oh, the comfort—the inexpressible comfort of feeling
safe with a person, having neither to weigh thoughts, nor
measure words, but pouring them all out, just as they are,
chaff and grain together; knowing that a faithful hand will
take and sift them—keep what is worth keeping—and with
the breath of kindness blow the rest away.

Dinah Mulock Craik 1826–87 English novelist

The only reward of virtue is virtue; the only way to have a
friend is to be one.

Ralph Waldo Emerson 1803–82 American writer

Of all the means which wisdom acquires to ensure
happiness throughout the whole of life, by far the most
important is friendship.

Epicurus 341–271 BC Greek philosopher

HUMPHREY BOGART: Louis, I think this is the beginning of a
beautiful friendship.

Julius J. Epstein 1909–2001 and **others** American
screenwriters, *in the film* Casablanca

Friendship

Friends are the sunshine of life.

John Hay 1838–1905 American diplomat

My father always used to say that when you die, if you've got five real friends, you've had a great life.

Lee Iacocca 1924– American businessman

If a man does not make new acquaintance as he advances through life, he will soon find himself left alone. A man, Sir, should keep his friendship in constant repair.

Samuel Johnson 1709–84 English lexicographer

However rare true love may be, true friendship is rarer.

Duc de la Rochefoucauld 1613–80 French moralist

Oh I get by with a little help from my friends,
Mm, I get high with a little help from my friends.

John Lennon 1940–80 and **Paul McCartney** 1942– English pop singers

To like and dislike the same things, that is indeed true friendship.

Sallust 86–35 BC Roman historian

Friendship is constant in all other things
Save in the office and affairs of love.

William Shakespeare 1564–1616 English dramatist

The holy passion of friendship is of so sweet and steady and loyal and enduring a nature that it will last through a whole lifetime, if not asked to lend money.

Mark Twain 1835–1910 American writer

I do not believe that friends are necessarily the people you like best, they are merely the people who got there first.

Peter Ustinov 1921–2004 British actor

The Future

'We are always doing', says he, 'something for Posterity, but I would fain see Posterity do something for us.'
   Joseph Addison 1672–1719 English writer

The future ain't what it used to be.
   Yogi Berra 1925–2015 American baseball player

Predictions can be very difficult—especially about the future.
   Niels Bohr 1885–1962 Danish physicist

You can never plan the future by the past.
   Edmund Burke 1729–97 Irish-born politician

I look to the future, because that's where I'm going to spend the rest of my life.
   George Burns 1896–1996 American comedian

The empires of the future are the empires of the mind.
   Winston Churchill 1874–1965 British statesman

The future belongs to crowds.
   Don DeLillo 1936–   American novelist

I never think of the future. It comes soon enough.
   Albert Einstein 1879–1955 German-born theoretical physicist

You cannot fight against the future. Time is on our side.
   W. E. Gladstone 1809–98 British statesman

The best way to predict the future is to invent it.
   Alan Kay 1940–   American computer scientist

We have trained them [men] to think of the Future as a promised land which favoured heroes attain—not as something which everyone reaches at the rate of sixty minutes an hour, whatever he does, whoever he is.
   C. S. Lewis 1898–1963 English literary scholar

Gardens

If you want a picture of the future, imagine a boot stamping on a human face—for ever.
George Orwell 1903–50 English novelist

Lord! we know what we are, but know not what we may be.
William Shakespeare 1564–1616 English dramatist

Gardens

I value my garden more for being full of blackbirds than of cherries, and very frankly give them fruit for their songs.
Joseph Addison 1672–1719 English writer

Nothing is more pleasant to the eye than green grass kept finely shorn.
Francis Bacon 1561–1626 English courtier

A garden is a lovesome thing, God wot!
T. E. Brown 1830–97 Manx schoolmaster

What is a weed? A plant whose virtues have not been discovered.
Ralph Waldo Emerson 1803–82 American writer

He that plants trees loves others beside himself.
Thomas Fuller 1654–1734 English physician

The kiss of the sun for pardon,
The song of the birds for mirth,
One is nearer God's Heart in a garden
Than anywhere else on earth.
Dorothy Frances Gurney 1858–1932 English poet

But though an old man, I am but a young gardener.
Thomas Jefferson 1743–1826 American statesman

The Glory of the Garden lies in more than meets the eye.
Rudyard Kipling 1865–1936 English writer

The Generation Gap

A garden was the primitive prison till man with
Promethean felicity and boldness luckily sinned himself
out of it.
> **Charles Lamb** 1775–1834 English writer

He who plants a tree
Plants a hope.
> **Lucy Larcom** 1824–93 American writer

Annihilating all that's made
To a green thought in a green shade.
> **Andrew Marvell** 1621–78 English poet

Come into the garden, Maud,
I am here at the gate alone.
> **Alfred, Lord Tennyson** 1809–92 English poet

What a man needs in gardening is a cast iron back, with a
hinge in it.
> **Charles Dudley Warner** 1829–1900 American writer

The Generation Gap see also **Youth**

The dead might as well try to speak to the living as the old
to the young.
> **Willa Cather** 1873–1947 American novelist

Come mothers and fathers,
Throughout the land
And don't criticize
What you can't understand.
> **Bob Dylan** 1941– American singer

Si jeunesse savait; si vieillesse pouvait.
If youth knew; if age could.
> **Henri Estienne** 1531–98 French printer

Genius

Every generation revolts against its fathers and makes
friends with its grandfathers.
Lewis Mumford 1895–1982 American sociologist

Crabbed age and youth cannot live together:
Youth is full of pleasance, age is full of care.
William Shakespeare 1564–1616 English dramatist

It's all that the young can do for the old, to shock them and
keep them up to date.
George Bernard Shaw 1856–1950 Irish dramatist

Nothing so dates a man as to decry the younger
generation.
Adlai Stevenson 1900–65 American politician

Hope I die before I get old.
Pete Townshend 1945– British rock musician

When I was a boy of 14, my father was so ignorant I could
hardly stand to have the old man around. But when I got
to be 21, I was astonished at how much the old man had
learned in seven years.
Mark Twain 1835–1910 American writer

The old believe everything: the middle-aged suspect
everything: the young know everything.
Oscar Wilde 1854–1900 Irish dramatist

 # Genius

Genius is only a greater aptitude for patience.
Comte de Buffon 1707–88 French naturalist

Everybody has talent at twenty-five. The difficult thing is to
have it at fifty.
Edgar Degas 1834–1917 French artist

Mediocrity knows nothing higher than itself, but talent instantly recognizes genius.

Arthur Conan Doyle 1859–1930 Scottish-born writer

Great wits are sure to madness near allied,
And thin partitions do their bounds divide.

John Dryden 1631–1700 English poet

Genius is one per cent inspiration, ninety-nine per cent perspiration.

Thomas Alva Edison 1847–1931 American inventor

Little minds are interested in the extraordinary; great minds in the commonplace.

Elbert Hubbard 1859–1915 American writer

The true genius is a mind of large general powers, accidentally determined to some particular direction.

Samuel Johnson 1709–84 English lexicographer

Genius does what it must, and Talent does what it can.

Owen Meredith 1831–91 English statesman

Every positive value has its price in negative terms…The genius of Einstein leads to Hiroshima.

Pablo Picasso 1881–1973 Spanish painter

Genius is always allowed some leeway, once the hammer has been pried from its hands and the blood has been cleaned up.

Terry Pratchett 1948–2015 English novelist

It takes a lot of time to be a genius, you have to sit around so much doing nothing, really doing nothing.

Gertrude Stein 1874–1946 American writer

When a true genius appears in the world, you may know him by this sign, that the dunces are all in confederacy against him.

Jonathan Swift 1667–1745 Irish poet and satirist

Gifts

I know of no genius but the genius of hard work.
J. M. W. Turner 1775–1851 English painter

I have nothing to declare except my genius.
Oscar Wilde 1854–1900 Irish dramatist, *at the New York Custom House*

 Gifts see also **Charity**

Surprises are foolish things. The pleasure is not enhanced, and the inconvenience is often considerable.
Jane Austen 1775–1817 English novelist

It is more blessed to give than to receive.
Bible

They gave it me,—for an un-birthday present.
Lewis Carroll 1832–98 English writer

One must be poor to know the luxury of giving.
George Eliot 1819–80 English novelist

Generosity is giving more than you can, and pride is taking less than you need.
Kahlil Gibran 1883–1931 Lebanese-born American writer

A gift though small is welcome.
Homer fl. 8th century BC Greek poet

I know it's not much, but it's the best I can do,
My gift is my song and this one's for you.
Elton John 1947– and **Bernie Taupin** 1950– English pop singer and English songwriter English pop singer and English songwriter

Presents, I often say, endear Absents.
Charles Lamb 1775–1834 English writer

Why is it no one ever sent me yet
One perfect limousine, do you suppose?

Ah no, it's always just my luck to get
One perfect rose.
Dorothy Parker 1893–1967 American critic

SEAN CONNERY: The key to a woman's heart is an
unexpected gift at an unexpected time.
Mike Rich 1959– American screenwriter, *in the film* Finding
Forrester

I am not in the giving vein to-day.
William Shakespeare 1564–1616 English dramatist

God see also **Religion**

The nature of God is a circle of which the centre is
everywhere and the circumference is nowhere.
Anonymous

There's probably no God. Now stop worrying and enjoy
your life.
Anonymous, *advertisement on London buses, supported by
English evolutionary biologist Richard Dawkins (1941–)*

In the beginning was the Word, and the Word was with
God, and the Word was God.
Bible

He that loveth not knoweth not God; for God is love.
Bible

When men stop believing in God they don't believe in
nothing; they believe in anything.
G. K. Chesterton 1874–1936 English writer

God moves in a mysterious way
His wonders to perform.
William Cowper 1731–1800 English poet

God

God is subtle but he is not malicious.
Albert Einstein 1879–1955 German-born theoretical physicist

Operationally, God is beginning to resemble not a ruler but the last fading smile of a cosmic Cheshire cat.
Julian Huxley 1887–1975 English biologist

An honest God is the noblest work of man.
Robert G. Ingersoll 1833–99 American agnostic

Many roads lead to God. I have chosen that of music and dance.
Jalal ad-Din ar-Rumi 1207–73 Persian poet

God is the breath of all breath.
Kabir c.1398–c.1448 North Indian poet and mystic

God seems to have left the receiver off the hook, and time is running out.
Arthur Koestler 1905–83 Hungarian-born writer

Praise belongs to God, the Lord of all Being,
the All-merciful, the All-compassionate.
The Koran

Though the mills of God grind slowly, yet they grind
  exceeding small;
Though with patience He stands waiting, with exactness
  grinds He all.
Henry Wadsworth Longfellow 1807–82 American poet

Whatever your heart clings to and confides in, that is really your God.
Martin Luther 1483–1546 German theologian

If the triangles were to make a God they would give him three sides.
Montesquieu 1689–1755 French political philosopher

The Buddha, the Godhead, resides quite as comfortably
in the circuits of a digital computer or the gears of a cycle
transmission as he does at the top of a mountain or in the
petals of a flower.
Robert M. Pirsig 1928–2017 American writer

Hear, O Israel: the Lord our God, the Lord is One.
The Siddur

O Lord, to what a state dost Thou bring those who love
Thee!
St Teresa of Ávila 1512–82 Spanish mystic

For man proposes, but God disposes.
Thomas à Kempis c.1380–1471 German writer

If God did not exist, it would be necessary to invent him.
Voltaire 1694–1778 French writer

Our God, our help in ages past
Our hope for years to come,
Our shelter from the stormy blast,
And our eternal home.
Isaac Watts 1674–1748 English hymn-writer

Golf

If you watch a game, it's fun. If you play it, it's recreation. If
you work at it, it's golf.
Bob Hope 1903–2003 American comedian

Golf is so popular simply because it is the best game in the
world at which to be bad.
A. A. Milne 1882–1956 English writer

Golf is a good walk spoiled.
Mark Twain 1835–1910 American writer

Good Looks

The least thing upset him on the links. He missed short putts because of the uproar of the butterflies in the adjoining meadows.

P. G. Wodehouse 1881–1975 English writer

Golf…is the infallible test. The man who can go into a patch of rough alone, with the knowledge that only God is watching him, and play his ball where it lies, is the man who will serve you faithfully and well.

P. G. Wodehouse 1881–1975 English writer

 # Good Looks

A pretty girl is like a melody
That haunts you night and day.

Irving Berlin 1888–1989 American songwriter

And she was fayr as is the rose in May.

Geoffrey Chaucer c.1343–1400 English poet

When a woman isn't beautiful, people always say, 'You have lovely eyes, you have lovely hair.'

Anton Chekhov 1860–1904 Russian writer

Beauty is the lover's gift.

William Congreve 1670–1729 English dramatist

Is it too much to ask that women be spared the daily struggle for superhuman beauty in order to offer it to the caresses of a subhumanly ugly mate?

Germaine Greer 1939– Australian feminist

I'm tired of all this nonsense about beauty being only skin-deep. That's deep enough. What do you want—an adorable pancreas?

Jean Kerr 1923–2003 American writer

The Lord prefers common-looking people. That is why he makes so many of them.
  Abraham Lincoln 1809–65 American statesman

A beautiful face is a mute recommendation.
  Publilius Syrus fl. 1st century BC Roman writer

Shall I compare thee to a summer's day?
Thou art more lovely and more temperate.
  William Shakespeare 1564–1616 English dramatist

Goodness see also Evil

Every art and every investigation, and likewise every practical pursuit or undertaking, seems to aim at some good: hence it has been well said that the Good is That at which all things aim.
  Aristotle 384–322 BC Greek philosopher

He who would do good to another, must do it in minute particulars.
  William Blake 1757–1827 English poet

No one can be good for long if goodness is not in demand.
  Bertolt Brecht 1898–1956 German dramatist

Integrity has no need of rules.
  Albert Camus 1913–60 French writer

No people do so much harm as those who go about doing good.
  Mandell Creighton 1843–1901 English prelate

        What after all
Is a halo? It's only one more thing to keep clean.
  Christopher Fry 1907–2005 English dramatist

I expect to pass through this world but once; any good thing therefore that I can do, or any kindness that I can show to

Goodness

any fellow-creature, let me do it now; let me not defer or neglect it, for I shall not pass this way again.
Stephen Grellet 1773–1855 French missionary

Be good, sweet maid, and let who will be clever.
Charles Kingsley 1819–75 English writer

Good and evil shall not be held equal. Turn away evil with that which is better; and behold the man between whom and thyself there was enmity, shall become, as it were, thy warmest friend.
The Koran

A man who wants to act virtuously in every way necessarily comes to grief among so many who are not virtuous.
Niccolò Machiavelli 1469–1527 Italian political philosopher

Virtue she finds too painful an endeavour,
Content to dwell in decencies for ever.
Alexander Pope 1688–1744 English poet

Dost thou think, because thou art virtuous, there shall be no more cakes and ale?
William Shakespeare 1564–1616 English dramatist

How far that little candle throws his beams!
So shines a good deed in a naughty world.
William Shakespeare 1564–1616 English dramatist

Our goodness derives not from our capacity to think but to love.
St Teresa of Ávila 1512–82 Spanish mystic

Would that we had spent one whole day well in this world!
Thomas à Kempis c.1380–1471 German writer

Virtue knows to a farthing what it has lost by not having been vice.
Horace Walpole 1717–97 English connoisseur

'Goodness, what beautiful diamonds!'
'Goodness had nothing to do with it.'
Mae West 1892–1980 American film actress

That best portion of a good man's life,
His little, nameless, unremembered, acts
Of kindness and of love.
William Wordsworth 1770–1850 English poet

Gossip

There is so much good in the worst of us,
And so much bad in the best of us,
That it hardly becomes any of us
To talk about the rest of us.
Anonymous

Careless talk costs lives.
Anonymous, *Second World War security slogan*

Every man is surrounded by a neighbourhood of voluntary
spies.
Jane Austen 1775–1817 English novelist

They come together like the Coroner's Inquest, to sit upon
the murdered reputations of the week.
William Congreve 1670–1729 English dramatist

Gossip is a sort of smoke that comes from the dirty tobacco-
pipes of those who diffuse it: it proves nothing but the bad
taste of the smoker.
George Eliot 1819–80 English novelist

Love and scandal are the best sweeteners of tea.
Henry Fielding 1707–54 English novelist

Like all gossip—it's merely one of those half-alive things
that try to crowd out real life.
E. M. Forster 1879–1970 English novelist

Government

No one gossips about other people's secret virtues.
Bertrand Russell 1872–1970 British philosopher

It takes your enemy and your friend, working together, to hurt you to the heart: the one to slander you and the other to get the news to you.
Mark Twain 1835–1910 American writer

There is only one thing in the world worse than being talked about, and that is not being talked about.
Oscar Wilde 1854–1900 Irish dramatist

 Government see also **Politics**

Let them hate, so long as they fear.
Accius 170–c.86 BC Roman poet

The happiness of society is the end of government.
John Adams 1735–1826 American statesman

Dullness in matters of government is a good sign, and not a bad one.
Walter Bagehot 1826–77 English economist

The object of government in peace and in war is not the glory of rulers or of races, but the happiness of the common man.
William Henry Beveridge 1879–1963 British economist

England is the mother of Parliaments.
John Bright 1811–89 English politician

Dear Chief Secretary, I'm afraid there is no money.
Liam Byrne 1970– British politician, *letter left for his successor as Chief Secretary to the Treasury*

The poor have sometimes objected to being governed badly; the rich have always objected to being governed at all.
G. K. Chesterton 1874–1936 English writer

It is a 'beautiful maxim' that it is necessary to save five *sous* on unessential things, and to pour out millions when it is a question of your glory.
Jean-Baptiste Colbert 1619–83 French statesman

No Government can be long secure without a formidable Opposition.
Benjamin Disraeli 1804–81 British statesman

Though God hath raised me high, yet this I count the glory of my crown: that I have reigned with your loves.
Elizabeth I 1533–1603 English monarch

If the Government is big enough to give you everything you want, it is big enough to take away everything you have.
Gerald Ford 1909–2006 American statesman

The state is like the human body. Not all of its functions are dignified.
Anatole France 1844–1924 French man of letters

My people and I have come to an agreement which satisfies us both. They are to say what they please, and I am to do what I please.
Frederick the Great 1712–86 Prussian monarch

Your business is not to govern the country but it is, if you think fit, to call to account those who do govern it.
W. E. Gladstone 1809–98 British statesman, *to the House of Commons*

Many journalists have fallen for the conspiracy theory of government. I do assure you that they would produce more accurate work if they adhered to the cock-up theory.
Bernard Ingham 1932– British journalist

The important thing for Government is not to do things which individuals are doing already, and to do them a little

Greatness

better or a little worse; but to do those things which at present are not done at all.
John Maynard Keynes 1883–1946 English economist

To govern is to choose.
Duc de Lévis 1764–1830 French soldier

It is much safer for a prince to be feared than loved, if he is to fail in one of the two.
Niccolò Machiavelli 1469–1527 Italian political philosopher

If men were angels, no government would be necessary.
James Madison 1751–1836 American statesman

BIG BROTHER IS WATCHING YOU.
George Orwell 1903–50 English novelist

The best government is that which governs least.
John L. O'Sullivan 1813–95 American journalist

For forms of government let fools contest;
Whate'er is best administered is best.
Alexander Pope 1688–1744 English poet

Wherever you have an efficient government you have a dictatorship.
Harry S. Truman 1884–1972 American statesman

Governments need both shepherds and butchers.
Voltaire 1694–1778 French writer

 # Greatness

The beauty of Israel is slain upon thy high places: how are the mighty fallen!
Bible

JOHN CUSACK: I'm looking for a dare-to-be-great situation.
Cameron Crowe 1957– American film director, *in the film* Say Anything

To be great is to be misunderstood.
> **Ralph Waldo Emerson** 1803–82 American writer

A man does not attain the status of Galileo merely because he is persecuted; he must also be right.
> **Stephen Jay Gould** 1941–2002 American palaeontologist

The glory of great men should always be measured against the means they used to acquire it.
> **Duc de la Rochefoucauld** 1613–80 French moralist

If any man seeks for greatness, let him forget greatness, and ask for truth, and he will find both.
> **Horace Mann** 1796–1859 American educationist

The first test of a truly great man is his humility.
> **John Ruskin** 1819–1900 English critic

But be not afraid of greatness: some men are born great, some achieve greatness, and some have greatness thrust upon them.
> **William Shakespeare** 1564–1616 English dramatist

Habit

The less of routine, the more of life.
> **Amos Bronson Alcott** 1799–1888 American reformer

Routine, in an intelligent man, is a sign of ambition.
> **W. H. Auden** 1907–73 English poet

Habit is a great deadener.
> **Samuel Beckett** 1906–89 Irish writer

Habit with him was all the test of truth,
'It must be right: I've done it from my youth.'
> **George Crabbe** 1754–1832 English poet

Happiness

Habit and routine have an unbelievable power to waste and destroy.
Henri de Lubac 1896–1991 French theologian

Sow an act, and you reap a habit. Sow a habit and you reap a character. Sow a character, and you reap a destiny.
Charles Reade 1814–84 English writer

Good habits: they are never good, because they are habits.
Jean-Paul Sartre 1905–80 French philosopher

 # Happiness

Mirth is like a flash of lightning that breaks through a gloom of clouds, and glitters for a moment: cheerfulness keeps up a kind of day-light in the mind.
Joseph Addison 1672–1719 English writer

A large income is the best recipe for happiness I ever heard of. It certainly may secure all the myrtle and turkey part of it.
Jane Austen 1775–1817 English novelist

There may be Peace without Joy, and Joy without Peace, but the two combined make Happiness.
John Buchan 1875–1940 Scottish novelist

Happiness is…finding two olives in your martini when you're hungry.
Johnny Carson 1925–2005 American comedian

Happiness is a mystery like religion, and should never be rationalized.
G. K. Chesterton 1874–1936 English writer

If you want others to be happy, practise compassion. If you want to be happy, practise compassion.
Dalai Lama 1935–   Tibetan monk

Happiness

Happiness resides not in possessions and not in gold,
the feeling of happiness dwells in the soul.
Democritus c.460–c.370 BC Greek philosopher

To be stupid, and selfish, and to have good health are the
three requirements for happiness, though if stupidity is
lacking, the others are useless.
Gustave Flaubert 1821–80 French novelist

Happiness makes up in height for what it lacks in length.
Robert Frost 1874–1963 American poet

Point me out the happy man and I will point you out
either egotism, selfishness, evil—or else an absolute
ignorance.
Graham Greene 1904–91 English novelist

Happiness is a how, not a what; a talent, not an object.
Hermann Hesse 1877–1962 German writer

I can sympathize with people's pains, but not with their
pleasures. There is something curiously boring about
somebody else's happiness.
Aldous Huxley 1894–1963 English novelist

Happiness is not an ideal of reason but of imagination.
Immanuel Kant 1724–1804 German philosopher

A man enjoys the happiness he feels, a woman the
happiness she gives.
Pierre Choderlos de Laclos 1741–1803 French soldier

Happiness writes white.
Philip Larkin 1922–85 English poet

Happiness is a warm gun.
John Lennon 1940–80 English pop singer

Happiness

Ask yourself whether you are happy, and you cease to be so.
John Stuart Mill 1806–73 English philosopher

Not to admire, is all the art I know,
To make men happy, and to keep them so.
Alexander Pope 1688–1744 English poet

To be without some of the things you want is an indispensable part of happiness.
Bertrand Russell 1872–1970 British philosopher

Freude, schöner Götterfunken,
Tochter aus Elysium.

Joy, beautiful radiance of the gods, daughter of Elysium.
Friedrich von Schiller 1759–1805 German poet

But a lifetime of happiness! No man alive could bear it: it would be hell on earth.
George Bernard Shaw 1856–1950 Irish dramatist

Call no man happy before he dies, he is at best but fortunate.
Solon c.640–after 556 BC Greek statesman

It is not how much we have, but how much we enjoy, that makes happiness.
C. H. Spurgeon 1834–92 English preacher

There's only one way of being comfortable, and that is to stop running round after happiness. If you make up your mind not to be happy there's no reason why you shouldn't have a fairly good time.
Edith Wharton 1862–1937 American novelist, *often quoted as 'If only we'd stop trying to be happy we could have a pretty good time'*

Hatred ✻

Better is a dinner of herbs where love is, than a stalled ox
and hatred therewith.
> **Bible**

I do not love thee, Dr Fell.
The reason why I cannot tell;
But this I know, and know full well,
I do not love thee, Dr Fell.
> **Thomas Brown** 1663–1704 English satirist

Now hatred is by far the longest pleasure;
Men love in haste, but they detest at leisure.
> **Lord Byron** 1788–1824 English poet

Love, friendship, respect do not unite people as much as
common hatred for something.
> **Anton Chekhov** 1860–1904 Russian writer

I never hated a man enough to give him diamonds back.
> **Zsa Zsa Gabor** 1919–2016 Hungarian-born film actress

We can scarcely hate any one that we know.
> **William Hazlitt** 1778–1830 English essayist

If you hate a person, you hate something in him that is part
of yourself. What isn't part of ourselves doesn't disturb us.
> **Hermann Hesse** 1877–1962 German writer

Returning hate for hate multiplies hate, adding deeper
darkness to a night already devoid of stars. Darkness cannot
drive out darkness; only light can do that. Hate cannot drive
out hate; only love can do that.
> **Martin Luther King** 1929–68 American civil rights leader

No one is born hating another person because of the colour
of his skin, or his background, or his religion. People must

learn to hate, and if they can learn to hate, they can be
taught to love, for love comes more naturally to the human
heart than its opposite.

Nelson Mandela 1918–2013 South African statesman

Always remember, others may hate you. Those who hate
you don't win unless you hate them. And then you destroy
yourself.

Richard Nixon 1913–94 American statesman

For hate is not conquered by hate: hate is conquered by love.
This is a law eternal.

Pali Tripitaka c. 2nd century BC Buddhist sacred texts

 # Health see also **Exercise**, **Sickness**

The first law of dietetics seems to be: if it tastes good, it's bad
for you.

Isaac Asimov 1920–92 Russian-born science fiction writer

The first wealth is health.

Ralph Waldo Emerson 1803–82 American writer

Health is worth more than learning.

Thomas Jefferson 1743–1826 American statesman

Mens sana in corpore sano.
A sound mind in a sound body.

Juvenal c.AD 60–c.140 Roman satirist

Life's not just being alive, but being well.

Martial c.AD 40–c.104 Roman epigrammatist

The best doctors are Dr Diet, Dr Quiet, and Dr Merryman.

Proverb

Choose rather to be strong in soul than strong of body.

Pythagoras 580–500 BC Greek philosopher

Look to your health; and if you have it, praise God, and value it next to a good conscience; for health is the second blessing that we mortals are capable of; a blessing that money cannot buy.
Izaak Walton 1593–1683 English writer

The Heart

The desires of the heart are as crooked as corkscrews
Not to be born is the best for man.
W. H. Auden 1907–73 English poet

There is a road from the eye to the heart that does not go through the intellect.
G. K. Chesterton 1874–1936 English writer

The human heart likes a little disorder in its geometry.
Louis de Bernières 1954– British novelist

A man who has not passed through the inferno of his passions has never overcome them.
Carl Gustav Jung 1875–1961 Swiss psychologist

Calm of mind, all passion spent.
John Milton 1608–74 English poet

The heart is an organ of fire.
Michael Ondaatje 1943– Canadian writer

The heart has its reasons which reason knows nothing of.
Blaise Pascal 1623–62 French scientist and philosopher

Unlearn'd, he knew no schoolman's subtle art,
No language, but the language of the heart.
Alexander Pope 1688–1744 English poet

    A man whose blood
Is very snow-broth; one who never feels
The wanton stings and motions of the sense.
William Shakespeare 1564–1616 English dramatist

Heaven

The heart of another is a dark forest.
Ivan Turgenev 1818–83 Russian novelist

Now that my ladder's gone
I must lie down where all ladders start
In the foul rag and bone shop of the heart.
W. B. Yeats 1865–1939 Irish poet

 # Heaven

And I saw a new heaven and a new earth: for the first
heaven and the first earth were passed away; and there was
no more sea.
Bible

The true paradises are the paradises that we have lost.
Marcel Proust 1871–1922 French novelist

HENRY LUTTRELL: My idea of heaven is, eating *pâté de foie
gras* to the sound of trumpets.
Sydney Smith 1771–1845 English essayist

I will spend my heaven doing good on earth.
St Teresa of Lisieux 1873–97 French nun

Heaven for climate, and hell for society.
Mark Twain 1835–1910 American writer

 # Hell

Hell, madam, is to love no more.
Georges Bernanos 1888–1948 French writer

Abandon all hope, you who enter!
Dante Alighieri 1265–1321 Italian poet, *inscription at the
entrance to Hell*

What is hell?
Hell is oneself,
Hell is alone, the other figures in it
Merely projections.
> **T. S. Eliot** 1888–1965 American-born British poet

Hell is other people.
> **Jean-Paul Sartre** 1905–80 French philosopher

A perpetual holiday is a good working definition of hell.
> **George Bernard Shaw** 1856–1950 Irish dramatist

Hell is a city much like London.
> **Percy Bysshe Shelley** 1792–1822 English poet

Heroes

We can be heroes
Just for one day.
> **David Bowie** 1947–2016 English rock musician

ANDREA: Unhappy the land that has no heroes!…
GALILEO: No. Unhappy the land that needs heroes.
> **Bertolt Brecht** 1898–1956 German dramatist

No man is a hero to his valet.
> **Mme Cornuel** 1605–94 French society hostess

Every hero becomes a bore at last.
> **Ralph Waldo Emerson** 1803–82 American writer

Ultimately a hero is a man who would argue with the Gods, and so awakens devils to contest his vision.
> **Norman Mailer** 1923–2007 American writer

Heroing is one of the shortest-lived professions there is.
> **Will Rogers** 1879–1935 American actor

A hero is the one who does what he can. The others don't.
> **Romain Rolland** 1866–1944 French writer

In this world I would rather live two days like a tiger,
than two hundred years like a sheep.
Tipu Sultan c.1750–99

 History

If history records good things of good men, the thoughtful
hearer is encouraged to imitate what is good.
The Venerable Bede AD 673–735 English historian

History repeats itself; historians repeat one another.
Rupert Brooke 1887–1915 English poet

History is the essence of innumerable biographies.
Thomas Carlyle 1795–1881 Scottish historian

To be ignorant of what occurred before you were born is to
remain forever a child.
Cicero 106–43 BC Roman statesman

History is philosophy from examples.
Dionysius of Halicarnassus fl. 30–7 BC Greek historian

History is more or less bunk.
Henry Ford 1863–1947 American car manufacturer

History is past politics, and politics is present history.
E. A. Freeman 1823–92 English historian

History…is, indeed, little more than the register of the
crimes, follies, and misfortunes of mankind.
Edward Gibbon 1737–94 English historian

War makes rattling good history; but Peace is poor reading.
Thomas Hardy 1840–1928 English novelist

Hegel says somewhere that all great events and personalities
in world history reappear in one fashion or another. He
forgot to add: the first time as tragedy, the second as farce.
Karl Marx 1818–83 German philosopher

Happy the people whose annals are blank in history-books!
Montesquieu 1689–1755 French political philosopher

History is not what you thought. *It is what you can remember.*
W. C. Sellar 1898–1951 and **R. J. Yeatman** 1898–1968 British writers

Human history becomes more and more a race between education and catastrophe.
H. G. Wells 1866–1946 English novelist

Home see also **Houses, Housework**

Home is home, though it be never so homely.
John Clarke d. 1658 English schoolmaster

'Home is the place where, when you have to go there,
They have to take you in.'
'I should have called it
Something you somehow haven't to deserve.'
Robert Frost 1874–1963 American poet

What's the good of a home if you are never in it?
George Grossmith 1847–1912 and **Weedon Grossmith** 1854–1919 English writers

One never reaches home. But wherever friendly paths intersect the whole world looks like home for a time.
Hermann Hesse 1877–1962 German writer

Any old place I can hang my hat is home sweet home to me.
William Jerome 1865–1932 American songwriter

The accent of one's birthplace lingers in the mind and in the heart as it does in one's speech.
Duc de la Rochefoucauld 1613–80 French moralist

Honesty

E.T. phone home.
> **Melissa Mathison** 1950– American screenwriter, *in the film* E.T.

Mid pleasures and palaces though we may roam,
Be it ever so humble, there's no place like home.
> **J. H. Payne** 1791–1852 American actor

Home is where you come to when you have nothing better to do.
> **Margaret Thatcher** 1925–2013 British stateswoman

 # Honesty see also **Deceit**

Honesty is praised and left to shiver.
> **Juvenal** C.AD 60–c.140 Roman satirist

honesty is a good
thing but
it is not profitable to
its possessor
unless it is
kept under control.
> **Don Marquis** 1878–1937 American poet and journalist

An honest man's the noblest work of God.
> **Alexander Pope** 1688–1744 English poet

Speak what we feel, not what we ought to say.
> **William Shakespeare** 1564–1616 English dramatist

It is dangerous to be sincere unless you are also stupid.
> **George Bernard Shaw** 1856–1950 Irish dramatist

I am afraid we must make the world honest before we can honestly say to our children that honesty is the best policy.
> **George Bernard Shaw** 1856–1950 Irish dramatist

Honour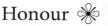

The louder he talked of his honour, the faster we counted
our spoons.

> **Ralph Waldo Emerson** 1803–82 American writer

GROUCHO MARX: Remember, you're fighting for this woman's
honour…which is probably more than she ever did.

> **Bert Kalmar** 1884–1947 and **others** American screenwriters,
> *in the film* Duck Soup

I could not love thee, Dear, so much,
Loved I not honour more.

> **Richard Lovelace** 1618–58 English poet

But he that filches from me my good name
Robs me of that which not enriches him,
And makes me poor indeed.

> **William Shakespeare** 1564–1616 English dramatist

O! I have lost my reputation. I have lost the immortal part
of myself, and what remains is bestial.

> **William Shakespeare** 1564–1616 English dramatist

His honour rooted in dishonour stood,
And faith unfaithful kept him falsely true.

> **Alfred, Lord Tennyson** 1809–92 English poet

Honours

The rank is but the guinea's stamp,
The man's the gowd for a' that!

> **Robert Burns** 1759–96 Scottish poet

A medal glitters, but it also casts a shadow.

> **Winston Churchill** 1874–1965 British statesman, *on the envy
> caused by the award of honours*

Hope

What I like about the Order of the Garter is that there is no damned merit about it.
Lord Melbourne 1779–1848 British statesman

When I want a peerage, I shall buy it like an honest man.
Lord Northcliffe 1865–1922 British newspaper proprietor

There is no stronger craving in the world than that of the rich for titles, except perhaps that of the titled for riches.
Hesketh Pearson 1887–1964 English biographer

Titles distinguish the mediocre, embarrass the superior, and are disgraced by the inferior.
George Bernard Shaw 1856–1950 Irish dramatist

What harm have I ever done to the Labour Party?
R. H. Tawney 1880–1962 British economic historian, *on declining the offer of a peerage*

Kind hearts are more than coronets,
And simple faith than Norman blood.
Alfred, Lord Tennyson 1809–92 English poet

 # Hope see also **Despair**, **Optimism**

Hope is a good breakfast, but it is a bad supper.
Francis Bacon 1561–1626 English courtier

Hope deferred maketh the heart sick: but when the desire cometh, it is a tree of life.
Bible

He that lives upon hope will die fasting.
Benjamin Franklin 1706–90 American statesman and scientist

Walk on, walk on, with hope in your heart,
And you'll never walk alone.
Oscar Hammerstein II 1895–1960 American songwriter

Hope is definitely not the same thing as optimism. It is not the conviction that something will turn out well, but the certainty that something makes sense, regardless of how it turns out.

Václav Havel 1936–2011 Czech statesman

He that lives in hope danceth without music.

George Herbert 1593–1633 English poet

Nil desperandum.

Never despair.

Horace 65–8 BC Roman poet

Plenty of hope—for God—an abundance of hope—only not for us.

Franz Kafka 1883–1924 Czech novelist, *often quoted as 'There is hope but not for us'*

Hope is like a road in the country; there was never a road, but when many people walk on it, the road comes into existence.

Lu Xun 1881–1936 Chinese writer

After all, tomorrow is another day.

Margaret Mitchell 1900–49 American novelist

Hope springs eternal in the human breast:
Man never Is, but always To be blest.

Alexander Pope 1688–1744 English poet

Hospitality

It was a delightful visit;– perfect, in being much too short.

Jane Austen 1775–1817 English novelist

Be not forgetful to entertain strangers: for thereby some have entertained angels unawares.

Bible

Houses

Come in the evening, or come in the morning,
Come when you're looked for, or come without warning.
Thomas Davis 1814–45 Irish poet

Hospitality consists in a little fire, a little food, and an immense quiet.
Ralph Waldo Emerson 1803–82 American writer

A host is like a general: misfortunes often reveal his genius.
Horace 65–8 BC Roman poet

Some people can stay longer in an hour than others can in a week.
William Dean Howells 1837–1920 American writer

For I, who hold sage Homer's rule the best,
Welcome the coming, speed the going guest.
Alexander Pope 1688–1744 English poet

       Unbidden guests
Are often welcomest when they are gone.
William Shakespeare 1564–1616 English dramatist

This door will open at a touch to welcome every friend.
Henry Van Dyke 1852–1933 American minister

 Houses see also **Home**

Houses are built to live in and not to look on; therefore let use be preferred before uniformity, except where both may be had.
Francis Bacon 1561–1626 English courtier

For a man's house is his castle, *et domus sua cuique est tutissimum refugium* [and each man's home is his safest refuge].
Edward Coke 1552–1634 English jurist

It takes a heap o' livin' in a house t' make it home.
Edgar A. Guest 1881–1959 American writer

A house is a machine for living in.
Le Corbusier 1887–1965 French architect

Have nothing in your houses that you do not know to be
useful, or believe to be beautiful.
William Morris 1834–96 English artist

Does anybody mind if I don't live in a house that is quaint?
Because, for one thing, quaint houses are generally houses
    where plumbing ain't.
Ogden Nash 1902–71 American humorist

A comfortable house is a great source of happiness. It ranks
immediately after health and a good conscience.
Sydney Smith 1771–1845 English essayist

But every house where Love abides
And Friendship is a guest,
Is surely home, and home, sweet home,
For there the heart can rest.
Henry Van Dyke 1852–1933 American minister

Housework see also **Home**

Conran's Law of Housework—it expands to fill the time
available plus half an hour.
Shirley Conran 1932–   English writer

There was no need to do any housework at all. After the first
four years the dirt doesn't get any worse.
Quentin Crisp 1908–99 English writer

Cleaning your house while your kids are still growing is like
shovelling the walk before it stops snowing.
Phyllis Diller 1917–2012 American actress

Housework

'I hate discussions of feminism that end up with who does the dishes,' she said. So do I. But at the end, there are always the damned dishes.
Marilyn French 1929–2009 American writer

Dirt is only matter out of place.
John Chipman Gray 1839–1915 American lawyer

At the worst, a house unkempt cannot be so distressing as a life unlived.
Rose Macaulay 1881–1958 English novelist

The dust comes secretly day after day,
Lies on my ledge and dulls my shining things.
But O this dust that I shall drive away
Is flowers and Kings,
Is Solomon's temple, poets, Nineveh.
Viola Meynell 1886–1956 English writer

There is scarcely any less bother in the running of a family than in that of an entire state. And domestic business is no less importunate for being less important.
Montaigne 1533–92 French moralist

God walks among the pots and pans.
St Teresa of Ávila 1512–82 Spanish mystic

MR PRITCHARD: I must dust the blinds and then I must raise them.
MRS OGMORE-PRITCHARD: And before you let the sun in, mind it wipes its shoes.
Dylan Thomas 1914–53 Welsh poet

Hatred of domestic work is a natural and admirable result of civilization.
Rebecca West 1892–1983 English writer

The Human Race

We are born of risen apes, not fallen angels, and the apes
were armed killers beside.
> **Robert Ardrey** 1908–80 American dramatist

There's a man all over for you, blaming on his boots the
faults of his feet.
> **Samuel Beckett** 1906–89 Irish writer

We carry within us the wonders we seek without us: there is
all Africa and her prodigies in us.
> **Sir Thomas Browne** 1605–82 English writer

By nature men are alike. Through practice they have
become far apart.
> **Confucius** 551–479 BC Chinese philosopher

What is man, when you come to think upon him, but a
minutely set, ingenious machine for turning, with infinite
artfulness, the red wine of Shiraz into urine?
> **Isak Dinesen** 1885–1962 Danish writer

Is man an ape or an angel? Now I am on the side of the
angels.
> **Benjamin Disraeli** 1804–81 British statesman

Man is a tool-making animal.
> **Benjamin Franklin** 1706–90 American statesman and scientist

Man is the only animal that laughs and weeps; for he is the
only animal that is struck with the difference between what
things are and what they ought to be.
> **William Hazlitt** 1778–1830 English essayist

The life of man is of no greater importance to the universe
than that of an oyster.
> **David Hume** 1711–76 Scottish philosopher

The Human Race

Out of the crooked timber of humanity no straight thing
can ever be made.
Immanuel Kant 1724–1804 German philosopher

In the final analysis, our most basic common link is that
we all inhabit this small planet. We all breathe the same air.
We all cherish our children's future. And we are all mortal.
John F. Kennedy 1917–63 American statesman

O mankind, We have created you
male and female, and appointed you
races and tribes, that you may know
one another.
The Koran

To say, for example, that a man is made up of certain
chemical elements is a satisfactory description only for
those who intend to use him as a fertilizer.
H. J. Muller 1890–1967 American geneticist

I teach you the superman. Man is something to be
surpassed.
Friedrich Nietzsche 1844–1900 German philosopher

Man is only a reed, the weakest thing in nature; but he is a
thinking reed.
Blaise Pascal 1623–62 French scientist and philosopher

Man is the measure of all things.
Protagoras b. c.485 BC Greek sophist

The children of Adam are limbs to each other, having been
created of one essence.
Sadi c.1213–c.91 Persian poet

How beauteous mankind is! O brave new world,
That has such people in't.
William Shakespeare 1564–1616 English dramatist

What a piece of work is a man! How noble in reason! how infinite in faculty! in form, in moving, how express and admirable! in action how like an angel! in apprehension how like a god! the beauty of the world! the paragon of animals!
William Shakespeare 1564–1616 English dramatist

Man is the Only Animal that Blushes. Or needs to.
Mark Twain 1835–1910 American writer

We're all of us guinea pigs in the laboratory of God. Humanity is just a work in progress.
Tennessee Williams 1911–83 American dramatist

Human Rights

We hold these truths to be self-evident, that all men are created equal, that they are endowed by their Creator with certain unalienable rights, that among these are life, liberty and the pursuit of happiness.
American Declaration of Independence 1776

Liberté! Égalité! Fraternité!
Freedom! Equality! Brotherhood!
Anonymous, *motto of the French Revolution*

Men, their rights, and nothing more; women, their rights, and nothing less.
Susan Brownell Anthony 1820–1906 American feminist

Natural rights is simple nonsense: natural and imprescriptible rights, rhetorical nonsense—nonsense upon stilts.
Jeremy Bentham 1748–1832 English philosopher

No man can put a chain about the ankle of his fellow man without at last finding the other end fastened about his own neck.
Frederick Douglass c.1818–95 American former slave

Humour

The rights of man come not from the generosity of the state,
but from the hand of God.
    John F. Kennedy 1917–63 American statesman

To no man will we sell, or deny, or delay, right or justice.
    Magna Carta 1215

The poorest he that is in England hath a life to live as the
greatest he.
    Thomas Rainborowe d. 1648 English soldier

We look forward to a world founded upon four essential
human freedoms. The first is freedom of speech and
expression—everywhere in the world. The second is
freedom of every person to worship God in his own way—
everywhere in the world. The third is freedom from want…
The fourth is freedom from fear.
    Franklin D. Roosevelt 1882–1945 American statesman

That little man…he says women can't have as much rights as
men, cause Christ wasn't a woman. Where did your Christ
come from? From God and a woman. Man had nothing to
do with Him.
    Sojourner Truth c.1797–1883 American evangelist

All human beings are born free and equal in dignity and
rights.
    Universal Declaration of Human Rights 1948

 # Humour see also **Wit**

Among those whom I like or admire, I can find no common
denominator, but among those whom I love, I can: all of
them make me laugh.
    W. H. Auden 1907–73 English poet

For what do we live, but to make sport for our neighbours, and laugh at them in our turn?
Jane Austen 1775–1817 English novelist

I make myself laugh at everything, for fear of having to weep at it.
Pierre-Augustin Caron de Beaumarchais 1732–99 French dramatist

Comedy is tragedy plus time.
Carol Burnett 1936– American comedienne

Of all days, the one most surely wasted is the one on which one has not laughed.
Nicolas-Sébastien Chamfort 1741–94 French writer

A difference of taste in jokes is a great strain on the affections.
George Eliot 1819–80 English novelist

The funniest thing about comedy is that you never know why people laugh. I know *what* makes them laugh but trying to get your hands on the *why* of it is like trying to pick an eel out of a tub of water.
W. C. Fields 1880–1946 American humorist

What do you mean, funny? Funny-peculiar or funny ha-ha?
Ian Hay 1876–1952 Scottish writer

[A pun] is a pistol let off at the ear; not a feather to tickle the intellect.
Charles Lamb 1775–1834 English writer

Every joke is a tiny revolution.
George Orwell 1903–50 English novelist

Laughter is pleasant, but the exertion is too much for me.
Thomas Love Peacock 1785–1866 English writer

Hypocrisy

Everything is funny as long as it is happening to Somebody Else.
Will Rogers 1879–1935 American actor

Humour is emotional chaos remembered in tranquillity.
James Thurber 1894–1961 American humorist

Against the assault of laughter nothing can stand.
Mark Twain 1835–1910 American writer

We are not amused.
Queen Victoria 1819–1901 British monarch

It's hard to be funny when you have to be clean.
Mae West 1892–1980 American film actress

 # Hypocrisy

Ye are like unto whited sepulchres, which indeed appear beautiful outward, but are within full of dead men's bones, and of all uncleanness.
Bible

Compound for sins, they are inclined to,
By damning those they have no mind to.
Samuel Butler 1612–80 English poet

The smylere with the knyf under the cloke.
Geoffrey Chaucer c.1343–1400 English poet

Keep up appearances; there lies the test;
The world will give thee credit for the rest.
Outward be fair, however foul within;
Sin if thou wilt, but then in secret sin.
Charles Churchill 1731–64 English poet

Hypocrisy is a tribute which vice pays to virtue.
Duc de la Rochefoucauld 1613–80 French moralist

Hypocrisy, the only evil that walks
Invisible, except to God alone.
> **John Milton** 1608–74 English poet

       I want that glib and oily art
To speak and purpose not.
> **William Shakespeare** 1564–1616 English dramatist

All Reformers, however strict their social conscience, live in
houses just as big as they can pay for.
> **Logan Pearsall Smith** 1865–1946 American writer

I sit on a man's back, choking him and making him carry
me, and yet assure myself and others that I am very sorry
for him and wish to ease his lot by all possible means—
except by getting off his back.
> **Leo Tolstoy** 1828–1910 Russian novelist

Idealism

A cause may be inconvenient, but it's magnificent. It's like
champagne or high heels, and one must be prepared to
suffer for it.
> **Arnold Bennett** 1867–1931 English novelist

Where there is no vision, the people perish.
> **Bible**

Oh, the vision thing.
> **George Bush** 1924– American statesman, *responding to the
> suggestion that he turn his attention from short-term campaign
> objectives and look to the longer term*

There's only one corner of the universe you can be certain of
improving, and that's your own self.
> **Aldous Huxley** 1894–1963 English novelist

Ideas

Each time a man stands up for an ideal…he sends forth
a tiny ripple of hope, and…those ripples build a current
which can sweep down the mightiest walls of oppression
and resistance.
Robert Kennedy 1925–68 American politician

If a man hasn't discovered something he will die for, he isn't
fit to live.
Martin Luther King 1929–68 American civil rights leader

The first thing a man will do for his ideals is lie.
J. A. Schumpeter 1883–1950 American economist

We are all in the gutter, but some of us are looking at the
stars.
Oscar Wilde 1854–1900 Irish dramatist

I have spread my dreams under your feet;
Tread softly because you tread on my dreams.
W. B. Yeats 1865–1939 Irish poet

 # Ideas see also **Thinking**

There is one thing stronger than all the armies in the world;
and that is an idea whose time has come.
Anonymous

Probable impossibilities are to be preferred to improbable
possibilities.
Aristotle 384–322 BC Greek philosopher

It isn't that they can't see the solution. It is that they can't see
the problem.
G. K. Chesterton 1874–1936 English writer

The value of an idea lies in the using of it.
Thomas Alva Edison 1847–1931 American inventor

I think that only daring speculation can lead us further and not accumulation of facts.

Albert Einstein 1879–1955 German-born theoretical physicist

Every now and then a man's mind is stretched by a new idea or sensation, and never shrinks back to its former dimensions.

Oliver Wendell Holmes 1809–94 American physician

A stand can be made against invasion by an army; no stand can be made against invasion by an idea.

Victor Hugo 1802–85 French writer

He who receives an idea from me, receives instruction himself without lessening mine; as he who lights his taper at mine, receives light without darkening me.

Thomas Jefferson 1743–1826 American statesman

MICHAEL CAINE: Hang on a minute lads, I've got a great idea.

Troy Kennedy-Martin 1932–2009 British screenwriter, *in the film* The Italian Job

When you are a Bear of Very Little Brain, and you Think of Things, you find sometimes that a Thing which seemed very Thingish inside you is quite different when it gets out into the open and has other people looking at it.

A. A. Milne 1882–1956 English writer

You see things; and you say 'Why?' But I dream things that never were; and I say 'Why not?'

George Bernard Shaw 1856–1950 Irish dramatist

Ideas won't keep. Something must be done about them.

Alfred North Whitehead 1861–1947 English philosopher

 Idleness

A man who has nothing to do with his own time has no conscience in his intrusion on that of others.
Jane Austen 1775–1817 English novelist

Go to the ant thou sluggard; consider her ways, and be wise.
Bible

The foul sluggard's comfort: 'It will last my time.'
Thomas Carlyle 1795–1881 Scottish historian

Idleness is only the refuge of weak minds.
Lord Chesterfield 1694–1773 English writer

It is better to wear out than to rust out.
Richard Cumberland 1631–1718 English divine

It is impossible to enjoy idling thoroughly unless one has plenty of work to do.
Jerome K. Jerome 1859–1927 English writer

I was raised to feel that doing nothing was a sin. I had to learn to do nothing.
Jenny Joseph 1932– English poet

Far from idleness being the root of evil, rather it is the true good.
Sören Kierkegaard 1813–55 Danish philosopher

Inactivity is death.
Benito Mussolini 1883–1945 Italian dictator

The time you enjoy wasting is not wasted time.
Laurence Peter 1919–90 Canadian writer, *commenting on a remark by Bertrand Russell*

For Satan finds some mischief still
For idle hands to do.
Isaac Watts 1674–1748 English hymn-writer

Procrastination is the thief of time.
Edward Young 1683–1765 English poet

Ignorance

Ignorance is not innocence but sin.
Robert Browning 1812–89 English poet

Ignorance more frequently begets confidence than does knowledge: it is those who know little, and not those who know much, who so positively assert that this or that problem will never be solved by science.
Charles Darwin 1809–82 English naturalist

To be conscious that you are ignorant is a great step to knowledge.
Benjamin Disraeli 1804–81 British statesman

Whatever Nature has in store for mankind, unpleasant as it may be, men must accept, for ignorance is never better than knowledge.
Enrico Fermi 1901–54 Italian-born American physicist

      Where ignorance is bliss,
'Tis folly to be wise.
Thomas Gray 1716–71 English poet

Ignorance, madam, pure ignorance.
Samuel Johnson 1709–84 English lexicographer, *on being asked why he had defined* pastern *as the 'knee' of a horse*

You know everybody is ignorant, only on different subjects.
Will Rogers 1879–1935 American actor

Learn to say, 'I don't know'. If used when appropriate, it will be often.
Donald Rumsfeld 1932– American politician

Imagination

If one does not know to which port one is sailing, no wind is favourable.
Seneca ('the Younger') C.4 BC–AD 65 Roman philosopher

As any fule kno.
Geoffrey Willans 1911–58 and **Ronald Searle** 1920–2011 English writers

 # Imagination

Imagination is the highest kite that can fly.
Lauren Bacall 1924–2014 American actress

All fantasy should have a solid base in reality.
Max Beerbohm 1872–1956 English critic

To see a world in a grain of sand
And a heaven in a wild flower
Hold infinity in the palm of your hand
And eternity in an hour.
William Blake 1757–1827 English poet

Go, and catch a falling star,
Get with child a mandrake root,
Tell me, where all past years are,
Or who cleft the Devil's foot.
Teach me to hear mermaids singing.
John Donne 1572–1631 English poet

Where there is no imagination there is no horror.
Arthur Conan Doyle 1859–1930 Scottish-born writer

Imagination is more important than knowledge. Knowledge is limited. Imagination encircles the world.
Albert Einstein 1879–1955 German-born theoretical physicist

Were it not for imagination, Sir, a man would be as happy in the arms of a chambermaid as of a Duchess.
Samuel Johnson 1709–84 English lexicographer

Heard melodies are sweet, but those unheard
Are sweeter.
   John Keats 1795–1821 English poet

Imagine there's no heaven
It's easy if you try.
   John Lennon 1940–80 English pop singer

His imagination resembled the wings of an ostrich.
It enabled him to run, though not to soar.
   Lord Macaulay 1800–59 English historian

Fantasy is like an exercise bicycle for the mind.
   Terry Pratchett 1948–2015 English novelist

The lunatic, the lover, and the poet,
Are of imagination all compact.
   William Shakespeare 1564–1616 English dramatist

Must then a Christ perish in torment in every age to save
those that have no imagination?
   George Bernard Shaw 1856–1950 Irish dramatist

Whither is fled the visionary gleam?
Where is it now, the glory and the dream?
   William Wordsworth 1770–1850 English poet

India

Nothing in India is identifiable, the mere asking of a
question causes it to disappear or to merge in something
else.
   E. M. Forster 1879–1970 English novelist

The brightest jewel that now remained in his Majesty's
crown.
   Charles James Fox 1749–1806 English politician, *on India*

Indifference

If there is a paradise on earth, it is this, it is this, it is this.
Amir Khusrau 1253–1325 Persian poet, *inscribed on the wall of the Diwan-i-Khas [the hall of special audience] in the Red Fort at Delhi*

India will go on.
R. K. Narayan 1906–2001 Indian novelist

At the stroke of the midnight hour, while the world sleeps, India will awake to life and freedom. A moment comes, which comes but rarely in history, when we step out from the old to the new, when an age ends, and when the soul of a nation, long suppressed, finds utterance.
Jawaharlal Nehru 1889–1964 Indian statesman

If there is one place on the face of the earth where all the dreams of living men have found a home from the very earliest days when man began the dream of existence, it is India.
Romain Rolland 1866–1944 French writer

Nothing has been left undone, either by man or Nature, to make India the most extraordinary country that the sun visits on his rounds.
Mark Twain 1835–1910 American writer

Indifference

All colours will agree in the dark.
Francis Bacon 1561–1626 English courtier

Because thou art lukewarm, and neither cold nor hot, I will spew thee out of my mouth.
Bible

Catholics and Communists have committed great crimes, but at least they have not stood aside, like an established

Indifference

society, and been indifferent. I would rather have blood on
my hands than water like Pilate.
Graham Greene 1904–91 English novelist

Let them eat cake.
Marie-Antoinette 1755–93 French queen, *on being told that her
people had no bread; the saying is of older origin*

I wish I could care what you do or where you go but
I can't…My dear, I don't give a damn.
Margaret Mitchell 1900–49 American novelist, *'Frankly,
my dear, I don't give a damn!' in Sidney Howard's screenplay for*
Gone With the Wind

Vacant heart and hand, and eye,—
Easy live and quiet die.
Sir Walter Scott 1771–1832 Scottish novelist

It is the disease of not listening, the malady of not marking,
that I am troubled withal.
William Shakespeare 1564–1616 English dramatist

The worst sin towards our fellow creatures is not to hate
them, but to be indifferent to them: that's the essence of
inhumanity.
George Bernard Shaw 1856–1950 Irish dramatist

I was much further out than you thought
And not waving but drowning.
Stevie Smith 1902–71 English poet

The opposite of love is not hate, it's indifference. The
opposite of art is not ugliness, it's indifference. The opposite
of faith is not heresy, it's indifference. And the opposite of
life is not death, it's indifference.
Elie Wiesel 1928–2016 Romanian-born American writer

Individuality

Cast a cold eye
On life, on death.
Horseman pass by!
W. B. Yeats 1865–1939 Irish poet

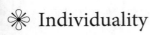# Individuality

A dead thing can go with the stream, but only a living thing
can go against it.
G. K. Chesterton 1874–1936 English writer

It is easier to live through someone else than to become
complete yourself.
Betty Friedan 1921–2006 American feminist

In friendship or in love, the two side by side raise hands
together to find what one cannot reach alone.
Kahlil Gibran 1883–1931 Lebanese-born American writer

I'm not alone, I'm free. I no longer have to be a credit,
I don't have to be a symbol to anybody, I don't have to be a
first to anybody. I don't have to be an imitation of a white
woman that Hollywood sort of hoped I'd become. I'm me,
and I'm like nobody else.
Lena Mary Calhoun Horne 1917–2010 American singer and
actor

That so few now dare to be eccentric marks the chief danger
of the time.
John Stuart Mill 1806–73 English philosopher

I am not an eccentric. It's just that I am more alive than
most people. I am an unpopular electric eel in a pool of
catfish.
Edith Sitwell 1887–1964 English poet

Most people are other people. Their thoughts are someone else's opinions, their lives a mimicry, their passions a quotation.
Oscar Wilde 1854–1900 Irish dramatist

Insight ✳

[See] things not as they are, but as they might be.
Felix Adler 1851–1933 American philosopher

If the doors of perception were cleansed everything would appear to man as it is, infinite.
William Blake 1757–1827 English poet

One sees great things from the valley; only small things from the peak.
G. K. Chesterton 1874–1936 English writer

If we had a keen vision and feeling of all ordinary human life, it would be like hearing the grass grow and the squirrel's heart beat, and we should die of that roar which lies on the other side of silence.
George Eliot 1819–80 English novelist

The crown of life is neither happiness nor annihilation; it is understanding.
Winifred Holtby 1898–1935 British novelist

Come to the edge.
We might fall.
Come to the edge.
It's too high!
COME TO THE EDGE!
And they came
and he pushed
and they flew…
Christopher Logue 1926–2011 English poet

Intelligence

To understand just one life, you have to swallow the world.
Salman Rushdie 1947– Indian-born British novelist

It is only with the heart that one can see rightly; what is essential is invisible to the eye.
Antoine de Saint-Exupéry 1900–44 French novelist

Every man takes the limits of his own field of vision for the limits of the world.
Arthur Schopenhauer 1788–1860 German philosopher

Tout comprendre rend très indulgent.
To be totally understanding makes one very indulgent.
Mme de Staël 1766–1817 French writer

Everything I have written seems like straw by comparison with what I have seen and what has been revealed to me.
St Thomas Aquinas c.1225–74 Italian theologian, *following a mystical experience, after which he did no more teaching or writing*

 # Intelligence

To the man-in-the-street, who, I'm sorry to say,
Is a keen observer of life,
The word 'Intellectual' suggests straight away
A man who's untrue to his wife.
W. H. Auden 1907–73 English poet

A man is not necessarily intelligent because he has plenty of ideas, any more than he is a good general because he has plenty of soldiers.
Nicolas-Sébastien Chamfort 1741–94 French writer

'Excellent,' I cried. 'Elementary,' said he.
Arthur Conan Doyle 1859–1930 Scottish-born writer, *commonly quoted as 'Elementary, my dear Watson'*

Intelligence

As a human being, one has been endowed with just enough intelligence to be able to see clearly how utterly inadequate that intelligence is when confronted with what exists.
Albert Einstein 1879–1955 German-born theoretical physicist

The test of a first-rate intelligence is the ability to hold two opposed ideas in the mind at the same time, and still retain the ability to function.
F. Scott Fitzgerald 1896–1940 American novelist

So dumb he can't fart and chew gum at the same time.
Lyndon Baines Johnson 1908–73 American statesman,
of Gerald Ford

Sir, I have found you an argument; but I am not obliged to find you an understanding.
Samuel Johnson 1709–84 English lexicographer

I think, therefore I am is the statement of an intellectual who underrates toothaches.
Milan Kundera 1929– Czech novelist

No one in this world, so far as I know—and I have searched the records for years, and employed agents to help me—has ever lost money by underestimating the intelligence of the great masses of the plain people.
H. L. Mencken 1880–1956 American journalist

You beat your pate, and fancy wit will come:
Knock as you please, there's nobody at home.
Alexander Pope 1688–1744 English poet

With stupidity the gods themselves struggle in vain.
Friedrich von Schiller 1759–1805 German poet

Rule no. 11: Be nice to nerds. Chances are you'll end up working for one.
Charles J. Sykes 1954– American writer, *often wrongly attributed to the American computer entrepreneur Bill Gates*

Invention and Discovery

When man wanted to make a machine that would walk he created the wheel, which does not resemble a leg.
Guillaume Apollinaire 1880–1918 French poet

Eureka!
I've got it!
Archimedes c.287–212 BC Greek mathematician

Printing, gunpowder, and the mariner's needle [compass]… these three have changed the whole face and state of things throughout the world.
Francis Bacon 1561–1626 English courtier

Through the unknown, we'll find the new.
Charles Baudelaire 1821–67 French poet

The discovery of a new dish does more for human happiness than the discovery of a star.
Anthelme Brillat-Savarin 1755–1826 French gourmet

LORD CARNARVON: Can you see anything?
CARTER: Yes, wonderful things.
Howard Carter 1874–1939 English archaeologist, *on first looking into the tomb of Tutankhamun*

Why sir, there is every possibility that you will soon be able to tax it!
Michael Faraday 1791–1867 English scientist, *to Gladstone, when asked about the usefulness of electricity*

What is the use of a new-born child?
Benjamin Franklin 1706–90 American statesman and scientist, *when asked what was the use of a new invention*

Invention and Discovery

SALVIATI: Now you see how easy it is to understand.
SAGREDO: So are all truths, once they are discovered.

Galileo Galilei 1564–1642 Italian astronomer, *often quoted as 'All truths are easy to understand, once they are discovered; the point is, to discover them'*

Then felt I like some watcher of the skies
When a new planet swims into his ken.

John Keats 1795–1821 English poet

Praise without end the go-ahead zeal
of whoever it was invented the wheel;
but never a word for the poor soul's sake
that thought ahead, and invented the brake.

Howard Nemerov 1920–91 American writer

I don't know what I may seem to the world, but as to myself, I seem to have been only like a boy playing on the sea-shore and diverting myself in now and then finding a smoother pebble or a prettier shell than ordinary, whilst the great ocean of truth lay all undiscovered before me.

Isaac Newton 1642–1727 English mathematician

I remembered the line from the Hindu scripture, the *Bhagavad Gita*…'I am become death, the destroyer of worlds.'

J. Robert Oppenheimer 1904–67 American physicist, *on the explosion of the first atomic bomb near Alamogordo, New Mexico*

If you wish to make an apple pie from scratch, you must first invent the universe.

Carl Sagan 1934–96 American astronomer

Discovery consists of seeing what everybody has seen and thinking what nobody has thought.

Albert von Szent-Györgyi 1893–1986 Hungarian-born biochemist

Name the greatest of all the inventors. Accident.

Mark Twain 1835–1910 American writer

Ireland

For the great Gaels of Ireland
Are the men that God made mad,
For all their wars are merry,
And all their songs are sad.
> **G. K. Chesterton** 1874–1936 English writer

Ulster will fight; Ulster will be right.
> **Lord Randolph Churchill** 1849–94 British politician

       The famous
Northern reticence, the tight gag of place
And times.
> **Seamus Heaney** 1939–2013 Irish poet

Ireland is the old sow that eats her farrow.
> **James Joyce** 1882–1941 Irish novelist

Ireland is a small but insuppressible island half an hour
nearer the sunset than Great Britain.
> **Thomas Kettle** 1880–1916 Irish economist

In Ireland the inevitable never happens and the unexpected
constantly occurs.
> **John Pentland Mahaffy** 1839–1919 Irish writer

Spenser's Ireland
has not altered;—
a place as kind as it is green,
the greenest place I've never seen.
> **Marianne Moore** 1887–1972 American poet

To be Irish is to know that in the end the world will break
your heart.
> **Daniel P. Moynihan** 1927–2003 American politician

Romantic Ireland's dead and gone,
It's with O'Leary in the grave.
W. B. Yeats 1865–1939 Irish poet

Jealousy see Envy

Journalism see also News

The Times has made many ministries.
Walter Bagehot 1826–77 English economist

I read the newspapers avidly. It is my one form of
continuous fiction.
Aneurin Bevan 1897–1960 British politician

When seagulls follow a trawler, it is because they think
sardines will be thrown into the sea.
Eric Cantona 1966– French footballer, *at a press conference*

When the legend becomes fact, print the legend.
Willis Goldbeck and **James Warner Bellah** American
screenwriters, *in the film* The Man Who Shot Liberty Valance

You furnish the pictures and I'll furnish the war.
William Randolph Hearst 1863–1951 American newspaper
publisher, *message to the artist Frederic Remington in Havana,
Cuba, during the Spanish-American War of 1898*

Power without responsibility: the prerogative of the harlot
throughout the ages.
Rudyard Kipling 1865–1936 English writer, *summing up Lord
Beaverbrook's political standpoint* vis-à-vis *the* Daily Express

A good newspaper, I suppose, is a nation talking to itself.
Arthur Miller 1915–2005 American dramatist

Journalism

All the news that's fit to print.
Adolph S. Ochs 1858–1935 American publisher, *motto of the*
New York Times

A cynical, mercenary, demagogic, corrupt press will
produce in time a people as base as itself.
Joseph Pulitzer 1847–1911 Hungarian-born American editor

The men with the muck-rakes are often indispensable to the
well-being of society; but only if they know when to stop
raking the muck.
Theodore Roosevelt 1858–1919 American statesman

Comment is free, but facts are sacred.
C. P. Scott 1846–1932 British journalist

Ever noticed that no matter what happens in one day,
it exactly fits in the newspaper?
Jerry Seinfeld 1954– American comedian

Comment is free but facts are on expenses.
Tom Stoppard 1937– British dramatist

We must try to find ways to starve the terrorist and the
hijacker of the oxygen of publicity on which they depend.
Margaret Thatcher 1925–2013 British stateswoman

The report of my death was an exaggeration.
Mark Twain 1835–1910 American writer, *usually quoted as
'Reports of my death have been greatly exaggerated'*

Journalism—an ability to meet the challenge of filling the
space.
Rebecca West 1892–1983 English writer

Rock journalism is people who can't write interviewing
people who can't talk for people who can't read.
Frank Zappa 1940–93 American rock musician

Justice see also **Law**

Jedem das Seine.

To each his own.

> **Anonymous**, *inscription on the gate of Buchenwald concentration camp; often quoted as 'Everyone gets what he deserves'*

Audi partem alteram.

Hear the other side.

> **St Augustine of Hippo** AD 354–430 Roman theologian

Publicity is the very soul of justice. It is the keenest spur to exertion, and the surest of all guards against improbity.

> **Jeremy Bentham** 1748–1832 English philosopher

Life for life,
Eye for eye, tooth for tooth.

> **Bible**

It is better that ten guilty persons escape than one innocent suffer.

> **William Blackstone** 1723–80 English jurist

When I hear of an 'equity' in a case like this, I am reminded of a blind man in a dark room—looking for a black hat—which isn't there.

> **Lord Bowen** 1835–94 English judge

No! No! Sentence first—verdict afterwards.

> **Lewis Carroll** 1832–98 English writer

Justice is truth in action.

> **Benjamin Disraeli** 1804–81 British statesman

All sensible people are selfish, and nature is tugging at every contract to make the terms of it fair.

> **Ralph Waldo Emerson** 1803–82 American writer

Justice

Fiat justitia et pereat mundus.
Let justice be done, though the world perish.
Ferdinand I 1503–64 Holy Roman emperor

Justice should not only be done, but should manifestly and undoubtedly be seen to be done.
Lord Hewart 1870–1943 British lawyer

Injustice anywhere is a threat to justice everywhere.
Martin Luther King 1929–68 American civil rights leader

I have always found that mercy bears richer fruits than strict justice.
Abraham Lincoln 1809–65 American statesman

In England, justice is open to all—like the Ritz Hotel.
James Mathew 1830–1908 Irish judge

Here [Paris] they hang a man first, and try him afterwards.
Molière 1622–73 French comic dramatist

The quality of mercy is not strained,
It droppeth as the gentle rain from heaven
Upon the place beneath: it is twice blessed;
It blesseth him that gives and him that takes.
William Shakespeare 1564–1616 English dramatist

Thrice is he armed that hath his quarrel just.
William Shakespeare 1564–1616 English dramatist

Two wrongs don't make a right, but they make a good excuse.
Thomas Szasz 1920–2012 Hungarian-born psychiatrist

It is justice, not charity, that is wanting in the world.
Mary Wollstonecraft 1759–97 English feminist

218

Kissing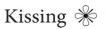

A kiss is a lovely trick designed by nature to stop speech
when words become superfluous.
    Ingrid Bergman 1915–82 Swedish actress

It's like kissing Hitler.
    Tony Curtis 1925–2010 American actor, *when asked what it was
    like to kiss Marilyn Monroe*

A fine romance with no kisses.
A fine romance, my friend, this is.
    Dorothy Fields 1905–74 American songwriter

To let a fool kiss you is stupid,
To let a kiss fool you is worse.
    E. Y. ('Yip') Harburg 1898–1981 American songwriter

Where do the noses go? I always wondered where the noses
would go.
    Ernest Hemingway 1899–1961 American novelist

You must remember this, a kiss is still a kiss,
A sigh is just a sigh;
The fundamental things apply,
As time goes by.
    Herman Hupfeld 1894–1951 American songwriter

A kiss can be a comma, a question mark or an exclamation
point. That's basic spelling that every woman ought to know.
    Mistinguett 1875–1956 French actress

O Love, O fire! once he drew
With one long kiss my whole soul through
My lips, as sunlight drinketh dew.
    Alfred, Lord Tennyson 1809–92 English poet

Knowledge

 Knowledge see also **Facts**, **Wisdom**

Everyman, I will go with thee, and be thy guide,
In thy most need to go by thy side.
Anonymous, Everyman (c.1509–19) *spoken by Knowledge*

The fox knows many things—the hedgehog one *big* one.
Archilochus Greek poet of the 7th century BC

All men by nature desire knowledge.
Aristotle 384–322 BC Greek philosopher

For also knowledge itself is power.
Francis Bacon 1561–1626 English courtier

For now we see through a glass, darkly; but then face to
face: now I know in part; but then shall I know even as also
I am known.
Bible

It is better to know nothing than to know what ain't so.
Josh Billings 1818–85 American humorist

The place to observe nature is where you are: the walk to
take to-day is the walk you took yesterday. You will not find
just the same things.
John Burroughs 1837–1921 American naturalist, *often quoted as
'To learn something new, take the path that you took yesterday'*

An expert is one who knows more and more about less and
less.
Nicholas Murray Butler 1862–1947 American philosopher

Knowledge may give weight, but accomplishments give
lustre, and many more people see than weigh.
Lord Chesterfield 1694–1773 English writer

Knowledge

There is no such thing on earth as an uninteresting subject;
the only thing that can exist is an uninterested person.
G. K. Chesterton 1874–1936 English writer

Where is the wisdom we have lost in knowledge?
Where is the knowledge we have lost in information?
T. S. Eliot 1888–1965 American-born British poet

Knowledge is of two kinds. We know a subject ourselves,
or we know where we can find information upon it.
Samuel Johnson 1709–84 English lexicographer

All wish to possess knowledge, but no one is willing to pay
the price.
Juvenal C.AD 60–c.140 Roman satirist

Dare to know! Have the courage to use your own reason!
This is the motto of the Enlightenment.
Immanuel Kant 1724–1804 German philosopher

The motto of all the mongoose family is, 'Run and find out.'
Rudyard Kipling 1865–1936 English writer

We have learned the answers, all the answers:
It is the question that we do not know.
Archibald MacLeish 1892–1982 American poet

Que sais-je?
What do I know?
Montaigne 1533–92 French moralist

Satisfaction of one's curiosity is one of the greatest sources
of happiness in life.
Linus Pauling 1901– 94 American chemist

A little learning is a dangerous thing;
Drink deep, or taste not the Pierian spring.
Alexander Pope 1688–1744 English poet

Knowledge

Knowledge without conscience is but the ruin of the soul.
François Rabelais c.1494–c.1553 French humanist

There are known knowns; there are things we know we know. We also know there are known unknowns; that is to say we know there are some things we do not know. But there are also unknown unknowns—the ones we don't know we don't know.
Donald Rumsfeld 1932– American politician

The larger the island of knowledge, the longer the shoreline of wonder.
Ralph W. Sockman 1889–1970 American clergyman

I know nothing except the fact of my ignorance.
Socrates 469–399 BC Greek philosopher

Everybody gets so much information all day long that they lose their common sense.
Gertrude Stein 1874–1946 American writer

Knowledge is good. It does not have to look good or sound good or even do good. It is good just by being knowledge. And the only thing that makes it knowledge is that it is true. You can't have too much of it and there is no little too little to be worth having.
Tom Stoppard 1937– British dramatist

UMA THURMAN: That was a little bit more information than I needed to know.
Quentin Tarantino 1963– American film director, *in the film* Pulp Fiction

All the business of war, and indeed all the business of life, is to endeavour to find out what you don't know by what you do; that's what I called 'guessing what was at the other side of the hill'.
Duke of Wellington 1769–1852 British general

Language see also **Meaning**, **Words**

One picture is worth ten thousand words.
Frederick R. Barnard

A word fitly spoken is like apples of gold in pictures of silver.
Bible

A definition is the enclosing a wilderness of idea within a wall of words.
Samuel Butler 1835–1902 English novelist

Take care of the sense, and the sounds will take care of themselves.
Lewis Carroll 1832–98 English writer

Colourless green ideas sleep furiously.
Noam Chomsky 1928– American linguist, *illustrating that grammatical structure is independent of meaning*

This is the sort of English up with which I will not put.
Winston Churchill 1874–1965 British statesman, *on prepositions*

He who understands baboon would do more towards metaphysics than Locke.
Charles Darwin 1809–82 English naturalist

Language is fossil poetry.
Ralph Waldo Emerson 1803–82 American writer

My pedantry is your scholarship, his reasonable accuracy, her irreducible minimum of education, and someone else's ignorance.
H. W. Fowler 1858–1933 English lexicographer

Language

Merely corroborative detail, intended to give artistic
verisimilitude to an otherwise bald and unconvincing
narrative.
W. S. Gilbert 1836–1911 English writer

The only person entitled to use the imperial 'we' in speaking
of himself is a king, an editor, and a man with a tapeworm.
Robert G. Ingersoll 1833–99 American agnostic

Language is the dress of thought.
Samuel Johnson 1709–84 English lexicographer

The mystery of language was revealed to me. I knew then
that 'w-a-t-e-r' meant the wonderful cool something that
was flowing over my hand. That living word awakened my
soul, gave it light, joy, set it free!
Helen Keller 1880–1968 American writer

All that is not prose is verse; and all that is not verse is
prose.
Molière 1622–73 French comic dramatist

Good heavens! For more than forty years I have been
speaking prose without knowing it.
Molière 1622–73 French comic dramatist

Slang is a language that rolls up its sleeves, spits on its hands
and goes to work.
Carl Sandburg 1878–1967 American poet

You taught me language; and my profit on't
Is, I know how to curse.
William Shakespeare 1564–1616 English dramatist

A language is a dialect with an army and a navy.
Max Weinreich 1894–1969 American Yiddish scholar

The limits of my language mean the limits of my world.
Ludwig Wittgenstein 1889–1951 Austrian-born philosopher

Languages

The inherited and permanent fact that North America speaks English.
> **Otto von Bismarck** 1815–98 German statesman, *when asked what was the greatest political fact of modern times*

If I'm selling to you, I speak your language; if I'm buying *dann mussen Sie Deutsch sprechen* [then you must speak German].
> **Willy Brandt** 1913–92 German statesman

To God I speak Spanish, to women Italian, to men French, and to my horse—German.
> **Charles V** 1500–58 Holy Roman emperor

I like to be beholden to the great metropolitan English speech, the sea which receives tributaries from every region under heaven.
> **Ralph Waldo Emerson** 1803–82 American writer

My English text is chaste, and all licentious passages are left in the obscurity of a learned language.
> **Edward Gibbon** 1737–94 English historian, *parodied as 'decent obscurity' in the* Anti-Jacobin

He who does not know foreign languages knows nothing of his own.
> **Johann Wolfgang von Goethe** 1749–1832 German writer

I am always sorry when any language is lost, because languages are the pedigree of nations.
> **Samuel Johnson** 1709–84 English lexicographer

What is not clear is not French.
> **Antoine de Rivarol** 1753–1801 French man of letters

The Law

It is impossible for an Englishman to open his mouth
without making some other Englishman hate or despise
him.
George Bernard Shaw 1856–1950 Irish dramatist

England and America are two countries divided by a
common language.
George Bernard Shaw 1856–1950 Irish dramatist

The English language is nobody's special property. It is
the property of the imagination: it is the property of the
language itself.
Derek Walcott 1930–2017 West Indian writer

 The Law see also **Crime, Justice**

Written laws are like spider's webs; they will catch, it is true,
the weak and poor, but would be torn in pieces by the rich
and powerful.
Anacharsis Scythian prince of the 6th century BC

Law is a bottomless pit.
Dr Arbuthnot 1667–1735 Scottish physician

Bad laws are the worst sort of tyranny.
Edmund Burke 1729–97 Irish-born politician

The good of the people is the chief law.
Cicero 106–43 BC Roman statesman

Cui bono?
To whose profit?
Cicero 106–43 BC Roman statesman

If the law supposes that…the law is a ass—a idiot.
Charles Dickens 1812–70 English novelist

The Law

'You must not tell us what the soldier, or any other man, said, sir,' interposed the judge; 'it's not evidence.'
Charles Dickens 1812–70 English novelist

Be you never so high, the law is above you.
Thomas Fuller 1654–1734 English physician

No poet ever interpreted nature as freely as a lawyer interprets the truth.
Jean Giraudoux 1882–1944 French dramatist

Laws grind the poor, and rich men rule the law.
Oliver Goldsmith 1728–74 Irish writer

A verbal contract isn't worth the paper it is written on.
Sam Goldwyn 1882–1974 American film producer

I know no method to secure the repeal of bad or obnoxious laws so effective as their stringent execution.
Ulysses S. Grant 1822–85 American statesman

English law does not permit good persons, as such, to strangle bad persons, as such.
T. H. Huxley 1825–95 English biologist

The more laws and orders are made prominent,
The more thieves and bandits there will be.
Lao Tzu c.604–c.531 BC Chinese philosopher

I don't know as I want a lawyer to tell me what I cannot do. I hire him to tell me how to do what I want to do.
John Pierpont Morgan 1837–1913 American financier

Laws were made to be broken.
Christopher North 1785–1854 Scottish critic

A lawyer with his briefcase can steal more than a hundred men with guns.
Mario Puzo 1920–99 American novelist

Leadership

Ignorance of the law excuses no man; not that all men know
the law, but because 'tis an excuse every man will plead,
and no man can tell how to confute him.
   John Selden 1584–1654 English historian

The first thing we do, let's kill all the lawyers.
   William Shakespeare 1564–1616 English dramatist

The big print giveth, and the fine print taketh away.
   Fulton J. Sheen 1895–1979 American bishop

Everything not forbidden is compulsory.
   T. H. White 1906–64 English novelist

Asking the ignorant to use the incomprehensible to decide
the unknowable.
   Hiller B. Zobel 1932–   American judge, *on the jury system*

 # Leadership

By the structure of the world we often want, at the sudden
occurrence of a grave tempest, to change the helmsman—to
replace the pilot of the calm by the pilot of the storm.
   Walter Bagehot 1826–77 English economist

If the blind lead the blind, both shall fall into the ditch.
   Bible

The art of leadership is saying no, not yes. It is very easy to
say yes.
   Tony Blair 1953–   British statesman

If you desire what is good, the people will be good. The
character of a ruler is like wind and that of the people is like
grass. In whatever direction the wind blows the grass always
bends.
   Confucius 551–479 BC Chinese philosopher

Leadership

The art of leadership…consists in consolidating the attention of the people against a single adversary and taking care that nothing will split up that attention.
   Adolf Hitler 1889–1945 German dictator

Ultimately a genuine leader is not a searcher for consensus, but a moulder of consensus.
   Martin Luther King 1929–68 American civil rights leader

A leader is best when people barely know he exists…He acts without unnecessary speech, and when the work is done the people say 'We did it ourselves'.
   Lao Tzu c.604–c.531 BC Chinese philosopher

The final test of a leader is that he leaves behind him in other men the conviction and the will to carry on.
   Walter Lippmann 1889–1974 American journalist

The first method for estimating the intelligence of a ruler is to look at the men he has around him.
   Niccolò Machiavelli 1469–1527 Italian political philosopher

A leader who doesn't hesitate before he sends his nation into battle is not fit to be a leader.
   Golda Meir 1898–1978 Israeli stateswoman

I don't mind how much my Ministers talk, so long as they do what I say.
   Margaret Thatcher 1925–2013 British stateswoman

The buck stops here.
   Harry S. Truman 1884–1972 American statesman

You can't lead the people if you don't love the people, and you can't save the people if you won't serve the people.
   Cornel West 1953– American academic

 Leisure

We are closer to the ants than to the butterflies. Very few
people can endure much leisure.
Gerald Brenan 1894–1987 British writer

There's sand in the porridge and sand in the bed,
And if this is pleasure we'd rather be dead.
Noël Coward 1899–1973 English dramatist

What is this life if, full of care,
We have no time to stand and stare.
W. H. Davies 1871–1940 Welsh poet

Man is so made that he can only find relaxation from one
kind of labour by taking up another.
Anatole France 1844–1924 French man of letters

Take rest; a field that has rested gives a bountiful crop.
Ovid 43 BC–c.AD 17 Roman poet

To be able to fill leisure intelligently is the last product of
civilization.
Bertrand Russell 1872–1970 British philosopher

If all the year were playing holidays,
To sport would be as tedious as to work;
But when they seldom come, they wished for come.
William Shakespeare 1564–1616 English dramatist

Repose is a good thing, but boredom is its brother.
Voltaire 1694–1778 French writer

We're all going on a summer holiday,
No more worries for a week or two.
Bruce Welch 1941– and **Brian Bennett** 1940– English
musicians

The world is too much with us; late and soon,
Getting and spending, we lay waste our powers.
   William Wordsworth 1770–1850 English poet

Letters

Letters of thanks, letters from banks,
Letters of joy from girl and boy.
   W. H. Auden 1907–73 English poet

She'll vish there wos more, and that's the great art o' letter writin'.
   Charles Dickens 1812–70 English novelist

Sir, more than kisses, letters mingle souls.
   John Donne 1572–1631 English poet

It is wonderful how much news there is when people write every other day; if they wait for a month, there is nothing that seems worth telling.
   O. Douglas 1877–1948 Scottish writer

All letters, methinks, should be free and easy as one's discourse, not studied as an oration, nor made up of hard words like a charm.
   Dorothy Osborne 1627–95

Don't think that this is a letter. It is only a small eruption of a disease called friendship.
   Jean Renoir 1894–1979 French film director

A woman seldom writes her mind but in her postscript.
   Richard Steele 1672–1729 Irish-born essayist

The humane art which owes its origin to the love of friends.
   Virginia Woolf 1882–1941 English novelist, *on letter-writing*

 # Liberty

Liberty is always unfinished business.
    Anonymous

Real freedom is freedom from fear, and unless you can live
free from fear you cannot live a dignified human life.
    Aung San Suu Kyi 1945– Burmese political leader

Liberty is liberty, not equality or fairness or justice or
human happiness or a quiet conscience.
    Isaiah Berlin 1909–97 British philosopher

The people never give up their liberties except under some
delusion.
    Edmund Burke 1729–97 Irish-born politician

The condition upon which God hath given liberty to man is
eternal vigilance.
    John Philpot Curran 1750–1817 Irish judge

The cost of liberty is less than the price of repression.
    W. E. B. Du Bois 1868–1963 American political activist

I know not what course others may take; but as for me,
give me liberty, or give me death!
    Patrick Henry 1736–99 American statesman

It is better to die on your feet than to live on your knees.
    Dolores Ibarruri 1895–1989 Spanish communist leader

The enemies of Freedom do not argue; they shout and they
shoot.
    Dean Inge 1860–1954 English writer

We shall pay any price, bear any burden, meet any hardship,
support any friend, oppose any foe to assure the survival
and the success of liberty.
    John F. Kennedy 1917–63 American statesman

Liberty is precious—so precious that it must be rationed.
  Lenin 1870–1924 Russian revolutionary

Stone walls do not a prison make,
Nor iron bars a cage.
  Richard Lovelace 1618–58 English poet

Freedom is always and exclusively freedom for the one who thinks differently.
  Rosa Luxemburg 1871–1919 German revolutionary

If men are to wait for liberty till they become wise and good in slavery, they may indeed wait for ever.
  Lord Macaulay 1800–59 English historian

The liberty of the individual must be thus far limited;
he must not make himself a nuisance to other people.
  John Stuart Mill 1806–73 English philosopher

Freedom is the freedom to say that two plus two make four. If that is granted, all else follows.
  George Orwell 1903–50 English novelist

O liberty! what crimes are committed in thy name!
  Mme Roland 1754–93 French revolutionary

Man was born free, and everywhere he is in chains.
  Jean-Jacques Rousseau 1712–78 French philosopher

What is freedom of expression? Without the freedom to offend, it ceases to exist.
  Salman Rushdie 1947– Indian-born British novelist

Liberty means responsibility. That is why most men dread it.
  George Bernard Shaw 1856–1950 Irish dramatist

A free society is a society where it is safe to be unpopular.
  Adlai Stevenson 1900–65 American politician

Libraries see also **Books**, **Reading**

I have always imagined Paradise as a kind of library.
Jorge Luis Borges 1899–1986 Argentinian writer

The true University of these days is a collection of books.
Thomas Carlyle 1795–1881 Scottish historian

A man should keep his little brain attic stocked with all the furniture that he is likely to use, and the rest he can put away in the lumber room of his library, where he can get it if he wants it.
Arthur Conan Doyle 1859–1930 Scottish-born writer

No place affords a more striking conviction of the vanity of human hopes, than a public library.
Samuel Johnson 1709–84 English lexicographer

Your *borrowers of books*—those mutilators of collections, spoilers of the symmetry of shelves, and creators of odd volumes.
Charles Lamb 1775–1834 English writer

A library is thought in cold storage.
Lord Samuel 1870–1963 British politician

Come, and take choice of all my library,
And so beguile thy sorrow.
William Shakespeare 1564–1616 English dramatist

 # Lies see also **Deceit**, **Truth**

An abomination unto the Lord, but a very present help in time of trouble.
Anonymous, *definition of a lie, an amalgamation of two biblical verses*

234

Lies

Truth, like light, blinds. Falsehood, on the contrary, is a beautiful twilight, that enhances every object.
Albert Camus 1913–60 French writer

Great is the power of steady misrepresentation.
Charles Darwin 1809–82 English naturalist

There are three kinds of lies: lies, damned lies and statistics.
Benjamin Disraeli 1804–81 British statesman

Without lies humanity would perish of despair and boredom.
Anatole France 1844–1924 French man of letters

In human relations kindness and lies are worth a thousand truths.
Graham Greene 1904–91 English novelist

Whoever would lie usefully should lie seldom.
Lord Hervey 1696–1743 English politician

The broad mass of a nation…will more easily fall victim to a big lie than to a small one.
Adolf Hitler 1889–1945 German dictator

There is no worse lie than a truth misunderstood by those who hear it.
William James 1842–1910 American philosopher

He would, wouldn't he?
Mandy Rice-Davies 1944–2014 English model, *on hearing that Lord Astor denied her allegations*

It is well said in the old proverb, 'a lie will go round the world while truth is pulling its boots on'.
C. H. Spurgeon 1834–92 English preacher

The cruellest lies are often told in silence.
Robert Louis Stevenson 1850–94 Scottish novelist

Life

One of the most striking differences between a cat and a lie is that a cat has only nine lives.
> **Mark Twain** 1835–1910 American writer

 # Life see also **Life Sciences**, **Lifestyles**

The Answer to the Great Question Of…Life, the Universe and Everything…[is] Forty-two.
> **Douglas Adams** 1952–2001 English writer

'Such,' he said, 'O King, seems to me the present life of men on earth, in comparison with that time which to us is uncertain, as if when on a winter's night you sit feasting with your ealdormen and thegns,—a single sparrow should fly swiftly into the hall, and coming in at one door, instantly fly out through another'.
> **The Venerable Bede** AD 673–735 English historian

Man that is born of a woman is of few days, and full of trouble.
> **Bible**

All that a man hath will he give for his life.
> **Bible**

Life is just a bowl of cherries.
> **Lew Brown** 1893–1958 American songwriter

Life is a tragedy when seen in close-up, but a comedy in long-shot.
> **Charlie Chaplin** 1889–1977 English film actor

W. C. FIELDS: It's a funny old world—a man's lucky if he gets out of it alive.
> **Walter de Leon** and **Paul M. Jones** American screenwriters, *in the film* You're Telling Me

All that matters is love and work.
Sigmund Freud 1856–1939 Austrian psychoanalyst

No arts; no letters; no society; and which is worst of all,
continual fear and danger of violent death; and the life of
man, solitary, poor, nasty, brutish, and short.
Thomas Hobbes 1588–1679 English philosopher

Life is just one damned thing after another.
Elbert Hubbard 1859–1915 American writer

As far as we can discern, the sole purpose of human
existence is to kindle a light in the darkness of mere being.
Carl Gustav Jung 1875–1961 Swiss psychologist

Life is either a daring adventure or nothing.
Helen Keller 1880–1968 American writer

Life must be understood backwards; but…it must be lived
forwards.
Sören Kierkegaard 1813–55 Danish philosopher

Life is first boredom, then fear.
Philip Larkin 1922–85 English poet

Life is like a sewer. What you get out of it depends on what
you put into it.
Tom Lehrer 1928–   American humorist

Life is just what happens to you,
while you're busy making other plans.
John Lennon 1940–80 English pop singer

Life well spent is long.
Leonardo da Vinci 1452–1519 Italian painter

Life is real! Life is earnest!
And the grave is not its goal;

Life

Dust thou art, to dust returnest,
Was not spoken of the soul.
   Henry Wadsworth Longfellow 1807–82 American poet

What, knocked a tooth out? Never mind, dear, laugh it off,
laugh it off; it's all part of life's rich pageant.
   Arthur Marshall 1910–89 British journalist

We live, not as we wish to, but as we can.
   Menander 342–c.292 BC Greek comic dramatist

I've looked at life from both sides now,
From win and lose and still somehow
It's life's illusions I recall;
I really don't know life at all.
   Joni Mitchell 1945– Canadian singer

Man is born to live, not to prepare for life.
   Boris Pasternak 1890–1960 Russian novelist

Real life is elsewhere.
   Arthur Rimbaud 1854–91 French poet

TOM HANKS: My momma always said life was like a box of
chocolates…you never know what you're gonna get.
   Eric Roth 1945– American screenwriter, *in the film* Forrest
   Gump

All the world's a stage,
And all the men and women merely players:
They have their exits and their entrances;
And one man in his time plays many parts,
His acts being seven ages.
   William Shakespeare 1564–1616 English dramatist

Life is not meant to be easy, my child; but take courage:
it can be delightful.
   George Bernard Shaw 1856–1950 Irish dramatist

Not to be born is, past all prizing, best.
> **Sophocles** c.496–406 BC Greek dramatist

The same stream of life that runs through my veins night and day runs through the world and dances in rhythmic measures.
It is the same life that shoots in joy through the dust of the earth into numberless blades of grass and breaks into tumultuous waves of leaves and flowers.
> **Rabindranath Tagore** 1861–1941 Bengali poet

Our life is frittered away by detail…Simplify, simplify.
> **Henry David Thoreau** 1817–62 American writer

Expect nothing. Live frugally
on surprise.
> **Alice Walker** 1944– American poet

This world is a comedy to those that think, a tragedy to those that feel.
> **Horace Walpole** 1717–97 English connoisseur

Never to have lived is best, ancient writers say;
Never to have drawn the breath of life, never to have looked
    into the eye of day;
The second best's a gay goodnight and quickly turn away.
> **W. B. Yeats** 1865–1939 Irish poet

Life Sciences see also Science

The Microbe is so very small
You cannot make him out at all.
> **Hilaire Belloc** 1870–1953 British writer

Men will not be content to manufacture life: they will want to improve on it.
> **J. D. Bernal** 1901–71 Irish-born physicist

Life Sciences

It has, I believe, been often remarked that a hen is only an egg's way of making another egg.
Samuel Butler 1835–1902 English novelist

We have discovered the secret of life!
Francis Crick 1916–2004 English biophysicist, *on the discovery of the structure of DNA*

Almost all aspects of life are engineered at the molecular level, and without understanding molecules we can only have a very sketchy understanding of life itself.
Francis Crick 1916–2004 English biophysicist

I have called this principle, by which each slight variation, if useful, is preserved, by the term of Natural Selection.
Charles Darwin 1809–82 English naturalist

From so simple a beginning endless forms most beautiful and most wonderful have been, and are being, evolved.
Charles Darwin 1809–82 English naturalist

I'd lay down my life for two brothers or eight cousins.
J. B. S. Haldane 1892–1964 Scottish mathematical biologist

Life exists in the universe only because the carbon atom possesses certain exceptional properties.
James Jeans 1877–1946 Scottish astronomer

The biologist passes, the frog remains.
Jean Rostand 1894–1977 French biologist, *sometimes quoted as 'Theories pass. The frog remains'*

So, naturalists observe, a flea
Hath smaller fleas that on him prey;
And these have smaller fleas to bite 'em,
And so proceed *ad infinitum*.
Jonathan Swift 1667–1745 Irish poet and satirist

Water is life's *mater* and *matrix*, mother and medium. There is no life without water.
> **Albert von Szent-Györgyi** 1893–1986 Hungarian-born biochemist

Biology is the search for the chemistry that works.
> **R. J. P. Williams** 1926–2015 British chemist

Lifestyles see also Life

What is the secret of my long life? I really don't know—cigarettes, whisky and wild, wild women!
> **Henry Allingham** 1896–2009, *the oldest British survivor of the First World War*

I've lived a life that's full, I've travelled each and ev'ry highway
And more, much more than this. I did it my way.
> **Paul Anka** 1941– Canadian singer

Love and do what you will.
> **St Augustine of Hippo** AD 354–430 Roman theologian

A man hath no better thing under the sun, than to eat, and to drink, and to be merry.
> **Bible**

Thou shalt love thy neighbour as thyself.
> **Bible**

The hippies wanted peace and love. We wanted Ferraris, blondes and switchblades.
> **Alice Cooper** 1948– American rock singer

Dream as if you'll live forever. Live as if you'll die today.
> **James Dean** 1931–55 American actor

Lifestyles

Live in the sunshine, swim the sea,
Drink the wild air's salubrity.
   Ralph Waldo Emerson 1803–82 American writer

RUSSELL CROWE: What we do in life echoes in eternity.
   David Franzoni 1947–   American screenwriter, *in the film*
   Gladiator

Just trust yourself and you'll learn the art of living.
   Johann Wolfgang von Goethe 1749–1832 German writer

If I had but two loaves of bread I would sell one of them,
and buy White Hyacinths to feed my soul.
   Elbert Hubbard 1859–1915 American writer

Live all you can; it's a mistake not to. It doesn't so much
matter what you do in particular, so long as you have your
life. If you haven't had that, what *have* you had?
   Henry James 1843–1916 American novelist

Your time is limited, so don't waste it living someone else's
life…Stay hungry. Stay foolish.
   Steve Jobs 1955–2011 American computer executive

Turn on, tune in and drop out.
   Timothy Leary 1920–96 American psychologist

Believe me! The secret of reaping the greatest fruitfulness
and the greatest enjoyment from life is *to live dangerously*!
   Friedrich Nietzsche 1844–1900 German philosopher

To live at all is miracle enough.
   Mervyn Peake 1911–68 British novelist

Fais ce que voudras.
Do what you like.
   François Rabelais *c.*1494–*c.*1553 French humanist

You only live once, and the way I live, once is enough.
Frank Sinatra 1915–98 American singer and actor

Take short views, hope for the best, and trust in God.
Sydney Smith 1771–1845 English essayist

Keep your eyes open and your mouth shut.
John Steinbeck 1902–68 American novelist

It's better to burn out
Than to fade away.
Neil Young 1945– Canadian singer

Literature see also **Writing**

A losing trade, I assure you, sir: literature is a drug.
George Borrow 1803–81 English writer

All tragedies are finished by a death,
All comedies are ended by a marriage;
The future states of both are left to faith.
Lord Byron 1788–1824 English poet

Literature is a luxury; fiction is a necessity.
G. K. Chesterton 1874–1936 English writer

The greatest masterpiece in literature is only a dictionary
out of order.
Jean Cocteau 1889–1963 French film director

Yes—oh dear yes—the novel tells a story.
E. M. Forster 1879–1970 English novelist

Works of serious purpose and grand promises often have a
purple patch or two stitched on, to shine far and wide.
Horace 65–8 BC Roman poet

It takes a great deal of history to produce a little literature.
Henry James 1843–1916 American novelist

London

Never trust the artist. Trust the tale.
D. H. Lawrence 1885–1930 English writer

Literature is news that STAYS news.
Ezra Pound 1885–1972 American poet

'Thou shalt not' might reach the head, but it takes 'Once upon a time' to reach the heart.
Philip Pullman 1946– English writer

Remarks are not literature.
Gertrude Stein 1874–1946 American writer

A novel is a mirror which passes over a highway. Sometimes it reflects to your eyes the blue of the skies, at others the churned-up mud of the road.
Stendhal 1783–1842 French novelist

The good ended happily, and the bad unhappily. That is what fiction means.
Oscar Wilde 1854–1900 Irish dramatist

 # London

Was für Plunder!
What rubbish!
Gebhard Lebrecht Blücher 1742–1819 Prussian field marshal, *often misquoted as 'Was für plündern [What a place to plunder]!'*

The great wen of all.
William Cobbett 1762–1835 English political reformer

Crowds without company, and dissipation without pleasure.
Edward Gibbon 1737–94 English historian

Maybe it's because I'm a Londoner
That I love London so.
Hubert Gregg 1914–2004 English songwriter

When a man is tired of London, he is tired of life.
Samuel Johnson 1709–84 English lexicographer

I thought of London spread out in the sun,
Its postal districts packed like squares of wheat.
Philip Larkin 1922–85 English poet

Earth has not anything to show more fair:
Dull would he be of soul who could pass by
A sight so touching in its majesty.
William Wordsworth 1770–1850 English poet

Love see also **Lovers, Marriage, Sex**

Love is, above all, the gift of oneself!
Jean Anouilh 1910–87 French dramatist

With love, you see, even too much is not enough.
Pierre-Augustin Caron de Beaumarchais 1732–99 French dramatist

Love is free; it is not practised as a way of achieving other ends.
Benedict XVI 1927– German pope

Many waters cannot quench love, neither can the floods drown it.
Bible

Greater love hath no man than this, that a man lay down his life for his friends.
Bible

Though I speak with the tongues of men and of angels, and have not charity, I am become as sounding brass, or a tinkling cymbal…

Love

And though I have all faith; so that I could remove mountains; and have not charity, I am nothing.
Bible

And now abideth faith, hope, charity, these three; but the greatest of these is charity.
Bible

There is no fear in love; but perfect love casteth out fear.
Bible

Love seeketh not itself to please,
Nor for itself hath any care;
But for another gives its ease,
And builds a Heaven in Hell's despair.
William Blake 1757–1827 English poet

When love is not madness, it is not love.
Pedro Calderón de La Barca 1600–81 Spanish dramatist

Say what you will, 'tis better to be left than never to have been loved.
William Congreve 1670–1729 English dramatist

The love that moves the sun and the other stars.
Dante Alighieri 1265–1321 Italian poet

Much love much trial, but what an utter desert is life without love.
Charles Darwin 1809–82 English naturalist

Selfhood begins with a walking away,
And love is proved in the letting go.
C. Day-Lewis 1904–72 English poet

Love itself is what is left over when being in love has burned away.
Louis de Bernières 1954– British novelist

Love

Love built on beauty, soon as beauty, dies.
John Donne 1572–1631 English poet

I am the Love that dare not speak its name.
Lord Alfred Douglas 1870–1945 English poet

Oh, if only we could lean over the soul we love and see as in a mirror the image we cast there!
André Gide 1869–1951 French novelist

If I love you, what does that matter to you!
Johann Wolfgang von Goethe 1749–1832 German writer

There is no disguise which can hide love for long where it exists, or feign it where it does not.
Duc de la Rochefoucauld 1613–80 French moralist

Only the flow matters; live and let live, love and let love. There is no point to love.
D. H. Lawrence 1885–1930 English writer

Where both deliberate, the love is slight;
Who ever loved that loved not at first sight?
Christopher Marlowe 1564–93 English dramatist

The love that lasts longest is the love that is never returned.
W. Somerset Maugham 1874–1965 English novelist

Love is the triumph of imagination over intelligence.
H. L. Mencken 1880–1956 American journalist

If I am pressed to say why I loved him, I feel it can only be explained by replying: 'Because it was he; because it was me.'
Montaigne 1533–92 French moralist

No, there's nothing half so sweet in life
As love's young dream.
Thomas Moore 1779–1852 Irish musician

Love is so short, forgetting is so long.
Pablo Neruda 1904–73 Chilean poet

Love

I find no peace, and I am not at war,
I fear and hope, and burn and I am ice.
Petrarch 1304–74 Italian poet

Birds do it, bees do it,
Even educated fleas do it.
Let's do it, let's fall in love.
Cole Porter 1891–1964 American songwriter

Love consists in this, that two solitudes protect and touch
and greet each other.
Rainer Maria Rilke 1875–1926 German poet

Life has taught us that love does not consist in gazing at
each other but in looking together in the same direction.
Antoine de Saint-Exupéry 1900–44 French novelist

Love rules the court, the camp, the grove
And men below and saints above
For love is heaven, and heaven is love.
Sir Walter Scott 1771–1832 Scottish novelist

Love means never having to say you're sorry.
Erich Segal 1937–2010 American writer

The course of true love never did run smooth.
William Shakespeare 1564–1616 English dramatist

Then, must you speak
Of one that loved not wisely but too well.
William Shakespeare 1564–1616 English dramatist

For stony limits cannot hold love out,
And what love can do that dares love attempt.
William Shakespeare 1564–1616 English dramatist

To be wise, and love,
Exceeds man's might.
William Shakespeare 1564–1616 English dramatist

Let me not to the marriage of true minds
Admit impediments. Love is not love
Which alters when it alteration finds.
William Shakespeare 1564–1616 English dramatist

We cease loving ourselves if no one loves us.
Mme de Staël 1766–1817 French writer

'Tis better to have loved and lost
Than never to have loved at all.
Alfred, Lord Tennyson 1809–92 English poet

Love conquers all things: let us too give in to Love.
Virgil 70–19 BC Roman poet

Yet each man kills the thing he loves,
By each let this be heard,
Some do it with a bitter look,
Some with a flattering word.
The coward does it with a kiss,
The brave man with a sword!
Oscar Wilde 1854–1900 Irish dramatist

A pity beyond all telling,
Is hid in the heart of love.
W. B. Yeats 1865–1939 Irish poet

Lovers

If equal affection cannot be,
Let the more loving one be me.
W. H. Auden 1907–73 English poet

One is never too old for romance.
Ingrid Bergman 1915–82 Swedish actress

A man chases a girl (until she catches him).
Irving Berlin 1888–1989 American songwriter

Lovers

To fall in love is to create a religion that has a fallible god.
Jorge Luis Borges 1899–1986 Argentinian writer

He's more myself than I am. Whatever our souls are made of his and mine are the same.
Emily Brontë 1818–48 English writer

If thou must love me, let it be for nought
Except for love's sake only.
Elizabeth Barrett Browning 1806–61 English poet

How do I love thee? Let me count the ways.
Elizabeth Barrett Browning 1806–61 English poet

O, my Luve's like a red, red rose
That's newly sprung in June;
O my Luve's like the melodie
That's sweetly play'd in tune.
Robert Burns 1759–96 Scottish poet

My heart has made its mind up
And I'm afraid it's you.
Wendy Cope 1945–   English poet

My soul is so knit to yours that it is but a divided life I live without you.
George Eliot 1819–80 English novelist

BILLY CRYSTAL: When you realize you want to spend the rest of your life with somebody, you want the rest of your life to start as soon as possible.
Nora Ephron 1941–2012 American screenwriter, *in the film* When Harry Met Sally

Stay, little Valentine, stay,
Each day is Valentine's day.
Lorenz Hart 1895–1943 American songwriter

I was more pleased with possessing your heart than with any other happiness.

Héloise c.1098–1164 French abbess

All you need is love.

John Lennon 1940–80 and **Paul McCartney** 1942– English pop singers

The life that I have
Is all that I have
And the life that I have
Is yours.

The love that I have
Of the life that I have
Is yours and yours and yours.

Leo Marks 1920–2001 English cryptographer, *given to the British secret agent Violette Szabo (1921–45), for use with the Special Operations Executive*

Difficult or easy, pleasant or bitter, you are the same you: I cannot live with you—or without you.

Martial c.AD 40–c.104 Roman epigrammatist

Love is never any better than the lover. Wicked people love wickedly, violent people love violently, weak people love weakly, stupid people love stupidly, but the love of a free man is never safe. There is no gift for the beloved.

Toni Morrison 1931– American novelist

I want to do with you
what spring does with the cherry trees.

Pablo Neruda 1904–73 Chilean poet

　　　　It were all one
That I should love a bright particular star
And think to wed it, he is so above me.

William Shakespeare 1564–1616 English dramatist

Luck

The fickleness of the women I love is only equalled by the infernal constancy of the women who love me.
George Bernard Shaw 1856–1950 Irish dramatist

Why so pale and wan, fond lover?
Prithee, why so pale?
Will, when looking well can't move her,
Looking ill prevail?
John Suckling 1609–42 English poet

Why is it that the most unoriginal thing we can say to one another is still the thing we long to hear? 'I love you' is always a quotation.
Jeanette Winterson 1959– English novelist

 # Luck

What we call luck is the inner man externalized. We make things happen to us.
Robertson Davies 1913–95 Canadian novelist

The best mascot is a good mechanic.
Amelia Earhart 1898–1937 American aviator

There is much good luck in the world, but it is luck. We are none of us safe. We are children, playing or quarrelling on the line.
E. M. Forster 1879–1970 English novelist

Care and diligence bring luck.
Thomas Fuller 1654–1734 English physician

Some folk want their luck buttered.
Thomas Hardy 1840–1928 English novelist

Watch out w'en you'er gittin all you want. Fattenin' hogs ain't in luck.
Joel Chandler Harris 1848–1908 American writer

All you know about it [luck] for certain is that it's bound to change.

Bret Harte 1836–1902 American poet

Is he lucky?

Cardinal Mazarin 1602–61 Italian-born French statesman, *first question on being requested to take anyone into his service, later associated with Napoleon*

Miracles do happen, but one has to work very hard for them.

Chaim Weizmann 1874–1952 Russian-born Israeli statesman

Luck is preparation meeting opportunity.

Oprah Winfrey 1954– American talk show hostess

Madness

Babylon in all its desolation is a sight not so awful as that of the human mind in ruins.

Scrope Davies c.1783–1852 English conversationalist

Whom God would destroy He first sends mad.

James Duport 1606–79 English scholar, *summarizing a Greek original*

Mad, is he? Then I hope he will *bite* some of my other generals.

George II 1683–1760 British monarch, *replying to the Duke of Newcastle, who had complained that General Wolfe was a madman*

There was only one catch and that was Catch-22…Orr would be crazy to fly more missions and sane if he didn't, but if he was sane he had to fly them. If he flew them he was crazy and didn't have to; but if he didn't want to he was sane and had to.

Joseph Heller 1923–99 American novelist

Management

Every one is more or less mad on one point.
Rudyard Kipling 1865–1936 English writer

Madness need not be all breakdown. It may also be break-through.
R. D. Laing 1927–89 Scottish psychiatrist

They called me mad, and I called them mad, and damn them, they outvoted me.
Nathaniel Lee c.1653–92 English dramatist

Is there no way out of the mind?
Sylvia Plath 1932–63 American poet

Though this be madness, yet there is method in't.
William Shakespeare 1564–1616 English dramatist

O! let me not be mad, not mad, sweet heaven;
Keep me in temper; I would not be mad!
William Shakespeare 1564–1616 English dramatist

 Management see also **Careers, Planning**

Committee—a group of men who individually can do nothing but as a group decide that nothing can be done.
Fred Allen 1894–1956 American humorist

A place for everything and everything in its place.
Mrs Beeton 1836–65 English cookery writer

You're either part of the solution or you're part of the problem.
Eldridge Cleaver 1935–98 American political activist

Meetings are a great trap…However, they are indispensable when you don't want to do anything.
J. K. Galbraith 1908–2006 American economist

If you want people motivated to do a good job, give them a good job to do.

Frederick Herzberg 1923–2000 American management researcher

A camel is a horse designed by a committee.

Alec Issigonis 1906–88 British engineer

There cannot be a crisis next week. My schedule is already full.

Henry Kissinger 1923– American politician

If it ain't broke, don't fix it.

Bert Lance 1931–2013 American government official

Every time I create an appointment, I create a hundred malcontents and one ingrate.

Louis XIV 1638–1715 French monarch

There is always a well-known solution to every human problem—neat, plausible, and wrong.

H. L. Mencken 1880–1956 American journalist

Time spent on any item of the agenda will be in inverse proportion to the sum involved.

C. Northcote Parkinson 1909–93 English writer

In a hierarchy every employee tends to rise to his level of incompetence.

Laurence Peter 1919–90 Canadian writer

Surround yourself with the best people you can find, delegate authority, and don't interfere.

Ronald Reagan 1911–2004 American statesman

There is nothing in the world which does not have its decisive moment, and the masterpiece of good management is to recognize and grasp this moment.

Cardinal de Retz 1613–79 French cardinal

Manners

A problem left to itself dries up or goes rotten. But fertilize a problem with a solution—you'll hatch out dozens.
N. F. Simpson 1919–2011 English dramatist

The shortest way to do many things is to do only one thing at once.
Samuel Smiles 1812–1904 English writer

Dans ce pays-ci il est bon de tuer de temps en temps un amiral pour encourager les autres.
In this country [England] it is thought well to kill an admiral from time to time to encourage the others.
Voltaire 1694–1778 French writer

 # Manners see also **Behaviour**, **Punctuality**

Evil communications corrupt good manners.
Bible

Curtsey while you're thinking what to say. It saves time.
Lewis Carroll 1832–98 English writer

Take the tone of the company that you are in.
Lord Chesterfield 1694–1773 English writer

It is wise to apply the oil of refined politeness to the mechanism of friendship.
Colette 1873–1954 French novelist

It's not a slam at *you* when people are rude—it's a slam at the people they've met before.
F. Scott Fitzgerald 1896–1940 American novelist

The art of pleasing consists in being pleased.
William Hazlitt 1778–1830 English essayist

An insolent reply from a polite person is a bad sign.
Hippocrates c.460–357 BC Greek physician

To Americans, English manners are far more frightening than none at all.
> **Randall Jarrell** 1914–65 American poet

THUMPER: If you can't say something nice…don't say nothing at all.
> **Larry Morey** 1905–71, *in the film* Bambi

Manners maketh man.
> **Proverb**, *motto of William of Wykeham (1324–1404)*

Stand not upon the order of your going.
> **William Shakespeare** 1564–1616 English dramatist

He is the very pineapple of politeness!
> **Richard Brinsley Sheridan** 1751–1816 Irish dramatist

Manners are especially the need of the plain. The pretty can get away with anything.
> **Evelyn Waugh** 1903–66 English novelist

Marriage see also **Love**, **Weddings**

It is a truth universally acknowledged, that a single man in possession of a good fortune, must be in want of a wife.
> **Jane Austen** 1775–1817 English novelist

Wives are young men's mistresses, companions for middle age, and old men's nurses.
> **Francis Bacon** 1561–1626 English courtier

Being a husband is a whole-time job. That is why so many husbands fail. They cannot give their entire attention to it.
> **Arnold Bennett** 1867–1931 English novelist

What therefore God hath joined together, let not man put asunder.
> **Bible**

Marriage

To have and to hold from this day forward, for better for worse, for richer for poorer, in sickness and in health, to love, cherish, and to obey, till death us do part.
> **Book of Common Prayer** 1662

The deep, deep peace of the double-bed after the hurly-burly of the chaise-longue.
> **Mrs Patrick Campbell** 1865–1940 English actress, *on her recent marriage*

Oh! how many torments lie in the small circle of a wedding-ring!
> **Colley Cibber** 1671–1757 English dramatist

I learnt a long time ago that the only people who count in any marriage are the two that are in it.
> **Hillary Rodham Clinton** 1947– American lawyer

Marriage is a wonderful invention; but, then again, so is a bicycle repair kit.
> **Billy Connolly** 1942– Scottish comedian

The heart of marriage is memories.
> **Bill Cosby** 1937– American actor

I would be married, but I'd have no wife,
I would be married to a single life.
> **Richard Crashaw** c.1612–49 English poet

The chains of marriage are so heavy that it takes two to bear them, and sometimes three.
> **Alexandre Dumas** 1824–95 French writer

Man's best possession is a sympathetic wife.
> **Euripides** c.485–c.406 BC Greek dramatist

Keep your eyes wide open before marriage, half shut afterwards.
> **Benjamin Franklin** 1706–90 American statesman and scientist

Always remember that the most important thing in a good marriage is not happiness, but stability.
> **Gabriel García Márquez** 1927–2014 Colombian novelist

Do you think your mother and I should have lived comfortably so long together, if ever we had been married?
> **John Gay** 1685–1732 English writer

You shall be together when the white wings of death scatter
  your days.
Ay, you shall be together even in the silent memory of God.
But let there be spaces in your togetherness,
And let the winds of the heavens dance between you.
> **Kahlil Gibran** 1883–1931 Lebanese-born American writer

The triumph of hope over experience.
> **Samuel Johnson** 1709–84 English lexicographer, *of a man who remarried immediately after the death of a wife with whom he had been unhappy*

Marriage is one long fit of compromise, deep and wide.
> **Barbara Kingsolver** 1955– American writer

I am your clay.
You are my clay.
In life we share a single quilt.
In death we will share one coffin.
> **Kuan Tao-sheng** 1262–1319 Chinese poet

A happy marriage is a long conversation that always seems too short.
> **André Maurois** 1885–1967 French writer

One doesn't have to get anywhere in a marriage. It's not a public conveyance.
> **Iris Murdoch** 1919–99 English novelist

The great secret of a successful marriage is to treat all disasters as incidents and none of the incidents as disasters.
> **Harold Nicolson** 1886–1968 English diplomat

Mathematics

Tolerance is the one essential ingredient.
> **Philip, Duke of Edinburgh** 1921– Greek-born husband of
> Elizabeth II, *his recipe for a successful marriage*

It doesn't much signify whom one marries, for one is sure to
find next morning that it was someone else.
> **Samuel Rogers** 1763–1855 English poet

A young man married is a man that's marred.
> **William Shakespeare** 1564–1616 English dramatist

Marriage is popular because it combines the maximum of
temptation with the maximum of opportunity.
> **George Bernard Shaw** 1856–1950 Irish dramatist

Chains do not hold a marriage together. It is threads,
hundreds of tiny threads which sew people together
through the years. That is what makes a marriage last—
more than passion or even sex!
> **Simone Signoret** 1921–85 French actress

Marriage is like life in this—that it is a field of battle,
and not a bed of roses.
> **Robert Louis Stevenson** 1850–94 Scottish novelist

Marriage isn't a word…it's a *sentence*!
> **King Vidor** 1895–1982 American film director

In married life three is company and two none.
> **Oscar Wilde** 1854–1900 Irish dramatist

 # Mathematics

Let no one enter who does not know geometry
[mathematics].
> **Anonymous**, *inscription on Plato's door, probably at the Academy
> at Athens*

Mathematics

If in other sciences we should arrive at certainty without doubt and truth without error, it behoves us to place the foundations of knowledge in mathematics.
Roger Bacon c.1220–c.92 English philosopher and friar

They are neither finite quantities, or quantities infinitely small, nor yet nothing. May we not call them the ghosts of departed quantities?
Bishop George Berkeley 1685–1753 Irish philosopher, *on Newton's infinitesimals*

I never could make out what those damned dots meant.
Lord Randolph Churchill 1849–94 British politician, *on decimal points*

Equations are more important to me, because politics is for the present, but an equation is something for eternity.
Albert Einstein 1879–1955 German-born theoretical physicist

There is no 'royal road' to geometry.
Euclid fl. 300 BC Greek mathematician

This book is written in mathematical language and its characters are triangles, circles and other geometrical figures, without whose help…one wanders in vain through a dark labyrinth.
Galileo Galilei 1564–1642 Italian astronomer, *often quoted as 'The book of nature is written...'*

Prime numbers are what is left when you have taken all the patterns away. I think prime numbers are like life.
Mark Haddon 1962– British novelist

Beauty is the first test: there is no permanent place in the world for ugly mathematics.
Godfrey Harold Hardy 1877–1947 English mathematician

Meaning

Someone told me that each equation I included in the book would halve the sales.
Stephen Hawking 1942– English theoretical physicist

God made the integers, all the rest is the work of man.
Leopold Kronecker 1823–91 German mathematician

In mathematics you don't understand things. You just get used to them.
John von Neumann 1903–57 American mathematician

There are 10 types of people in the country: those who understand binary and those who don't.
Jeremy Paxman 1950– British journalist

God is always doing geometry.
Plato 429–347 BC Greek philosopher

An equation for me has no meaning unless it expresses a thought of God.
Srinivasa Ramanujan 1887–1920 Indian mathematician

What would life be without arithmetic, but a scene of horrors?
Sydney Smith 1771–1845 English essayist

 ## Meaning see also **Words**

No one means all he says, and yet very few say all they mean, for words are slippery and thought is viscous.
Henry Brooks Adams 1838–1918 American historian

'Then you should say what you mean,' the March Hare went on. 'I do,' Alice hastily replied; 'at least—at least I mean what I say—that's the same thing, you know.' 'Not the same thing a bit!' said the Hatter. 'Why, you might just as well say that "I see what I eat" is the same thing as "I eat what I see!" '
Lewis Carroll 1832–98 English writer

It depends on what the meaning of 'is' is.
Bill Clinton 1946– American statesman

The meaning doesn't matter if it's only idle chatter of a transcendental kind.
W. S. Gilbert 1836–1911 English writer

It all depends what you mean by…
C. E. M. Joad 1891–1953 English philosopher, *characteristic response to questions*

God and I both knew what it meant once; now God alone knows.
Friedrich Klopstock 1724–1803 German poet

I pray thee, understand a plain man in his plain meaning.
William Shakespeare 1564–1616 English dramatist

The little girl had the making of a poet in her who, being told to be sure of her meaning before she spoke, said, 'How can I know what I think till I see what I say?'
Graham Wallas 1858–1932 British political scientist

Medicine see also **Health**, **Sickness**

Cure the disease and kill the patient.
Francis Bacon 1561–1626 English courtier

The remedy is worse than the disease.
Francis Bacon 1561–1626 English courtier

Physician, heal thyself.
Bible

He that sinneth before his Maker, let him fall into the hand of the physician.
Bible (Apocrypha)

Medicine

We all labour against our own cure, for death is the cure of all diseases.
Sir Thomas Browne 1605–82 English writer

Every day, in every way, I am getting better and better.
Émile Coué 1857–1926 French psychologist, *to be said 15 to 20 times, morning and evening*

Life is short, the art long.
Hippocrates c.460–357 BC Greek physician, *often quoted as* 'Ars longa, vita brevis'

As to diseases, make a habit of two things—to help, or at least to do no harm.
Hippocrates c.460–357 BC Greek physician

It may seem a strange principle to enunciate as the very first requirement in a Hospital that it should do the sick no harm.
Florence Nightingale 1820–1910 English nurse

One finger in the throat and one in the rectum makes a good diagnostician.
William Osler 1849–1919 Canadian-born physician

By medicine life may be prolonged, yet death
Will seize the doctor too.
William Shakespeare 1564–1616 English dramatist

Throw physic to the dogs; I'll none of it.
William Shakespeare 1564–1616 English dramatist

Formerly, when religion was strong and science weak, men mistook magic for medicine; now, when science is strong and religion weak, men mistake medicine for magic.
Thomas Szasz 1920–2012 Hungarian-born psychiatrist

Meeting see also **Parting**

Gin a body meet a body
Comin thro' the rye,
Gin a body kiss a body
Need a body cry?
Robert Burns 1759–96 Scottish poet

'Is there anybody there?' said the Traveller,
Knocking on the moonlit door.
Walter de la Mare 1873–1956 English poet

HUMPHREY BOGART: Of all the gin joints in all the towns in
all the world, she walks into mine.
Julius J. Epstein 1909–2001 and **others** American
screenwriters, *in the film* Casablanca

Some enchanted evening,
You may see a stranger,
You may see a stranger,
Across a crowded room.
Oscar Hammerstein II 1895–1960 American songwriter

Not many sounds in life, and I include all urban and all
rural sounds, exceed in interest a knock at the door.
Charles Lamb 1775–1834 English writer

How d'ye do, and how is the old complaint?
Lord Palmerston 1784–1865 British statesman, *reputed to be his
greeting to all those he did not know*

We'll meet again, don't know where,
Don't know when,
But I know we'll meet again some sunny day.
Ross Parker 1914–74 and **Hugh Charles** 1907–95 British
songwriters

Memory

When shall we three meet again
In thunder, lightning, or in rain?
William Shakespeare 1564–1616 English dramatist

Ill met by moonlight, proud Titania.
William Shakespeare 1564–1616 English dramatist

Dr Livingstone, I presume?
Henry Morton Stanley 1841–1904 British explorer

Why don't you come up sometime, and see me?
Mae West 1892–1980 American film actress

 # Memory

And we forget because we must
And not because we will.
Matthew Arnold 1822–88 English poet

Someone said that God gave us memory so that we might
have roses in December.
J. M. Barrie 1860–1937 Scottish writer

Nobody can remember more than seven of anything.
St Robert Bellarmine 1542–1621 Italian cardinal, *reason for
omitting the eight beatitudes from his catechism*

We'll tak a cup o' kindness yet,
For auld lang syne.
Robert Burns 1759–96 Scottish poet

Our memories are card-indexes consulted, and then put
back in disorder by authorities whom we do not control.
Cyril Connolly 1903–74 English writer

Memory

Everyone seems to remember with great clarity what
they were doing on November 22nd, 1963, at the precise
moment they heard President Kennedy was dead.

Frederick Forsyth 1938- English novelist

The heart's memory eliminates the bad and magnifies the
good, and…thanks to this artifice we manage to endure the
burden of the past.

Gabriel García Márquez 1927–2014 Colombian novelist

What are those blue remembered hills,
What spires, what farms are those?

A. E. Housman 1859–1936 English poet

The true art of memory is the art of attention.

Samuel Johnson 1709–84 English lexicographer

A cigarette that bears a lipstick's traces,
An airline ticket to romantic places;
And still my heart has wings
These foolish things
Remind me of you.

Holt Marvell 1901–69 English songwriter

You may break, you may shatter the vase, if you will,
But the scent of the roses will hang round it still.

Thomas Moore 1779–1852 Irish musician

Better by far you should forget and smile
Than that you should remember and be sad.

Christina Rossetti 1830–94 English poet

There's rosemary, that's for remembrance; pray, love,
remember.

William Shakespeare 1564–1616 English dramatist

Men

Are all men in disguise except those crying?
Dannie Abse 1923–2014 Welsh-born poet

ANTHONY QUINN: Am I not a man? And is not a man
stupid? I'm a man, so I married. Wife, children, house,
everything, the full catastrophe.
Michael Cacoyannis 1922–2011 Cypriot-born film director, *in the
film* Zorba the Greek

Older men treat women like possessions, which is why I like
younger men.
Joan Collins 1933– British actress

A man…is *so* in the way in the house!
Elizabeth Gaskell 1810–65 English novelist

Man is Nature's sole mistake!
W. S. Gilbert 1836–1911 English writer

Years ago, manhood was an opportunity for achievement,
and now it is a problem to be overcome.
Garrison Keillor 1942– American writer

Why can't a woman be more like a man?
Men are so honest, so thoroughly square;
Eternally noble, historically fair.
Alan Jay Lerner 1918–86 American songwriter

Give me macho, or give me death.
Madonna 1958– American pop singer

Somehow a bachelor never quite gets over the idea that he is
a thing of beauty and a boy forever.
Helen Rowland 1875–1950 American writer

Sigh no more, ladies, sigh no more,
Men were deceivers ever.
> **William Shakespeare** 1564–1616 English dramatist

It's not the men in my life that counts—it's the life in
my men.
> **Mae West** 1892–1980 American film actress

Men and Women see also **Woman's Role**

Women are really much nicer than men:
No wonder we like them.
> **Kingsley Amis** 1922–95 English novelist

In societies where men are truly confident of their own
worth, women are not merely tolerated but valued.
> **Aung San Suu Kyi** 1945– Burmese political leader

Men look at women. Women watch themselves being
looked at.
> **John Berger** 1926–2017 British writer

Man's love is of man's life a thing apart,
'Tis woman's whole existence.
> **Lord Byron** 1788–1824 English poet

The man's desire is for the woman; but the woman's desire is
rarely other than for the desire of the man.
> **Samuel Taylor Coleridge** 1772–1834 English poet

Any woman who is sure of her own wits is a match at any
time for a man who is not sure of his own temper.
> **Wilkie Collins** 1824–89 English novelist

There is more difference within the sexes than between
them.
> **Ivy Compton-Burnett** 1884–1969 English novelist

Men and Women

In the sex-war thoughtlessness is the weapon of the male, vindictiveness of the female.
Cyril Connolly 1903–74 English writer

[Woman] is defined and differentiated with reference to man and not he with reference to her; she is the incidental, the inessential as opposed to the essential.
Simone de Beauvoir 1908–86 French novelist

A woman needs a man like a fish needs a bicycle.
Irina Dunn 1948– Australian writer and politician

Men are from Mars, women are from Venus.
John Gray 1951– American writer

Women have very little idea of how much men hate them.
Germaine Greer 1939– Australian feminist

The female of the species is more deadly than the male.
Rudyard Kipling 1865–1936 English writer

A woman can forgive a man for the harm he does her, but she can never forgive him for the sacrifices he makes on her account.
W. Somerset Maugham 1874–1965 English novelist

He for God only, she for God in him.
John Milton 1608–74 English poet

I admit it is better fun to punt than to be punted, and that a desire to have all the fun is nine-tenths of the law of chivalry.
Dorothy L. Sayers 1893–1957 English writer

'Tis strange what a man may do, and a woman yet think him an angel.
William Makepeace Thackeray 1811–63 English novelist

After all these years, I see that I was mistaken about Eve in the beginning; it is better to live outside the Garden with her than inside it without her.
Mark Twain 1835–1910 American writer

Me Tarzan, you Jane.
Johnny Weissmuller 1904–84 American film actor

Whatever women do they must do twice as well as men to be thought half as good.
Charlotte Whitton 1896–1975 Canadian writer

All women become like their mothers. That is their tragedy. No man does. That's his.
Oscar Wilde 1854–1900 Irish dramatist

Middle Age

Years ago we discovered the exact point, the dead centre of middle age. It occurs when you are too young to take up golf and too old to rush up to the net.
Franklin P. Adams 1881–1960 American journalist

You are living in a land you no longer recognize. You don't know the language.
Martin Amis 1949– English novelist

I am past thirty, and three parts iced over.
Matthew Arnold 1822–88 English poet

Nel mezzo del cammin di nostra vita.
Midway along the path of our life.
Dante Alighieri 1265–1321 Italian poet

At eighteen our convictions are hills from which we look; at forty-five they are caves in which we hide.
F. Scott Fitzgerald 1896–1940 American novelist

Middle Age

The afternoon of human life must also have a significance of its own and cannot be merely a pitiful appendage to life's morning.
Carl Gustav Jung 1875–1961 Swiss psychologist

Men at forty
Learn to close softly
The doors to rooms they will not be
Coming back to.
Donald Justice 1925–2004 American poet

At forty-five,
What next, what next?
At every corner,
I meet my Father,
my age, still alive.
Robert Lowell 1917–77 American poet

The lovely thing about being forty is that you can appreciate twenty-five-year-old men more.
Colleen McCullough 1937–2015 Australian writer

Middle age is when you've met so many people that every new person you meet reminds you of someone else.
Ogden Nash 1902–71 American humorist

Do you think my mind is maturing late,
Or simply rotted early?
Ogden Nash 1902–71 American humorist, *on facing forty*

One of the pleasures of middle age is to *find out* that one WAS right, and that one was much righter than one knew at say 17 or 23.
Ezra Pound 1885–1972 American poet

One's prime is elusive. You little girls, when you grow up, must be on the alert to recognise your prime at whatever time of your life it may occur.
Muriel Spark 1918–2006 British novelist

By the time you hit 50, I reckon you've earned your
wrinkles, so why not be proud of them?
Twiggy 1949– English model

The Mind ✳

Our modern skulls house a Stone Age mind.
Leda Cosmides 1957– and **John Tooby** – American
psychologist and American anthropologist

It is not enough to have a good mind; the main thing is to
use it well.
René Descartes 1596–1650 French philosopher

On earth there is nothing great but man; in man there is
nothing great but mind.
William Hamilton 1788–1856 Scottish metaphysician

O the mind, mind has mountains; cliffs of fall
Frightful, sheer, no-man-fathomed.
Gerard Manley Hopkins 1844–89 English poet

Everyone complains of his memory, and no one complains
of his judgement.
Duc de la Rochefoucauld 1613–80 French moralist

The mind loves the unknown. It loves images whose
meaning is unknown, since the meaning of the mind itself
is unknown.
René Magritte 1898–1967 Belgian surrealist painter

The mind of man is capable of anything.
Guy de Maupassant 1850–93 French writer

The mind is its own place, and in itself
Can make a heaven of hell, a hell of heaven.
John Milton 1608–74 English poet

Misfortune

Those who are caught in mental cages can often picture
freedom, it just has no attractive power.
  Iris Murdoch 1919–99 English novelist

That's the classical mind at work, runs fine inside but looks
dingy on the surface.
  Robert M. Pirsig 1928–2017 American writer

Why waste money on psychotherapy when you can listen to
the B Minor Mass?
  Michael Torke 1961– American composer

 # Misfortune

Prosperity doth best discover vice, but adversity doth best
discover virtue.
  Francis Bacon 1561–1626 English courtier

And always keep a-hold of Nurse
For fear of finding something worse.
  Hilaire Belloc 1870–1953 British writer

Man is born unto trouble, as the sparks fly upward.
  Bible

There is no greater pain than to remember a happy time
when one is in misery.
  Dante Alighieri 1265–1321 Italian poet

In the words of one of my more sympathetic correspondents,
it has turned out to be an 'annus horribilis'.
  Elizabeth II 1926– British monarch

I left the room with silent dignity, but caught my foot in
the mat.
  George Grossmith 1847–1912 and **Weedon Grossmith**
1854–1919 English writers

Misfortune

Man needs difficulties; they are necessary for health.
Carl Gustav Jung 1875–1961 Swiss psychologist

In the misfortune of our best friends, we always find
something which is not displeasing to us.
Duc de la Rochefoucauld 1613–80 French moralist

Into each life some rain must fall,
Some days must be dark and dreary.
Henry Wadsworth Longfellow 1807–82 American poet

When fortune empties her chamberpot on your head,
smile—and say 'we are going to have a summer shower'.
John A. Macdonald 1815–91 Canadian statesman

now and then
there is a person born
who is so unlucky
that he runs into accidents
which started to happen
to somebody else.
Don Marquis 1878–1937 American poet

All the misfortunes of men derive from one single thing,
which is their inability to be at ease in a room.
Blaise Pascal 1623–62 French scientist and philosopher

I had never had a piece of toast
Particularly long and wide,
But fell upon the sanded floor,
And always on the buttered side.
James Payn 1830–98 English writer

Sweet are the uses of adversity,
Which like the toad, ugly and venomous,
Wears yet a precious jewel in his head.
William Shakespeare 1564–1616 English dramatist

Mistakes

One likes people much better when they're battered
down by a prodigious siege of misfortune than when they
triumph.

Virginia Woolf 1882–1941 English novelist

 # Mistakes

Truth lies within a little and certain compass, but error is
immense.

Henry St John, 1st Viscount Bolingbroke 1678–1751 English
politician

It is worse than a crime, it is a blunder.

Antoine Boulay de la Meurthe 1761–1840 French statesman,
on hearing of the execution of the Duc d'Enghien

I would rather be wrong, by God, with Plato…than be
correct with those men.

Cicero 106–43 BC Roman statesman, *of Pythagoreans*

I beseech you, in the bowels of Christ, think it possible you
may be mistaken.

Oliver Cromwell 1599–1658 English statesman

If all else fails, immortality can always be assured by
adequate error.

J. K. Galbraith 1908–2006 American economist

Mistakes are a fact of life
It is the response to error that counts.

Nikki Giovanni 1943– American poet

An expert is someone who knows some of the worst
mistakes that can be made in his subject and who manages
to avoid them.

Werner Heisenberg 1901–76 German mathematical physicist

Sometimes even excellent Homer nods.
Horace 65–8 BC Roman poet

Crooked things may be as stiff and unflexible as straight:
and men may be as positive in error as in truth.
John Locke 1632–1704 English philosopher

I don't like people who have never fallen or stumbled.
Their virtue is lifeless and it isn't of much value. Life hasn't
revealed its beauty to them.
Boris Pasternak 1890–1960 Russian novelist

To err is human, but it feels divine.
Dolly Parton 1946– American singer

The man who makes no mistakes does not usually make
anything.
Edward John Phelps 1822–1900 American lawyer

One Galileo in two thousand years is enough.
Pius XII 1876–1958 Italian pope, *on being asked to proscribe the works of Teilhard de Chardin*

A man should never be ashamed to own he has been in the
wrong, which is but saying, in other words, that he is wiser
to-day than he was yesterday.
Alexander Pope 1688–1744 English poet

It is better to be vaguely right than exactly wrong.
Carveth Read 1848–1931 English philosopher

'Forward, the Light Brigade!'
Was there a man dismayed?
Not though the soldier knew
Some one had blundered.
Alfred, Lord Tennyson 1809–92 English poet

Moderation

To lose one parent, Mr Worthing, may be regarded as a misfortune; to lose both looks like carelessness.
Oscar Wilde 1854–1900 Irish dramatist

 # Moderation

Nothing in excess.
Anonymous, *inscribed on the temple of Apollo at Delphi*

To many, total abstinence is easier than perfect moderation.
St Augustine of Hippo AD 354–430 Roman theologian

We know what happens to people who stay in the middle of the road. They get run down.
Aneurin Bevan 1897–1960 British politician

There's nothing in the middle of the road but yellow stripes and dead armadillos.
Jim Hightower 1943– American writer

There is moderation in everything.
Horace 65–8 BC Roman poet

You will go most safely by the middle way.
Ovid 43 BC–c.AD 17 Roman poet

To gild refinèd gold, to paint the lily…
Is wasteful and ridiculous excess.
William Shakespeare 1564–1616 English dramatist

Above all, gentlemen, not the slightest zeal.
Charles-Maurice de Talleyrand 1754–1838 French statesman

Use, do not abuse…Neither abstinence nor excess ever renders man happy.
Voltaire 1694–1778 French writer

Too much of a good thing can be wonderful.
Mae West 1892–1980 American film actress

Money see also **Poverty**, **Wealth**

Nothing that costs only a dollar is worth having.
Elizabeth Arden 1876–1966 American businesswoman

Money is like muck, not good except it be spread.
Francis Bacon 1561–1626 English courtier

Money, it turned out, was exactly like sex, you thought of nothing else if you didn't have it and thought of other things if you did.
James Baldwin 1924–87 American writer

Money speaks sense in a language all nations understand.
Aphra Behn 1640–89 English writer

The love of money is the root of all evil.
Bible

The sinews of war, unlimited money.
Cicero 106–43 BC Roman statesman

MR MICAWBER: Annual income twenty pounds, annual expenditure nineteen nineteen six, result happiness. Annual income twenty pounds, annual expenditure twenty pounds ought and six, result misery.
Charles Dickens 1812–70 English novelist

Money doesn't talk, it swears.
Bob Dylan 1941–   American singer

Money makes the world go around.
Fred Ebb 1932–2004 American songwriter

Money without brains is always dangerous.
Napoleon Hill 1883–1970 American writer

Put not your trust in money, but put your money in trust.
Oliver Wendell Holmes 1809–94 American physician

Money

A bank is a place that will lend you money if you can prove that you don't need it.
Bob Hope 1903–2003 American comedian

If possible honestly, if not, somehow, make money.
Horace 65–8 BC Roman poet

When a feller says, 'It hain't the money, but th' principle o' th' thing,' it's the money.
Frank McKinney ('Kin') Hubbard 1868–1930 American humorist

Economy does not lie in sparing money, but in spending it wisely.
T. H. Huxley 1825–95 English biologist

For I don't care too much for money,
For money can't buy me love.
John Lennon 1940–80 and **Paul McCartney** 1942– English pop singers

Take care of the pence, and the pounds will take care of themselves.
William Lowndes 1652–1724 English politician

Money is like a sixth sense without which you cannot make a complete use of the other five.
W. Somerset Maugham 1874–1965 English novelist

Money couldn't buy friends but you got a better class of enemy.
Spike Milligan 1918–2002 Irish comedian

I want to spend, and spend, and spend.
Vivian Nicholson 1936–2015 British pools winner, *said to reporters on arriving to collect her winnings of £152,000*

Expenditure rises to meet income.
C. Northcote Parkinson 1909–93 English writer

'My boy,' he says, 'always try to rub up against money, for if you rub up against money long enough, some of it may rub off on you.'
Damon Runyon 1884–1946 American writer

Money is always there but the pockets change.
Gertrude Stein 1874–1946 American writer

Pennies don't fall from heaven. They have to be earned on earth.
Margaret Thatcher 1925–2013 British stateswoman

You can be young without money but you can't be old without it.
Tennessee Williams 1911–83 American dramatist

Morality ✳

Morality is a private and costly luxury.
Henry Brooks Adams 1838–1918 American historian

Waste no more time arguing what a good man should be. Be one.
Marcus Aurelius AD 121–180 Roman emperor

Standards are always out of date. That is what makes them standards.
Alan Bennett 1934–   English writer

Food comes first, then morals.
Bertolt Brecht 1898–1956 German dramatist

The end justifies the means.
Hermann Busenbaum 1600–68 German theologian

What I know most surely about morality and the duty of man I owe to sport.
Albert Camus 1913–60 French writer, *often quoted as '...I owe to football'*

Morality

The last temptation is the greatest treason:
To do the right deed for the wrong reason.
T. S. Eliot 1888–1965 American-born British poet

I know only that what is moral is what you feel good after
and what is immoral is what you feel bad after.
Ernest Hemingway 1899–1961 American novelist

State a moral case to a ploughman and a professor. The
former will decide it as well, and often better than the latter,
because he has not been led astray by artificial rules.
Thomas Jefferson 1743–1826 American statesman

Two things fill the mind with ever new and increasing
wonder and awe, the more often and the more seriously
reflection concentrates upon them: the starry heaven above
me and the moral law within me.
Immanuel Kant 1724–1804 German philosopher

We know no spectacle so ridiculous as the British public in
one of its periodical fits of morality.
Lord Macaulay 1800–59 English historian

If people want a sense of purpose, they should get it from
their archbishops. They should not hope to receive it from
their politicians.
Harold Macmillan 1894–1986 British statesman

The most useful thing about a principle is that it can always
be sacrificed to expediency.
W. Somerset Maugham 1874–1965 English novelist

Morality is the herd-instinct in the individual.
Friedrich Nietzsche 1844–1900 German philosopher

There is no good or evil, there is only power, and those too
weak to seek it.
J. K. Rowling 1965– English novelist

There is nothing either good or bad, but thinking makes it so.
William Shakespeare 1564–1616 English dramatist

We know that a man can read Goethe or Rilke in the evening, that he can play Bach and Schubert, and go to his day's work at Auschwitz in the morning.
George Steiner 1929– American critic

If your morals make you dreary, depend upon it they are wrong.
Robert Louis Stevenson 1850–94 Scottish novelist

The more things are forbidden, the more popular they become.
Mark Twain 1835–1910 American writer

Moral indignation is jealousy with a halo.
H. G. Wells 1866–1946 English novelist

Mothers

What *do* girls do who haven't any mothers to help them through their troubles?
Louisa May Alcott 1832–88 American novelist

I have reached the age when a woman begins to perceive that she is growing into the person she least plans to resemble: her mother.
Anita Brookner 1928–2016 British novelist

The mother's yearning, that completest type of the life in another life which is the essence of real human love, feels the presence of the cherished child even in the debased, degraded man.
George Eliot 1819–80 English novelist

Mountains

A mother's arms are made of tenderness, and children sleep soundly in them.
Victor Hugo 1802–85 French writer

If I were damned of body and soul,
I know whose prayers would make me whole,
Mother o' mine, O mother o' mine.
Rudyard Kipling 1865–1936 English writer

Here's to the happiest years of our lives
Spent in the arms of other men's wives.
Gentlemen!—Our mothers!
Edwin Lutyens 1869–1944 English architect, *proposing a toast*

My mother had a good deal of trouble with me, but I think she enjoyed it.
Mark Twain 1835–1910 American writer

The hand that rocks the cradle
Is the hand that rules the world.
William Ross Wallace 1819–81 American poet

Guilt is to motherhood as grapes are to wine.
Fay Weldon 1931– British novelist

 # Mountains

The Alps, the Rockies and all other mountains are related to the earth, the Himalayas to the heavens.
J. K. Galbraith 1908–2006 American economist

There are other Annapurnas in the lives of men.
Maurice Herzog 1919–2012 French mountaineer

Well, we knocked the bastard off!
Edmund Hillary 1919–2008 New Zealand mountaineer,
on conquering Mount Everest, 1953

It is a fine thing to be out on the hills alone. A man can hardly be a beast or a fool alone on a great mountain.
Francis Kilvert 1840–79 English clergyman

Because it's there.
George Leigh Mallory 1886–1924 British mountaineer, *on being asked why he wanted to climb Mount Everest*

Climb the mountains and get their good tidings.
John Muir 1838–1914 Scottish-born American naturalist

My mountain did not seem to me a lifeless thing of rock and ice, but warm and friendly and living. She was a mother hen, and the other mountains were chicks under her wings.
Tenzing Norgay 1914–86 Sherpa mountaineer, *on Everest*

Mountains are the beginning and the end of all natural scenery.
John Ruskin 1819–1900 English critic

Do nothing in haste, look well to each step, and from the beginning think what may be the end.
Edward Whymper 1840–1911 English mountaineer

Murder ✳

Thou shalt not kill.
Bible

Mordre wol out; that se we day by day.
Geoffrey Chaucer c.1343–1400 English poet

Thou shalt not kill; but need'st not strive
Officiously to keep alive.
Arthur Hugh Clough 1819–61 English poet

Murder considered as one of the fine arts.
Thomas De Quincey 1785–1859 English essayist

Music

Kill a man, and you are an assassin. Kill millions of men,
and you are a conqueror. Kill everyone, and you are a god.
Jean Rostand 1894–1977 French biologist

Murder most foul, as in the best it is;
But this most foul, strange, and unnatural.
William Shakespeare 1564–1616 English dramatist

I don't think a man who has watched the sun going down
could walk away and commit a murder.
Laurens van der Post 1906–96 South African explorer

 Music see also **Singing**

Beethoven tells you what it's like to be Beethoven and
Mozart tells you what it's like to be human. Bach tells you
what it's like be the universe.
Douglas Adams 1952–2001 English writer

Please do not shoot the pianist. He is doing his best.
Anonymous, *printed notice in a dancing saloon, c.1882*

If you still have to ask…shame on you.
Louis Armstrong 1901–71 American jazz musician, *when asked
what jazz is; sometimes quoted as 'Man, if you gotta ask you'll
never know'*

All music is folk music, I ain't never heard no horse sing a
song.
Louis Armstrong 1901–71 American jazz musician

There are two golden rules for an orchestra: start together
and finish together. The public doesn't give a damn what
goes on in between.
Thomas Beecham 1879–1961 English conductor

Music is a higher revelation than all wisdom and philosophy.
Ludwig van Beethoven 1770–1827 German composer

Music…can name the unnameable, and communicate the unknowable.
Leonard Bernstein 1918–90 American composer

Music has charms to sooth a savage breast.
William Congreve 1670–1729 English dramatist

Extraordinary how potent cheap music is.
Noël Coward 1899–1973 English dramatist

It is only that which cannot be expressed otherwise that is worth expressing in music.
Frederick Delius 1862–1934 English composer

There is music in the air.
Edward Elgar 1857–1934 English composer

The hills are alive with the sound of music,
With songs they have sung for a thousand years.
Oscar Hammerstein II 1895–1960 American songwriter

Music is the pleasure the human mind experiences from counting without being aware that it is counting.
Gottfried Wilhelm Leibniz 1646–1716 German philosopher

Down the road someone is practising scales,
The notes like little fishes vanish with a wink of tails.
Louis MacNeice 1907–63 British poet

Fortissimo at last!
Gustav Mahler 1860–1911 Austrian composer, *on seeing Niagara Falls*

The symphony must be like the world. It must embrace everything.
Gustav Mahler 1860–1911 Austrian composer

Art is not national. It is international. Music is not written in red, white and blue; it is written with the heart's blood of the composer.
Nellie Melba 1861–1931 Australian operatic soprano

Music

Music is spiritual. The music business is not.
Van Morrison 1945- Irish musician

Melody is the essence of music. I compare a good melodist to a fine racer, and counterpoints to hack post-horses.
Wolfgang Amadeus Mozart 1756–91 Austrian composer

If I don't practise for one day, I know it; if I don't practise for two days, the critics know it; if I don't practise for three days, the audience knows it.
Ignacy Jan Paderewski 1860–1941 Polish pianist and statesman

Music is your own experience, your thoughts, your wisdom. If you don't live it, it won't come out of your horn.
Charlie Parker 1920–55 American jazz saxophonist

Music begins to atrophy when it departs too far from the dance…poetry begins to atrophy when it gets too far from music.
Ezra Pound 1885–1972 American poet

Applause is a receipt, not a note of demand.
Artur Schnabel 1882–1951 Austrian-born pianist

If music be the food of love, play on.
William Shakespeare 1564–1616 English dramatist

Hell is full of musical amateurs: music is the brandy of the damned.
George Bernard Shaw 1856–1950 Irish dramatist

Music is feeling, then, not sound.
Wallace Stevens 1879–1955 American poet

A good composer does not imitate; he steals.
Igor Stravinsky 1882–1971 Russian composer

You just pick a chord, go twang, and you've got music.
Sid Vicious 1957–79 British rock musician

Names

Proper names are poetry in the raw. Like all poetry they are untranslatable.

> **W. H. Auden** 1907–73 English poet

With a name like yours, you might be any shape, almost.

> **Lewis Carroll** 1832–98 English writer, *Humpty Dumpty to Alice*

Colin is the sort of name you give your goldfish for a joke.

> **Colin Firth** 1960– British actor

A self-made man may prefer a self-made name.

> **Learned Hand** 1872–1961 American judge, *on Samuel Goldfish changing his name to Samuel Goldwyn*

A nickname is the heaviest stone that the devil can throw at a man.

> **William Hazlitt** 1778–1830 English essayist

What's in a name? that which we call a rose
By any other name would smell as sweet.

> **William Shakespeare** 1564–1616 English dramatist

JAQUES: I do not like her name.
ORLANDO: There was no thought of pleasing you when she was christened.

> **William Shakespeare** 1564–1616 English dramatist

Nature

KATHARINE HEPBURN: Nature, Mr Allnutt, is what we are put into this world to rise above.

> **James Agee** 1909–55 American writer, *in the film* The African Queen

Nature does nothing without purpose or uselessly.

> **Aristotle** 384–322 BC Greek philosopher

Nature

A culture is no better than its woods.
W. H. Auden 1907–73 English poet

The subtlety of nature is greater many times over than the subtlety of the senses and understanding.
Francis Bacon 1561–1626 English courtier

The tree which moves some to tears of joy is in the eyes of others only a green thing that stands in the way.
William Blake 1757–1827 English poet

All things are artificial, for nature is the art of God.
Sir Thomas Browne 1605–82 English writer

I love not man the less, but nature more.
Lord Byron 1788–1824 English poet

What a book a devil's chaplain might write on the clumsy, wasteful, blundering, low, and horridly cruel works of nature!
Charles Darwin 1809–82 English naturalist

You may drive out nature with a pitchfork, yet she'll be constantly running back.
Horace 65–8 BC Roman poet

In her [Nature's] inventions nothing is lacking, and nothing is superfluous.
Leonardo da Vinci 1452–1519 Italian painter

It is far from easy to judge whether she [Nature] has proved a kind parent to man or a harsh step-mother.
Pliny the Elder AD 23–79 Roman senator

And this our life, exempt from public haunt,
Finds tongues in trees, books in the running brooks,
Sermons in stones, and good in everything.
William Shakespeare 1564–1616 English dramatist

Nature, red in tooth and claw.
Alfred, Lord Tennyson 1809–92 English poet

Nature is not a temple, but a workshop, and man's the workman in it.
Ivan Turgenev 1818–83 Russian novelist

One impulse from a vernal wood
May teach you more of man,
Of moral evil and of good,
Than all the sages can.
William Wordsworth 1770–1850 English poet

News see also **Journalism**

Tell it not in Gath, publish it not in the streets of Askelon.
Bible

How beautiful upon the mountains are the feet of him that bringeth good tidings.
Bible

If a dog bites a man it is not news, but if a man bites a dog it is.
Charles A. Dana 1819–97 American newspaper editor, *often attributed to the American journalist John B. Bogart*

Ill news hath wings, and with the wind doth go,
Comfort's a cripple and comes ever slow.
Michael Drayton 1563–1631 English poet

News is something which somebody wants suppressed—all the rest is advertising.
William Randolph Hearst 1863–1951 American newspaper publisher

What news on the Rialto?
William Shakespeare 1564–1616 English dramatist

Night

The nature of bad news infects the teller.
William Shakespeare 1564–1616 English dramatist

A squirrel dying in front of your house may be more relevant to your interests right now than people dying in Africa.
Mark Zuckerberg 1984– American computer entrepreneur

 # Night see also **Day**

Lighten our darkness, we beseech thee, O Lord; and by thy great mercy defend us from all perils and dangers of this night.
Book of Common Prayer 1662

I cannot walk through the suburbs in the solitude of the night without thinking that the night pleases us because it suppresses idle details, just as our memory does.
Jorge Luis Borges 1899–1986 Argentinian writer

The Sun's rim dips; the stars rush out;
At one stride comes the dark.
Samuel Taylor Coleridge 1772–1834 English poet

The curfew tolls the knell of parting day,
The lowing herd wind slowly o'er the lea,
The ploughman homeward plods his weary way,
And leaves the world to darkness and to me.
Thomas Gray 1716–71 English poet

The cares that infest the day
Shall fold their tents, like the Arabs,
And as silently steal away.
Henry Wadsworth Longfellow 1807–82 American poet

Night came down, and enfolded the earth in her dusky wings.
Virgil 70–19 BC Roman poet

Old Age ✳

Age is whatever you think it is. You are as old as you think you are.
> **Muhammad Ali** 1942–2016 American boxer

Age will not be defied.
> **Francis Bacon** 1561–1626 English courtier

To me old age is always fifteen years older than I am.
> **Bernard Baruch** 1870–1965 American financier

The days of our age are threescore years and ten; and though men be so strong that they come to fourscore years: yet is their strength then but labour and sorrow; so soon passeth it away, and we are gone.
> **Bible**

If I'd known I was gonna live this long, I'd have taken better care of myself.
> **Eubie Blake** 1883–1983 American ragtime pianist, *on reaching the age of 100*

What is called the serenity of age is only perhaps a euphemism for the fading power to feel the sudden shock of joy or sorrow.
> **Arthur Bliss** 1891–1975 English composer

The man who works and is not bored is never old.
> **Pablo Casals** 1876–1973 Spanish cellist

Considering the alternative, it's not too bad at all.
> **Maurice Chevalier** 1888–1972 French actor, *when asked what he felt about the advancing years on his 72nd birthday*

Oh, to be seventy again!
> **Georges Clemenceau** 1841–1929 French statesman, *on seeing a pretty girl on his eightieth birthday*

Old Age

It's a good thing to be old, because that means you haven't died yet, right?
Penelope Cruz 1974– Spanish actress

We turn not older with years, but newer every day.
Emily Dickinson 1830–86 American poet

While there's snow on the roof, it doesn't mean the fire has gone out in the furnace.
John G. Diefenbaker 1895–1979 Canadian statesman, *approaching his 80th birthday*

As Groucho Marx once said, 'Anyone can get old—all you have to do is to live long enough.'
Elizabeth II 1926– British monarch

Age does not make us childish, as men tell,
It merely finds us children still at heart.
Johann Wolfgang von Goethe 1749–1832 German writer

You will recognize, my boy, the first sign of old age: it is when you go out into the streets of London and realize for the first time how young the policemen look.
Seymour Hicks 1871–1949 English actor-manager

A person is always startled when he hears himself seriously called an old man for the first time.
Oliver Wendell Holmes 1809–94 American physician

When I am an old woman I shall wear purple
With a red hat which doesn't go, and doesn't suit me.
Jenny Joseph 1932– English poet

Perhaps being old is having lighted rooms
Inside your head, and people in them, acting.
People you know, yet can't quite name.
Philip Larkin 1922–85 English poet

Will you still need me, will you still feed me,
When I'm sixty four?
> **John Lennon** 1940–80 and **Paul McCartney** 1942–   English
> pop singers

Growing old is no more than a bad habit which a busy man
has no time to form.
> **André Maurois** 1885–1967 French writer

The unending problem of growing old was not how he
changed, but how things did.
> **Toni Morrison** 1931–   American novelist

Growing old is like being increasingly penalized for a crime
you haven't committed.
> **Anthony Powell** 1905–2000 English novelist

In a dream you are never eighty.
> **Anne Sexton** 1928–74 American poet

Second childishness, and mere oblivion,
Sans teeth, sans eyes, sans taste, sans everything.
> **William Shakespeare** 1564–1616 English dramatist

Every man desires to live long; but no man would be old.
> **Jonathan Swift** 1667–1745 Irish poet and satirist

Do not go gentle into that good night,
Old age should burn and rave at close of day;
Rage, rage against the dying of the light.
> **Dylan Thomas** 1914–53 Welsh poet

Old age is the most unexpected of all things that happen to
a man.
> **Leon Trotsky** 1879–1940 Russian revolutionary

When you are old and grey and full of sleep,
And nodding by the fire, take down this book

Opinion

And slowly read and dream of the soft look
Your eyes had once, and of their shadows deep.
    W. B. Yeats 1865–1939 Irish poet

 Opinion

Why should you mind being wrong if someone can show
you that you are?
    A. J. Ayer 1910–89 English philosopher

I've never had a humble opinion. If you've got an opinion,
why be humble about it?
    Joan Baez 1941– American singer

He that complies against his will,
Is of his own opinion still.
    Samuel Butler 1612–80 English poet

People seem not to see that their opinion of the world is
also a confession of character.
    Ralph Waldo Emerson 1803–82 American writer

Every man has a right to utter what he thinks truth, and
every other man has a right to knock him down for it.
Martyrdom is the test.
    Samuel Johnson 1709–84 English lexicographer

There are nine and sixty ways of constructing tribal lays,
And—every—single—one—of—them—is—right!
    Rudyard Kipling 1865–1936 English writer

Thank God, in these days of enlightenment and
establishment, everyone has a right to his own opinions,
and chiefly to the opinion that nobody else has a right to
theirs.
    Ronald Knox 1888–1957 English writer

New opinions are always suspected, and usually opposed, without any other reason but because they are not already common.
John Locke 1632–1704 English philosopher

There never were in the world two opinions alike, no more than two hairs or two grains; the most universal quality is diversity.
Montaigne 1533–92 French moralist

Some praise at morning what they blame at night;
But always think the last opinion right.
Alexander Pope 1688–1744 English poet

Optimism see also **Hope, Pessimism**

The lark's on the wing;
The snail's on the thorn:
God's in his heaven—
All's right with the world!
Robert Browning 1812–89 English poet

In the depths of winter, I finally learned that within me there lay an invincible summer.
Albert Camus 1913–60 French writer

I have known him come home to supper with a flood of tears, and a declaration that nothing was now left but a jail; and go to bed making a calculation of the expense of putting bow-windows to the house, 'in case anything turned up,' which was his favourite expression.
Charles Dickens 1812–70 English novelist, *of Mr Micawber*

Grab your coat, and get your hat,
Leave your worry on the doorstep,
Just direct your feet

Originality

To the sunny side of the street.
Dorothy Fields 1905–74 American songwriter

Cheer up! the worst is yet to come!
Philander Chase Johnson 1866–1939

Sin is behovely, but all shall be well and all shall be well and all manner of thing shall be well.
Julian of Norwich 1343–after 1416 English anchoress

an optimist is a guy
that has never had
much experience.
Don Marquis 1878–1937 American poet

You've got to ac-cent-tchu-ate the positive
Elim-my-nate the negative
Latch on to the affirmative
Don't mess with Mister In-between.
Johnny Mercer 1909–76 American songwriter

In this best of possible worlds…all is for the best.
Voltaire 1694–1778 French writer

 # Originality

Be daring, be different, be impractical, be anything that will assert integrity of purpose and imaginative vision against the play-it-safers, the creatures of the commonplace, the slaves of the ordinary.
Cecil Beaton 1904–80 English photographer

The original writer is not he who refrains from imitating others, but he who can be imitated by none.
François-René Chateaubriand 1768–1848 French writer

What is originality? Undetected plagiarism.
Dean Inge 1860–1954 English writer

If you steal from one author, it's plagiarism; if you steal from many, it's research.
    Wilson Mizner 1876–1933 American dramatist

It could be said of me that in this book I have only made up a bunch of other men's flowers, providing of my own only the string that ties them together.
    Montaigne 1533–92 French moralist

Posterity weaves no garlands for imitators.
    Friedrich von Schiller 1759–1805 German poet

Painting ✺

Good painters imitate nature, bad ones spew it up.
    Cervantes 1547–1616 Spanish novelist

The sound of water escaping from mill-dams, etc., willows, old rotten planks, slimy posts, and brickwork...those scenes made me a painter and I am grateful.
    John Constable 1776–1837 English painter

Remark all these roughnesses, pimples, warts, and everything as you see me; otherwise I will never pay a farthing for it.
    Oliver Cromwell 1599–1658 English statesman, *to Lely, on the painting of his portrait; commonly quoted as 'warts and all'*

I don't want justice, I want mercy.
    William Morris 'Billy' Hughes 1862–1952 British-born Australian statesman, *on having his portrait painted*

Art does not reproduce the visible; rather, it makes visible.
    Paul Klee 1879–1940 German-Swiss painter

This is not a pipe.
    René Magritte 1898–1967 Belgian surrealist painter, *on a painting of a tobacco pipe*

Parents

I paint objects as I think them, not as I see them.
Pablo Picasso 1881–1973 Spanish painter

No, painting is not made to decorate apartments. It's an offensive and defensive weapon against the enemy.
Pablo Picasso 1881–1973 Spanish painter

I have seen, and heard, much of Cockney impudence before now; but never expected to hear a coxcomb ask two hundred guineas for flinging a pot of paint in the public's face.
John Ruskin 1819–1900 English critic, *on Whistler's Nocturne in Black and Gold*

Every time I paint a portrait I lose a friend.
John Singer Sargent 1856–1925 American painter

A good picture is equivalent to a good deed.
Vincent Van Gogh 1853–90 Dutch painter

No, I ask it for the knowledge of a lifetime.
James McNeill Whistler 1834–1903 American-born painter, *in his case against Ruskin, replying to the question: 'For two days' labour, you ask two hundred guineas?'*

 # Parents see also **Children**, **Family**

The joys of parents are secret, and so are their griefs and fears.
Francis Bacon 1561–1626 English courtier

Honour thy father and thy mother.
Bible

A wise son maketh a glad father: but a foolish son is the heaviness of his mother.
Bible

Parents

Having one child makes you a parent; having two you are a referee.
David Frost 1939–2013 English broadcaster

The father is always a Republican toward his son, and his mother's always a Democrat.
Robert Frost 1874–1963 American poet

Your children are not your children.
They are the sons and daughters of Life's longing for itself.
They came through you but not from you
And though they are with you yet they belong not to you.
Kahlil Gibran 1883–1931 Lebanese-born American writer

They fuck you up, your mum and dad.
They may not mean to, but they do.
They fill you with the faults they had
And add some extra, just for you.
Philip Larkin 1922–85 English poet

Parents can plant magic in a child's mind through certain words spoken with some thrilling quality of voice, some uplift of the heart and spirit.
Robert MacNeil 1931– Canadian writer

Love crawls with the baby, walks with the toddler, runs with the child, then stands aside to let the youth walk into adulthood.
Jo Ann Merrell

Children aren't happy with nothing to ignore,
And that's what parents were created for.
Ogden Nash 1902–71 American humorist

If you bungle raising your children I don't think whatever else you do well matters very much.
Jacqueline Kennedy Onassis 1929–94 American First Lady

Parties

No matter how old a mother is she watches her middle-aged children for signs of improvement.
Florida Scott-Maxwell 1883–1979 American writer

Parentage is a very important profession, but no test of fitness for it is ever imposed in the interest of the children.
George Bernard Shaw 1856–1950 Irish dramatist

The natural term of the affection of the human animal for its offspring is six years.
George Bernard Shaw 1856–1950 Irish dramatist

Parents learn a lot from their children about coping with life.
Muriel Spark 1918–2006 British novelist

You shouldn't sit in judgment of your parents. We did the best we could while being people too.
John Updike 1932–2009 American writer

Parents are the bones on which children sharpen their teeth.
Peter Ustinov 1921–2004 British actor

My children are ungrateful: they don't care. That is my great reward. They are free.
Fay Weldon 1931– British novelist

Children begin by loving their parents; after a time they judge them; rarely, if ever, do they forgive them.
Oscar Wilde 1854–1900 Irish dramatist

 Parties

The sooner every party breaks up the better.
Jane Austen 1775–1817 English novelist

Like other parties of the kind, it was first silent, then talky, then argumentative, then disputatious, then unintelligible, then altogethery, then inarticulate, and then drunk.
Lord Byron 1788–1824 English poet

At every party there are two kinds of people—those who want to go home and those who don't. The trouble is, they are usually married to each other.
Ann Landers 1918–2002 American advice columnist

At a dinner party one should eat wisely but not too well, and talk well but not too wisely.
W. Somerset Maugham 1874–1965 English novelist

He showed me his bill of fare to tempt me to dine with him; poh, said I, I value not your bill of fare, give me your bill of company.
Jonathan Swift 1667–1745 Irish poet and satirist

If one plays good music, people don't listen and if one plays bad music people don't talk.
Oscar Wilde 1854–1900 Irish dramatist

Parting see also **Meeting**

CORBETT: It's goodnight from me.
BARKER: And it's goodnight from him.
Ronnie Barker 1929–2005 and **Ronnie Corbett** 1930–2016 English comedians

I wish everyone, friend or foe, well. That is that. The end.
Tony Blair 1953– British statesman, *leaving the House of Commons*

ARNOLD SCHWARZENEGGER: I'll be back.
James Cameron 1954– Canadian film director, *in the film* The Terminator

Atque in perpetuum, frater, ave atque vale.
And so, my brother, hail, and farewell evermore!
Catullus c.84–c.54 BC Roman poet

Parting

You have sat too long here for any good you have been doing. Depart, I say, and let us done with you. In the name of God, go!

Oliver Cromwell 1599–1658 English statesman, *addressing the Rump Parliament*

Parting is all we know of heaven,
And all we need of hell.

Emily Dickinson 1830–86 American poet

Since there's no help, come let us kiss and part,
Nay, I have done: you get no more of me.

Michael Drayton 1563–1631 English poet

And ever has it been that love knows not its own depth until the hour of separation.

Kahlil Gibran 1883–1931 Lebanese-born American writer

GROUCHO MARX: If you can't leave in a taxi you can leave in a huff. If that's too soon, you can leave in a minute and a huff.

Bert Kalmar 1884–1947 and **others** American screenwriters, *in the film* Duck Soup

Leave them while you're looking good.

Anita Loos 1893–1981 American writer

Fare well my dear child and pray for me, and I shall for you and all your friends that we may merrily meet in heaven.

Thomas More 1478–1535 English scholar and saint

Good-night, good-night! parting is such sweet sorrow
That I shall say good-night till it be morrow.

William Shakespeare 1564–1616 English dramatist

The Past

Even a god cannot change the past.
Agathon b. c.445 BC Greek tragic poet

Nostalgia isn't what it used to be.
Anonymous

In every age 'the good old days' were a myth. No one ever
thought they were good at the time. For every age has
consisted of crises that seemed intolerable to the people
who lived through them.
Brooks Atkinson 1894–1984 American writer

Think only of the past as its remembrance gives you
pleasure.
Jane Austen 1775–1817 English novelist

Stands the Church clock at ten to three?
And is there honey still for tea?
Rupert Brooke 1887–1915 English poet

The moving finger writes; and, having writ,
Moves on: nor all thy piety nor wit
Shall lure it back to cancel half a line,
Nor all thy tears wash out a word of it.
Edward Fitzgerald 1809–83 English poet

The past is a foreign country: they do things differently
there.
L. P. Hartley 1895–1972 English novelist

O God! Put back Thy universe and give me yesterday.
Henry Arthur Jones 1851–1929 and **Henry Herman** 1832–94
English dramatists

Yesterday, all my troubles seemed so far away,
Now it looks as though they're here to stay.

Patience

Oh I believe in yesterday.
John Lennon 1940–80 and **Paul McCartney** 1942– English pop singers

Think of it, soldiers; from the summit of these pyramids, forty centuries look down upon you.
Napoleon I 1769–1821 French emperor

Things ain't what they used to be.
Ted Persons

I tell you the past is a bucket of ashes.
Carl Sandburg 1878–1967 American poet

Those who cannot remember the past are condemned to repeat it.
George Santayana 1863–1952 Spanish-born philosopher

What's gone and what's past help
Should be past grief.
William Shakespeare 1564–1616 English dramatist

O! call back yesterday, bid time return.
William Shakespeare 1564–1616 English dramatist

The past is the only dead thing that smells sweet.
Edward Thomas 1878–1917 English poet

But where are the snows of yesteryear?
François Villon c.1431–after 63 French poet

 ## Patience

We had better wait and see.
Herbert Asquith 1852–1928 British statesman

Our patience will achieve more than our force.
Edmund Burke 1729–97 Irish-born politician

Beware the fury of a patient man.
John Dryden 1631–1700 English poet

All human wisdom is contained in these two words, Wait and Hope.
Alexandre Dumas 1802–70 French novelist

They also serve who only stand and wait.
John Milton 1608–74 English poet

Patience is a bitter thing, but its fruit is sweet.
Sadi c.1213–c.91 Persian poet

Let nothing trouble you, nothing frighten you. All things are passing; God never changes. Patient endurance attains all things.
St Teresa of Ávila 1512–82 Spanish mystic

I am extraordinarily patient, provided I get my own way in the end.
Margaret Thatcher 1925–2013 British stateswoman

The strongest of all warriors are these two—time and patience.
Leo Tolstoy 1828–1910 Russian novelist

Patriotism

What pity is it
That we can die but once to serve our country!
Joseph Addison 1672–1719 English writer

Patriotism is a lively sense of collective responsibility. Nationalism is a silly cock crowing on its own dunghill.
Richard Aldington 1892–1962 English writer

A steady patriot of the world alone,
The friend of every country but his own.
George Canning 1770–1827 British statesman

Patriotism

Patriotism is not enough. I must have no hatred or
bitterness towards anyone.
> **Edith Cavell** 1865–1915 English nurse, *on the eve of her execution*

> Be England what she will,
With all her faults, she is my country still.
> **Charles Churchill** 1731–64 English poet

Our country! In her intercourse with foreign nations, may
she always be in the right; but our country, right or wrong.
> **Stephen Decatur** 1779–1820 American naval officer

If I had to choose between betraying my country and betraying
my friend, I hope I should have the guts to betray my country.
> **E. M. Forster** 1879–1970 English novelist

That this House will in no circumstances fight for its King
and Country.
> **D. M. Graham** 1911–99 British broadcaster, *motion for a debate
at the Oxford Union, 1933*

I only regret that I have but one life to lose for my country.
> **Nathan Hale** 1755–76 American revolutionary, *prior to his
execution by the British for spying*

Dulce et decorum est pro patria mori.

Lovely and honourable it is to die for one's country.
> **Horace** 65–8 BC Roman poet

Patriotism is the last refuge of a scoundrel.
> **Samuel Johnson** 1709–84 English lexicographer

And so, my fellow Americans: ask not what your country
can do for you—ask what you can do for your country.
> **John F. Kennedy** 1917–63 American statesman

I fell in love with my country when I was a prisoner in
someone else's.
> **John McCain** 1936– American politician

My country, right or wrong; if right, to be kept right; and if wrong, to be set right!
Carl Schurz 1829–1906 American soldier

Breathes there the man, with soul so dead,
Who never to himself hath said,
This is my own, my native land!
Sir Walter Scott 1771–1832 Scottish novelist

You'll never have a quiet world till you knock the patriotism out of the human race.
George Bernard Shaw 1856–1950 Irish dramatist

I vow to thee, my country—all earthly things above—
Entire and whole and perfect, the service of my love.
Cecil Spring-Rice 1859–1918 British diplomat

The cricket test—which side do they cheer for?…Are you still looking back to where you came from or where you are?
Norman Tebbit 1931– British politician, *on the loyalties of Britain's immigrant population*

Peace

They shall beat their swords into plowshares, and their spears into pruninghooks: nation shall not lift up sword against nation, neither shall they learn war any more.
Bible

The peace of God, which passeth all understanding, shall keep your hearts and minds through Christ Jesus.
Bible

Give peace in our time, O Lord.
Book of Common Prayer 1662

Peace

This is the second time in our history that there has come back from Germany to Downing Street peace with honour. I believe it is peace for our time.
Neville Chamberlain 1869–1940 British statesman

In His will is our peace.
Dante Alighieri 1265–1321 Italian poet

Lord Salisbury and myself have brought you back peace— but a peace I hope with honour.
Benjamin Disraeli 1804–81 British statesman

Go placidly amid the noise and the haste, and remember what peace there may be in silence.
Max Ehrmann 1872–1945 American writer

I think that people want peace so much that one of these days governments had better get out of the way and let them have it.
Dwight D. Eisenhower 1890–1969 American statesman

If we are to reach real peace in this world, and if we are to carry on a real war against war, we shall have to begin with the children.
Mahatma Gandhi 1869–1948 Indian statesman

Give peace a chance.
John Lennon 1940–80 and **Paul McCartney** 1942– English pop singers

A war can perhaps be won single-handedly. But peace— lasting peace—cannot be secured without the support of all.
Luiz Inácio Lula da Silva 1945– Brazilian statesman

War appears to be as old as mankind, but peace is a modern invention.
Henry Maine 1822–88 English jurist

You can't separate peace from freedom because no one can be at peace unless he has his freedom.
Malcolm X 1925–65 American civil rights campaigner

…Peace hath her victories
No less renowned than war.
John Milton 1608–74 English poet

Enough of blood and tears. Enough.
Yitzhak Rabin 1922–95 Israeli statesman

They make a wilderness and call it peace.
Tacitus C.AD 56–after 117 Roman historian

Shantih, shantih, shantih.
Peace! Peace! Peace!
The Upanishads 800–200 BC Hindu sacred treatises

Let him who desires peace, prepare for war.
Vegetius fl. AD 379–395 Roman military writer

Perfection

The pursuit of perfection, then, is the pursuit of sweetness and light.
Matthew Arnold 1822–88 English poet

Pictures of perfection as you know make me sick and wicked.
Jane Austen 1775–1817 English novelist

Faultless to a fault.
Robert Browning 1812–89 English poet

Forget your perfect offering
There is a crack in everything
That's how the light gets in.
Leonard Cohen 1934–2016 Canadian singer

Persistence

Trifles make perfection, and perfection is no trifle.
Michelangelo 1475–1564 Italian artist

The best is the best, though a hundred judges have declared
it so.
Arthur Quiller-Couch 1863–1944 English critic

Perfection is finally attained not when there is no longer
anything to add but when there is no longer anything to
take away, when a body has been stripped down to its
nakedness.
Antoine de Saint-Exupéry 1900–44 French novelist

How many things by season seasoned are
To their right praise and true perfection!
William Shakespeare 1564–1616 English dramatist

Finality is death. Perfection is finality.
Nothing is perfect. There are lumps in it.
James Stephens 1882–1950 Irish poet

The best is the enemy of the good.
Voltaire 1694–1778 French writer

The intellect of man is forced to choose
Perfection of the life, or of the work.
W. B. Yeats 1865–1939 Irish poet

 Persistence see also **Determination**

Nothing in the world can take the place of persistence.
Talent will not; nothing is more common than unsuccessful
men with talent. Genius will not; unrewarded genius is
almost a proverb. Education will not; the world is full
of educated derelicts. Persistence and determination are

omnipotent. The slogan 'press on' has solved and always will
solve the problems of the human race.
Calvin Coolidge 1872–1933 American statesman

There must be a beginning of any great matter, but the
continuing unto the end until it be thoroughly finished
yields the true glory.
Francis Drake c.1540–96 English sailor

Pick yourself up,
Dust yourself off,
Start all over again.
Dorothy Fields 1905–74 American songwriter

The drop of rain maketh a hole in the stone, not by violence,
but by oft falling.
Hugh Latimer c.1485–1555 English martyr

Keep right on to the end of the road,
Keep right on to the end.
Tho' the way be long, let your heart be strong,
Keep right on round the bend.
Harry Lauder 1870–1950 Scottish music-hall entertainer

Either don't attempt it, or carry it through to the end.
Ovid 43 BC–c.AD 17 Roman poet

Perseverance, dear my lord,
Keeps honour bright.
William Shakespeare 1564–1616 English dramatist

'Tis known by the name of perseverance in a good cause,—
and of obstinacy in a bad one.
Laurence Sterne 1713–68 English novelist

What is the victory of a cat on a hot tin roof?—I wish
I knew…Just staying on it, I guess, as long as she can.
Tennessee Williams 1911–83 American dramatist

Pessimism

 Pessimism see also **Despair**, **Optimism**

WOODY ALLEN: I feel that life is—is divided up into the horrible and the miserable.
Woody Allen 1935- and **Marshall Brickman** 1941-
American film director and American screenwriter, *in the film* Annie Hall

The optimist proclaims that we live in the best of all possible worlds; and the pessimist fears this is true.
James Branch Cabell 1879-1958 American writer

I don't consider myself a pessimist. I think of a pessimist as someone who is waiting for it to rain. And I feel soaked to the skin.
Leonard Cohen 1934-2016 Canadian singer

If way to the Better there be, it exacts a full look at the worst.
Thomas Hardy 1840-1928 English novelist

Man hands on misery to man.
It deepens like a coastal shelf.
Get out as early as you can,
And don't have any kids yourself.
Philip Larkin 1922-85 English poet

If we see light at the end of the tunnel,
It's the light of the oncoming train.
Robert Lowell 1917-77 American poet

The nice part about being a pessimist is that you are constantly being either proven right or pleasantly surprised.
George F. Will 1941- American columnist

'Twixt the optimist and pessimist
The difference is droll:

The optimist sees the doughnut
But the pessimist sees the hole.
McLandburgh Wilson b. 1892

Philosophy ✳

Metaphysics is the finding of bad reasons for what we
believe upon instinct.
F. H. Bradley 1846–1924 English philosopher

If it was so, it might be; and if it were so, it would be: but as
it isn't, it ain't. That's logic.
Lewis Carroll 1832–98 English writer

There is nothing so absurd but some philosopher has said it.
Cicero 106–43 BC Roman statesman

I refute it *thus*.
Samuel Johnson 1709–84 English lexicographer, *kicking a
large stone by way of refuting Bishop Berkeley's theory of the non-
existence of matter*

The philosophers have only interpreted the world in various
ways; the point is to change it.
Karl Marx 1818–83 German philosopher

No more things should be presumed to exist than are
absolutely necessary.
William of Occam c.1285–1349 English philosopher, 'Occam's
razor', not found in this form in his writings, although he frequently
used similar expressions

The point of philosophy is to start with something so simple
as not to seem worth stating, and to end with something so
paradoxical that no one will believe it.
Bertrand Russell 1872–1970 British philosopher

The unexamined life is not worth living.
Socrates 469–399 BC Greek philosopher

Photography

The safest general characterization of the European philosophical tradition is that it consists of a series of footnotes to Plato.
Alfred North Whitehead 1861–1947 English philosopher

Philosophy is a battle against the bewitchment of our intelligence by means of language.
Ludwig Wittgenstein 1889–1951 Austrian-born philosopher

 # Photography

There are always two people in every picture: the photographer and the viewer.
Ansel Adams 1902–84 American photographer

A photograph is a secret about a secret. The more it tells you the less you know.
Diane Arbus 1923–71 American photographer

Most things in life are moments of pleasure and a lifetime of embarrassment; photography is a moment of embarrassment and a lifetime of pleasure.
Tony Benn 1925–2014 British politician

In photography you've got to be quick, quick, quick, like an animal and a prey.
Henri Cartier-Bresson 1908–2004 French photographer

You press the button, we do the rest.
George Eastman 1854–1932 American inventor, *advertising slogan to launch the Kodak camera, 1888*

The important thing is not the camera but the eye.
Alfred Eisenstaedt 1898–1995 American photographer

Photography deals exquisitely with appearances, but nothing is what it appears to be.
Duane Michals 1932– American photographer

The photographer is like the cod which produces a million eggs in order that one may reach maturity.
George Bernard Shaw 1856–1950 Irish dramatist

My idea of a good picture is one that's in focus and of a famous person doing something unfamous. It's being in the right place at the wrong time.
Andy Warhol 1927–87 American artist

Planning ✳

Be prepared.
Lord Baden-Powell 1857–1941 English soldier, *motto of the Scout Association*

We are ready for any unforeseen event which may or may not happen.
George W. Bush 1946– American statesman

Probability is the very guide of life.
Joseph Butler 1692–1752 English bishop

First things first, second things never.
Shirley Conran 1932– English writer

In preparing for battle I have always found that plans are useless, but planning is indispensable.
Dwight D. Eisenhower 1890–1969 American statesman

No plan of operations reaches with any certainty beyond the first encounter with the enemy's main force.
Helmuth von Moltke 1800–91 Prussian military commander, *often quoted as 'no plan survives first contact with the enemy'*

A good plan violently executed *Now* is better than a perfect plan next week.
George S. Patton 1885–1945 American general

Pleasure

There are no small steps in great affairs.
Cardinal de Retz 1613–79 French cardinal

The thing that is important is the thing that is not seen.
Antoine de Saint-Exupéry 1900–44 French novelist

If we had had more time for discussion we should probably
have made a great many more mistakes.
Leon Trotsky 1879–1940 Russian revolutionary

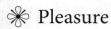 # Pleasure

One half of the world cannot understand the pleasures of
the other.
Jane Austen 1775–1817 English novelist

The great pleasure in life is doing what people say you
cannot do.
Walter Bagehot 1826–77 English economist

I'm tired of Love: I'm still more tired of Rhyme.
But Money gives me pleasure all the time.
Hilaire Belloc 1870–1953 British writer

Let us have wine and women, mirth and laughter,
Sermons and soda-water the day after.
Lord Byron 1788–1824 English poet

The essence of pleasure is spontaneity.
Germaine Greer 1939–   Australian feminist

Speed, it seems to me, provides the one genuinely modern
pleasure.
Aldous Huxley 1894–1963 English novelist

The less we indulge our pleasures the more we enjoy them.
Juvenal c.AD 60–c.140 Roman satirist

Ever let the fancy roam,
Pleasure never is at home.
John Keats 1795–1821 English poet

The greatest pleasure I know, is to do a good action by stealth, and to have it found out by accident.
Charles Lamb 1775–1834 English writer

Who loves not woman, wine, and song
Remains a fool his whole life long.
Martin Luther 1483–1546 German theologian

Pleasure is nothing else but the intermission of pain.
John Selden 1584–1654 English historian

Life would be very pleasant if it were not for its enjoyments.
R. S. Surtees 1805–64 English novelist

All the things I really like to do are either illegal, immoral, or fattening.
Alexander Woollcott 1887–1943 American writer

Poetry

A poet's hope: to be,
like some valley cheese,
local, but prized elsewhere.
W. H. Auden 1907–73 English poet

Prose is when all the lines except the last go on to the end. Poetry is when some of them fall short of it.
Jeremy Bentham 1748–1832 English philosopher

The reason Milton wrote in fetters when he wrote of Angels and God, and at liberty when of Devils and Hell, is because he was a true Poet, and of the Devil's party without knowing it.
William Blake 1757–1827 English poet

Poetry

All poets are mad.
Robert Burton 1577–1640 English clergyman

That willing suspension of disbelief for the moment, which constitutes poetic faith.
Samuel Taylor Coleridge 1772–1834 English poet

Prose = words in their best order;—poetry = the *best* words in the best order.
Samuel Taylor Coleridge 1772–1834 English poet

I used to think all poets were Byronic.
They're mostly wicked as a ginless tonic
And wild as pension plans.
Wendy Cope 1945– English poet

If I read a book [and] it makes my whole body so cold no fire can ever warm me, I know *that* is poetry. If I feel physically as if the top of my head were taken off, I know *that* is poetry. These are the only way I know it. Is there any other way.
Emily Dickinson 1830–86 American poet

Immature poets imitate; mature poets steal.
T. S. Eliot 1888–1965 American-born British poet

Poetry is a subject as precise as geometry.
Gustave Flaubert 1821–80 French novelist

Like a piece of ice on a hot stove the poem must ride on its own melting.
Robert Frost 1874–1963 American poet

As soon as war is declared it will be impossible to hold the poets back. Rhyme is still the most effective drum.
Jean Giraudoux 1882–1944 French dramatist

Skilled or unskilled, we all scribble poems.
Horace 65–8 BC Roman poet

Poetry

[BOSWELL:] Sir, what is poetry?
[JOHNSON:] Why Sir, it is much easier to say what it is not.
We all *know* what light is; but it is not easy to *tell* what it is.
    Samuel Johnson 1709–84 English lexicographer

If poetry comes not as naturally as the leaves to a tree it had
better not come at all.
    John Keats 1795–1821 English poet

A poem should not mean
But be.
    Archibald MacLeish 1892–1982 American poet

Writing a book of poetry is like dropping a rose petal down
the Grand Canyon and waiting for the echo.
    Don Marquis 1878–1937 American poet

Rhyme being…but the invention of a barbarous age, to set
off wretched matter and lame metre.
    John Milton 1608–74 English poet

Most people ignore most poetry
because
most poetry ignores most people.
    Adrian Mitchell 1932–2008 English writer

All a poet can do today is warn.
    Wilfred Owen 1893–1918 English poet

Poets are the unacknowledged legislators of the world.
    Percy Bysshe Shelley 1792–1822 English poet

Poetry is the spontaneous overflow of powerful feelings: it
takes its origin from emotion recollected in tranquillity.
    William Wordsworth 1770–1850 English poet

We make out of the quarrel with others, rhetoric, but of the
quarrel with ourselves, poetry.
    W. B. Yeats 1865–1939 Irish poet

Politicians see also **Politics**

A constitutional statesman is in general a man of common
opinion and uncommon abilities.
>   **Walter Bagehot** 1826–77 English economist

I am not going to spend any time whatsoever in attacking
the Foreign Secretary…If we complain about the tune, there
is no reason to attack the monkey when the organ grinder
is present.
>   **Aneurin Bevan** 1897–1960 British politician

Your representative owes you, not his industry only, but
his judgement; and he betrays, instead of serving you, if he
sacrifices it to your opinion.
>   **Edmund Burke** 1729–97 Irish-born politician

An honest politician is one who when he's bought stays
bought.
>   **Simon Cameron** 1799–1889 American politician

A minister who moves about in society is in a position to
read the signs of the times even in a festive gathering, but
one who remains shut up in his office learns nothing.
>   **Duc de Choiseul** 1719–85 French politician

It is the ability to foretell what is going to happen tomorrow,
next week, next month, and next year. And to have the
ability afterwards to explain why it didn't happen.
>   **Winston Churchill** 1874–1965 British statesman, *on the
>   qualifications for becoming a politician*

There are no true friends in politics. We are all sharks
circling, and waiting, for traces of blood to appear in the
water.
>   **Alan Clark** 1928–99 British politician

Definition of an independent Member of Parliament, viz. one that could not be depended upon.

> **Edward Stanley, 14th Earl of Derby** 1799–1869 British Conservative statesman

'Do you pray for the senators, Dr Hale?' 'No, I look at the senators and I pray for the country.'

> **Edward Everett Hale** 1822–1909 American clergyman

Politicians are the same all over. They promise to build a bridge where there is no river.

> **Nikita Khrushchev** 1894–1971 Soviet statesman

Forever poised between a cliché and an indiscretion.

> **Harold Macmillan** 1894–1986 British statesman, *on the life of a Foreign Secretary*

What I want is men who will support me when I am in the wrong.

> **Lord Melbourne** 1779–1848 British statesman, *replying to a politician who said 'I will support you as long as you are in the right'*

A statesman is a politician who places himself at the service of the nation. A politician is a statesman who places the nation at his service.

> **Georges Pompidou** 1911–74 French statesman

A statesman is a politician who's been dead 10 or 15 years.

> **Harry S. Truman** 1884–1972 American statesman

If you want a friend in Washington, get a dog.

> **Harry S. Truman** 1884–1972 American statesman

All those men have their price.

> **Robert Walpole** 1676–1745 English statesman, *of fellow parliamentarians*

Politics see also **Democracy**, **Government**

In politics the middle way is none at all.
John Adams 1735–1826 American statesman

Man is by nature a political animal.
Aristotle 384–322 BC Greek philosopher

Politics is the art of looking for trouble, finding it
everywhere, diagnosing it wrongly and applying unsuitable
remedies.
Ernest Benn 1875–1954 English publisher

Politics is the art of the possible.
Otto von Bismarck 1815–98 German statesman

A statesman…must wait until he hears the steps of God
sounding through events; then leap up and grasp the hem
of his garment.
Otto von Bismarck 1815–98 German statesman

Magnanimity in politics is not seldom the truest wisdom;
and a great empire and little minds go ill together.
Edmund Burke 1729–97 Irish-born politician

In politics, there is no use looking beyond the next
fortnight.
Joseph Chamberlain 1836–1914 British politician

In politics, what begins in fear usually ends in folly.
Samuel Taylor Coleridge 1772–1834 English poet

You campaign in poetry. You govern in prose.
Mario Cuomo 1932–2015 American politician

International life is right-wing, like nature. The social
contract is left-wing, like humanity.
Régis Debray 1940– French Marxist theorist

'Two nations; between whom there is no intercourse and
no sympathy; who are as ignorant of each other's habits,
thoughts, and feelings, as if they were dwellers in different
zones, or inhabitants of different planets...' 'You speak of—'
said Egremont, hesitatingly, 'THE RICH AND THE POOR.'

Benjamin Disraeli 1804–81 British statesman

Damn your principles! Stick to your party.

Benjamin Disraeli 1804–81 British statesman

I never dared be radical when young
For fear it would make me conservative when old.

Robert Frost 1874–1963 American poet

Politics is not the art of the possible. It consists in choosing
between the disastrous and the unpalatable.

J. K. Galbraith 1908–2006 American economist

If I could not go to Heaven but with a party, I would not go
there at all.

Thomas Jefferson 1743–1826 American statesman

The great nations have always acted like gangsters, and the
small nations like prostitutes.

Stanley Kubrick 1928–99 American film director

Who? Whom?

Lenin 1870–1924 Russian revolutionary, *definition of political
science, meaning 'Who will outstrip whom?'*

Politics is a marathon, not a sprint.

Ken Livingstone 1945– British politician

If you want to succeed in politics, you must keep your
conscience well under control.

David Lloyd George 1863–1945 British statesman

The opposition of events.

Harold Macmillan 1894–1986 British statesman, *on his biggest
problem; popularly quoted as 'Events, dear boy. Events'*

Pollution

Politics is war without bloodshed while war is politics with bloodshed.
Mao Zedong 1893–1976 Chinese statesman

Never doubt that a small group of thoughtful committed citizens can change the world. In fact, it's the only thing that ever has.
Margaret Mead 1901–78 American anthropologist

Political language…is designed to make lies sound truthful and murder respectable, and to give an appearance of solidity to pure wind.
George Orwell 1903–50 English novelist

Socialism can only arrive by bicycle.
José Antonio Viera Gallo 1943– Chilean politician

A week is a long time in politics.
Harold Wilson 1916–95 British statesman

A liberal is a conservative who's been arrested.
Tom Wolfe 1931– American writer

 ## Pollution see also **Environment**

Woe to her that is filthy and polluted, to the oppressing city!
Bible

NOISE, *n*. A stench in the ear…The chief product and authenticating sign of civilization.
Ambrose Bierce 1842–c.1914 American writer

Over increasingly large areas of the United States, spring now comes unheralded by the return of the birds, and the early mornings are strangely silent where once they were filled with the beauty of bird song.
Rachel Carson 1907–64 American zoologist

Man has been endowed with reason, with the power to
create, so that he can add to what he's been given. But up
to now he hasn't been a creator, only a destroyer. Forests
keep disappearing, rivers dry up, wild life's become extinct,
the climate's ruined and the land grows poorer and uglier
every day.

Anton Chekhov 1860–1904 Russian writer

The river Rhine, it is well known,
Doth wash your city of Cologne;
But tell me, Nymphs, what power divine
Shall henceforth wash the river Rhine?

Samuel Taylor Coleridge 1772–1834 English poet

The sea is the universal sewer.

Jacques Cousteau 1910–97 French underwater explorer

Clear the air! clean the sky! wash the wind!

T. S. Eliot 1888–1965 American-born British poet

The sanitary and mechanical age we are now entering
makes up for the mercy it grants to our sense of smell by the
ferocity with which it assails our sense of hearing. As usual,
what we call 'progress' is the exchange of one nuisance for
another nuisance.

Havelock Ellis 1859–1939 English sexologist

And all is seared with trade; bleared, smeared with toil;
And wears man's smudge and shares man's smell.

Gerard Manley Hopkins 1844–89 English poet

It goes so heavily with my disposition that this goodly
frame, the earth, seems to me a sterile promontory;
this most excellent canopy, the air, look you, this brave
o'erhanging firmament, this majestical roof fretted with
golden fire, why, it appears no other thing to me but a foul
and pestilent congregation of vapours.

William Shakespeare 1564–1616 English dramatist

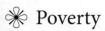

Poverty

✳ Poverty

Make poverty history.
Anonymous, *campaign slogan, 2005*

The poor have the sufferings to which they are fairly
accustomed.
W. H. Auden 1907–73 English poet

Anyone who has ever struggled with poverty knows how
extremely expensive it is to be poor.
James Baldwin 1924–87 American writer

The poor always ye have with you.
Bible

When I give food to the poor they call me a saint. When
I ask why the poor have no food they call me a communist.
Helder Camara 1909–99 Brazilian priest

There is no scandal like rags, nor any crime so shameful as
poverty.
George Farquhar 1678–1707 Irish dramatist

I want there to be no peasant in my kingdom so poor that
he is unable to have a chicken in his pot every Sunday.
Henri IV 1553–1610 French monarch

Oh! God! that bread should be so dear,
And flesh and blood so cheap!
Thomas Hood 1799–1845 English poet

It's easy to be independent when you've got money. But to
be independent when you haven't got a thing—that's the
Lord's test.
Mahalia Jackson 1911–72 American singer

Resolve not to be poor: whatever you have, spend less.
Poverty is a great enemy to human happiness; it certainly

destroys liberty, and it makes some virtues impracticable, and others extremely difficult.

Samuel Johnson 1709-84 English lexicographer

The misfortunes of poverty carry with them nothing harder to bear than that it makes men ridiculous.

Juvenal c.AD 60-c.140 Roman satirist

Overcoming poverty is not a gesture of charity. It is an act of justice.

Nelson Mandela 1918-2013 South African statesman

The greatest of evils and the worst of crimes is poverty.

George Bernard Shaw 1856-1950 Irish dramatist

Poverty is no disgrace to a man, but it is confoundedly inconvenient.

Sydney Smith 1771-1845 English essayist

A hungry man is not a free man.

Adlai Stevenson 1900-65 American politician

Sixteen tons, what do you get?
Another day older and deeper in debt.
Say brother, don't you call me 'cause I can't go
I owe my soul to the company store.

Merle Travis 1917-83 American singer

Power

Power tends to corrupt and absolute power corrupts absolutely.

Lord Acton 1834-1902 British historian

Every dictator uses religion as a prop to keep himself in power.

Benazir Bhutto 1953-2007 Pakistani stateswoman

Power

The most potent weapon in the hands of the oppressor is the mind of the oppressed.
Steve Biko 1946–77 South African anti-apartheid campaigner

A man may build himself a throne of bayonets, but he cannot sit on it.
Dean Inge 1860–1954 English writer, *quoted by Boris Yeltsin at the time of the failed military coup in Russia, 1991*

Power without love is reckless and abusive, and love without power is sentimental and anaemic. Power at its best is love implementing the demands of justice, and justice at its best is power correcting everything that stands against love.
Martin Luther King 1929–68 American civil rights leader

Power is the great aphrodisiac.
Henry Kissinger 1923– American politician

Power? It's like a Dead Sea fruit. When you achieve it, there is nothing there.
Harold Macmillan 1894–1986 British statesman

Political power grows out of the barrel of a gun.
Mao Zedong 1893–1976 Chinese statesman

On the highest throne in the world, we still sit only on our bottom.
Montaigne 1533–92 French moralist

Who controls the past controls the future: who controls the present controls the past.
George Orwell 1903–50 English novelist

You only have power over people as long as you don't take *everything* away from them. But when you've robbed a man of *everything* he's no longer in your power—he's free again.
Alexander Solzhenitsyn 1918–2008 Russian novelist

The Pope! How many divisions has *he* got?
> **Joseph Stalin** 1879–1953 Soviet dictator, *on being asked to encourage Catholicism in Russia by way of conciliating the Pope*

Practicality

Put your trust in God, my boys, and keep your powder dry.
> **Valentine Blacker** 1728–1823 Irish soldier, *'Oliver's Advice', often attributed to Oliver Cromwell himself*

The colour of the cat doesn't matter as long as it catches the mice.
> **Deng Xiaoping** 1904–97 Chinese statesman

Common sense is the best distributed commodity in the world, for every man is convinced that he is well supplied with it.
> **René Descartes** 1596–1650 French philosopher

Common sense is nothing more than a deposit of prejudices laid down in the mind before you reach eighteen.
> **Albert Einstein** 1879–1955 German-born theoretical physicist

Praise the Lord and pass the ammunition.
> **Howell Forgy** 1908–83 American naval chaplain, *at Pearl Harbor, while sailors passed ammunition by hand to the deck*

So I really think that American gentlemen are the best after all, because kissing your hand may make you feel very very good but a diamond and safire bracelet lasts forever.
> **Anita Loos** 1893–1981 American writer

Be nice to people on your way up because you'll meet 'em on your way down.
> **Wilson Mizner** 1876–1933 American dramatist

Common sense is not so common.
> **Voltaire** 1694–1778 French writer

Praise

The flattery of posterity is not worth much more than
contemporary flattery, which is worth nothing.
Jorge Luis Borges 1899–1986 Argentinian writer

The advantage of doing one's praising for oneself is that one
can lay it on so thick and exactly in the right places.
Samuel Butler 1835–1902 English novelist

Imitation is the sincerest of flattery.
Charles Caleb Colton c.1780–1832 English clergyman

How light, how small is the thing which casts down or
restores a mind greedy for praise.
Horace 65–8 BC Roman poet

All censure of a man's self is oblique praise. It is in order to
shew how much he can spare.
Samuel Johnson 1709–84 English lexicographer

And even the ranks of Tuscany
Could scarce forbear to cheer.
Lord Macaulay 1800–59 English historian

Damn with faint praise, assent with civil leer,
And without sneering, teach the rest to sneer.
Alexander Pope 1688–1744 English poet

But when I tell him he hates flatterers,
He says he does, being then most flattered.
William Shakespeare 1564–1616 English dramatist

I suppose flattery hurts no one, that is, if he doesn't inhale.
Adlai Stevenson 1900–65 American politician

Prayer

O Lord! thou knowest how busy I must be this day:
if I forget thee, do not thou forget me.
> **Jacob Astley** 1579–1652 English soldier, *before the Battle of Edgehill*

The wish for prayer is a prayer in itself.
> **Georges Bernanos** 1888–1948 French writer

Ask, and it shall be given you; seek, and ye shall find; knock,
and it shall be opened unto you.
> **Bible**

And lips say, 'God be pitiful,'
Who ne'er said, 'God be praised.'
> **Elizabeth Barrett Browning** 1806–61 English poet

Prayer is translation. A man translates himself into a child
asking for all there is in a language he has barely mastered.
> **Leonard Cohen** 1934–2016 Canadian singer

He prayeth best, who loveth best
All things both great and small.
> **Samuel Taylor Coleridge** 1772–1834 English poet

One single grateful thought raised to heaven is the most
perfect prayer.
> **G. E. Lessing** 1729–81 German dramatist

Often when I pray I wonder if I am not posting letters to a
non-existent address.
> **C. S. Lewis** 1898–1963 English literary scholar

The family that prays together stays together.
> **Al Scalpone** fl. 1947

Prejudice

My words fly up, my thoughts remain below:
Words without thoughts never to heaven go.
William Shakespeare 1564–1616 English dramatist

More things are wrought by prayer
Than this world dreams of.
Alfred, Lord Tennyson 1809–92 English poet

Whatever a man prays for, he prays for a miracle. Every
prayer reduces itself to this: Great God, grant that twice two
be not four.
Ivan Turgenev 1818–83 Russian novelist

You can't pray a lie.
Mark Twain 1835–1910 American writer

 Prejudice see also **Race**

Prejudices, it is well known, are most difficult to eradicate
from the heart whose soil has never been loosened or
fertilised by education.
Charlotte Brontë 1816–55 English novelist

Bigotry may be roughly defined as the anger of men who
have no opinions.
G. K. Chesterton 1874–1936 English writer

Being a star has made it possible for me to get insulted in
places where the average Negro could never *hope* to go and
get insulted.
Sammy Davis Jnr. 1925–90 American entertainer

Minds are like parachutes. They only function when they
are open.
James Dewar 1842–1923 Scottish physicist

Human diversity makes tolerance more than a virtue, it
makes it a requirement for survival.
   René Dubos 1901–82 French-born American microbiologist

If my theory of relativity is proven correct, Germany will
claim me as a German and France will declare that I am a
citizen of the world. Should my theory prove untrue, France
will say that I am a German and Germany will declare that
I am a Jew.
   Albert Einstein 1879–1955 German-born theoretical physicist

Make hatred hated!
   Anatole France 1844–1924 French man of letters

Drive out prejudices through the door, and they will return
through the window.
   Frederick the Great 1712–86 Prussian monarch

Without the aid of prejudice and custom, I should not be
able to find my way across the room.
   William Hazlitt 1778–1830 English essayist

The mind of the bigot [is like] the pupil of the eye; the more
light you pour on it, the more it contracts.
   Oliver Wendell Holmes 1809–94 American physician

Four legs good, two legs bad.
   George Orwell 1903–50 English novelist

We should therefore claim, in the name of tolerance, the
right not to tolerate the intolerant.
   Karl Popper 1902–94 Austrian-born philosopher

The only good Indian is a dead Indian.
   Philip Henry Sheridan 1831–88 American cavalry commander

Bigotry tries to keep truth safe in its hand
With a grip that kills it.
   Rabindranath Tagore 1861–1941 Bengali poet

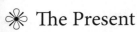 The Present

Can ye not discern the signs of the times?
   Bible

Take therefore no thought for the morrow: for the morrow shall take thought for the things of itself. Sufficient unto the day is the evil thereof.
   Bible

Few people can say: I am here. They look for themselves in the past and see themselves in the future.
   Georges Braque 1882–1963 French painter

Exhaust the little moment. Soon it dies.
And be it gash or gold it will not come
Again in this identical disguise.
   Gwendolyn Brooks 1917–2000 American poet

The rule is, jam to-morrow and jam yesterday—but never jam today.
   Lewis Carroll 1832–98 English writer

Forever—is composed of nows.
   Emily Dickinson 1830–86 American poet

Unborn TO-MORROW, and dead YESTERDAY,
Why fret about them if TO-DAY be sweet!
   Edward Fitzgerald 1809–83 English poet

Carpe diem, quam minimum credula postero.
Seize the day, put no trust in the future.
   Horace 65–8 BC Roman poet

Things are both more trivial than they ever were, and more important than they ever were, and the difference between

336

the trivial and the important doesn't seem to matter. But the nowness of everything is absolutely wondrous.

Dennis Potter 1935–94 English dramatist, *on his approaching death*

What is love? 'tis not hereafter;
Present mirth hath present laughter;
What's to come is still unsure.

William Shakespeare 1564–1616 English dramatist

Our work is for today, yesterday has gone, tomorrow has not yet come. We have only today.

Mother Teresa 1910–97 Roman Catholic nun

The Presidency

My country has in its wisdom contrived for me the most insignificant office that ever the invention of man contrived or his imagination conceived.

John Adams 1735–1826 American statesman, *of the vice-presidency*

To those of you who received honours, awards and distinctions, I say well done. And to the C students, I say you, too, can be president of the United States.

George W. Bush 1946– American statesman

When I was a boy I was told that anybody could become President. I'm beginning to believe it.

Clarence Darrow 1857–1938 American lawyer

No easy problems ever come to the President of the United States. If they are easy to solve, somebody else has solved them.

Dwight D. Eisenhower 1890–1969 American statesman

Pride

When the President does it, that means that it is not illegal.
Richard Nixon 1913–94 American statesman

I have got such a bully pulpit!
Theodore Roosevelt 1858–1919 American statesman

To announce that there must be no criticism of the president, or that we are to stand by the president, right or wrong, is not only unpatriotic and servile, but is morally treasonable to the American public.
Theodore Roosevelt 1858–1919 American statesman

 # Pride

Pride goeth before destruction, and an haughty spirit before a fall.
Bible

For whosoever exalteth himself shall be abased; and he that humbleth himself shall be exalted.
Bible

Proud people breed sad sorrows for themselves.
Emily Brontë 1818–48 English writer

He that is down needs fear no fall,
He that is low no pride.
He that is humble ever shall
Have God to be his guide.
John Bunyan 1628–88 English writer

URIAH HEEP: We are so very 'umble.
Charles Dickens 1812–70 English novelist

Pride helps us; and pride is not a bad thing when it only urges us to hide our own hurts, not to hurt others.
George Eliot 1819–80 English novelist

I can trace my ancestry back to a protoplasmal primordial atomic globule. Consequently, my family pride is something in-conceivable. I can't help it. I was born sneering.

   W. S. Gilbert 1836–1911 English writer

PLEASE ACCEPT MY RESIGNATION. I DON'T WANT TO BELONG TO ANY CLUB THAT WILL ACCEPT ME AS A MEMBER.

   Groucho Marx 1890–1977 American film comedian

No one can make you feel inferior without your consent.

   Eleanor Roosevelt 1884–1962 American humanitarian

As for conceit, what man will do any good who is not conceited? Nobody holds a good opinion of a man who has a low opinion of himself.

   Anthony Trollope 1815–82 English novelist

Progress

Want is one only of five giants on the road of reconstruction…the others are Disease, Ignorance, Squalor and Idleness.

   William Henry Beveridge 1879–1963 British economist

The thing that hath been, it is that which shall be; and that which is done is that which shall be done: and there is no new thing under the sun.

   Bible

pity this busy monster, manunkind,
not. Progress is a comfortable disease.

   e. e. cummings 1894–1962 American poet

Progress doesn't come from early risers—progress is made by lazy men looking for easier ways to do things.

   Robert Heinlein 1907–88 American science fiction writer

Progress

Is it progress if a cannibal uses knife and fork?
   Stanislaw Lec 1909–66 Polish writer

One step forward two steps back.
   Lenin 1870–1924 Russian revolutionary

Oui, cela était autrefois ainsi, mais nous avons changé tout cela.
Yes, in the old days that was so, but we have changed all that.
   Molière 1622–73 French comic dramatist

JOHN CLEESE: What have the Romans ever done for us?
   Monty Python's Flying Circus 1969–74 British television programme, *in the film* Monty Python's Life of Brian

If I have seen further it is by standing on the shoulders of giants.
   Isaac Newton 1642–1727 English mathematician

Forward ever, backward never.
   Kwame Nkrumah 1900–72 Ghanaian statesman

'Change' is scientific, 'progress' is ethical; change is indubitable, whereas progress is a matter of controversy.
   Bertrand Russell 1872–1970 British philosopher

The reasonable man adapts himself to the world: the unreasonable one persists in trying to adapt the world to himself. Therefore all progress depends on the unreasonable man.
   George Bernard Shaw 1856–1950 Irish dramatist

And he gave it for his opinion, that whoever could make two ears of corn or two blades of grass to grow upon a spot of ground where only one grew before, would deserve better

of mankind, and do more essential service to his country
than the whole race of politicians put together.
Jonathan Swift 1667–1745 Irish poet and satirist

Without deviation from the norm, progress is not possible.
Frank Zappa 1940–93 American rock musician

Promises

If [human life] depends on anything, it is on this frail cord,
flung from the forgotten hills of yesterday to the invisible
mountains of tomorrow.
G. K. Chesterton 1874–1936 English writer, *on the promise*

My tongue swore, but my mind's unsworn.
Euripides c.485–c.406 BC Greek dramatist, *lamenting the
breaking of an oath*

I believe that it is better to light one candle than promise a
million light bulbs.
Stephen Harper 1959– Canadian statesman

You always pay too much. Particularly for promises.
There ain't no such thing as a bargain promise.
Cormac McCarthy 1933– American novelist

A promise made is a debt unpaid.
Robert W. Service 1874–1958 Canadian poet

Promises and pie-crust are made to be broken.
Jonathan Swift 1667–1745 Irish poet and satirist

To promise not to do a thing is the surest way in the world
to make a body want to go and do that very thing.
Mark Twain 1835–1910 American writer

Protest

'It's always best on these occasions to do what the mob do.'
'But suppose there are two mobs?' suggested Mr Snodgrass.
'Shout with the largest,' replied Mr Pickwick.
   Charles Dickens 1812–70 English novelist

Making noise is an effective means of opposition.
   Joseph Goebbels 1897–1945 German Nazi leader

The citizen's first duty is unrest.
   Günter Grass 1927–2015 German writer

Even a purely moral act that has no hope of any immediate
and visible political effect can gradually and indirectly, over
time, gain in political significance.
   Václav Havel 1936–2011 Czech statesman

Ev'rywhere I hear the sound of marching, charging feet, boy,
'Cause summer's here and the time is right for fighting in
   the street, boy.
   Mick Jagger 1943–   and **Keith Richards** 1943–   English rock
   musicians

One-fifth of the people are against everything all the time.
   Robert Kennedy 1925–68 American politician

A riot is at bottom the language of the unheard.
   Martin Luther King 1929–68 American civil rights leader

The lady doth protest too much, methinks.
   William Shakespeare 1564–1616 English dramatist

Minorities…are almost always in the right.
   Sydney Smith 1771–1845 English essayist

I've always had the impression that real militants are like
cleaning women, doing a thankless, daily but necessary job.
   François Truffaut 1932–84 French film director

Punctuality

I love deadlines. I love the whooshing noise they make as they go by.
Douglas Adams 1952–2001 English writer

Punctuality is the politeness of kings.
Louis XVIII 1755–1824 French monarch

People who are late are often so much jollier than the people who have to wait for them.
E. V. Lucas 1868–1938 English writer

We must leave exactly on time…From now on everything must function to perfection.
Benito Mussolini 1883–1945 Italian dictator, *to a station-master*

You come most carefully upon your hour.
William Shakespeare 1564–1616 English dramatist

Punctuality is the virtue of the bored.
Evelyn Waugh 1903–66 English novelist

Punishment see also **Crime**

All punishment is mischief: all punishment in itself is evil.
Jeremy Bentham 1748–1832 English philosopher

He that spareth his rod hateth his son.
Bible

He that is without sin among you, let him first cast a stone at her.
Bible

Hanging is too good for him, said Mr Cruelty.
John Bunyan 1628–88 English writer

Punishment

It is one thing to praise discipline, and another to submit to it.
Cervantes 1547–1616 Spanish novelist

Excessive bail shall not be required, nor excessive fines imposed, nor cruel and unusual punishment inflicted.
Constitution of the United States 1787

Punishment is not for revenge, but to lessen crime and reform the criminal.
Elizabeth Fry 1780–1845 English prison reformer

My object all sublime
I shall achieve in time—
To let the punishment fit the crime—
The punishment fit the crime.
W. S. Gilbert 1836–1911 English writer

Awaiting the sensation of a short, sharp shock,
From a cheap and chippy chopper on a big black block.
W. S. Gilbert 1836–1911 English writer

Men are not hanged for stealing horses, but that horses may not be stolen.
Lord Halifax 1633–95 English politician

If my life teaches the public that men are made mad by bad treatment, and if the police are taught that they may not exasperate to madness men they persecute and ill treat, my life will not be entirely thrown away.
Ned Kelly 1855–80 Australian outlaw

Society needs to condemn a little more and understand a little less.
John Major 1943– British statesman

I went out to Charing Cross, to see Major-general Harrison hanged, drawn, and quartered; which was done there, he looking as cheerful as any man could do in that condition.
Samuel Pepys 1633–1703 English diarist

Quotations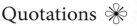

The surest way to make a monkey of a man is to quote him.
Robert Benchley 1889–1945 American humorist

It is a good thing for an uneducated man to read books of quotations.
Winston Churchill 1874–1965 British statesman

I hate quotation. Tell me what you know.
Ralph Waldo Emerson 1803–82 American writer

When a thing has been said and well said, have no scruple: take it and copy it.
Anatole France 1844–1924 French man of letters

I quote others only the better to express myself.
Montaigne 1533–92 French moralist

I always have a quotation for everything—it saves original thinking.
Dorothy L. Sayers 1893–1957 English writer

Famous remarks are very seldom quoted correctly.
Simeon Strunsky 1879–1948 American writer

What a good thing Adam had. When he said a good thing he knew nobody had said it before.
Mark Twain 1835–1910 American writer

OSCAR WILDE: How I wish I had said that.
WHISTLER: You will, Oscar, you will.
James McNeill Whistler 1834–1903 American-born painter

Some for renown on scraps of learning dote,
And think they grow immortal as they quote.
Edward Young 1683–1765 English poet

Race

 Race see also **Equality**, **Prejudice**

Black is beautiful.
Anonymous, *slogan of American civil rights campaigners, mid-1960s*

You have seen how a man was made a slave; you shall see how a slave was made a man.
Frederick Douglass c.1818–95 American former slave

I herewith commission you to carry out all preparations with regard to…a *total solution* of the Jewish question in those territories of Europe which are under German influence.
Hermann Goering 1893–1946 German Nazi leader

Though it be a thrilling and marvellous thing to be merely young and gifted in such times, it is doubly so, doubly dynamic—to be young, gifted and *black*.
Lorraine Hansberry 1930–65 American dramatist

When I look out at this convention, I see the face of America, red, yellow, brown, black, and white. We are all precious in God's sight—the real rainbow coalition.
Jesse Jackson 1941-   American clergyman

There are no 'white' or 'coloured' signs on the foxholes or graveyards of battle.
John F. Kennedy 1917–63 American statesman

I have a dream that my four little children will one day live in a nation where they will not be judged by the colour of their skin but by the content of their character.
Martin Luther King 1929–68 American civil rights leader

My son, your troubled eyes search mine,
Puzzled and hurt by colour line.

Your black skin as soft as velvet shine;
What can I tell you, son of mine?
Oodgeroo Noonuccal 1920–93 Australian poet

Our mistreatment was just not right, and I was tired of it.
Rosa Parks 1913–2005 American civil rights activist, *of her refusal to surrender her seat on a segregated bus in Alabama to a white man*

Where today are the Pequot? Where are the Narragansett, the Mohican, the Pokanoket, and many other once powerful tribes of our people? They have vanished before the avarice and oppression of the white man, as snow before the summer sun.
Tecumseh 1768–1813 Shawnee chief

Am I not a man and a brother.
Josiah Wedgwood 1730–95 English potter, *legend on Wedgwood cameo, depicting a kneeling African slave in chains*

Remember, Christians, Negroes black as Cain
May be refined, and join th' angelic train.
Phillis Wheatley c.1753–84 American poet

Growing up, I came up with this name: I'm a Cablinasian.
Tiger Woods 1975–   American golfer, *explaining his rejection of 'African-American' as the term to describe his Caucasian, Afro-American, Native American, Thai, and Chinese ancestry*

Railways

This is the Night Mail crossing the Border,
Bringing the cheque and the postal order,
Letters for the rich, letters for the poor,
The shop at the corner, the girl next door.
W. H. Auden 1907–73 English poet

Reading

Railways and the Church have their critics, but both are the best ways of getting a man to his ultimate destination.

Revd W. Awdry 1911–97 English writer

The only way of catching a train I have ever discovered is to miss the train before.

G. K. Chesterton 1874–1936 English writer

Railway termini. They are our gates to the glorious and the unknown. Through them we pass out into adventure and sunshine, to them, alas! we return.

E. M. Forster 1879–1970 English novelist

Sir, Saturday morning, although recurring at regular and well-foreseen intervals, always seems to take this railway by surprise.

W. S. Gilbert 1836–1911 English writer, *letter to the station-master at Baker Street, on the Metropolitan line*

That life-quickening atmosphere of a big railway station where everything is something trembling on the brink of something else.

Vladimir Nabokov 1899–1977 Russian novelist

 Reading see also **Books**

In science, read, by preference, the newest works; in literature, the oldest.

Edward Bulwer-Lytton 1803–73 British novelist

Choose an author as you choose a friend.

Wentworth Dillon, Earl of Roscommon c.1633–85 Irish poet

What do we ever get nowadays from reading to equal the excitement and the revelation in those first fourteen years?

Graham Greene 1904–91 English novelist

A man ought to read just as inclination leads him; for what he reads as a task will do him little good.
  Samuel Johnson 1709–84 English lexicographer

Curiously enough, one cannot *read* a book: one can only reread it. A good reader, a major reader, an active and creative reader is a rereader.
  Vladimir Nabokov 1899–1977 Russian novelist

Much reading is an oppression of the mind, and extinguishes the natural candle, which is the reason of so many senseless scholars in the world.
  William Penn 1644–1718 English Quaker

The bookful blockhead, ignorantly read,
With loads of learned lumber in his head.
  Alexander Pope 1688–1744 English poet

POLONIUS: What do you read, my lord?
HAMLET: Words, words, words.
  William Shakespeare 1564–1616 English dramatist

People say that life is the thing, but I prefer reading.
  Logan Pearsall Smith 1865–1946 American writer

Reading is to the mind what exercise is to the body.
  Richard Steele 1672–1729 Irish-born essayist

Reality ✳

It's as large as life, and twice as natural!
  Lewis Carroll 1832–98 English writer

Reality is that which, when you stop believing in it, doesn't go away.
  Philip K. Dick 1928–82 American writer

Relationships

> Human kind
> Cannot bear very much reality.
> **T. S. Eliot** 1888–1965 American-born British poet

All theory, dear friend, is grey, but the golden tree of actual life springs ever green.
Johann Wolfgang von Goethe 1749–1832 German writer

What is rational is actual and what is actual is rational.
G. W. F. Hegel 1770–1831 German philosopher

The camera makes everyone a tourist in other people's reality, and eventually in one's own.
Susan Sontag 1933–2004 American writer

> They said, 'You have a blue guitar,
> You do not play things as they are.'
>
> The man replied, 'Things as they are
> Are changed upon the blue guitar.'
> **Wallace Stevens** 1879–1955 American poet

The nineteenth century dislike of Realism is the rage of Caliban seeing his own face in the glass.
Oscar Wilde 1854–1900 Irish dramatist

BLANCHE: I don't want realism.
MITCH: Naw, I guess not.
BLANCHE: I'll tell you what I want. Magic!
Tennessee Williams 1911–83 American dramatist

 # Relationships

> Love is like the wild rose-briar;
> Friendship like the holly-tree:
> The holly is dark when the rose-briar blooms,
> But which will bloom most constantly?
> **Emily Brontë** 1818–48 English writer

Men love women, women love children; children love
hamsters—it's quite hopeless.
>**Alice Thomas Ellis** 1932–2005 English novelist

The ones we choose to love become our anchor
when the hawser of the blood-tie's hacked, or frays.
>**Tony Harrison** 1937– British poet

Three things in human life are important. The first is to be
kind. The second is to be kind. And the third is to be kind.
>**Henry James** 1843–1916 American novelist

Marriage may often be a stormy lake, but celibacy is almost
always a muddy horsepond.
>**Thomas Love Peacock** 1785–1866 English writer

Human relationships don't belong to engineering,
mathematics, chess, which offer problems that can be
perfectly solved. Human relationships grow, like trees.
>**J. B. Priestley** 1894–1984 English writer

KATHARINE HEPBURN: The time to make up your mind
about people is never.
>**Donald Ogden Stewart** 1894–1980 American humorist, *in the
film* The Philadelphia Story

By loving people without cause he discovered indubitable
causes for loving them.
>**Leo Tolstoy** 1828–1910 Russian novelist

Religion see also **Church**, **God**, **Prayer**

Render therefore unto Caesar the things which are Caesar's;
and unto God the things that are God's.
>**Bible**

One religion is as true as another.
>**Robert Burton** 1577–1640 English clergyman

Religion

Christians have burnt each other, quite persuaded
That all the Apostles would have done as they did.
Lord Byron 1788–1824 English poet

Putting moral virtues at the highest, and religion at the
lowest, religion must still be allowed to be a collateral
security, at least, to virtue; and every prudent man will
sooner trust to two securities than to one.
Lord Chesterfield 1694–1773 English writer

Science without religion is lame, religion without science
is blind.
Albert Einstein 1879–1955 German-born theoretical physicist

The various modes of worship, which prevailed in the
Roman world, were all considered by the people as equally
true; by the philosopher, as equally false; and by the
magistrate, as equally useful. And thus toleration produced
not only mutual indulgence, but even religious concord.
Edward Gibbon 1737–94 English historian

In all ages of the world, priests have been enemies of liberty.
David Hume 1711–76 Scottish philosopher

I go into the Muslim mosque and the Jewish synagogue and
the Christian church and I see one altar.
Jalal ad-Din ar-Rumi 1207–73 Persian poet

Religion's in the heart, not in the knee.
Douglas Jerrold 1803–57 English writer

No compulsion is there in religion.
The Koran

I count religion but a childish toy,
And hold there is no sin but ignorance.
Christopher Marlowe 1564–93 English dramatist

Religion…is the opium of the people.
Karl Marx 1818–83 German philosopher

Things have come to a pretty pass when religion is allowed to invade the sphere of private life.
Lord Melbourne 1779–1848 British statesman, *on hearing an evangelical sermon*

My country is the world, and my religion is to do good.
Thomas Paine 1737–1809 English political theorist

Is that which is holy loved by the gods because it is holy, or is it holy because it is loved by the gods?
Plato 429–347 BC Greek philosopher

Religion to me has always been the wound, not the bandage.
Dennis Potter 1935–94 English dramatist

'Men of sense are really but of one religion.'…'Pray, my lord, what religion is that which men of sense agree in?' 'Madam,' says the earl immediately, 'men of sense never tell it.'
Lord Shaftesbury 1621–83 English statesman

We have just enough religion to make us hate, but not enough to make us love one another.
Jonathan Swift 1667–1745 Irish poet and satirist

India has 2,000,000 gods, and worships them all. In religion all other countries are paupers; India is the only millionaire.
Mark Twain 1835–1910 American writer

Orthodoxy is my doxy; heterodoxy is another man's doxy.
William Warburton 1698–1779 English theologian

I went to America to convert the Indians; but oh, who shall convert me?
John Wesley 1703–91 English preacher

Retirement

So many gods, so many creeds,
So many paths that wind and wind,
While just the art of being kind
Is all the sad world needs.
> **Ella Wheeler Wilcox** 1855–1919 American poet

 # Retirement

Once I leave, I leave. I am not going to speak to the man on
the bridge, and I am not going to spit on the deck.
> **Stanley Baldwin** 1867–1947 British statesman, *on resigning*

If anything could have pulled me out of retirement, it would
have been an Indiana Jones film. But in the end, retirement
is just too damned much fun.
> **Sean Connery** 1930– Scottish actor

The most horrifying thing in the world is to be without an
adventure.
> **George Foreman** 1948– American boxer, *considering a
> comeback at 55*

The transition from Who's Who to Who's He.
> **Eddie George** 1938–2009 English banker

Learn to live well, or fairly make your will;
You've played, and loved, and ate, and drunk your fill:
Walk sober off; before a sprightlier age
Comes tittering on, and shoves you from the stage.
> **Alexander Pope** 1688–1744 English poet

As to that leisure evening of life, I must say that I do not
want it. I can conceive of no contentment of which toil is
not to be the immediate parent.
> **Anthony Trollope** 1815–82 English novelist

Revenge ✳

Revenge is a kind of wild justice, which the more man's nature runs to, the more ought law to weed it out.
Francis Bacon 1561–1626 English courtier

Vengeance is mine; I will repay, saith the Lord.
Bible

Sweet is revenge—especially to women.
Lord Byron 1788–1824 English poet

It may be that vengeance is sweet, and that the gods forbade vengeance to men because they reserved for themselves so delicious and intoxicating a drink. But no one should drain the cup to the bottom. The dregs are often filthy-tasting.
Winston Churchill 1874–1965 British statesman

Heaven has no rage, like love to hatred turned,
Nor Hell a fury, like a woman scorned.
William Congreve 1670–1729 English dramatist

RUSSELL CROWE: And I will have my vengeance, in this life or the next.
David Franzoni 1947– American screenwriter, *in the film* Gladiator

The Germans…are going to be squeezed as a lemon is squeezed—until the pips squeak.
Eric Geddes 1875–1937 British politician

Nobody ever forgets where he buried a hatchet.
Frank McKinney ('Kin') Hubbard 1868–1930 American humorist

Get your retaliation in first.
Carwyn James 1929–83 Welsh rugby player

Revolution

Men should be either treated generously or destroyed,
because they take revenge for slight injuries—for heavy ones
they cannot.
Niccolò Machiavelli 1469–1527 Italian political philosopher

Don't get mad, get everything.
Ivana Trump 1949– Czech model, *advice to wronged wives*

Revolution

Better to abolish serfdom from above than to wait till it
begins to abolish itself from below.
Alexander II 1818–81 Russian tsar

The most radical revolutionary will become a conservative
on the day after the revolution.
Hannah Arendt 1906–75 American philosopher

Those who have served the cause of the revolution have
ploughed the sea.
Simón Bolívar 1783–1830 Venezuelan statesman

Revolutions are celebrated when they are no longer
dangerous.
Pierre Boulez 1925–2016 French composer

Rebellion to tyrants is obedience to God.
John Bradshaw 1602–59 English judge

Would it not be easier
In that case for the government
To dissolve the people
And elect another?
Bertolt Brecht 1898–1956 German dramatist, *on the 1953
uprising in East Germany*

Revolution

All modern revolutions have ended in a reinforcement of the State.

> **Albert Camus** 1913–60 French writer

A desperate disease requires a dangerous remedy.

> **Guy Fawkes** 1570–1606 English conspirator

I will die like a true-blue rebel. Don't waste any time in mourning—organize.

> **Joe Hill** 1879–1915 American labour leader, *farewell telegram prior to his death by firing squad*

The generation which commences a revolution can rarely complete it.

> **Thomas Jefferson** 1743–1826 American statesman

When smashing monuments, save the pedestals—they always come in handy.

> **Stanislaw Lec** 1909–66 Polish writer

Après nous le déluge.

After us the deluge.

> **Madame de Pompadour** 1721–64 French courtesan

J'ai vécu.

I survived.

> **Abbé Emmanuel Joseph Sieyès** 1748–1836 French politician, *when asked what he had done during the French Revolution*

I have seen the future; and it works.

> **Lincoln Steffens** 1866–1936 American journalist, *following a visit to the Soviet Union in 1919*

Bliss was it in that dawn to be alive,
But to be young was very heaven!

> **William Wordsworth** 1770–1850 English poet, *on the French revolution*

Royalty

[A king] is the fountain of honour.
Francis Bacon 1561–1626 English courtier

Its mystery is its life. We must not let in daylight upon magic.
Walter Bagehot 1826–77 English economist, *on royalty*

The Sovereign has, under a constitutional monarchy such as ours, three rights—the right to be consulted, the right to encourage, the right to warn.
Walter Bagehot 1826–77 English economist

To be Prince of Wales is not a position. It is a predicament.
Alan Bennett 1934– English writer

A subject and a sovereign are clean different things.
Charles I 1600–49 British monarch

I'd like to be a queen in people's hearts but I don't see myself being Queen of this country.
Diana, Princess of Wales 1961–97 British princess

Everyone likes flattery; and when you come to Royalty you should lay it on with a trowel.
Benjamin Disraeli 1804–81 British statesman

I have found it impossible to carry the heavy burden of responsibility and to discharge my duties as King as I would wish to do without the help and support of the woman I love.
Edward VIII 1894–1972 British monarch, *radio broadcast following his abdication*

I know I have the body of a weak and feeble woman, but I have the heart and stomach of a king, and of a king of England too.
Elizabeth I 1533–1603 English monarch

L'État c'est moi.
I am the State.
>   **Louis XIV** 1638–1715 French monarch

Royalty is the gold filling in a mouthful of decay.
>   **John Osborne** 1929– English dramatist

Uneasy lies the head that wears a crown.
>   **William Shakespeare** 1564–1616 English dramatist

Monarchy is only the string that ties the robber's bundle.
>   **Percy Bysshe Shelley** 1792–1822 English poet

I will be good.
>   **Queen Victoria** 1819–1901 British monarch, *on being shown a chart of the line of succession*

Satisfaction see also **Discontent**

You never know what is enough unless you know what is more than enough.
>   **William Blake** 1757–1827 English poet

He is a wise man who does not grieve for the things which he has not, but rejoices for those which he has.
>   **Epictetus** C.AD 50–120 Phrygian philosopher

A book of verses underneath the bough,
A jug of wine, a loaf of bread—and Thou
Beside me singing in the wilderness—
And wilderness were paradise enow.
>   **Edward Fitzgerald** 1809–83 English poet

I can't get no satisfaction.
>   **Mick Jagger** 1943– and **Keith Richards** 1943– English rock musicians

Science

If one cannot catch the bird of paradise, better take a wet hen.
Nikita Khrushchev 1894–1971 Soviet statesman

So long as the great majority of men are not deprived of either property or honour, they are satisfied.
Niccolò Machiavelli 1469–1527 Italian political philosopher

He is well paid that is well satisfied.
William Shakespeare 1564–1616 English dramatist

As long as I have a want, I have a reason for living. Satisfaction is death.
George Bernard Shaw 1856–1950 Irish dramatist

Content is disillusioning to behold: what is there to be content about?
Virginia Woolf 1882–1941 English novelist

 # Science see also **Life Sciences**, **Technology**

When I find myself in the company of scientists, I feel like a shabby curate who has strayed by mistake into a drawing room full of dukes.
W. H. Auden 1907–73 English poet

Anybody who is not shocked by this subject has failed to understand it.
Niels Bohr 1885–1962 Danish physicist, *of quantum mechanics*

Basic research is what I am doing when I don't know what I am doing.
Wernher von Braun 1912–77 German-born rocket engineer

The aim of science is not to open the door to infinite wisdom, but to set a limit to infinite error.
Bertolt Brecht 1898–1956 German dramatist

Science

The essence of science: ask an impertinent question, and you are on the way to a pertinent answer.
Jacob Bronowski 1908–74 Polish-born scientist

If an elderly but distinguished scientist says that something is possible he is almost certainly right, but if he says that it is impossible he is very probably wrong.
Arthur C. Clarke 1917–2008 English science fiction writer

In science the credit goes to the man who convinces the world, not to the man to whom the idea first occurs.
Francis Darwin 1848–1925 English botanist

It is more important to have beauty in one's equations than to have them fit experiment.
Paul Dirac 1902–84 British theoetical physicist

I ask you to look both ways. For the road to a knowledge of the stars leads through the atom; and important knowledge of the atom has been reached through the stars.
Arthur Eddington 1882–1944 British astrophysicist

The grand aim of all science [is] to cover the greatest number of empirical facts by logical deduction from the smallest possible number of hypotheses or axioms.
Albert Einstein 1879–1955 German-born theoretical physicist

It can scarcely be denied that the supreme goal of all theory is to make the irreducible basic elements as simple and as few as possible without having to surrender the adequate representation of a single datum of experience.
Albert Einstein 1879–1955 German-born theoretical physicist, *often quoted as 'Everything should be made as simple as possible, but not simpler'*

Nothing is too wonderful to be true, if it be consistent with the laws of nature, and in such things as these, experiment is the best test of such consistency.
Michael Faraday 1791–1867 English scientist

Science

The great tragedy of Science—the slaying of a beautiful hypothesis by an ugly fact.
T. H. Huxley 1825–95 English biologist

Where observation is concerned, chance favours only the prepared mind.
Louis Pasteur 1822–95 French chemist

Science knows no country, because knowledge belongs to humanity.
Louis Pasteur 1822–95 French chemist

I almost think it is the ultimate destiny of science to exterminate the human race.
Thomas Love Peacock 1785–1866 English writer

A new scientific truth does not triumph by convincing its opponents and making them see the light, but rather because its opponents eventually die, and a new generation grows up that is familiar with it.
Max Planck 1858–1947 German physicist

Science is built up of facts, as a house is built of stones; but an accumulation of facts is no more a science than a heap of stones is a house.
Henri Poincaré 1854–1912 French mathematician

Nature, and Nature's laws lay hid in night.
God said, *Let Newton be!* and all was light.
Alexander Pope 1688–1744 English poet

Aristotle maintained that women have fewer teeth than men; although he was twice married, it never occurred to him to verify this statement by examining his wives' mouths.
Bertrand Russell 1872–1970 British philosopher

All science is either physics or stamp collecting.
Ernest Rutherford 1871–1937 New Zealand physicist

We haven't got the money, so we've got to think!
Ernest Rutherford 1871–1937 New Zealand physicist

Science is always wrong; it is the very artifice of men.
Science can never solve one problem without raising ten
more problems.
George Bernard Shaw 1856–1950 Irish dramatist

It did not last: the Devil howling 'Ho!
Let Einstein be!' restored the status quo.
J. C. Squire 1884–1958 English man of letters, *responding to
Pope's lines on Newton*

Scotland

There are few more impressive sights in the world than a
Scotsman on the make.
J. M. Barrie 1860–1937 Scottish writer

My heart's in the Highlands, my heart is not here;
My heart's in the Highlands a-chasing the deer.
Robert Burns 1759–96 Scottish poet

Scots, wha hae wi' Wallace bled,
Scots, wham Bruce has aften led,
Welcome to your gory bed,—
Or to victorie.
Robert Burns 1759–96 Scottish poet

From the lone shieling of the misty island
Mountains divide us, and the waste of seas—
Yet still the blood is strong, the heart is Highland,
And we in dreams behold the Hebrides!
John Galt 1779–1839 Scottish writer

The noblest prospect which a Scotchman ever sees, is the
high road that leads him to England!
Samuel Johnson 1709–84 English lexicographer

Sculpture

O Caledonia! stern and wild,
Meet nurse for a poetic child!
    Sir Walter Scott 1771–1832 Scottish novelist

Stands Scotland where it did?
    William Shakespeare 1564–1616 English dramatist

O flower of Scotland, when will we see your like again,
that fought and died for your wee bit hill and glen
and stood against him, proud Edward's army,
and sent him homeward tae think again.
    Roy Williamson 1936–90 Scottish musician

It is never difficult to distinguish between a Scotsman with a
grievance and a ray of sunshine.
    P. G. Wodehouse 1881–1975 English writer

 Sculpture

Most statues seem sad and introspective,
they hold their breath between coming and going,
They lament their devoured, once shuddering stone.
    Dannie Abse 1923–2014 Welsh-born poet

Carving is interrelated masses conveying an emotion: a
perfect relationship between the mind and the colour, light
and weight which is the stone, made by the hand which feels.
    Barbara Hepworth 1903–75 English sculptor

It's amazing what you can do with an E in A-level art,
twisted imagination and a chainsaw.
    Damien Hirst 1965– English artist, *after winning the 1995 Turner Prize*

The marble not yet carved can hold the form
Of every thought the greatest artist has.
    Michelangelo 1475–1564 Italian artist

The first hole made through a piece of stone is a revelation.
    Henry Moore 1898–1986 English sculptor

The Sea ❋

A willing foe and sea room.
    Anonymous, *naval toast in the time of Nelson*

They that go down to the sea in ships: and occupy their
business in great waters.
    Bible

Don't talk to me about naval tradition. It's nothing but rum,
sodomy, and the lash.
    Winston Churchill 1874–1965 British statesman

Water, water, everywhere,
And all the boards did shrink;
Water, water, everywhere,
Nor any drop to drink.
    Samuel Taylor Coleridge 1772–1834 English poet

No man will be a sailor who has contrivance enough to get
himself into a jail; for being in a ship is being in a jail, with
the chance of being drowned…A man in a jail has more
room, better food, and commonly better company.
    Samuel Johnson 1709–84 English lexicographer

It is an interesting biological fact that all of us have in our
veins the exact same percentage of salt in our blood that
exists in the ocean, and therefore, we have salt in our blood,
in our sweat, in our tears. We are tied to the ocean. And
when we go back to the sea—whether it is to sail or to watch
it—we are going back from whence we came.
    John F. Kennedy 1917–63 American statesman

Secrecy

I must go down to the seas again, to the lonely sea and
  the sky,
And all I ask is a tall ship and a star to steer her by.
> **John Masefield** 1878–1967 English poet

Meditation and water are wedded for ever.
> **Herman Melville** 1819–91 American novelist

The sea hates a coward!
> **Eugene O'Neill** 1888–1953 American dramatist

Whosoever commands the sea commands the trade;
whosoever commands the trade of the world commands
the riches of the world, and consequently the world itself.
> **Walter Ralegh** c.1552–1618 English courtier

Full fathom five thy father lies;
Of his bones are coral made:
Those are pearls that were his eyes:
Nothing of him that doth fade,
But doth suffer a sea-change
Into something rich and strange.
> **William Shakespeare** 1564–1616 English dramatist

Rocked in the cradle of the deep.
> **Emma Hart Willard** 1787–1870 American educationist

 # Secrecy

I shall be but a short time tonight. I have seldom spoken
with greater regret, for my lips are not yet unsealed.
> **Stanley Baldwin** 1867–1947 British statesman, *usually quoted
> as 'My lips are sealed'*

When thou doest alms, let not thy left hand know what thy
right hand doeth.
> **Bible**

Secrecy

The truth is out there.
> **Chris Carter** 1957– American screenwriter, *catchphrase;*
> The X Files

The small man said to the other: 'Where does a wise man
hide a pebble?' And the tall man answered in a low voice:
'On the beach.'
> **G. K. Chesterton** 1874–1936 English writer

I would not open windows into men's souls.
> **Elizabeth I** 1533–1603 English monarch

A secret in the Oxford sense: you may tell it to only one
person at a time.
> **Lord Franks** 1905–92 British philosopher

We dance round in a ring and suppose,
But the Secret sits in the middle and knows.
> **Robert Frost** 1874–1963 American poet

Once the toothpaste is out of the tube, it is awfully hard to
get it back in.
> **H. R. Haldeman** 1929–93 American Presidential assistant,
> *comment on the Watergate affair*

Love and a cough cannot be hid.
> **George Herbert** 1593–1633 English poet

Nothing weighs so heavy as a secret; women find it difficult
to carry one far. And I know a lot of men who are just like
women about this.
> **Jean de la Fontaine** 1621–95 French poet

It is wise to disclose what cannot be concealed.
> **Friedrich von Schiller** 1759–1805 German poet

A secret may be sometimes best kept by keeping the secret
of its being a secret.
> **Henry Taylor** 1800–86 British writer

 # The Self

Whatever you are is never enough; you must find a way to accept something however small from the other to make you whole.
Chinua Achebe 1930–2013 Nigerian novelist

Some thirty inches from my nose
The frontier of my Person goes,
And all the untilled air between
Is private *pagus* or demesne.
W. H. Auden 1907–73 English poet

Through the Thou a person becomes I.
Martin Buber 1878–1965 Austrian-born philosopher

Be who God meant you to be and you will set the world on fire.
St Catherine of Siena c.1347–80 Italian mystic

'You' your joys and your sorrows, your memories and ambitions, your sense of personal identity and free will, are in fact no more than the behaviour of a vast assembly of nerve cells and their associated molecules.
Francis Crick 1916–2004 English biophysicist

To study the self is to forget the self. To forget the self is to be authenticated by the myriad things.
Dogen Kigen 1200–53 Japanese Buddhist monk, *often quoted as '…to become one with the ten thousand things'*

If you have no confidence in self you are twice defeated in the race of life. With confidence you have won even before you have started.
Marcus Garvey 1887–1940 Jamaican political activist

I am the master of my fate:
I am the captain of my soul.
W. E. Henley 1849–1903 English poet

It is not contrary to reason to prefer the destruction of the whole world to the scratching of my finger.
David Hume 1711–76 Scottish philosopher

I am not a number, I am a free man!
Patrick McGoohan 1928–2009 English actor, *Number Six,* in The Prisoner

When a man points a finger at someone else, he should remember that four of his fingers are pointing to himself.
Louis Nizer 1902–94 American lawyer

The self is hateful.
Blaise Pascal 1623–62 French scientist and philosopher

Thus God and nature linked the gen'ral frame,
And bade self-love and social be the same.
Alexander Pope 1688–1744 English poet

Personal isn't the same as important.
Terry Pratchett 1948–2015 English novelist

Who is it that can tell me who I am?
William Shakespeare 1564–1616 English dramatist

It is easy—terribly easy—to shake a man's faith in himself. To take advantage of that to break a man's spirit is devil's work.
George Bernard Shaw 1856–1950 Irish dramatist

Whatever people think I am or say I am, that's what I'm not.
Alan Sillitoe 1928–2010 English writer

Rose is a rose is a rose, is a rose.
Gertrude Stein 1874–1946 American writer

If a man does not keep pace with his companions, perhaps it is because he hears a different drummer. Let him step to the music which he hears, however measured or far away.
Henry David Thoreau 1817–62 American writer

Self-Knowledge

Do I contradict myself?
Very well then I contradict myself,
(I am large, I contain multitudes.)
Walt Whitman 1819–92 American poet

 # Self-Knowledge

Know thyself.
Anonymous, *inscribed on the temple of Apollo at Delphi*

The image of myself which I try to create in my own mind
in order that I may love myself is very different from the
image which I try to create in the minds of others in order
that they may love me.
W. H. Auden 1907–73 English poet

Why beholdest thou the mote that is in thy brother's eye,
but considerest not the beam that is in thine own eye?
Bible

The one self-knowledge worth having is to know one's own
mind.
F. H. Bradley 1846–1924 English philosopher

O wad some Pow'r the giftie gie us
To see oursels as others see us!
It wad frae mony a blunder free us,
And foolish notion.
Robert Burns 1759–96 Scottish poet

How little do we know that which we are!
How less what we may be!
Lord Byron 1788–1824 English poet

I do not know whether I was then a man dreaming I was a
butterfly, or whether I am now a butterfly dreaming I am
a man.
Chuang-tzu (Zhuangzi) c.369–286 BC Chinese philosopher

I do not know myself, and God forbid that I should.
Johann Wolfgang von Goethe 1749–1832 German writer

He who knows others is wise;
He who knows himself is enlightened.
He who conquers others has physical strength.
He who conquers himself is strong.
Lao Tzu c.604–c.531 BC Chinese philosopher

All our knowledge is, ourselves to know.
Alexander Pope 1688–1744 English poet

This above all: to thine own self be true,
And it must follow, as the night the day,
Thou canst not then be false to any man.
William Shakespeare 1564–1616 English dramatist

Sex see also **Love**, **Marriage**

That [sex] was the most fun I ever had without laughing.
Woody Allen 1935– American film director

Don't knock masturbation. It's sex with someone I love.
Woody Allen 1935– American film director

On bisexuality: It immediately doubles your chances for a date on Saturday night.
Woody Allen 1935– American film director

Give me chastity and continency—but not yet!
St Augustine of Hippo AD 354–430 Roman theologian

It doesn't matter what you do in the bedroom as long as you don't do it in the street and frighten the horses.
Mrs Patrick Campbell 1865–1940 English actress

The pleasure is momentary, the position ridiculous, and the expense damnable.
Lord Chesterfield 1694–1773 English writer

Sex

Licence my roving hands, and let them go,
Behind, before, above, between, below.
O my America, my new found land,
My kingdom, safeliest when with one man manned.
>**John Donne** 1572–1631 English poet

I'll have what she's having.
>**Nora Ephron** 1941–2012 American screenwriter, *said by woman to waiter, seeing Sally acting an orgasm, in the film* When Harry Met Sally

BILLY CRYSTAL: Women need a reason to have sex, men just need a place.
>**Lowell Ganz** 1948– and **Babaloo Mandel** 1949– American screenwriters, *in the film* City Slickers

But did thee feel the earth move?
>**Ernest Hemingway** 1899–1961 American novelist

When I hear his steps outside my door I lie down on my bed, close my eyes, open my legs, and think of England.
>**Lady Hillingdon** 1857–1940

The only unnatural sex act is that which you cannot perform.
>**Alfred Kinsey** 1894–1956 American sex researcher

'Tisn't beauty, so to speak, nor good talk necessarily. It's just It. Some women'll stay in a man's memory if they once walked down a street.
>**Rudyard Kipling** 1865–1936 English writer

The Duke returned from the wars today and did pleasure me in his top-boots.
>**Sarah, Duchess of Marlborough** 1660–1744

Not tonight, Josephine.
>**Napoleon I** 1769–1821 French emperor

Love is two minutes fifty-two seconds of squishing noises.
        Johnny Rotten 1957– English pop singer

Is it not strange that desire should so many years outlive
performance?
        William Shakespeare 1564–1616 English dramatist

Someone asked Sophocles, 'How is your sex-life now?
Are you still able to have a woman?' He replied, 'Hush,
man; most gladly indeed am I rid of it all, as though I had
escaped from a mad and savage master.'
        Sophocles c.496–406 BC Greek dramatist

Is that a gun in your pocket, or are you just glad to see me?
        Mae West 1892–1980 American film actress

Sickness see also **Medicine**

A man's illness is his private territory and, no matter how
much he loves you and how close you are, you stay an
outsider. You are healthy.
        Lauren Bacall 1924–2014 American actress

If a lot of cures are suggested for a disease, it means that the
disease is incurable.
        Anton Chekhov 1860–1904 Russian writer

All diseases run into one, old age.
        Ralph Waldo Emerson 1803–82 American writer

Did God who gave us flowers and trees,
Also provide the allergies?
        E. Y. ('Yip') Harburg 1898–1981 American songwriter

It is a most extraordinary thing, but I never read a patent
medicine advertisement without being impelled to the

Sickness

conclusion that I am suffering from the particular disease therein dealt with in its most virulent form.

Jerome K. Jerome 1859–1927 English writer

I told you I was ill.

Spike Milligan 1918–2002 Irish comedian, *inscription on his gravestone*

The desire to take medicine is perhaps the greatest feature which distinguishes man from animals.

William Osler 1849–1919 Canadian-born physician

Cured yesterday of my disease,
I died last night of my physician.

Matthew Prior 1664–1721 English poet

Illness is the doctor to whom we pay most heed; to kindness, to knowledge, we make promise only; pain we obey.

Marcel Proust 1871–1922 French novelist

I now begin the journey that will lead me into the sunset of my life.

Ronald Reagan 1911–2004 American statesman, *statement to the American people revealing that he had Alzheimer's disease*

You matter because you are you, and you matter to the last moment of your life. We will do all that we can not only to help you die peacefully, but also to live until you die.

Cicely Saunders 1916–2005 English founder of hospice movement

Diseases desperate grown,
By desperate appliances are relieved
Or not at all.

William Shakespeare 1564–1616 English dramatist

Illness is the night-side of life, a more onerous citizenship.
Everyone who is born holds dual citizenship, in the
kingdom of the well and in the kingdom of the sick.
   Susan Sontag 1933-2004 American writer

The biggest disease today is not leprosy or tuberculosis,
but rather the feeling of being unwanted, uncared for and
deserted by everybody.
   Mother Teresa 1910-97 Roman Catholic nun

To know ourselves diseased, is half our cure.
   Edward Young 1683-1765 English poet

Silence

Silence is the virtue of fools.
   Francis Bacon 1561-1626 English courtier

Blessed is the man who, having nothing to say, abstains
from giving us wordy evidence of the fact.
   George Eliot 1819-80 English novelist

Thou still unravished bride of quietness,
Thou foster-child of silence and slow time.
   John Keats 1795-1821 English poet

People talking without speaking
People hearing without listening...
'Fools,' said I, 'You do not know
Silence like a cancer grows.'
   Paul Simon 1942-   American singer

The sound of Brahman is OM. At the end of OM is silence.
It is a silence of joy.
   The Upanishads 800-200 BC Hindu sacred treatises

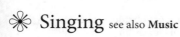 # Singing see also **Music**

Nothing is capable of being well set to music that is not nonsense.
Joseph Addison 1672–1719 English writer

Today if something is not worth saying, people sing it.
Pierre-Augustin Caron de Beaumarchais 1732–99 French dramatist

The exercise of singing is delightful to Nature, and good to preserve the health of man. It doth strengthen all parts of the breast, and doth open the pipes.
William Byrd 1543–1623 English composer

Swans sing before they die: 'twere no bad thing
Should certain persons die before they sing.
Samuel Taylor Coleridge 1772–1834 English poet

Every tone [of the songs of the slaves] was a testimony against slavery, and a prayer to God for deliverance from chains.
Frederick Douglass c.1818–95 American former slave

In writing songs I've learned as much from Cézanne as I have from Woody Guthrie.
Bob Dylan 1941– American singer

If a man were permitted to make all the ballads, he need not care who should make the laws of a nation.
Andrew Fletcher of Saltoun 1655–1716 Scottish patriot

Opera is when a guy gets stabbed in the back and, instead of bleeding, he sings.
Ed Gardner 1901–63 American comedian

Words make you think a thought. Music makes you feel a feeling. A song makes you feel a thought.
E. Y. ('Yip') Harburg 1898–1981 American songwriter

You think that's noise—you ain't heard nuttin' yet!
> **Al Jolson** 1886–1950 American singer, *in a café, competing with the din from a neighbouring building site*

The Skies

Beautiful! Beautiful! Magnificent desolation.
> **Buzz Aldrin** 1930– American astronaut, *on landing on the moon*

Looking up at the stars, I know quite well
That for all they care, I can go to hell.
> **W. H. Auden** 1907–73 English poet

The heavens declare the glory of God: and the firmament sheweth his handy-work.
> **Bible**

Slowly, silently, now the moon
Walks the night in her silver shoon.
> **Walter de la Mare** 1873–1956 English poet

Busy old fool, unruly sun,
Why dost thou thus,
Through windows, and through curtains call on us?
> **John Donne** 1572–1631 English poet

Eppur si muove.
But it does move.
> **Galileo Galilei** 1564–1642 Italian astronomer, *after his recantation, that the earth moves around the sun*

It may be that the stars of heaven appear to us fair and pure simply because we are at such a distance from them, and know nothing of their private life.
> **Heinrich Heine** 1797–1856 German poet

Sleep

Look at the stars! look, look up at the skies!
O look at all the fire-folk sitting in the air!
The bright boroughs, the circle-citadels there!
Gerard Manley Hopkins 1844–89 English poet

…The evening star,
Love's harbinger.
John Milton 1608–74 English poet

The eternal silence of these infinite spaces [the heavens]
terrifies me.
Blaise Pascal 1623–62 French scientist and philosopher

       The moon's an arrant thief,
And her pale fire she snatches from the sun.
William Shakespeare 1564–1616 English dramatist

I have loved the stars too truly to be fearful of the night.
Sarah Williams 1837–68 British writer

 Sleep see also **Dreams**

The sleep of a labouring man is sweet.
Bible

…The cool kindliness of sheets, that soon
Smooth away trouble; and the rough male kiss
Of blankets.
Rupert Brooke 1887–1915 English poet

When you're lying awake with a dismal headache, and
   repose is taboo'd by anxiety,
I conceive you may use any language you choose to indulge
   in, without impropriety.
W. S. Gilbert 1836–1911 English writer

Sleep is when all the unsorted stuff comes flying out as from a dustbin upset in a high wind.
    William Golding 1911–93 English novelist

What hath night to do with sleep?
    John Milton 1608–74 English poet

Sleeping is no mean art: for its sake one must stay awake all day.
    Friedrich Nietzsche 1844–1900 German philosopher

And so to bed.
    Samuel Pepys 1633–1703 English diarist

Methought I heard a voice cry, 'Sleep no more!
Macbeth does murder sleep,' the innocent sleep,
Sleep that knits up the ravelled sleave of care.
    William Shakespeare 1564–1616 English dramatist

In winter I get up at night
And dress by yellow candle-light.
In summer, quite the other way,—
I have to go to bed by day.
    Robert Louis Stevenson 1850–94 Scottish novelist

Early to rise and early to bed makes a male healthy and wealthy and dead.
    James Thurber 1894–1961 American humorist

Tired Nature's sweet restorer, balmy sleep!
    Edward Young 1683–1765 English poet

Society ✱

Hunger allows no choice
To the citizen or the police;
We must love one another or die.
    W. H. Auden 1907–73 English poet

Society

We started off trying to set up a small anarchist community, but people wouldn't obey the rules.
Alan Bennett 1934- English writer

The greatest happiness of the greatest number is the foundation of morals and legislation.
Jeremy Bentham 1748-1832 English philosopher

Society is indeed a contract…it becomes a partnership not only between those who are living, but between those who are living, those who are dead, and those who are to be born.
Edmund Burke 1729-97 Irish-born politician

The Big Society is our big idea.
David Cameron 1966- British Conservative statesman

No man is an Island, entire of it self.
John Donne 1572-1631 English poet

Economics is all about how people make choices. Sociology is all about why they don't have any choices to make.
James Stemble Duesenberry 1918-2009 American economist

Only in the state does man have a rational existence…Man owes his entire existence to the state, and has his being within it alone.
G. W. F. Hegel 1770-1831 German philosopher

In a consumer society there are inevitably two kinds of slaves: the prisoners of addiction and the prisoners of envy.
Ivan Illich 1926-2002 American sociologist

From each according to his abilities, to each according to his needs.
Karl Marx 1818-83 German philosopher

The city is not a concrete jungle, it is a human zoo.
Desmond Morris 1928- English anthropologist

There is no such thing as Society. There are individual men and women, and there are families.

Margaret Thatcher 1925-2013 British stateswoman

The Social Contract is nothing more or less than a vast conspiracy of human beings to lie to and humbug themselves and one another for the general Good. Lies are the mortar that bind the savage individual man into the social masonry.

H. G. Wells 1866-1946 English novelist

Solitude

He who is unable to live in society, or who has no need because he is sufficient for himself, must be either a beast or a god.

Aristotle 384-322 BC Greek philosopher

It is not good that the man should be alone; I will make him an help meet for him.

Bible

I want to be alone.

Greta Garbo 1905-90 Swedish actress

Conversation enriches the understanding, but solitude is the school of genius.

Edward Gibbon 1737-94 English historian

If you are idle, be not solitary; if you are solitary, be not idle.

Samuel Johnson 1709-84 English lexicographer

Down to Gehenna or up to the Throne,
He travels the fastest who travels alone.

Rudyard Kipling 1865-1936 English writer

All the lonely people, where do they all come from?

John Lennon 1940-80 and **Paul McCartney** 1942- English pop singers

Sorrow

Ships that pass in the night, and speak each other in
    passing;
Only a signal shown and a distant voice in the darkness;
So on the ocean of life we pass and speak one another,
Only a look and a voice; then darkness again and a silence.
    Henry Wadsworth Longfellow 1807–82 American poet

Never less alone than when alone.
    Samuel Rogers 1763–1855 English poet

Loneliness is the poverty of self; solitude is the richness
of self.
    May Sarton 1912–95 American writer

Man goes into the noisy crowd to drown his own clamour
of silence.
    Rabindranath Tagore 1861–1941 Bengali poet

One may have a blazing hearth in one's soul, and yet no one
ever comes to sit by it.
    Vincent Van Gogh 1853–90 Dutch painter

We're born alone, we live alone, we die alone. Only through
our love and friendship can we create the illusion for the
moment that we're not alone.
    Orson Welles 1915–85 American film director, *words added by
    Welles to Henry Jaglom's script for the film* Someone to Love

 Sorrow see also Bereavement, Suffering

By the waters of Babylon we sat down and wept: when we
remembered thee, O Sion.
    Bible

I tell you, hopeless grief is passionless.
    Elizabeth Barrett Browning 1806–61 English poet

Sorrow

We do not expect people to be deeply moved by what is not unusual. That element of tragedy which lies in the very fact of frequency, has not yet wrought itself into the coarse emotion of mankind.

George Eliot 1819–80 English novelist

Yes, he thought, between grief and nothing I will take grief.

William Faulkner 1897–1962 American novelist

Now laughing friends deride tears I cannot hide,
So I smile and say 'When a lovely flame dies,
Smoke gets in your eyes.'

Otto Harbach 1873–1963 American songwriter

No one ever told me that grief felt so like fear.

C. S. Lewis 1898–1963 English literary scholar

Sorrow and silence are strong, and patient endurance is godlike.

Henry Wadsworth Longfellow 1807–82 American poet

The pain of grief is just as much a part of life as the joy of love; it is, perhaps, the price we pay for love, the cost of commitment .

Colin Murray Parkes 1928– English psychiatrist, *usually quoted as 'Grief is the price we pay for love'*

Small sorrows speak; great ones are silent.

Seneca ('the Younger') c.4 BC–AD 65 Roman philosopher

When sorrows come, they come not single spies,
But in battalions.

William Shakespeare 1564–1616 English dramatist

Give sorrow words: the grief that does not speak
Whispers the o'er-fraught heart, and bids it break.

William Shakespeare 1564–1616 English dramatist

Speechmaking

Tears, idle tears, I know not what they mean,
Tears from the depth of some divine despair.
Alfred, Lord Tennyson 1809–92 English poet

Pure and complete sorrow is as impossible as pure and
complete joy.
Leo Tolstoy 1828–1910 Russian novelist

Sunt lacrimae rerum et mentem mortalia tangunt.
There are tears shed for things and mortality touches the
heart.
Virgil 70–19 BC Roman poet

For of all sad words of tongue or pen,
The saddest are these: 'It might have been!'
John Greenleaf Whittier 1807–92 American poet

Laugh and the world laughs with you;
Weep, and you weep alone;
For the sad old earth must borrow its mirth,
But has trouble enough of its own.
Ella Wheeler Wilcox 1855–1919 American poet

 Speechmaking see also **Conversation**

I do not object to people looking at their watches when
I am speaking. But I strongly object when they start shaking
them to make certain they are still going.
Lord Birkett 1883–1962 English judge

Grasp the subject, the words will follow.
Cato the Elder 234–149 BC Roman statesman

He [Lord Charles Beresford] is one of those orators of
whom it was well said, 'Before they get up, they do not
know what they are going to say; when they are speaking,

they do not know what they are saying; and when they have sat down, they do not know what they have said.'
Winston Churchill 1874–1965 British statesman

When you have nothing to say, say nothing.
Charles Caleb Colton c.1780–1832 English clergyman

When asked what was first in oratory, [he] replied to his questioner, 'action,' what second, 'action,' and again third, 'action'.
Demosthenes c.384–c.322 BC Greek statesman

Human speech is like a cracked kettle on which we tap crude rhythms for bears to dance to, while we long to make music that will melt the stars.
Gustave Flaubert 1821–80 French novelist

But all was false and hollow; though his tongue
Dropped manna, and could make the worse appear
The better reason.
John Milton 1608–74 English poet

Be silent, unless your speech is better than silence.
Salvator Rosa 1615–73 Italian painter, *inscription on self portrait*

I do not much dislike the matter, but
The manner of his speech.
William Shakespeare 1564–1616 English dramatist

Friends, Romans, countrymen, lend me your ears.
William Shakespeare 1564–1616 English dramatist

If I reprehend any thing in this world, it is the use of my oracular tongue, and a nice derangement of epitaphs!
Richard Brinsley Sheridan 1751–1816 Irish dramatist

Do you remember that in classical times when Cicero had finished speaking, the people said, 'How well he spoke',

Sport

but when Demosthenes had finished speaking, they said,
'Let us march.'
Adlai Stevenson 1900–65 American politician

What can be said at all can be said clearly; and whereof one
cannot speak thereof one must be silent.
Ludwig Wittgenstein 1889–1951 Austrian-born philosopher

The reason why we have two ears and only one mouth is
that we may listen the more and talk the less.
Zeno c.335–c.263 BC Greek philosopher

 Sport see also **Baseball, Cricket, Football, Golf, Tennis**

Citius, altius, fortius.
Swifter, higher, stronger.
Anonymous, *motto of the Olympic Games*

This is a hard tour and hard work wins it. Vive Le Tour.
Lance Armstrong 1971– American cyclist, *on winning his
seventh consecutive Tour de France*

I just blew my mind. And I blew the world's mind.
Usain Bolt 1986– Jamaican athlete, *on winning the 200m at the
Beijing Olympics*

Sports do not build character. They reveal it.
Heywood Hale Broun 1918–2001 American sports
commentator

The important thing in life is not the victory but the contest;
the essential thing is not to have won but to have fought
well.
Baron Pierre de Coubertin 1863–1937 French sportsman,
on the Olympic Games

There is plenty of time to win this game, and to thrash the Spaniards too.

> **Francis Drake** c.1540–96 English sailor, *receiving news of the Armada while playing bowls on Plymouth Hoe*

Nice guys. Finish last.

> **Leo Durocher** 1906–91 American baseball coach, *usually quoted as 'Nice guys finish last'*

He shoots! He scores!

> **Foster William Hewitt** 1902–85 Canadian broadcaster, *catchphrase used at ice-hockey games*

Only two things does he [the modern citizen] anxiously wish for—bread and circuses.

> **Juvenal** c.AD 60–c.140 Roman satirist

The flannelled fools at the wicket or the muddied oafs at the goals.

> **Rudyard Kipling** 1865–1936 English writer

A royal sport for the natural kings of earth.

> **Jack London** 1876–1916 American novelist, *on surfing*

> Chaos umpire sits,
And by decision more embroils the fray.

> **John Milton** 1608–74 English poet

Play up! play up! and play the game!

> **Henry Newbolt** 1862–1938 English writer

Eclipse first, the rest nowhere.

> **Dennis O'Kelly** c.1720–87 Irish racehorse-owner, *comment on a horse race*

Serious sport has nothing to do with fair play. It is bound up with hatred, jealousy, boastfulness, and disregard of all the rules.

> **George Orwell** 1903–50 English novelist

Spring

For when the One Great Scorer comes to mark against
   your name,
He writes—not that you won or lost—but how you played
   the Game.
   Grantland Rice 1880–1954 American sports writer

To play billiards well is a sign of an ill-spent youth.
   Charles Roupell British lawyer

Sure, winning isn't everything. It's the only thing.
   Henry 'Red' Sanders 1905–58 American football coach

Ka mate! Ka mate! Ka ora! Ka ora!
I die! I die! I live! I live!
   Te Rauparaha –d. 1849 Maori chief, *haka, now particularly
   associated with the New Zealand All Blacks rugby union team*

 Spring

In fact, it is about five o'clock in an evening that the
first hour of spring strikes—autumn arrives in the early
morning, but spring at the close of a winter day.
   Elizabeth Bowen 1899–1973 Anglo-Irish novelist

Whan that Aprill with his shoures soote
The droghte of March hath perced to the roote.
   Geoffrey Chaucer c.1343–1400 English poet

April is the cruellest month, breeding
Lilacs out of the dead land.
   T. S. Eliot 1888–1965 American-born British poet

And since to look at things in bloom
Fifty springs are little room,
About the woodlands I will go
To see the cherry hung with snow.
   A. E. Housman 1859–1936 English poet

Work seethes in the hands of spring,
That strapping dairymaid.
    Boris Pasternak 1890–1960 Russian novelist

Statistics

Statistics are the triumph of the quantitative method, and
the quantitative method is the victory of sterility and death.
    Hilaire Belloc 1870–1953 British writer

All models are wrong but some are useful.
    George Box 1919–2013 English statistician

A witty statesman said, you might prove anything by
figures.
    Thomas Carlyle 1795–1881 Scottish historian

Long and painful experience has taught me one great
principle in managing business for other people, viz., if you
want to inspire confidence, *give plenty of statistics.*
    Lewis Carroll 1832–98 English writer

There are three kinds of lies: lies, damned lies and statistics.
    Benjamin Disraeli 1804–81 British statesman

From the fact that there are 400,000 species of beetles
on this planet, but only 8,000 species of mammals, he
[Haldane] concluded that the Creator, if He exists, has a
special preference for beetles.
    J. B. S. Haldane 1892–1964 Scottish mathematical biologist

We are just statistics, born to consume resources.
    Horace 65–8 BC Roman poet

He uses statistics as a drunken man uses lampposts—for
support rather than for illumination.
    Andrew Lang 1844–1912 Scottish man of letters

Strength

If your experiment needs statistics, you ought to have done a better experiment.

Ernest Rutherford 1871–1937 New Zealand physicist

 Strength

The weak have one weapon: the errors of those who think they are strong.

Georges Bidault 1899–1983 French politician

You cannot strengthen the weak by weakening the strong.

William J. H. Boetcker 1873–1962 American Presbyterian minister, *often wrongly attributed to Abraham Lincoln*

It is the nature, and the advantage, of strong people that they can bring out the crucial questions and form a clear opinion about them. The weak always have to decide between alternatives that are not their own.

Dietrich Bonhoeffer 1906–45 German theologian

Toughness doesn't have to come in a pinstripe suit.

Dianne Feinstein 1933– American politician

A weak man has doubts before a decision; a strong man has them afterwards.

Karl Kraus 1874–1936 Austrian satirist

You are the weakest link...goodbye.

Anne Robinson 1944– English television presenter

A house built on granite and strong foundations, not even the onslaught of pouring rain, gushing torrents and strong winds will be able to pull down.

Haile Selassie 1892–1975 Ethiopian emperor

This is the law of the Yukon, that only the Strong shall thrive; That surely the Weak shall perish, and only the Fit survive.

Robert W. Service 1874–1958 Canadian poet

The gods are on the side of the stronger.
Tacitus c.AD 56–after 117 Roman historian

Style see also **Brevity**

Have something to say, and say it as clearly as you can. That is the only secret of style.
Matthew Arnold 1822–88 English poet

Style is the man.
Comte de Buffon 1707–88 French naturalist

Words easy to be understood do often hit the mark; when high and learned ones do only pierce the air.
John Bunyan 1628–88 English writer

I'm just trying to change the world one sequin at a time.
Lady Gaga 1986– American singer

When we see a natural style, we are quite surprised and delighted, for we expected to see an author and we find a man.
Blaise Pascal 1623–62 French scientist and philosopher

Good design is intelligence made visible.
Frank Pick 1878–1941 British transport administrator

True wit is Nature to advantage dressed,
What oft was thought, but ne'er so well expressed.
Alexander Pope 1688–1744 English poet

Proper words in proper places, make the true definition of a style.
Jonathan Swift 1667–1745 Irish poet and satirist

'Feather-footed through the plashy fen passes the questing vole'…'Yes,' said the Managing Editor. 'That must be good style.'
Evelyn Waugh 1903–66 English novelist

Success

In matters of grave importance, style, not sincerity is the vital thing.
Oscar Wilde 1854–1900 Irish dramatist

 ## Success see also **Failure**, **Winning**

'Tis not in mortals to command success,
But we'll do more, Sempronius; we'll deserve it.
Joseph Addison 1672–1719 English writer

For what shall it profit a man, if he shall gain the whole world, and lose his own soul?
Bible

Pourvu que ça dure!
Let's hope it lasts!
Laetitia Bonaparte 1750–1836, *on her son Napoleon becoming Emperor, 1804*

Veni, vidi, vici.
I came, I saw, I conquered.
Julius Caesar 100–44 BC Roman statesman

Success is not the key to happiness. Happiness is the key to success.
Herman Cain 1945– American businessman

I have climbed to the top of the greasy pole.
Benjamin Disraeli 1804–81 British statesman

If *A* is a success in life, then *A* equals *x* plus *y* plus *z*. Work is *x*; *y* is play; and *z* is keeping your mouth shut.
Albert Einstein 1879–1955 German-born theoretical physicist

Success is relative:
It is what we can make of the mess we have made of things.
T. S. Eliot 1888–1965 American-born British poet

Success is more dangerous than failure, the ripples break over a wider coastline.
Graham Greene 1904–91 English novelist

In most things success depends on knowing how long it takes to succeed.
Montesquieu 1689–1755 French political philosopher

Success makes life easier. It doesn't make *living* easier.
Bruce Springsteen 1949– American rock singer

He has achieved success who has lived well, laughed often, and loved much; who has enjoyed the trust of pure women, the respect of intelligent men, and the love of little children;…whose life was an inspiration, whose memory a benediction.
Bessie Anderson Stanley fl. 1905 American writer, *often wrongly attributed to Ralph Waldo Emerson or Robert Louis Stevenson*

All you need in this life is ignorance and confidence; then success is sure.
Mark Twain 1835–1910 American writer

It is not enough to succeed. Others must fail.
Gore Vidal 1925–2012 American writer

Suffering see also **Sympathy**

Justice inclines her scales so that wisdom comes at the price of suffering.
Aeschylus c.525–456 BC Greek tragedian

Children's talent to endure stems from their ignorance of alternatives.
Maya Angelou 1928–2014 American writer

Suffering

Even the dreadful martyrdom must run its course
Anyhow in a corner, some untidy spot
Where the dogs go on with their doggy life and the
    torturer's horse
Scratches its innocent behind on a tree.
    W. H. Auden 1907–73 English poet

Nothing happens to anybody which he is not fitted by
nature to bear.
    Marcus Aurelius AD 121–180 Roman emperor

The number of casualties will be more than any of us can
bear.
    Rudolph Giuliani 1944–   American politician, *in the aftermath
    of the terrorist attacks of 11 September 2001*

To each his suff'rings, all are men,
Condemned alike to groan;
The tender for another's pain,
Th' unfeeling for his own.
    Thomas Gray 1716–71 English poet

If suffer we must, let's suffer on the heights.
    Victor Hugo 1802–85 French writer

Scars have the strange power to remind us that our past
is real.
    Cormac McCarthy 1933–   American novelist

It is not true that suffering ennobles the character;
happiness does that sometimes, but suffering, for the most
part, makes men petty and vindictive.
    W. Somerset Maugham 1874–1965 English novelist

A man who fears suffering is already suffering from what
he fears.
    Montaigne 1533–92 French moralist

What does not kill me makes me stronger.
Friedrich Nietzsche 1844–1900 German philosopher

Pain of mind is worse than pain of body.
Publilius Syrus fl. 1st century BC Roman writer

The worst is not,
So long as we can say, 'This is the worst.'
William Shakespeare 1564–1616 English dramatist

He jests at scars, that never felt a wound.
William Shakespeare 1564–1616 English dramatist

I am a man
More sinned against than sinning.
William Shakespeare 1564–1616 English dramatist

Nothing begins, and nothing ends,
That is not paid with moan;
For we are born in other's pain,
And perish in our own.
Francis Thompson 1859–1907 English poet

Those who have courage to love should have courage to suffer.
Anthony Trollope 1815–82 English novelist

Too long a sacrifice
Can make a stone of the heart.
W. B. Yeats 1865–1939 Irish poet

Summer

Sumer is icumen in,
Lhude sing cuccu!
Groweth sed, and bloweth med,
And springeth the wude nu.
Anonymous, *'Cuckoo Song'* (c.1250)

The Supernatural

June is bustin' out all over.
Oscar Hammerstein II 1895–1960 American songwriter

Summer time an' the livin' is easy,
Fish are jumpin' an' the cotton is high.
Du Bose Heyward 1885–1940 and **Ira Gershwin** 1896–1983 American songwriters

Summer afternoon—summer afternoon…the two most beautiful words in the English language.
Henry James 1843–1916 American novelist

The way to ensure summer in England is to have it framed and glazed in a comfortable room.
Horace Walpole 1717–97 English connoisseur

 # The Supernatural

Up the airy mountain,
Down the rushy glen,
We daren't go a-hunting,
For fear of little men.
William Allingham 1824–89 Irish poet

From ghoulies and ghosties and long-leggety beasties
And things that go bump in the night,
Good Lord, deliver us!
Anonymous, *The Cornish or West Country Litany*

Then a spirit passed before my face; the hair of my flesh stood up.
Bible

For we wrestle not against flesh and blood, but against principalities, against powers, against the rulers of the darkness of this world, against spiritual wickedness in high places.
Bible

The Supernatural

Black magic operates most effectively in preconscious,
marginal areas. Casual curses are the most effective.
  William S. Burroughs 1914–97 American novelist

THE FAT BOY: I wants to make your flesh creep.
  Charles Dickens 1812–70 English novelist

There are fairies at the bottom of our garden!
  Rose Fyleman 1877–1957 English writer

Superstition is the poetry of life.
  Johann Wolfgang von Goethe 1749–1832 German writer

All argument is against it; but all belief is for it.
  Samuel Johnson 1709–84 English lexicographer, *of the
  existence of ghosts*

If there's something strange in your neighbourhood,
Who you gonna call? Ghostbusters.
  Ray Parker Jr. 1954– American musician

Mr Geller may have psychic powers by means of which
he can bend spoons; if so, he appears to be doing it the
hard way.
  James Randi 1928– Canadian-born American conjuror

Double, double toil and trouble;
Fire burn and cauldron bubble.
  William Shakespeare 1564–1616 English dramatist

There are more things in heaven and earth, Horatio,
Than are dreamt of in your philosophy.
  William Shakespeare 1564–1616 English dramatist

Superstition sets the whole world in flames; philosophy
quenches them.
  Voltaire 1694–1778 French writer

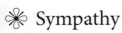

Sympathy

Nobody can tell what I suffer! But it is always so. Those who do not complain are never pitied.
>**Jane Austen** 1775-1817 English novelist

O divine Master, grant that I may not so much seek
To be consoled as to console;
To be understood as to understand.
>**St Francis of Assisi** 1181-1226 Italian monk

Our sympathy is cold to the relation of distant misery.
>**Edward Gibbon** 1737-94 English historian

True kindness presupposes the faculty of imagining as one's own the sufferings and joys of others.
>**André Gide** 1869-1951 French novelist

But yet the pity of it, Iago! O! Iago, the pity of it, Iago!
>**William Shakespeare** 1564-1616 English dramatist

Honest plain words best pierce the ears of grief.
>**William Shakespeare** 1564-1616 English dramatist

When times get rough,
And friends just can't be found
Like a bridge over troubled water
I will lay me down.
>**Paul Simon** 1942- American singer

Taxes

To tax and to please, no more than to love and to be wise, is not given to men.
>**Edmund Burke** 1729-97 Irish-born politician

Read my lips: no new taxes.
>**George Bush** 1924- American statesman

Taxes

The art of taxation consists in so plucking the goose as to obtain the largest possible amount of feathers with the smallest possible amount of hissing.

Jean-Baptiste Colbert 1619–83 French statesman

In this world nothing can be said to be certain, except death and taxes.

Benjamin Franklin 1706–90 American statesman and scientist

Only the little people pay taxes.

Leona Helmsley c.1920–2007 American hotelier, *reported at her trial for tax evasion*

Excise. A hateful tax levied upon commodities.

Samuel Johnson 1709–84 English lexicographer

Taxation without representation is tyranny.

James Otis 1725–83 American politician

Taxation is just a sophisticated way of demanding money with menaces.

Terry Pratchett 1948–2015 English novelist

Income Tax has made more Liars out of the American people than Golf.

Will Rogers 1879–1935 American actor

There is no art which one government sooner learns of another than that of draining money from the pockets of the people.

Adam Smith 1723–90 Scottish economist

Pecunia non olet.

Money has no smell.

Vespasian AD 9–79 Roman emperor, *quashing an objection to a tax on public lavatories*

The art of government is to make two-thirds of a nation pay all it possibly can pay for the benefit of the other third.

Voltaire 1694–1778 French writer

✳ Teaching see also **Education**

A teacher affects eternity; he can never tell where his influence stops.
Henry Brooks Adams 1838–1918 American historian

There is no such whetstone, to sharpen a good wit and encourage a will to learning, as is praise.
Roger Ascham 1515–68 English scholar

For precept must be upon precept, precept upon precept; line upon line, line upon line; here a little, and there a little.
Bible

The task of the modern educator is not to cut down jungles but to irrigate deserts.
C. S. Lewis 1898–1963 English literary scholar

We teachers can only help the work going on, as servants wait upon a master.
Maria Montessori 1870–1952 Italian educationist

Men must be taught as if you taught them not,
And things unknown proposed as things forgot.
Alexander Pope 1688–1744 English poet

For every person who wants to teach there are approximately thirty who don't want to learn—much.
W. C. Sellar 1898–1951 and **R. J. Yeatman** 1898–1968 British writers

Even while they teach, men learn.
Seneca ('the Younger') c.4 BC–AD 65 Roman philosopher

He who can, does. He who cannot, teaches.
George Bernard Shaw 1856–1950 Irish dramatist

Give me a girl at an impressionable age, and she is mine for life.

Muriel Spark 1918–2006 British novelist

Delightful task! to rear the tender thought,
To teach the young idea how to shoot.

James Thomson 1700–48 Scottish poet

Technology see also **Invention**

Science finds, industry applies, man conforms.

Anonymous, *guidebook to 1933 Chicago World's Fair*

Give me but one firm spot on which to stand, and I will move the earth.

Archimedes *c.*287–212 BC Greek mathematician, *on the action of a lever*

I sell here, Sir, what all the world desires to have—POWER.

Matthew Boulton 1728–1809 British engineer, *speaking of his engineering works*

Any sufficiently advanced technology is indistinguishable from magic.

Arthur C. Clarke 1917–2008 English science fiction writer

For a successful technology, reality must take precedence over public relations, for nature cannot be fooled.

Richard Feynman 1918–88 American physicist

Technology happens. It's not good, it's not bad. Is steel good or bad?

Andrew Grove 1936–2016 American businessman

The thing with high-tech is that you always end up using scissors.

David Hockney 1937– British artist

Technology

One machine can do the work of fifty ordinary men.
No machine can do the work of one extraordinary man.
Elbert Hubbard 1859–1915 American writer

Communism is Soviet power plus the electrification of the whole country.
Lenin 1870–1924 Russian revolutionary

The new electronic interdependence recreates the world in the image of a global village.
Marshall McLuhan 1911–80 Canadian communications scholar

The medium is the message.
Marshall McLuhan 1911–80 Canadian communications scholar

It is questionable if all the mechanical inventions yet made have lightened the day's toil of any human being.
John Stuart Mill 1806–73 English philosopher

When you see something that is technically sweet, you go ahead and do it and you argue about what to do about it only after you have had your technical success. That is the way it was with the atomic bomb.
J. Robert Oppenheimer 1904–67 American physicist

One of the universal rules of happiness is: always be wary of any helpful item that weighs less than its operating manual.
Terry Pratchett 1948–2015 English novelist

It has been said that an engineer is a man who can do for ten shillings what any fool can do for a pound.
Nevil Shute 1899–1960 British novelist

The Britain that is going to be forged in the white heat of this revolution will be no place for restrictive practices or for outdated methods on either side of industry.
Harold Wilson 1916–95 British statesman, *usually quoted as 'the white heat of the technological revolution'*

Television ✳

Those who say they give the public what it wants begin by underestimating public taste, and end by debauching it.
   T. S. Eliot 1888–1965 American-born British poet

Television has brought back murder into the home—where it belongs.
   Alfred Hitchcock 1899–1980 British-born film director

Anyone afraid of what he thinks television does to the world is probably just afraid of the world.
   Clive James 1939–   Australian critic

Television brought the brutality of war into the comfort of the living room. Vietnam was lost in the living rooms of America—not the battlefields of Vietnam.
   Marshall McLuhan 1911–80 Canadian communications scholar

Television is actually closer to reality than anything in books. The madness of TV is the madness of human life.
   Camille Paglia 1947–   American writer

Television has made dictatorship impossible, but democracy unbearable.
   Shimon Peres 1923–2016 Israeli statesman

Nation shall speak peace unto nation.
   Montague John Rendall 1862–1950 English headmaster, *motto of the BBC*

It's just like having a licence to print your own money.
   Roy Thomson 1894–1976 Canadian-born British newspaper proprietor, *on the profitability of commercial television in Britain*

Never miss a chance to have sex or appear on television.
   Gore Vidal 1925–2012 American writer

Temptation

I hate television. I hate it as much as peanuts. But I can't
stop eating peanuts.
Orson Welles 1915–85 American film director

Television contracts the imagination and radio expands it.
Terry Wogan 1938–2016 Irish broadcaster

 # Temptation

Watch and pray, that ye enter not into temptation: the spirit
indeed is willing but the flesh is weak.
Bible

For the good that I would I do not: but the evil which
I would not, that I do.
Bible

From all the deceits of the world, the flesh, and the devil,
Good Lord, deliver us.
Book of Common Prayer 1662

What's done we partly may compute,
But know not what's resisted.
Robert Burns 1759–96 Scottish poet

The Lord above made liquor for temptation—but
With a little bit of luck…
When temptation comes you'll give right in!
Alan Jay Lerner 1918–86 American songwriter

If we are to be punished for the sins we have committed,
at least we should be praised for our yearning for the sins
we have not committed.
Jawaharlal Nehru 1889–1964 Indian statesman

Is this her fault or mine?
The tempter or the tempted, who sins most?
William Shakespeare 1564–1616 English dramatist

There are several good protections against temptations,
but the surest is cowardice.

    Mark Twain 1835–1910 American writer

I can resist everything except temptation.

    Oscar Wilde 1854–1900 Irish dramatist

Tennis

I call tennis the McDonald's of sport—you go in, they make
a quick buck out of you, and you're out.

    Pat Cash 1965-　Australian tennis player

New Yorkers love it when you spill your guts out there.
Spill your guts at Wimbledon and they make you stop and
clean it up.

    Jimmy Connors 1952-　American tennis player

You cannot be serious!

    John McEnroe 1959-　American tennis player, *said to tennis
umpire at Wimbledon*

I can cry like Roger, it's a shame I can't play like him.

    Andy Murray 1987-　Scottish tennis player, *after losing to
Roger Federer in the final of the Australian Open*

Do what you love and love what you do and everything else
is detail.

    Martina Navratilova 1956-　Czech-born American tennis
player

When we have matched our rackets to these balls,
We will in France, by God's grace, play a set
Shall strike his father's crown into the hazard.

    William Shakespeare 1564–1616 English dramatist

Thanks

If you can keep playing tennis when somebody is shooting a gun down the street, that's concentration. I didn't grow up playing at the country club.

Serena Williams 1981– American tennis player

 # Thanks

No duty is more urgent than that of returning thanks.

St Ambrose c.339–397 French-born bishop of Milan

They say late thanks are ever best.

Francis Bacon 1561–1626 English courtier

A joyful and pleasant thing it is to be thankful.

Bible

When I'm not thanked at all, I'm thanked enough,
I've done my duty, and I've done no more.

Henry Fielding 1707–54 English novelist

For this relief much thanks.

William Shakespeare 1564–1616 English dramatist

 # The Theatre

I go to the theatre to be entertained, I want to be taken out of myself, I don't want to see lust and rape and incest and sodomy and so on, I can get all that at home.

Alan Bennett 1934– English writer

There's no business like show business.

Irving Berlin 1888–1989 American songwriter

Things on stage should be as complicated and as simple as in life. People dine, just dine, while their happiness is made and their lives are smashed. If in Act 1 you have a pistol hanging on the wall, then it must fire in the last act.

Anton Chekhov 1860–1904 Russian writer

JOSEPHINE HULL: Shakespeare is so tiring. You never get a chance to sit down unless you're a king.

George S. Kaufman 1889–1961 and **Howard Teichmann** 1916–87 American dramatists, *in the film* The Solid Gold Cadillac

O! for a Muse of fire, that would ascend
The brightest heaven of invention;
A kingdom for a stage, princes to act
And monarchs to behold the swelling scene.

William Shakespeare 1564–1616 English dramatist

Four trestles, four boards, two actors, a passion.

Lope de Vega 1562–1635 Spanish dramatist and poet, *on all he needed to create a play*

It's a sound you can't get in the movies or television…the sound of a wonderful, deep silence that means you've hit them where they live.

Shelley Winters 1922–2006 American actress

Thinking see also **Ideas, Mind**

Think different.

Anonymous, *advertising slogan for Apple Computers*

To change your mind and to follow him who sets you right is to be nonetheless the free agent that you were before.

Marcus Aurelius AD 121–180 Roman emperor

Never express yourself more clearly than you think.

Niels Bohr 1885–1962 Danish physicist

Thinking

Learning without thought is labour lost; thought without learning is perilous.

Confucius 551–479 BC Chinese philosopher

Cogito, ergo sum.

I think, therefore I am.

René Descartes 1596–1650 French philosopher

It is a capital mistake to theorize before you have all the evidence. It biases the judgement.

Arthur Conan Doyle 1859–1930 Scottish-born writer

What was once thought can never be unthought.

Friedrich Dürrenmatt 1921–90 Swiss writer

I'll not listen to reason…Reason always means what someone else has got to say.

Elizabeth Gaskell 1810–65 English novelist

Logical consequences are the scarecrows of fools and the beacons of wise men.

T. H. Huxley 1825–95 English biologist

Doublethink means the power of holding two contradictory beliefs in one's mind simultaneously, and accepting both of them.

George Orwell 1903–50 English novelist

I don't mind your thinking slowly: I mind your publishing faster than you think.

Wolfgang Pauli 1900–58 Austrian-born American physicist

Most people would sooner die than think—in fact they do so.

Bertrand Russell 1872–1970 British philosopher

Yond Cassius has a lean and hungry look;
He thinks too much: such men are dangerous.

William Shakespeare 1564–1616 English dramatist

The real question is not whether machines think but whether men do.
B. F. Skinner 1904–90 American psychologist

The important thing is not to think much but to love much.
St Teresa of Ávila 1512–82 Spanish mystic

Time ✳

Time is an illusion. Lunchtime doubly so.
Douglas Adams 1952–2001 English science fiction writer

Every instant of time is a pinprick of eternity.
Marcus Aurelius AD 121–180 Roman emperor

VLADIMIR: That passed the time.
ESTRAGON: It would have passed in any case.
VLADIMIR: Yes, but not so rapidly.
Samuel Beckett 1906–89 Irish writer

Time is a great teacher but unfortunately it kills all its pupils.
Hector Berlioz 1803–69 French composer

I am Time grown old to destroy the world,
Embarked on the course of world annihilation.
Bhagavad Gita 250 BC–AD 250 Hindu poem

To every thing there is a season, and a time to every purpose under the heaven:
A time to be born, and a time to die…
A time to weep, and a time to laugh; a time to mourn, and a time to dance.
Bible

Men talk of killing time, while time quietly kills them.
Dion Boucicault 1820–90 Irish dramatist

Time

I recommend to you to take care of minutes: for hours will take care of themselves.
Lord Chesterfield 1694–1773 English writer

I shall use the phrase 'time's arrow' to express this one-way property of time which has no analogue in space.
Arthur Eddington 1882–1944 British astrophysicist

The distinction between past, present and future is only an illusion, however persistent.
Albert Einstein 1879–1955 German-born theoretical physicist

Time is…Time was…Time is past.
Robert Greene c.1560–92 English dramatist

In the long run we are all dead.
John Maynard Keynes 1883–1946 English economist

Nothing puzzles me more than time and space; and yet nothing troubles me less, as I never think about them.
Charles Lamb 1775–1834 English writer

But at my back I always hear
Time's wingèd chariot hurrying near:
And yonder all before us lie
Deserts of vast eternity.
Andrew Marvell 1621–78 English poet

Time the devourer of everything.
Ovid 43 BC–C.AD 17 Roman poet

Even such is Time, which takes in trust
Our youth, our joys, and all we have,
And pays us but with age and dust.
Walter Ralegh c.1552–1618 English courtier

Half our life is spent trying to find something to do with the time we have rushed through life trying to save.
Will Rogers 1879–1935 American actor

Three o'clock is always too late or too early for anything you want to do.
Jean-Paul Sartre 1905–80 French philosopher

Ah! the clock is always slow;
It is later than you think.
Robert W. Service 1874–1958 Canadian poet

To-morrow, and to-morrow, and to-morrow,
Creeps in this petty pace from day to day,
To the last syllable of recorded time;
And all our yesterdays have lighted fools
The way to dusty death.
William Shakespeare 1564–1616 English dramatist

Time hath, my lord, a wallet at his back,
Wherein he puts alms for oblivion.
William Shakespeare 1564–1616 English dramatist

As if you could kill time without injuring eternity.
Henry David Thoreau 1817–62 American writer

Time is
Too slow for those who wait,
Too swift for those who fear,
Too long for those who grieve,
Too short for those who rejoice;
But for those who love,
Time is eternity.
Henry Van Dyke 1852–1933 American minister

Sed fugit interea, fugit inreparabile tempus.
But meanwhile it is flying, irretrievable time is flying.
Virgil 70–19 BC Roman poet

Time, like an ever-rolling stream,
Bears all its sons away.
Isaac Watts 1674–1748 English hymn-writer

Toasts

Here's tae us; wha's like us?
Gey few, and they're a' deid.
Anonymous

HUMPHREY BOGART: Here's looking at you, kid.
Julius J. Epstein 1909–2001 and **others** American
screenwriters, *in the film* Casablanca

Lang may yer lum reek!
Scottish Proverb, *long may your chimney smoke*

May you live all the days of your life.
Jonathan Swift 1667–1745 Irish poet and satirist

 The Town see also **Country**

We do not look in great cities for our best morality.
Jane Austen 1775–1817 English novelist

If you would be known, and not know, vegetate in a village;
if you would know, and not be known, live in a city.
Charles Caleb Colton c.1780–1832 English clergyman

Slums may well be breeding-grounds of crime, but middle-
class suburbs are incubators of apathy and delirium.
Cyril Connolly 1903–74 English writer

The materials of city planning are sky, space, trees, steel and
cement in that order and in that hierarchy.
Le Corbusier 1887–1965 French architect

The fields and trees won't teach me anything, and the people
in the city do.
Socrates 469–399 BC Greek philosopher

There is no there there.
Gertrude Stein 1874–1946 American writer, *on her hometown of Oakland, California, often misquoted as being said of Los Angeles*

Commuters give the city its tidal restlessness; natives give it solidity and continuity; but the settlers give it passion.
E. B. White 1899–1985 American humorist

The modern city is a place for banking and prostitution and very little else.
Frank Lloyd Wright 1867–1959 American architect

Transience

Sic transit gloria mundi.
Thus passes the glory of the world.
Anonymous, *said at the coronation of a new Pope, while flax is burned*

All flesh is as grass, and all the glory of man as the flower of grass. The grass withereth, and the flower thereof falleth away.
Bible

He who binds to himself a joy
Doth the winged life destroy
But he who kisses the joy as it flies
Lives in Eternity's sunrise.
William Blake 1757–1827 English poet

Look thy last on all things lovely,
Every hour.
Walter de la Mare 1873–1956 English poet

Gather ye rosebuds while ye may,
Old Time is still a-flying:

413

Travel

And this same flower that smiles to-day,
To-morrow will be dying.
Robert Herrick 1591–1674 English poet

Like that of leaves is a generation of men.
Homer fl. 8th century BC Greek poet

Ceaselessly the river flows, and yet the water is never the
same, while in the still pools the shifting foam gathers and
is gone, never staying for a moment. Even so is man and his
habitation.
Kamo no Chomei 1155–1216 Japanese poet

The butterfly counts not months but moments, and has time
enough.
Rabindranath Tagore 1861–1941 Bengali poet

 # Travel

Travel, in the younger sort, is a part of education; in the
elder, a part of experience. He that travelleth into a country
before he hath some entrance into the language, goeth to
school, and not to travel.
Francis Bacon 1561–1626 English courtier

See one promontory (said Socrates of old), one mountain,
one sea, one river, and see all.
Robert Burton 1577–1640 English clergyman

Men travel faster now, but I do not know if they go to better
things.
Willa Cather 1873–1947 American novelist

The whole object of travel is not to set foot on foreign land;
it is at last to set foot on one's own country as a foreign land.
G. K. Chesterton 1874–1936 English writer

Wherever you go, go with all your heart.
Confucius 551–479 BC Chinese philosopher

Like all great travellers, I have seen more than I remember,
and remember more than I have seen.
Benjamin Disraeli 1804–81 British statesman

Worth seeing, yes; but not worth going to see.
Samuel Johnson 1709–84 English lexicographer, *of the Giant's
Causeway*

A good traveller has no fixed plans.
Lao Tzu c.604–c.531 BC Chinese philosopher

A good traveller is one who does not know where he is
going to, and a perfect traveller does not know where he
came from.
Lin Yutang 1895–1976 Chinese writer

Traveller, there is no path. Paths are made by walking.
Antonio Machado 1875–1939 Spanish poet

I have not told even half of the things that I have seen.
Marco Polo c.1254–c.1324 Italian traveller, *when asked if he
wished to deny any of his stories of his travels*

A man travels the world in search of what he needs and
returns home to find it.
George Moore 1852–1933 Irish novelist

The real voyage of discovery…consists not in seeking new
landscapes but in having new eyes.
Marcel Proust 1871–1922 French novelist

To travel hopefully is a better thing than to arrive, and the
true success is to labour.
Robert Louis Stevenson 1850–94 Scottish novelist

Travel is fatal to prejudice, bigotry, and narrow-mindedness.
Mark Twain 1835–1910 American writer

Trust and Treachery

He that is surety for a stranger shall smart for it.
> **Bible**

Just for a handful of silver he left us,
Just for a riband to stick in his coat.
> **Robert Browning** 1812–89 English poet, *of Wordsworth accepting the Laureateship*

Anyone can rat, but it takes a certain amount of ingenuity to re-rat.
> **Winston Churchill** 1874–1965 British statesman, *on rejoining the Conservatives twenty years after leaving them for the Liberals*

I know what it is to be a subject, and what to be a Sovereign. Good neighbours I have had, and I have met with bad: and in trust I have found treason.
> **Elizabeth I** 1533–1603 English monarch

Anyone who hasn't experienced the ecstasy of betrayal knows nothing about ecstasy at all.
> **Jean Genet** 1910–86 French writer

Treason doth never prosper, what's the reason?
For if it prosper, none dare call it treason.
> **John Harington** 1561–1612 English courtier

And I said to the man who stood at the gate of the year:
'Give me a light that I may tread safely into the unknown.'
    And he replied:
    'Go out into the darkness and put your hand into the Hand of God. That shall be to you better than light and safer than a known way.'
> **Minnie Louise Haskins** 1875–1957 English writer, *quoted by George VI in his Christmas broadcast, 1939*

It is better to suffer wrong than to do it, and happier to be sometimes cheated than not to trust.
Samuel Johnson 1709–84 English lexicographer

Quis custodiet ipsos custodes?
Who is to guard the guards themselves?
Juvenal c.AD 60–c.140 Roman satirist

To betray, you must first belong.
Kim Philby 1912–88 British intelligence officer and Soviet spy

But I'm always true to you, darlin', in my fashion.
Yes I'm always true to you, darlin', in my way.
Cole Porter 1891–1964 American songwriter

I fear the Greeks even when they bring gifts.
Virgil 70–19 BC Roman poet

Truth see also Lies

The truth is often a terrible weapon of aggression. It is possible to lie, and even to murder, for the truth.
Alfred Adler 1870–1937 Austrian psychologist

The truth which makes men free is for the most part the truth which men prefer not to hear.
Herbert Agar 1897–1980 American writer

Plato is dear to me, but dearer still is truth.
Aristotle 384–322 BC Greek philosopher

It contains a misleading impression, not a lie. It was being economical with the truth.
Robert Armstrong 1927– British civil servant

What is truth? said jesting Pilate; and would not stay for an answer.
Francis Bacon 1561–1626 English courtier

Truth

And ye shall know the truth, and the truth shall make you free.
Bible

Great is Truth, and mighty above all things.
Bible (Apocrypha)

A truth that's told with bad intent
Beats all the lies you can invent.
William Blake 1757–1827 English poet

One of the favourite maxims of my father was the distinction between the two sorts of truths, profound truths recognized by the fact that the opposite is also a profound truth, in contrast to trivialities where opposites are obviously absurd.
Niels Bohr 1885–1962 Danish physicist

'Tis strange—but true; for truth is always strange; Stranger than fiction.
Lord Byron 1788–1824 English poet

What I tell you three times is true.
Lewis Carroll 1832–98 English writer

It is commonly said, and more particularly by Lord Shaftesbury, that ridicule is the best test of truth.
Lord Chesterfield 1694–1773 English writer

When you have eliminated the impossible, whatever remains, *however improbable*, must be the truth.
Arthur Conan Doyle 1859–1930 Scottish-born writer

A Hair perhaps divides the False and True.
Edward Fitzgerald 1809–83 English poet

An exaggeration is a truth that has lost its temper.
Kahlil Gibran 1883–1931 Lebanese-born American writer

Believe those who are seeking the truth; doubt those who find it.

André Gide 1869–1951 French novelist

True and False are attributes of speech, not of things. And where speech is not, there is neither Truth nor Falsehood.

Thomas Hobbes 1588–1679 English philosopher

It is the customary fate of new truths to begin as heresies and to end as superstitions.

T. H. Huxley 1825–95 English biologist

But, my dearest Agathon, it is truth which you cannot contradict; you can without any difficulty contradict Socrates.

Socrates 469–399 BC Greek philosopher

Rather than love, than money, than fame, give me truth.

Henry David Thoreau 1817–62 American writer

There was things which he stretched, but mainly he told the truth.

Mark Twain 1835–1910 American writer

I can't tell a lie, Pa; you know I can't tell a lie. I did cut it with my hatchet.

George Washington 1732–99 American statesman

The truth is rarely pure, and never simple.

Oscar Wilde 1854–1900 Irish dramatist

A thing is not necessarily true because a man dies for it.

Oscar Wilde 1854–1900 Irish dramatist

The Universe

Had I been present at the Creation, I would have given some useful hints for the better ordering of the universe.

Alfonso 'the Wise', King of Castile 1221–84, *on studying the Ptolemaic system*

The Universe

'Gad! she'd better!'
> **Thomas Carlyle** 1795–1881 Scottish historian, *on hearing that
> Margaret Fuller 'accept[ed] the universe'*

The eternal mystery of the world is its comprehensibility…
The fact that it is comprehensible is a miracle.
> **Albert Einstein** 1879–1955 German-born theoretical physicist,
> *usually quoted as 'The most incomprehensible fact about the
> universe is that it is comprehensible'*

Now, my own suspicion is that the universe is not only
queerer than we suppose, but queerer than we *can* suppose.
> **J. B. S. Haldane** 1892–1964 Scottish mathematical biologist

If we find the answer to that [why it is that we and the
universe exist], it would be the ultimate triumph of human
reason—for then we would know the mind of God.
> **Stephen Hawking** 1942– English theoretical physicist

This, now, is the judgement of our scientific age—the third
reaction of man upon the universe! This universe is not
hostile, nor yet is it friendly. It is simply indifferent.
> **John H. Holmes** 1879–1964 American Unitarian minister

From the intrinsic evidence of his creation, the Great
Architect of the Universe now begins to appear as a pure
mathematician.
> **James Jeans** 1877–1946 Scottish astronomer

How is it that hardly any major religion has looked at
science and concluded, 'This is better than we thought!
The Universe is much bigger than our prophets said,
grander, more subtle, more elegant'?
> **Carl Sagan** 1934–96 American astronomer

Sometimes I think the surest sign that intelligent life exists
elsewhere in the universe is that none of it has tried to
contact us.
> **Bill Watterson** 1958– American cartoonist

The world is everything that is the case.
Ludwig Wittgenstein 1889–1951 Austrian-born philosopher

Violence ✳

Keep violence in the mind
Where it belongs.
Brian Aldiss 1925– English writer

Violence is the last refuge of the incompetent.
Isaac Asimov 1920–92 Russian-born science fiction writer

All they that take the sword shall perish with the sword.
Bible

I say violence is necessary. It is as American as cherry pie.
H. Rap Brown 1943– American Black Power leader

Victory attained by violence is tantamount to a defeat, for it
is momentary.
Mahatma Gandhi 1869–1948 Indian statesman

What has violence ever accomplished? What has it ever
created? No martyr's cause has ever been stilled by an
assassin's bullet.
Robert Kennedy 1925–68 American politician

Who overcomes
By force, hath overcome but half his foe.
John Milton 1608–74 English poet

If you strike a child take care that you strike it in anger,
even at the risk of maiming it for life. A blow in cold blood
neither can nor should be forgiven.
George Bernard Shaw 1856–1950 Irish dramatist

Where force is necessary, there it must be applied boldly,
decisively and completely. But one must know the

limitations of force; one must know when to blend force
with a manoeuvre, a blow with an agreement.

Leon Trotsky 1879–1940 Russian revolutionary

The quietly pacifist peaceful
always die
to make room for men
who shout.

Alice Walker 1944– American poet

 # Wales

It profits a man nothing to give his soul for the whole
world…But for Wales—!

Robert Bolt 1924–95 English dramatist

The English have forgot that they ever conquered the Welsh,
but some ages will elapse before the Welsh forget that the
English have conquered them.

George Borrow 1803–81 English writer

Who dare compare the English, the most degraded of all the
races under heaven, with the Welsh?

Giraldus Cambrensis 1146?–1220? Welsh historian

The land of my fathers, how fair is thy fame.

Evan James 1809–78 Welsh bard

Everyday when I wake up, I thank the Lord I'm Welsh.

Cerys Matthews 1969– Welsh singer

Though it appear a little out of fashion,
There is much care and valour in this Welshman.

William Shakespeare 1564–1616 English dramatist

The land of my fathers. My fathers can have it.

Dylan Thomas 1914–53 Welsh poet

War see also **Armed Forces**

We make war that we may live in peace.
Aristotle 384–322 BC Greek philosopher

The bomber will always get through. The only defence is in offence, which means that you have to kill more women and children more quickly than the enemy if you want to save yourselves.
Stanley Baldwin 1867–1947 British statesman

Not worth the healthy bones of a single Pomeranian grenadier.
Otto von Bismarck 1815–98 German statesman, *of possible German involvement in the Balkans*

This policy cannot succeed through speeches, and shooting-matches, and songs; it can only be carried out through blood and iron.
Otto von Bismarck 1815–98 German statesman

C'est magnifique, mais ce n'est pas la guerre.
It is magnificent, but it is not war.
Pierre Bosquet 1810–61 French general, *on the charge of the Light Brigade at Balaclava, 1854*

As you know, God is usually on the side of the big squadrons against the small.
Comte de Bussy-Rabutin 1618–93 French soldier and poet

In war, whichever side may call itself the victor, there are no winners, but all are losers.
Neville Chamberlain 1869–1940 British statesman

War is a game that is played with a smile. If you can't smile grin. If you can't grin keep out of the way till you can.
Winston Churchill 1874–1965 British statesman

War

We shall fight on the beaches, we shall fight on the landing grounds, we shall fight in the fields and in the streets, we shall fight in the hills; we shall never surrender.

Winston Churchill 1874–1965 British statesman

Let us therefore brace ourselves to our duty, and so bear ourselves that, if the British Empire and its Commonwealth lasts for a thousand years, men will still say, 'This was their finest hour.'

Winston Churchill 1874–1965 British statesman

Never in the field of human conflict was so much owed by so many to so few.

Winston Churchill 1874–1965 British statesman

Laws are silent in time of war.

Cicero 106–43 BC Roman statesman

War is nothing but a continuation of politics with the admixture of other means.

Karl von Clausewitz 1780–1831 Prussian military theorist, *commonly rendered 'War is the continuation of politics by other means'*

War is too serious a matter to entrust to military men.

Georges Clemenceau 1841–1929 French statesman

ROBERT DUVALL: I love the smell of napalm in the morning. It smells like victory.

Francis Ford Coppola 1939–   American film director, *in the film* Apocalypse Now

I am not only a pacifist but a militant pacifist. I am willing to fight for peace. Nothing will end war unless the people themselves refuse to go to war.

Albert Einstein 1879–1955 German-born theoretical physicist

There never was a good war, or a bad peace.

Benjamin Franklin 1706–90 American statesman and scientist

War

If we are attacked we can only defend ourselves with guns not with butter.

Joseph Goebbels 1897–1945 German Nazi leader

Would you rather have butter or guns?…preparedness makes us powerful. Butter merely makes us fat.

Hermann Goering 1893–1946 German Nazi leader

War is hell, and all that, but it has a good deal to recommend it. It wipes out all the small nuisances of peace-time.

Ian Hay 1876–1952 Scottish writer

War is the father of all and the king of all.

Heraclitus c.540–c.480 BC Greek philosopher

Always mystify, mislead, and surprise the enemy, if possible.

Thomas Jonathan 'Stonewall' Jackson 1824–63 American general, *his strategic motto during the Civil War*

Among the calamities of war may be jointly numbered the diminution of the love of truth, by the falsehoods which interest dictates and credulity encourages.

Samuel Johnson 1709–84 English lexicographer, *possibly the source of 'When war is declared, Truth is the first casualty'; attributed also to Hiram Johnson*

It is well that war is so terrible. We should grow too fond of it.

Robert E. Lee 1807–70 American general

Rule 1, on page 1 of the book of war, is: 'Do not march on Moscow'…[Rule 2] is: 'Do not go fighting with your land armies in China.'

Lord Montgomery of Alamein 1887–1976 British field marshal

War

Probably the battle of Waterloo *was* won on the playing-fields of Eton, but the opening battles of all subsequent wars have been lost there.
>   **George Orwell** 1903–50 English novelist

My subject is War, and the pity of War.
The Poetry is in the pity.
>   **Wilfred Owen** 1893–1918 English poet

Little girl…Sometime they'll give a war and nobody will come.
>   **Carl Sandburg** 1878–1967 American poet

Once more unto the breach, dear friends, once more;
Or close the wall up with our English dead!
In peace there's nothing so becomes a man
As modest stillness and humility:
But when the blast of war blows in our ears,
Then imitate the action of the tiger.
>   **William Shakespeare** 1564–1616 English dramatist

There is many a boy here to-day who looks on war as all glory, but, boys, it is all hell.
>   **William Tecumseh Sherman** 1820–91 American general

War is capitalism with the gloves off.
>   **Tom Stoppard** 1937–   British dramatist

To win one hundred victories in one hundred battles is not the acme of skill. To subdue the enemy without fighting is the acme of skill.
>   **Sun Tzu** fl. c.400–320 BC Chinese general

The battle of Waterloo was won on the playing fields of Eton.
>   **Duke of Wellington** 1769–1852 British general

Next to a battle lost, the greatest misery is a battle gained.
>   **Duke of Wellington** 1769–1852 British general

Wealth see also **Money**

It is easier for a camel to go through the eye of a needle,
than for a rich man to enter into the kingdom of God.
>   **Bible**

Greed is all right…Greed is healthy. You can be greedy and
still feel good about yourself.
>   **Ivan F. Boesky** 1937– American businessman

My riches consist, not in the extent of my possessions, but
in the fewness of my wants.
>   **Joseph Brotherton** 1783–1857 English politician, *responding
>   to a slighting reference to the fortune that he had amassed in
>   manufacturing*

A very rich person should leave his kids enough to do
anything but not enough to do nothing.
>   **Warren Buffett** 1930– American businessman

The man who dies…rich dies disgraced.
>   **Andrew Carnegie** 1835–1919 American industrialist

Let me tell you about the very rich. They are different from
you and me.
>   **F. Scott Fitzgerald** 1896–1940 American novelist, *to which
>   Ernest Hemingway replied, 'Yes, they have more money'*

In every well-governed state, wealth is a sacred thing; in
democracies it is the only sacred thing.
>   **Anatole France** 1844–1924 French man of letters

If you would be wealthy, think of saving as well as of
getting.
>   **Benjamin Franklin** 1706–90 American statesman and scientist

If you can actually count your money, then you are not
really a rich man.
>   **J. Paul Getty** 1892–1976 American industrialist

Wealth

We are not here to sell a parcel of boilers and vats, but the potentiality of growing rich, beyond the dreams of avarice.
Samuel Johnson 1709–84 English lexicographer, *at the sale of Thrale's brewery*

I've been rich and I've been poor: rich is better.
Beatrice Kaufman 1895–1945 American writer

Let us be frank about it: most of our people have never had it so good.
Harold Macmillan 1894–1986 British statesman

[New Labour] is intensely relaxed about people getting filthy rich.
Peter Mandelson 1953– British politician

A kiss on the hand may be quite continental,
But diamonds are a girl's best friend.
Leo Robin 1900–84 American songwriter

Wealth is like sea-water; the more we have, the thirstier we become, and the same is true of fame.
Arthur Schopenhauer 1788–1860 German philosopher

The chief enjoyment of riches consists in the parade of riches.
Adam Smith 1723–90 Scottish economist

How many things I can do without!
Socrates 469–399 BC Greek philosopher, *on looking at a multitude of goods exposed for sale*

The only way not to think about money is to have a great deal of it.
Edith Wharton 1862–1937 American novelist

I am grateful for the blessings of wealth, but it hasn't changed who I am. My feet are still on the ground. I'm just wearing better shoes.
Oprah Winfrey 1954– American talk show hostess

Weather ✳

What dreadful hot weather we have! It keeps one in a continual state of inelegance.

Jane Austen 1775–1817 English novelist

The rain, it raineth on the just
And also on the unjust fella:
But chiefly on the just, because
The unjust steals the just's umbrella.

Lord Bowen 1835–94 English judge

Every time it rains, it rains
Pennies from heaven.
Don't you know each cloud contains
Pennies from heaven?

Johnny Burke 1908–64 American songwriter

This is a London particular…A fog, miss.

Charles Dickens 1812–70 English novelist

A woman rang to say she heard there was a hurricane on the way. Well don't worry, there isn't.

Michael Fish 1944– British weather forecaster, *weather forecast on the night before serious gales in southern England*

The weather is like the Government, always in the wrong.

Jerome K. Jerome 1859–1927 English writer

When two Englishmen meet, their first talk is of the weather.

Samuel Johnson 1709–84 English lexicographer

No one can tell me,
Nobody knows,
Where the wind comes from,
Where the wind goes.

A. A. Milne 1882–1956 English writer

Weddings

The first fall of snow is not only an event, but it is a magical event. You go to bed in one kind of world and wake up to find yourself in another quite different, and if this is not enchantment, then where is it to be found?

J. B. Priestley 1894–1984 English writer

The fog comes
on little cat feet.

Carl Sandburg 1878–1967 American poet

So foul and fair a day I have not seen.

William Shakespeare 1564–1616 English dramatist

There is no such thing as bad weather. All weather is good because it is God's.

St Teresa of Ávila 1512–82 Spanish mystic

Rain is grace; rain is the sky condescending to the earth; without rain, there would be no life.

John Updike 1932–2009 American writer

It was the wrong kind of snow.

Terry Worrall British railway spokesman, *popular summary of his explanation of disruption on British Rail*

 # Weddings

If it were not for the presents, an elopement would be preferable.

George Ade 1866–1944 American humorist

Now you will feel no rain, for each of you will be shelter for the other. Now you will feel no cold, for each of you will be warmth for the other.

Anonymous, *from the saying known as the 'Apache Blessing'*

As the bridegroom rejoiceth over the bride.

Bible

Wilt thou love her, comfort her, honour, and keep her in
sickness and in health; and, forsaking all other, keep thee
only unto her, so long as ye both shall live?
Book of Common Prayer 1662

Why am I always the bridesmaid,
Never the blushing bride?
Fred W. Leigh d. 1924 and **others** British songwriters

I'm getting married in the morning,
Ding dong! The bells are gonna chime.
Pull out the stopper;
Let's have a whopper;
But get me to the church on time!
Alan Jay Lerner 1918–86 American songwriter

Happy is the bride that the sun shines on.
Proverb

Winning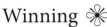

The race is not to the swift, nor the battle to the strong.
Bible

You ask, what is our aim? I can answer in one word:
Victory, victory at all costs, victory in spite of all terror;
victory, however long and hard the road may be; for
without victory, there is no survival.
Winston Churchill 1874–1965 British statesman

Victory has a hundred fathers, but no-one wants to
recognise defeat as his own.
Count Galeazzo Ciano 1903–44 Italian politician

STEERFORTH: Ride on! Rough-shod if need be, smooth-shod
if that will do, but ride on! Ride on over all obstacles, and
win the race!
Charles Dickens 1812–70 English novelist

Winter

Winning is everything. The only ones who remember you
when you come second are your wife and your dog.
Damon Hill 1960–   English motor-racing driver

The moment of victory is much too short to live for that and
nothing else.
Martina Navratilova 1956–   Czech-born American tennis
player

We are not interested in the possibilities of defeat; they do
not exist.
Queen Victoria 1819–1901 British monarch

 # Winter

The English winter—ending in July,
To recommence in August.
Lord Byron 1788–1824 English poet

Winter lies too long in country towns; hangs on until it is
stale and shabby, old and sullen.
Willa Cather 1873–1947 American novelist

No shade, no shine, no butterflies, no bees,
No fruits, no flowers, no leaves, no birds,—
November!
Thomas Hood 1799–1845 English poet

The most serious charge which can be brought against New
England is not Puritanism but February.
Joseph Wood Krutch 1893–1970 American critic and naturalist

Winter is icummen in,
Lhude sing Goddamm,
Raineth drop and staineth slop,
And how the wind doth ramm!
Ezra Pound 1885–1972 American poet

O, Wind,
If Winter comes, can Spring be far behind?
Percy Bysshe Shelley 1792–1822 English poet

Let no man boast himself that he has got through the perils
of winter till at least the seventh of May.
Anthony Trollope 1815–82 English novelist

Wisdom see also **Knowledge**

In our sleep, pain which cannot forget falls drop by drop
upon the heart until, in our own despair, against our will,
comes wisdom through the awful grace of God.
Aeschylus c.525–456 BC Greek tragedian, *quoted by Robert
Kennedy on the night of the assassination of Martin Luther King*

The price of wisdom is above rubies.
Bible

Authority without wisdom is like a heavy axe without an
edge, fitter to bruise than polish.
Anne Bradstreet c.1612–72 English-born American poet

The fool wonders, the wise man asks.
Benjamin Disraeli 1804–81 British statesman

Mere cleverness is not wisdom.
Euripides c.485–c.406 BC Greek dramatist

The art of being wise is the art of knowing what to
overlook.
William James 1842–1910 American philosopher

Wisdom is not the purchase of a day.
Thomas Paine 1737–1809 English political theorist

No man is wise at all times.
Pliny the Elder AD 23–79 Roman senator

Wit

One would need to be already wise, in order to love wisdom.
Friedrich von Schiller 1759–1805 German poet

 # Wit see also **Humour**

Wit is educated insolence.
Aristotle 384–322 BC Greek philosopher

A thing well said will be wit in all languages.
John Dryden 1631–1700 English poet

Wit is the salt of conversation, not the food.
William Hazlitt 1778–1830 English essayist

Wit is the epitaph of an emotion.
Friedrich Nietzsche 1844–1900 German philosopher

I am not only witty in myself, but the cause that wit is in other men.
William Shakespeare 1564–1616 English dramatist

Brevity is the soul of wit.
William Shakespeare 1564–1616 English dramatist

There's no possibility of being witty without a little ill-nature; the malice of a good thing is the barb that makes it stick.
Richard Brinsley Sheridan 1751–1816 Anglo-Irish dramatist

 # Woman's Role see also **Men and Women**

If all men are born free, how is it that all women are born slaves?
Mary Astell 1668–1731 English poet

The freedom women were supposed to have found in the Sixties largely boiled down to easy contraception and abortion: things to make life easier for men, in fact.
Julie Burchill 1960– English journalist

Woman's Role

I could have stayed home and baked cookies and had teas. But what I decided was to fulfil my profession, which I entered before my husband was in public life.
    Hillary Rodham Clinton 1947– American lawyer

One is not born a woman: one becomes one.
    Simone de Beauvoir 1908–86 French novelist

Today the problem that has no name is how to juggle work, love, home and children.
    Betty Friedan 1921–2006 American feminist

I didn't fight to get women out from behind the vacuum cleaner to get them onto the board of Hoover.
    Germaine Greer 1939– Australian feminist

My mother said it was simple to keep a man, you must be a maid in the living room, a cook in the kitchen and a whore in the bedroom. I said I'd hire the other two and take care of the bedroom bit.
    Jerry Hall 1956– American model

A woman's preaching is like a dog's walking on his hinder legs. It is not done well; but you are surprised to find it done at all.
    Samuel Johnson 1709–84 English lexicographer

The first blast of the trumpet against the monstrous regiment of women.
    John Knox c.1505–72 Scottish Protestant reformer

But if God had wanted us to think just with our wombs, why did He give us a brain?
    Clare Booth Luce 1903–87 American writer and politician

Well-behaved women seldom make history.
    Laurel Thatcher Ulrich 1938– American historian

Women

The Queen is most anxious to enlist every one who can speak or write to join in checking this mad, wicked folly of 'Woman's Rights', with all its attendant horrors, on which her poor feeble sex is bent, forgetting every sense of womanly feeling and propriety.
Queen Victoria 1819–1901 British monarch

Womanist is to feminist as purple to lavender.
Alice Walker 1944– American poet

I do not wish them [women] to have power over men; but over themselves.
Mary Wollstonecraft 1759–97 English feminist

 # Women see also **Men and Women**

There's a special place in hell for women who don't help other women.
Madeleine Albright 1937– American diplomat

The weaker sex, to piety more prone.
William Alexander, Earl of Stirling c.1567–1640 Scottish poet

All the privilege I claim for my own sex…is that of loving longest, when existence or when hope is gone.
Jane Austen 1775–1817 English novelist

Who can find a virtuous woman? for her price is far above rubies.
Bible

Good women always think it is their fault when someone else is being offensive. Bad women never take the blame for anything.
Anita Brookner 1928–2016 British novelist

Women

In her first passion woman loves her lover,
In all the others all she loves is love.
Lord Byron 1788–1824 English poet

The prime truth of woman, the universal mother…that if a
thing is worth doing, it is worth doing badly.
G. K. Chesterton 1874–1936 English writer

She knows her man, and when you rant and swear,
Can draw you to her *with a single hair*.
John Dryden 1631–1700 English poet

The happiest women, like the happiest nations, have no
history.
George Eliot 1819–80 English novelist

What does a woman want?
Sigmund Freud 1856–1939 Austrian psychoanalyst

Show me a woman who doesn't feel guilty and I'll show you
a man.
Erica Jong 1942–   American novelist

Being a woman is of special interest only to aspiring male
transsexuals. To actual women, it is merely a good excuse
not to play football.
Fran Lebowitz 1950–   American writer

She's the sort of woman who lives for others—you can
always tell the others by their hunted expression.
C. S. Lewis 1898–1963 English literary scholar

Woman was God's second blunder.
Friedrich Nietzsche 1844–1900 German philosopher

Woman is the nigger of the world.
Yoko Ono 1933– Japanese poet

Women

The greatest glory of a woman is to be least talked about by men.

Pericles c.495-429 BC Greek statesman

Every woman adores a Fascist,
The boot in the face, the brute
Brute heart of a brute like you.

Sylvia Plath 1932–63 American poet

She floats, she hesitates; in a word, she's a woman.

Jean Racine 1639–99 French tragedian

O Woman! in our hours of ease,
Uncertain, coy, and hard to please…
When pain and anguish wring the brow,
A ministering angel thou!

Sir Walter Scott 1771–1832 Scottish novelist

Frailty, thy name is woman!

William Shakespeare 1564–1616 English dramatist

Here's to the maiden of bashful fifteen
Here's to the widow of fifty
Here's to the flaunting, extravagant quean;
And here's to the housewife that's thrifty.

Richard Brinsley Sheridan 1751–1816 Irish dramatist

The great and almost only comfort about being a woman is that one can always pretend to be more stupid than one is and no one is surprised.

Freya Stark 1893–1993 English traveller

We are becoming the men we wanted to marry.

Gloria Steinem 1934–   American journalist

From birth to 18 a girl needs good parents. From 18 to 35, she needs good looks. From 35 to 55, good personality. From 55 on, she needs good cash.

Sophie Tucker 1884–1966 American vaudeville artist

When once a woman has given you her heart, you can never get rid of the rest of her body.
John Vanbrugh 1664–1726 English architect and dramatist

Words see also **Language**, **Meaning**

The Greeks had a word for it.
Zoë Akins 1886–1958 American writer

'When *I* use a word,' Humpty Dumpty said in a rather scornful tone, 'it means just what I choose it to mean—neither more nor less.'
Lewis Carroll 1832–98 English writer

It cannot in the opinion of His Majesty's Government be classified as slavery in the extreme acceptance of the word without some risk of terminological inexactitude.
Winston Churchill 1874–1965 British statesman

A man who could make so vile a pun would not scruple to pick a pocket.
John Dennis 1657–1734 English writer

> Words strain,
> Crack and sometimes break, under the burden,
> Under the tension, slip, slide, perish,
> Decay with imprecision, will not stay in place,
> Will not stay still.

T. S. Eliot 1888–1965 American-born British poet

The chief merit of language is clearness, and we know that nothing detracts so much from this as do unfamiliar terms.
Galen AD 129–199 Greek physician

Words without actions are the assassins of idealism.
Herbert Hoover 1874–1964 American statesman

Work

And once sent out, a word takes wing beyond recall.
Horace 65–8 BC Roman poet

Lexicographer. A writer of dictionaries, a harmless drudge.
Samuel Johnson 1709–84 English lexicographer

I am not yet so lost in lexicography as to forget that words are the daughters of earth, and that things are the sons of heaven. Language is only the instrument of science, and words are but the signs of ideas.
Samuel Johnson 1709–84 English lexicographer

Words are, of course, the most powerful drug used by mankind.
Rudyard Kipling 1865–1936 English writer

Whatever we have words for, that we have already got beyond.
Friedrich Nietzsche 1844–1900 German philosopher

'Refudiate', 'misunderestimate', 'weewee'd up'. English is a living language. Shakespeare liked to coin words, too.
Sarah Palin 1964–   American politician, *following controversy over her use of the word 'refudiate'*

Syllables govern the world.
John Selden 1584–1654 English historian

Was there anything so real as words?
Oscar Wilde 1854–1900 Irish dramatist

 # Work see also **Careers**

In the sweat of thy face shalt thou eat bread.
Bible

For the labourer is worthy of his hire.
Bible

Work is much more fun than fun.
Noël Coward 1899–1973 English dramatist

Work is love made visible.
Kahlil Gibran 1883–1931 Lebanese-born American writer

I have long been of the opinion that if work were such
a splendid thing the rich would have kept more of it for
themselves.
Bruce Grocott 1940– British politician

I like work: it fascinates me. I can sit and look at it for hours.
I love to keep it by me: the idea of getting rid of it nearly
breaks my heart.
Jerome K. Jerome 1859–1927 English writer

Why should I let the toad *work*
Squat on my life?
Can't I use my wit as a pitchfork
And drive the brute off?
Philip Larkin 1922–85 English poet

Blessèd are the horny hands of toil!
James Russell Lowell 1819–91 American poet

Work expands so as to fill the time available for its
completion.
C. Northcote Parkinson 1909–93 English writer

It's true hard work never killed anybody, but I figure why
take the chance?
Ronald Reagan 1911–2004 American statesman

If you have great talents, industry will improve them: if
you have but moderate abilities, industry will supply their
deficiency.
Joshua Reynolds 1723–92 English painter

Writing

Far and away the best prize that life offers is the chance to work hard at work worth doing.
Theodore Roosevelt 1858–1919 American statesman

Which of us…is to do the hard and dirty work for the rest— and for what pay? Who is to do the pleasant and clean work, and for what pay?
John Ruskin 1819–1900 English critic

One of the symptoms of approaching nervous breakdown is the belief that one's work is terribly important, and that to take a holiday would bring all kinds of disaster.
Bertrand Russell 1872–1970 British philosopher

The labour we delight in physics pain.
William Shakespeare 1564–1616 English dramatist

O God, give me work till the end of my life
And life till the end of my work.
Annie S. Swan 1859–1943 Scottish-born novelist

Work saves us from three great evils: boredom, vice and need.
Voltaire 1694–1778 French writer

 # Writing see also **Literature**, **Style**

Writers don't give prescriptions. They give headaches.
Chinua Achebe 1930–2013 Nigerian novelist

If you can't annoy somebody with what you write, I think there's little point in writing.
Kingsley Amis 1922–95 English novelist

Let other pens dwell on guilt and misery. I quit such odious subjects as soon as I can.
Jane Austen 1775–1817 English novelist

Writing

Writers, like teeth, are divided into incisors and grinders.
Walter Bagehot 1826–77 English economist

Manuscripts don't burn.
Mikhail Bulgakov 1891–1940 Russian writer

Beneath the rule of men entirely great
The pen is mightier than the sword.
Edward Bulwer-Lytton 1803–73 British novelist

When in doubt have a man come through the door with a gun in his hand.
Raymond Chandler 1888–1959 American writer

A writer must be as objective as a chemist: he must abandon the subjective line; he must know that dung-heaps play a very reasonable part in a landscape, and that evil passions are as inherent in life as good ones.
Anton Chekhov 1860–1904 Russian writer

We must beat the iron while it is hot, but we may polish it at leisure.
John Dryden 1631–1700 English poet

The writer's only responsibility is to his art. He will be completely ruthless if he is a good one…If a writer has to rob his mother, he will not hesitate; the *Ode on a Grecian Urn* is worth any number of old ladies.
William Faulkner 1897–1962 American novelist

Only connect!…Only connect the prose and the passion.
E. M. Forster 1879–1970 English novelist

The business of the poet and novelist is to show the sorriness underlying the grandest things, and the grandeur underlying the sorriest things.
Thomas Hardy 1840–1928 English novelist

Writing

The most essential gift for a good writer is a built-in, shock-proof shit detector. This is the writer's radar and all great writers have had it.

Ernest Hemingway 1899–1961 American novelist

No man but a blockhead ever wrote, except for money.

Samuel Johnson 1709–84 English lexicographer

Read over your compositions, and where ever you meet with a passage which you think is particularly fine, strike it out.

Samuel Johnson 1709–84 English lexicographer

When my sonnet was rejected, I exclaimed, 'Damn the age; I will write for Antiquity!'

Charles Lamb 1775–1834 English writer

What in me is dark
Illumine, what is low raise and support;
That to the height of this great argument
I may assert eternal providence,
And justify the ways of God to men.

John Milton 1608–74 English poet

The last thing one knows in constructing a work is what to put first.

Blaise Pascal 1623–62 French scientist and philosopher

But those who cannot write, and those who can,
All rhyme, and scrawl, and scribble, to a man.

Alexander Pope 1688–1744 English poet

And, as imagination bodies forth
The forms of things unknown, the poet's pen
Turns them to shapes, and gives to airy nothing
A local habitation and a name.

William Shakespeare 1564–1616 English dramatist

Learn to write well, or not to write at all.

John Sheffield 1648–1721 English politician

Writing is not a profession but a vocation of unhappiness.
Georges Simenon 1903–89 Belgian novelist

Not that the story need be long, but it will take a long while to make it short.
Henry David Thoreau 1817–62 American writer

How vain it is to sit down to write when you have not stood up to live.
Henry David Thoreau 1817–62 American writer

I have written my work, not as an essay which is to win the applause of the moment, but as a possession for all time.
Thucydides c.455–c.400 BC Greek historian

Writing saved me from the sin and *inconvenience* of violence.
Alice Walker 1944–   American poet

A woman must have money and a room of her own if she is to write fiction.
Virginia Woolf 1882–1941 English novelist

Never forget what I believe was observed to you by Coleridge, that every great and original writer, in proportion as he is great and original, must himself create the taste by which he is to be relished.
William Wordsworth 1770–1850 English poet

Youth see also **Generation Gap**

I'm not young enough to know everything.
J. M. Barrie 1860–1937 Scottish writer

Youth is something very new: twenty years ago no one mentioned it.
Coco Chanel 1883–1971 French couturière

Youth

It is better to waste one's youth than to do nothing with it at all.
Georges Courteline 1858–1929 French writer

Youth is happy because it has the ability to see beauty.
Franz Kafka 1883–1924 Czech novelist

A boy's will is the wind's will
And the thoughts of youth are long, long thoughts.
Henry Wadsworth Longfellow 1807–82 American poet

Youth is vivid rather than happy, but memory always remembers the happy things.
Bernard Lovell 1913–2012 British astronomer

Whom the gods love dies young.
Menander 342–c.292 BC Greek comic dramatist

The atrocious crime of being a young man…I shall neither attempt to palliate nor deny.
William Pitt 1708–78 British statesman

My salad days,
When I was green in judgement.
William Shakespeare 1564–1616 English dramatist

Maturity is a high price to pay for growing up.
Tom Stoppard 1937– British dramatist

The force that through the green fuse drives the flower
Drives my green age.
Dylan Thomas 1914–53 Welsh poet

Make me young, make me young, make me young!
Kurt Vonnegut 1922–2007 American novelist

Youth is the one thing worth having.
Oscar Wilde 1854–1900 Irish dramatist

Youth

Heaven lies about us in our infancy!
Shades of the prison-house begin to close
Upon the growing boy.
   William Wordsworth 1770–1850 English poet

Index of Authors

Abse, Dannie
Men, Sculpture

Accius
Government

Achebe, Chinua
Self, Writing

Acheson, Dean
Britain,
Bureaucracy,
Careers

Acton, Lord
Power

Adams, Abigail
Character, Fashion

Adams, Ansel
Photography

Adams, Douglas
Crises, Life, Music,
Punctuality, Time

Adams, Franklin P.
Middle Age

**Adams, Henry
Brooks**
Education,
Experience,
Meaning, Morality,
Teaching

Adams, John
Democracy,
Government,
Politics, Presidency

Adamson, Harold
Crises

Addison, Joseph
Business,
Education,
Future, Gardens,
Happiness,
Patriotism, Singing,
Success

Ade, George
Weddings

Adenauer, Konrad
Character

Adler, Alfred
Truth

Adler, Felix
Insight

Aeschylus
Deceit, Suffering,
Wisdom

Agar, Herbert
Truth

Agate, James
Certainty

Agathon
Past

Agee, James
Nature

Akins, Zoë
Words

**Albright,
Madeleine**
Women

**Alcott, Amos
Bronson**
Habit

Alcott, Louisa May
Christmas, Mothers

Aldington, Richard
Patriotism

Aldiss, Brian
Violence

Aldrin, Buzz
Skies

Alexander II
Revolution

**Alexander, Cecil
Frances**
Animals, Class

**Alexander,
William, Earl of
Stirling**
Women

**Alfonso 'the Wise',
King of Castile**
Universe

Ali, Muhammad
Boxing, Old Age

Ali ibn-Abi-Talib
Enemies

Allen, Fred
Management

Allen, Woody
Death, Sex

Allen, Woody and
Brickman, Marshall
Pessimism

Allingham, Henry
Lifestyles

Allingham, William
Supernatural

Ambrose, St
Behaviour, Thanks

**American
Declaration of
Independence**
Human Rights

Amies, Hardy
Clothes

Amis, Kingsley
Men and Women,
Writing

Amis, Martin
Middle Age

Anacharsis
Law

**Andersen, Hans
Christian**
Birth

449

Index of Authors

Andrewes, Bishop Lancelot
  Church
Angelou, Maya
  *Experience,
  Suffering*
Anka, Paul
  Lifestyles
Anonymous
  *Armed Forces,
  Bereavement,
  Computers,
  Crises, Death,
  Determination,
  Economics,
  Education,
  Effort, Elections,
  Environment,
  Experience, Fame,
  Foolishness, God,
  Gossip, Human
  Rights, Ideas,
  Justice, Knowledge,
  Liberty, Lies,
  Mathematics,
  Moderation,
  Music, Past,
  Poverty, Race, Sea,
  Self-Knowledge,
  Sport, Summer,
  Supernatural,
  Technology,
  Thinking, Toasts,
  Transience,
  Weddings*
Anouilh, Jean
  Deceit, France, Love
**Anthony, Susan
Brownell**
  Human Rights
Apelles
  Drawing
**Apollinaire,
Guillaume**
  Custom, Invention
**Appleton, Thomas
Gold**
  America

Arbus, Diane
  Photography
Arbuthnot, Dr
  Law
Archilochus
  Knowledge
Archimedes
  *Invention,
  Technology*
Arden, Elizabeth
  Money
Ardrey, Robert
  Human Race
Arendt, Hannah
  Evil, Revolution
Aristophanes
  Character
Aristotle
  *Democracy,
  Education,
  Goodness, Ideas,
  Knowledge, Nature,
  Politics, Solitude,
  Truth, War, Wit*
Armour, Richard
  Food
Armstrong, Lance
  Sport
Armstrong, Louis
  Music
Armstrong, Neil
  Achievement
Armstrong, Robert
  Truth
Arnald-Amaury
  Cynicism
Arnold, Matthew
  *Memory, Middle
  Age, Perfection,
  Style*
Asaf, George
  Anxiety
Ascham, Roger
  *Education,
  Teaching*
Asimov, Isaac
  Health, Violence

Asquith, Herbert
  Patience
Astell, Mary
  Woman's Role
Astley, Jacob
  Prayer
Astor, Nancy
  Drink
Atkinson, Brooks
  Past
Attlee, Clement
  Democracy
Auden, W. H.
  *Behaviour,
  Bereavement,
  Books, Evil,
  Failure, Habit,
  Heart, Humour,
  Intelligence, Letters,
  Lovers, Names,
  Nature, Poetry,
  Poverty, Railways,
  Science, Self-
  Knowledge, Skies,
  Society, Suffering*
**Augustine, St of
Hippo**
  *Evil, Justice,
  Lifestyles,
  Moderation, Sex*
Aung San Suu Kyi
  *Liberty, Men and
  Women*
Aurelius, Marcus
  *Anger, Morality,
  Suffering, Thinking,
  Time*
Austen, Jane
  *Conversation, Gifts,
  Gossip, Happiness,
  Hospitality,
  Humour, Idleness,
  Marriage, Parties,
  Past, Perfection,
  Pleasure, Sympathy,
  Town, Weather,
  Women, Writing*

Index of Authors

Awdry, Revd W.
Railways

Ayer, A. J.
Opinion

Bacall, Lauren
Imagination,
Sickness

Bach, Richard
Achievement

Bacon, Francis
Ability, Action,
Advice, Anger,
Belief, Books,
Certainty, Change,
Character,
Children, Dance,
Education,
Family, Gardens,
Hope, Houses,
Indifference,
Invention,
Knowledge,
Marriage, Medicine,
Misfortune, Money,
Nature, Old Age,
Parents, Revenge,
Royalty, Silence,
Thanks, Travel,
Truth

Bacon, Francis
Friendship

Bacon, Roger
Mathematics

Baden-Powell, Lord
Planning

Baez, Joan
Opinion

Bagehot, Walter
Bureaucracy,
Government,
Journalism,
Leadership,
Pleasure,
Politicians, Royalty,
Writing

Bailey, David
Fashion

Bairnsfather, Bruce
Advice

Baldwin, James
Money, Poverty

Baldwin, Stanley
Retirement, Secrecy,
War

Balfour, Arthur
James
Cynicism

Balzac, Honoré de
Equality

Banks, Joseph
Australia

Barker, Joel Arthur
Action

Barker, Ronnie and
Corbett, Ronnie
Parting

Barkley, Alben W.
Apology

Barnard,
Frederick R.
Language

Barnes, Julian
Books, Britain,
Children

Barnum, Phineas T.
Foolishness

Barrie, J. M.
Belief, Charm,
Death, Festivals,
Memory, Scotland,
Youth

Barton, Edmund
Australia

Baruch, Bernard
Elections,
Old Age

Basho, Matsuo
Autumn

Bates, Katherine
Lee
America

Batten, Jean
Flight

Battle of Maldon,
The
Determination

Baudelaire, Charles
Class, Invention

Baxter, Richard
Behaviour

Beamer, Todd
Action

Beaton, Cecil
Originality

Beaumarchais,
Pierre-Augustin
Caron de
Humour, Love,
Singing

Beckett, Samuel
Boredom, Failure,
Habit, Human
Race, Time

Becon, Thomas
Drink

Bede, The
Venerable
History, Life

Beecham, Thomas
Music

Beerbohm, Max
Dreams,
Imagination

Beethoven, Ludwig
van
Cookery, Fate, Music

Beeton, Mrs
Management

Behan, Brendan
Fame

Behn, Aphra
Money

Bellah, James
Warner *see*
Goldbeck, Willis
and Bellah, James
Warner

Bellarmine,
St Robert
Memory

Index of Authors

Belloc, Hilaire
Class, Cookery,
Doubt, Life
Sciences,
Misfortune,
Pleasure, Statistics
Benchley, Robert
Quotations
Benedict XVI
Love
Benenson, Peter
Action
Benn, Ernest
Politics
Benn, Tony
Photography
Bennett, Alan
Art, Behaviour,
Examinations,
Morality, Royalty,
Society, Theatre
Bennett, Arnold
Idealism, Marriage
Bennett, Brian see
Welch, Bruce and
Bennett, Brian
Bentham, Jeremy
Animals, Human
Rights, Justice,
Poetry, Punishment,
Society
**Beresford, Lord
Charles**
Apology
Berger, John
Men and Women
Bergman, Ingrid
Kissing, Lovers
**Berkeley, Bishop
George**
Mathematics
Berlin, Irving
America, Christmas,
Dance, Good Looks,
Lovers, Theatre
Berlin, Isaiah
Liberty

Berlioz, Hector
Time
Bernal, J. D.
Life Sciences
Bernanos, Georges
Hell, Prayer
Bernbach, Bill
Advertising
Bernstein, Leonard
Music
Berra, Yogi
Baseball, Ending,
Future
Berry, Halle
Beauty
Berry, Wendell
Earth
Berryman, John
Boredom, Fear
Betjeman, John
Children,
Christmas,
Education,
Environment
Bevan, Aneurin
Journalism,
Moderation,
Politicians
**Beveridge, William
Henry**
Government,
Progress
Bevin, Ernest
Enemies
Bhagavad Gita
Time
Bhutto, Benazir
Democracy, Power
Bibesco, Elizabeth
Certainty
Bible
Absence,
Achievement,
Advice, Anger,
Animals,
Appearance,
Beauty, Beginning,

Belief, Bereavement,
Birth, Body, Books,
Brevity, Careers,
Chance, Change,
Charity, Children,
Christmas,
Cooperation,
Day, Death, Debt,
Despair, Doubt,
Drink, Earth,
Ending, Enemies,
Environment,
Envy, Equality,
Evil, Fame, Family,
Fate, Foolishness,
Forgiveness, Gifts,
God, Greatness,
Hatred, Heaven,
Hope, Hospitality,
Hypocrisy,
Idealism, Idleness,
Indifference,
Justice, Knowledge,
Language,
Leadership, Life,
Lifestyles, Love,
Manners, Marriage,
Medicine,
Misfortune, Money,
Murder, News, Old
Age, Parents, Peace,
Pollution, Poverty,
Prayer, Present,
Pride, Progress,
Punishment,
Religion, Revenge,
Sea, Secrecy, Self-
Knowledge, Skies,
Sleep, Solitude,
Sorrow, Success,
Supernatural,
Teaching,
Temptation,
Thanks, Time,
Transience, Trust,
Truth, Violence,
Wealth, Weddings,
Winning, Wisdom,
Women, Work

Index of Authors

Bible (Apocrypha)
Business, Medicine, Truth

Bidault, Georges
Strength

Bierce, Ambrose
Pollution

Biko, Steve
Power

Billings, Josh
Dogs, Knowledge

Binyon, Laurence
Autumn

Bion
Cruelty

Birkett, Lord
Speechmaking

Bishop, Elizabeth
Dreams, Earth

Bismarck, Otto von
Europe, Languages, Politics, War

Blacker, Valentine
Practicality

Blackstone, William
Justice

Blair, Tony
Africa, Crime, Determination, Education, Leadership, Parting

Blake, Eubie
Old Age

Blake, William
Ambition, Animals, Cruelty, England, Environment, Forgiveness, Goodness, Imagination, Insight, Love, Nature, Poetry, Satisfaction, Transience, Truth

Blanchflower, Danny
Football

Bliss, Arthur
Old Age

Blücher, Gebhard Lebrecht
London

Boesky, Ivan F.
Wealth

Boetcker, William J. H.
Strength

Bohr, Niels
Belief, Future, Science, Thinking, Truth

Bolingbroke, Henry St John, 1st Viscount
Mistakes

Bolívar, Simón
Revolution

Bolt, Robert
Wales

Bolt, Usain
Sport

Bonaparte, Laetitia
Success

Bonhoeffer, Dietrich
Strength

Book of Common Prayer
Conscience, Death, Environment, Marriage, Night, Peace, Temptation, Weddings

Boren, James H.
Bureaucracy

Borges, Jorge Luis
Libraries, Lovers, Night, Praise

Borgia, Cesare
Ambition

Borrow, George
Literature, Wales

Bosquet, Pierre
War

Boswell, James
Friendship

Boucicault, Dion
Time

Boulay, Antoine de la Meurthe
Mistakes

Boulez, Pierre
Revolution

Boulton, Matthew
Technology

Bowen, Elizabeth
Absence, Envy, Experience, Fate, Spring

Bowen, Lord
Justice, Weather

Bowie, David
Heroes

Box, George
Statistics

Brabazon, Tara
Computers

Brackett, Charles and Wilder, Billy
Cinema

Bradford, John
Chance

Bradley, F. H.
Philosophy, Self-Knowledge

Bradman, Don
Cricket

Bradshaw, John
Revolution

Bradstreet, Anne
Wisdom

Bramah, Ernest
Conversation

Brando, Marlon
Acting

Index of Authors

Brandt, Willy
Languages

Braque, Georges
Art, Present

Braun, Wernher von
Science

Brautigan, Richard
Computers

Brebner, John Bartlet
Canada

Brecht, Bertolt
Clothes, Goodness, Heroes, Morality, Revolution, Science

Brenan, Gerald
Boredom, Leisure

Brickman, Marshall
see Allen, Woody and Brickman, Marshall

Bright, John
Government

Brillat-Savarin, Anthelme
Cookery, Eating, Invention

Brockbank, Russell
Europe

Brokaw, Tom
Fishing

Bronowski, Jacob
Action, Science

Brontë, Charlotte
Anxiety, Prejudice

Brontë, Emily
Courage, Lovers, Pride, Relationships

Brooke, Rupert
Death, Flowers, History, Past, Sleep

Brookner, Anita
Mothers, Women

Brooks, Gwendolyn
Present

Brooks, J.
Animals

Brotherton, Joseph
Wealth

Broun, Heywood Hale
Sport

Brown, Gordon
Experience, Family

Brown, H. Rap
Violence

Brown, Lew
Life

Brown, T. E.
Gardens

Brown, Thomas
Hatred

Browne, Sir Thomas
Human Race, Medicine, Nature

Browning, Elizabeth Barrett
Lovers, Prayer, Sorrow

Browning, Robert
Ambition, Beauty, Birds, Choice, Cynicism, England, Ignorance, Optimism, Perfection, Trust

Bruce, Lenny
Drugs

Brummell, Beau
Clothes

Brundtland, Gro Harlem
Environment

Bruno, Frank
Boxing

Buber, Martin
Self

Buchan, John
Happiness

Buchman, Frank
Economics

Buffett, Warren
Business, Danger, Wealth

Buffon, Comte de
Genius, Style

Bulgakov, Mikhail
Writing

Bulwer-Lytton, Edward
Friendship, Reading, Writing

Bunyan, John
Pride, Punishment, Style

Burchill, Julie
Woman's Role

Burke, Edmund
Ambition, Cooperation, Custom, Danger, Evil, Family, Fear, Future, Law, Liberty, Patience, Politicians, Politics, Society, Taxes

Burke, Johnny
Weather

Burnett, Carol
Humour

Burns, George
Future

Burns, John
England

Burns, Robert
Animals, Chance, Cruelty, Drink, Eating, Equality, Friendship, Honours, Lovers, Meeting, Memory, Scotland, Self-Knowledge, Temptation

Burroughs, John
Knowledge

Index of Authors

Burroughs, William S.
Drugs, Evil, Supernatural

Burton, Robert
Poetry, Religion, Travel

Busenbaum, Hermann
Morality

Bush, George
America, Boredom, Family, Food, Idealism, Taxes

Bush, George W.
Planning, Presidency

Bussy-Rabutin, Comte de
War

Butler, Joseph
Planning

Butler, Nicholas Murray
Knowledge

Butler, Samuel
Cynicism, Hypocrisy, Opinion

Butler, Samuel
Canada, Conscience, Dogs, Friendship, Language, Life Sciences, Praise

Butler, William
Food

Byrd, William
Singing

Byrne, Liam
Government

Byron, Lord
Criticism, Dance, Dogs, Fame, Hatred, Literature, Men and Women, Nature, Parties, Pleasure, Religion, Revenge, Self-Knowledge, Truth, Winter, Women

Cabell, James Branch
Pessimism

Cacoyannis, Michael
Men

Caesar, Julius
Ambition, Behaviour, Choice, Success

Cain, Herman
Success

Calderón, Pedro de La Barca
Love

Callimachus
Books

Calonne, Charles Alexandre de
Effort

Calvino, Italo
Books

Camara, Helder
Poverty

Cameron, David
Society

Cameron, James
Parting

Cameron, Simon
Politicians

Campbell, Mrs Patrick
Marriage, Sex

Campbell, Thomas
Country

Camus, Albert
Autumn, Charm, Goodness, Lies, Morality, Optimism, Revolution

Canetti, Elias
Dreams

Canning, George
Friendship, Patriotism

Cantona, Eric
Journalism

Capone, Al
Crime

Capp, Al
Art

Capra, Frank
Cinema

Caracciolo, Francesco
England

Carlyle, Thomas
Biography, Civilization, Experience, France, History, Idleness, Libraries, Statistics, Universe

Carnegie, Andrew
Wealth

Carr, Emily
Drawing

Carroll, Lewis
Beginning, Behaviour, Belief, Books, Conversation, Effort, Gifts, Justice, Language, Manners, Meaning, Names, Philosophy, Present, Reality, Statistics, Truth, Words

Carson, Johnny
Happiness

Carson, Rachel
Earth, Pollution

Carter, Chris
Secrecy

Carter, Henry
Australia

Carter, Howard
Invention

455

Index of Authors

Cartier, Jacques
Canada
Cartier-Bresson, Henri
Photography
Cartwright, John
Democracy, Elections
Casals, Pablo
Old Age
Cash, Pat
Tennis
Castro, Fidel
Economics
Cather, Willa
Generation Gap, Travel, Winter
Catherine, St of Siena
Self
Catherine the Great
Forgiveness
Cato the Elder
Speechmaking
Catullus
Parting
Cavell, Edith
Patriotism
Cervantes
Eating, Painting, Punishment
Cézanne, Paul
Drawing
Chamberlain, Joseph
Politics
Chamberlain, Neville
Peace, War
Chamfort, Nicolas-Sébastien
Humour, Intelligence
Chandler, Raymond
Creativity, Crime, Writing

Chanel, Coco
Clothes, Fashion, Youth
Channon, Henry 'Chips'
Diaries
Chaplin, Charlie
Cinema, Life
Charles I
Apology, Royalty
Charles V
Languages
Charles, Hugh see Parker, Ross and Charles, Hugh
Charles, Prince of Wales
Architecture
Chateaubriand, François-René
Originality
Chatwin, Bruce
Exercise
Chaucer, Geoffrey
Behaviour, Birds, Education, Good Looks, Hypocrisy, Murder, Spring
Chekhov, Anton
Friendship, Good Looks, Hatred, Pollution, Sickness, Theatre, Writing
Chesterfield, Lord
Advice, Behaviour, Chance, Conversation, Enemies, Idleness, Knowledge, Manners, Religion, Sex, Time, Truth
Chesterton, G. K.
Animals, Chance, Crime, Custom, God, Government, Happiness, Heart, Ideas, Individuality,

Insight, Ireland, Knowledge, Literature, Prejudice, Promises, Railways, Secrecy, Travel, Women
Chevalier, Maurice
Old Age
Child, Lydia Maria
Festivals
Chirac, Jacques
Britain
Choiseul, Duc de
Politicians
Chomsky, Noam
Brevity, Language
Chuang-tzu
Self-Knowledge
Church, Francis Pharcellus
Christmas
Churchill, Charles
Envy, Hypocrisy, Patriotism
Churchill, Lord Randolph
Ireland, Mathematics
Churchill, Winston
Achievement, Animals, Architecture, Art, Babies, Britain, Courage, Crime, Custom, Danger, Democracy, Determination, Diplomacy, Drink, Ending, Europe, Food, Future, Honours, Language, Politicians, Quotations, Revenge, Sea, Speechmaking, Trust, War, Winning, Words

Index of Authors

Ciano, Count Galeazzo
Winning

Cibber, Colley
Fashion, Marriage

Cicero
Behaviour, History, Law, Mistakes, Money, Philosophy, War

Clark, Alan
Politicians

Clarke, Arthur C.
Earth, Science, Technology

Clarke, John
Home

Clausewitz, Karl von
War

Clayton, Tubby
Charity

Cleaver, Eldridge
Conversation, Management

Clemenceau, Georges
Old Age, War

Clifford, William
Belief

Clinton, Bill
America, Drugs, Meaning

Clinton, Hillary Rodham
Children, Marriage, Woman's Role

Clough, Arthur Hugh
Crime, Determination, Envy, Fear, Murder

Cobbett, William
London

Cocteau, Jean
Art, Literature

Coetzee, J. M.
Dreams

Cohen, Leonard
Body, Canada, Perfection, Pessimism, Prayer

Coke, Edward
Business, Houses

Colbert, Jean-Baptiste
Government, Taxes

Colbert, Stephen
Books

Coleridge, Samuel Taylor
Babies, Chance, Men and Women, Night, Poetry, Politics, Pollution, Prayer, Sea, Singing

Colette
Manners

Collins, Joan
Men

Collins, Wilkie
Men and Women

Colton, Charles Caleb
Examinations, Praise, Speechmaking, Town

Comden, Betty and **Green, Adolph**
Ending

Compton-Burnett, Ivy
Men and Women

Confucius
Education, Human Race, Leadership, Thinking, Travel

Congreve, William
Good Looks, Gossip, Love, Music, Revenge

Connery, Sean
Retirement

Connolly, Billy
Fishing, Marriage

Connolly, Cyril
Charm, Memory, Men and Women, Town

Connors, Jimmy
Tennis

Conrad, Joseph
Action

Conran, Shirley
Housework, Planning

Constable, John
Beauty, Painting

Constant, Benjamin
Art

Constitution of the United States
Punishment

Cook, James
Ambition

Coolidge, Calvin
Civilization, Persistence

Cooper, Alice
Lifestyles

Cope, Wendy
Lovers, Poetry

Coppola, Francis Ford
War

Coppola, Francis Ford see Puzo, Mario and Coppola, Francis Ford

Corbett, Ronnie see Barker, Ronnie and Corbett, Ronnie

Corneille, Pierre
Danger

Cornuel, Mme
Heroes

Cory, William
Boats

457

Index of Authors

Cosby, Bill
Marriage

Cosmides, Leda and **Tooby, John**
Mind

Coubertin, Baron Pierre de
Sport

Coué, Émile
Medicine

Coupland, Douglas
Careers

Courteline, Georges
Youth

Cousteau, Jacques
Pollution

Coward, Noël
Acting, Class, England, Leisure, Music, Work

Cowper, William
Change, Country, God

Crabbe, George
Habit

Craik, Dinah Mulock
Friendship

Crashaw, Richard
Marriage

Crawford, Cindy
Appearance

Creighton, Mandell
Goodness

Crick, Francis
Life Sciences, Self

Crisp, Quentin
Biography, Diplomacy, Housework

Cromwell, Oliver
Achievement, Mistakes, Painting, Parting

Cronenberg, David
Fear

Crossman, Richard
Bureaucracy

Crowe, Cameron
Greatness

Cruz, Penelope
Old Age

Cumberland, Richard
Idleness

cummings, e. e.
Body, Progress

Cunningham, Allan
Boats

Cuomo, Mario
Politics

Cupitt, Don
Christmas

Curie, Marie
Family, Fear

Curran, John Philpot
Liberty

Curtis, Tony
Kissing

Cyprian, St
Church

Dalai Lama
Happiness

Dali, Salvador
Ambition

Dana, Charles A.
News

Dante Alighieri
Conscience, Hell, Love, Middle Age, Misfortune, Peace

Danton, Georges Jacques
Courage

Darrow, Clarence
Presidency

Darwin, Charles
Animals, Appearance, Ignorance, Language, Lies, Life Sciences, Love, Nature

Darwin, Erasmus
Facts

Darwin, Francis
Science

David, Elizabeth
Cookery

Davies, John
Dance

Davies, Robertson
Canada, Luck

Davies, Scrope
Madness

Davies, W. H.
Birds, Leisure

Davis, Sammy Jnr.
Prejudice

Davis, Thomas
Hospitality

Dawkins, Richard
Africa, Death

Dawson, Christopher
Evil

Day-Lewis, C.
Love

Dean, James
Cars, Lifestyles

de Beauvoir, Simone
Men and Women, Woman's Role

de Bernières, Louis
Heart, Love

Debray, Régis
Politics

Decatur, Stephen
Patriotism

Defoe, Daniel
Anxiety, Custom

Degas, Edgar
Genius

de Gaulle, Charles
Canada, Diplomacy, France

Index of Authors

de la Mare, Walter
Eating, Meeting, Skies, Transience

de Leon, Walter and **Jones, Paul M.**
Life

DeLillo, Don
Future

Delius, Frederick
Music

Della Femina, Jerry
Advertising

de Mille, Agnes
Dance

Democritus
Happiness

Demosthenes
Speechmaking

Dempsey, Jack
Boxing

Deng Xiaoping
Practicality

Dennis, John
Words

De Quincey, Thomas
Conscience, Drugs, Murder

Derby, Edward Stanley, 14th Earl of
Politicians

Descartes, René
Mind, Practicality, Thinking

Destouches, Philippe Néricault
Absence

De Vries, Peter
Eating

Dewar, James
Prejudice

Dewar, Lord
Cars

Diana, Princess of Wales
Royalty

Dick, Philip K.
Reality

Dickens, Charles
Babies, Business, Chance, Christmas, Class, Education, Facts, Food, Law, Letters, Money, Optimism, Pride, Protest, Supernatural, Weather, Winning

Dickinson, Emily
Fame, Old Age, Parting, Poetry, Present

Diefenbaker, John G.
Old Age

Diller, Phyllis
Housework

Dillon, Wentworth, Earl of Roscommon
Reading

DiMaggio, Joe
Baseball

Dinesen, Isak
Human Race

Diogenes
Cynicism

Dionysius of Halicarnassus
History

Dirac, Paul
Science

Disney, Walt
Books, Children

Disraeli, Benjamin
Apology, Careers, Democracy, Education, Government, Human Race, Ignorance, Justice, Lies, Peace, Politics, Royalty, Statistics, Success, Wisdom

Dogen Kigen
Self

Donleavy, J. P.
Discontent

Donne, John
Death, Imagination, Letters, Love, Sex, Skies, Society

Dostoevsky, Fedor
Beauty

Douglas, Lord Alfred
Love

Douglas, O.
Letters

Douglass, Frederick
Human Rights, Race, Singing

Doyle, Arthur Conan
Country, Crime, Facts, Genius, Imagination, Intelligence, Libraries, Thinking, Truth

Drake, Francis
Persistence, Sport

Drayton, Michael
News, Parting

Dryden, John
Discontent, Exercise, Genius, Patience, Wit, Women, Writing

Du Bellay, Joachim
France

Du Bois, W. E. B.
Liberty

Dubos, René
Prejudice

Du Deffand, Mme
Achievement

Duesenberry, James Stemble
Society

Index of Authors

Dumas, Alexandre
  Cooperation, Patience

Dumas, Alexandre
  Marriage

Dumouriez, Charles
  Experience

Duncan, Ronald
  Animals

Dunn, Irina
  Men and Women

Duport, James
  Madness

Durocher, Leo
  Sport

Dürrenmatt, Friedrich
  Thinking

Dury, Ian
  Body

Dworkin, Andrea
  Birth

Dylan, Bob
  Change, Failure, Generation Gap, Money, Singing

Earhart, Amelia
  Courage, Luck

Eastman, George
  Photography

Ebb, Fred
  Money

Eddington, Arthur
  Chance, Science, Time

Edison, Thomas Alva
  Cars, Genius, Ideas

Edmund, St of Abingdon
  Education

Edward VIII
  Royalty

Edwards, Jonathan
  Death

Ehrenreich, Barbara
  Exercise

Ehrmann, Max
  Peace

Einstein, Albert
  Chance, Education, Future, God, Ideas, Imagination, Intelligence, Mathematics, Practicality, Prejudice, Religion, Science, Success, Time, Universe, War

Eisenhower, Dwight D.
  Armed Forces, Courage, Peace, Planning, Presidency

Eisenstaedt, Alfred
  Photography

Elgar, Edward
  Art, Music

Eliot, George
  Animals, Cruelty, Despair, Discontent, Eating, Gifts, Gossip, Humour, Insight, Lovers, Mothers, Pride, Silence, Sorrow, Women

Eliot, T. S.
  Beginning, Cats, Ending, Experience, Fear, Forgiveness, Hell, Knowledge, Morality, Poetry, Pollution, Reality, Spring, Success, Television, Words

Elizabeth I
  Forgiveness, Government,

Royalty, Secrecy, Trust

Elizabeth II
  France, Misfortune, Old Age

Ellis, Alice Thomas
  Relationships

Ellis, Havelock
  Pollution

Elyot, Thomas
  Football

Emanuel, Rahm
  Crises

Emerson, Ralph Waldo
  Ability, Achievement, Ambition, Babies, Biography, Danger, Education, Flowers, Friendship, Gardens, Greatness, Health, Heroes, Honour, Hospitality, Justice, Language, Languages, Lifestyles, Opinion, Quotations, Sickness

Engels, Friedrich
  see **Marx, Karl and Engels, Friedrich**

Enright, Anne
  Cats

Ephron, Nora
  Lovers, Sex

Epictetus
  Satisfaction

Epicurus
  Death, Friendship

Epstein, Julius J.
  Friendship, Meeting, Toasts

Equiano, Olaudah
  Africa

Erhard, Ludwig
  Europe

Index of Authors

Ertz, Susan
Boredom
Estienne, Henri
Generation Gap
Euclid
Mathematics
Euripides
Fate, Marriage, Promises, Wisdom
Fadiman, Clifton
Food
Falkland, Lucius Cary, Viscount
Change
Fanon, Frantz
Africa
Faraday, Michael
Invention, Science
Farjeon, Eleanor
Day
Farquhar, George
Poverty
Faulkner, William
Drink, Sorrow, Writing
Fawkes, Guy
Revolution
Feinstein, Dianne
Strength
Fellini, Federico
Art
Ferdinand I
Justice
Fermi, Enrico
Ignorance
Feynman, Richard
Technology
Field, Frank
Certainty
Fielding, Henry
Envy, Gossip, Thanks
Fields, Dorothy
Kissing, Optimism, Persistence

Fields, W. C.
Elections, Foolishness, Humour
Firth, Colin
Names
Fish, Michael
Weather
Fitzgerald, Edward
Day, Drink, Flowers, Past, Present, Satisfaction, Truth
Fitzgerald, F. Scott
Despair, Intelligence, Manners, Middle Age, Wealth
Fitzsimmons, Robert
Boxing
Flaubert, Gustave
Art, Enemies, Happiness, Poetry, Speechmaking
Fleming, Ian
Chance
Fletcher, Andrew of Saltoun
Singing
Foley, J.
Armed Forces
Foot, Alistair *see* **Marriott, Anthony and Foot, Alistair**
Forbes, Miss C. F.
Clothes
Ford, Gerald
Government
Ford, Henry
Choice, Evil, Exercise, History
Foreman, George
Retirement
Forgy, Howell
Practicality

Forster, E. M.
Creativity, Criticism, Cynicism, Death, Democracy, Gossip, India, Literature, Luck, Patriotism, Railways, Writing
Forsyth, Frederick
Memory
Foster, Charles
America
Fowler, H. W.
Language
Fox, Charles James
India
France, Anatole
Government, Leisure, Lies, Prejudice, Quotations, Wealth
Francis, St of Assisi
Sympathy
Franklin, Benjamin
Advice, Business, Conscience, Cooperation, Debt, Hope, Human Race, Invention, Marriage, Taxes, War, Wealth
Franklin, Miles
Conversation
Franks, Lord
Secrecy
Franzoni, David
Lifestyles, Revenge
Frederick the Great
Government, Prejudice
Freeman, E. A.
History
French, Marilyn
Housework
Freud, Sigmund
America, Body, Dreams, Life, Women

Index of Authors

Friedan, Betty
*Individuality,
Woman's Role*
Friedman, Milton
Economics
Frost, David
Parents
Frost, Robert
*Birthdays, Careers,
Change, Choice,
Determination,
Happiness, Home,
Parents, Poetry,
Politics, Secrecy*
Fry, Christopher
Goodness
Fry, Elizabeth
Punishment
Fry, Stephen
Computers
Frye, Mary E.
Bereavement
**Fuller, R.
Buckminster**
Earth
Fuller, Thomas
Architecture
Fuller, Thomas
*Gardens, Law,
Luck*
Fyleman, Rose
Supernatural
Gabor, Zsa Zsa
Hatred
Gaga, Lady
Style
Gaitskell, Hugh
Country, Europe
Galbraith, J. K.
*Management,
Mistakes,
Mountains, Politics*
Galen
Words
Galileo Galilei
*Invention,
Mathematics, Skies*

Galsworthy, John
Beauty
Galt, John
Scotland
Gandhi, Mahatma
*Change,
Civilization,
Country, Peace,
Violence*
**Ganz, Lowell and
Mandel, Babaloo**
Sex
Garbo, Greta
Solitude
**García Márquez,
Gabriel**
Marriage, Memory
Gardner, Ed
Singing
Garrick, David
Cookery
Garvey, Marcus
Self
Gaskell, Elizabeth
*Foolishness, Men,
Thinking*
Gauguin, Paul
Art
Gay, John
*Choice, Deceit,
Marriage*
Geddes, Eric
Revenge
Genet, Jean
Trust
George II
Madness
George VI
Diplomacy
George, Eddie
Retirement
Gershwin, Ira *see*
**Heyward, Du Bose
and Gershwin, Ira**
Getty, J. Paul
*Business, Charity,
Wealth*

Gibbon, Edward
*Armed Forces,
Country, History,
Languages, London,
Religion, Solitude,
Sympathy*
Gibran, Kahlil
*Gifts, Individuality,
Marriage, Parents,
Parting, Truth, Work*
Gide, André
*Experience, Love,
Sympathy, Truth*
Gilbert, Elizabeth
Babies
Gilbert, W. S.
*Certainty, Elections,
Equality, Language,
Meaning, Men,
Pride, Punishment,
Railways, Sleep*
Giovanni, Nikki
Mistakes
**Giraldus
Cambrensis**
Wales
Giraudoux, Jean
Law, Poetry
Giuliani, Rudolph
Suffering
Gladstone, W. E.
*Democracy, Future,
Government*
Gloucester, Duke of
Books
Godard, Jean-Luc
Cinema
Godwin, William
Crises
Goebbels, Joseph
Protest, War
Goering, Hermann
Race, War
**Goethe, Johann
Wolfgang von**
*Art, Character,
Effort, Fame,*

Index of Authors

*Languages,
Lifestyles, Love,
Old Age, Reality,
Self-Knowledge,
Supernatural*

**Goldbeck, Willis
and Bellah, James
Warner**
Journalism

Golding, William
Sleep

Goldman, William
Cinema

Goldsmith, Oliver
Law

Goldwyn, Sam
*Certainty, Cinema,
Law*

Gorky, Maxim
Art

Gould, Stephen Jay
Greatness

Goya
Dreams

Grace, W. G.
Cricket

Graham, D. M.
Patriotism

Graham, Martha
Body, Dance

Grahame, Kenneth
Boats, Cars

Grant, Ulysses S.
Law

Grass, Günter
Protest

Gray, John
Men and Women

Gray, John Chipman
Housework

Gray, Thomas
*Children,
Ignorance, Night,
Suffering*

Greeley, Horace
America

Green, Adolph *see*
**Comden, Betty and
Green, Adolph**

Greene, Graham
*Happiness,
Indifference, Lies,
Reading, Success*

Greene, Robert
Time

Greer, Germaine
*Football, Good
Looks, Men and
Women, Pleasure,
Woman's Role*

Gregg, Hubert
London

Gregory, Dick
Baseball

Grellet, Stephen
Goodness

**Griffith-Jones,
Mervyn**
Censorship

Grocott, Bruce
Work

Groening, Matt
Effort, France

**Grossmith, George
and Grossmith,
Weedon**
Home, Misfortune

**Grossmith,
Weedon** *see*
**Grossmith, George
and Grossmith,
Weedon**

Grove, Andrew
*Business,
Technology*

Guest, Edgar A.
Houses

**Gurney, Dorothy
Frances**
Gardens

Haddon, Mark
Mathematics

Hakuin
Cooperation

Haldane, J. B. S.
*Life Sciences,
Statistics, Universe*

Haldeman, H. R.
Secrecy

**Hale, Edward
Everett**
Politicians

Hale, Nathan
Patriotism

Halifax, Lord
Anger, Punishment

Hall, Jerry
Woman's Role

Hamilton, Alex
Character

Hamilton, William
Mind

**Hammerstein II,
Oscar**
*Hope, Meeting,
Music, Summer*

**Hampton,
Christopher**
Doubt

Hand, Learned
Names

Hannibal
Determination

**Hansberry,
Lorraine**
Race

Harbach, Otto
Sorrow

**Harburg, E. Y.
('Yip')**
*Kissing, Sickness,
Singing*

**Hardy, Godfrey
Harold**
Mathematics

Hardy, Thomas
*Appearance,
History, Luck,
Pessimism, Writing*

Index of Authors

Hare, Maurice Evan
Fate
Harington, John
Trust
Harper, Stephen
Promises
Harris, Joel Chandler
Luck
Harris, Thomas and **Tally, Ted**
Eating
Harrison, Tony
Relationships
Hart, Lorenz
Behaviour, Lovers
Harte, Bret
Luck
Hartley, L. P.
Past
Haskins, Minnie Louise
Trust
Havel, Václav
Hope, Protest
Hawking, Stephen
Computers, Mathematics, Universe
Hay, Ian
Humour, War
Hay, John
Friendship
Hazlitt, William
Country, Hatred, Human Race, Manners, Names, Prejudice, Wit
Heaney, Seamus
Ireland
Hearst, William Randolph
Journalism, News
Hegel, G. W. F.
Reality, Society
Heine, Heinrich
Censorship, Skies

Heinlein, Robert
Progress
Heisenberg, Werner
Mistakes
Heller, Joseph
Madness
Hellman, Lillian
Conscience, Cynicism
Helmsley, Leona
Taxes
Héloïse
Lovers
Hemingway, Ernest
Africa, Courage, Evil, Failure, Kissing, Morality, Sex, Writing
Henley, W. E.
Determination, Self
Henri IV
Cynicism, Poverty
Henry, O.
Deceit
Henry, Patrick
Liberty
Hepworth, Barbara
Drawing, Sculpture
Heraclitus
Change, Character, War
Herbert, A. P.
Country
Herbert, George
Drink, Fathers, Hope, Secrecy
Herman, Henry see **Jones, Henry Arthur** and **Herman, Henry**
Herrick, Robert
Clothes, Transience
Hervey, Lord
Lies
Herzberg, Frederick
Management

Herzog, Maurice
Mountains
Hesiod
Effort
Hesse, Hermann
Happiness, Hatred, Home
Hewart, Lord
Justice
Hewitt, Foster William
Sport
Heyward, Du Bose and **Gershwin, Ira**
Summer
Hicks, J. R.
Business
Hicks, Seymour
Old Age
Hightower, Jim
Moderation
Hill, Aaron
Courage
Hill, Damon
Winning
Hill, Joe
Revolution
Hill, Napoleon
Money
Hillary, Edmund
Mountains
Hillingdon, Lady
Sex
Hilton, Paris
Clothes
Hippocrates
Art, Manners, Medicine
Hirst, Damien
Sculpture
Hitchcock, Alfred
Acting, Cinema, Fear, Television
Hitchens, Christopher
Facts

Index of Authors

Hitler, Adolf
  Leadership, Lies
Hobbes, Thomas
  Life, Truth
Hockney, David
  *Criticism,
  Technology*
Holiday, Billie
  Drugs
**Holland, Henry
Scott**
  Death
Holmes, John H.
  Universe
**Holmes, Oliver
Wendell**
  *Conversation,
  Festivals, Ideas,
  Money, Old Age,
  Prejudice*
Holtby, Winifred
  Insight
Home, Lord
  Fishing
Homer
  *Death, Gifts,
  Transience*
Hood, Thomas
  Poverty, Winter
Hoover, Herbert
  Fishing, Words
Hope, Bob
  *Birthdays, Golf,
  Money*
**Hopkins, Gerard
Manley**
  *Beauty, Birds,
  Despair,
  Environment,
  Mind, Pollution,
  Skies*
Horace
  *Anger, Birthdays,
  Brevity, Crises,
  Death, Effort,
  Foolishness,*

*Hope, Hospitality,
Literature,
Mistakes,
Moderation,
Money, Nature,
Patriotism, Poetry,
Praise, Present,
Statistics, Words*
Hornby, Nick
  Cynicism, Football
**Horne, Donald
Richmond**
  Australia
**Horne, Lena Mary
Calhoun**
  Individuality
Housman, A. E.
  *Drink, Memory,
  Spring*
**Howells, William
Dean**
  Hospitality
Hubbard, Elbert
  *Genius, Life,
  Lifestyles,
  Technology*
**Hubbard, Frank
McKinney ('Kin')**
  *Economics, Money,
  Revenge*
Hughes, Thomas
  Cricket
**Hughes, William
Morris 'Billy'**
  Painting
Hugo, Victor
  *Church, Fame,
  France, Ideas,
  Mothers, Suffering*
Hume, David
  *Character, Custom,
  Human Race,
  Religion, Self*
Huntington, Samuel
  America
Hupfeld, Herman
  Kissing

Huxley, Aldous
  *Achievement,
  Apology, Change,
  Criticism, Dogs,
  Education,
  Experience,
  Facts, Happiness,
  Idealism, Pleasure*
Huxley, Julian
  God
Huxley, T. H.
  *Doubt, Law, Money,
  Science, Thinking,
  Truth*
Iacocca, Lee
  Friendship
Ibarruri, Dolores
  Liberty
Ibsen, Henrik
  Clothes
Illich, Ivan
  Society
Inge, Dean
  *Argument, Liberty,
  Originality, Power*
Ingersoll, Robert G.
  God, Language
Ingham, Bernard
  Government
Ingres, J. A. D.
  Drawing
Irving, Washington
  Conversation
Issigonis, Alec
  Management
Jackson, Jesse
  Race
Jackson, Mahalia
  Poverty
**Jackson, Thomas
Jonathan
'Stonewall'**
  War
Jacobs, Joe
  Boxing

Index of Authors

Jagger, Mick and
Richards, Keith
Protest, Satisfaction
**Jalal ad-Din
ar-Rumi**
God, Religion
James, Carwyn
Revenge
James, Clive
Television
**James, Cyril Lionel
Robert**
Cricket
James, Evan
Wales
James, Henry
*Criticism, Lifestyles,
Literature,
Relationships,
Summer*
James, P. D.
Autumn
James, William
Lies, Wisdom
Jarrell, Randall
*Discontent,
Manners*
Jay, Antony *see
Lynn, Jonathan* and
Jay, Antony
Jeans, James
*Life Sciences,
Universe*
Jefferson, Thomas
*Anger, Character,
Civilization,
Exercise, Gardens,
Health, Ideas,
Morality, Politics,
Revolution*
Jeffrey, Francis, Lord
Criticism
Jennings, Elizabeth
Animals
Jerome, Jerome K.
*Idleness, Sickness,
Weather, Work*

Jerome, William
Home
Jerrold, Douglas
Religion
Joad, C. E. M.
Meaning
Jobs, Steve
*Achievement,
Death, Lifestyles*
John XXIII
Church
John, Elton and
Taupin, Bernie
Gifts
John Paul II
Church
Johnson, Amy
Flight
Johnson, Boris
*Crises,
Examinations*
**Johnson, Lyndon
Baines**
*Enemies,
Intelligence*
**Johnson, Philander
Chase**
Optimism
Johnson, Samuel
*Achievement,
Advertising,
Biography, Careers,
Change, Children,
Conversation,
Criticism, Death,
Effort, Equality,
Evil, Fishing,
Food, Friendship,
Genius, Ignorance,
Imagination,
Intelligence,
Knowledge,
Language,
Languages,
Libraries, London,
Marriage,
Memory, Opinion,
Patriotism,*

*Philosophy, Poetry,
Poverty, Praise,
Reading, Scotland,
Sea, Solitude,
Supernatural,
Taxes, Travel,
Trust, War, Wealth,
Weather, Woman's
Role, Words,
Writing*
Johst, Hanns
Civilization
Jolson, Al
Singing
**Jones, Henry
Arthur** and
Herman, Henry
Past
Jones, Paul M. *see
De Leon, Walter and
Jones, Paul M.*
Jong, Erica
Women
Joseph, Jenny
Idleness, Old Age
Joyce, James
Ireland
Julian of Norwich
Optimism
Jung, Carl Gustav
*Belief, Children,
Cruelty, Drugs,
Heart, Life, Middle
Age, Misfortune*
Justice, Donald
Middle Age
Juvenal
*Children,
Conversation, Evil,
Health, Honesty,
Knowledge,
Pleasure, Poverty,
Sport, Trust*
Kabir
God
Kafka, Franz
*Books, Despair,
Hope, Youth*

Index of Authors

Kalmar, Bert
 Honour, Parting
Kamo no Chomei
 Transience
Kant, Immanuel
 Happiness, Human Race, Knowledge, Morality
Karr, Alphonse
 Change
Kaufman, Beatrice
 Wealth
Kaufman, George S. and Teichmann, Howard
 Theatre
Kautilya
 Deceit
Kay, Alan
 Future
Keats, John
 Autumn, Beauty, Creativity, Death, Discontent, Dreams, Imagination, Invention, Pleasure, Poetry, Silence
Keillor, Garrison
 Christmas, Men
Keller, Helen
 Body, Language, Life
Kelley, Earl C.
 Certainty
Kelly, Ned
 Punishment
Kennedy, John F.
 Beginning, Cooperation, Diplomacy, Forgiveness, Human Race, Human Rights, Liberty, Patriotism, Race, Sea

Kennedy, Joseph P.
 Business, Determination
Kennedy, Robert
 Economics, Idealism, Protest, Violence
Kennedy-Martin, Troy
 Ideas
Kerr, Jean
 Flight, Good Looks
Kerry, John
 Armed Forces, Certainty
Kettle, Thomas
 Ireland
Keynes, John Maynard
 Examinations, Facts, Government, Time
Khrushchev, Nikita
 Politicians, Satisfaction
Khusrau, Amir
 India
Kierkegaard, Sören
 Idleness, Life
Kilmer, Joyce
 Creativity
Kilvert, Francis
 Mountains
King, David
 Earth
King, Martin Luther
 Conscience, Cooperation, Equality, Hatred, Idealism, Justice, Leadership, Power, Protest, Race
King, William Lyon Mackenzie
 Canada

Kingsley, Charles
 Goodness
Kingsolver, Barbara
 Marriage
Kinsey, Alfred
 Sex
Kipling, Rudyard
 Armed Forces, Art, Cats, Character, Crises, Dogs, England, Gardens, Journalism, Knowledge, Madness, Men and Women, Mothers, Opinion, Sex, Solitude, Sport, Words
Kissinger, Henry
 Europe, Management, Power
Klee, Paul
 Drawing, Painting
Klopstock, Friedrich
 Meaning
Knox, John
 Woman's Role
Knox, Ronald
 Babies, Opinion
Koestler, Arthur
 God
Kohl, Helmut
 Europe
Koran, The
 God, Goodness, Human Race, Religion
Kranz, Gene
 Failure
Kraus, Karl
 Cars, Strength
Kronecker, Leopold
 Mathematics

Index of Authors

Krutch, Joseph Wood
Cats, Winter

Kuan Tao-sheng
Marriage

Kubrick, Stanley
Politics

Kundera, Milan
Intelligence

Laclos, Pierre Choderlos de
Happiness

Lacroix, Christian
Fashion

la Fontaine, Jean de
Fame, Secrecy

Lahr, John
Advertising

Laing, R. D.
Madness

Lamb, Charles
Belief, Debt, Gardens, Gifts, Humour, Libraries, Meeting, Pleasure, Time, Writing

Lamont, Norman
Economics

Lampedusa, Giuseppe di
Change

Lance, Bert
Management

Landers, Ann
Parties

Lang, Andrew
Statistics

Lang, Julia
Beginning

Langley, Noel
Change

Lao Tzu
Beginning, Law, Leadership, Self-Knowledge, Travel

Larcom, Lucy
Gardens

Larkin, Philip
Birthdays, Boredom, Day, Happiness, Life, London, Old Age, Parents, Pessimism, Work

la Rochefoucauld, Duc de
Absence, Boredom, Friendship, Greatness, Home, Hypocrisy, Love, Mind, Misfortune

Latimer, Hugh
Persistence

Lauder, Harry
Persistence

Lauren, Ralph
Fashion

Lawrence, D. H.
Australia, Autumn, Behaviour, Literature, Love

Lazarus, Emma
America

Leacock, Stephen
Advertising

Leary, Timothy
Computers, Lifestyles

Lebowitz, Fran
Conversation, Women

Lec, Stanislaw
Censorship, Progress, Revolution

le Carré, John
Bureaucracy

Le Corbusier
Houses, Town

Lee, Harper
Conscience, Courage

Lee, Nathaniel
Madness

Lee, Robert E.
War

Lehrer, Tom
Achievement, Life

Leibniz, Gottfried Wilhelm
Music

Leigh, Fred W.
Weddings

Lenin
Liberty, Politics, Progress, Technology

Lennon, John
Fame, Happiness, Imagination, Life

Lennon, John and McCartney, Paul
Friendship, Lovers, Money, Old Age, Past, Peace, Solitude

Leonardo da Vinci
Life, Nature

Lerner, Alan Jay
Charm, Men, Temptation, Weddings

Lessing, Doris
Cats

Lessing, G. E.
Prayer

Leverhulme, Lord
Advertising

Levi, Primo
Cruelty

Lévis, Duc de
Government

Lewis, C. S.
Bereavement, Courage, Forgiveness, Future, Prayer, Sorrow, Teaching, Women

Liberace
Criticism

Index of Authors

Lincoln, Abraham
*Achievement,
Change, Criticism,
Deceit, Democracy,
Determination,
Elections, Good
Looks, Justice*
Lindbergh, Charles
Flight
Lineker, Gary
Football
Lin Yutang
Travel
Lippmann, Walter
Leadership
Livingstone, Ken
Elections, Politics
Livy
Failure
**Lloyd George,
David**
*Britain, Charity,
Politics*
Locke, John
Mistakes, Opinion
Lodge, David
Children
Logue, Christopher
Insight
Lombardi, Vince
Failure
London, Jack
Sport
**Longfellow, Henry
Wadsworth**
*Biography,
Festivals, God, Life,
Misfortune, Night,
Solitude, Sorrow,
Youth*
Loos, Anita
Parting, Practicality
Lorenz, Edward N.
Chance
Louis XIV
*Management,
Royalty*

Louis XVIII
*Armed Forces,
Punctuality*
Louis, Joe
Boxing
Lovelace, Richard
Honour, Liberty
Lovell, Bernard
Youth
**Lowell, James
Russell**
Argument, Work
Lowell, Robert
*Middle Age,
Pessimism*
Lowndes, William
Money
Lubac, Henri de
Habit
Lucas, E. V.
Punctuality
Lucas, George
Experience
Lucas, Matt and
Walliams, David
Computers
Luce, Clare Booth
Woman's Role
Lucretius
Creativity
**Lula da Silva, Luiz
Inácio**
Peace
Luther, Martin
God, Pleasure
Lutyens, Edwin
Mothers
Luxemburg, Rosa
Liberty
Lu Xun
Hope
Lynch, Peter
Business
Lynn, Jonathan and
Jay, Antony
Cynicism

Lyte, Henry Francis
Change
Macaulay, Lord
*Imagination,
Liberty, Morality,
Praise*
Macaulay, Rose
Housework
McCain, John
Patriotism
McCarthy, Cormac
Promises, Suffering
McCartney, Linda
Eating
McCartney, Paul see
Lennon, John and
McCartney, Paul
McCormick, P. D.
Australia
**McCullough,
Colleen**
Middle Age
Macdonald, John A.
Misfortune
McEnroe, John
Tennis
McGoohan, Patrick
Self
McGregor, Jimmie
Football
Machado, Antonio
Travel
Machiavelli, Niccolò
*Goodness,
Government,
Leadership,
Revenge,
Satisfaction*
**Maclaren,
Alexander**
Church
MacLeish, Archibald
Knowledge, Poetry
McLuhan, Marshall
*Babies, Cars,
Technology,
Television*

Index of Authors

Macmillan, Harold
Africa, Morality,
Politicians, Politics,
Power, Wealth
McNealy, Scott
Computers
MacNeice, Louis
Birth, Music
MacNeil, Robert
Parents
Madison, James
Government
Madonna
Men
Magee, John Gillespie
Flight
Magna Carta
Human Rights
Magnusson, Magnus
Beginning
Magritte, René
Mind, Painting
Mahaffy, John Pentland
Ireland
Mahler, Gustav
Music
Mailer, Norman
Fashion, Heroes
Maine, Henry
Peace
Major, John
Britain, Economics,
Punishment
Malcolm X
Anger, Peace
Mallory, George Leigh
Mountains
Mancroft, Lord
Cricket
Mandel, Babaloo
see Ganz, Lowell and
Mandel, Babaloo

Mandela, Nelson
Africa, Diplomacy,
Education,
Forgiveness, Hatred,
Poverty
Mandelson, Peter
Wealth
Manikan, Ruby
Education
Mann, Horace
Greatness
Mann, Thomas
Bereavement,
Festivals
Mao Zedong
Armed Forces,
Politics, Power
Maradona, Diego
Football
Marco Polo
Travel
Marie-Antoinette
Indifference
Marks, Leo
Lovers
Marlborough, Sarah, Duchess of
Sex
Marlowe, Christopher
Love, Religion
Marquis, Don
Honesty,
Misfortune,
Optimism, Poetry
Marriott, Anthony and Foot, Alistair
Britain
Marshall, Arthur
Life
Martel, Yann
Clothes
Martial
Birthdays, Health,
Lovers
Martin, Dean
Drink

Marvell, Andrew
Gardens, Time
Marvell, Holt
Memory
Marx, Groucho
Pride
Marx, Karl
Custom, History,
Philosophy,
Religion, Society
Marx, Karl and Engels, Friedrich
Class
Mary, Queen of Scots
Ending
Masefield, John
Boats, Sea
Mathew, James
Justice
Mathison, Melissa
Home
Matlovich, Leonard
Armed Forces
Matthews, Cerys
Wales
Maugham, W. Somerset
Charity, Love,
Men and Women,
Money, Morality,
Parties, Suffering
Maupassant, Guy de
Mind
Maurois, André
Marriage, Old Age
Mayer, Louis B.
Cinema
Mazarin, Cardinal
Luck
Mead, Margaret
Politics
Medici, Cosimo de'
Forgiveness
Meir, Golda
Leadership

Index of Authors

Melba, Nellie
Music

Melbourne, Lord
Certainty, Honours, Politicians, Religion

Melville, Herman
Achievement, Books, Sea

Menander
Life, Youth

Mencken, H. L.
Conscience, Intelligence, Love, Management

Menzies, Robert Gordon
Australia

Mercer, Johnny
Optimism

Meredith, George
Certainty, Cookery

Meredith, Owen
Genius

Merrell, Jo Ann
Parents

Merritt, Dixon Lanier
Birds

Meynell, Viola
Housework

Michals, Duane
Photography

Michelangelo
Perfection, Sculpture

Mies van der Rohe, Ludwig
Architecture

Mill, John Stuart
Discontent, Happiness, Individuality, Liberty, Technology

Millay, Edna St Vincent
Bereavement

Miller, Arthur
Business, Journalism

Milligan, Spike
Money, Sickness

Milne, A. A.
Birthdays, Eating, Education, Exercise, Golf, Ideas, Weather

Milton, John
Ambition, Books, Change, Conversation, Dance, Evil, Fame, Heart, Hypocrisy, Men and Women, Mind, Patience, Peace, Poetry, Skies, Sleep, Speechmaking, Sport, Violence, Writing

Mistinguett
Kissing

Mitchell, Adrian
Poetry

Mitchell, Joni
Life

Mitchell, Margaret
Birth, Hope, Indifference

Mizner, Wilson
Conversation, Doubt, Originality, Practicality

Molière
Criticism, Custom, Eating, Foolishness, Justice, Language, Progress

Moltke, Helmuth von
Planning

Montagu, Lady Mary Wortley
Enemies

Montaigne
Belief, Cats, Children, Failure, Housework, Knowledge, Love, Opinion, Originality, Power, Quotations, Suffering

Montesquieu
Birth, God, History, Success

Montessori, Maria
Teaching

Montgomery, Lord of Alamein
War

Monty Python's Flying Circus
Change, Death, Progress

Moore, Clement C.
Christmas

Moore, George
Travel

Moore, Henry
Sculpture

Moore, Marianne
Ireland

Moore, Thomas
Love, Memory

More, Thomas
Parting

Morey, Larry
Manners

Morgan, John Pierpont
Law

Morris, Desmond
Society

Morris, William
Houses

Morrison, Toni
Beauty, Choice, Lovers, Old Age

Morrison, Van
Music

Index of Authors

Moser, Claus
Education
Moss, Kate
Body
Mountbatten, Lord
Bereavement
Moynihan, Daniel P.
Ireland
Mozart, Wolfgang Amadeus
Music
Mugabe, Robert
Cricket
Muggeridge, Malcolm
Evil
Muir, John
Mountains
Muller, H. J.
Human Race
Mulroney, Brian
Canada
Mumford, Lewis
Generation Gap
Murdoch, Iris
Flowers, Marriage, Mind
Murray, Andy
Tennis
Mussolini, Benito
Idleness, Punctuality
Nabokov, Vladimir
Railways, Reading
Napoleon I
Armed Forces, Courage, England, Europe, Failure, Past, Sex
Narayan, R. K.
India
Narváez, Ramón María
Enemies
Nash, Ogden
Cars, Cats, Dogs, Drink, Family,

Fathers, Festivals, Houses, Middle Age, Parents
Navratilova, Martina
Tennis, Winning
Nehru, Jawaharlal
India, Temptation
Nelson, Horatio, Lord
England
Nemerov, Howard
Invention
Neruda, Pablo
Love, Lovers
Nesbit, Edith
Children
Neumann, John von
Mathematics
Newbolt, Henry
Cricket, Sport
Newman, John Henry
Belief, Change, Doubt
Newton, Isaac
Invention, Progress
Nicholson, Vivian
Money
Nicolson, Harold
Diaries, Marriage
Niebuhr, Reinhold
Change
Niemöller, Martin
Cooperation
Nietzsche, Friedrich
Discontent, Human Race, Lifestyles, Morality, Sleep, Suffering, Wit, Women, Words
Nightingale, Florence
Discontent, Medicine
Nin, Anaïs
Anxiety, Courage

Nixon, Richard
Hatred, Presidency
Nizer, Louis
Self
Nkrumah, Kwame
Progress
Nobbs, David
Careers
Noonuccal, Oodgeroo
Race
North, Christopher
Law
Northcliffe, Lord
Censorship, Honours
Norton, Caroline
Death
Norworth, Jack
Baseball
Nyerere, Julius
Debt
Obama, Barack
America, Determination, Diplomacy
Occam, William of
Philosophy
Ochs, Adolph S.
Journalism
Ogilvy, David
Advertising
O'Kelly, Dennis
Sport
Oldfield, Bruce
Fashion
Olivier, Laurence
Acting
Omar, Caliph
Censorship
Onassis, Aristotle
Business
Onassis, Jacqueline Kennedy
Parents

Index of Authors

Ondaatje, Michael
Heart

O'Neill, Eugene
Crime, Sea

Ono, Yoko
Women

**Oppenheimer,
J. Robert**
*Invention,
Technology*

O'Rourke, P. J.
Debt

**Ortega y Gasset,
José**
Environment

Orwell, George
*Advertising,
Appearance,
Argument, Body,
Censorship,
Equality, Future,
Government,
Humour, Liberty,
Politics, Power,
Prejudice, Sport,
Thinking, War*

Osborne, Dorothy
Letters

Osborne, John
Royalty

Osler, William
Medicine, Sickness

O'Sullivan, John L.
Government

Otis, James
Taxes

O'Toole, Peter
Exercise

Ovid
*Character,
Envy, Leisure,
Moderation,
Persistence, Time*

Owen, Wilfred
*Armed Forces,
Poetry, War*

**Paderewski, Ignacy
Jan**
Music

Paglia, Camille
*Civilization,
Television*

**Paige, Leroy
('Satchel')**
Exercise

Paine, Thomas
Religion, Wisdom

Paley, William
Argument

Palin, Sarah
*Determination,
Words*

Pali Tripitaka
Hatred

Palmerston, Lord
Death, Meeting

**Pankhurst,
Emmeline**
Argument

Parker, Charlie
Music

Parker, Dorothy
*Acting, Appearance,
Birth, Death, Gifts*

Parker, Ray Jr.
Supernatural

**Parker, Ross and
Charles, Hugh**
England, Meeting

**Parkes, Colin
Murray**
Sorrow

Parkes, Henry
Australia

**Parkinson,
C. Northcote**
*Bureaucracy,
Management,
Money, Work*

Parks, Rosa
Race

**Parnell, Charles
Stewart**
Advice

Parton, Dolly
*Appearance,
Mistakes*

Pascal, Blaise
*Appearance,
Brevity, Crises,
Death, Heart,
Human Race,
Misfortune, Self,
Skies, Style,
Writing*

Pasternak, Boris
*Life, Mistakes,
Spring*

Pasteur, Louis
Science

Paton, Alan
Forgiveness

Patton, George S.
*Armed Forces,
Planning*

Pauli, Wolfgang
Thinking

Pauling, Linus
Knowledge

Paxman, Jeremy
Mathematics

Payn, James
Misfortune

Payne, J. H.
Home

**Peacock, Thomas
Love**
*Humour,
Relationships,
Science*

Peake, Mervyn
Lifestyles

Pearson, Hesketh
Honours

Pearson, Lester
Canada

Pelé
Football

Index of Authors

Penn, William
Reading
Pepys, Samuel
Punishment, Sleep
Peres, Shimon
Television
Pericles
Bereavement, Fame, Women
Persons, Ted
Past
Pétain, Marshal
Biography
Peter, Laurence
Idleness, Management
Petrarch
Love
Petronius
Death
Phelps, Edward John
Mistakes
Philby, Kim
Trust
Philip, Duke of Edinburgh
Cookery, Marriage
Phillips, Arthur Angell
Australia
Picasso, Pablo
Art, Genius, Painting
Pick, Frank
Style
Pirsig, Robert M.
God, Mind
Pitt, William
Environment, Youth
Pius VII
Diplomacy
Pius XII
Mistakes
Planck, Max
Science

Plath, Sylvia
Birth, Madness, Women
Plato
Children, Mathematics, Religion
Pliny the Elder
Africa, Books, Certainty, Nature, Wisdom
Poe, Edgar Allan
Dreams
Poincaré, Henri
Science
Pompadour, Madame de
Revolution
Pompidou, Georges
Politicians
Pope, Alexander
Brevity, Charity, Children, Conversation, Dogs, Education, Environment, Foolishness, Forgiveness, Goodness, Government, Happiness, Heart, Honesty, Hope, Hospitality, Intelligence, Knowledge, Mistakes, Opinion, Praise, Reading, Retirement, Science, Self, Self-Knowledge, Style, Teaching, Writing
Popper, Karl
Prejudice
Porter, Cole
Country, Love, Trust

Potter, Dennis
Flight, Present, Religion
Pound, Ezra
Literature, Middle Age, Music, Winter
Powell, Anthony
Old Age
Pratchett, Terry
Advice, Genius, Imagination, Self, Taxes, Technology
Priestley, J. B.
Football, Relationships, Weather
Prior, Matthew
Sickness
Pritchett, V. S.
Books
Protagoras
Human Race
Proust, Marcel
Day, Heaven, Sickness, Travel
Proverb
Absence, Advertising, Anger, Crime, Ending, Enemies, Exercise, Health, Manners, Weddings
Publilius Syrus
Charity, Good Looks, Suffering
Pulitzer, Joseph
Journalism
Pullman, Philip
Literature
Punch
Behaviour, Choice, Diplomacy
Pushkin, Alexander
Deceit
Puzo, Mario
Choice, Law

Index of Authors

Puzo, Mario and **Coppola, Francis Ford**
Enemies

Pythagoras
Health

Quiller-Couch, Arthur
Perfection

Rabelais, François
Children, Eating, Knowledge, Lifestyles

Rabin, Yitzhak
Peace

Racine, Jean
Women

Radcliffe, Paula
Exercise

Rainborowe, Thomas
Human Rights

Ralegh, Walter
Ambition, Sea, Time

Raleigh, Walter
Examinations

Ramanujan, Srinivasa
Mathematics

Randi, James
Supernatural

Raposo, Joe
Environment

Read, Carveth
Mistakes

Reade, Charles
Habit

Reagan, Ronald
Character, Economics, Management, Sickness, Work

Reger, Max
Criticism

Rendall, Montague John
Television

Renoir, Jean
Letters

Retz, Cardinal de
Fear, Management, Planning

Reynolds, Joshua
Work

Rhodes, Cecil
Achievement, England

Rice, Grantland
Sport

Rice-Davies, Mandy
Lies

Rich, Mike
Gifts

Richards, Keith *see* **Jagger, Mick** and **Richards, Keith**

Richardson, Ralph
Acting

Richter, Jean Paul
Birthdays

Rilke, Rainer Maria
Fate, Love

Rimbaud, Arthur
Life

Ritz, César
Business

Rivarol, Antoine de
Languages

Robin, Leo
Wealth

Robinson, Anne
Strength

Robinson, Bruce
Flowers

Roddick, Anita
Business

Rogers, Samuel
Action, Marriage, Solitude

Rogers, Will
Civilization, Heroes, Humour, Ignorance, Taxes, Time

Roland, Mme
Liberty

Rolland, Romain
Heroes, India

Rolle, Richard de Hampole
Class

Roosevelt, Eleanor
Pride

Roosevelt, Franklin D.
Economics, Fear, Human Rights

Roosevelt, Theodore
Armed Forces, Diplomacy, Fathers, Journalism, Presidency, Work

Rosa, Salvator
Speechmaking

Rossetti, Christina
Memory

Rostand, Jean
Life Sciences, Murder

Rosten, Leo
Children

Roth, Eric
Life

Rotten, Johnny
Sex

Roupell, Charles
Sport

Rousseau, Jean-Jacques
Books, Liberty

Rowland, Helen
Foolishness, Men

Rowling, J. K.
Ability, Morality

Royden, Maude
Church

Rumbold, Richard
Democracy

Index of Authors

Rumsfeld, Donald
*Advice, Criticism,
Europe, Ignorance,
Knowledge*
Runyon, Damon
Money
Rushdie, Salman
*Absence, Insight,
Liberty*
Rusk, Dean
Crises
Ruskin, John
*Architecture, Art,
Beauty, Books,
Cooperation,
Greatness,
Mountains,
Painting, Work*
Russell, Bertrand
*Belief, Boredom,
Censorship, Fathers,
Gossip, Happiness,
Leisure, Philosophy,
Progress, Science,
Thinking, Work*
Rutherford, Ernest
Science, Statistics
Sadi
*Human Race,
Patience*
Sagan, Carl
*Earth, Invention,
Universe*
Sagan, Françoise
Envy
**Saint-Exupéry,
Antoine de**
*Children, Fear,
Insight, Love,
Perfection,
Planning*
Saint Laurent, Yves
Clothes
Saki
Clothes, Cookery
Salisbury, Lord
Elections

Sallust
Friendship
Samuel, Lord
Libraries
Samuelson, Paul A.
Economics
Sandburg, Carl
*Babies, Language,
Past, War, Weather*
**Sanders, Henry
'Red'**
Sport
Santayana, George
Past
**Sargent, John
Singer**
Painting
Sarton, May
Solitude
Sartre, Jean-Paul
*Despair, Habit,
Hell, Time*
Saunders, Cicely
Sickness
Sayers, Dorothy L.
*Men and Women,
Quotations*
Scalpone, Al
Prayer
**Schelling, Friedrich
von**
Architecture
**Schiller, Friedrich
von**
*Happiness,
Intelligence,
Originality, Secrecy,
Wisdom*
Schmidt, Eric
Computers
Schnabel, Artur
Music
**Schopenhauer,
Arthur**
Insight, Wealth
Schulberg, Budd
Ability

Schumacher, E. F.
*Economics,
Environment*
Schumpeter, J. A.
Idealism
Schurz, Carl
Patriotism
Scott, C. P.
Journalism
**Scott, Robert
Falcon**
Experience
Scott, Sir Walter
*Chance, Deceit,
Indifference,
Love, Patriotism,
Scotland, Women*
Scottish Proverb
Toasts
**Scott-Maxwell,
Florida**
Parents
Searle, Ronald see
**Willans, Geoffrey
and Searle, Ronald**
Seeger, Pete
Experience
Segal, Erich
Love
Seinfeld, Jerry
Journalism
Sei Shōnagon
Enemies
Selassie, Haile
Strength
Selden, John
*Law, Pleasure,
Words*
**Sellar, W. C. and
Yeatman, R. J.**
*Examinations,
History, Teaching*
**Seneca ('the
Younger')**
*Death, Debt,
Ignorance, Sorrow,
Teaching*

Index of Authors

Service, Robert W.
Promises, Strength, Time

Sexton, Anne
Fathers, Old Age

Shackleton, Ernest
Determination, Effort

Shaftesbury, Lord
Religion

Shakespeare, William
Acting, Action, Ambition, Anxiety, Appearance, Bereavement, Body, Careers, Chance, Character, Charity, Choice, Clothes, Conscience, Conversation, Courage, Cruelty, Custom, Danger, Day, Death, Debt, Diplomacy, Doubt, Dreams, Eating, Education, Effort, Ending, England, Envy, Equality, Evil, Failure, Fame, Family, Fate, Fathers, Fear, Flowers, Food, Friendship, Future, Generation Gap, Gifts, Good Looks, Goodness, Greatness, Heart, Honesty, Honour, Hospitality, Human Race, Hypocrisy, Imagination, Indifference, Justice, Language, Law, Leisure, Libraries, Life, Love, Lovers, Madness, Manners, Marriage, Meaning, Medicine, Meeting, Memory, Men, Misfortune, Moderation, Morality, Murder, Music, Names, Nature, News, Old Age, Parting, Past, Perfection, Persistence, Pollution, Praise, Prayer, Present, Protest, Punctuality, Reading, Royalty, Satisfaction, Scotland, Sea, Self, Self-Knowledge, Sex, Sickness, Skies, Sleep, Sorrow, Speechmaking, Suffering, Supernatural, Sympathy, Temptation, Tennis, Thanks, Theatre, Thinking, Time, Wales, War, Weather, Wit, Women, Work, Writing, Youth

Shankly, Bill
Football

Shaw, George Bernard
Armed Forces, Beauty, Choice, Cinema, Dance, Democracy, Determination, Drink, Fame, Food, Forgiveness, Generation Gap, Happiness, Hell, Honesty, Honours, Ideas, Imagination, Indifference, Languages, Liberty, Life, Lovers, Marriage, Music, Parents, Patriotism, Photography, Poverty, Progress, Satisfaction, Science, Self, Teaching, Violence

Sheen, Fulton J.
Law

Sheffield, John
Writing

Shelley, Percy Bysshe
Autumn, Dreams, Hell, Poetry, Royalty, Winter

Sheridan, Philip Henry
Prejudice

Sheridan, Richard Brinsley
Manners, Speechmaking, Wit, Women

Sherman, William Tecumseh
War

Shute, Nevil
Technology

Sibelius, Jean
Criticism

Siddur, The
God

Sidney, Philip
Charity

Sieyès, Abbé Emmanuel Joseph
Revolution

Signoret, Simone
Marriage

Sill, Edward Rowland
Drink

Sillitoe, Alan
Self

Simenon, Georges
Writing

Simon, Paul
Silence, Sympathy

Index of Authors

Simpson, N. F.
Management

Simpson, Wallis
Body

Sinatra, Frank
Lifestyles

Sinclair, Upton
Careers

Sitwell, Edith
Individuality

Skinner, B. F.
*Education,
Thinking*

Smart, Christopher
Cats

Smiles, Samuel
*Eating,
Management*

Smith, Adam
*Business, Taxes,
Wealth*

Smith, Delia
Food, Football

Smith, F. E.
Ambition

Smith, Iain Duncan
Determination

**Smith, Logan
Pearsall**
*Careers, Hypocrisy,
Reading*

Smith, Stevie
Death, Indifference

Smith, Sydney
*Books, Country,
Criticism, Death,
Food, Heaven,
Houses, Lifestyles,
Mathematics,
Poverty, Protest*

Sockman, Ralph W.
Knowledge

Socrates
*Knowledge,
Philosophy, Town,
Truth, Wealth*

Solon
Happiness

**Solzhenitsyn,
Alexander**
*Censorship,
Democracy, Evil,
Power*

Sondheim, Stephen
America

Sontag, Susan
Reality, Sickness

Sophocles
Life, Sex

Spark, Muriel
*Middle Age,
Parents, Teaching*

Spencer, Herbert
Foolishness

Spock, Benjamin
Babies

Spring-Rice, Cecil
Patriotism

Springsteen, Bruce
Success

Spurgeon, C. H.
Happiness, Lies

Squire, J. C.
Drink, Science

Staël, Mme de
Insight, Love

Stalin, Joseph
Class, Death, Power

**Stanley, Bessie
Anderson**
Success

**Stanley, Henry
Morton**
Meeting

Stark, Freya
Women

Steele, Richard
Letters, Reading

Steffens, Lincoln
Revolution

Stein, Gertrude
*Danger, Genius,
Knowledge,*
*Literature, Money,
Self, Town*

Steinbeck, John
Fishing, Lifestyles

Steinem, Gloria
Women

Steiner, George
Morality

Steiner, Peter
Computers

Stendhal
Beauty, Literature

Stengel, Casey
Baseball

Stephens, James
Perfection

Stern, Nicholas
Environment

Sterne, Laurence
France, Persistence

Stevens, Wallace
Music, Reality

Stevenson, Adlai
*Generation
Gap, Liberty,
Poverty, Praise,
Speechmaking*

**Stevenson, Robert
Louis**
*Brevity, Drink,
Eating, Failure,
Food, Lies,
Marriage, Morality,
Sleep, Travel*

**Stewart, Donald
Ogden**
Relationships

Stone, Oliver *see*
Weiser, Stanley and
Stone, Oliver

Stoppard, Tom
*Bureaucracy,
Elections,
Journalism,
Knowledge, War,
Youth*

Stowe, Harriet Beecher
Bereavement

Strachey, Lytton
Biography

Stravinsky, Igor
Music

Strunsky, Simeon
Quotations

Suckling, John
Lovers

Sullivan, Louis Henri
Architecture

Sun Tzu
War

Surtees, R. S.
Eating, Pleasure

Swan, Annie S.
Work

Swift, Jonathan
Church, Criticism, Genius, Life Sciences, Old Age, Parties, Progress, Promises, Religion, Style, Toasts

Sykes, Charles J.
Intelligence

Szasz, Thomas
Forgiveness, Justice, Medicine

Szent-Györgyi, Albert von
Invention, Life Sciences

Tacitus
Peace, Strength

Tagore, Rabindranath
Life, Prejudice, Solitude, Transience

Talleyrand, Charles-Maurice de
Ending, Moderation

Tally, Ted *see* Harris, Thomas and Tally, Ted

Tarantino, Quentin
Knowledge

Taupin, Bernie *see* John, Elton and Taupin, Bernie

Tawney, R. H.
Honours

Taylor, Henry
Secrecy

Teale, Edwin Way
Autumn

Tebbit, Norman
Patriotism

Tecumseh
Race

Teichmann, Howard *see* Kaufman, George S. and Teichmann, Howard

Temple, William
Cricket

Tennyson, Alfred, Lord
Armed Forces, Belief, Birds, Change, Death, Determination, Europe, Festivals, Gardens, Honour, Honours, Kissing, Love, Mistakes, Nature, Prayer, Sorrow

Tenzing Norgay
Mountains

Te Rauparaha
Sport

Teresa, Mother
Charity, Present, Sickness

Teresa, St of Ávila
God, Goodness, Housework,

Patience, Thinking, Weather

Teresa, St of Lisieux
Heaven

Tertullian
Belief, Church

Thackeray, William Makepeace
Family, Men and Women

Thatcher, Margaret
Charity, Choice, Determination, Home, Journalism, Leadership, Money, Patience, Society

Thomas à Kempis
God, Goodness

Thomas Aquinas, St
Insight

Thomas, Dylan
Death, Housework, Old Age, Wales, Youth

Thomas, Edward
Past

Thompson, Francis
Suffering

Thomson, James
Britain, Teaching

Thomson, Roy
Television

Thoreau, Henry David
Birds, Body, Clothes, Education, Environment, Evil, Fashion, Life, Self, Time, Truth, Writing

Thucydides
Writing

Thurber, James
Humour, Sleep

Thurlow, Edward, 1st Baron
Conscience

Index of Authors

Tillich, Paul
  Anxiety
Tipu Sultan
  Heroes
Titus
  Charity
Tocqueville, Alexis de
  Class
Tolstoy, Leo
  Art, Beauty, Body, Family, Hypocrisy, Patience, Relationships, Sorrow
Tooby, John *see* **Cosmides, Leda and Tooby, John**
Torke, Michael
  Mind
Toussenel, A.
  Dogs
Townshend, Pete
  Generation Gap
Travis, Merle
  Poverty
Trevelyan, G. M.
  France
Trinder, Tommy
  America
Trollope, Anthony
  Equality, Pride, Retirement, Suffering, Winter
Trollope, Frances
  Autumn
Trotsky, Leon
  Civilization, Old Age, Planning, Violence
Trudeau, Pierre
  Censorship
Truffaut, François
  Protest
Truman, Harry S.
  Economics, Government,

  Leadership, Politicians
Trump, Donald
  Business
Trump, Ivana
  Revenge
Truth, Sojourner
  Human Rights
Tubman, Harriet
  Determination
Tucker, Sophie
  Women
Tupper, Martin
  Books
Turgenev, Ivan
  Beginning, Heart, Nature, Prayer
Turner, J. M. W.
  Genius
Twain, Mark
  Anger, Books, Custom, Dogs, Doubt, Facts, Festivals, Food, Foolishness, Friendship, Generation Gap, Golf, Gossip, Heaven, Human Race, Humour, India, Invention, Journalism, Lies, Men and Women, Morality, Mothers, Prayer, Promises, Quotations, Religion, Success, Temptation, Travel, Truth
Twiggy
  Middle Age
Tynan, Kenneth
  Criticism
Ulrich, Laurel Thatcher
  Woman's Role

Unamuno, Miguel de
  Doubt
Universal Declaration of Human Rights
  Human Rights
Upanishads, The
  Peace, Silence
Updike, John
  America, Boredom, Fame, Fathers, Parents, Weather
Ustinov, Peter
  Computers, Friendship, Parents
Vanbrugh, John
  Women
Vanderbilt, William H.
  Business
van der Post, Laurens
  Murder
Van Dyke, Henry
  Hospitality, Houses, Time
Van Gogh, Vincent
  Painting, Solitude
Vaughan, Harry
  Character
Vega, Lope de
  Theatre
Vegetius
  Peace
Vespasian
  Taxes
Vicious, Sid
  Music
Victoria, Queen
  Birth, Humour, Royalty, Winning, Woman's Role
Vidal, Gore
  Business, Success, Television

Index of Authors

Vidor, King
Marriage
Viera Gallo, José Antonio
Politics
Vigneault, Gilles
Canada
Villon, François
Past
Virgil
Ability, Courage, Love, Night, Sorrow, Time, Trust
Voltaire
Boredom, Canada, Censorship, Change, Democracy, Doubt, Enemies, England, God, Government, Leisure, Management, Moderation, Optimism, Perfection, Practicality, Supernatural, Taxes, Work
Vonnegut, Kurt
Character, Death, Youth
Walcott, Derek
Creativity, Languages
Walker, Alice
Life, Violence, Woman's Role, Writing
Wallace, William Ross
Mothers
Wallas, Graham
Meaning
Walliams, David
see **Lucas, Matt and Walliams, David**
Walpole, Horace
Fashion, Goodness, Life, Summer

Walpole, Robert
Politicians
Walton, Izaak
Fishing, Health
Walton, Sam
Business
Warburton, William
Religion
Warhol, Andy
Fame, Photography
Warner, Charles Dudley
Gardens
Warner, Sylvia Townsend
Diaries
Washington, George
Armed Forces, Truth
Watson, Thomas Snr.
Business
Watterson, Bill
Universe
Watts, Isaac
God, Idleness, Time
Waugh, Evelyn
Britain, England, Manners, Punctuality, Style
Webster, Daniel
Ambition
Webster, John
Death, Discontent, Fate
Wedgwood, Josiah
Race
Weil, Simone
Economics
Weinreich, Max
Language
Weir, Robert Stanley
Canada

Weiser, Stanley and Stone, Oliver
Eating, Economics
Weissmuller, Johnny
Men and Women
Weizmann, Chaim
Luck
Welch, Bruce and Bennett, Brian
Leisure
Weldon, Fay
Mothers, Parents
Welles, Orson
Cinema, Civilization, Flight, Solitude, Television
Wellington, Duke of
Armed Forces, Books, Knowledge, War
Wells, H. G.
History, Morality, Society
Wesley, John
Church, Religion
West, Cornel
Leadership
West, Mae
Choice, Diaries, Goodness, Humour, Meeting, Men, Moderation, Sex
West, Rebecca
Housework, Journalism
Wharton, Edith
Happiness, Wealth
Whately, Richard
Economics
Wheatley, Phillis
Race
Whistler, James McNeill
Argument, Criticism,

Index of Authors

*Examinations,
Painting,
Quotations*

White, E. B.
Town

White, T. H.
Education, Law

**Whitehead, Alfred
North**
*Ability, Ideas,
Philosophy*

Whitman, Walt
*America, Body,
Charity, Creativity,
Self*

**Whittier, John
Greenleaf**
Food, Sorrow

Whitton, Charlotte
Men and Women

Whymper, Edward
Mountains

Wiesel, Elie
Indifference

**Wilcox, Ella
Wheeler**
Religion, Sorrow

Wilde, Oscar
*Advice, Appearance,
Biography,
Country, Cynicism,
Diaries, England,
Experience,
Fashion, Generation
Gap, Genius,
Gossip, Idealism,
Individuality,
Literature, Love,
Marriage, Men and
Women, Mistakes,
Parents, Parties,
Reality, Style,
Temptation, Truth,
Words, Youth*

Wilder, Billy *see*
**Brackett, Charles
and Wilder, Billy**

Wilder, Thornton
Bereavement

Wilensky, Robert
Computers

Will, George F.
Baseball, Pessimism

**Willans, Geoffrey
and Searle, Ronald**
Ignorance

**Willard, Emma
Hart**
Sea

William III
Fate

Williams, R. J. P.
Life Sciences

Williams, Sarah
Skies

Williams, Serena
Tennis

**Williams,
Tennessee**
*Cruelty, Human
Race, Money,
Persistence, Reality*

**Williams, William
Carlos**
Certainty

**Williamson,
Marianne**
Fear

Williamson, Roy
Scotland

Wilson, Harold
*Crises, Politics,
Technology*

**Wilson,
McLandburgh**
Pessimism

Wilson, Woodrow
*Cinema,
Democracy*

Windsor, Barbara
Acting

Winfrey, Oprah
*Exercise, Luck,
Wealth*

Winters, Shelley
Theatre

**Winterson,
Jeanette**
Lovers

**Wittgenstein,
Ludwig**
*Body, Language,
Philosophy,
Speechmaking,
Universe*

Wodehouse, P. G.
*Apology,
Discontent, Family,
Golf, Scotland*

Wogan, Terry
Television

Wolfe, Tom
Politics

**Wollstonecraft,
Mary**
*Justice, Woman's
Role*

**Wolstenholme,
Kenneth**
Ending

Wooden, John
Failure

Woods, Tiger
Race

Woolf, Virginia
*Eating, Letters,
Misfortune,
Satisfaction,
Writing*

**Woollcott,
Alexander**
Pleasure

**Wordsworth,
William**
*Bereavement,
Birth, Children,
Death, England,
Flowers, Goodness,
Imagination,
Leisure, London,
Nature, Poetry,*

Revolution,
Writing, Youth
Worrall, Terry
Weather
Wotton, Henry
Architecture,
Bereavement,
Diplomacy
Wright, Frank Lloyd
Architecture, Town
Yāqūt
Earth
Yeatman, R. J. *see*
Sellar, W. C. and
Yeatman, R. J.

Yeats, W. B.
Change, Death,
Heart, Idealism,
Indifference,
Ireland, Life, Love,
Old Age, Perfection,
Poetry, Suffering
Young, Edward
Foolishness,
Idleness,
Quotations,
Sickness, Sleep
Young, George W.
Drink
Young, Neil
Lifestyles

Zangwill, Israel
America
Zappa, Frank
Drugs, Journalism,
Progress
Zeno
Speechmaking
Zephaniah,
Benjamin
Christmas
Zobel, Hiller B.
Law
Zuckerberg, Mark
News

List of Articles